Programming in D

Programming in D

Ali Çehreli

Edited by Luís Marques

Programming in D

D version: 2.098.1
Book revision: 2022-01-07 [1]

The most recent electronic versions of this book are available online[2].

Edited by Luís Marques[3]

Cover design by İzgi Yapıcı[4]

Cover illustration by Sarah Reece[5]

Published by Ali Çehreli[6]

Fonts:

 Andada by Carolina Giovagnoli for Huerta Tipográfica
 Open Sans by Steve Matteson
 DejaVu Mono by DejaVu Fonts

PDF version is generated with Prince XML
Other ebook versions are generated with Calibre

ISBNs:

 978-0-692-59943-3 hardcover by IngramSpark
 978-0-692-52957-7 paperback by IngramSpark
 978-1-515-07460-1 paperback by CreateSpace
 978-1-519-95441-1 ePUB by Draft2Digital

---

1. https://bitbucket.org/acehreli/ddili
2. http://ddili.org/ders/d.en
3. http://www.luismarques.eu
4. http://izgiyapici.com
5. mailto:sarah@reeceweb.com
6. mailto:acehreli@yahoo.com

Contents

Those of us who know Ali might notice his book on D is imbued with its author's personality: straightforward, patient, and nice without being pandering.

There is purpose in every sentence, and with each, a step forward is being made; not too fast, and not too slow. "Note that `opApply()` itself is implemented by a `foreach` loop. As a result, the `foreach` inside `main()` ends up making indirect use of a `foreach` over the `points` member." And so it goes, in just as many words as needed. And in the right order, too; Ali does an admirable job at presenting language concepts – which especially to a beginner overwhelmingly come "in parallel" – in a sequential manner.

But there's another thing I like most about "Programming in D": it's a good book for learning programming *in general*. See, a good introductory book on Haskell implicitly teaches functional programming along the way; one on C would come with systems programming notions in tow; one on Python with scripting, and so on. What would, then, a good introductory text to D teach in subtext? At best, Programming with a capital P.

D fosters a "use the right tool for the job" attitude, and allows its user to tap into a wide range of programming techniques, without throwing too many idiosyncrasies in the way. The most fun way to approach coding in D is with an open mind, because for each design that starts to get stilted there is opportunity to mold it into the right design choosing a different implementation, approach, or paradigm altogether. To best choose what's most fitting, the engineer must know the gamut of what's possible – and "Programming in D" is a great way to equip one's intellect with that knowledge. Internalizing it helps not only writing good code in D, but writing good code, period.

There's good tactical advice, too, to complement the teaching of programming and language concepts. Timeless teaching on avoiding code duplication, choosing good names, aiming for good decomposition, and more – it's all there, quick-and-dirty hacks iteratively annealed into robust solutions, just as they should in normal practice. Instead of falling for getting things done quickly, "Programming in D" focuses on getting things done properly, to the lasting benefit of its reader.

I've long suspected D is a good first programming language to learn. It exposes its user to a variety of concepts – systems, functional, object oriented, generic, generative – candidly and without pretense. And so does Ali's book, which seems to me an excellent realization of that opportunity.

Andrei Alexandrescu
San Francisco, *May 2015*

Preface

D is a multi-paradigm system programming language that combines a wide range of powerful programming concepts from the lowest to the highest levels. It emphasizes memory safety, program correctness, and pragmatism.

The main aim of this book is to teach D to readers who are new to computer programming. Although having experience in other programming languages is certainly helpful, this book starts from the basics.

In order for this book to be useful, you will need an environment to write, compile, and run your D programs. This *development environment* must include at least a D compiler and a text editor. We will learn how to install a compiler and how to compile programs in the next chapter.

Each chapter is based on the contents of the previous ones, introducing as few new concepts as possible. I recommend that you read the book in linear fashion, without skipping chapters. Although this book was written with beginners in mind, it covers almost all features of D. More experienced programmers can use the book as a D language reference by starting from the index section.

Some chapters include exercises and their solutions so that you can write small programs and compare your methods to mine.

Computer programming is a satisfying craft that involves continuously discovering and learning new tools, techniques, and concepts. I am sure you will enjoy programming in D at least as much as I do. Learning to program is easier and more fun when shared with others. Take advantage of the D.learn newsgroup[1] to follow discussions and to ask and answer questions.

This book is available in Turkish[2] as well.

Acknowledgments
I am indebted to the following people who have been instrumental during the evolution of this book:

Mert Ataol, Zafer Çelenk, Salih Dinçer, Can Alpay Çiftçi, Faruk Erdem Öncel, Muhammet Aydın (aka Mengü Kağan), Ergin Güney, Jordi Sayol, David Herberth, Andre Tampubolon, Gour-Gadadhara Dasa, Raphaël Jakse, Andrej Mitrović, Johannes Pfau, Jerome Sniatecki, Jason Adams, Ali H. Çalışkan, Paul Jurczak, Brian Rogoff, Михаил Страшун (Mihails Strasuns), Joseph Rushton Wakeling, Tove, Hugo Florentino, Satya Pothamsetti, Luís Marques, Christoph Wendler, Daniel Nielsen, Ketmar Dark, Pavel Lukin, Jonas Fiala, Norman Hardy, Rich Morin, Douglas Foster, Paul Robinson, Sean Garratt, Stéphane Goujet, Shammah Chancellor, Steven Schveighoffer, Robbin Carlson, Bubnenkov Dmitry Ivanovich, Bastiaan Veelo, Olivier Pisano, Dave Yost, Tomasz Miazek-Mioduszewski, Gerard Vreeswijk, Justin Whear, Gerald Jansen, Sylvain Gault, Shriramana Sharma, Jay Norwood, Henri Menke, Chen Lejia, Vladimir Panteleev, Martin Tschierschke, ag0aep6g, Andrew Edwards, Steve White, Mark Schwarzmann, Thibaut Charles, Richard Palme, Don Grant, Goksan Kadir, Aleksandr Treyger, Michael Siegel, Quirin Schroll, Don Allen, Krasimir Berov, Chibisi Chima-Okereke, Xavier Gachon, and Paul Hines.

Thanks especially to Luís Marques and Steven Schveighoffer who, through their hard work, improved every chapter of the book. If you find any part of this book useful, it is likely due to their diligent editing.

---

1. http://forum.dlang.org/group/digitalmars.D.learn/
2. http://ddili.org/ders/d/

Thanks to Luís Marques, Steven Schveighoffer, Andrej Mitrović, Robbin Carlson, Ergin Güney, and Andrew Edwards for their suggestions that elevated this book from my Inglish to English.

I am grateful to the entire D community for keeping my enthusiasm and motivation high. D has an amazing community of tireless individuals like bearophile and Kenji Hara.

Ebru, Damla, and Derin, thank you for being so patient and supportive while I was lost writing these chapters.

Ali Çehreli
Mountain View, *May 2017*

This revision of the book contains many corrections, improvements[1], and a new chapter: `static foreach` (page 602).

Ali Çehreli
Mountain View, *February 2019*

The main addition to this revision is Copy Constructors (page 279).

Ali Çehreli
Mountain View, *January 2022*

---

1. https://bitbucket.org/acehreli/ddili/commits/all

1 The Hello World Program

The first program to show in most programming language books is the *hello world* program. This very short and simple program merely writes "Hello, World!" and finishes. This program is important because it includes some of the essential concepts of that language.

Here is a *hello world* program in D:

```d
import std.stdio;

void main() {
    writeln("Hello, World!");
}
```

The *source code* above needs to be compiled by a D compiler to produce an executable program.

1.1 Compiler installation

At the time of writing this chapter, there are three D compilers to choose from: dmd, the Digital Mars compiler; gdc, the D compiler of GCC; and ldc, the D compiler that targets the LLVM compiler infrastructure.

dmd is the D compiler that has been used during the design and development of the language over the years. All of the examples in this book have been tested with dmd. For that reason, it would be the easiest for you to start with dmd and try other compilers only if you have a specific need to. The code samples in this book were compiled with dmd version 2.098.1.

To install the latest version of dmd, go to the download page at Digital Mars[1] and select the compiler build that matches your computer environment. You must select the dmd build that is for your operating system and package management system, and whether you have a 32-bit or a 64-bit CPU and operating system. Do not install a D1 compiler. This book covers only *D version two*.

The installation steps are different on different environments but it should be as easy as following simple on-screen instructions and clicking a couple of buttons.

1.2 Source file

The file that the programmer writes for the D compiler to compile is called the *source file*. Since D is usually used as a compiled language, the source file itself is not an executable program. The source file must be converted to an executable program by the compiler.

As with any file, the source file must have a name. Although the name can be anything that is legal on the file system, it is customary to use the .d *file extension* for D source files because development environments, programming tools, and programmers all expect this to be the case. For example, test.d, game.d, invoice.d, etc. are appropriate D source file names.

1.3 Compiling the hello world program

You will write the source file in a text editor[2] (or an *IDE* as mentioned below). Copy or type the hello world program above into a text file and save it under the name hello.d.

---

1. http://www.dlang.org/download.html
2. http://wiki.dlang.org/Editors

The compiler will soon check that the syntax of this source code is correct (i.e. it is valid according to the language rules) and make a program out of it by translating it into machine code. Follow these steps to compile the program:

1. Open a terminal window.
2. Go to the directory where you saved hello.d.
3. Enter the following command. (Do not type the $ character; it is there to indicate the command line prompt.)

```
$ dmd hello.d
```

If you did not make any mistake, you may think that nothing has happened. To the contrary, it means that everything went well. There should be an executable file named hello (or hello.exe under Windows) that has just been created by the compiler.

If the compiler has instead printed some messages, you probably have made a mistake when copying the program code. Try to identify the mistake, correct it, and retry compiling. You will routinely make many mistakes when programming, so the process of correcting and compiling will become familiar to you.

Once the program has been created successfully, type the name of the executable program to run it. You should see that the program prints "Hello, World!":

```
$ ./hello        ← running the program
Hello, World!    ← the message that it prints
```

Congratulations! Your first D program works as expected.

1.4 Compiler switches

The compiler has many command line switches that are used for influencing how it compiles the program. To see a list of compiler switches enter just the name of the compiler:

```
$ dmd        ← enter just the name
DMD64 D Compiler v2.098.1
...
  -de            show use of deprecated features as errors (halt compilation)
...
  -unittest      compile in unit tests
...
  -w             warnings as errors (compilation will halt)
...
```

The abbreviated output above shows only the command line switches that I recommend that you always use. Although it makes no difference with the hello world program in this chapter, the following command line would compile the program by enabling unit tests and not allowing any warnings or deprecated features. We will see these and other switches in more detail in later chapters:

```
$ dmd hello.d -de -w -unittest
```

The complete list of dmd command line switches can be found in the DMD Compiler documentation[1].

One other command line switch that you may find useful is -run. It compiles the source code, produces the executable program, and runs it with a single

---

1. http://dlang.org/dmd-linux.html

command. `-run` must be the last of compiler switches, specified right before the name of the source file:

```
$ dmd -de -w -unittest -run hello.d
Hello, World!   ← the program is automatically executed
```

1.5 IDE

In addition to the compiler, you may also consider installing an IDE (integrated development environment). IDEs are designed to make program development easier by simplifying the steps of writing, compiling, and debugging.

If you do install an IDE, compiling and running the program will be as simple as pressing a key or clicking a button on the IDE. I still recommend that you familiarize yourself with compiling programs manually in a terminal window.

If you decide to install an IDE, go to the IDEs page at dlang.org[1] to see a list of available IDEs.

1.6 Contents of the hello world program

Here is a quick list of the many D concepts that have appeared in this short program:

Core feature: Every language defines its syntax, fundamental types, keywords, rules, etc. All of these make the *core features* of that language. The parentheses, semicolons, and words like `main` and `void` are all placed according to the rules of D. These are similar to the rules of English: subject, verb, punctuation, sentence structure, etc.

Library and function: The core features define only the structure of the language. They are used for defining functions and user types, and those in turn are used for building libraries. Libraries are collections of reusable program parts that get *linked* with your programs to help them achieve their purposes.

`writeln` above is a *function* in D's standard *library*. It is used for printing a line of text, as its name suggests: write line.

Module: Library contents are grouped by types of tasks that they intend to help with. Such a group is called a module. The only module that this program uses is `std.stdio`, which handles data input and output.

Character and string: Expressions like `"Hello, World!"` are called *strings*, and the elements of strings are called *characters*. The only string in this program contains characters `'H'`, `'e'`, `'!'`, and others.

Order of operations: Programs complete their tasks by executing operations in a certain order. These tasks start with the operations that are written in the function named `main`. The only operation in this program writes "Hello world!".

Significance of uppercase and lowercase letters: You can choose to type any character inside strings, but you must type the other characters exactly as they appear in the program. This is because lowercase vs. uppercase is significant in D programs. For example, `writeln` and `Writeln` are two different names.

Keyword: Special words that are a part of the core features of the language are *keywords*. Such words are reserved for the language itself, and cannot be used for any other purpose in a D program. There are two keywords in this program: `import`, which is used to introduce a module to the program; and `void`, which here means "not returning anything".

The complete list of D keywords is `abstract`, `alias`, `align`, `asm`, `assert`, `auto`, `body`, `bool`, `break`, `byte`, `case`, `cast`, `catch`, `cdouble`, `cent`, `cfloat`, `char`, `class`,

---

1. http://wiki.dlang.org/IDEs

const, continue, creal, dchar, debug, default, delegate, delete, deprecated, do, double, else, enum, export, extern, false, final, finally, float, for, foreach, foreach_reverse, function, goto, idouble, if, ifloat, immutable, import, in, inout, int, interface, invariant, ireal, is, lazy, long, macro, mixin, module, new, nothrow, null, out, override, package, pragma, private, protected, public, pure, real, ref, return, scope, shared, short, static, struct, super, switch, synchronized, template, this, throw, true, try, typedef, typeid, typeof, ubyte, ucent, uint, ulong, union, unittest, ushort, version, void, volatile, wchar, while, with, __FILE__, __FILE_FULL_PATH__, __MODULE__, __LINE__, __FUNCTION__, __PRETTY_FUNCTION__, __gshared, __traits, __vector, and __parameters.

We will cover these keywords in the upcoming chapters with the exception of the following ones: asm[1] and __vector[2] are outside of the scope of this book; body, delete, typedef, and volatile are deprecated; and macro is unused by D at this time.

1.7 Exercises

1. Make the program output something else.
2. Change the program to output more than one line. You can do this by adding one more writeln line to the program.
3. Try to compile the program after making other changes; e.g. remove the semicolon at the end of the line with writeln and observe a compilation error.

The solutions are on page 695.

---

1. http://dlang.org/statement.html#AsmStatement
2. http://dlang.org/phobos/core_simd.html#.Vector

2 writeln and write

In the previous chapter we have seen that `writeln` takes a string within parentheses and prints the string.

The parts of programs that actually do work are called *functions* and the information that they need to complete their work are called *parameters*. The act of giving such information to functions is called *passing parameter values* to them. Parameters are passed to functions within parentheses, separated by commas.

Note: *The word* parameter *describes the information that is passed to a function at the conceptual level. The concrete information that is actually passed during the execution of the program is called an* argument. *Although not technically the same, these terms are sometimes used interchangably in the software industry.*

`writeln` can take more than one argument. It prints them one after the other on the same line:

```
import std.stdio;

void main() {
    writeln("Hello, World!", "Hello, fish!");
}
```

Sometimes, not all of the information that is to be printed on the same line may be readily available to be passed to `writeln`. In such cases, the first parts of the line may be printed by `write` and the last part of the line may be printed by `writeln`.

`writeln` advances to the next line, `write` stays on the same line:

```
import std.stdio;

void main() {
    // Let's first print what we have available:
    write("Hello,");

    // ... let's assume more operations at this point ...

    write("World!");

    // ... and finally:
    writeln();
}
```

Calling `writeln` without any parameter merely completes the current line, or if nothing has been written, outputs a blank line.

Lines that start with `//` are called *comment lines* or briefly *comments*. A comment is not a part of the program code in the sense that it doesn't affect the behavior of the program. Its only purpose is to explain what the code does in that particular section of the program. The audience of a comment is anybody who may be reading the program code later, including the programmer who wrote the comment in the first place.

2.1 Exercises

1. Both of the programs in this chapter print the strings without any spaces between them. Change the programs so that there is space between the arguments as in "Hello, World!".

2. Try calling `write` with more than one parameter as well.

The solutions are on page 695.

3 Compilation

We have seen that the two tools that are used most in D programming are *the text editor* and *the compiler*. D programs are written in text editors.

The concept of compilation and the function of the compiler must also be understood when using *compiled* languages like D.

3.1 Machine code

The brain of the computer is the microprocessor (or the CPU, short for *central processing unit*). Telling the CPU what to do is called *coding*, and the instructions that are used when doing so are called *machine code*.

Most CPU architectures use machine code specific to that particular architecture. These machine code instructions are determined under hardware constraints during the design stage of the architecture. At the lowest level these machine code instructions are implemented as electrical signals. Because the ease of coding is not a primary consideration at this level, writing programs directly in the form of the machine code of the CPU is a very difficult task.

These machine code instructions are special numbers, which represent various operations supported by the CPU. For example, for an imaginary 8-bit CPU, the number 4 might represent the operation of loading, the number 5 might represent the operation of storing, and the number 6 might represent the operation of incrementing. Assuming that the leftmost 3 bits are the operation number and the rightmost 5 bits are the value that is used in that operation, a sample program in machine code for this CPU might look like the following:

```
Operation   Value           Meaning
      100   11110      LOAD      11110
      101   10100      STORE     10100
      110   10100      INCREMENT 10100
      000   00000      PAUSE
```

Being so close to hardware, machine code is not suitable for representing higher level concepts like *a playing card* or *a student record*.

3.2 Programming language

Programming languages are designed as efficient ways of programming a CPU, capable of representing higher-level concepts. Programming languages do not have to deal with hardware constraints; their main purposes are ease of use and expressiveness. Programming languages are easier for humans to understand, closer to natural languages:

```
if (a_card_has_been_played()) {
    display_the_card();
}
```

However, programming languages adhere to much more strict and formal rules than any spoken language.

3.3 Interpreter

An interpreter is a tool (a program) that reads the instructions from source code and executes them. For example, for the code above, an interpreter would understand to first execute a_card_has_been_played() and then conditionally execute display_the_card(). From the point of view of the programmer, executing with an interpreter involves just two steps: writing the source code and giving it to the interpreter.

The interpreter must read and understand the instructions every time the program is executed. For that reason, running a program with an interpreter is usually slower than running the compiled version of the same program. Additionally, interpreters usually perform very little analysis on the code before executing it. As a result, most interpreters discover programming errors only after they start executing the program.

Some languages like Perl, Python and Ruby have been designed to be very flexible and dynamic, making code analysis harder. These languages have traditionally been used with an interpreter.

3.4 Compiler

A compiler is another tool that reads the instructions of a program from source code. Different from an interpreter, it does not execute the code; rather, it produces a program written in another language (usually machine code). This produced program is responsible for the execution of the instructions that were written by the programmer. From the point of view of the programmer, executing with a compiler involves three steps: writing the source code, compiling it, and running the produced program.

Unlike an interpreter, the compiler reads and understands the source code only once, during compilation. For that reason and in general, a compiled program runs faster compared to executing that program with an interpreter. Compilers usually perform advanced analysis on the code, which help with producing fast programs and catching programming errors before the program even starts running. On the other hand, having to compile the program every time it is changed is a complication and a potential source of human errors. Moreover, the programs that are produced by a compiler can usually run only on a specific platform; to run on a different kind of processor or on a different operating system, the program would have to be recompiled. Additionally, the languages that are easy to compile are usually less dynamic than those that run in an interpreter.

For reasons like safety and performance, some languages have been designed to be compiled. Ada, C, C++, and D are some of them.

Compilation error

As the compiler compiles a program according to the rules of the language, it stops the compilation as soon as it comes across *illegal* instructions. Illegal instructions are the ones that are outside the specifications of the language. Problems like a mismatched parenthesis, a missing semicolon, a misspelled keyword, etc. all cause compilation errors.

The compiler may also emit a *compilation warning* when it sees a suspicious piece of code that may cause concern but not necessarily an error. However, warnings almost always indicate an actual error or bad style, so it is a common practice to consider most or all warnings as errors. The dmd compiler switch to enable warnings as errors is -w.

4 Fundamental Types

We have seen that the brain of a computer is the CPU. Most of the tasks of a program are performed by the CPU and the rest are dispatched to other parts of the computer.

The smallest unit of data in a computer is called *a bit*. The value of a bit can be either 0 or 1.

Since a type of data that can hold only the values 0 and 1 would have very limited use, the CPU supports larger data types that are combinations of more than one bit. As an example, a *byte* usually consists of 8 bits. If an N-bit data type is the most efficient data type supported by a CPU, we consider it to be an *N-bit CPU*: as in 32-bit CPU, 64-bit CPU, etc.

The data types that the CPU supports are still not sufficient: they can't represent higher level concepts like *name of a student* or *a playing card*. Likewise, D's fundamental data types are not sufficient to represent many higher level concepts. Such concepts must be defined by the programmer as *structs* and *classes*, which we will see in later chapters.

D's *fundamental types* are very similar to the fundamental types of many other languages, as seen in the following table. The terms that appear in the table are explained below:

D's Fundamental Data Types

Type	Definition	Initial Value
bool	Boolean type	false
byte	signed 8 bits	0
ubyte	unsigned 8 bits	0
short	signed 16 bits	0
ushort	unsigned 16 bits	0
int	signed 32 bits	0
uint	unsigned 32 bits	0
long	signed 64 bits	0L
ulong	unsigned 64 bits	0LU
float	32-bit floating point	float.nan
double	64-bit floating point	double.nan
real	either the largest floating point type that the hardware supports, or double; whichever is larger	real.nan
ifloat	imaginary value type of float	float.nan * 1.0i
idouble	imaginary value type of double	double.nan * 1.0i
ireal	imaginary value type of real	real.nan * 1.0i
cfloat	complex number type made of two floats	float.nan + float.nan * 1.0i
cdouble	complex number type made of two doubles	double.nan + double.nan * 1.0i
creal	complex number type made of two reals	real.nan + real.nan * 1.0i
char	UTF-8 code unit	0xFF
wchar	UTF-16 code unit	0xFFFF
dchar	UTF-32 code unit and Unicode code point	0x0000FFFF

In addition to the above, the keyword void represents *having no type*. The keywords cent and ucent are reserved for future use to represent signed and unsigned 128 bit values.

Unless there is a specific reason not to, you can use int to represent whole values. To represent concepts that can have fractional values, consider double.

The following are the terms that appeared in the table:

- **Boolean:** The type of logical expressions, having the value t rue for truth and false for falsity.
- **Signed type:** A type that can have negative and positive values. For example, byte can have values from -128 to 127. The names of these types come from the negative *sign*.
- **Unsigned type:** A type that can have only positive values. For example, ubyte can have values from 0 to 255. The u at the beginning of the name of these types comes from *unsigned*.
- **Floating point:** The type that can represent values with fractions as in 1.25. The precision of floating point calculations are directly related to the bit count of the type: higher the bit count, more precise the results are. Only floating point types can represent fractions; integer types like int can only represent whole values like 1 and 2.
- **Complex number type:** The type that can represent the complex numbers of mathematics.
- **Imaginary number type:** The type that represents only the imaginary part of complex numbers. The i that appears in the Initial Value column is the square root of -1 in mathematics.
- **nan:** Short for "not a number", representing *invalid floating point value*.

4.1 Properties of types

D types have *properties*. Properties are accessed with a dot after the name of the type. For example, the sizeof property of int is accessed as int.sizeof. We will see only some of type properties in this chapter:

- .stringof is the name of the type
- .sizeof is the length of the type in terms of bytes. (In order to determine the bit count, this value must be multiplied by 8, the number of bits in a byte.)
- .min is short for "minimum"; this is the smallest value that the type can have
- .max is short for "maximum"; this is the largest value that the type can have
- .init is short for "initial value" (default value); this is the value that D assigns to a type when an initial value is not specified

Here is a program that prints these properties for int:

```
import std.stdio;

void main() {
    writeln("Type            : ", int.stringof);
    writeln("Length in bytes: ", int.sizeof);
    writeln("Minimum value  : ", int.min);
    writeln("Maximum value  : ", int.max);
    writeln("Initial value  : ", int.init);
}
```

The output of the program is the following:

```
Type            : int
Length in bytes: 4
Minimum value  : -2147483648
Maximum value  : 2147483647
Initial value  : 0
```

4.2 `size_t`

You will come across the `size_t` type as well. `size_t` is not a separate type but an alias of an existing unsigned type. Its name comes from "size type". It is the most suitable type to represent concepts like *size* or *count*.

`size_t` is large enough to represent the number of bytes of the memory that a program can potentially be using. Its actual size depends on the system: `uint` on a 32-bit system and `ulong` on a 64-bit system. For that reason, `ulong` is larger than `size_t` on a 32-bit system.

You can use the `.stringof` property to see what `size_t` is an alias of on your system:

```d
import std.stdio;

void main() {
    writeln(size_t.stringof);
}
```

The output of the program is the following on my system:

```
ulong
```

4.3 Exercise

Print the properties of other types.

Note: *You can't use the reserved types* cent *and* ucent *in any program; and as an exception,* void *does not have the properties* .min, .max *and* .init.

Additionally, the .min *property is deprecated for floating point types. (You can see all the various properties for the fundamental types in the D property specification[1]). If you use a floating point type in this exercise, you would be warned by the compiler that* .min *is not valid for that type. Instead, as we will see later in the Floating Point Types chapter (page 42), you must use the negative of the* .max *property e.g. as* -double.max.

The solution is on page 695.

---

1. http://dlang.org/property.html

5 Assignment and Order of Evaluation

The first two difficulties that most students face when learning to program involve the assignment operation and the order of evaluation.

5.1 The assignment operation

You will see lines similar to the following in almost every program in almost every programming language:

```
a = 10;
```

The meaning of that line is "make a's value become 10". Similarly, the following line means "make b's value become 20":

```
b = 20;
```

Based on that information, what can be said about the following line?

```
a = b;
```

Unfortunately, that line is not about the equality concept of mathematics that we all know. The expression above **does not** mean "a is equal to b"! When we apply the same logic from the earlier two lines, the expression above must mean "make a's value become the same as b's value".

The well-known = symbol of mathematics has a completely different meaning in programming: make the left side's value the same as the right side's value.

5.2 Order of evaluation

In general, the operations of a program are applied step by step in the order that they appear in the program. (There are exceptions to this rule, which we will see in later chapters.) We may see the previous three expressions in a program in the following order:

```
a = 10;
b = 20;
a = b;
```

The meaning of those three lines altogether is this: "make a's value become 10, *then* make b's value become 20, *then* make a's value become the same as b's value". Accordingly, after those three operations are performed, the value of both a and b would be 20.

5.3 Exercise

Observe that the following three operations swap the values of a and b. If at the beginning their values are 1 and 2 respectively, after the operations the values become 2 and 1:

```
c = a;
a = b;
b = c;
```

The solution is on page 695.

6 Variables

Concrete concepts that are represented in a program are called *variables*. A value like *air temperature* and a more complicated object like *a car engine* can be variables of a program.

The main purpose of a variable is to represent a value in the program. The value of a variable is the last value that has been assigned to that variable. Since every value is of a certain type, every variable is of a certain type as well. Most variables have names as well, but some variables are anonymous.

As an example of a variable, we can think of the concept of *the number of students* at a school. Since the number of students is a whole number, int is a suitable type, and studentCount would be a sufficiently descriptive name.

According to D's syntax rules, a variable is introduced by its type followed by its name. The introduction of a variable to the program is called its *definition*. Once a variable is defined, its name represents its value.

```
import std.stdio;

void main() {
    // The definition of the variable; this definition
    // specifies that the type of studentCount is int:
    int studentCount;

    // The name of the variable becomes its value:
    writeln("There are ", studentCount, " students.");
}
```

The output of this program is the following:

```
There are 0 students.
```

As seen from that output, the value of studentCount is 0. This is according to the fundamental types table from the previous chapter: the initial value of int is 0.

Note that studentCount does not appear in the output as its name. In other words, the output of the program is not "There are studentCount students".

The values of variables are changed by the = operator. The = operator assigns new values to variables, and for that reason is called the *assignment operator*:

```
import std.stdio;

void main() {
    int studentCount;
    writeln("There are ", studentCount, " students.");

    // Assigning the value 200 to the studentCount variable:
    studentCount = 200;
    writeln("There are now ", studentCount, " students.");
}
```

```
There are 0 students.
There are now 200 students.
```

When the value of a variable is known at the time of the variable's definition, the variable can be defined and assigned at the same time. This is an important guideline; it makes it impossible to use a variable before assigning its intended value:

```
import std.stdio;

void main() {
    // Definition and assignment at the same time:
```

```
    int studentCount = 100;

    writeln("There are ", studentCount, " students.");
}
```

```
There are 100 students.
```

6.1 Exercise

Define two variables to print "I have exchanged 20 Euros at the rate of 2.11". You can use the floating point type double for the decimal value.

The solution is on page 696.

7 Standard Input and Output Streams

So far, the printed output of our programs has been appearing on the *terminal window* (or *screen*). Although the terminal is often the ultimate target of output, this is not always the case. The objects that can accept output are called *standard output streams*.

The standard output is character based; everything to be printed is first converted to the corresponding character representation and then sent to the output as characters. For example, the integer value 100 that we've printed in the last chapter is not sent to the output as the value 100, but as the three characters 1, 0, and 0.

Similarly, what we normally perceive as the *keyboard* is actually the *standard input stream* of a program and is also character based. The information always comes as characters to be converted to data. For example, the integer value 42 actually comes through the standard input as the characters 4 and 2.

These conversions happen automatically.

This concept of consecutive characters is called a *character stream*. As D's standard input and standard output fit this description, they are character streams.

The names of the standard input and output streams in D are stdin and stdout, respectively.

Operations on these streams normally require the name of the stream, a dot, and the operation; as in stream.operation(). Because stdin's reading methods and stdout's writing methods are used very commonly, those operations can be called without the need of the stream name and the dot.

writeln that we've been using in the previous chapters is actually short for stdout.writeln. Similarly, write is short for stdout.write. Accordingly, the *hello world* program can also be written as follows:

```d
import std.stdio;

void main() {
    stdout.writeln("Hello, World!");
}
```

7.1 Exercise

Observe that stdout.write works the same as write.

The solution is on page 696.

8 Reading from the Standard Input

Any data that is read by the program must first be stored in a variable. For example, a program that reads the number of students from the input must store this information in a variable. The type of this specific variable can be `int`.

As we've seen in the previous chapter, we don't need to type `stdout` when printing to the output, because it is implied. Further, what is to be printed is specified as the argument. So, `write(studentCount)` is sufficient to print the value of `studentCount`. To summarize:

```
stream:      stdout
operation:   write
data:        the value of the studentCount variable
target:      commonly the terminal window
```

The reverse of `write` is `readf`; it reads from the standard input. The "f" in its name comes from "formatted" as what it reads must always be presented in a certain format.

We've also seen in the previous chapter that the standard input stream is `stdin`.

In the case of reading, one piece of the puzzle is still missing: where to store the data. To summarize:

```
stream:      stdin
operation:   readf
data:        some information
target:      ?
```

The location of where to store the data is specified by the address of a variable. The address of a variable is the exact location in the computer's memory where its value is stored.

In D, the & character that is typed before a name is the address of what that name represents. For example, the address of `studentCount` is `&studentCount`. Here, `&studentCount` can be read as "the address of `studentCount`" and is the missing piece to replace the question mark above:

```
stream:      stdin
operation:   readf
data:        some information
target:      the location of the studentCount variable
```

Typing a & in front of a name means *pointing* at what that name represents. This concept is the foundation of references and pointers that we will see in later chapters.

I will leave one peculiarity about the use of `readf` for later; for now, let's accept as a rule that the first argument to `readf` must be `"%s"`:

```
    readf("%s", &studentCount);
```

Actually, `readf` can work without the & character as well:

```
    readf("%s", studentCount);    // same as above
```

Although the code is cleaner and safer without the & character, I will continue to use `readf` with pointers partly to prepare you to the concepts of references (page 159) and reference function parameters (page 168).

"%s" indicates that the data should automatically be converted in a way that is suitable to the type of the variable. For example, when the '4' and '2' characters are read to a variable of type int, they are converted to the integer value 42.

The program below asks the user to enter the number of students. You must press the Enter key after typing the input:

```
import std.stdio;

void main() {
    write("How many students are there? ");

    /* The definition of the variable that will be used to
     * store the information that is read from the input. */
    int studentCount;

    // Storing the input data to that variable
    readf("%s", &studentCount);

    writeln("Got it: There are ", studentCount, " students.");
}
```

8.1 Skipping the whitespace characters

Even the Enter key that we press after typing the data is stored as a special code and is placed into the stdin stream. This is useful to the programs to detect whether the information has been input on a single line or multiple lines.

Although sometimes useful, such special codes are mostly not important for the program and must be filtered out from the input. Otherwise they *block* the input and prevent reading other data.

To see this *problem* in a program, let's also read the number of teachers from the input:

```
import std.stdio;

void main() {
    write("How many students are there? ");
    int studentCount;
    readf("%s", &studentCount);

    write("How many teachers are there? ");
    int teacherCount;
    readf("%s", &teacherCount);

    writeln("Got it: There are ", studentCount, " students",
            " and ", teacherCount, " teachers.");
}
```

Unfortunately, the program cannot use that special code when expecting an int value:

```
How many students are there? 100
How many teachers are there? 20
    ← An exception is thrown here
```

Although the user enters the number of teachers as 20, the special code(s) that represents the Enter key that has been pressed when entering the previous 100 is still in the input stream and is blocking it. The characters that appeared in the input stream are similar to the following representation:

```
100[EnterCode]20[EnterCode]
```

I have highlighted the Enter code that is blocking the input.

The solution is to use a space character before %s to indicate that the Enter code that appears before reading the number of teachers is not important: " %s".

Spaces that are in the format strings are used to read and ignore zero or more invisible characters that would otherwise appear in the input. Such characters include the actual space character, the code(s) that represent the Enter key, the Tab character, etc. and are called the *whitespace characters*.

As a general rule, you can use " %s" for every data that is read from the input. The program above works as expected with the following changes:

```
// ...
    readf(" %s", &studentCount);
// ...
    readf(" %s", &teacherCount);
// ...
```

The output:

```
How many students are there? 100
How many teachers are there? 20
Got it: There are 100 students and 20 teachers.
```

8.2 Additional information

- Lines that start with // are useful for single lines of comments. To write multiple lines as a single comment, enclose the lines within /* and */ markers.

  In order to be able to comment even other comments, use /+ and +/:

  ```
  /+
  // A single line of comment

  /*
    A comment that spans
    multiple lines
  */

  /+
    It can even include nested /+ comments +/
  +/

  A comment block that includes other comments
  +/
  ```

- Most of the whitespace in the source code is insignificant. It is good practice to write longer expressions as multiple lines or add extra whitespace to make the code more readable. Still, as long as the syntax rules of the language are observed, the programs can be written without any extra whitespace:

  ```
  import std.stdio;void main(){writeln("Hard to read!");}
  ```

  It can be hard to read source code with small amounts of whitespace.

8.3 Exercise

Enter non-numerical characters when the program is expecting integer values and observe that the program does not work correctly.

The solution is on page 696.

The actual work that a program performs is accomplished by *expressions*. Any part of a program that produces a value or a side effect is called an expression. It has a very wide definition because even a constant value like 42 and a string like "hello" are expressions, since they produce the respective constant values 42 and "hello".

Note: *Don't confuse producing a value with defining a variable. Values need not be associated with variables.*

Function calls like writeln are expressions as well because they have side effects. In the case of writeln, the effect is on the output stream by the placement of characters on it. Another example from the programs that we have written so far would be the assignment operation, which affects the variable that is on its left-hand side.

Because of producing values, expressions can take part in other expressions. This allows us to form more complex expressions from simpler ones. For example, assuming that there is a function named currentTemperature that produces the value of the current air temperature, the value that it produces may directly be used in a writeln expression:

```
writeln("It's ", currentTemperature(),
        " degrees at the moment.");
```

That line consists of four expressions:

1. "It's "
2. currentTemperature()
3. " degrees at the moment."
4. The writeln() expression that makes use of the other three

In this chapter we will cover the particular type of expression that is used in conditional statements.

Before going further though, I would like to repeat the assignment operator once more, this time emphasizing the two expressions that appear on its left and right sides: the assignment operator (=) assigns the value of the expression on its right-hand side to the expression on its left-hand side (e.g. to a variable).

```
temperature = 23      // temperature's value becomes 23
```

9.1 Logical Expressions
Logical expressions are the expressions that are used in Boolean arithmetic. Logical expressions are what makes computer programs make decisions like "if the answer is yes, I will save the file".

Logical expressions can have one of only two values: false that indicates falsity, and true that indicates truth.

I will use writeln expressions in the following examples. If a line has true printed at the end, it will mean that what is printed on the line is true. Similarly, false will mean that what is on the line is false. For example, if the output of a program is the following,

```
There is coffee: true
```

then it will mean that "there is coffee". Similarly,

```
There is coffee: false
```

will mean that "there is no coffee". I use the "... is ...: false" construct to mean "is not" or "is false".

Logical expressions are used extensively in *conditional statements, loops, function parameters*, etc. It is essential to understand how they work. Luckily, logical expressions are easy to explain and use.

The logical operators that are used in logical expressions are the following:

- The == operator answers the question "is equal to?". It compares the expression on its left side to the one on its right side and produces true if they are equal and false if they are not. By definition, the value that == produces is a logical expression.

  As an example, let's assume that we have the following two variables:

  ```
  int daysInWeek = 7;
  int monthsInYear = 12;
  ```

  The following are two logical expressions that use those values:

  ```
  daysInWeek == 7          // true
  monthsInYear == 11       // false
  ```

- The != operator answers the question "is not equal to?". It compares the two expressions on its sides and produces the opposite of ==.

  ```
  daysInWeek != 7          // false
  monthsInYear != 11       // true
  ```

- The || operator means "or", and produces true if any one of the logical expressions is true.

  If the value of the left-hand expression is true, it produces true without even looking at the expression that is on the right-hand side. If the left-hand side is false, then it produces the value of the right-hand side. This operator is similar to the "or" in English: if the left one, the right one, or both are true, then it produces true.

  The following table presents all of the possible values for both sides of this operator and its result:

Left expression	Operator	Right expression	Result
false	||	false	false
false	||	true	true
true	||	false (not evaluated)	true
true	||	true (not evaluated)	true

```d
import std.stdio;

void main() {
    // false means "no", true means "yes"

    bool existsCoffee = false;
    bool existsTea = true;

    writeln("There is warm drink: ",
            existsCoffee || existsTea);
}
```

Because at least one of the two expressions is true, the logical expression above produces true.

- The && operator means "and", and produces true if both of the expressions are true.

  If the value of the left-hand expression is false, it produces false without even looking at the expression that is on the right-hand side. If the left-hand side is true, then it produces the value of the right-hand side. This operator is similar to the "and" in English: if the left value and the right value are true, then it produces true.

Left expression	Operator	Right expression	Result
false	&&	false (not evaluated)	false
false	&&	true (not evaluated)	false
true	&&	false	false
true	&&	true	true

```
writeln("I will drink coffee: ",
        wantToDrinkCoffee && existsCoffee);
```

Note: *The fact that the || and && operators may not evaluate the right-hand expression is called their* short-circuit behavior*. The ternary operator ?:, which we will see in a later chapter, is similar in that it never evaluates one of its three expressions. All of the other operators always evaluate and use all of their expressions.*

- The ^ operator answers the question "is one or the other but not both?". This operator produces true if only one expression is true, but not both.

  Warning: In reality, this operator is not a logical operator but an arithmetic one. It behaves like a logical operator only if both of the expressions are bool.

Left expression	Operator	Right expression	Result
false	^	false	false
false	^	true	true
true	^	false	true
true	^	true	false

For example, the logic that represents my playing chess if *only one* of my two friends shows up can be coded like this:

```
writeln("I will play chess: ", jimShowedUp ^ bobShowedUp);
```

- The < operator answers the question "is less than?" (or "does come before in sort order?").

```
writeln("We beat: ", theirScore < ourScore);
```

- The > operator answers the question "is greater than?" (or "does come after in sort order?").

```
writeln("They beat: ", theirScore > ourScore);
```

- The <= operator answers the question "is less than or equal to?" (or "does come before or the same in sort order?"). This operator is the opposite of the > operator.

```
writeln("We were not beaten: ", theirScore <= ourScore);
```

- The >= operator answers the question "is greater than or equal to?" (or "does come after or the same in sort order?"). This operator is the opposite of the < operator.

```
    writeln("We did not beat: ", theirScore >= ourScore);
```

- The ! operator means "the opposite of". Different from the other logical operators, it takes just one expression and produces true if that expression is false, and false if that expression is true.

```
    writeln("I will walk: ", !existsBicycle);
```

9.2 Grouping expressions

The order in which the expressions are evaluated can be specified by using parentheses to group them. When parenthesized expressions appear in more complex expressions, the parenthesized expressions are evaluated before they can be used in the expressions that they appear in. For example, the expression "if there is coffee or tea, and also cookie or scone; then I am happy" can be coded as follows:

```
writeln("I am happy: ",
(existsCoffee || existsTea) && (existsCookie || existsScone));
```

If the sub expressions were not parenthesized, the expressions would be evaluated according to *operator precedence* rules of D (which have been inherited from the C language). Since in these rules && has a higher precedence than ||, writing the expression without parentheses would not be evaluated as intended:

```
writeln("I am happy: ",
existsCoffee || existsTea && existsCookie || existsScone);
```

The && operator would be evaluated first and the whole expression would be the semantic equivalent of the following expression:

```
writeln("I am happy: ",
existsCoffee || (existsTea && existsCookie) || existsScone);
```

That has a totally different meaning: "if there is coffee, or tea and cookie, or scone; then I am happy".

The operator precedence table will be presented later in the book (page 692).

9.3 Reading bool input

All of the bool values above are automatically printed as "false" or "true". It is the same in the opposite direction: readf() automatically converts strings "false" and "true" to bool values false and true, respectively. It accepts any combination of lower and uppercase letters as well. For example, "False" and "FALSE" are converted to false and "True" and "TRUE" are converted to true.

Note that this is the case only when reading into bool variables. Otherwise, the input would be read as-is without conversion when reading into a string variable. (As we will see later in the strings chapter (page 75), one must use readln() when reading strings.)

9.4 Exercises

1. We've seen above that the < and the > operators are used to determine whether a value is less than or greater than another value; but there is no operator that answers the question "is between?" to determine whether a value is between two other values.

Let's assume that a programmer has written the following code to determine whether value is between 10 and 20. Observe that the program cannot be compiled as written:

```
import std.stdio;

void main() {
    int value = 15;

    writeln("Is between: ",
            10 < value < 20);          // ← compilation ERROR
}
```

Try using parentheses around the whole expression:

```
    writeln("Is between: ",
            (10 < value < 20));        // ← compilation ERROR
```

Observe that it still cannot be compiled.

2. While searching for a solution to this problem, the same programmer discovers that the following use of parentheses now enables the code to be compiled:

```
    writeln("Is between: ",
            (10 < value) < 20);        // ← compiles but WRONG
```

Observe that the program now works as expected and prints "true". Unfortunately, that output is misleading because the program has a bug. To see the effect of that bug, replace 15 with a value greater than 20:

```
    int value = 21;
```

Observe that the program still prints "true" even though 21 is not less than 20.

Hint: Remember that the type of a logical expression is bool. It shouldn't make sense whether a bool value is less than 20. The reason it compiles is due to the compiler converting the boolean expression to a 1 or 0, and then evaluating that against 20 to see if it is less.

3. The logical expression that answers the question "is between?" must instead be coded like this: "is greater than the lower value and less than the upper value?".

    Change the expression in the program according to that logic and observe that it now prints "true" as expected. Additionally, test that the logical expression works correctly for other values as well: for example, when value is 50 or 1, the program should print "false"; and when it is 12, the program should print "true".

4. Let's assume that we can go to the beach when one of the following conditions is true:

    ◦ If the distance to the beach is less than 10 miles and there is a bicycle for everyone

    ◦ If there is fewer than 6 of us, and we have a car, and at least one of us has a driver license

    As written, the following program always prints "true". Construct a logical expression that will print "true" when one of the conditions above is true. (When trying the program, enter "false" or "true" for questions that start with "Is there a".).

```
import std.stdio;

void main() {
    write("How many are we? ");
    int personCount;
    readf(" %s", &personCount);

    write("How many bicycles are there? ");
    int bicycleCount;
    readf(" %s", &bicycleCount);

    write("What is the distance to the beach? ");
    int distance;
    readf(" %s", &distance);

    write("Is there a car? ");
    bool existsCar;
    readf(" %s", &existsCar);

    write("Is there a driver license? ");
    bool existsLicense;
    readf(" %s", &existsLicense);

    /* Replace the 'true' below with a logical expression that
     * produces the value 'true' when one of the conditions
     * listed in the question is satisfied: */
    writeln("We are going to the beach: ", true);
}
```

Enter various values and test that the logical expression that you wrote works correctly.

The solutions are on page 696.

10 `if` Statement

We've learned that the actual work in a program is performed by expressions. All of the expressions of all of the programs that we've seen so far have started with the `main()` function and were executed until the end of `main`.

Statements, on the other hand, are features that affect the execution of expressions. Statements don't produce values and don't have side effects themselves. They determine whether and in what order the expressions are executed. Statements sometimes use logical expressions when making such decisions.

Note: *Other programming languages may have different definitions for expression and statement, while some others may not have a distinction at all.*

10.1 The `if` block and its scope

The `if` statement determines whether one or more expressions would be executed. It makes this decision by evaluating a logical expression. It has the same meaning as the English word "if", as in the phrase "if there is coffee then I will drink coffee".

`if` takes a logical expression in parentheses. If the value of that logical expression is `true`, then it executes the expressions that are within the following curly brackets. Conversely, if the logical expression is `false`, it does not execute the expressions within the curly brackets.

The area within the curly brackets is called a *scope* and all of the code that is in that scope is called a *block of code*.

Here is the syntax of the `if` statement:

```
if (a_logical_expression) {
    // ... expression(s) to execute if true
}
```

For example, the program construct that represents "if there is coffee then drink coffee and wash the cup" can be written as in the following program:

```
import std.stdio;

void main() {
    bool existsCoffee = true;

    if (existsCoffee) {
        writeln("Drink coffee");
        writeln("Wash the cup");
    }
}
```

If the value of `existsCoffee` is `false`, then the expressions that are within the block would be skipped and the program would not print anything.

10.2 The `else` block and its scope

Sometimes there are operations to execute for when the logical expression of the `if` statement is `false`. For example, there is always an operation to execute in a decision like "if there is coffee I will drink coffee, else I will drink tea".

The operations to execute in the `false` case are placed in a scope after the `else` keyword:

```
if (a_logical_expression) {
    // ... expression(s) to execute if true
```

```
    } else {
        // ... expression(s) to execute if false
    }
```

For example, under the assumption that there is always tea:

```
    if (existsCoffee) {
        writeln("Drink coffee");

    } else {
        writeln("Drink tea");
    }
```

In that example, either the first or the second string would be printed depending on the value of existsCoffee.

else itself is not a statement but an optional *clause* of the if statement; it cannot be used alone.

Note the placement of curly brackets of the if and else blocks above. Although it is official D style[1] to place curly brackets on separate lines, this book uses a common style of inline curly brackets throughout.

10.3 Always use the scope curly brackets

It is not recommended but is actually possible to omit the curly brackets if there is only one statement within a scope. As both the if and the else scopes have just one statement above, that code can also be written as the following:

```
    if (existsCoffee)
        writeln("Drink coffee");

    else
        writeln("Drink tea");
```

Most experienced programmers use curly brackets even for single statements. (One of the exercises of this chapter is about omitting them.) Having said that, I will now show the only case where omitting the curly brackets is actually better.

10.4 The "if, else if, else" chain

One of the powers of statements and expressions is the ability to use them in more complex ways. In addition to expressions, scopes can contain other statements. For example, an else scope can contain an if statement. Connecting statements and expressions in different ways allows us to make programs behave intelligently according to their purposes.

The following is a more complex example written under the agreement that riding to a good coffee shop is preferred over walking to a bad one:

```
    if (existsCoffee) {
        writeln("Drink coffee at home");

    } else {

        if (existsBicycle) {
            writeln("Ride to the good place");

        } else {
            writeln("Walk to the bad place");
        }
    }
```

---

1. http://dlang.org/dstyle.html

The code above represents the sentences "If there is coffee, drink at home. Else, if there is a bicycle, ride to the good place. Otherwise, walk to the bad place."

Let's complicate this decision process further: instead of having to walk to the bad place, let's first try the neighbor:

```
if (existsCoffee) {
    writeln("Drink coffee at home");

} else {

    if (existsBicycle) {
        writeln("Ride to the good place");

    } else {

        if (neighborIsHome) {
            writeln("Have coffee at neighbor's");

        } else {
            writeln("Walk to the bad place");
        }
    }
}
```

Such decisions like "if this case, else if that other case, else if that even other case, etc." are common in programs. Unfortunately, when the guideline of always using curly brackets is followed obstinately, the code ends up having too much horizontal and vertical space: ignoring the empty lines, the 3 if statements and the 4 writeln expressions above occupy a total of 13 lines.

In order to write such constructs in a more compact way, when an else scope contains only one if statement, then the curly brackets of that else scope are omitted as an exception to this guideline.

I am leaving the following code untidy as an intermediate step before showing the better form of it. No code should be written in such an untidy way.

The following is what the code looks like after removing the curly brackets of the two else scopes that contain just a single if statement:

```
if (existsCoffee) {
    writeln("Drink coffee at home");

} else

    if (existsBicycle) {
        writeln("Ride to the good place");

    } else

        if (neighborIsHome) {
            writeln("Have coffee at neighbor's");

        } else {
            writeln("Walk to the bad place");
        }
```

If we now move those if statements up to the same lines as their enclosing else clauses and tidy up the code, we end up with the following more readable format:

```
if (existsCoffee) {
    writeln("Drink coffee at home");

} else if (existsBicycle) {
    writeln("Ride to the good place");

} else if (neighborIsHome) {
    writeln("Have coffee at neighbor's");
```

```
    } else {
        writeln("Walk to the bad place");
    }
```

Removing the curly brackets allows the code to be more compact and lines up all of the expressions for easier readability. The logical expressions, the order that they are evaluated, and the operations that are executed when they are true are now easier to see at a glance.

This common programming construct is called the "if, else if, else" chain.

10.5 Exercises

1. Since the logical expression below is t rue, we would expect this program to *drink lemonade and wash the cup*:

```
import std.stdio;

void main() {
    bool existsLemonade = true;

    if (existsLemonade) {
        writeln("Drinking lemonade");
        writeln("Washing the cup");

    } else
        writeln("Eating pie");
        writeln("Washing the plate");
}
```

But when you run that program you will see that it *washes the plate* as well:

```
Drinking lemonade
Washing the cup
Washing the plate
```

Why? Correct the program to wash the plate only when the logical expression is false.

2. Write a program that plays a game with the user (obviously with trust). The user throws a die and enters its value. Either the user or the program wins according to the value of the die:

```
Value of the die       Output of the program
       1                    You won
       2                    You won
       3                    You won
       4                    I won
       5                    I won
       6                    I won
 Any other value            ERROR: Invalid value
```

Bonus: Have the program also mention the value when the value is invalid. For example:

```
ERROR: 7 is invalid
```

3. Let's change the game by having the user enter a value from 1 to 1000. Now the user wins when the value is in the range 1-500 and the computer wins when the value is in the range 501-1000. Can the previous program be easily modified to work in this way?

The solutions are on page 697.

11 while Loop

The `while` loop is similar to the `if` statement and essentially works as a repeated `if` statement. Just like `if`, `while` also takes a logical expression and evaluates the block when the logical expression is `true`. The difference is that the `while` statement evaluates the logical expression and executes the expressions in the block repeatedly, as long as the logical expression is `true`, not just once. Repeating a block of code this way is called *looping*.

Here is the syntax of the `while` statement:

```
while (a_logical_expression) {
    // ... expression(s) to execute while true
}
```

For example, the code that represents *eat cookies as long as there is cookie* can be coded like this:

```
import std.stdio;

void main() {
    bool existsCookie = true;

    while (existsCookie) {
        writeln("Take cookie");
        writeln("Eat cookie");
    }
}
```

That program would continue repeating the loop because the value of `existsCookie` never changes from `true`.

`while` is useful when the value of the logical expression changes during the execution of the program. To see this, let's write a program that takes a number from the user as long as that number is zero or greater. Remember that the initial value of `int` variables is 0:

```
import std.stdio;

void main() {
    int number;

    while (number >= 0) {
        write("Please enter a number: ");
        readf(" %s", &number);

        writeln("Thank you for ", number);
    }

    writeln("Exited the loop");
}
```

The program thanks for the provided number and exits the loop only when the number is less than zero.

11.1 The continue statement

The continue statement starts the next iteration of the loop right away, instead of executing the rest of the expressions of the block.

Let's modify the program above to be a little picky: instead of thanking for any number, let's not accept 13. The following program does not thank for 13 because in that case the `continue` statement makes the program go to the beginning of the loop to evaluate the logical expression again:

```
import std.stdio;

void main() {
    int number;

    while (number >= 0) {
        write("Please enter a number: ");
        readf(" %s", &number);

        if (number == 13) {
            writeln("Sorry, not accepting that one...");
            continue;
        }

        writeln("Thank you for ", number);
    }

    writeln("Exited the loop");
}
```

We can define the behavior of that program as *take numbers as long as they are greater than or equal to 0 but skip 13*.

continue works with do-while, for, and foreach statements as well. We will see these features in later chapters.

11.2 The break statement

Sometimes it becomes obvious that there is no need to stay in the while loop any longer. break allows the program to exit the loop right away. The following program exits the loop as soon as it finds a special number:

```
import std.stdio;

void main() {
    int number;

    while (number >= 0) {
        write("Please enter a number: ");
        readf(" %s", &number);

        if (number == 42) {
            writeln("FOUND IT!");
            break;
        }

        writeln("Thank you for ", number);
    }

    writeln("Exited the loop");
}
```

We can summarize this behavior as *take numbers as long as they are greater than or equal to 0 or until a number is 42*.

break works with do-while, for, foreach, and switch statements as well. We will see these features in later chapters.

11.3 Unconditional loop

Sometimes the logical expression is intentionally made a constant true. The break statement is a common way of exiting such *unconditional loops*. (*Infinite loop* is an alternative but not completely accurate term that means unconditional loop.)

The following program prints a menu in an unconditional loop; the only way of exiting the loop is a break statement:

```
import std.stdio;

void main() {
    /* Unconditional loop, because the logical expression is always
     * true */
    while (true) {
        write("0:Exit, 1:Turkish, 2:English - Your choice? ");

        int choice;
        readf(" %s", &choice);

        if (choice == 0) {
            writeln("See you later...");
            break;    // The only exit of this loop

        } else if (choice == 1) {
            writeln("Merhaba!");

        } else if (choice == 2) {
            writeln("Hello!");

        } else {
            writeln("Sorry, I don't know that language. :/");
        }
    }
}
```

Note: Exceptions *can terminate an unconditional loop as well. We will see exceptions in a later chapter.*

11.4 Exercises

1. The following program is designed to stay in the loop as long as the input is 3, but there is a bug: it doesn't ask for any input:

```
import std.stdio;

void main() {
    int number;

    while (number == 3) {
        write("Number? ");
        readf(" %s", &number);
    }
}
```

Fix the bug. The program should stay in the loop as long as the input is 3.

2. Make the computer help Anna and Bill play a game. First, the computer should take a number from Anna in the range from 1 to 10. The program should not accept any other number; it should ask again.

   Once the program takes a valid number from Anna, it should start taking numbers from Bill until he guesses Anna's number correctly.

   Note: *The numbers that Anna enters obviously stay on the terminal and can be seen by Bill. Let's ignore this fact and write the program as an exercise of the* whi le *statement.*

   The solutions are on page 698.

12 Integers and Arithmetic Operations

We have seen that the `if` and `while` statements allow programs to make decisions by using the `bool` type in the form of logical expressions. In this chapter, we will see arithmetic operations on the *integer* types of D. These features will allow us to write much more useful programs.

Although arithmetic operations are a part of our daily lives and are actually simple, there are very important concepts that a programmer must be aware of in order to produce correct programs: the *bit length of a type*, *overflow* (wrap), and *truncation*.

Before going further, I would like to summarize the arithmetic operations in the following table as a reference:

Operator	Effect	Sample
++	increments by one	++variable
--	decrements by one	--variable
+	the result of adding two values	first + second
-	the result of subtracting 'second' from 'first'	first - second
*	the result of multiplying two values	first * second
/	the result of dividing 'first' by 'second'	first / second
%	the remainder of dividing 'first' by 'second'	first % second
^^	the result of raising 'first' to the power of 'second' (multiplying 'first' by itself 'second' times)	first ^^ second

Most of those operators have counterparts that have an = sign attached: +=, -=, *=, /=, %=, and ^^=. The difference with these operators is that they assign the result to the left-hand side:

```
variable += 10;
```

That expression adds the value of `variable` and 10 and assigns the result to `variable`. In the end, the value of `variable` would be increased by 10. It is the equivalent of the following expression:

```
variable = variable + 10;
```

I would like also to summarize two important concepts here before elaborating on them below.

Overflow: Not all values can fit in a variable of a given type. If the value is too big for the variable we say that the variable *overflows*. For example, a variable of type `ubyte` can have values only in the range of 0 to 255; so when assigned 260, the variable overflows, wraps around, and its value becomes 4. (**Note:** *Unlike some other languages like C and C++, overflow for signed types is legal in D. It has the same wrap around behavior of unsigned types.*)

Similarly, a variable cannot have a value that is less than the minimum value of its type.

Truncation: Integer types cannot have values with fractional parts. For example, the value of the `int` expression 3/2 is 1, not 1.5.

We encounter arithmetic operations daily without many surprises: if a bagel is $1, two bagels are $2; if four sandwiches are $15, one sandwich is $3.75, etc.

Unfortunately, things are not as simple with arithmetic operations in computers. If we don't understand how values are stored in a computer, we may be surprised to see that a company's debt is *reduced* to $1.7 billion when it borrows $3 billion more on top of its existing debt of $3 billion! Or when a box of ice cream serves 4 kids, an arithmetic operation may claim that 2 boxes would be sufficient for 11 kids!

Programmers must understand how integers are stored in computers.

Integer types

Integer types are the types that can have only whole values like -2, 0, 10, etc. These types cannot have fractional parts, as in 2.5. All of the integer types that we saw in the Fundamental Types chapter (page 8) are the following:

Type	Number of Bits	Initial Value
byte	8	0
ubyte	8	0
short	16	0
ushort	16	0
int	32	0
uint	32	0
long	64	0L
ulong	64	0LU

The u at the beginning of the type names stands for "unsigned" and indicates that such types cannot have values less than zero.

Although they are equal to 0; 0L and 0LU are *manifest constants* typed as long and ulong, respectively.

Number of bits of a type

In today's computer systems, the smallest unit of information is called a *bit*. At the physical level, a bit is represented by electrical signals around certain points in the circuitry of a computer. A bit can be in one of two states that correspond to different voltages in the area that defines that particular bit. These two states are arbitrarily defined to have the values 0 and 1. As a result, a bit can have one of these two values.

As there aren't many concepts that can be represented by just two states, a bit is not a very useful type. It can only be useful for concepts with two states like heads or tails or whether a light switch is on or off.

If we consider two bits together, the total amount of information that can be represented multiplies. Based on each bit having a value of 0 or 1 individually, there are a total of 4 possible states. Assuming that the left and right digits represent the first and second bit respectively, these states are 00, 01, 10, and 11. Let's add one more bit to see this effect better; three bits can be in 8 different states: 000, 001, 010, 011, 100, 101, 110, 111. As can be seen, each added bit doubles the total number of states that can be represented.

The values to which these eight states correspond are defined by conventions. The following table shows these values for the signed and unsigned representations of 3 bits:

Bit State	Unsigned Value	Signed Value
000	0	0
001	1	1
010	2	2
011	3	3

100	4	-4
101	5	-3
110	6	-2
111	7	-1

We can construct the following table by adding more bits:

Bits	Number of Distinct Values	D Type	Minimum Value	Maximum Value
1	2			
2	4			
3	8			
4	16			
5	32			
6	64			
7	128			
8	256	byte	-128	127
		ubyte	0	255
...	...			
16	65536	short	-32768	32767
		ushort	0	65535
...	...			
32	4294967296	int	-2147483648	2147483647
		uint	0	4294967295
...	...			
64	18446744073709551616	long	-9223372036854775808	9223372036854775807
		ulong	0	18446744073709551615
...	...			

I skipped many rows in the table and indicated the signed and unsigned versions of the D types that have the same number of bits on the same row (e.g. int and uint are both on the 32-bit row).

Choosing a type

D has no 3-bit type. But such a hypothetical type could only have 8 distinct values. It could only represent concepts such as the value of a die, or the week's day number.

On the other hand, although uint is a very large type, it cannot represent the concept of an ID number for each living person, as its maximum value is less than the world population of 7 billion. long and ulong would be more than enough to represent many concepts.

As a general rule, as long as there is no specific reason not to, you can use int for integer values.

Overflow

The fact that types can only hold values within a limited range may cause unexpected results. For example, although adding two uint variables with values of 3 billion each should produce 6 billion, because that sum is greater than the maximum value that a uint variable can hold (about 4 billion), this sum *overflows*. Without any warning, only the difference of 6 and 4 billion gets stored. (A little more accurately, 6 minus 4.3 billion.)

Truncation

Since integers cannot have values with fractional parts, they lose the part after the decimal point. For example, assuming that a box of ice cream serves 4 kids, although 11 kids would actually need 2.75 boxes, the fractional part of that value cannot be stored in an integer type, so the value becomes 2.

I will show limited techniques to help reduce the risk of overflow and truncation later in the chapter.

.min and .max

I will take advantage of the `.min` and `.max` properties below, which we have seen in the Fundamental Types chapter (page 8). These properties provide the minimum and maximum values that an integer type can have.

Increment: ++

This operator is used with a single variable (more generally, with a single expression) and is written before the name of that variable. It increments the value of that variable by 1:

```
import std.stdio;

void main() {
    int number = 10;
    ++number;
    writeln("New value: ", number);
}
```

```
New value: 11
```

The increment operator is the equivalent of using the *add-and-assign* operator with the value of 1:

```
    number += 1;      // same as ++number
```

If the result of the increment operation is greater than the maximum value of that type, the result *overflows* and becomes the minimum value. We can see this effect by incrementing a variable that initially has the value `int.max`:

```
import std.stdio;

void main() {
    writeln("minimum int value   : ", int.min);
    writeln("maximum int value   : ", int.max);

    int number = int.max;
    writeln("before the increment: ", number);
    ++number;
    writeln("after the increment : ", number);
}
```

The value becomes `int.min` after the increment:

```
minimum int value   : -2147483648
maximum int value   : 2147483647
before the increment: 2147483647
after the increment : -2147483648
```

This is a very important observation because the value changes from the maximum to the minimum as a result of *incrementing* and without any warning! This effect is called *overflow*. We will see similar effects with other operations.

Decrement: --

This operator is similar to the increment operator; the difference is that the value is decreased by 1:

```
    --number;    // the value decreases by 1
```

The decrement operation is the equivalent of using the *subtract-and-assign* operator with the value of 1:

```
    number -= 1;      // same as --number
```

Similar to the ++ operator, if the value is the minimum value to begin with, it becomes the maximum value. This effect is called *overflow* as well.

Addition: +

This operator is used with two expressions and adds their values:

```
import std.stdio;

void main() {
    int number_1 = 12;
    int number_2 = 100;

    writeln("Result: ", number_1 + number_2);
    writeln("With a constant expression: ", 1000 + number_2);
}
```

```
Result: 112
With a constant expression: 1100
```

If the sum of the two expressions is greater than the maximum value of that type, it overflows and becomes a value that is less than both of the expressions:

```
import std.stdio;

void main() {
    // 3 billion each
    uint number_1 = 3000000000;
    uint number_2 = 3000000000;

    writeln("maximum value of uint: ", uint.max);
    writeln("              number_1: ", number_1);
    writeln("              number_2: ", number_2);
    writeln("                   sum: ", number_1 + number_2);
    writeln("OVERFLOW! The result is not 6 billion!");
}
```

```
maximum value of uint: 4294967295
              number_1: 3000000000
              number_2: 3000000000
                   sum: 1705032704
OVERFLOW! The result is not 6 billion!
```

Subtraction: -

This operator is used with two expressions and gives the difference between the first and the second:

```
import std.stdio;

void main() {
    int number_1 = 10;
    int number_2 = 20;

    writeln(number_1 - number_2);
    writeln(number_2 - number_1);
}
```

```
-10
10
```

It is again surprising if the actual result is less than zero and is stored in an unsigned type. Let's rewrite the program using the uint type:

```
import std.stdio;

void main() {
    uint number_1 = 10;
```

```
    uint number_2 = 20;

    writeln("PROBLEM! uint cannot have negative values:");
    writeln(number_1 - number_2);
    writeln(number_2 - number_1);
}
```

```
PROBLEM! uint cannot have negative values:
4294967286
10
```

It is a good guideline to use signed types to represent concepts that may ever be subtracted. As long as there is no specific reason not to, you can choose int.

Multiplication: *

This operator multiplies the values of two expressions; the result is again subject to overflow:

```
import std.stdio;

void main() {
    uint number_1 = 6;
    uint number_2 = 7;

    writeln(number_1 * number_2);
}
```

```
42
```

Division: /

This operator divides the first expression by the second expression. Since integer types cannot have fractional values, the fractional part of the value is discarded. This effect is called *truncation*. As a result, the following program prints 3, not 3.5:

```
import std.stdio;

void main() {
    writeln(7 / 2);
}
```

```
3
```

For calculations where fractional parts matter, *floating point types* must be used instead of integers. We will see floating point types in the next chapter.

Remainder (modulus): %

This operator divides the first expression by the second expression and produces the remainder of the division:

```
import std.stdio;

void main() {
    writeln(10 % 6);
}
```

```
4
```

A common application of this operator is to determine whether a value is odd or even. Since the remainder of dividing an even number by 2 is always 0, comparing the result against 0 is sufficient to make that distinction:

```
    if ((number % 2) == 0) {
        writeln("even number");
```

```
    } else {
        writeln("odd number");
    }
```

Power: ^^

This operator raises the first expression to the power of the second expression. For example, raising 3 to the power of 4 is multiplying 3 by itself 4 times:

```
import std.stdio;

void main() {
    writeln(3 ^^ 4);
}
```

```
81
```

Arithmetic operations with assignment

All of the operators that take two expressions have *assignment* counterparts. These operators assign the result back to the expression that is on the left-hand side:

```
import std.stdio;

void main() {
    int number = 10;

    number += 20;   // same as number = number + 20; now 30
    number -= 5;    // same as number = number - 5;  now 25
    number *= 2;    // same as number = number * 2;  now 50
    number /= 3;    // same as number = number / 3;  now 16
    number %= 7;    // same as number = number % 7;  now  2
    number ^^= 6;   // same as number = number ^^ 6; now 64

    writeln(number);
}
```

```
64
```

Negation: -

This operator converts the value of the expression from negative to positive or positive to negative:

```
import std.stdio;

void main() {
    int number_1 = 1;
    int number_2 = -2;

    writeln(-number_1);
    writeln(-number_2);
}
```

```
-1
2
```

The type of the result of this operation is the same as the type of the expression. Since unsigned types cannot have negative values, the result of using this operator with unsigned types can be surprising:

```
    uint number = 1;
    writeln("negation: ", -number);
```

The type of `-number` is `uint` as well, which cannot have negative values:

```
negation: 4294967295
```

Plus sign: +

This operator has no effect and exists only for symmetry with the negation operator. Positive values stay positive and negative values stay negative:

```d
import std.stdio;

void main() {
    int number_1 = 1;
    int number_2 = -2;

    writeln(+number_1);
    writeln(+number_2);
}
```

```
1
-2
```

Post-increment: ++

Note: *Unless there is a strong reason not to, always use the regular increment operator (which is sometimes called the pre-increment operator).*

Contrary to the regular increment operator, it is written after the expression and still increments the value of the expression by 1. The difference is that the post-increment operation produces the old value of the expression. To see this difference, let's compare it with the regular increment operator:

```d
import std.stdio;

void main() {
    int incremented_regularly = 1;
    writeln(++incremented_regularly);      // prints 2
    writeln(incremented_regularly);        // prints 2

    int post_incremented = 1;

    // Gets incremented, but its old value is used:
    writeln(post_incremented++);           // prints 1
    writeln(post_incremented);             // prints 2
}
```

```
2
2
1
2
```

The `writeln(post_incremented++);` statement above is the equivalent of the following code:

```d
    int old_value = post_incremented;
    ++post_incremented;
    writeln(old_value);                    // prints 1
```

Post-decrement: --

Note: *Unless there is a strong reason not to, always use the regular decrement operator (which is sometimes called the pre-decrement operator).*

This operator behaves the same way as the post-increment operator except that it decrements.

Operator precedence

The operators we've discussed above have all been used in operations on their own with only one or two expressions. However, similar to logical expressions, it is common to combine these operators to form more complex arithmetic expressions:

```
int value = 77;
int result = (((value + 8) * 3) / (value - 1)) % 5;
```

As with logical operators, arithmetic operators also obey operator precedence rules. For example, the * operator has precedence over the + operator. For that reason, when parentheses are not used (e.g. in the value + 8 * 3 expression), the * operator is evaluated before the + operator. As a result, that expression becomes the equivalent of value + 24, which is quite different from (value + 8) * 3.

Using parentheses is useful both for ensuring correct results and for communicating the intent of the code to programmers who may work on it in the future.

The operator precedence table will be presented later in the book (page 692).

Detecting overflow

Although it uses functions (page 136) and ref parameters (page 168), which we have not covered yet, I would like to mention here that the core.checkedint module[1] contains arithmetic functions that detect overflow. Instead of operators like + and -, this module uses functions: adds and addu for signed and unsigned addition, muls and mulu for signed and unsigned multiplication, subs and subu for signed and unsigned subtraction, and negs for negation.

For example, assuming that a and b are two int variables, the following code would detect whether adding them has caused an overflow:

```
import core.checkedint;

void main() {
    // Let's cause overflow for test purposes
    int a = int.max - 1;
    int b = 2;

    // This variable will become 'true' if the addition
    // operation inside the 'adds' function overflows:
    bool hasOverflowed = false;
    int result = adds(a, b, hasOverflowed);

    if (hasOverflowed) {
        // We must not use 'result' because it has overflowed
        // ...

    } else {
        // We can use 'result'
        // ...
    }
}
```

There is also the std.experimental.checkedint[2] module that defines the Checked template but both its usage and its implementation are too advanced at this point in the book.

---

1. http://dlang.org/phobos/core_checkedint.html
2. https://dlang.org/phobos/std_experimental_checkedint.html

Preventing overflow

If the result of an operation cannot fit in the type of the result, then there is nothing that can be done. Sometimes, although the ultimate result would fit in a certain type, the intermediate calculations may overflow and cause incorrect results.

As an example, let's assume that we need to plant an apple tree per 1000 square meters of an area that is 40 by 60 kilometers. How many trees are needed?

When we solve this problem on paper, we see that the result is 40000 times 60000 divided by 1000, being equal to 2.4 million trees. Let's write a program that executes this calculation:

```d
import std.stdio;

void main() {
    int width  = 40000;
    int length = 60000;
    int areaPerTree = 1000;

    int treesNeeded = width * length / areaPerTree;

    writeln("Number of trees needed: ", treesNeeded);
}
```

```
Number of trees needed: -1894967
```

Not to mention it is not even close, the result is also less than zero! In this case, the intermediate calculation width * length overflows and the subsequent calculation of / areaPerTree produces an incorrect result.

One way of avoiding the overflow in this example is to change the order of operations:

```d
    int treesNeeded = width / areaPerTree * length ;
```

The result would now be correct:

```
Number of trees needed: 2400000
```

The reason this method works is the fact that all of the steps of the calculation now fit the int type.

Please note that this is not a complete solution because this time the intermediate value is prone to truncation, which may affect the result significantly in certain other calculations. Another solution might be to use a floating point type instead of an integer type: float, double, or real.

Preventing truncation

Changing the order of operations may be a solution to truncation as well. An interesting example of truncation can be seen by dividing and multiplying a value with the same number. We would expect the result of 10/9*9 to be 10, but it comes out as 9:

```d
import std.stdio;

void main() {
    writeln(10 / 9 * 9);
}
```

```
9
```

The result is correct when truncation is avoided by changing the order of operations:

```
    writeln(10 * 9 / 9);
```

```
10
```

This too is not a complete solution: This time the intermediate calculation could be prone to overflow. Using a floating point type may be another solution to truncation in certain calculations.

12.1 Exercises

1. Write a program that takes two integers from the user, prints the integer quotient resulting from the division of the first by the second, and also prints the remainder. For example, when 7 and 3 are entered, have the program print the following equation:

   ```
   7 = 3 * 2 + 1
   ```

2. Modify the program to print a shorter output when the remainder is 0. For example, when 10 and 5 are entered, it should not print "10 = 5 * 2 + 0" but just the following:

   ```
   10 = 5 * 2
   ```

3. Write a simple calculator that supports the four basic arithmetic operations. Have the program let the operation to be selected from a menu and apply that operation to the two values that are entered. You can ignore overflow and truncation in this program.

4. Write a program that prints the values from 1 to 10, each on a separate line, with the exception of value 7. Do not use repeated lines as in the following code:

   ```
   import std.stdio;

   void main() {
       // Do not do this!
       writeln(1);
       writeln(2);
       writeln(3);
       writeln(4);
       writeln(5);
       writeln(6);
       writeln(8);
       writeln(9);
       writeln(10);
   }
   ```

   Instead, imagine a variable whose value is incremented in a loop. You may need to take advantage of the *is not equal to* operator != here.

The solutions are on page 699.

13 Floating Point Types

In the previous chapter, we have seen that despite their ease of use, arithmetic operations on integers are prone to programming errors due to overflow and truncation. We have also seen that integers cannot have values with fractional parts, as in 1.25.

Floating point types are designed to support fractional parts. The "point" in their name comes from the *radix point*, which separates the integer part from the fractional part, and "floating" refers to a detail in how these types are implemented: the decimal point *floats* left and right as appropriate. (This detail is not important when using these types.)

We must cover important details in this chapter as well. Before doing that, I would like to give a list of some of the interesting aspects of floating point types:

- Adding 0.001 a thousand times is not the same as adding 1.
- Using the logical operators == and != with floating point types is erroneous in most cases.
- The initial value of floating point types is .nan, not 0. .nan may not be used in expressions in any meaningful way. When used in comparison operations, .nan is not less than nor greater than any value.
- The two overflow values are .infinity and negative .infinity.

Although floating point types are more useful in some cases, they have peculiarities that every programmer must know. Compared to integers, they are very good at avoiding truncation because their main purpose is to support fractional values. Like any other type, being based on a certain number of bits, they too are prone to overflow, but compared to integers, the range of values that they can support is vast. Additionally, instead of being silent in the case of overflow, they get the special values of positive and negative *infinity*.

As a reminder, the floating point types are the following:

Type	Number of Bits	Initial Value
float	32	float.nan
double	64	double.nan
real	at least 64, maybe more (e.g. 80, depending on hardware support)	real.nan

13.1 Floating point type properties

Floating point types have more properties than other types:

- .stringof is the name of the type.
- .sizeof is the length of the type in terms of bytes. (In order to determine the bit count, this value must be multiplied by 8, the number of bits in a byte.)
- .max is the short for "maximum" and is the maximum value that the type can have. There is no separate .min property for floating types; the negative of .max is the minimum value that the type can have. For example, the minimum value of double is -double.max.
- .min_normal is the smallest positive value that this type can represent with its normal precision. (Precision is explained below.) The type can represent smaller values than .min_normal but those values cannot be as precise as other values of the type and are generally slower to compute. The condition of

a floating point value being between negative .min_normal and positive .min_normal (excluding 0) is called *underflow*.

- .dig is short for "digits" and specifies the number of digits that signify the precision of the type.
- .infinity is the special value used to denote overflow.

Other properties of floating point types are used less commonly. You can see all of them at Properties for Floating Point Types at dlang.org[1].

The properties of floating point types and their relations can be shown on a number line like the following:

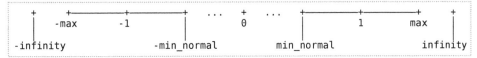

Other than the two special infinity values, the line above is to scale: the number of values that can be represented between min_normal and 1 is equal to the number of values that can be represented between 1 and max. This means that the precision of the fractional parts of the values that are between min_normal and 1 is very high. (The same is true for the negative side as well.)

13.2 .nan

We have already seen that this is the default value of floating point variables.
.nan may appear as a result of meaningless floating point expressions as well. For example, the floating point expressions in the following program all produce double.nan:

```d
import std.stdio;

void main() {
    double zero = 0;
    double infinity = double.infinity;

    writeln("any expression with nan: ", double.nan + 1);
    writeln("zero / zero          : ", zero / zero);
    writeln("zero * infinity      : ", zero * infinity);
    writeln("infinity / infinity  : ", infinity / infinity);
    writeln("infinity - infinity  : ", infinity - infinity);
}
```

.nan is not useful just because it indicates an uninitialized value. It is also useful because it is propagated through computations, making it easier and earlier to detect errors.

13.3 Specifying floating point values

Floating point values can be built from integer values without a decimal point, like 123, or created directly with a decimal point, like 123.0.

Floating point values can also be specified with the special floating point syntax, as in 1.23e+4. The e+ part in that syntax can be read as "times 10 to the power of". According to that reading, the previous value is "1.23 times 10 to the power of 4", which is the same as "1.23 times 10^4", which in turn is the same as 1.23x10000, being equal to 12300.

---

1. http://dlang.org/property.html

If the value after e is negative, as in 5.67e-3, then it is read as "divided by 10 to the power of". Accordingly, this example is "5.67 divided by 10³", which in turn is the same as 5.67/1000, being equal to 0.00567.

The floating point format is apparent in the output of the following program that prints the properties of the three floating point types:

```d
import std.stdio;

void main() {
    writeln("Type                   : ", float.stringof);
    writeln("Precision              : ", float.dig);
    writeln("Minimum normalized value: ", float.min_normal);
    writeln("Minimum value          : ", -float.max);
    writeln("Maximum value          : ", float.max);
    writeln();

    writeln("Type                   : ", double.stringof);
    writeln("Precision              : ", double.dig);
    writeln("Minimum normalized value: ", double.min_normal);
    writeln("Minimum value          : ", -double.max);
    writeln("Maximum value          : ", double.max);
    writeln();

    writeln("Type                   : ", real.stringof);
    writeln("Precision              : ", real.dig);
    writeln("Minimum normalized value: ", real.min_normal);
    writeln("Minimum value          : ", -real.max);
    writeln("Maximum value          : ", real.max);
}
```

The output of the program is the following in my environment. Since real depends on the hardware, you may get a different output:

```
Type                   : float
Precision              : 6
Minimum normalized value: 1.17549e-38
Minimum value          : -3.40282e+38
Maximum value          : 3.40282e+38

Type                   : double
Precision              : 15
Minimum normalized value: 2.22507e-308
Minimum value          : -1.79769e+308
Maximum value          : 1.79769e+308

Type                   : real
Precision              : 18
Minimum normalized value: 3.3621e-4932
Minimum value          : -1.18973e+4932
Maximum value          : 1.18973e+4932
```

Note: *Although double and real have more precision than float, writeln prints all floating point values with 6 digits of precision. (Precision is explained below.)*

Observations

As you will remember from the previous chapter, the maximum value of ulong has 20 digits: 18,446,744,073,709,551,616. That value looks small when compared to even the smallest floating point type: float can have values up to the 10^{38} range, e.g. 340,282,000,000,000,000,000,000,000,000,000,000,000. The maximum value of real is in the range 10^{4932}, a value with more than 4900 digits!

As another observation, let's look at the minimum value that double can represent with 15-digit precision:

```
0.000...(there are 300 more zeroes here)...0000222507385850720
```

13.4 Overflow is not ignored

Despite being able to take very large values, floating point types are prone to overflow as well. The floating point types are safer than integer types in this regard because overflow is not ignored. The values that overflow on the positive side become .infinity, and the values that overflow on the negative side become -.infinity. To see this, let's increase the value of .max by 10%. Since the value is already at the maximum, increasing by 10% would overflow:

```
import std.stdio;

void main() {
    real value = real.max;

    writeln("Before         : ", value);

    // Multiplying by 1.1 is the same as adding 10%
    value *= 1.1;
    writeln("Added 10%       : ", value);

    // Let's try to reduce its value by dividing in half
    value /= 2;
    writeln("Divided in half: ", value);
}
```

Once the value overflows and becomes real.infinity, it remains that way even after being divided in half:

```
Before         : 1.18973e+4932
Added 10%       : inf
Divided in half: inf
```

13.5 Precision

Precision is a concept that we come across in daily life but do not talk about much. Precision is the number of digits that is used when specifying a value. For example, when we say that the third of 100 is 33, the precision is 2 because 33 has 2 digits. When the value is specified more precisely as 33.33, then the precision is 4 digits.

The number of bits that each floating type has, not only affects its maximum value, but also its precision. The greater the number of bits, the more precise the values are.

13.6 There is no truncation in division

As we have seen in the previous chapter, integer division cannot preserve the fractional part of a result:

```
int first = 3;
int second = 2;
writeln(first / second);
```

Output:

```
1
```

Floating point types don't have this *truncation* problem; they are specifically designed for preserving the fractional parts:

```
double first = 3;
double second = 2;
writeln(first / second);
```

Output:

The accuracy of the fractional part depends on the precision of the type: real has the highest precision and float has the lowest precision.

13.7 Which type to use

Unless there is a specific reason not to, you can choose double for floating point values. float has low precision but due to being smaller than the other types it may be useful when memory is limited. On the other hand, since the precision of real is higher than double on some hardware, it would be preferable for high precision calculations.

13.8 Cannot represent all values

We cannot represent certain values in our daily lives. In the decimal system that we use daily, the digits before the decimal point represent ones, tens, hundreds, etc. and the digits after the decimal point represent tenths, hundredths, thousandths, etc.

If a value is created from a combination of these values, it can be represented exactly. For example, because the value 0.23 consists of 2 tenths and 3 hundredths it is represented exactly. On the other hand, the value 1/3 cannot be exactly represented in the decimal system because the number of digits is always insufficient, no matter how many are specified: 0.33333...

The situation is very similar with the floating point types. Because these types are based on a certain number of bits, they cannot represent every value exactly.

The difference with the binary system that the computers use is that the digits before the decimal point are ones, twos, fours, etc. and the digits after the decimal point are halves, quarters, eighths, etc. Only the values that are exact combinations of those digits can be represented exactly.

A value that cannot be represented exactly in the binary system used by computers is 0.1, as in 10 cents. Although this value can be represented exactly in the decimal system, its binary representation never ends and continuously repeats four digits: 0.0001100110011... (Note that the value is written in binary system, not decimal.) It is always inaccurate at some level depending on the precision of the floating point type that is used.

The following program demonstrates this problem. The value of a variable is being incremented by 0.001 a thousand times in a loop. Surprisingly, the result is not 1:

```
import std.stdio;

void main() {
    float result = 0;

    // Adding 0.001 for a thousand times:
    int counter = 1;
    while (counter <= 1000) {
        result += 0.001;
        ++counter;
    }

    if (result == 1) {
        writeln("As expected: 1");

    } else {
        writeln("DIFFERENT: ", result);
    }
}
```

Because 0.001 cannot be represented exactly, that inaccuracy affects the result at every iteration:

```
DIFFERENT: 0.999991
```

Note: *The variable* `counter` *above is a loop counter. Defining a variable explicitly for that purpose is not recommended. Instead, a common approach is to use a* `foreach` *loop, which we will see in a later chapter (page 121).*

13.9 Unorderedness

The same comparison operators that we have covered with integers are used with floating point types as well. However, since the special value .nan represents invalid floating point values, comparing .nan to other values is not meaningful. For example, it does not make sense to ask whether .nan or 1 is greater.

For that reason, floating point values introduce another comparison concept: unorderedness. Being unordered means that at least one of the values is .nan.

The following table lists all the floating point comparison operators. All of them are binary operators (meaning that they take two operands) and used as in left == right. The columns that contain false and true are the results of the comparison operations.

The last column indicates whether the operation is meaningful if one of the operands is .nan. For example, even though the result of the expression 1.2 < real.nan is false, that result is meaningless because one of the operands is real.nan. The result of the reverse comparison real.nan < 1.2 would produce false as well. The abreviation lhs stands for *left-hand side*, indicating the expression on the left-hand side of each operator.

Operator	Meaning	If lhs is greater	If lhs is less	If both are equal	If at least one is .nan	Meaningful with .nan
==	is equal to	false	false	true	false	yes
!=	is not equal to	true	true	false	true	yes
>	is greater than	true	false	false	false	no
>=	is greater than or equal to	true	false	true	false	no
<	is less than	false	true	false	false	no
<=	is less than or equal to	false	true	true	false	no

Although meaningful to use with .nan, the == operator always produces false when used with a .nan value. This is the case even when both values are .nan:

```
import std.stdio;

void main() {
    if (double.nan == double.nan) {
        writeln("equal");

    } else {
        writeln("not equal");
    }
}
```

Although one would expect double.nan to be equal to itself, the result of the comparison is false:

```
not equal
```

isNaN() for .nan equality comparison

As we have seen above, it is not possible to use the == operator to determine whether the value of a floating point variable is .nan:

```
    if (variable == double.nan) {     // ← WRONG
        // ...
    }
```

isNaN() function from the std.math module is for determining whether a value is .nan:

```
import std.math;
// ...
    if (isNaN(variable)) {             // ← correct
        // ...
    }
```

Similarly, to determine whether a value is *not* .nan, one must use !isNaN() because otherwise the != operator would always produce true.

13.10 Exercises

1. Instead of float, use double (or real) in the program above which added 0.001 a thousand times:

   ```
       double result = 0;
   ```

   This exercise demonstrates how misleading floating point equality comparisons can be.

2. Modify the calculator from the previous chapter to support floating point types. The new calculator should work more accurately with that change. When trying the calculator, you can enter floating point values in various formats, as in 1000, 1.23, and 1.23e4.

3. Write a program that reads 5 floating point values from the input. Make the program first print twice of each value and then one fifth of each value.

   This exercise is a preparation for the array concept of the next chapter. If you write this program with what you have seen so far, you will understand arrays more easily and will better appreciate them.

The solutions are on page 700.

We have defined five variables in one of the exercises of the last chapter, and used them in certain calculations. The definitions of those variables were the following:

```
double value_1;
double value_2;
double value_3;
double value_4;
double value_5;
```

This method of defining variables individually does not scale to cases where even more variables are needed. Imagine needing a thousand values; it is almost impossible to define a thousand variables from `value_1` to `value_1000`.

Arrays are useful in such cases: the array feature allows us to define a single variable that stores multiple values together. Although simple, arrays are the most common data structure used to store a collection of values.

This chapter covers only some of the features of arrays. More features will be introduced later in the Slices and Other Array Features chapter (page 65).

14.1 Definition

The definition of array variables is very similar to the definition of normal variables. The only difference is that the number of values associated with the variable is specified in square brackets. We can contrast the two definitions as follows:

```
int      singleValue;
int[10] arrayOfTenValues;
```

The first line above is the definition of a variable which stores a single value, just like the variables that we have defined so far. The second line is the definition of a variable which stores ten consecutive values. In other words, it stores an array of ten integer values. You can also think of it as defining ten variables of the same type, or as defining an array, for short.

Accordingly, the equivalent of the five separate variables above can be defined as an array of five values using the following syntax:

```
double[5] values;
```

That definition can be read as 5 *double values*. Note that I have chosen the name of the array variable as plural to avoid confusing it with a single-valued variable. Variables which only store a single value are called scalar variables.

In summary, the definition of an array variable consists of the type of the values, the number of values, and the name of the variable that refers to the array of values:

```
type_name[value_count] variable_name;
```

The type of the values can also be a user-defined type. (We will see user-defined types later.) For example:

```
// An array that holds the weather information of all
// cities. Here, the bool values may mean
//    false: overcast
//    true : sunny
bool[cityCount] weatherConditions;
```

```
// An array that holds the weights of a hundred boxes
double[100] boxWeights;

// Information about the students of a school
StudentInformation[studentCount] studentInformation;
```

14.2 Containers and elements

Data structures that bring elements of a certain type together are called *containers*. According to this definition, arrays are containers. For example, an array that holds the air temperatures of the days in July can bring 31 `double` values together and form *a container of elements of type double*.

The variables of a container are called *elements*. The number of elements of an array is called the *length* of the array.

14.3 Accessing the elements

In order to differentiate the variables in the exercise of the previous chapter, we appended an underscore and a number to their names as in `value_1`. This is not possible nor necessary when a single array stores all the values under a single name. Instead, the elements are accessed by specifying the *element number* within square brackets:

```
values[0]
```

That expression can be read as *the element with the number 0 of the array named values*. In other words, instead of typing `value_1` one must type `values[0]` with arrays.

There are two important points worth stressing here:

- **The numbers start with zero:** Although humans assign numbers to items starting with 1, the numbers in arrays start at 0. The values that we have numbered as 1, 2, 3, 4, and 5 before are numbered as 0, 1, 2, 3, and 4 in the array. This variation can confuse new programmers.

- **Two different uses of the [ ] characters:** Don't confuse the two separate uses of the [ ] characters. When defining arrays, the [ ] characters are written after the type of the elements and specify the number of elements. When accessing elements, the [ ] characters are written after the name of the array and specify the number of the element that is being accessed:

```
// This is a definition. It defines an array that consists
// of 12 elements. This array is used to hold the number
// of days in each month.
int[12] monthDays;

// This is an access. It accesses the element that
// corresponds to December and sets its value to 31.
monthDays[11] = 31;

// This is another access. It accesses the element that
// corresponds to January, the value of which is passed to
// writeln.
writeln("January has ", monthDays[0], " days.");
```

Reminder: The element numbers of January and December are 0 and 11 respectively; not 1 and 12.

14.4 Index

The number of an element is called its *index* and the act of accessing an element is called *indexing*.

An index need not be a constant value; the value of a variable can also be used as an index, making arrays even more useful. For example, the month can be determined by the value of the monthIndex variable below:

```
writeln("This month has ", monthDays[monthIndex], " days.");
```

When the value of monthIndex is 2, the expression above would print the value of monthDays[2], the number of days in March.

Only the index values between zero and one less than the length of the array are valid. For example, the valid indexes of a three-element array are 0, 1, and 2. Accessing an array with an invalid index causes the program to be terminated with an error.

Arrays are containers where the elements are placed side by side in the computer's memory. For example, the elements of the array holding the number of days in each month can be shown as follows (assuming a year when February has 28 days):

```
indexes →    0    1    2    3    4    5    6    7    8    9   10   11
elements →  | 31 | 28 | 31 | 30 | 31 | 30 | 31 | 31 | 30 | 31 | 30 | 31 |
```

Note: *The indexes above are for demonstration purposes only; they are not stored in the computer's memory.*

The element at index 0 has the value 31 (number of days in January); the element at index 1 has the value of 28 (number of days in February), etc.

14.5 Fixed-length arrays vs. dynamic arrays

When the length of an array is specified when the program is written, that array is a *fixed-length array*. When the length can change during the execution of the program, that array is a *dynamic array*.

Both of the arrays that we have defined above are fixed-length arrays because their element counts are specified as 5 and 12 at the time when the program is written. The lengths of those arrays cannot be changed during the execution of the program. To change their lengths, the source code must be modified and the program must be recompiled.

Defining dynamic arrays is simpler than defining fixed-length arrays because omitting the length makes a dynamic array:

```
int[] dynamicArray;
```

The length of such an array can increase or decrease during the execution of the program.

Fixed-length arrays are also known as static arrays.

14.6 Using .length to get or set the number of elements

Arrays have properties as well, of which we will see only .length here. .length returns the number of elements of the array:

```
writeln("The array has ", array.length, " elements.");
```

Additionally, the length of dynamic arrays can be changed by assigning a value to this property:

```
int[] array;          // initially empty
array.length = 5;     // now has 5 elements
```

14.7 An array example

Let's now revisit the exercise with the five values and write it again by using an array:

```
import std.stdio;

void main() {
    // This variable is used as a loop counter
    int counter;

    // The definition of a fixed-length array of five
    // elements of type double
    double[5] values;

    // Reading the values in a loop
    while (counter < values.length) {
        write("Value ", counter + 1, ": ");
        readf(" %s", &values[counter]);
        ++counter;
    }

    writeln("Twice the values:");
    counter = 0;
    while (counter < values.length) {
        writeln(values[counter] * 2);
        ++counter;
    }

    // The loop that calculates the fifths of the values would
    // be written similarly
}
```

Observations: The value of counter determines how many times the loops are repeated (iterated). Iterating the loop while its value is less than values.length ensures that the loops are executed once per element. As the value of that variable is incremented at the end of each iteration, the values[counter] expression refers to the elements of the array one by one: values[0], values[1], etc.

To see how this program is better than the previous one, imagine needing to read 20 values. The program above would require a single change: replacing 5 with 20. On the other hand, a program that did not use an array would have to have 20 variable definitions. Furthermore, since you would be unable to use a loop to iterate the 20 values, you would also have to repeat several lines 20 times, one time for each single-valued variable.

14.8 Initializing the elements

Like every variable in D, the elements of arrays are automatically initialized. The initial value of the elements depends on the type of the elements: 0 for int, double.nan for double, etc.

All of the elements of the values array above are initialized to double.nan:

```
double[5] values;      // elements are all double.nan
```

Obviously, the values of the elements can be changed later during the execution of the program. We have already seen this above when assigning to an element of an array:

```
monthDays[11] = 31;
```

That also happened when reading a value from the input:

```
        readf(" %s", &values[counter]);
```

Sometimes the desired values of the elements are known at the time when the array is defined. In such cases, the initial values of the elements can be specified on the right-hand side of the assignment operator, within square brackets. Let's see this in a program that reads the number of the month from the user, and prints the number of days in that month:

```
import std.stdio;

void main() {
    // Assuming that February has 28 days
    int[12] monthDays =
        [ 31, 28, 31, 30, 31, 30, 31, 31, 30, 31, 30, 31 ];

    write("Please enter the number of the month: ");
    int monthNumber;
    readf(" %s", &monthNumber);

    int index = monthNumber - 1;
    writeln("Month ", monthNumber, " has ",
            monthDays[index], " days.");
}
```

As you can see, the monthDays array is defined and initialized at the same time. Also note that the number of the month, which is in the range 1-12, is converted to a valid array index in the range 0-11. Any value that is entered outside of the 1-12 range would cause the program to be terminated with an error.

When initializing arrays, it is possible to use a single value on the right-hand side. In that case all of the elements of the array are initialized to that value:

```
    int[10] allOnes = 1;    // All of the elements are set to 1
```

14.9 Basic array operations
Arrays provide convenience operations that apply to all of their elements.

Copying fixed-length arrays
The assignment operator copies all of the elements from the right-hand side to the left-hand side:

```
    int[5] source = [ 10, 20, 30, 40, 50 ];
    int[5] destination;

    destination = source;
```

Note: *The meaning of the assignment operation is completely different for dynamic arrays. We will see this in a later chapter.*

Adding elements to dynamic arrays
The ~= operator adds new elements to the end of a dynamic array:

```
    int[] array;            // empty
    array ~= 7;             // array is now equal to [7]
    array ~= 360;           // array is now equal to [7, 360]
    array ~= [ 30, 40 ];    // array is now equal to [7, 360, 30, 40]
```

It is not possible to add elements to fixed-length arrays:

```
    int[10] array;
    array ~= 7;             // ← compilation ERROR
```

Removing elements from dynamic arrays

Array elements can be removed with the `remove()` function from the `std.algorithm` module. Because there may be more than one *slice* to the same elements, `remove()` cannot actually change the number of element of the array. Rather, it has to move some of the elements of the array one or more positions to the left. For that reason, the result of the remove operation must be assigned back to the same array variable.

There are two different ways of using `remove()`:

1. Providing the index of the element to remove. For example, the following code removes the element at index 1.

```
import std.stdio;
import std.algorithm;

void main() {
    int[] array = [ 10, 20, 30, 40 ];
    array = array.remove(1);            // Assigned back to array
    writeln(array);
}
```

```
[10, 30, 40]
```

2. Specifying the elements to remove with a *lambda function*, which we will cover in a later chapter (page 475). For example, the following code removes the elements of the array that are equal to 42.

```
import std.stdio;
import std.algorithm;

void main() {
    int[] array = [ 10, 42, 20, 30, 42, 40 ];
    array = array.remove!(a => a == 42);    // Assigned back to array
    writeln(array);
}
```

```
[10, 20, 30, 40]
```

Combining arrays

The ~ operator creates a new array by combining two arrays. Its ~= counterpart combines the two arrays and assigns the result back to the left-hand side array:

```
import std.stdio;

void main() {
    int[10] first = 1;
    int[10] second = 2;
    int[] result;

    result = first ~ second;
    writeln(result.length);     // prints 20

    result ~= first;
    writeln(result.length);     // prints 30
}
```

The ~= operator cannot be used when the left-hand side array is a fixed-length array:

```
    int[20] result;
    // ...
    result ~= first;            // ← compilation ERROR
```

If the array sizes are not equal, the program is terminated with an error during assignment:

```
    int[10] first = 1;
    int[10] second = 2;
    int[21] result;

    result = first ~ second;
```

```
object.Error@(0): Array lengths don't match for copy: 20 != 21
```

Sorting the elements

`std.algorithm.sort` can sort the elements of many types of collections. In the case of integers, the elements get sorted from the smallest value to the greatest value. In order to use the `sort()` function, one must import the `std.algorithm` module first. (We will see functions in a later chapter.)

```
import std.stdio;
import std.algorithm;

void main() {
    int[] array = [ 4, 3, 1, 5, 2 ];
    sort(array);
    writeln(array);
}
```

The output:

```
[1, 2, 3, 4, 5]
```

Reversing the elements

`std.algorithm.reverse` reverses the elements in place (the first element becomes the last element, etc.):

```
import std.stdio;
import std.algorithm;

void main() {
    int[] array = [ 4, 3, 1, 5, 2 ];
    reverse(array);
    writeln(array);
}
```

The output:

```
[2, 5, 1, 3, 4]
```

14.10 Exercises

1. Write a program that asks the user how many values will be entered and then reads all of them. Have the program sort the elements using `sort()` and then reverse the sorted elements using `reverse()`.

2. Write a program that reads numbers from the input, and prints the odd and even ones separately but in order. Treat the value -1 specially to determine the end of the numbers; do not process that value.

    For example, when the following numbers are entered,

```
1 4 7 2 3 8 11 -1
```

have the program print the following:

```
1 3 7 11 2 4 8
```

Hint: You may want to put the elements in separate arrays. You can determine whether a number is odd or even using the % (remainder) operator.

3. The following is a program that does not work as expected. The program is written to read five numbers from the input and to place the squares of those numbers into an array. The program then attempts to print the squares to the output. Instead, the program terminates with an error.

Fix the bugs of this program and make it work as expected:

```
import std.stdio;

void main() {
    int[5] squares;

    writeln("Please enter 5 numbers");

    int i = 0;
    while (i <= 5) {
        int number;
        write("Number ", i + 1, ": ");
        readf(" %s", &number);

        squares[i] = number * number;
        ++i;
    }

    writeln("=== The squares of the numbers ===");
    while (i <= squares.length) {
        write(squares[i], " ");
        ++i;
    }

    writeln();
}
```

The solutions are on page 701.

Characters are building blocks of strings. Any symbol of a writing system is called a character: letters of alphabets, numerals, punctuation marks, the space character, etc. Confusingly, building blocks of characters themselves are called characters as well.

Arrays of characters make up *strings*. We have seen arrays in the previous chapter; strings will be covered two chapters later.

Like any other data, characters are also represented as integer values that are made up of bits. For example, the integer value of the lowercase `'a'` is 97 and the integer value of the numeral `'1'` is 49. These values are merely a convention, assigned when the ASCII standard was designed.

In many programming languages, characters are represented by the char type, which can hold only 256 distinct values. If you are familiar with the char type from other languages, you may already know that it is not large enough to support the symbols of many writing systems. Before getting to the three distinct character types of D, let's first take a look at the history of characters in computer systems.

15.1 History

ASCII Table

The ASCII table was designed at a time when computer hardware was very limited compared to modern systems. Having been based on 7 bits, the ASCII table can have 128 distinct code values. That many distinct values are sufficient to represent the lowercase and uppercase versions of the 26 letters of the basic Latin alphabet, numerals, commonly used punctuation marks, and some terminal control characters.

As an example, the ASCII codes of the characters of the string `"hello"` are the following (the commas are inserted just to make it easier to read):

```
104, 101, 108, 108, 111
```

Every code above represents a single letter of `"hello"`. For example, there are two 108 values corresponding to the two `'l'` letters.

The codes of the ASCII table were later increased to 8 bits to become the Extended ASCII table. The Extended ASCII table has 256 distinct codes.

IBM Code Pages

IBM Corporation has defined a set of tables, each one of which assign the codes of the Extended ASCII table from 128 to 255 to one or more writing systems. These code tables allowed supporting the letters of many more alphabets. For example, the special letters of the Turkish alphabet are a part of IBM's code page 857.

Despite being much more useful than ASCII, code pages have some problems and limitations: In order to display text correctly, it must be known what code page a given text was originally written in. This is because the same code corresponds to a different character in most other tables. For example, the code that represents `'ğ'` in table 857 corresponds to `'ª'` in table 437.

In addition to the difficulty in supporting multiple alphabets in a single document, alphabets that have more than 128 non-ASCII characters cannot be supported by an IBM table at all.

ISO/IEC 8859 Code Pages

The ISO/IEC 8859 code pages are a result of international standardization efforts. They are similar to IBM's code pages in how they assign codes to characters. As an example, the special letters of the Turkish alphabet appear in code page 8859-9. These tables have the same problems and limitations as IBM's tables. For example, the Dutch digraph ij does not appear in any of these tables.

Unicode

Unicode solves all problems and limitations of previous solutions. Unicode includes more than a hundred thousand characters and symbols of the writing systems of many human languages, current and old. (New ones are constantly under review for addition to the table.) Each of these characters has a unique code. Documents that are encoded in Unicode can include all characters of separate writing systems without any confusion or limitation.

15.2 Unicode encodings

Unicode assigns a unique code for each character. Since there are more Unicode characters than an 8-bit value can hold, some characters must be represented by at least two 8-bit values. For example, the Unicode character code of 'Ğ' (286) is greater than the maximum value of a ubyte.

The way characters are represented in electronic mediums is called their *encoding*. We have seen above how the string "hello" is encoded in ASCII. We will now see three Unicode encodings that correspond to D's character types.

UTF-32: This encoding uses 32 bits (4 bytes) for every Unicode character. The UTF-32 encoding of "hello" is similar to its ASCII encoding, but every character is represented with 4 bytes:

```
0,0,0,104, 0,0,0,101, 0,0,0,108, 0,0,0,108, 0,0,0,111
```

As another example, the UTF-32 encoding of "aĞ" is the following:

```
0,0,0,97, 0,0,1,30
```

Note: *The order of the bytes of UTF-32 may be different on different computer systems.*

'a' and 'Ğ' are represented by 1 and 2 significant bytes respectively, and the values of the other 5 bytes are all zeros. These zeros can be thought of as filler bytes to make every Unicode character occupy 4 bytes each.

For documents based on the basic Latin alphabet, this encoding always uses 4 times as many bytes as the ASCII encoding. When most of the characters of a given document have ASCII equivalents, the 3 filler bytes for each of those characters make this encoding more wasteful compared to other encodings.

On the other hand, there are benefits of representing every character by an equal number of bytes. For example, the next Unicode character is always exactly four bytes away.

UTF-16: This encoding uses 16 bits (2 bytes) to represent most of the Unicode characters. Since 16 bits can have about 65 thousand unique values, the other (less commonly used) 35 thousand Unicode characters must be represented using additional bytes.

As an example, "aĞ" is encoded by 4 bytes in UTF-16:

```
0,97, 1,30
```

Note: *The order of the bytes of UTF-16 may be different on different computer systems.*

Compared to UTF-32, this encoding takes less space for most documents, but because some characters must be represented by more than 2 bytes, UTF-16 is more complicated to process.

UTF-8: This encoding uses 1 to 4 bytes for every character. If a character has an equivalent in the ASCII table, it is represented by 1 byte, with the same numeric code as in the ASCII table. The rest of the Unicode characters are represented by 2, 3, or 4 bytes. Most of the special characters of the European writing systems are among the group of characters that are represented by 2 bytes.

For most documents in western countries, UTF-8 is the encoding that takes the least amount of space. Another benefit of UTF-8 is that the documents that were produced using ASCII can be opened directly (without conversion) as UTF-8 documents. UTF-8 also does not waste any space with filler bytes, as every character is represented by significant bytes. As an example, the UTF-8 encoding of "ağ" is:

```
97, 196,158
```

15.3 The character types of D

There are three D types to represent characters. These characters correspond to the three Unicode encodings mentioned above. Copying from the Fundamental Types chapter (page 8):

Type	Definition	Initial Value
char	UTF-8 code unit	0xFF
wchar	UTF-16 code unit	0xFFFF
dchar	UTF-32 code unit and Unicode code point	0x0000FFFF

Contrary to some other programming languages, characters in D may consist of different numbers of bytes. For example, because 'ğ' must be represented by at least 2 bytes in Unicode, it doesn't fit in a variable of type char. On the other hand, because dchar consists of 4 bytes, it can hold any Unicode character.

15.4 Character literals

Literals are constant values that are written in the program as a part of the source code. In D, character literals are specified within single quotes:

```
char  letter_a = 'a';
wchar letter_e_acute = 'é';
```

Double quotes are not valid for characters because double quotes are used when specifying *strings*, which we will see in a later chapter (page 75). 'a' is a character literal and "a" is a string literal that consists of a single character.

Variables of type char can only hold letters that are in the ASCII table.

There are many ways of inserting characters in code:

- Most naturally, typing them on the keyboard.
- Copying from another program or another text. For example, you can copy and paste from a web site, or from a program that is specifically for displaying Unicode characters. (One such program in most Linux environments is *Character Map* (charmap on the terminal).)
- Using short names of the characters. The syntax for this feature is \&*character_name*;. For example, the name of the Euro sign is euro and it can be specified in the program as follows:

```
    wchar currencySymbol = '\&euro;';
```

See the list of named characters[1] for all characters that can be specified this way.

- Specifying characters by their integer Unicode values:

```
    char a = 97;
    wchar Ğ = 286;
```

- Specifying the codes of the characters of the ASCII table either by *value_in_octal* or \\x*value_in_hexadecimal* syntax:

```
    char questionMarkOctal = '\77';
    char questionMarkHexadecimal = '\x3f';
```

- Specifying the Unicode values of the characters by using the \\u*four_digit_value* syntax for wchar, and the \\U*eight_digit_value* syntax for dchar (note u versus U). The Unicode values must be specified in hexadecimal:

```
    wchar Ğ_w = '\u011e';
    dchar Ğ_d = '\U0000011e';
```

These methods can be used to specify the characters within strings as well. For example, the following two lines have the same string literals:

```
    writeln("Résumé preparation: 10.25€");
    writeln("\x52\&eacute;sum\u00e9 preparation: 10.25\&euro;");
```

15.5 Control characters

Some characters only affect the formatting of the text, they don't have a visual representation themselves. For example, the *new-line* character, which specifies that the output should continue on a new line, does not have a visual representation. Such characters are called *control characters*. Some common control characters can be specified with the *control_character* syntax.

Syntax	Name	Definition
\n	new line	Moves the printing to a new line
\r	carriage return	Moves the printing to the beginning of the current line
\t	tab	Moves the printing to the next tab stop

For example, the write() function, which does not start a new line automatically, would do so for every \n character. Every occurrence of the \n control character within the following literal represents the start of a new line:

```
    write("first line\nsecond line\nthird line\n");
```

The output:

```
first line
second line
third line
```

15.6 Single quote and backslash

The single quote character itself cannot be written within single quotes because the compiler would take the second one as the closing character of the first one:

---

1. http://dlang.org/entity.html

''' . The first two would be the opening and closing quotes, and the third one would be left alone, causing a compilation error.

Similarly, since the backslash character has a special meaning in the control character and literal syntaxes, the compiler would take it as the start of such a syntax: '\'. The compiler then would be looking for a closing single quote character, not finding one, and emitting a compilation error.

For those reasons, the single quote and the backslash characters are *escaped* by a preceding backslash character:

Syntax	Name	Definition
\'	single quote	Allows specifying the single quote character:'\''
\\	backslash	Allows specifying the backslash character: '\\' or "\\"

15.7 The std.uni module

The std.uni module includes functions that are useful for working with Unicode characters. You can see this module at its documentation[1].

The functions that start with is answer certain questions about characters. The result is false or true depending on whether the answer is no or yes, respectively. These functions are useful in logical expressions:

- isLower: is it a lowercase character?
- isUpper: is it an uppercase character?
- isAlpha: is it a Unicode alphabetic character?
- isWhite: is it a whitespace character?

The functions that start with to produce new characters from existing ones:

- toLower: produces the lowercase version of the given character
- toUpper: produces the uppercase version of the given character

Here is a program that uses all those functions:

```
import std.stdio;
import std.uni;

void main() {
    writeln("Is ğ lowercase? ", isLower('ğ'));
    writeln("Is Ş lowercase? ", isLower('Ş'));

    writeln("Is İ uppercase? ", isUpper('İ'));
    writeln("Is ç uppercase? ", isUpper('ç'));

    writeln("Is z alphabetic? ",      isAlpha('z'));
    writeln("Is \&euro; alphabetic? ", isAlpha('\&euro;'));

    writeln("Is new-line whitespace? ",   isWhite('\n'));
    writeln("Is the underscore whitespace? ", isWhite('_'));

    writeln("The lowercase of Ğ: ", toLower('Ğ'));
    writeln("The lowercase of İ: ", toLower('İ'));

    writeln("The uppercase of ş: ", toUpper('ş'));
    writeln("The uppercase of ı: ", toUpper('ı'));
}
```

The output:

---

1. http://dlang.org/phobos/std_uni.html

```
Is ğ lowercase? true
Is Ş lowercase? false
Is İ uppercase? true
Is ç uppercase? false
Is z alphabetic? true
Is € alphabetic? false
Is new-line whitespace? true
Is the underscore whitespace? false
The lowercase of Ğ: ğ
The lowercase of İ: i
The uppercase of ş: Ş
The uppercase of ı: I
```

15.8 Limited support for ı and i

The lowercase and uppercase versions of the letters 'ı' and 'i' are consistently dotted or undotted in some alphabets (e.g. the Turkish alphabet). Most other aphabets are inconsistent in this regard: the uppercase of the dotted 'i' is undotted 'I'.

Because the computer systems have started with the ASCII table, traditionally the uppercase of 'i' is 'I' and the lowercase of 'I' is 'i'. For that reason, these two letters may need special attention. The following program demonstrates this problem:

```
import std.stdio;
import std.uni;

void main() {
    writeln("The uppercase of i: ", toUpper('i'));
    writeln("The lowercase of I: ", toLower('I'));
}
```

The output is according to the basic Latin alphabet:

```
The uppercase of i: I
The lowercase of I: i
```

Characters are converted between their uppercase and lowercase versions normally by their Unicode character codes. This method is problematic for many alphabets. For example, the Azeri and Celt alphabets are subject to the same problem of producing the lowercase of 'I' as 'i'.

There are similar problems with sorting: Many letters like 'ğ' and 'á' may be sorted after 'z' even for the basic Latin alphabet.

15.9 Problems with reading characters

The flexibility and power of D's Unicode characters may cause unexpected results when reading characters from an input stream. This contradiction is due to the multiple meanings of the term *character*. Before expanding on this further, let's look at a program that exhibits this problem:

```
import std.stdio;

void main() {
    char letter;
    write("Please enter a letter: ");
    readf(" %s", &letter);
    writeln("The letter that has been read: ", letter);
}
```

If you try that program in an environment that does not use Unicode, you may see that even the non-ASCII characters are read and printed correctly.

On the other hand, if you start the same program in a Unicode environment (e.g. a Linux terminal), you may see that the character printed on the output is not the same character that has been entered. To see this, let's enter a non-ASCII character in a terminal that uses the UTF-8 encoding (like most Linux terminals):

```
Please enter a letter: ğ
The letter that has been read:    ← no letter on the output
```

The reason for this problem is that the non-ASCII characters like 'ğ' are represented by two codes, and reading a char from the input reads only the first one of those codes. Since that single char is not sufficient to represent the whole Unicode character, the program does not have a complete character to display.

To show that the UTF-8 codes that make up a character are indeed read one char at a time, let's read two char variables and print them one after the other:

```d
import std.stdio;

void main() {
    char firstCode;
    char secondCode;

    write("Please enter a letter: ");
    readf(" %s", &firstCode);
    readf(" %s", &secondCode);

    writeln("The letter that has been read: ",
            firstCode, secondCode);
}
```

The program reads two char variables from the input and prints them in the same order that they are read. When those codes are sent to the terminal in that same order, they complete the UTF-8 encoding of the Unicode character on the terminal and this time the Unicode character is printed correctly:

```
Please enter a letter: ğ
The letter that has been read: ğ
```

These results are also related to the fact that the standard inputs and outputs of programs are char streams.

We will see later in the Strings chapter (page 75) that it is easier to read characters as strings, instead of dealing with UTF codes individually.

15.10 D's Unicode support

Unicode is a large and complicated standard. D supports a very useful subset of it.

A Unicode-encoded document consists of the following levels of concepts, from the lowermost to the uppermost:

- **Code unit**: The values that make up the UTF encodings are called code units. Depending on the encoding and the characters themselves, Unicode characters are made up of one or more code units. For example, in the UTF-8 encoding the letter 'a' is made up of a single code unit and the letter 'ğ' is made up of two code units.

  D's character types char, wchar, and dchar correspond to UTF-8, UTF-16, and UTF-32 code units, respectively.

- **Code point**: Every letter, numeral, symbol, etc. that the Unicode standard defines is called a code point. For example, the Unicode code values of 'a' and 'ğ' are two distinct code points.

Depending on the encoding, code points are represented by one or more code units. As mentioned above, in the UTF-8 encoding 'a' is represented by a single code unit, and 'ğ' is represented by two code units. On the other hand, both 'a' and 'ğ' are represented by a single code unit in both UTF-16 and UTF-32 encodings.

The D type that supports code points is dchar. char and wchar can only be used as code units.

- **Character**: Any symbol that the Unicode standard defines and what we call "character" or "letter" in daily talk is a character.

  This definition of character is flexible in Unicode, which brings a complication. Some characters can be formed by more than one code point. For example, the letter 'ğ' can be specified in two ways:

  - as the single code point for 'ğ'
  - as the two code points for 'g' and '˘' (combining breve)

Although they would mean the same character to a human reader, the single code point 'ğ' is different from the two consecutive code points 'g' and '˘'.

15.11 Summary

- Unicode supports all characters of all writing systems.
- char is for UTF-8 encoding; although it is not suitable to represent characters in general, it supports the ASCII table.
- wchar is for UTF-16 encoding; although it is not suitable to represent characters in general, it can support letters of multiple alphabets.
- dchar is for UTF-32 encoding; as it is 32 bits, it can also represent code points.

16 Slices and Other Array Features

We have seen in the Arrays chapter (page 49) how elements are grouped as a collection in an array. That chapter was intentionally brief, leaving most of the features of arrays to this chapter.

Before going any further, here are a few brief definitions of some of the terms that happen to be close in meaning:

- **Array:** The general concept of a group of elements that are located side by side and are accessed by indexes.
- **Fixed-length array (static array):** An array with a fixed number of elements. This type of array owns its elements.
- **Dynamic array:** An array that can gain or lose elements. This type of array provides access to elements that are owned by the D runtime environment.
- **Slice:** Another name for *dynamic array*.

When I write *slice* I will specifically mean a slice; and when I write *array*, I will mean either a slice or a fixed-length array, with no distinction.

16.1 Slices

Slices are the same feature as dynamic arrays. They are called *dynamic arrays* for being used like arrays, and are called *slices* for providing access to portions of other arrays. They allow using those portions as if they are separate arrays.

Slices are defined by the *number range* syntax that correspond to the indexes that specify the beginning and the end of the range:

```
beginning_index .. one_beyond_the_end_index
```

In the number range syntax, the beginning index is a part of the range but the end index is outside of the range:

```
/* ... */ = monthDays[0 .. 3];   // 0, 1, and 2 are included; but not 3
```

Note: *Number ranges are different from Phobos ranges. Phobos ranges are about struct and class interfaces. We will see these features in later chapters.*

As an example, we can *slice* the monthDays array to be able to use its parts as four smaller arrays:

```
int[12] monthDays =
    [ 31, 28, 31, 30, 31, 30, 31, 31, 30, 31, 30, 31 ];

int[] firstQuarter  = monthDays[0 .. 3];
int[] secondQuarter = monthDays[3 .. 6];
int[] thirdQuarter  = monthDays[6 .. 9];
int[] fourthQuarter = monthDays[9 .. 12];
```

The four variables in the code above are slices; they provide access to four parts of an already existing array. An important point worth stressing here is that those slices do not have their own elements. They merely provide access to the elements of the actual array. Modifying an element of a slice modifies the element of the actual array. To see this, let's modify the first elements of each slice and then print the actual array:

```
firstQuarter[0]  = 1;
secondQuarter[0] = 2;
thirdQuarter[0]  = 3;
```

```
    fourthQuarter[0] = 4;

    writeln(monthDays);
```

The output:

```
[1, 28, 31, 2, 31, 30, 3, 31, 30, 4, 30, 31]
```

Each slice modifies its first element, and the corresponding element of the actual array is affected.

We have seen earlier that valid array indexes are from 0 to one less than the length of the array. For example, the valid indexes of a 3-element array are 0, 1, and 2. Similarly, the end index in the slice syntax specifies one beyond the last element that the slice will be providing access to. For that reason, when the last element of an array needs to be included in a slice, the length of the array must be specified as the end index. For example, a slice of all elements of a 3-element array would be array[0..3].

An obvious limitation is that the beginning index cannot be greater than the end index:

```
    int[3] array = [ 0, 1, 2 ];
    int[] slice = array[2 .. 1];   // ← run-time ERROR
```

It is legal to have the beginning and the end indexes to be equal. In that case the slice is empty. Assuming that index is valid:

```
    int[] slice = anArray[index .. index];
    writeln("The length of the slice: ", slice.length);
```

The output:

```
The length of the slice: 0
```

16.2 Using $, instead of array.length

When indexing, $ is a shorthand for the length of the array:

```
    writeln(array[array.length - 1]);   // the last element
    writeln(array[$ - 1]);              // the same thing
```

16.3 Using .dup to copy

Short for "duplicate", the .dup property makes a new array from the copies of the elements of an existing array:

```
    double[] array = [ 1.25, 3.75 ];
    double[] theCopy = array.dup;
```

As an example, let's define an array that contains the number of days of the months of a leap year. A method is to take a copy of the non-leap-year array and then to increment the element that corresponds to February:

```
import std.stdio;

void main() {
    int[12] monthDays =
        [ 31, 28, 31, 30, 31, 30, 31, 31, 30, 31, 30, 31 ];

    int[] leapYear = monthDays.dup;

    ++leapYear[1];    // increments the days in February

    writeln("Non-leap year: ", monthDays);
```

```
        writeln("Leap year    : ", leapYear);
}
```

The output:

```
Non-leap year: [31, 28, 31, 30, 31, 30, 31, 31, 30, 31, 30, 31]
Leap year    : [31, 29, 31, 30, 31, 30, 31, 31, 30, 31, 30, 31]
```

16.4 Assignment

We have seen so far that the assignment operator *modifies* values of variables. It is the same with fixed-length arrays:

```
    int[3] a = [ 1, 1, 1 ];
    int[3] b = [ 2, 2, 2 ];

    a = b;          // the elements of 'a' become 2
    writeln(a);
```

The output:

```
[2, 2, 2]
```

The assignment operation has a completely different meaning for slices: It makes the slice start providing access to new elements:

```
    int[] odds = [ 1, 3, 5, 7, 9, 11 ];
    int[] evens = [ 2, 4, 6, 8, 10 ];

    int[] slice;    // not providing access to any elements yet

    slice = odds[2 .. $ - 2];
    writeln(slice);

    slice = evens[1 .. $ - 1];
    writeln(slice);
```

Above, slice does not provide access to any elements when it is defined. It is then used to provide access to some of the elements of odds, and later to some of the elements of evens:

```
[5, 7]
[4, 6, 8]
```

16.5 Making a slice longer may terminate sharing

Since the length of a fixed-length array cannot be changed, the concept of *termination of sharing* is only about slices.

It is possible to access the same elements by more than one slice. For example, the first two of the eight elements below are being accessed through three slices:

```
import std.stdio;

void main() {
    int[] slice = [ 1, 3, 5, 7, 9, 11, 13, 15 ];
    int[] half = slice[0 .. $ / 2];
    int[] quarter = slice[0 .. $ / 4];

    quarter[1] = 0;      // modify through one slice

    writeln(quarter);
    writeln(half);
    writeln(slice);
}
```

The effect of the modification to the second element of quarter is seen through all slices:

```
[1, 0]
[1, 0, 5, 7]
[1, 0, 5, 7, 9, 11, 13, 15]
```

When viewed this way, slices provide *shared* access to elements. This sharing opens the question of what happens when a new element is added to one of the slices. Since multiple slices can provide access to same elements, there may not be room to add elements to a slice without *stomping* on the elements of others.

D disallows element stomping and answers this question by terminating the sharing relationship if there is no room for the new element: The slice that has no room to grow leaves the sharing. When this happens, all of the existing elements of that slice are copied to a new place automatically and the slice starts providing access to these new elements.

To see this in action, let's add an element to quarter before modifying its second element:

```
quarter ~= 42;      // this slice leaves the sharing because
                    // there is no room for the new element

quarter[1] = 0;     // for that reason this modification
                    // does not affect the other slices
```

The output of the program shows that the modification to the quarter slice does not affect the others:

```
[1, 0, 42]
[1, 3, 5, 7]
[1, 3, 5, 7, 9, 11, 13, 15]
```

Explicitly increasing the length of a slice makes it leave the sharing as well:

```
++quarter.length;        // leaves the sharing
```

or

```
quarter.length += 5;     // leaves the sharing
```

On the other hand, shortening a slice does not affect sharing. Shortening the slice merely means that the slice now provides access to fewer elements:

```
int[] a = [ 1, 11, 111 ];
int[] d = a;

d = d[1 .. $];   // shortening from the beginning
d[0] = 42;       // modifying the element through the slice

writeln(a);      // printing the other slice
```

As can be seen from the output, the modification through d is seen through a; the sharing is still in effect:

```
[1, 42, 111]
```

Reducing the length in different ways does not terminate the sharing either:

```
d = d[0 .. $ - 1];       // shortening from the end
--d.length;              // same thing
d.length = d.length - 1; // same thing
```

Sharing of elements is still in effect.

Using capacity to determine whether sharing will be terminated

There are cases when slices continue sharing elements even after an element is added to one of them. This happens when the element is added to the longest slice and there is room at the end of it:

```d
import std.stdio;

void main() {
    int[] slice = [ 1, 3, 5, 7, 9, 11, 13, 15 ];
    int[] half = slice[0 .. $ / 2];
    int[] quarter = slice[0 .. $ / 4];

    slice ~= 42;        // adding to the longest slice ...
    slice[1] = 0;       // ... and then modifying an element

    writeln(quarter);
    writeln(half);
    writeln(slice);
}
```

As seen in the output, although the added element increases the length of a slice, the sharing has not been terminated, and the modification is seen through all slices:

```
[1, 0]
[1, 0, 5, 7]
[1, 0, 5, 7, 9, 11, 13, 15, 42]
```

The `capacity` property of slices determines whether the sharing will be terminated if an element is added to a particular slice. (`capacity` is actually a function but this distinction does not have any significance in this discussion.)

The value of `capacity` has the following meanings:

- When its value is 0, it means that this is not the longest original slice. In this case, adding a new element would definitely relocate the elements of the slice and the sharing would terminate.

- When its value is nonzero, it means that this is the longest original slice. In this case `capacity` denotes the total number of elements that this slice can hold without needing to be copied. The number of *new elements* that can be added can be calculated by subtracting the actual length of the slice from the capacity value. If the length of the slice equals its capacity, then the slice will be copied to a new location if one more element is added.

Accordingly, a program that needs to determine whether the sharing will terminate should use a logic similar to the following:

```d
    if (slice.capacity == 0) {
        /* Its elements would be relocated if one more element
         * is added to this slice. */

        // ...

    } else {
        /* This slice may have room for new elements before
         * needing to be relocated. Let's calculate how
         * many: */
        auto howManyNewElements = slice.capacity - slice.length;

        // ...
    }
```

An interesting corner case is when there are more than one slice to *all elements*. In such a case all slices report to have capacity:

```d
import std.stdio;

void main() {
    // Three slices to all elements
    int[] s0 = [ 1, 2, 3, 4 ];
    int[] s1 = s0;
    int[] s2 = s0;

    writeln(s0.capacity);
    writeln(s1.capacity);
    writeln(s2.capacity);
}
```

All three have capacity:

```
7
7
7
```

However, as soon as an element is added to one of the slices, the capacity of the others drop to 0:

```d
    s1 ~= 42;      // ← s1 becomes the longest

    writeln(s0.capacity);
    writeln(s1.capacity);
    writeln(s2.capacity);
```

Since the slice with the added element is now the longest, it is the only one with capacity:

```
0
7          ← now only s1 has capacity
0
```

Reserving room for elements

Both copying elements and allocating new memory to increase capacity have some cost. For that reason, appending an element can be an expensive operation. When the number of elements to append is known beforehand, it is possible to reserve capacity for the elements:

```d
import std.stdio;

void main() {
    int[] slice;

    slice.reserve(20);
    writeln(slice.capacity);

    foreach (element; 0 .. 17) {
        slice ~= element;  // ← these elements will not be moved
    }
}
```

```
31          ← Capacity for at least 20 elements
```

The elements of `slice` would be moved only after there are more than 31 elements.

16.6 Operations on all elements

This feature is for both fixed-length arrays and slices.

The [ ] characters written after the name of an array means *all elements*. This feature simplifies the program when certain operations need to be applied to all of the elements of an array.

```
import std.stdio;

void main() {
    double[3] a = [ 10, 20, 30 ];
    double[3] b = [  2,  3,  4 ];

    double[3] result = a[] + b[];

    writeln(result);
}
```

The output:

```
[12, 23, 34]
```

The addition operation in that program is applied to the corresponding elements of both of the arrays in order: First the first elements are added, then the second elements are added, etc. A natural requirement is that the lengths of the two arrays must be equal.

The operator can be one of the arithmetic operators +, -, *, /, %, and ^^; one of the binary operators ^, &, and |; as well as the unary operators - and ~ that are typed in front of an array. We will see some of these operators in later chapters.

The assignment versions of these operators can also be used: =, +=, -=, *=, /=, %=, ^^=, ^=, &=, and |=.

This feature works not only using two arrays; it can also be used with an array and a compatible expression. For example, the following operation divides all elements of an array by four:

```
    double[3] a = [ 10, 20, 30 ];
    a[] /= 4;

    writeln(a);
```

The output:

```
[2.5, 5, 7.5]
```

To assign a specific value to all elements:

```
    a[] = 42;
    writeln(a);
```

The output:

```
[42, 42, 42]
```

This feature requires great attention when used with slices. Although there is no apparent difference in element values, the following two expressions have very different meanings:

```
    slice2 = slice1;       // ← slice2 starts providing access
                           //    to the same elements that
                           //    slice1 provides access to

    slice3[] = slice1;     // ← the values of the elements of
                           //    slice3 change .
```

The assignment of slice2 makes it share the same elements as slice1. On the other hand, since slice3[] means *all elements of slice3*, the values of its elements become the same as the values of the elements of slice1. The effect of the presence or absence of the [ ] characters cannot be ignored.

We can see an example of this difference in the following program:

```
import std.stdio;

void main() {
    double[] slice1 = [ 1, 1, 1 ];
    double[] slice2 = [ 2, 2, 2 ];
    double[] slice3 = [ 3, 3, 3 ];

    slice2 = slice1;        // ← slice2 starts providing access
                            //    to the same elements that
                            //    slice1 provides access to

    slice3[] = slice1;      // ← the values of the elements of
                            //    slice3 change

    writeln("slice1 before: ", slice1);
    writeln("slice2 before: ", slice2);
    writeln("slice3 before: ", slice3);

    slice2[0] = 42;         // ← the value of an element that
                            //    it shares with slice1 changes

    slice3[0] = 43;         // ← the value of an element that
                            //    only it provides access to
                            //    changes

    writeln("slice1 after : ", slice1);
    writeln("slice2 after : ", slice2);
    writeln("slice3 after : ", slice3);
}
```

The modification through slice2 affects slice1 too:

```
slice1 before: [1, 1, 1]
slice2 before: [1, 1, 1]
slice3 before: [1, 1, 1]
slice1 after : [42, 1, 1]
slice2 after : [42, 1, 1]
slice3 after : [43, 1, 1]
```

The danger here is that the potential bug may not be noticed until after the value of a shared element is changed.

16.7 Multi-dimensional arrays

So far we have used arrays with only fundamental types like int and double. The element type can actually be any other type, including other arrays. This enables the programmer to define complex containers like *array of arrays*. Arrays of arrays are called *multi-dimensional arrays*.

The elements of all of the arrays that we have defined so far have been written in the source code from left to right. To help us understand the concept of a two-dimensional array, let's define an array from top to bottom this time:

```
    int[] array = [
                10,
                20,
                30,
                40
            ];
```

As you remember, most spaces in the source code are used to help with readability and do not change the meaning of the code. The array above could have been defined on a single line and would have the same meaning.

Let's now replace every element of that array with another array:

```
/* ... */ array = [
                    [ 10, 11, 12 ],
                    [ 20, 21, 22 ],
                    [ 30, 31, 32 ],
                    [ 40, 41, 42 ]
                  ];
```

We have replaced elements of type int with elements of type int[]. To make the code conform to the array definition syntax, we must now specify the type of the elements as int[] instead of int:

```
int[][] array = [
                  [ 10, 11, 12 ],
                  [ 20, 21, 22 ],
                  [ 30, 31, 32 ],
                  [ 40, 41, 42 ]
                ];
```

Such arrays are called *two-dimensional arrays* because they can be seen as having rows and columns.

Two-dimensional arrays are used the same way as any other array as long as we remember that each element is an array itself and is used in array operations:

```
array ~= [ 50, 51 ]; // adds a new element (i.e. a slice)
array[0] ~= 13;      // adds to the first element
```

The new state of the array:

```
[[10, 11, 12, 13], [20, 21, 22], [30, 31, 32], [40, 41, 42], [50, 51]]
```

Arrays and elements can be fixed-length as well. The following is a three-dimensional array where all dimensions are fixed-length:

```
int[2][3][4] array;  // 2 columns, 3 rows, 4 pages
```

The definition above can be seen as *four pages of three rows of two columns of integers*. As an example, such an array can be used to represent a 4-story building in an adventure game, each story consisting of 2x3=6 rooms.

For example, the number of items in the first room of the second floor can be incremented as follows:

```
// The index of the second floor is 1, and the first room
// of that floor is accessed by [0][0]
++itemCounts[1][0][0];
```

In addition to the syntax above, the new expression can also be used to create a *slice of slices*. The following example uses only two dimensions:

```
import std.stdio;

void main() {
    int[][] s = new int[][](2, 3);
    writeln(s);
}
```

The new expression above creates 2 slices containing 3 elements each and returns a slice that provides access to those slices and elements. The output:

```
[[0, 0, 0], [0, 0, 0]]
```

16.8 Summary

- Fixed-length arrays own their elements; slices provide access to elements that don't belong exclusively to them.
- Within the [] operator, $ is the equivalent of *array_name*.length.
- .dup makes a new array that consists of the copies of the elements of an existing array.
- With fixed-length arrays, the assignment operation changes the values of elements; with slices, it makes the slices start providing access to other elements.
- Slices that get longer *may* stop sharing elements and start providing access to newly copied elements. capacity determines whether this will be the case.
- The syntax array[] means *all elements of the array*; the operation that is applied to it is applied to each element individually.
- Arrays of arrays are called multi-dimensional arrays.

16.9 Exercise

Iterate over the elements of an array of doubles and halve the ones that are greater than 10. For example, given the following array:

```
double[] array = [ 1, 20, 2, 30, 7, 11 ];
```

Modify it as the following:

```
[1, 10, 2, 15, 7, 5.5]
```

Although there are many solutions of this problem, try to use only the features of slices. You can start with a slice that provides access to all elements. Then you can shorten the slice from the beginning and always use the first element.

The following expression shortens the slice from the beginning:

```
slice = slice[1 .. $];
```

The solution is on page 703.

17 Strings

We have used strings in many programs that we have seen so far. Strings are a combination of the two features that we have covered in the last three chapters: characters and arrays. In the simplest definition, strings are nothing but arrays of characters. For example, `char[]` is a type of string.

This simple definition may be misleading. As we have seen in the Characters chapter (page 57), D has three separate character types. Arrays of these character types lead to three separate string types, some of which may have surprising outcomes in some string operations.

17.1 `readln` and `strip`, instead of `readf`

There are surprises even when reading strings from the terminal.

Being character arrays, strings can contain control characters like '\n' as well. When reading strings from the input, the control character that corresponds to the Enter key that is pressed at the end of the input becomes a part of the string as well. Further, because there is no way to tell `readf()` how many characters to read, it continues to read until the end of the entire input. For these reasons, `readf()` does not work as intended when reading strings:

```
import std.stdio;

void main() {
    char[] name;

    write("What is your name? ");
    readf(" %s", &name);

    writeln("Hello ", name, "!");
}
```

The Enter key that the user presses after the name does not terminate the input. `readf()` continues to wait for more characters to add to the string:

```
What is your name? Mert
    ← The input is not terminated although Enter has been pressed
    ← (Let's assume that Enter is pressed a second time here)
```

One way of terminating the standard input stream in a terminal is pressing Ctrl-D under Unix-based systems and Ctrl-Z under Windows systems. If the user eventually terminates the input that way, we see that the new-line characters have been read as parts of the string as well:

```
Hello Mert
    ← new-line character after the name
!   ← (one more before the exclamation mark)
```

The exclamation mark appears after those characters instead of being printed right after the name.

`readln()` is more suitable when reading strings. Short for "read line", `readln()` reads until the end of the line. It is used differently because the " %s " format string and the & operator are not needed:

```
import std.stdio;

void main() {
    char[] name;

    write("What is your name? ");
    readln(name);
```

```
    writeln("Hello ", name, "!");
}
```

readln() stores the new-line character as well. This is so that the program has a way of determining whether the input consisted of a complete line or whether the end of input has been reached:

```
What is your name? Mert
Hello Mert
!    ← new-line character before the exclamation mark
```

Such control characters as well as all whitespace characters at both ends of strings can be removed by std.string.strip:

```
import std.stdio;
import std.string;

void main() {
    char[] name;

    write("What is your name? ");
    readln(name);
    name = strip(name);

    writeln("Hello ", name, "!");
}
```

The strip() expression above returns a new string that does not contain the trailing control characters. Assigning that return value back to name produces the intended output:

```
What is your name? Mert
Hello Mert!    ← no new-line character
```

readln() can be used without a parameter. In that case it *returns* the line that it has just read. Chaining the result of readln() to strip() enables a shorter and more readable syntax:

```
    string name = strip(readln());
```

I will start using that form after introducing the string type below.

17.2 formattedRead for parsing strings

Once a line is read from the input or from any other source, it is possible to parse and convert separate data that it may contain with formattedRead() from the std.format module. Its first parameter is the line that contains the data, and the rest of the parameters are used exacly like readf():

```
import std.stdio;
import std.string;
import std.format;

void main() {
    write("Please enter your name and age," ~
          " separated with a space: ");

    string line = strip(readln());

    string name;
    int age;
    formattedRead(line, " %s %s", name, age);

    writeln("Your name is ", name,
```

```
            ", and your age is ", age, '.');
}
```

```
Please enter your name and age, separated with a space: Mert 30
Your name is Mert, and your age is 30.
```

Both readf() and formattedRead() *return* the number of items that they could parse and convert successfully. That value can be compared against the expected number of data items so that the input can be validated. For example, as the formattedRead() call above expects to read *two* items (a string as name and an int as age), the following check ensures that it really is the case:

```
    uint items = formattedRead(line, " %s %s", name, age);

    if (items != 2) {
        writeln("Error: Unexpected line.");

    } else {
        writeln("Your name is ", name,
                ", and your age is ", age, '.');
    }
```

When the input cannot be converted to name and age, the program prints an error:

```
Please enter your name and age, separated with a space: Mert
Error: Unexpected line.
```

17.3 Double quotes, not single quotes

We have seen that single quotes are used to define character literals. String literals are defined with double quotes. 'a' is a character; "a" is a string that contains a single character.

17.4 string, wstring, and dstring are immutable

There are three string types that correspond to the three character types: char[], wchar[], and dchar[].

There are three *aliases* of the *immutable* versions of those types: string, wstring, and dstring. The characters of the variables that are defined by these aliases cannot be modified. For example, the characters of a wchar[] can be modified but the characters of a wstring cannot be modified. (We will see D's *immutability* concept in later chapters.)

For example, the following code that tries to capitalize the first letter of a string would cause a compilation error:

```
    string cannotBeMutated = "hello";
    cannotBeMutated[0] = 'H';          // ← compilation ERROR
```

We may think of defining the variable as a char[] instead of the string alias but that cannot be compiled either:

```
    char[] a_slice = "hello";  // ← compilation ERROR
```

This time the compilation error is due to the combination of two factors:

1. The type of string literals like "hello" is string, not char[], so they are immutable.
2. The char[] on the left-hand side is a slice, which, if the code compiled, would provide access to all of the characters of the right-hand side.

Since char[] is mutable and string is not, there is a mismatch. The compiler does not allow accessing characters of an immutable array through a mutable slice.

The solution here is to take a copy of the immutable string by using the .dup property:

```
import std.stdio;

void main() {
    char[] s = "hello".dup;
    s[0] = 'H';
    writeln(s);
}
```

The program can now be compiled and will print the modified string:

```
Hello
```

Similarly, char[] cannot be used where a string is needed. In such cases, the .idup property can be used to produce an immutable string variable from a mutable char[] variable. For example, if s is a variable of type char[], the following line will fail to compile:

```
    string result = s ~ '.';          // ←  compilation ERROR
```

When the type of s is char[], the type of the expression on the right-hand side of the assignment above is char[] as well. .idup is used for producing immutable strings from existing strings:

```
    string result = (s ~ '.').idup;   // ← now compiles
```

17.5 Potentially confusing length of strings

We have seen that some Unicode characters are represented by more than one byte. For example, the character 'é' (the latin letter 'e' combined with an acute accent) is represented by Unicode encodings using at least two bytes. This fact is reflected in the .length property of strings:

```
    writeln("résumé".length);
```

Although "résumé" contains six *letters*, the length of the string is the number of UTF-8 code units that it contains:

```
8
```

The type of the elements of string literals like "hello" is char and each char value represents a UTF-8 code unit. A problem that this may cause is when we try to replace a two-code-unit character with a single-code-unit character:

```
    char[] s = "résumé".dup;
    writeln("Before: ", s);
    s[1] = 'e';
    s[5] = 'e';
    writeln("After : ", s);
```

The two 'e' characters do not replace the two 'é' characters; they replace single code units, resulting in an invalid UTF-8 encoding:

```
Before: résumé
After : reͼsueé        ← INCORRECT
```

When dealing with letters, symbols, and other Unicode characters directly, as in the code above, the correct type to use is dchar:

```
    dchar[] s = "résumé"d.dup;
    writeln("Before: ", s);
    s[1] = 'e';
    s[5] = 'e';
    writeln("After : ", s);
```

The output:

```
Before: résumé
After : resume
```

Please note the two differences in the new code:

1. The type of the string is dchar[].
2. There is a d at the end of the literal "résumé"d, specifying its type as an array of dchars.

In any case, keep in mind that the use of dchar[] and dstring does not solve all of the problems of manipulating Unicode characters. For instance, if the user inputs the text "résumé" you and your program cannot assume that the string length will be 6 even for dchar strings. It might be greater if e.g. at least one of the 'é' characters is not encoded as a single code point but as the combination of an 'e' and a combining accute accent. To avoid dealing with this and many other Unicode issues, consider using a Unicode-aware text manipulation library in your programs.

17.6 String literals

The optional character that is specified after string literals determines the type of the elements of the string:

```
import std.stdio;

void main() {
    string s = "résumé"c;    // same as "résumé"
    wstring w = "résumé"w;
    dstring d = "résumé"d;

    writeln(s.length);
    writeln(w.length);
    writeln(d.length);
}
```

The output:

```
8
6
6
```

Because all of the Unicode characters of "résumé" can be represented by a single wchar or dchar, the last two lengths are equal to the number of characters.

17.7 String concatenation

Since they are actually arrays, all of the array operations can be applied to strings as well. ~ concatenates two strings and ~= appends to an existing string:

```
import std.stdio;
import std.string;

void main() {
```

```
    write("What is your name? ");
    string name = strip(readln());

    // Concatenate:
    string greeting = "Hello " ~ name;

    // Append:
    greeting ~= "! Welcome...";

    writeln(greeting);
}
```

The output:

```
What is your name? Can
Hello Can! Welcome...
```

17.8 Comparing strings

Note: *Unicode does not define how the characters are ordered other than their Unicode codes. For that reason, you may get results that don't match your expectations below.*

We have used comparison operators <, >=, etc. with integer and floating point values before. The same operators can be used with strings as well, but with a different meaning: strings are ordered *lexicographically*. This ordering takes each character's Unicode code to be its place in a hypothetical grand Unicode alphabet. The concepts of *less* and *greater* are replaced with *before* and *after* in this hypothetical alphabet:

```
import std.stdio;
import std.string;

void main() {
    write("      Enter a string: ");
    string s1 = strip(readln());

    write("Enter another string: ");
    string s2 = strip(readln());

    if (s1 == s2) {
        writeln("They are the same!");

    } else {
        string former;
        string latter;

        if (s1 < s2) {
            former = s1;
            latter = s2;

        } else {
            former = s2;
            latter = s1;
        }

        writeln("'", former, "' comes before '", latter, "'.");
    }
}
```

Because Unicode adopts the letters of the basic Latin alphabet from the ASCII table, the strings that contain only the letters of the ASCII table will always be ordered correctly.

17.9 Lowercase and uppercase are different

Because each character has a unique code, every letter variant is different from the others. For example, 'A' and 'a' are different letters, when directly comparing Unicode strings.

Additionally, as a consequence of their ASCII code values, all of the latin uppercase letters are sorted before all of the lowercase letters. For example, 'B' comes before 'a'. The `icmp()` function of the `std.string` module can be used when strings need to be compared regardless of lowercase and uppercase. You can see the functions of this module at its online documentation[1].

Because strings are arrays (and as a corollary, *ranges*), the functions of the `std.array`, `std.algorithm`, and `std.range` modules are very useful with strings as well.

17.10 Exercises

1. Browse the documentations of the `std.string`, `std.array`, `std.algorithm`, and `std.range` modules.

2. Write a program that makes use of the ~ operator: The user enters the first name and the last name, all in lowercase letters. Produce the full name that contains the proper capitalization of the first and last names. For example, when the strings are "ebru" and "domates" the program should print "Ebru Domates".

3. Read a line from the input and print the part between the first and last 'e' letters of the line. For example, when the line is "this line has five words" the program should print "e has five".

   You may find the `indexOf()` and `lastIndexOf()` functions useful to get the two indexes needed to produce a slice.

   As it is indicated in their documentation, the return types of `indexOf()` and `lastIndexOf()` are not `int` nor `size_t`, but `ptrdiff_t`. You may have to define variables of that exact type:

   ```
   ptrdiff_t first_e = indexOf(line, 'e');
   ```

   It is possible to define variables with the `auto` keyword, which we will see in a later chapter:

   ```
   auto first_e = indexOf(line, 'e');
   ```

The solutions are on page 704.

---

1. http://dlang.org/phobos/std_string.html

18 Redirecting the Standard Input and Output Streams

All of the programs that we have seen so far have interacted through stdin and stdout, the standard input and output streams. Input and output functions like readf and writeln operate on these streams by default.

While using these streams, we assumed that the standard input comes from the keyboard and that the standard output goes to the screen.

We will start writing programs that deal with files in later chapters. We will see that, just like the standard input and output streams, files are character streams as well; so they are used in almost the same way as stdin and stdout.

But before seeing how files are accessed from within programs, I would like to show how the standard inputs and outputs of programs can be redirected to files or piped to other programs. Existing programs can, without their source code being changed, be made to print to files instead of the screen, and read from files instead of the keyboard. Although these features are not directly related to programming languages, they are useful tools that are available in nearly all modern shells.

18.1 Redirecting the standard output to a file with operator >

When starting the program from the terminal, typing a > character and a file name at the end of the command line redirects the standard output of that program to the specified file. Everything that the program prints to its standard output will be written to that file instead.

Let's test this with a program that reads a floating point number from its input, multiplies that number by two, and prints the result to its standard output:

```
import std.stdio;

void main() {
    double number;
    readf(" %s", &number);

    writeln(number * 2);
}
```

If the name of the program is by_two, its output will be written to a file named by_two_result.txt when the program is started on the command line as in the following line:

```
./by_two > by_two_result.txt
```

For example, if we enter 1.2 at the terminal, the result 2.4 will appear in by_two_result.txt. (**Note:** *Although the program does not display a prompt like "Please enter a number", it still expects a number to be entered.*)

18.2 Redirecting the standard input from a file with operator <

Similarly to redirecting the standard output by using the > operator, the standard input can be redirected from a file by using the < operator. In this case, the program reads from the specified file instead of from the keyboard.

To test this, let's use a program that calculates one tenth of a number:

```
import std.stdio;

void main() {
    double number;
    readf(" %s", &number);
```

```
    writeln(number / 10);
}
```

Assuming that the file by_two_result.txt still exists and contains 2.4 from the previous output, and that the name of the new program is one_tenth, we can redirect the new program's standard input from that file as in the following line:

```
./one_tenth < by_two_result.txt
```

This time the program will read from by_two_result.txt and print the result to the terminal as 0.24.

18.3 Redirecting both standard streams

The operators > and < can be used at the same time:

```
./one_tenth < by_two_result.txt > one_tenth_result.txt
```

This time the standard input will be read from by_two_result.txt and the standard output will be written to one_tenth_result.txt.

18.4 Piping programs with operator |

Note that by_two_result.txt is an intermediary between the two programs; by_two writes to it and one_tenth reads from it.

The | operator pipes the standard output of the program that is on its left-hand side to the standard input of the program that is on its right-hand side without the need for an intermediary file. For example, when the two programs above are piped together as in the following line, they collectively calculate *one fifth* of the input:

```
./by_two | ./one_tenth
```

First by_two reads a number from its input. (Remember that although it does not prompt for one, it still waits for a number.) Then by_two writes the result to its standard output. This result of by_two will appear on the standard input of one_tenth, which in turn will calculate and print one tenth of that result.

18.5 Exercise

Pipe more than one program:

```
./one | ./two | ./three
```

The solution is on page 704.

19 Files

We have seen in the previous chapter that the standard input and output streams can be redirected to and from files and other programs with the >, <, and | operators on the terminal. Despite being very powerful, these tools are not suitable in every situation because in many cases programs can not complete their tasks simply by reading from their input and writing to their output.

For example, a program that deals with student records may use its standard output to display the program menu. Such a program would need to write the student records to an actual file instead of to stdout.

In this chapter, we will cover reading from and writing to files of file systems.

19.1 Fundamental concepts

Files are represented by the File *struct* of the std.stdio module. Since I haven't introduced structs yet, we will have to accept the syntax of struct construction as is for now.

Before getting to code samples we have to go through fundamental concepts about files.

The producer and the consumer

Files that are created on one platform may not be readily usable on other platforms. Merely opening a file and writing data to it may not be sufficient for that data to be available on the consumer's side. The producer and the consumer of the data must have already agreed on the format of the data that is in the file. For example, if the producer has written the id and the name of the student records in a certain order, the consumer must read the data back in the same order.

Additionally, the code samples below do not write a *byte order mark* (BOM) to the beginning of the file. This may make your files incompatible with systems that require a BOM. (The BOM specifies in what order the UTF code units of characters are arranged in a file.)

Access rights

File systems present files to programs under certain access rights. Access rights are important for both data integrity and performance.

When it comes to reading, allowing multiple programs to read from the same file can improve performance, because the programs will not have to wait for each other to perform the read operation. On the other hand, when it comes to writing, it is often beneficial to prevent concurrent accesses to a file, even when only a single program wants to write to it. By locking the file, the operating system can prevent other programs from reading partially written files, from overwriting each other's data and so on.

Opening a file

The standard input and output streams stdin and stdout are already *open* when programs start running. They are ready to be used.

On the other hand, normal files must first be opened by specifying the name of the file and the access rights that are needed. As we will see in the examples below, creating a File object is sufficient to open the file specified by its name:

```
File file = File("student_records", "r");
```

Closing a file

Any file that has been opened by a program must be closed when the program finishes using that file. In most cases the files need not be closed explicitly; they are closed automatically when File objects are terminated automatically:

```
if (aCondition) {

    // Assume a File object has been created and used here.
    // ...

} // ← The actual file would be closed automatically here
  //   when leaving this scope. No need to close explicitly.
```

In some cases a file object may need to be re-opened to access a different file or the same file with different access rights. In such cases the file must be closed and re-opened:

```
    file.close();
    file.open("student_records", "r");
```

Writing to and reading from files

Since files are character streams, input and output functions writeln, readf, etc. are used exactly the same way with them. The only difference is that the name of the File variable and a dot must be typed:

```
    writeln("hello");          // writes to the standard output
    stdout.writeln("hello"); // same as above
    file.writeln("hello");   // writes to the specified file
```

eof() to determine the end of a file

The eof() member function determines whether the end of a file has been reached while reading from a file. It returns true if the end of the file has been reached.

For example, the following loop will be active until the end of the file:

```
    while (!file.eof()) {
        // ...
    }
```

The std.file module

The std.file module[1] contains functions and types that are useful when working with contents of directories. For example, exists can be used to determine whether a file or a directory exists on the file systems:

```
import std.file;

// ...

    if (exists(fileName)) {
        // there is a file or directory under that name

    } else {
        // no file or directory under that name
    }
```

---

1. http://dlang.org/phobos/std_file.html

19.2 `std.stdio.File` struct

The `File` struct is included in the `std.stdio` module[1]. To use it you specify the name of the file you want to open and the desired access rights, or mode. It uses the same mode characters that are used by `fopen` of the C programming language:

Mode	Definition
r	**read** access the file is opened to be read from the beginning
r+	**read and write** access the file is opened to be read from and written at the beginning
w	**write** access if the file does not exist, it is created as empty if the file already exists, its contents are cleared
w+	**read and write** access if the file does not exist, it is created as empty if the file already exists, its contents are cleared
a	**append** access if the file does not exist, it is created as empty if the file already exists, its contents are preserved and it is opened to be written at the end
a+	**read and append** access if the file does not exist, it is created as empty if the file already exists, its contents are preserved and the file is opened to be read from the beginning and written at the end

A 'b' character may be added to the mode string, as in "rb". This may have an effect on platforms that support the *binary mode*, but it is ignored on all POSIX systems.

Writing to a file

The file must have been opened in one of the write modes first:

```
import std.stdio;

void main() {
    File file = File("student_records", "w");

    file.writeln("Name   : ", "Zafer");
    file.writeln("Number: ", 123);
    file.writeln("Class : ", "1A");
}
```

As you remember from the Strings chapter (page 75), the type of literals like `"student_records"` is `string`, consisting of immutable characters. For that reason, it is not possible to construct `File` objects by using mutable text to specify the file name (e.g. `char[]`). When needed, call the `.idup` property of the mutable string to get an immutable copy.

The program above creates or overwrites the contents of a file named `student_records` in the directory that it has been started under (in the program's *working directory*).

Note: *File names can contain any character that is legal for that file system. To be portable, I will use only the commonly supported ASCII characters.*

Reading from a file

To read from a file the file must first have been opened in one of the read modes:

```
import std.stdio;
import std.string;
```

---

1. http://dlang.org/phobos/std_stdio.html

```
void main() {
    File file = File("student_records", "r");

    while (!file.eof()) {
        string line = strip(file.readln());
        writeln("read line -> |", line);
    }
}
```

The program above reads all of the lines of the file named student_records and prints those lines to its standard output.

19.3 Exercise

Write a program that takes a file name from the user, opens that file, and writes all of the non-empty lines of that file to another file. The name of the new file can be based on the name of the original file. For example, if the original file is foo.txt, the new file can be foo.txt.out.

The solution is on page 704.

20 auto and typeof

20.1 auto

When defining `File` variables in the previous chapter, we have repeated the name of the type on both sides of the = operator:

```
File file = File("student_records", "w");
```

It feels redundant. It would also be cumbersome and especially error-prone if the type name were longer:

```
VeryLongTypeName var = VeryLongTypeName(/* ... */);
```

Fortunately, the type name on the left-hand side is not necessary because the compiler can infer the type of the left-hand side from the expression on the right-hand side. For the compiler to infer the type, the `auto` keyword can be used:

```
auto var = VeryLongTypeName(/* ... */);
```

`auto` can be used with any type even when the type is not spelled out on the right-hand side:

```
auto duration = 42;
auto distance = 1.2;
auto greeting = "Hello";
auto vehicle = BeautifulBicycle("blue");
```

Although "auto" is the abbreviation of *automatic*, it does not come from *automatic type inference*. It comes from *automatic storage class*, which is a concept about the life times of variables. `auto` is used when no other specifier is appropriate. For example, the following definition does not use `auto`:

```
immutable i = 42;
```

The compiler infers the type of `i` as `immutable int` above. (We will see `immutable` in a later chapter.)

20.2 typeof

`typeof` provides the type of an expression (including single variables, objects, literals, etc.) without actually evaluating that expression.

The following is an example of how `typeof` can be used to specify a type without explicitly spelling it out:

```
int value = 100;      // already defined as 'int'

typeof(value) value2; // means "type of value"
typeof(100) value3;   // means "type of literal 100"
```

The last two variable definitions above are equivalent to the following:

```
int value2;
int value3;
```

It is obvious that `typeof` is not needed in situations like above when the actual types are known. Instead, you would typically use it in more elaborate scenarios, where you want the type of your variables to be consistent with some other piece of code whose type can vary. This keyword is especially useful in templates (page 399) and mixins (page 560), both of which will be covered in later chapters.

20.3 Exercise

As we have seen above, the type of literals like 100 is `int` (as opposed to `short`, `long`, or any other type). Write a program to determine the type of floating point literals like 1.2. `typeof` and `.stringof` would be useful in this program.

The solution is on page 705.

21 Name Scope

Any name is accessible from the point where it has been defined to the point where its scope ends, as well as in all of the scopes that its scope includes. In this regard, every scope defines a *name scope*.

Names are not available beyond the end of their scope:

```
void main() {
    int outer;

    if (aCondition) {  // ← curly bracket starts a new scope
        int inner = 1;
        outer = 2;      // ← 'outer' is available here

    } // ← 'inner' is not available beyond this point

    inner = 3;  // ← compilation ERROR
                //    'inner' is not available in the outer scope
}
```

Because `inner` is defined within the scope of the `if` condition it is available only in that scope. On the other hand, `outer` is available in both the outer scope and the inner scope.

It is not legal to define the same name in an inner scope:

```
size_t length = oddNumbers.length;

if (aCondition) {
    size_t length = primeNumbers.length; // ← compilation ERROR
}
```

Scopes need not be associated with statements; they can be defined by a free pair of curly braces inside functions (and most other constructs):

```
void main() {
    // This scope is not associated with any statement:
    {
        int a;
    }

    // Another one:
    {
        int a;     // This 'a' is different from the previous one
    }
}
```

However, such unassociated scopes cannot be defined at module scope (at the top level of the source code):

```
void main() {
    // ...
}

{    // ← compilation ERROR
}
```

21.1 Defining names closest to their first use

As we have been doing in all of the programs so far, variables must be defined before their first use:

```
writeln(number);   // ← compilation ERROR
                   //    number is not known yet
int number = 42;
```

For that code to be acceptable by the compiler, number must be defined before it is used with writeln. Although there is no restriction on how many lines earlier it should be defined, it is accepted as good programming practice that variables be defined closest to where they are first used.

Let's see this in a program that prints the average of the numbers that it takes from the user. Programmers who are experienced in some other programming languages may be used to defining variables at tops of scopes:

```
    int count;                                    // ← HERE
    int[] numbers;                                // ← HERE
    double averageValue;                          // ← HERE

    write("How many numbers are there? ");

    readf(" %s", &count);

    if (count >= 1) {
        numbers.length = count;

        // ... assume the calculation is here ...

    } else {
        writeln("ERROR: You must enter at least one number!");
    }
```

Contrast the code above to the one below that defines the variables later, as each variable actually starts taking part in the program:

```
    write("How many numbers are there? ");

    int count;                                    // ← HERE
    readf(" %s", &count);

    if (count >= 1) {
        int[] numbers;                            // ← HERE
        numbers.length = count;

        double averageValue;                      // ← HERE

        // ... assume that the calculation is here ...

    } else {
        writeln("ERROR: You must enter at least one number!");
    }
```

Although defining all of the variables at the top may look better structurally, there are several benefits of defining them as late as possible:

- **Speed:** Every variable definition tends to add a small speed cost to the program. As every variable is initialized in D, defining variables at the top will result in them always being initialized, even if they are only sometimes used later, wasting resources.

- **Risk of mistakes:** Every line between the definition and use of a variable carries a higher risk of programming mistakes. As an example of this, consider a variable using the common name length. It is possible to confuse that variable with some other length and use it inadvertently before reaching the line of its first intended use. When that line is finally reached the variable may no longer have the desired value.

- **Readability:** As the number of lines in a scope increase, it becomes more likely that the definition of a variable is too far up in the source code, forcing the programmer to scroll back in order to look at its definition.

- **Code maintenance:** Source code is in constant modification and improvement: new features are added, old features are removed, bugs are fixed, etc. These changes sometimes make it necessary to extract a group of lines altogether into a new function.

  When that happens, having all of the variables defined close to the lines that use them makes it easier to move them as a coherent bunch.

  For example, in the latter code above that followed this guideline, all of the lines within the if statement can be moved to a new function in the program.

  On the other hand, when the variables are always defined at the top, if some lines ever need to be moved, the variables that are used in those lines must be identified one by one.

22 for Loop

The `for` loop serves the same purpose as the `while` loop (page 28). `for` makes it possible to put the definitions and expressions concerning the loop's iteration on the same line.

Although `for` is used much less than `foreach` in practice, it is important to understand the `for` loop first. We will see `foreach` in a later chapter (page 121).

22.1 The sections of the `while` loop

The `while` loop evaluates the loop condition and continues executing the loop as long as that condition is `true`. For example, a loop to print the numbers between 1 and 10 may check the condition *less than 11*:

```
while (number < 11)
```

Iterating the loop can be achieved by incrementing `number` at the end of the loop:

```
++number;
```

To be compilable as D code, `number` must have been defined before its first use:

```
int number = 1;
```

Finally, there is the actual work within the loop body:

```
writeln(number);
```

These four sections can be combined into the desired loop as follows:

```
int number = 1;          // ← preparation

while (number < 11) {    // ← condition check
    writeln(number);     // ← actual work
    ++number;            // ← iteration
}
```

The sections of the `while` loop are executed in the following order during the iteration of the `while` loop:

```
preparation

condition check
actual work
iteration

condition check
actual work
iteration

...
```

A `break` statement or a thrown exception can terminate the loop as well.

22.2 The sections of the `for` loop

The `for` loop brings three of these sections onto a single line. They are written within the parentheses of the `for` loop, separated by semicolons. The loop body contains only the actual work:

```
for (/* preparation */; /* condition check */; /* iteration */) {
    /* actual work */
}
```

Here is the same code written as a for loop:

```
for (int number = 1; number < 11; ++number) {
    writeln(number);
}
```

The benefits of the for loop are more obvious when the loop body has a large number of statements. The expression that increments the loop variable is visible on the for line instead of being mixed with the other statements of the loop. It is also more clear that the declared variable is used only as part of the loop, and not by any other surrounding code.

The sections of the for loop are executed in the same order as in the while loop. The break and continue statements also work exactly the same way as they do in the for loop. The only difference between while and for loops is the name scope of the loop variable. This is explained below.

Although very common, the iteration variable need not be an integer, nor it is modified only by incrementing. For example, the following loop is used to print the halves of the previous floating point values:

```
for (double value = 1; value > 0.001; value /= 2) {
    writeln(value);
}
```

It is possible to define multiple loop variables by defining them inside curly braces. For example, the following loop defines two variables of different types:

```
for ({ int i = 0; double d = 0.5; } i < 10; ++i) {
    writeln("i: ", i, ", d: ", d);
    d /= 2;
}
```

Note that the preparation section is the area within the highlighted curly brackets and that there is no semicolon between the preparation section and the condition section.

22.3 The sections may be empty
All three of the for loop sections may be left empty:

- Sometimes a special loop variable is not needed, possibly because an already-defined variable would be used.
- Sometimes the loop would be exited by a break statement, instead of by relying on the loop condition.
- Sometimes the iteration expressions depend on certain conditions that would be checked within the loop body.

When all of the sections are emtpy, the for loop means *forever*:

```
for ( ; ; ) {
    // ...
}
```

Such a loop may be designed to never end or end with a break statement.

22.4 The name scope of the loop variable
The only difference between the for and while loops is the name scope of the variable defined during loop preparation: The variable is accessible only within the for loop, not outside of it:

```
    for (int i = 0; i < 5; ++i) {
        // ...
    }

    writeln(i);    // ← compilation ERROR
                   //   i is not accessible here
```

In contrast, when using a while loop the variable is defined in the same name scope as that which contains the loop, and therefore the name is accessible even after the loop:

```
    int i = 0;

    while (i < 5) {
        // ...
        ++i;
    }

    writeln(i);    // ← 'i' is accessible here
```

We have seen the guideline of *defining names closest to their first use* in the previous chapter. Similar to the rationale for that guideline, the smaller the name scope of a variable the better. In this regard, when the loop variable is not needed outside the loop, a for loop is better than a while loop.

22.5 Exercises

1. Print the following 9x9 table by using two for loops, one inside the other:

    ```
    0,0 0,1 0,2 0,3 0,4 0,5 0,6 0,7 0,8
    1,0 1,1 1,2 1,3 1,4 1,5 1,6 1,7 1,8
    2,0 2,1 2,2 2,3 2,4 2,5 2,6 2,7 2,8
    3,0 3,1 3,2 3,3 3,4 3,5 3,6 3,7 3,8
    4,0 4,1 4,2 4,3 4,4 4,5 4,6 4,7 4,8
    5,0 5,1 5,2 5,3 5,4 5,5 5,6 5,7 5,8
    6,0 6,1 6,2 6,3 6,4 6,5 6,6 6,7 6,8
    7,0 7,1 7,2 7,3 7,4 7,5 7,6 7,7 7,8
    8,0 8,1 8,2 8,3 8,4 8,5 8,6 8,7 8,8
    ```

2. Use one or more for loops to print the * character as needed to produce geometrical patterns:

    ```
    *
    **
    ***
    ****
    *****
    ```

    ```
    *******
     *******
      *******
       *******
        *******
    ```

    etc.

The solutions are on page 705.

The ?: operator works very similarly to an if-else statement:

```
if (/* condition check */) {
    /* ... expression(s) to execute if true */

} else {
    /* ... expression(s) to execute if false */
}
```

The if statement executes either the block for the case of true or the block for the case of false. As you remember, being a statement, it does not have a value; if merely affects the execution of code blocks.

On the other hand, the ?: operator is an expression. In addition to working similarly to the if-else statement, it produces a value. The equivalent of the above code is the following:

```
/* condition */ ? /* truth expression */ : /* falsity expression */
```

Because it uses three expressions, the ?: operator is called the ternary operator.

The value that is produced by this operator is either the value of the truth expression or the value of the falsity expression. Because it is an expression, it can be used anywhere that expressions can be used.

The following examples contrast the ?: operator to the if-else statement. The ternary operator is more concise for the cases that are similar to these examples.

- **Initialization**

    To initialize a variable with 366 if it is leap year, 365 otherwise:

    ```
    int days = isLeapYear ? 366 : 365;
    ```

    With an if statement, one way to do this is to define the variable without an explicit initial value and then assign the intended value:

    ```
    int days;

    if (isLeapYear) {
        days = 366;

    } else {
        days = 365;
    }
    ```

    An alternative also using an if is to initialize the variable with the non-leap year value and then increment it if it is a leap year:

    ```
    int days = 365;

    if (isLeapYear) {
        ++days;
    }
    ```

- **Printing**

    Printing part of a message differently depending on a condition:

    ```
    writeln("The glass is half ",
            isOptimistic ? "full." : "empty.");
    ```

    With an if, the first and last parts of the message may be printed separately:

```
    write("The glass is half ");

    if (isOptimistic) {
        writeln("full.");

    } else {
        writeln("empty.");
    }
```

Alternatively, the entire message can be printed separately:

```
    if (isOptimistic) {
        writeln("The glass is half full.");

    } else {
        writeln("The glass is half empty.");
    }
```

- **Calculation**

    Increasing the score of the winner in a backgammon game 2 points or 1 point depending on whether the game has ended with gammon:

```
    score += isGammon ? 2 : 1;
```

A straightforward equivalent using an if:

```
    if (isGammon) {
        score += 2;

    } else {
        score += 1;
    }
```

An alternative also using an if is to first increment by one and then increment again if gammon:

```
    ++score;

    if (isGammon) {
        ++score;
    }
```

As can be seen from the examples above, the code is more concise and clearer with the ternary operator in certain situations.

23.1 The type of the ternary expression

The value of the ?: operator is either the value of the truth expression or the value of the falsity expression. The types of these two expressions need not be the same but they must have a *common type*.

The common type of two expressions is decided by a relatively complicated algorithm, involving type conversions (page 237) and inheritance (page 328). Additionally, depending on the expressions, the *kind* of the result is either an lvalue or an rvalue (page 181). We will see these concepts in later chapters.

For now, accept common type as a type that can represent both of the values without requiring an explicit cast. For example, the integer types int and long have a common type because they can both be represented as long. On the other hand, int and string do not have a common type because neither int nor string can automatically be converted to the other type.

Remember that a simple way of determining the type of an expression is using typeof and then printing its .stringof property:

```
    int i;
    double d;

    auto result = someCondition ? i : d;
    writeln(typeof(result).stringof);
```

Because double can represent int but not the other way around, the common type of the ternary expression above is double:

```
double
```

To see an example of two expressions that do not have a common type, let's look at composing a message that reports the number of items to be shipped. Let's print "A dozen" when the value equals 12: "A **dozen** items will be shipped." Otherwise, let's have the message include the exact number: "**3** items will be shipped."

One might think that the varying part of the message can be selected with the ?: operator:

```
    writeln(
        (count == 12) ? "A dozen" : count, // ←  compilation ERROR
        " items will be shipped.");
```

Unfortunately, the expressions do not have a common type because the type of "A dozen" is string and the type of count is int.

A solution is to first convert count to string. The function to!string from the std.conv module produces a string value from the specified parameter:

```
import std.conv;
// ...
    writeln((count == 12) ? "A dozen" : to!string(count),
            " items will be shipped.");
```

Now, as both of the selection expressions of the ?: operator are of string type, the code compiles and prints the expected message.

23.2 Exercise

Have the program read a single int value as *the net amount* where a positive value represents a gain and a negative value represents a loss.

The program should print a message that contains "gained" or "lost" depending on whether the amount is positive or negative. For example, "$100 lost" or "$70 gained". Even though it may be more suitable, do not use the if statement in this exercise.

The solution is on page 706.

24 Literals

Programs achieve their tasks by manipulating the values of variables and objects. They produce new values and new objects by using them with functions and operators.

Some values need not be produced during the execution of the program; they are instead written directly into the source code. For example, the floating point value 0.75 and the string value "Total price: " below are not calculated by the program:

```
discountedPrice = actualPrice * 0.75;
totalPrice += count * discountedPrice;
writeln("Total price: ", totalPrice);
```

Such values that are directly typed into the source code are called literals. We have used many literals in the programs that we have written so far. We will cover all of the types of literals and their syntax rules.

24.1 Integer literals

Integer literals can be written in one of four ways: the decimal system that we use in our daily lives; the hexadecimal and binary systems, which are more suitable for certain computing tasks; and the octal system, which may be needed in very rare cases.

In order to make the code more readable, it is possible to insert _ characters anywhere after the first digit of integer literals. For example, we can use it to form groups of three digits, as in 1_234_567. Another example would be if we measured some value in cents of a currency, and used it to separate the currency units from the cents, as in 199_99. These characters are optional; they are ignored by the compiler.

In the decimal system: The literals are specified by the decimal numerals in exactly the same way as we are used to in our daily lives, such as 12. When using the decimal system in D the first digit cannot be 0. Such a leading zero digit is often used in other programming languages to indicate the octal system, so this constraint helps to prevent bugs that are caused by this easily overlooked difference. This does not preclude 0 on its own: 0 is zero.

In the hexadecimal system: The literals start with 0x or 0X and include the numerals of the hexadecimal system: "0123456789abcdef" and "ABCDEF" as in 0x12ab00fe.

In the octal system: The literals are specified using the octal template from the std.conv module and include the numerals of the octal system: "01234567" as in octal!576.

In the binary system: The literals start with 0b or 0B and include the numerals of the binary system: 0 and 1 as in 0b01100011.

The types of integer literals

Just like any other value, every literal is of a certain type. The types of literals are not specified explicitly as int, double, etc. The compiler infers the type from the value and syntax of the literal itself.

Although most of the time the types of literals are not important, sometimes the types may not match the expressions that they are used in. In such cases the type must be explicitly specified.

By default, integer literals are inferred to be of type int. When the value happens to be too large to be represented by an int, the compiler uses the following logic to decide on the type of the literal:

- If the value of the literal does not fit an int and it is specified in the decimal system, then its type is long.
- If the value of the literal does not fit an int and it is specified in any other system, then the type becomes the first of the following types that can accomodate the value: uint, long, and ulong.

To see this logic in action, let's try the following program that takes advantage of typeof and stringof:

```d
import std.stdio;

void main() {
    writeln("\n--- these are written in decimal ---");

    // fits an int, so the type is int
    writeln(        2_147_483_647, "\t\t",
            typeof(2_147_483_647).stringof);

    // does not fit an int and is decimal, so the type is long
    writeln(        2_147_483_648, "\t\t",
            typeof(2_147_483_648).stringof);

    writeln("\n--- these are NOT written in decimal ---");

    // fits an int, so the type is int
    writeln(        0x7FFF_FFFF, "\t\t",
            typeof(0x7FFF_FFFF).stringof);

    // does not fit an int and is not decimal, so the type is uint
    writeln(        0x8000_0000, "\t\t",
            typeof(0x8000_0000).stringof);

    // does not fit a uint and is not decimal, so the type is long
    writeln(        0x1_0000_0000, "\t\t",
            typeof(0x1_0000_0000).stringof);

    // does not fit a long and is not decimal, so the type is ulong
    writeln(        0x8000_0000_0000_0000, "\t\t",
            typeof(0x8000_0000_0000_0000).stringof);
}
```

The output:

```
--- these are written in decimal ---
2147483647              int
2147483648              long

--- these are NOT written in decimal ---
2147483647              int
2147483648              uint
4294967296              long
9223372036854775808             ulong
```

The L suffix
Regardless of the magnitude of the value, if it ends with L as in 10L, the type is long.

The U suffix
If the literal ends with U as in 10U, then its type is an unsigned type. Lowercase u can also be used.

The L and U specifiers can be used together in any order. For example, 7UL and 8LU are both of type ulong.

24.2 Floating point literals

The floating point literals can be specified in either the decimal system, as in 1.234, or in the hexadecimal system, as in 0x9a.bc.

In the decimal system: An exponent may be appended after the character e or E, meaning "times 10 to the power of". For example, 3.4e5 means "3.4 times 10 to the power of 5", or 340000.

The - character typed before the value of the exponent changes the meaning to be "divided by 10 to the power of". For example, 7.8e-3 means "7.8 divided by 10 to the power of 3". A + character may also be specified before the value of the exponent, but it has no effect. For example, 5.6e2 and 5.6e+2 are the same.

In the hexadecimal system: The value starts with either 0x or 0X and the parts before and after the point are specified in the numerals of the hexadecimal system. Since e and E are valid numerals in this system, the exponent is specified by p or P.

Another difference is that the exponent does not mean "10 to the power of", but instead "2 to the power of". For example, the P4 part in 0xabc.defP4 means "2 to the power of 4".

Floating point literals almost always have a point but it may be omitted if an exponent is specified. For example, 2e3 is a floating point literal with the value 2000.

The value before the point may be omitted if zero. For example, .25 is a literal having the value "quarter".

The optional _ characters may be used with floating point literals as well, as in 1_000.5.

The types of floating point literals

Unless explicitly specified, the type of a floating point literal is double. The f and F specifiers mean float, and the L specifier means real. For example; 1.2 is double, 3.4f is float, and 5.6L is real.

24.3 Character literals

Character literals are specified within single quotes as in 'a', '\n', '\x21', etc.

As the character itself: The character may be typed directly by the keyboard or copied from a separate text: 'a', 'ş', etc.

As the character specifier: The character literal may be specified by a backslash character followed by a special character. For example, the backslash character itself can be specified by '\\'. The following character specifiers are accepted:

Syntax	Definition
\'	single quote
\"	double quote
\?	question mark
\\	backslash
\a	alert (bell sound on some terminals)
\b	delete character
\f	new page
\n	new-line
\r	carriage return
\t	tab
\v	vertical tab

As the extended ASCII character code: Character literals can also be specified by their codes. The codes can be specified either in the hexadecimal system or in the octal system. When using the hexadecimal system, the literal must start with \x and must use two digits for the code, and when using the octal system the literal must start with \ and have up to three digits. For example, the literals '\x21' and '\41' are both the exclamation point.

As the Unicode character code: When the literal is specified with u followed by 4 hexadecimal digits, then its type is wchar. When it is specified with U followed by 8 hexadecimal digits, then its type is dchar. For example, '\u011e' and '\U0000011e' are both the Ğ character, having the type wchar and dchar, respectively.

As named character entity: Characters that have entity names can be specified by that name using the HTML character entity syntax '\&*name*;'. D supports all character entities from HTML 5[1]. For example, '\€' is €, '\♥' is ♥, and '\©' is ©.

24.4 String literals

String literals are a combination of character literals and can be specified in a variety of ways.

Double-quoted string literals

The most common way of specifying string literals is by typing their characters within double quotes as in "hello". Individual characters of string literals follow the rules of character literals. For example, the literal "A4 ka\u011fıt: 3\½TL" is the same as "A4 kağıt: 3½TL".

Wysiwyg string literals

When string literals are specified using back-quotes, the individual characters of the string do not obey the special syntax rules of character literals. For example, the literal `c:\nurten` can be a directory name on the Windows operating system. If it were written using double quotes, the '\n' part would mean the *new-line* character:

```
    writeln(`c:\nurten`);
    writeln("c:\nurten");
```

```
c:\nurten   ← wysiwyg (what you see is what you get)
c:          ← the character literal is taken as new-line
urten
```

Wysiwyg string literals can alternatively be specified using double quotes but prepended with the r character: r"c:\nurten" is also a wysiwyg string literal.

Delimited string literals

The string literal may contain delimiters that are typed right inside the double quotes. These delimiters are not considered to be parts of the value of the literal. Delimited string literals start with a q before the opening double quote. For example, the value of q".hello." is "hello"; the dots are not parts of the value. As long as it ends with a new-line, the delimiter can have more than one character:

```
writeln(q"MY_DELIMITER
first line
second line
MY_DELIMITER");
```

---

1. http://dlang.org/entity.html

MY_DELIMITER is not a part of the value:

```
first line
second line
```

Such a multi-line string literal including all the indentation is called a *heredoc*.

Token string literals

String literals that start with q and that use { and } as delimiters can contain only legal D source code:

```
    auto str = q{int number = 42; ++number;};
    writeln(str);
```

The output:

```
int number = 42; ++number;
```

This feature is particularly useful to help text editors display the contents of the string as syntax highlighted D code.

Types of string literals

By default the type of a string literal is immutable(char)[]. An appended c, w, or d character specifies the type of the string explicitly as immutable(char)[], immutable(wchar)[], or immutable(dchar)[], respectively. For example, the characters of "hello"d are of type immutable(dchar).

We have seen in the Strings chapter (page 75) that these three string types are aliased as string, wstring, and dstring, respectively.

24.5 Literals are calculated at compile time

It is possible to specify literals as expressions. For example, instead of writing the total number of seconds in January as 2678400 or 2_678_400, it is possible to specify it by the terms that make up that value, namely 60 * 60 * 24 * 31. The multiplication operations in that expression do not affect the run-time speed of the program; the program is compiled as if 2678400 were written instead.

The same applies to string literals. For example, the concatenation operation in "hello " ~ "world" is executed at compile time, not at run time. The program is compiled as if the code contained the single string literal "hello world".

24.6 Exercises

1. The following line causes a compilation error:

   ```
       int amount = 10_000_000_000;    // ← compilation ERROR
   ```

   Change the program so that the line can be compiled and that amount equals ten billions.

2. Write a program that increases the value of a variable and prints it continuously. Make the value always be printed on the same line, overwriting the previous value:

   ```
   Number: 25774   ← always on the same line
   ```

   A special character literal other than '\n' may be useful here.

The solutions are on page 706.

25 Formatted Output

This chapter is about features of the `std.format` module, not about the core features of the D language.

Like all modules that have the prefix `std`, `std.format` is a module inside Phobos, the standard library of D. There is not enough space to fully explore Phobos in this book.

D's input and output format specifiers are similar to the ones in the C language.

Before going further, I would like to summarize the format specifiers and flags, for your reference:

```
Flags (can be used together)
     -        flush left
     +        print the sign
     #        print in the alternative way
     0        print zero-filled
  space       print space-filled

Format Specifiers
     s         default
     b         binary
     d         decimal
     o         octal
   x,X         hexadecimal
   f,F         floating point in the standard decimal notation
   e,E         floating point in scientific notation
   a,A         floating point in hexadecimal notation
   g,G         as e or f

     ,         digit separators

     (         element format start
     )         element format end
     |         element delimiter
```

We have been using functions like `writeln` with multiple parameters as necessary to print the desired output. The parameters would be converted to their string representations and then sent to the output.

Sometimes this is not sufficient. The output may have to be in a very specific format. Let's look at the following code that is used to print items of an invoice:

```
items ~= 1.23;
items ~= 45.6;

for (int i = 0; i != items.length; ++i) {
    writeln("Item ", i + 1, ": ", items[i]);
}
```

The output:

```
Item 1: 1.23
Item 2: 45.6
```

Despite the information being correct, we may be required to print it in a different format. For example, maybe the decimal marks (the dots, in this case) must line up and we must ensure that there always are two digits after the decimal mark, as in the following output:

```
Item 1:     1.23
Item 2:    45.60
```

Formatted output is useful in such cases. The output functions that we have been using so far have counterparts that contain the letter f in their names: `writef()`

and `writefln()`. The letter f is short for *formatted*. The first parameter of these functions is a *format string* that describes how the other parameters should be printed.

For example, `writefln()` can produce the desired output above with the following format string:

```
writefln("Item %d:%9.02f", i + 1, items[i]);
```

The format string contains regular characters that are passed to the output as is, as well as special format specifiers that correspond to each parameter that is to be printed. Format specifiers start with the % character and end with a *format character*. The format string above has two format specifiers: %d and %9.02f.

Every specifier is associated with the respective parameter, usually in order of appearance. For example, %d is associated with i + 1 and %9.02f is associated with items[i]. Every specifier specifies the format of the parameter that it corresponds to. (Format specifiers may have parameter numbers as well. This will be explained later in the chapter.)

All of the other characters of the format string that are not part of format specifiers are printed as is. Such *regular* characters of the format specifier above are highlighted in `"Item %d:%9.02f"`.

Format specifiers consist of several parts, most of which are optional. The part named *position* will be explained later below. The others are the following: (**Note:** *The spaces between these parts are inserted here to help with readability; they are not part of the specifiers.*)

```
%   flags   width   separator   precision   format_character
```

The % character at the beginning and the format character at the end are required; the others are optional.

Because % has a special meaning in format strings, when we need to print a % as a regular character, we must type it as %%.

25.1 *format_character*

b: An integer argument is printed in the binary system.

o: An integer argument is printed in the octal system.

x and X: An integer argument is printed in the hexadecimal system; with lowercase letters when using x and with uppercase letters when using X.

d: An integer argument is printed in the decimal system; a negative sign is also printed if it is a signed type and the value is less than zero.

```
int value = 12;

writefln("Binary      : %b", value);
writefln("Octal       : %o", value);
writefln("Hexadecimal: %x", value);
writefln("Decimal     : %d", value);
```

```
Binary     : 1100
Octal      : 14
Hexadecimal: c
Decimal    : 12
```

e: A floating point argument is printed according to the following rules.

- a single digit before the decimal mark
- a decimal mark if *precision* is nonzero

- the required digits after the decimal mark, the number of which is determined by *precision* (default precision is 6)
- the e character (meaning "10 to the power of")
- the - or + character, depending on whether the exponent is less than or greater than zero
- the exponent, consisting of at least two digits

E: Same as e, with the exception of outputting the character E instead of e.

  f and F: A floating point argument is printed in the decimal system; there is at least one digit before the decimal mark and the default precision is 6 digits after the decimal mark.

  g: Same as f if the exponent is between -5 and *precision*; otherwise same as e. *precision* does not specify the number of digits after the decimal mark, but the significant digits of the entire value. If there are no significant digits after the decimal mark, then the decimal mark is not printed. The rightmost zeros after the decimal mark are not printed.

  G: Same as g, with the exception of outputting the character E.

  a: A floating point argument is printed in the hexadecimal floating point notation:

- the characters 0x
- a single hexadecimal digit
- a decimal mark if *precision* is nonzero
- the required digits after the decimal mark, the number of which is determined by *precision*; if no *precision* is specified, then as many digits as necessary
- the p character (meaning "2 to the power of")
- the - or + character, depending on whether the exponent is less than or greater than zero
- the exponent, consisting of at least one digit (the exponent of the value 0 is 0)

A: Same as a, with the exception of outputting the characters 0X and P.

```
    double value = 123.456789;

    writefln("with e: %e", value);
    writefln("with f: %f", value);
    writefln("with g: %g", value);
    writefln("with a: %a", value);
```

```
with e: 1.234568e+02
with f: 123.456789
with g: 123.457
with a: 0x1.edd3c07ee0b0bp+6
```

s: The value is printed in the same way as in regular output, according to the type of the argument:

- bool values as true or false
- integer values same as %d
- floating point values same as %g
- strings in UTF-8 encoding; *precision* determines the maximum number of bytes to use (remember that in UTF-8 encoding, the number of bytes is not the

same as the number of characters; for example, the string "ağ" has 2 characters, consisting a total of 3 bytes)

- struct and class objects as the return value of the toString() member functions of their types; *precision* determines the maximum number of bytes to use

- arrays as their element values, side by side

```
    bool b = true;
    int i = 365;
    double d = 9.87;
    string s = "formatted";
    auto o = File("test_file", "r");
    int[] a = [ 2, 4, 6, 8 ];

    writefln("bool  : %s", b);
    writefln("int   : %s", i);
    writefln("double: %s", d);
    writefln("string: %s", s);
    writefln("object: %s", o);
    writefln("array : %s", a);
```

```
bool  : true
int   : 365
double: 9.87
string: formatted
object: File(55738FA0)
array : [2, 4, 6, 8]
```

25.2 *width*

This part determines the width of the field that the argument is printed in. If the width is specified as the character *, then the actual width value is read from the next argument (that argument must be an int). If width is a negative value, then the - flag is assumed.

```
    int value = 100;

    writefln("In a field of 10 characters:%10s", value);
    writefln("In a field of 5 characters :%5s", value);
```

```
In a field of 10 characters:       100
In a field of 5 characters :  100
```

25.3 *separator*

The comma character specifies to separate digits of a number in groups. The default number of digits in a group is 3 but it can be specified after the comma:

```
    writefln("%,f", 1234.5678);        // Groups of 3
    writefln("%,s", 1000000);          // Groups of 3
    writefln("%,2s", 1000000);         // Groups of 2
```

```
1,234.567,800
1,000,000
1,00,00,00
```

If the number of digits is specified as the character *, then the actual number of digits is read from the next argument (that argument must be an int).

```
    writefln("%,*s", 1, 1000000);      // Groups of 1
```

```
1,0,0,0,0,0,0
```

Similarly, it is possible to specify the separator character by using a question mark after the comma and providing the character as an additional argument before the number:

```
writefln("%,?s", '.', 1000000);    // The separator is '.'
```

```
1.000.000
```

25.4 *precision*

Precision is specified after a dot in the format specifier. For floating point types, it determines the precision of the printed representation of the values. If the precision is specified as the character *, then the actual precision is read from the next argument (that argument must be an int). Negative precision values are ignored.

```
double value = 1234.56789;

writefln("%.8g", value);
writefln("%.3g", value);
writefln("%.8f", value);
writefln("%.3f", value);
```

```
1234.5679
1.23e+03
1234.56789000
1234.568
```

```
auto number = 0.123456789;
writefln("Number: %.*g", 4, number);
```

```
Number: 0.1235
```

25.5 *flags*

More than one flag can be specified.

-: the value is printed left-aligned in its field; this flag cancels the 0 flag

```
int value = 123;

writefln("Normally right-aligned:|%10d|", value);
writefln("Left-aligned           :|%-10d|", value);
```

```
Normally right-aligned:|       123|
Left-aligned           :|123       |
```

+: if the value is positive, it is prepended with the + character; this flag cancels the *space* flag

```
writefln("No effect for negative values    : %+d", -50);
writefln("Positive value with the + flag    : %+d", 50);
writefln("Positive value without the + flag: %d", 50);
```

```
No effect for negative values    : -50
Positive value with the + flag    : +50
Positive value without the + flag: 50
```

#: prints the value in an *alternate* form depending on the *format_character*

- o: the first character of the octal value is always printed as 0
- x and X: if the value is not zero, it is prepended with 0x or 0X

- floating points: a decimal mark is printed even if there are no significant digits after the decimal mark
- g and G: even the insignificant zero digits after the decimal mark are printed

```
writefln("Octal starts with 0                            : %#o", 1000);
writefln("Hexadecimal starts with 0x                     : %#x", 1000);
writefln("Contains decimal mark even when unnecessary: %#g", 1f);
writefln("Rightmost zeros are printed                    : %#g", 1.2);
```

```
Octal starts with 0                            : 01750
Hexadecimal starts with 0x                     : 0x3e8
Contains decimal mark even when unnecessary: 1.00000
Rightmost zeros are printed                    : 1.20000
```

0: the field is padded with zeros (unless the value is nan or infinity); if *precision* is also specified, this flag is ignored

```
writefln("In a field of 8 characters: %08d", 42);
```

```
In a field of 8 characters: 00000042
```

space character: if the value is positive, a space character is prepended to align the negative and positive values

```
writefln("No effect for negative values: % d", -34);
writefln("Positive value with space    : % d", 56);
writefln("Positive value without space : %d", 56);
```

```
No effect for negative values: -34
Positive value with space    :  56
Positive value without space : 56
```

25.6 Positional parameters

We have seen above that the arguments are associated one by one with the specifiers in the format string. It is also possible to use position numbers within format specifiers. This enables associating the specifiers with specific arguments. Arguments are numbered in increasing fashion, starting with 1. The argument numbers are specified immediately after the % character, followed by a $:

```
% position$ flags width precision format_character
```

An advantage of positional parameters is being able to use the same argument in more than one place in the same format string:

```
writefln("%1$d %1$x %1$o %1$b", 42);
```

The format string above uses the argument numbered 1 within four specifiers to print it in decimal, hexadecimal, octal, and binary formats:

```
42 2a 52 101010
```

Another application of positional parameters is supporting multiple natural languages. When referred by position numbers, arguments can be moved anywhere within the specific format string for a given human language. For example, the number of students of a given classroom can be printed as in the following:

```
writefln("There are %s students in room %s.", count, room);
```

```
There are 20 students in room 1A.
```

Let's assume that the program must also support Turkish. In this case the format string needs to be selected according to the active language. The following method takes advantage of the ternary operator:

```
auto format = (language == "en"
               ? "There are %s students in room %s."
               : "%s sınıfında %s öğrenci var.");

writefln(format, count, room);
```

Unfortunately, when the arguments are associated one by one, the classroom and student count information appear in reverse order in the Turkish message; the room information is where the count should be and the count is where the room should be:

```
20 sınıfında 1A öğrenci var.   ← Wrong: means "room 20", and "1A students"!
```

To avoid this, the arguments can be specified by numbers, such as 1$ and 2$, to associate each specifier with the exact argument:

```
auto format = (language == "en"
               ? "There are %1$s students in room %2$s."
               : "%2$s sınıfında %1$s öğrenci var.");

writefln(format, count, room);
```

Now the arguments appear in the proper order, regardless of the language selected:

```
There are 20 students in room 1A.
```

```
1A sınıfında 20 öğrenci var.
```

25.7 Formatted element output

Format specifiers between %(and %) are applied to every element of a container (e.g. an array or a range):

```
auto numbers = [ 1, 2, 3, 4 ];
writefln("%(%s%)", numbers);
```

The format string above consists of three parts:

- %(: Start of element format
- %s: Format for each element
- %): End of element format

Each being printed with the %s format, the elements appear one after the other:

```
1234
```

The regular characters before and after the element format are repeated for each element. For example, the {%s}, specifier would print each element between curly brackets separated by commas:

```
writefln("%({%s},%)", numbers);
```

However, regular characters to the right of the format specifier are considered to be element delimiters and are printed only between elements, not after the last one:

```
{1},{2},{3},{4   ← '}' and ',' are not printed after the last element
```

%| is used for specifying the characters that should be printed even for the last element. Characters that are to the right of %| are considered to be the delimiters and are not printed for the last element. Conversely, characters to the left of %| are printed even for the last element.

For example, the following format specifier would print the closing curly bracket after the last element but not the comma:

```
writefln("%({%s}%|,%)", numbers);
```

```
{1},{2},{3},{4}   ← '}' is printed after the last element as well
```

Unlike strings that are printed individually, strings that are printed as elements appear within double quotes:

```
auto vegetables = [ "spinach", "asparagus", "artichoke" ];
writefln("%(%s, %)", vegetables);
```

```
"spinach", "asparagus", "artichoke"
```

When the double quotes are not desired, the element format must be started with %-(instead of %(:

```
writefln("%-(%s, %)", vegetables);
```

```
spinach, asparagus, artichoke
```

The same applies to characters as well. %(prints them within single quotes:

```
writefln("%(%s%)", "hello");
```

```
'h''e''l''l''o'
```

%-(prints them without quotes:

```
writefln("%-(%s%)", "hello");
```

```
hello
```

There must be two format specifiers for associative arrays: one for the keys and one for the values. For example, the following %s (%s) specifier would print first the key and then the value in parentheses:

```
auto spelled = [ 1 : "one", 10 : "ten", 100 : "hundred" ];
writefln("%-(%s (%s)%|, %)", spelled);
```

Also note that, being specified to the right of %|, the comma is not printed for the last element:

```
1 (one), 100 (hundred), 10 (ten)
```

25.8 format

Formatted output is available through the format() function of the std.string module as well. format() works the same as writef() but it *returns* the result as a string instead of printing it to the output:

```
import std.stdio;
import std.string;
```

```
void main() {
    write("What is your name? ");
    auto name = strip(readln());

    auto result = format("Hello %s!", name);
}
```

The program can make use of that result in later expressions.

Checked format string

There is an alternative syntax for functions like format in the standard library that take a format string (writef, writefln, formattedWrite, readf, formattedRead, etc.). It is possible to provide the format string as a *template argument* to these functions so that the validity of the format string and the arguments are checked at compile time:

```
import std.stdio;

void main() {
    writefln!"%s %s"(1);      // ← compilation ERROR (extra %s)
    writefln!"%s"(1, 2);      // ← compilation ERROR (extra 2)
    writefln!"%s %d"(1, 2.5); // ← compilation ERROR (mismatched %d and 2.5)
}
```

The ! character above is the template instantiation operator, which we will see in a later chapter (page 399).

   (**Note:** *Although this snytax is safer because it catches potential programmer errors at compile time, it may also make compilation times longer.*)

25.9 Exercises

1. Write a program that reads a value and prints it in the hexadecimal system.
2. Write a program that reads a floating point value and prints it as percentage value with two digits after the decimal mark. For example, if the value is 1.2345, it should print %1.23.

   The solutions are on page 707.

It is possible to specify the format of the data that is expected at the input. The format specifies both the data that is to be read and the characters that should be ignored.

D's input format specifiers are similar to the ones present in the C language.

As we have already been using in the previous chapters, the format specifier "%s" reads the data according to the type of the variable. For example, as the type of the following variable is double, the characters at the input would be read as floating point number:

```
double number;

readf(" %s", &number);
```

The format string can contain three types of information:

- **The space character**: Indicates *zero* or more whitespace characters at the input and specifies that all of those characters should be read and ignored.
- **Format specifier**: Similar to the output format specifiers, input format specifiers start with the % character and determine the format of the data that is to be read.
- **Any other character**: Indicates the characters that are expected at the input as is, which should be read and ignored.

The format string makes it possible to select specific information from the input and ignore the others.

Let's have a look at an example that uses all of the three types of information in the format string. Let's assume that the student number and the grade are expected to appear at the input in the following format:

```
number:123 grade:90
```

Let's further assume that the tags number: and grade: must be ignored. The following format string would *select* the values of number and grade and would ignore the other characters:

```
int number;
int grade;
readf("number:%s grade:%s", &number, &grade);
```

The characters that are highlighted in "number:%s grade:%s" must appear at the input exactly as specified; readf() reads and ignores them.

The single space character that appears in the format string above would cause all of the whitespace characters that appear exactly at that position to be read and ignored.

As the % character has a special meaning in format strings, when that character itself needs to be read and ignored, it must be written twice in the format string as %%.

Reading a single line of data from the input has been recommended as strip(readln()) in the Strings chapter (page 75). Instead of that method, a \n character at the end of the format string can achieve a similar goal:

```
import std.stdio;

void main() {
```

```
    write("First name: ");
    string firstName;
    readf(" %s\n", &firstName);      // ← \n at the end

    write("Last name : ");
    string lastName;
    readf(" %s\n", &lastName);       // ← \n at the end

    write("Age        : ");
    int age;
    readf(" %s", &age);

    writefln("%s %s (%s)", firstName, lastName, age);
}
```

The \n characters at the ends of the format strings when reading firstName and lastName would cause the new-line characters to be read from the input and to be ignored. However, potential whitespace characters at the ends of the strings may still need to be removed by strip().

26.1 Format specifier characters

The way the data should be read is specified with the following format specifier characters:

d: Read an integer in the decimal system.

o: Read an integer in the octal system.

x: Read an integer in the hexadecimal system.

f: Read a floating point number.

s: Read according to the type of the variable. This is the most commonly used specifier.

c: Read a single character. This specifier allows reading whitespace characters as well. (It cancels the ignore behavior.)

For example, if the input contains "23 23 23", the values would be read differently according to different format specifiers:

```
    int number_d;
    int number_o;
    int number_x;

    readf(" %d %o %x", &number_d, &number_o, &number_x);

    writeln("Read with %d: ", number_d);
    writeln("Read with %o: ", number_o);
    writeln("Read with %x: ", number_x);
```

Although the input contains three sets of "23" characters, the values of the variables are different:

```
Read with %d: 23
Read with %o: 19
Read with %x: 35
```

Note: *Very briefly, "23" is equal to 2x8+3=19 in the octal system and to 2x16+3=35 in the hexadecimal system.*

26.2 Exercise

Assume that the input contains the date in the format *year.month.day*. Write a program that prints the number of the month. For example, if the input is 2009.09.30, the output should be 9.

The solution is on page 707.

In the for Loop chapter (page 93) we saw the steps in which the while loop (page 28) is executed:

```
preparation

condition check
actual work
iteration

condition check
actual work
iteration

...
```

The do-while loop is very similar to the while loop. The difference is that the *condition check* is performed at the end of each iteration of the do-while loop, so that the *actual work* is performed at least once:

```
preparation

actual work
iteration
condition check      ← at the end of the iteration

actual work
iteration
condition check      ← at the end of the iteration

...
```

For example, do-while may be more natural in the following program where the user guesses a number, as the user must guess at least once so that the number can be compared:

```d
import std.stdio;
import std.random;

void main() {
    int number = uniform(1, 101);

    writeln("I am thinking of a number between 1 and 100.");

    int guess;

    do {
        write("What is your guess? ");

        readf(" %s", &guess);

        if (number < guess) {
            write("My number is less than that. ");

        } else if (number > guess) {
            write("My number is greater than that. ");
        }

    } while (guess != number);

    writeln("Correct!");
}
```

The function uniform() that is used in the program is a part of the std.random module. It returns a random number in the specified range. The way it is used above, the second number is considered to be outside of the range. In other words, uniform() would not return 101 for that call.

27.1 Exercise

Write a program that plays the same game but have the program do the guessing. If the program is written correctly, it should be able to guess the user's number in at most 7 tries.

The solution is on page 708.

28 Associative Arrays

Associative arrays are a feature that is found in most modern high-level languages. They are very fast data structures that work like mini databases and are used in many programs.

We saw in the Arrays chapter (page 49) that plain arrays are containers that store their elements side-by-side and provide access to them by index. An array that stores the names of the days of the week can be defined like this:

```
string[] dayNames =
    [ "Monday", "Tuesday", "Wednesday", "Thursday",
        "Friday", "Saturday", "Sunday" ];
```

The name of a specific day can be accessed by its index in that array:

```
writeln(dayNames[1]);    // prints "Tuesday"
```

The fact that plain arrays provide access to their values through index numbers can be described as an *association* of indexes with values. In other words, arrays map indexes to values. Plain arrays can use only integers as indexes.

Associative arrays allow indexing not only using integers but also using any other type. They map the values of one type to the values of another type. The values of the type that associative arrays *map from* are called *keys*, rather than indexes. Associative arrays store their elements as key-value pairs.

Associative arrays are implemented in D using a *hash table*. Hash tables are among the fastest collections for storing and accessing elements. Other than in rare pathological cases, the time it takes to store or access an element is independent of the number of elements that are in the associative array.

The high performance of hash tables comes at the expense of storing the elements in an unordered way. Also, unlike arrays, the elements of hash tables are not stored side-by-side.

For plain arrays, index values are not stored at all. Because array elements are stored side-by-side in memory, index values are implicitly the relative positions of elements from the beginning of the array.

On the other hand, associative arrays do store both the keys and the values of elements. Although this difference makes associative arrays use more memory, it also allows them to use *sparse* key values. For example, when there are just two elements to store for keys 0 and 999, an associative array stores just two elements, not 1000 as a plain array has to.

28.1 Definition

The syntax of associative arrays is similar to the array syntax. The difference is that it is the type of the key that is specified within the square brackets, not the length of the array:

```
value_type[key_type] associative_array_name;
```

For example, an associative array that maps day names of type string to day numbers of type int can be defined like this:

```
int[string] dayNumbers;
```

The dayNumbers variable above is an associative array that can be used as a table that provides a mapping from day names to day numbers. In other words, it can be used as the opposite of the dayNames array at the beginning of this chapter. We will use the dayNumbers associative array in the examples below.

The keys of associative arrays can be of any type, including user-defined struct and class types. We will see user-defined types in later chapters.

The length of associative arrays cannot be specified when defined. They grow automatically as key-value pairs are added.

Note: *An associative array that is defined without any element is null (page 233), not empty. This distinction has an important consequence when passing associative arrays to functions (page 168). We will cover these concepts in later chapters.*

28.2 Adding key-value pairs

Using the assignment operator is sufficient to build the association between a key and a value:

```
// associates value 0 with key "Monday"
dayNumbers["Monday"] = 0;

// associates value 1 with key "Tuesday"
dayNumbers["Tuesday"] = 1;
```

The table grows automatically with each association. For example, dayNumbers would have two key-value pairs after the operations above. This can be demonstrated by printing the entire table:

```
writeln(dayNumbers);
```

The output indicates that the values 0 and 1 correspond to keys "Monday" and "Tuesday", respectively:

```
["Monday":0, "Tuesday":1]
```

There can be only one value per key. For that reason, when we assign a new key-value pair and the key already exists, the table does not grow; instead, the value of the existing key changes:

```
dayNumbers["Tuesday"] = 222;
writeln(dayNumbers);
```

The output:

```
["Monday":0, "Tuesday":222]
```

28.3 Initialization

Sometimes some of the mappings between the keys and the values are already known at the time of the definition of the associative array. Associative arrays are initialized similarly to regular arrays, using a colon to separate each key from its respective value:

```
// key : value
int[string] dayNumbers =
    [ "Monday"   : 0, "Tuesday" : 1, "Wednesday" : 2,
      "Thursday" : 3, "Friday"  : 4, "Saturday"  : 5,
      "Sunday"   : 6 ];

writeln(dayNumbers["Tuesday"]);     // prints 1
```

28.4 Removing key-value pairs

Key-value pairs can be removed by using .remove():

```
    dayNumbers.remove("Tuesday");
    writeln(dayNumbers["Tuesday"]);     // ← run-time ERROR
```

The first line above removes the key-value pair "Tuesday" / 1. Since that key is not in the container anymore, the second line would cause an exception to be thrown and the program to be terminated if that exception is not caught. We will see exceptions in a later chapter (page 192).

.clear removes all elements:

```
    dayNumbers.clear;     // The associative array becomes empty
```

28.5 Determining the presence of a key

The in operator determines whether a given key exists in the associative array:

```
    int[string] colorCodes = [ /* ... */ ];

    if ("purple" in colorCodes) {
        // key "purple" exists in the table

    } else {
        // key "purple" does not exist in the table
    }
```

Sometimes it makes sense to use a default value if a key does not exist in the associative array. For example, the special value of -1 can be used as the code for colors that are not in colorCodes. .get() is useful in such cases: it returns the value associated with the specified key if that key exists, otherwise it returns the default value. The default value is specified as the second parameter of .get():

```
    int[string] colorCodes = [ "blue" : 10, "green" : 20 ];
    writeln(colorCodes.get("purple", -1));
```

Since the array does not contain a value for the key "purple", .get() returns -1:

```
-1
```

28.6 Properties

- .length returns the number of key-value pairs.
- .keys returns a copy of all keys as a dynamic array.
- .byKey provides access to the keys without copying them; we will see how .byKey is used in foreach loops in the next chapter.
- .values returns a copy of all values as a dynamic array.
- .byValue provides access to the values without copying them.
- .byKeyValue provides access to the key-value pairs without copying them.
- .rehash may make the array more efficient in some cases, such as after inserting a large number of key-value pairs.
- .sizeof is the size of the array *reference* (it has nothing to do with the number of key-value pairs in the table and is the same value for all associative arrays).
- .get returns the value if it exists, the default value otherwise.
- .remove removes the specified key and its value from the array.
- .clear removes all elements.

28.7 Example

Here is a program that prints the Turkish names of colors that are specified in English:

```
import std.stdio;
import std.string;

void main() {
    string[string] colors = [ "black" : "siyah",
                              "white" : "beyaz",
                              "red"   : "kırmızı",
                              "green" : "yeşil",
                              "blue"  : "mavi" ];

    writefln("I know the Turkish names of these %s colors: %s",
            colors.length, colors.keys);

    write("Please ask me one: ");
    string inEnglish = strip(readln());

    if (inEnglish in colors) {
        writefln("\"%s\" is \"%s\" in Turkish.",
                inEnglish, colors[inEnglish]);

    } else {
        writeln("I don't know that one.");
    }
}
```

28.8 Exercises

1. How can all of the key-value pairs of an associative array be removed other than calling .clear? (.clear is the most natural method.) There are at least three methods:

   - Removing them one-by-one from the associative array.
   - Assigning an empty associative array.
   - Similar to the previous method, assigning the array's .init property.
     Note: *The .init property of any variable or type is the initial value of that type:*

     ```
     number = int.init;    // 0 for int
     ```

2. Just like with arrays, there can be only one value for each key. This may be seen as a limitation for some applications.

   Assume that an associative array is used for storing student grades. For example, let's assume that the grades 90, 85, 95, etc. are to be stored for the student named "emre".

   Associative arrays make it easy to access the grades by the name of the student as in grades["emre"]. However, the grades cannot be inserted as in the following code because each grade would overwrite the previous one:

   ```
   int[string] grades;
   grades["emre"] = 90;
   grades["emre"] = 85;    // ← Overwrites the previous grade!
   ```

   How can you solve this problem? Define an associative array that can store multiple grades per student.

   The solutions are on page 708.

29 foreach Loop

One of the most common statements in D is the `foreach` loop. It is used for applying the same operations to every element of a container (or a *range*).

Operations that are applied to elements of containers are very common in programming. We have seen in the `for` Loop chapter (page 93) that elements of an array are accessed in a `for` loop by an index value that is incremented at each iteration:

```
for (int i = 0; i != array.length; ++i) {
    writeln(array[i]);
}
```

The following steps are involved in iterating over all the elements:

- Defining a variable as a counter, which is conventionally named as i
- Iterating the loop up to the value of the `.length` property of the array
- Incrementing i
- Accessing the element

`foreach` has essentially the same behavior but it simplifies the code by handling those steps automatically:

```
foreach (element; array) {
    writeln(element);
}
```

Part of the power of `foreach` comes from the fact that it can be used the same way regardless of the type of the container. As we have seen in the previous chapter, one way of iterating over the values of an associative array in a `for` loop is by first calling the array's `.values` property:

```
auto values = aa.values;
for (int i = 0; i != values.length; ++i) {
    writeln(values[i]);
}
```

`foreach` does not require anything special for associative arrays; it is used exactly the same as with arrays:

```
foreach (value; aa) {
    writeln(value);
}
```

29.1 The foreach syntax

`foreach` consists of three sections:

```
foreach (names; container_or_range) {
    operations
}
```

- ***container_or_range*** specifies where the elements are.
- ***operations*** specifies the operations to apply to each element.
- ***names*** specifies the name of the element and potentially other variables depending on the type of the container or the range. Although the choice of names is up to the programmer, the number of and the types of these names depend on the type of the container.

29.2 `continue` and `break`

These keywords have the same meaning as they do for the `for` loop: `continue` moves to the next iteration before completing the rest of the operations for the current element, and `break` terminates the loop altogether.

29.3 `foreach` with arrays

When using `foreach` with plain arrays and there is a single name specified in the *names* section, that name represents the value of the element at each iteration:

```
foreach (element; array) {
    writeln(element);
}
```

When two names are specified in the *names* section, they represent an automatic counter and the value of the element, respectively:

```
foreach (i, element; array) {
    writeln(i, ": ", element);
}
```

The counter is incremented automatically by `foreach`. Although it can be named anything else, `i` is a very common name for the automatic counter.

29.4 `foreach` with strings and `std.range.stride`

Since strings are arrays of characters, `foreach` works with strings the same way as it does with arrays: A single name refers to the character, two names refer to the counter and the character, respectively:

```
foreach (c; "hello") {
    writeln(c);
}

foreach (i, c; "hello") {
    writeln(i, ": ", c);
}
```

However, being UTF code units, `char` and `wchar` iterate over UTF code units, not Unicode code points:

```
foreach (i, code; "abcçd") {
    writeln(i, ": ", code);
}
```

The two UTF-8 code units that make up ç would be accessed as separate elements:

```
0: a
1: b
2: c
3:
4: 
5: d
```

One way of iterating over Unicode characters of strings in a `foreach` loop is `stride` from the `std.range` module. `stride` presents the string as a container that consists of Unicode characters. Its second parameter is the number of steps that it should take as it *strides* over the characters:

```
import std.range;

// ...

    foreach (c; stride("abcçd", 1)) {
```

```
        writeln(c);
    }
```

Regardless of the character type of the string, `stride` always presents its elements as Unicode characters:

```
a
b
c
ç
d
```

I will explain below why this loop could not include an automatic counter.

29.5 foreach with associative arrays

When using `foreach` with associative arrays, a single name refers to the value, while two names refer to the key and the value, respectively:

```
foreach (value; aa) {
    writeln(value);
}

foreach (key, value; aa) {
    writeln(key, ": ", value);
}
```

Associative arrays can provide their keys and values as *ranges* as well. We will see ranges in a later chapter (page 569). `.byKey`, `.byValue`, and `.byKeyValue` return efficient range objects that are useful in contexts other than `foreach` loops as well.

`.byValue` does not bring any benefit in `foreach` loops over the regular value iteration above. On the other hand, `.byKey` is the only efficient way of iterating over *just* the keys of an associative array:

```
foreach (key; aa.byKey) {
    writeln(key);
}
```

`.byKeyValue` provides each key-value element through a variable that is similar to a tuple (page 513). The key and the value are accessed separately through the `.key` and `.value` properties of that variable:

```
foreach (element; aa.byKeyValue) {
    writefln("The value for key %s is %s",
             element.key, element.value);
}
```

29.6 foreach with number ranges

We have seen number ranges before, in the Slices and Other Array Features chapter (page 65). It is possible to specify a number range in the *container_or_range* section:

```
foreach (number; 10..15) {
    writeln(number);
}
```

Remember that 10 would be included in the range but 15 would not be.

29.7 foreach with structs, classes, and ranges

`foreach` can also be used with objects of user-defined types that define their own iteration in `foreach` loops. Structs and classes provide support for `foreach` iteration either by their opApply() member functions, or by a set of *range* member functions. We will see these features in later chapters.

29.8 The counter is automatic only for arrays

The automatic counter is provided only when iterating over arrays. There are two options for other containers

- Taking advantage of std.range.enumerate as we will see later in the foreach with Structs and Classes chapter (page 491).
- Defining and incrementing a counter variable explicitly:

```d
size_t i = 0;
foreach (element; container) {
    // ...
    ++i;
}
```

Such a variable is needed when counting a specific condition as well. For example, the following code counts only the values that are divisible by 10:

```d
import std.stdio;

void main() {
    auto numbers = [ 1, 0, 15, 10, 3, 5, 20, 30 ];

    size_t count = 0;
    foreach (number; numbers) {
        if ((number % 10) == 0) {
            ++count;
            write(count);

        } else {
            write(' ');
        }

        writeln(": ", number);
    }
}
```

The output:

```
 : 1
1: 0
 : 15
2: 10
 : 3
 : 5
3: 20
4: 30
```

29.9 The copy of the element, not the element itself

The foreach loop normally provides a copy of the element, not the actual element that is stored in the container. This may be a cause of bugs.

To see an example of this, let's have a look at the following program that is trying to double the values of the elements of an array:

```d
import std.stdio;

void main() {
    double[] numbers = [ 1.2, 3.4, 5.6 ];

    writefln("Before: %s", numbers);

    foreach (number; numbers) {
```

```
        number *= 2;
    }

    writefln("After : %s", numbers);
}
```

The output of the program indicates that the assignment made to each element inside the foreach body does not have any effect on the elements of the container:

```
Before: [1.2, 3.4, 5.6]
After : [1.2, 3.4, 5.6]
```

That is because number is not an actual element of the array, but a copy of each element. When the actual elements need to be operated on, the name must be defined as a *reference* of the actual element, by using the ref keyword:

```
    foreach (ref number; numbers) {
        number *= 2;
    }
```

The new output shows that the assignments now modify the actual elements of the array:

```
Before: [1.2, 3.4, 5.6]
After : [2.4, 6.8, 11.2]
```

The ref keyword makes number an *alias* of the actual element at each iteration. As a result, the modifications through number modify that actual element of the container.

29.10 The integrity of the container must be preserved

Although it is fine to modify the elements of a container through ref variables, the structure of a container must not be changed during its iteration. For example, elements must not be removed nor added to the container during a foreach loop.

Such modifications may confuse the inner workings of the loop iteration and result in incorrect program states.

29.11 foreach_reverse to iterate in the reverse direction

foreach_reverse works the same way as foreach except it iterates in the reverse direction:

```
    auto container = [ 1, 2, 3 ];

    foreach_reverse (element; container) {
        writefln("%s ", element);
    }
```

The output:

```
3
2
1
```

The use of foreach_reverse is not common because the range function retro() achieves the same goal. We will see retro() in a later chapter.

29.12 Exercise

We know that associative arrays provide a mapping from keys to values. This mapping is unidirectional: values are accessed by keys but not the other way around.

Assume that there is already the following associative array:

```
string[int] names = [ 1:"one", 7:"seven", 20:"twenty" ];
```

Use that associative array and a foreach loop to fill another associative array named values. The new associative array should provide values that correspond to names. For example, the following line should print 20:

```
writeln(values["twenty"]);
```

The solution is on page 709.

switch is a statement that allows comparing the value of an expression against multiple values. It is similar to but not the same as an "if, else if, else" chain. case is used for specifying the values that are to be compared with switch's expression. case is a part of the switch statement, not a statement itself.

switch takes an expression within parentheses, compares the value of that expression to the case values, and executes the operations of the case that is equal to the value of the expression. Its syntax consists of a switch block that contains one or more case sections and a default section:

```
switch (expression) {

case value_1:
    // operations to execute if the expression is equal to value_1
    // ...
    break;

case value_2:
    // operations to execute if the expression is equal to value_2
    // ...
    break;

// ... other cases ...

default:
    // operations to execute if the expression is not equal to any case
    // ...
    break;
}
```

The expression that switch takes is not used directly as a logical expression. It is not evaluated as "if this condition is true", as it would be in an if statement. The *value* of the switch expression is used in equality comparisons with the case values. It is similar to an "if, else if, else" chain that has only equality comparisons:

```
auto value = expression;

if (value == value_1) {
    // operations for value_1
    // ...

} else if (value == value_2) {
    // operations for value_2
    // ...
}

// ... other 'else if's ...

} else {
    // operations for other values
    // ...
}
```

However, the "if, else if, else" above is not an exact equivalent of the switch statement. The reasons why will be explained in the following sections.

If a case value matches the value of the switch expression, then the operations that are under the case are executed. If no value matches, then the operations that are under the default are executed.

30.1 The goto statement

The use of goto is generally advised against in most programming languages. However, goto is useful in switch statements in some situations, without being as problematic as in other uses. The goto statement will be covered in more detail in a later chapter (page 510).

case does not introduce a *scope* as the if statement does. Once the operations within an if or else scope are finished the evaluation of the entire if statement is also finished. That does not happen with the case sections; once a matching case is found, the execution of the program jumps to that case and executes the operations under it. When needed in rare situations, goto case makes the program execution jump to the next case:

```
    switch (value) {

    case 5:
        writeln("five");
        goto case;     // continues to the next case

    case 4:
        writeln("four");
        break;

    default:
        writeln("unknown");
        break;
    }
```

If value is 5, the execution continues under the case 5 line and the program prints "five". Then the goto case statement causes the execution to continue to the next case, and as a result "four" is also printed:

```
five
four
```

goto can appear in three ways under case sections:

- goto case causes the execution to continue (fallthrough) to the next case.
- goto default causes the execution to continue to the default section.
- goto case *expression* causes the execution to continue to the case that matches that expression.

The following program demonstrates these three uses by taking advantage of a foreach loop:

```
import std.stdio;

void main() {
    foreach (value; [ 1, 2, 3, 10, 20 ]) {
        writefln("--- value: %s ---", value);

        switch (value) {

        case 1:
            writeln("case 1");
            goto case;

        case 2:
            writeln("case 2");
            goto case 10;

        case 3:
            writeln("case 3");
            goto default;

        case 10:
            writeln("case 10");
            break;
```

```
        default:
            writeln("default");
            break;
        }
    }
}
```

The output:

```
--- value: 1 ---
case 1
case 2
case 10
--- value: 2 ---
case 2
case 10
--- value: 3 ---
case 3
default
--- value: 10 ---
case 10
--- value: 20 ---
default
```

30.2 The expression must be an integer, string, or bool type

Any type can be used in equality comparisons in if statements. On the other hand, the type of the switch expression is limited to all integer types, all string types, and bool.

```
    string op = /* ... */;
    // ...
    switch (op) {

    case "add":
        result = first + second;
        break;

    case "subtract":
        result = first - second;
        break;

    case "multiply":
        result = first * second;
        break;

    case "divide":
        result = first / second;
        break;

    default:
        throw new Exception(format("Unknown operation: %s", op));
    }
```

Note: *The code above throws an exception when the operation is not recognized by the program. We will see exceptions in a later chapter (page 192).*

Although it is possible to use bool expressions as well, because bool has only two values it may be more suitable to use an if statement or the ternary operator (?:) with that type.

30.3 Value ranges

Ranges of values can be specified by .. between cases:

```
    switch (dieValue) {

    case 1:
        writeln("You won");
        break;
```

```
    case 2: .. case 5:
        writeln("It's a draw");
        break;

    case 6:
        writeln("I won");
        break;

    default:
        /* The program should never get here because the cases
         * above cover the entire range of valid die values.
         * (See 'final switch' below.) */
        break;
    }
```

The code above determines that the game ends in a draw when the die value is 2, 3, 4, or 5.

30.4 Distinct values

Let's assume that it is a draw for the values 2 and 4, rather than for the values that are in the range [2, 5]. Distinct values of a case are separated by commas:

```
    case 2, 4:
        writeln("It's a draw");
        break;
```

30.5 The `final switch` statement

The `final switch` statement works similarly to the regular `switch` statement, with the following differences:

- It cannot have a `default` section. Note that this section is meaningless when the `case` sections cover the entire range of values anyway, as has been with the six values of the die above.
- Value ranges cannot be used with `cases` (distinct values can be).
- If the expression is of an enum type, all of the values of the type must be covered by the `cases` (we will see enum types in the next chapter).

```
    int dieValue = 1;

    final switch (dieValue) {

    case 1:
        writeln("You won");
        break;

    case 2, 3, 4, 5:
        writeln("It's a draw");
        break;

    case 6:
        writeln("I won");
        break;
    }
```

30.6 When to use

`switch` is suitable for comparing the value of an expression against a set of values that are known at compile time.

When there are only two values to compare, an `if` statement may make more sense. For example, to check whether it is heads or tails:

```
if (headsTailsResult == heads) {
    // ...

} else {
    // ...
}
```

As a general rule, switch is more suitable when there are three or more values to compare.

When all of the values need to be handled, then prefer final switch. This is especially the case for enum types.

30.7 Exercises

1. Write a calculator program that supports arithmetic operations. Have the program first read the operation as a string, then two values of type double from the input. The calculator should print the result of the operation. For example, when the operation and values are "add" and "5 7", respectively, the program should print 12.

    The input can be read as in the following code:

    ```
    string op;
    double first;
    double second;

    // ...

    op = strip(readln());
    readf(" %s %s", &first, &second);
    ```

2. Improve the calculator to support operators like "+" in addition to words like "add".

3. Have the program throw an exception for unknown operators. We will cover exceptions in a later chapter (page 192). For now, adapt the throw statement used above to your program.

    The solutions are on page 709.

31 enum

enum is the feature that enables defining named constant values.

31.1 Effects of magic constants on code quality

The following code appeared in the exercise solutions (page 699) of the Integers and Arithmetic Operations chapter:

```
if (operation == 1) {
    result = first + second;

} else if (operation == 2) {
    result = first - second;

} else if (operation == 3) {
    result = first * second;

} else if (operation == 4) {
    result = first / second;
}
```

The integer literals 1, 2, 3, and 4 in that piece of code are called *magic constants*. It is not easy to determine what each of those literals means in the program. One must examine the code in each scope to determine that 1 means *addition*, 2 means *subtraction*, etc. This task is relatively easy for the code above because all of the scopes contain just a single line. It would be considerably more difficult to decipher the meanings of magic constants in most other programs.

Magic constants must be avoided because they impair two important qualities of source code: readability and maintainability.

enum enables giving names to such constants and, as a consequence, making the code more readable and maintainable. Each condition would be readily understandable if the following enum constants were used:

```
if (operation == Operation.add) {
    result = first + second;

} else if (operation == Operation.subtract) {
    result = first - second;

} else if (operation == Operation.multiply) {
    result = first * second;

} else if (operation == Operation.divide) {
    result = first / second;
}
```

The enum type Operation above that obviates the need for magic constants 1, 2, 3, and 4 can be defined like this:

```
enum Operation { add = 1, subtract, multiply, divide }
```

31.2 The enum syntax

The common definition of an enum is the following:

```
enum TypeName { ValueName_1, ValueName_2, /* etc. */ }
```

Sometimes it is necessary to specify the actual type (the *base type*) of the values as well:

```
enum TypeName : base_type { ValueName_1, ValueName_2, /* etc. */ }
```

We will see how this is used in the next section.

TypeName defines what the constants collectively mean. All of the member constants of an enum *type* are listed within curly brackets. Here are some examples:

```
enum HeadsOrTails { heads, tails }
enum Suit { spades, hearts, diamonds, clubs }
enum Fare { regular, child, student, senior }
```

Each set of constants becomes part of a separate type. For example, heads and tails become members of the type HeadsOrTails. The new type can be used like other fundamental types when defining variables:

```
HeadsOrTails result;              // default initialized
auto ht = HeadsOrTails.heads;     // inferred type
```

As has been seen in the pieces of code above, the members of enum types are always specified by the name of their enum type:

```
if (result == HeadsOrTails.heads) {
    // ...
}
```

31.3 Actual values and base types

The member constants of enum types are by default implemented as int values. In other words, although on the surface they appear as just names such as heads and tails, they also have numerical values. (**Note:** *It is possible to choose a type other than int when needed.*).

Unless explicitly specified by the programmer, the numerical values of enum members start at 0 and are incremented by one for each member. For example, the two members of the HeadsOrTails enum have the numerical values 0 and 1:

```
writeln("heads is 0: ", (HeadsOrTails.heads == 0));
writeln("tails is 1: ", (HeadsOrTails.tails == 1));
```

The output:

```
heads is 0: true
tails is 1: true
```

It is possible to manually (re)set the values at any point in the enum. That was the case when we specified the value of Operation.add as 1 above. The following example manually sets a new count twice:

```
enum Test { a, b, c, ç = 100, d, e, f = 222, g, ğ }
writefln("%d %d %d", Test.b, Test.ç, Test.ğ);
```

The output:

```
1 100 224
```

If int is not suitable as the base type of the enum values, the base type can be specified explicitly after the name of the enum:

```
enum NaturalConstant : double { pi = 3.14, e = 2.72 }
enum TemperatureUnit : string { C = "Celsius", F = "Fahrenheit" }
```

31.4 enum values that are not of an enum type

We have discussed that it is important to avoid magic constants and instead to take advantage of the enum feature.

However, sometimes it may not be natural to come up with enum type names just to use named constants. Let's assume that a named constant is needed to represent the number of seconds per day. It should not be necessary to also define an enum *type* to contain this constant value. All that is needed is a constant value that can be referred to by its name. In such cases, the type name of the enum and the curly brackets are omitted:

```
enum secondsPerDay = 60 * 60 * 24;
```

The type of the constant can be specified explicitly, which would be required if the type cannot be inferred from the right hand side:

```
enum int secondsPerDay = 60 * 60 * 24;
```

Since there is no enum type to refer to, such named constants can be used in code simply by their names:

```
totalSeconds = totalDays * secondsPerDay;
```

enum can be used for defining named constants of other types as well. For example, the type of the following constant would be string:

```
enum fileName = "list.txt";
```

Such constants are *rvalues* (page 181) and they are called *manifest constants*.

It is possible to create manifest constants of arrays and associative arrays as well. However, as we will see later in the Immutability chapter (page 147), enum arrays and associative arrays may have hidden costs.

31.5 Properties

The .min and .max properties are the minimum and maximum values of an enum type. When the values of the enum type are consecutive, they can be iterated over in a for loop within these limits:

```
enum Suit { spades, hearts, diamonds, clubs }

for (auto suit = Suit.min; suit <= Suit.max; ++suit) {
    writefln("%s: %d", suit, suit);
}
```

Format specifiers "%s" and "%d" produce different outputs:

```
spades: 0
hearts: 1
diamonds: 2
clubs: 3
```

Note that a foreach loop over that range would leave the .max value out of the iteration:

```
foreach (suit; Suit.min .. Suit.max) {
    writefln("%s: %d", suit, suit);
}
```

The output:

```
spades: 0
hearts: 1
diamonds: 2
                    ← clubs is missing
```

For that reason, a correct way of iterating over all values of an enum is using the EnumMembers template from the `std.traits` module:

```
import std.traits;
// ...
    foreach (suit; EnumMembers!Suit) {
        writefln("%s: %d", suit, suit);
    }
```

Note: *The ! character above is for template instantiations, which will be covered in a later chapter (page 399).*

```
spades: 0
hearts: 1
diamonds: 2
clubs: 3          ← clubs is present
```

31.6 Converting from the base type

As we saw in the formatted outputs above, an enum value can automatically be converted to its base type (e.g. to `int`). The reverse conversion is not automatic:

```
    Suit suit = 1;        // ← compilation ERROR
```

One reason for this is to avoid ending up with invalid enum values:

```
    suit = 100;           // ← would be an invalid enum value
```

The values that are known to correspond to valid enum values of a particular enum type can still be converted to that type by an explicit *type cast*:

```
    suit = cast(Suit)1;  // now hearts
```

It would be the programmer's responsibility to ensure the validity of the values when an explicit cast is used. We will see type casting in a later chapter (page 237).

31.7 Exercise

Modify the calculator program from the exercises of the Integers and Arithmetic Operations chapter (page 31) to have the user select the arithmetic operation from a menu.

This program should be different from the previous one in at least the following areas:

- Use enum values, not magic constants.
- Use `double` instead of `int`.
- Use a `switch` statement instead of an "if, else if, else" chain.

The solution is on page 711.

Similarly to how fundamental types are building blocks of program data, functions are building blocks of program behavior.

Functions are also closely related to the craft aspect of programming. The functions that are written by experienced programmers are succinct, simple, and clear. This goes both ways: The mere act of trying to identify and write smaller building blocks of a program makes for a better programmer.

We have covered basic statements and expressions in previous chapters. Although there will be many more that we will see in later chapters, what we have seen so far are commonly-used features of D. Still, they are not sufficient on their own to write large programs. The programs that we have written so far have all been very short, each demonstrating just a simple feature of the language. Trying to write a program with any level of complexity without functions would be very difficult and prone to bugs.

This chapter covers only the basic features of functions. We will see more about functions later in the following chapters:

- Function Parameters (page 168)
- Function Overloading (page 265)
- Function Pointers, Delegates, and Lambdas (page 475)
- More Functions (page 547)

Functions are features that put statements and expressions together as units of program execution. Such statements and expressions altogether are given a name that describes what they collectively achieve. They can then be *called* (or *executed*) by using that name.

The concept of *giving names to a group of steps* is common in our daily lives. For example, the act of cooking an omelet can be described in some level of detail by the following steps:

- get a pan
- get butter
- get an egg
- turn on the stove
- put the pan on the fire
- put butter into the pan when it is hot
- put the egg into butter when it is melted
- remove the pan from the fire when the egg is cooked
- turn off the stove

Since that much detail is obviously excessive, steps that are related together would be combined under a single name:

- make preparations (get the pan, butter, and the egg)
- turn on the stove
- cook the egg (put the pan on the fire, etc.)
- turn off the stove

Going further, there can be a single name for all of the steps:

- make a one-egg omelet (all of the steps)

Functions are based on the same concept: steps that can collectively be named as a whole are put together to form a function. As an example, let's start with the following lines of code that achieve the task of printing a menu:

```
    writeln(" 0 Exit");
    writeln(" 1 Add");
    writeln(" 2 Subtract");
    writeln(" 3 Multiply");
    writeln(" 4 Divide");
```

Since it would make sense to name those combined lines as printMenu, they can be put together to form a function by using the following syntax:

```
void printMenu() {
    writeln(" 0 Exit");
    writeln(" 1 Add");
    writeln(" 2 Subtract");
    writeln(" 3 Multiply");
    writeln(" 4 Divide");
}
```

The contents of that function can now be executed from within main() simply by using its name:

```
void main() {
    printMenu();

    // ...
}
```

It may be obvious from the similarities of the definitions of printMenu() and main() that main() is a function as well. The execution of a D program starts with the function named main() and branches out to other functions from there.

32.1 Parameters

Some of the powers of functions come from the fact that their behaviors are adjustable through parameters.

Let's continue with the omelet example by modifying it to make an omelet of five eggs instead of always one. The steps would exactly be the same, the only difference being the number of eggs to use. We can change the more general description above accordingly:

- make preparations (get the pan, butter, and five eggs)
- turn on the stove
- cook the eggs (put the pan on the fire, etc.)
- turn off the stove

Likewise, the most general single step would become the following:

- make a five-egg omelet (all of the steps)

This time there is an additional information that concerns some of the steps: "get five eggs", "cook the eggs", and "make a five-egg omelet".

The behaviors of functions can be adjusted similarly to the omelet example. The information that functions use to adjust their behavior are called *parameters*. Parameters are specified in a comma separated *function parameter list*. The parameter list rests inside of the parentheses that comes after the name of the function.

The `printMenu()` function above was defined with an empty parameter list because that function always printed the same menu. Let's assume that sometimes the menu will need to be printed differently in different contexts. For example, it may make more sense to print the first entry as "Return" instead of "Exit" depending on the part of the program that is being executed at that time.

In such a case, the first entry of the menu can be *parameterized* by having been defined in the parameter list. The function then uses the value of that parameter instead of the literal `"Exit"`:

```
void printMenu(string firstEntry) {
    writeln(" 0 ", firstEntry);
    writeln(" 1 Add");
    writeln(" 2 Subtract");
    writeln(" 3 Multiply");
    writeln(" 4 Divide");
}
```

Notice that since the information that the `firstEntry` parameter conveys is a piece of text, its type has been specified as `string` in the parameter list. This function can now be *called* with different parameter values to print menus having different first entries. All that needs to be done is to use the appropriate `string` values depending on where the function is being called from:

```
    // At some place in the program:
    printMenu("Exit");
    // ...
    // At some other place in the program:
    printMenu("Return");
```

Note: When you write and use your own functions with parameters of type `string` you may encounter compilation errors. As written, `printMenu()` above cannot be called with parameter values of type `char[]`. For example, the following code would cause a compilation error:

```
    char[] anEntry;
    anEntry ~= "Take square root";
    printMenu(anEntry);  // ←  compilation ERROR
```

On the other hand, if `printMenu()` were defined to take its parameter as `char[]`, then it could not be called with `string`s like `"Exit"`. This is related to the concept of immutability and the `immutable` keyword, both of which will be covered in the next chapter.

Let's continue with the menu function and assume that it is not appropriate to always start the menu selection numbers with zero. In that case the starting number can also be passed to the function as its second parameter. The parameters of the function must be separated by commas:

```
void printMenu(string firstEntry, int firstNumber) {
    writeln(' ', firstNumber + 0, ' ', firstEntry);
    writeln(' ', firstNumber + 1, " Add");
    writeln(' ', firstNumber + 2, " Subtract");
    writeln(' ', firstNumber + 3, " Multiply");
    writeln(' ', firstNumber + 4, " Divide");
}
```

It is now possible to tell the function what number to start from:

```
    printMenu("Return", 1);
```

32.2 Calling a function

Starting a function so that it achieves its task is called *calling a function*. The function call syntax is the following:

```
function_name(parameter_values)
```

The actual parameter values that are passed to functions are called *function arguments*. Although the terms *parameter* and *argument* are sometimes used interchangeably in the literature, they signify different concepts.

The arguments are matched to the parameters one by one in the order that the parameters are defined. For example, the last call of `printMenu()` above uses the *arguments* "Return" and 1, which correspond to the *parameters* `firstEntry` and `firstNumber`, respectively.

The type of each argument must match the type of the corresponding parameter.

32.3 Doing work

In previous chapters, we have defined expressions as entities that do work. Function calls are expressions as well: they do some work. Doing work means producing a value or having a side effect:

- **Producing a value**: Some operations only produce values. For example, a function that adds numbers would be producing the result of that addition. As another example, a function that makes a `Student` object by using the student's name and address would be producing a `Student` object.

- **Having side effects**: Side effects are any change in the state of the program or its environment. Some operations have only side effects. An example is how the `printMenu()` function above changes `stdout` by printing to it. As another example, a function that adds a `Student` object to a student container would also have a side effect: it would be causing the container to grow.

  In summary, operations that cause a change in the state of the program have side effects.

- **Having side effects and producing a value**: Some operations do both. For example, a function that reads two values from `stdin` and returns their sum would be having side effects due to changing the state of `stdin` and also producing the sum of the two values.

- **No operation**: Although every function is designed as one of the three categories above, depending on certain conditions at compile time or at run time, some functions end up doing no work at all.

32.4 The return value

The value that a function produces as a result of its work is called its *return value*. This term comes from the observation that once the program execution branches into a function, it eventually *returns* back to where the function has been called. Functions get *called* and they *return* values.

Just like any other value, return values have types. The type of the return value is specified right before the name of the function, at the point where the function is defined. For example, a function that adds two values of type `int` and returns their sum also as an `int` would be defined as follows:

```
int add(int first, int second) {
    // ...   the actual work of the function ...
}
```

The value that a function returns takes the place of the function call itself. For example, assuming that the function call add(5, 7) produces the value 12, then the following two lines would be equivalent:

```
writeln("Result: ", add(5, 7));
writeln("Result: ", 12);
```

In the first line above, the add() function is called with the arguments 5 and 7 *before* writeln() gets called. The value 12 that the function returns is in turn passed to writeln() as its second argument.

This allows passing the return values of functions to other functions to form complex expressions:

```
writeln("Result: ", add(5, divide(100, studentCount())));
```

In the line above, the return value of studentCount() is passed to divide() as its second argument, the return value of divide() is passed to add() as its second argument, and eventually the return value of add() is passed to writeln() as its second argument.

32.5 The return statement
The return value of a function is specified by the return keyword:

```
int add(int first, int second) {
    int result = first + second;
    return result;
}
```

A function produces its return value by taking advantage of statements, expressions, and potentially by calling other functions. The function would then return that value by the return keyword, at which point the execution of the function ends.

It is possible to have more than one return statement in a function. The value of the first return statement that gets executed determines the return value of the function for a particular call:

```
int complexCalculation(int aParameter, int anotherParameter) {
    if (aParameter == anotherParameter) {
        return 0;
    }

    return aParameter * anotherParameter;
}
```

The function above returns 0 when the two parameters are equal, and the product of their values when they are different.

32.6 void functions
The return types of functions that do not produce values are specified as void. We have seen this many times with the main() function so far, as well as the printMenu() function above. Since they do not return any value to the caller, their return types have been defined as void. (**Note:** *main()* can also be defined as *returning* int. *We will see this in a later chapter (page 185).*)

32.7 The name of the function

The name of a function must be chosen to communicate the purpose of the function clearly. For example, the names add and printMenu were appropriate because their purposes were to add two values, and to print a menu, respectively.

A common guideline for function names is that they contain a verb like *add* or *print*. According to this guideline names like addition() and menu() would be less than ideal.

However, it is acceptable to name functions simply as nouns if those functions do not have any side effects. For example, a function that returns the current temperature can be named as currentTemperature() instead of getCurrentTemperature().

Coming up with names that are clear, short, and consistent is part of the subtle art of programming.

32.8 Code quality through functions

Functions can improve the quality of code. Smaller functions with fewer responsibilities lead to programs that are easier to maintain.

Code duplication is harmful

One of the aspects that is highly detrimental to program quality is code duplication. Code duplication occurs when there is more than one piece of code in the program that performs the same task.

Although this sometimes happens by copying lines of code around, it may also happen incidentally when writing separate pieces of code.

One of the problems with pieces of code that duplicate essentially the same functionality is that they present multiple chances for bugs to crop up. When such bugs do occur and we need to fix them, it can be hard to make sure that we have fixed all places where we introduced the problem, as they may be spread around. Conversely, when the code appears in only one place in the program, then we only need to fix it at that one place to get rid of the bug once and for all.

As I mentioned above, functions are closely related to the craft aspect of programming. Experienced programmers are always on the lookout for code duplication. They continually try to identify commonalities in code and move common pieces of code to separate functions (or to common structs, classes, templates, etc., as we will see in later chapters).

Let's start with a program that contains some code duplication. Let's see how that duplication can be removed by moving code into functions (i.e. by *refactoring* the code). The following program reads numbers from the input and prints them first in the order that they have arrived and then in numerical order:

```d
import std.stdio;
import std.algorithm;

void main() {
    int[] numbers;

    int count;
    write("How many numbers are you going to enter? ");
    readf(" %s", &count);

    // Read the numbers
    foreach (i; 0 .. count) {
        int number;
        write("Number ", i, "? ");
        readf(" %s", &number);

        numbers ~= number;
```

```
    }

    // Print the numbers
    writeln("Before sorting:");
    foreach (i, number; numbers) {
        writefln("%3d:%5d", i, number);
    }

    sort(numbers);

    // Print the numbers
    writeln("After sorting:");
    foreach (i, number; numbers) {
        writefln("%3d:%5d", i, number);
    }
}
```

Some of the duplicated lines of code are obvious in that program. The last two
foreach loops that are used for printing the numbers are exactly the same.
Defining a function that might appropriately be named as print() would remove
that duplication. The function could take a slice as a parameter and print it:

```
void print(int[] slice) {
    foreach (i, element; slice) {
        writefln("%3s:%5s", i, element);
    }
}
```

Notice that the parameter is now referred to using the more general name slice
instead of original and more specific name numbers. The reason for that is the
fact that the function would not know what the elements of the slice would
specifically represent. That can only be known at the place where the function
has been called from. The elements may be student IDs, parts of a password, etc.
Since that cannot be known in the print() function, general names like slice
and element are used in its implementation.

The new function can be called from the two places where the slice needs to be
printed:

```
import std.stdio;
import std.algorithm;

void print(int[] slice) {
    foreach (i, element; slice) {
        writefln("%3s:%5s", i, element);
    }
}

void main() {
    int[] numbers;

    int count;
    write("How many numbers are you going to enter? ");
    readf(" %s", &count);

    // Read the numbers
    foreach (i; 0 .. count) {
        int number;
        write("Number ", i, "? ");
        readf(" %s", &number);

        numbers ~= number;
    }

    // Print the numbers
    writeln("Before sorting:");
    print(numbers);
```

```
    sort(numbers);

    // Print the numbers
    writeln("After sorting:");
    print(numbers);
}
```

There is more to do. Notice that there is always a title line printed right before printing the elements of the slice. Although the title is different, the task is the same. If printing the title can be seen as a part of printing the slice, the title too can be passed as a parameter. Here are the new changes:

```
void print(string title, int[] slice) {
    writeln(title, ":");

    foreach (i, element; slice) {
        writefln("%3s:%5s", i, element);
    }
}

// ...

    // Print the numbers
    print("Before sorting", numbers);

// ...

    // Print the numbers
    print("After sorting", numbers);
```

This step has the added benefit of obviating the comments that appear right before the two print() calls. Since the name of the function already clearly communicates what it does, those comments are unnecessary:

```
    print("Before sorting", numbers);
    sort(numbers);
    print("After sorting", numbers);
```

Although subtle, there is more code duplication in this program: The values of count and number are read in exactly the same way. The only difference is the message that is printed to the user and the name of the variable:

```
    int count;
    write("How many numbers are you going to enter? ");
    readf(" %s", &count);

// ...

        int number;
        write("Number ", i, "? ");
        readf(" %s", &number);
```

The code would become even better if it took advantage of a new function that might be named appropriately as readInt(). The new function can take the message as a parameter, print that message, read an int from the input, and return that int:

```
int readInt(string message) {
    int result;
    write(message, "? ");
    readf(" %s", &result);
    return result;
}
```

count can now be initialized directly by the return value of a call to this new
function:

```
    int count =
        readInt("How many numbers are you going to enter");
```

number cannot be initialized in as straightforward a way because the loop
counter i happens to be a part of the message that is displayed when reading
number. This can be overcome by taking advantage of format:

```
import std.string;
// ...
        int number = readInt(format("Number %s", i));
```

Further, since number is used in only one place in the foreach loop, its definition
can be eliminated altogether and the return value of readInt() can directly be
used in its place:

```
    foreach (i; 0 .. count) {
        numbers ~= readInt(format("Number %s", i));
    }
```

Let's make a final modification to this program by moving the lines that read the
numbers to a separate function. This would also eliminate the need for the "Read
the numbers" comment because the name of the new function would already
carry that information.

The new readNumbers() function does not need any parameter to complete its
task. It reads some numbers and returns them as a slice. The following is the final
version of the program:

```
import std.stdio;
import std.string;
import std.algorithm;

void print(string title, int[] slice) {
    writeln(title, ":");

    foreach (i, element; slice) {
        writefln("%3s:%5s", i, element);
    }
}

int readInt(string message) {
    int result;
    write(message, "? ");
    readf(" %s", &result);
    return result;
}

int[] readNumbers() {
    int[] result;

    int count =
        readInt("How many numbers are you going to enter");

    foreach (i; 0 .. count) {
        result ~= readInt(format("Number %s", i));
    }

    return result;
}

void main() {
    int[] numbers = readNumbers();
    print("Before sorting", numbers);
    sort(numbers);
```

```
        print("After sorting", numbers);
}
```

Compare this version of the program to the first one. The major steps of the program are very clear in the `main()` function of the new program. In contrast, the `main()` function of the first program had to be carefully examined to understand the purpose of that program.

Although the total numbers of nontrivial lines of the two versions of the program ended up being equal in this example, functions make programs shorter in general. This effect is not apparent in this simple program. For example, before the `readInt()` function has been defined, reading an `int` from the input involved three lines of code. After the definition of `readInt()`, the same goal is achieved by a single line of code. Further, the definition of `readInt()` allowed removing the definition of the variable `number` altogether.

Commented lines of code as functions

Sometimes the need to write a comment to describe the purpose of a group of lines of code is an indication that those lines could better be moved to a newly defined function. If the name of the function is descriptive enough then there will be no need for the comment either.

The three commented groups of lines of the first version of the program have been used for defining new functions that achieved the same tasks.

Another important benefit of removing comment lines is that comments tend to become outdated as the code gets modified over time. When updating code, programmers sometimes forget to update associated comments thus these comments become either useless or, even worse, misleading. For that reason, it is beneficial to try to write programs without the need for comments.

32.9 Exercises

1. Modify the `printMenu()` function to take the entire set of menu items as a parameter. For example, the menu items can be passed to the function as in the following code:

   ```
   string[] items =
       [ "Black", "Red", "Green", "Blue", "White" ];
   printMenu(items, 1);
   ```

   Have the program produce the following output:

   ```
   1 Black
   2 Red
   3 Green
   4 Blue
   5 White
   ```

2. The following program uses a two dimensional array as a canvas. Start with that program and improve it by adding more functionality to it:

   ```
   import std.stdio;

   enum totalLines = 20;
   enum totalColumns = 60;

   /* The 'alias' in the next line makes 'Line' an alias of
    * dchar[totalColumns]. Every 'Line' that is used in the rest
    * of the program will mean dchar[totalColumns] from this
    * point on.
    *
    * Also note that 'Line' is a fixed-length array.   */
   ```

```
alias Line = dchar[totalColumns];

/* A dynamic array of Lines is being aliased as 'Canvas'. */
alias Canvas = Line[];

/* Prints the canvas line by line. */
void print(Canvas canvas) {
    foreach (line; canvas) {
        writeln(line);
    }
}

/* Places a dot at the specified location on the canvas. In a
 * sense, "paints" the canvas. */
void putDot(Canvas canvas, int line, int column) {
    canvas[line][column] = '#';
}

/* Draws a vertical line of the specified length from the
 * specified position. */
void drawVerticalLine(Canvas canvas,
                      int line,
                      int column,
                      int length) {
    foreach (lineToPaint; line .. line + length) {
        putDot(canvas, lineToPaint, column);
    }
}

void main() {
    Line emptyLine = '.';

    /* An empty canvas */
    Canvas canvas;

    /* Constructing the canvas by adding empty lines */
    foreach (i; 0 .. totalLines) {
        canvas ~= emptyLine;
    }

    /* Using the canvas */
    putDot(canvas, 7, 30);
    drawVerticalLine(canvas, 5, 10, 4);

    print(canvas);
}
```

The solutions are on page 712.

33 Immutability

Concepts are represented by the variables of a program. Interactions of concepts are commonly achieved by expressions that change the values of variables that represent those concepts. For example, the following code *changes* some variables that represent a purchase:

```
totalPrice = calculateAmount(itemPrices);
moneyInWallet -= totalPrice;
moneyAtMerchant += totalPrice;
```

Changing the value of a variable is called *modifying* or *mutating* that variable. Disallowing mutation of a variable is called *immutability*.

As mutation is essential for most tasks, deliberately disallowing it can be counter-intuitive but is a powerful and useful feature. The concept of immutability is based on experience gained by the programming community in general: Immutability helps with correctness and maintainability of programs. This idea is so powerful that some functional programming languages disallow mutation altogether.

Some benefits of immutability are the following:

- Some concepts are immutable by definition. For example, there are always seven days in a week, the math constant *pi* (π) never changes, the list of natural languages supported by a program may be fixed (e.g. only English and Turkish), etc.

- Even if they don't represent immutable concepts, some variables are not intended to be mutated after they are initialized; so it may be a programmer error to do so. For example, totalPrice in the code above likely should not be mutated after being assigned its initial value.

- By defining only some of its parameters as mutable, a function can dictate which of those parameters will be used *as-is* as its inputs and which parameters will be modified as side effects.

Immutability is so common in programming in general and widely adopted by D programmers that the following curiosities are accepted as consequences:

- As evidenced by the programs we have been writing so far, immutability is not absolutely necessary.

- The immutability concept is expressed in D by the const (short for "constant") and immutable keywords. Although the two words have the same meaning in English, their responsibilities in programs are different and they are sometimes incompatible. (Like inout (page 168) and shared (page 640), const and immutable are *type qualifiers*.)

- Both of the terms "immutable variable" and "constant variable" are nonsensical when the word "variable" is taken literally to mean *something that changes*. In a broader sense, the word "variable" is often understood to mean any concept of a program, either mutable or immutable.

- As an example of self-fulfilling prophecy, functions are forced to observe immutability (forced to be *const-correct*) and become more useful as a consequence. (This forced observance of const-correctness is sometimes described as being similar to a viral disease.)

33.1 Immutable variables

There are three ways of defining variables that cannot be mutated.

enum constants

We have seen earlier in the enum chapter (page 132) that enum defines named constant values:

```
enum fileName = "list.txt";
```

As long as their values can be determined at compile time, enum variables can be initialized with more complex expressions as well, including return values of functions:

```
int totalLines() {
    return 42;
}

int totalColumns() {
    return 7;
}

string name() {
    return "list";
}

void main() {
    enum fileName = name() ~ ".txt";
    enum totalSquares = totalLines() * totalColumns();
}
```

The D feature that enables such initialization is *compile time function execution* (CTFE), which we will see in a later chapter (page 547).

As expected, the values of enum constants cannot be modified:

```
++totalSquares;    // ← compilation ERROR
```

Although it is a very effective way of representing immutable values, enum can only be used with compile-time values.

An enum constant is *a manifest constant*, meaning that the program is compiled as if every mention of that constant had been replaced by its value. As an example, let's consider the following enum definition and the two expressions that make use of it:

```
enum i = 42;
writeln(i);
foo(i);
```

The code above is the exact equivalent of the one below, where every use of i is replaced with its value of 42:

```
writeln(42);
foo(42);
```

Although that replacement makes sense for simple types like int and makes no difference to the resulting program, enum constants can bring a hidden cost when they are used for arrays or associative arrays:

```
enum a = [ 42, 100 ];
writeln(a);
foo(a);
```

After replacing a with its value, the equivalent code that the compiler would be compiling is the following:

```
writeln([ 42, 100 ]); // an array is created at run time
foo([ 42, 100 ]);     // another array is created at run time
```

The hidden cost here is that there would be two separate arrays created for the two expressions above. For that reason, it makes more sense to define arrays and associative arrays as immutable variables if they are going to be mentioned more than once in the program.

const variables

Like enum, this keyword specifies that the value of a variable will never change. Unlike enum, a const variable is an actual variable with a memory address and const variables are commonly initialized during the execution of the program.

The compiler does not allow mutating a const variable:

```
const half = total / 2;
half = 10;     // ← compilation ERROR
```

The following program uses both enum and const. The program asks for the user to guess a number that has been picked randomly. Since the random number cannot be determined at compile time, it cannot be defined as an enum. Still, since the randomly picked value must never be changed after having been decided, it is suitable to specify that variable as const.

The program takes advantage of the readInt() function that was defined in the previous chapter:

```
import std.stdio;
import std.random;

int readInt(string message) {
    int result;
    write(message, "? ");
    readf(" %s", &result);
    return result;
}

void main() {
    enum min = 1;
    enum max = 10;

    const number = uniform(min, max + 1);

    writefln("I am thinking of a number between %s and %s.",
            min, max);

    auto isCorrect = false;
    while (!isCorrect) {
        const guess = readInt("What is your guess");
        isCorrect = (guess == number);
    }

    writeln("Correct!");
}
```

Observations:

- min and max are integral parts of the behavior of this program and their values are known at compile time. For that reason they are defined as enum constants.

- number is specified as const because it would not be appropriate to modify it after its initialization at run time. Likewise for each user guess: once read, the guess should not be modified.
- The types of those variables are not specified explicitly. As with the uses of auto, enum, etc.; the type of a const variable can be inferred from the expression on the right hand side.

Although it is not necessary to write the type fully, const normally takes the actual type within parentheses, e.g. const(int). The output of the following program demonstrates that the full names of the types of the three variables are in fact the same:

```
import std.stdio;

void main() {
    const       inferredType = 0;
    const int   explicitType = 1;
    const(int)  fullType     = 2;

    writeln(typeof(inferredType).stringof);
    writeln(typeof(explicitType).stringof);
    writeln(typeof(fullType).stringof);
}
```

The actual name of the type includes const:

```
const(int)
const(int)
const(int)
```

The use of parentheses has significance, and specifies which parts of the type are immutable. We will see this below when discussing the immutability of an entire slice vs. its elements.

immutable variables

When defining variables the immutable keyword has the same effect as const. immutable variables cannot be modified:

```
    immutable half = total / 2;
    half = 10;    // ←  compilation ERROR
```

Unless other parts of the program require a variable to be immutable, immutable variables can either be defined as const or immutable. When a function requires specifically that a parameter must be immutable, then a variable corresponding to that parameter must be defined as immutable. We will see this below.

33.2 Parameters

As we will see in the next two chapters, functions can mutate their parameters. For example, they can mutate the elements of slices that are passed as arguments to those functions.

As you would remember from the Slices and Other Array Features chapter (page 65), slices do not own elements but provide access to them. There may be more than one slice at a given time that provides access to the same elements.

Although the examples in this section focus only on slices, this topic is applicable to associative arrays and classes as well because they too are *reference types*.

A slice that is passed as a function argument is not the slice that the function is called with. The argument is a *copy* of the slice variable. (Only the slice *variable* is copied, not the elements.)

```d
import std.stdio;

void main() {
    int[] slice = [ 10, 20, 30, 40 ];   // 1
    halve(slice);
    writeln(slice);
}

void halve(int[] numbers) {             // 2
    foreach (ref number; numbers) {
        number /= 2;
    }
}
```

When program execution enters the halve() function, there are two slices that provide access to the same four elements:

1. The slice named slice that is defined in main(), which is passed to halve() as its parameter
2. The slice named numbers that halve() receives as its argument, which provides access to the same elements as slice

Since both slices refer to the same elements and that we use the ref keyword in the foreach loop, the values of the elements get halved:

```
[5, 10, 15, 20]
```

It is indeed useful for functions to be able to modify the elements of the slices that are passed as arguments. As we have seen in this example, some functions exist just for that purpose.

The compiler does not allow passing const variables as arguments to such functions:

```d
    const(int[]) slice = [ 10, 20, 30, 40 ];
    halve(slice);    // ← compilation ERROR
```

The compilation error indicates that a variable of type const(int[]) cannot be used as an argument of type int[]:

```
Error: function deneme.halve (int[] numbers) is not callable
using argument types (const(int[]))
```

const parameters

It is important and natural that const variables be prevented from being passed to functions like halve() that modify their arguments. However, it would be a limitation if they could not be passed to functions that do not intend to modify them like the print() function below:

```d
import std.stdio;

void main() {
    const(int[]) slice = [ 10, 20, 30, 40 ];
    print(slice);    // ← compilation ERROR
}

void print(int[] slice) {
    writefln("%s elements: ", slice.length);
```

```
    foreach (i, element; slice) {
        writefln("%s: %s", i, element);
    }
}
```

It does not make sense above that a slice is prevented from being printed just because it is const. The proper way of dealing with this situation is using const parameters. This is called making the function *const-correct*. (This is the self-fulfilling prophecy mentioned above that forces functions to observe immutability.)

The const keyword specifies that a variable is not modified through *that particular reference* (e.g. a slice) of that variable. Specifying a parameter as const guarantees that the elements of the slice are not modified inside the function. Once print() provides this guarantee, the program can now be compiled:

```
    print(slice);    // now compiles
// ...
void print(const int[] slice) {
    // ...
}
```

This guarantee of non-mutation provides flexibility because it allows passing *mutable*, const, and immutable variables as arguments:

```
    int[] mutableSlice = [ 7, 8 ];
    print(mutableSlice);    // compiles

    const int[] slice = [ 10, 20, 30, 40 ];
    print(slice);           // compiles

    immutable int[] immSlice = [ 1, 2 ];
    print(immSlice);        // compiles
```

Conversely, failing to define a parameter as const when that parameter is not modified in the function reduces the applicability of that function. Such functions are not const-correct.

Another benefit of const parameters is providing useful information to the programmer: Knowing that a variable will not be modified when passed to a function makes the code easier to understand.

The fact that const parameters can accept *mutable*, const, and immutable variables has an interesting consequence. This is explained in the "Should a parameter be const or immutable?" section below.

in parameters

As we will see in the next chapter, in implies const and is more useful with the -preview=in command line switch. For that reason, I recommend in parameters over const parameters.

immutable parameters

const parameters can be seen as *welcoming* because they accept *mutable*, const, and immutable variables as arguments.

In contrast, immutable parameters are *selective* because they bring a strong requirement: The argument must be immutable. While a const parameter communicates "I will not mutate", an immutable parameter adds "and you should not mutate either".

Only immutable variables can be passed to functions as their immutable parameters:

```
void func(immutable int[] slice) {
    // ...
}

void main() {
    immutable int[] immSlice = [ 1, 2 ];
            int[]    slice = [ 8, 9 ];

    func(immSlice);     // compiles
    func(slice);        // ← compilation ERROR
}
```

For that reason, the immutable specifier should be used only when this requirement is actually necessary. We have indeed been using the immutable specifier indirectly through certain string types. This will be covered below.

We have seen that the parameters that are specified as const or immutable promise not to modify *the actual variable* that is passed as an argument. This is relevant only for reference types because only then there is *the actual variable* to talk about the immutability of.

Reference types and *value types* will be covered in the next chapter. Among the types that we have seen so far, only slices and associative arrays are reference types; the others are value types.

Should a parameter be const or immutable?

Note: *As in implies const, this section is about in as well.*

The sections above may give the impression that, being more flexible, const parameters should be preferred over immutable parameters. This is not always true.

const *erases* the information of whether the original variable was *mutable*, const, or immutable. This information is hidden even from the compiler.

A consequence of this fact is that const parameters cannot be passed as arguments to functions that take immutable parameters. For example, the intermediate function foo() below cannot pass its const parameter to bar() even though the actual variable that is passed through the functions is defined as immutable to begin with in main:

```
void main() {
    /* The original variable is immutable */
    immutable int[] slice = [ 10, 20, 30, 40 ];
    foo(slice);
}

/* A function that takes its parameter as const, in order to
 * be more useful. */
void foo(const int[] slice) {
    bar(slice);     // ← compilation ERROR
}

/* A function that requires an immutable slice. */
void bar(immutable int[] slice) {
    // ...
}
```

bar() requires the parameter to be immutable. However, it is not known (in general) whether the original variable that foo()'s const parameter references was immutable or not.

Note: *It is clear to an observer in the code above that the original variable in main() is immutable. However, the compiler compiles functions individually, without regard to every place that function is called from. To the compiler, the slice parameter of foo() may refer to a mutable variable or an immutable one.*

A solution would be to call bar() with an immutable copy of the parameter:

```
void foo(const int[] slice) {
    bar(slice.idup);
}
```

Although that would make the code compile, it does incur into the cost of copying the slice and its contents, which would be wasteful in the case where the original variable was immutable to begin with.

After this analysis, it should be clear that always declaring parameters as const is not the best approach in every situation. After all, if foo()'s parameter had been defined as immutable there would be no need to copy it before calling bar():

```
void foo(immutable int[] slice) {  // This time immutable
    bar(slice);       // Copying is not needed anymore
}
```

Although the code compiles, defining the parameter as immutable has a similar cost: This time an immutable copy of the original variable is needed when calling foo(), if that variable was not immutable to begin with:

```
    foo(mutableSlice.idup);
```

Templates can help. (We will see templates in later chapters.) Although I don't expect you to fully understand the following function at this point in the book, I will present it as a solution to this problem. The following function template foo() can be called with *mutable*, const, and immutable variables. The parameter would be copied only if the original variable was mutable; no copying would take place if it were immutable:

```
import std.conv;
// ...

/* Because it is a template, foo() can be called with both mutable
 * and immutable variables. */
void foo(T)(T[] slice) {
    /* 'to()' does not make a copy if the original variable is
     * already immutable. */
    bar(to!(immutable T[])(slice));
}
```

33.3 Initialization

Disallowing mutations can be seen as a limitation when initial values of variables depend on non-trivial expressions. For example, the contents of the fruits array below depend on the value of addCitrus but the code fails to compile because the variable is const:

```
    const fruits = [ "apple", "pear" ];

    if (addCitrus) {
        fruits ~= [ "orange" ];    // ← compilation ERROR
    }
```

Although making the variable mutable e.g. by defining it with auto would allow the code to compile, it is still possible to define it as const by moving the initialization code to a function:

```
bool addCitrus;
```

```
string[] makeFruits() {
    auto result = [ "apple", "pear" ];

    if (addCitrus) {
        result ~= [ "orange" ];
    }

    return result;
}

void main() {
    const fruits = makeFruits();
}
```

Note how the local `result` array is mutable but the `fruits` is still `const` (presumably as desired by the programmer). When it is impossible or cumbersome to move the code to a named function, a lambda (page 475) can be used instead:

```
const fruits = {
  // Exactly the same code as 'makeFruits()'.
  auto result = [ "apple", "pear" ];

    if (addCitrus) {
        result ~= [ "orange" ];
    }

    return result;
}();
```

The lambda is defined by the highlighted curly braces and is executed by the parenteses at the end. Again, the `fruits` variable ends up being `const` as desired.

D allows assigning to `const` and `immutable` variables in special initialization blocks called `shared static this()` (and `static this()`). These blocks are for initializing variables defined at module scope (outside of any function). It is possible to mutate `const` and `immutable` variables in `shared static this()` blocks:

```
immutable int[] i;

shared static this() {
    // It is possible to mutate 'const' and 'immutable' module
    // variables in this block:
    i ~= 43;

    // The variables are still 'const' and 'immutable' for the
    // rest of the program.
}
```

`shared static this()` blocks are executed before the program starts running the body of the `main()` function.

33.4 Immutability of the slice versus the elements

We have seen above that the type of a `const` slice has been printed as `const(int[])`. As the parentheses after `const` indicate, it is the entire slice that is `const`. Such a slice cannot be modified in any way: elements may not be added or removed, their values may not be modified, and the slice may not start providing access to a different set of elements:

```
const int[] slice = [ 1, 2 ];
slice ~= 3;            // ← compilation ERROR
slice[0] = 3;          // ← compilation ERROR
slice.length = 1;      // ← compilation ERROR
```

```
        const int[] otherSlice = [ 10, 11 ];
        slice = otherSlice;         // ← compilation ERROR
```

Taking immutability to that extreme may not be suitable in every case. In most cases, what is important is the immutability of the elements themselves. Since a slice is just a tool to access the elements, it should not matter if we make changes to the slice itself as long as the elements are not modified. This is especially true in the cases we have seen so far, where the function receives a copy of the slice itself.

To specify that only the elements are immutable we use the const keyword with parentheses that enclose just the element type. Modifying the code accordingly, now only the elements are immutable, not the slice itself:

```
        const(int)[] slice = [ 1, 2 ];
        slice ~= 3;                 // can add elements
        slice[0] = 3;               // ← compilation ERROR
        slice.length = 1;           // can drop elements

        const int[] otherSlice = [ 10, 11 ];
        slice = otherSlice;         /* can provide access to
                                     * other elements */
```

Although the two syntaxes are very similar, they have different meanings. To summarize:

```
        const int[]   a = [1]; /* Neither the elements nor the
                                * slice can be modified */

        const(int[]) b = [1]; /* The same meaning as above */

        const(int)[] c = [1]; /* The elements cannot be
                                * modified but the slice can be */
```

This distinction has been in effect in some of the programs that we have written so far. As you may remember, the three string aliases involve immutability:

- `string` is an alias for `immutable(char)[]`
- `wstring` is an alias for `immutable(wchar)[]`
- `dstring` is an alias for `immutable(dchar)[]`

Likewise, string literals are immutable as well:

- The type of literal `"hello"c` is `string`
- The type of literal `"hello"w` is `wstring`
- The type of literal `"hello"d` is `dstring`

According to these definitions, D strings are normally arrays of *immutable characters*.

const and immutable are transitive

As mentioned in the code comments of slices a and b above, both those slices and their elements are immutable.

This is true for structs (page 246) and classes (page 322) as well, both of which will be covered in later chapters. For example, all members of a const struct variable are const and all members of an immutable struct variable are immutable. (Likewise for classes.)

`.dup` and `.idup`

There may be mismatches in immutability when strings are passed to functions as parameters. The `.dup` and `.idup` properties make copies of arrays with the desired mutability:

- `.dup` makes a mutable copy of the array ("dup" stands for "do duplicate")
- `.idup` makes an immutable copy of the array

For example, a function that insists on the immutability of a parameter may have to be called with an immutable copy of a mutable string:

```
void foo(string s) {
    // ...
}

void main() {
    char[] salutation;
    foo(salutation);           // ← compilation ERROR
    foo(salutation.idup);      // ← this compiles
}
```

33.5 How to use

- As a general rule, prefer immutable variables over mutable ones.
- Define constant values as enum if their values can be calculated at compile time. For example, the constant value of *seconds per minute* can be an enum:

  ```
  enum int secondsPerMinute = 60;
  ```

  There is no need to specify the type explicitly if it can be inferred from the right hand side:

  ```
  enum secondsPerMinute = 60;
  ```

- Consider the hidden cost of enum arrays and enum associative arrays. Define them as `immutable` variables if they are used more than once in the program.
- Specify variables as `const` if their values will never change but cannot be known at compile time. Again, the type can be inferred:

  ```
  const guess = readInt("What is your guess");
  ```

- If a function does not modify a parameter, specify that parameter as in. This would express programmer's intent and allow both mutable and `immutable` variables to be passed as arguments:

  ```
  void foo(in char[] s) {
      // ...
  }

  void main() {
      char[] mutableString;
      string immutableString;

      foo(mutableString);        // ← compiles
      foo(immutableString);      // ← compiles
  }
  ```

- Unlike most examples throughout this book, always specify what part of a parameter should be immutable:

```
// Only the elements may not be mutated (the slice can be)
void print_1(const(int)[] slice) {
    // ...
}

// Neither the slice variable nor the elements can be mutated
void print_2(const(int[]) slice) {
    // ...
}

// Same as print_2()  (Unlike most examples in this book, avoid this style)
void print_3(const int[] slice) {
    // ...
}
```

- Consider that const parameters cannot be passed to functions taking immutable. See the section "Should a parameter be const or immutable?" above.

- If the function modifies a parameter, leave that parameter as mutable (in, const, or immutable would not allow modifications anyway):

```
import std.stdio;

void reverse(dchar[] s) {
    foreach (i; 0 .. s.length / 2) {
        immutable temp = s[i];
        s[i] = s[$ - 1 - i];
        s[$ - 1 - i] = temp;
    }
}

void main() {
    dchar[] salutation = "hello"d.dup;
    reverse(salutation);
    writeln(salutation);
}
```

The output:

```
olleh
```

33.6 Summary

- enum variables represent immutable concepts that are known at compile time.
- enum arrays and associative arrays have the cost of creating a new array at every mention of that enum constant. Prefer immutable for arrays and associative arrays instead.
- Prefer in parameters over const parameters.
- const and immutable variables represent immutable concepts that can be known at run time (or somewhat obscurely, that must have some memory location that we can refer to).
- const parameters are the ones that functions do not modify. *Mutable*, const, and immutable variables can be passed as arguments of const parameters.
- immutable parameters are the ones that functions specifically require them to be so. Only immutable variables can be passed as arguments of immutable parameters.
- const(int[]) specifies that neither the slice nor its elements can be modified.
- const(int)[] specifies that only the elements cannot be modified.

34 Value Types and Reference Types

This chapter introduces the concepts of value types and reference types. These concepts are particularly important to understand the differences between structs and classes.

This chapter also gets into more detail with the & operator.

The chapter ends with a table that contains the outcomes of the following two concepts for different types of variables:

- Value comparison
- Address comparison

34.1 Value types

Value types are easy to describe: Variables of value types carry values. For example, all of the integer and floating point types are values types. Although not immediately obvious, fixed-length arrays are value types as well.

For example, a variable of type int has an integer value:

```
int speed = 123;
```

The number of bytes that the variable speed occupies is the size of an int. If we visualize the memory as a ribbon going from left to right, we can imagine the variable living on some part of it:

```
    speed
   ┌───────┐
   │  123  │
   └───────┘
```

When variables of value types are copied, they get their own values:

```
int newSpeed = speed;
```

The new variable would have a place and a value of its own:

```
    speed          newSpeed
   ┌───────┐      ┌───────┐
   │  123  │      │  123  │
   └───────┘      └───────┘
```

Naturally, modifications that are made to these variables are independent:

```
speed = 200;
```

The value of the other variable does not change:

```
    speed          newSpeed
   ┌───────┐      ┌───────┐
   │  200  │      │  123  │
   └───────┘      └───────┘
```

The use of assert checks below

The following examples contain assert checks to indicate that their conditions are true. In other words, they are not checks in the normal sense, rather my way of telling to the reader that "this is true".

For example, the check assert(speed == newSpeed) below means "speed is equal to newSpeed".

Value identity

As the memory representations above indicate, there are two types of equality that concern variables:

- **Value equality**: The == operator that appears in many examples throughout the book compares variables by their values. When two variables are said to be *equal* in that sense, their values are equal.
- **Value identity**: In the sense of owning separate values, speed and newSpeed have separate identities. Even when their values are equal, they are different variables.

```
int speed = 123;
int newSpeed = speed;
assert(speed == newSpeed);
speed = 200;
assert(speed != newSpeed);
```

Address-of operator, &

We have been using the & operator so far with readf(). The & operator tells readf() where to put the input data.

Note: *As we have seen in the Reading from the Standard Input chapter (page 15), readf() can be used without explicit pointers as well.*

The addresses of variables can be used for other purposes as well. The following code simply prints the addresses of two variables:

```
int speed = 123;
int newSpeed = speed;

writeln("speed    : ", speed,    " address: ", &speed);
writeln("newSpeed: ", newSpeed, " address: ", &newSpeed);
```

speed and newSpeed have the same value but their addresses are different:

```
speed   : 123 address: 7FFF4B39C738
newSpeed: 123 address: 7FFF4B39C73C
```

Note: *It is normal for the addresses to have different values every time the program is run. Variables live at parts of memory that happen to be available during that particular execution of the program.*

Addresses are normally printed in hexadecimal format.

Additionally, the fact that the two addresses are 4 apart indicates that those two integers are placed next to each other in memory. (Note that the value of hexadecimal C is 12, so the difference between 8 and 12 is 4.)

34.2 Reference variables

Before getting to reference types let's first define reference variables.

Terminology: We have been using the phrase *to provide access to* so far in several contexts throughout the book. For example, slices and associative arrays do not own any elements but provide access to elements that are owned by the D runtime. Another phrase that is identical in meaning is *being a reference of* as in "slices are references of zero or more elements", which is sometimes used even shorter as *to reference* as in "this slice references two elements". Finally, the act of accessing a value through a reference is called *dereferencing*.

Reference variables are variables that act like aliases of other variables. Although they look and are used like variables, they do not have values themselves. Modifications made on a reference variable change the value of the actual variable.

We have already used reference variables so far in two contexts:

- **`ref` in `foreach` loops**: The `ref` keyword makes the loop variable the *actual* element that corresponds to that iteration. When the `ref` keyword is not used, the loop variable is a *copy* of the actual element.

    This can be demonstrated by the & operator as well. If their addresses are the same, two variables would be referencing the same value (or the *same element* in this case):

    ```d
    int[] slice = [ 0, 1, 2, 3, 4 ];

    foreach (i, ref element; slice) {
        assert(&element == &slice[i]);
    }
    ```

    Although they are separate variables, the fact that the addresses of `element` and `slice[i]` are the same proves that they have the same value identity.

    In other words, `element` and `slice[i]` are references of the same value. Modifying either of those affects the actual value. The following memory layout indicates a snapshot of the iteration when `i` is 3:

    ```
    slice[0] slice[1] slice[2] slice[3] slice[4]
      ⋯→       ⋯→       ⋯→    (element)
    ┌────────┬────────┬────────┬────────┬────────┐
    │   0    │   1    │   2    │   3    │   4    │
    └────────┴────────┴────────┴────────┴────────┘
    ```

- **`ref` and `out` function parameters**: Function parameters that are specified as `ref` or `out` are aliases of the actual variable the function is called with.

    The following example demonstrates this case by passing the same variable to separate `ref` and `out` parameters of a function. Again, the & operator indicates that both parameters have the same value identity:

    ```d
    import std.stdio;

    void main() {
        int originalVariable;
        writeln("address of originalVariable: ", &originalVariable);
        foo(originalVariable, originalVariable);
    }

    void foo(ref int refParameter, out int outParameter) {
        writeln("address of refParameter    : ", &refParameter);
        writeln("address of outParameter    : ", &outParameter);
        assert(&refParameter == &outParameter);
    }
    ```

    Although they are defined as separate parameters, `refParameter` and `outParameter` are aliases of `originalVariable`:

    ```
    address of originalVariable: 7FFF24172958
    address of refParameter    : 7FFF24172958
    address of outParameter    : 7FFF24172958
    ```

34.3 Reference types

Variables of reference types have individual identities but they do not have individual values. They *provide access to* existing variables.

We have already seen this concept with slices. Slices do not own elements, they provide access to existing elements:

```
void main() {
    // Although it is named as 'array' here, this variable is
    // a slice as well. It provides access to all of the
    // initial elements:
    int[] array = [ 0, 1, 2, 3, 4 ];

    // A slice that provides access to elements other than the
    // first and the last:
    int[] slice = array[1 .. $ - 1];

    // At this point slice[0] and array[1] provide access to
    // the same value:
    assert(&slice[0] == &array[1]);

    // Changing slice[0] changes array[1]:
    slice[0] = 42;
    assert(array[1] == 42);
}
```

Contrary to reference variables, reference types are not simply aliases. To see this distinction, let's define another slice as a copy of one of the existing slices:

```
int[] slice2 = slice;
```

The two slices have their own adresses. In other words, they have separate identities:

```
assert(&slice != &slice2);
```

The following list is a summary of the differences between reference variables and reference types:

- Reference variables do not have identities, they are aliases of existing variables.
- Variables of reference types have identities but they do not own values; rather, they provide access to existing values.

The way slice and slice2 live in memory can be illustrated as in the following figure:

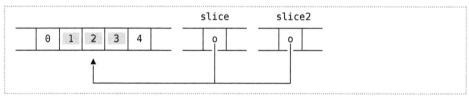

The three elements that the two slices both reference are highlighted.

One of the differences between C++ and D is that classes are reference types in D. Although we will cover classes in later chapters in detail, the following is a short example to demonstrate this fact:

```
class MyClass {
    int member;
}
```

Class objects are constructed by the new keyword:

```
auto variable = new MyClass;
```

variable is a reference to an anonymous MyClass object that has been constructed by new:

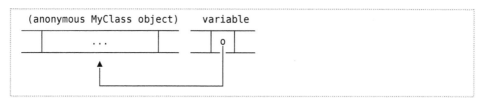

Just like with slices, when `variable` is copied, the copy becomes another reference to the same object. The copy has its own address:

```
auto variable = new MyClass;
auto variable2 = variable;
assert(variable == variable2);
assert(&variable != &variable2);
```

They are equal from the point of view of referencing the same object, but they are separate variables:

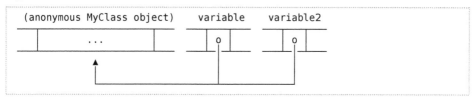

This can also be shown by modifying the member of the object:

```
auto variable = new MyClass;
variable.member = 1;

auto variable2 = variable;    // They share the same object
variable2.member = 2;

assert(variable.member == 2); // The object that variable
                              // provides access to has
                              // changed.
```

Another reference type is associative arrays. Like slices and classes, when an associative array is copied or assigned to another variable, both give access to the same set of elements:

```
string[int] byName =
[
    1   : "one",
    10  : "ten",
    100 : "hundred",
];

// The two associative arrays will be sharing the same
// set of elements
string[int] byName2 = byName;

// The mapping added through the second ...
byName2[4] = "four";

// ... is visible through the first.
assert(byName[4] == "four");
```

As it will be explained in the next chapter, there is no element sharing if the original associative array were `null` to begin with.

The difference in the assignment operation

With value types and reference variables, the assignment operation changes *the actual value*:

```
void main() {
    int number = 8;

    halve(number);        // The actual value changes
    assert(number == 4);
}

void halve(ref int dividend) {
    dividend /= 2;
}
```

On the other hand, with reference types, the assignment operation changes *which value is being accessed*. For example, the assignment of the slice3 variable below does not change the value of any element; rather, it changes what elements slice3 is now a reference of:

```
int[] slice1 = [ 10, 11, 12, 13, 14 ];
int[] slice2 = [ 20, 21, 22 ];

int[] slice3 = slice1[1 .. 3]; // Access to element 1 and
                               // element 2 of slice1

slice3[0] = 777;
assert(slice1 == [ 10, 777, 12, 13, 14 ]);

// This assignment does not modify the elements that
// slice3 is providing access to. It makes slice3 provide
// access to other elements.
slice3 = slice2[$ - 1 .. $]; // Access to the last element

slice3[0] = 888;
assert(slice2 == [ 20, 21, 888 ]);
```

Let's demonstrate the same effect this time with two objects of the MyClass type:

```
auto variable1 = new MyClass;
variable1.member = 1;

auto variable2 = new MyClass;
variable2.member = 2;

auto aCopy = variable1;
aCopy.member = 3;

aCopy = variable2;
aCopy.member = 4;

assert(variable1.member == 3);
assert(variable2.member == 4);
```

The aCopy variable above first references the same object as variable1, and then the same object as variable2. As a consequence, the .member that is modified through aCopy is first variable1's and then variable2's.

Variables of reference types may not be referencing any object

With a reference variable, there is always an actual variable that it is an alias of; it can not start its life without a variable. On the other hand, variables of reference types can start their lives without referencing any object.

For example, a MyClass variable can be defined without an actual object having been created by new:

```
MyClass variable;
```

Such variables have the special value of null. We will cover null and the is keyword in a later chapter (page 233).

34.4 Fixed-length arrays are value types, slices are reference types

D's arrays and slices diverge when it comes to value type versus reference type.

As we have already seen above, slices are reference types. On the other hand, fixed-length arrays are value types. They own their elements and behave as individual values:

```d
int[3] array1 = [ 10, 20, 30 ];

auto array2 = array1; // array2's elements are different
                      // from array1's
array2[0] = 11;

// First array is not affected:
assert(array1[0] == 10);
```

array1 is a fixed-length array because its length is specified when it has been defined. Since auto makes the compiler infer the type of array2, it is a fixed-length array as well. The values of array2's elements are copied from the values of the elements of array1. Each array has its own elements. Modifying an element through one does not affect the other.

34.5 Experiment

The following program is an experiment of applying the == operator to different types. It applies the operator to both variables of a certain type and to the addresses of those variables. The program produces the following output:

```
              Type of variable                    a == b  &a == &b
================================================================
        variables with equal values (value type)   true    false
    variables with different values (value type)   false   false
                   foreach with 'ref' variable      true    true
                foreach without 'ref' variable      true    false
                  function with 'out' parameter      true    true
                  function with 'ref' parameter      true    true
                   function with 'in' parameter      true    false
        slices providing access to same elements     true    false
   slices providing access to different elements    false   false
  MyClass variables to same object (reference type)  true    false
MyClass variables to different objects (reference type) false  false
```

The table above has been generated by the following program:

```d
import std.stdio;
import std.array;

int moduleVariable = 9;

class MyClass {
    int member;
}

void printHeader() {
    immutable dchar[] header =
        "                       Type of variable" ~
        "                       a == b  &a == &b";

    writeln();
    writeln(header);
    writeln(replicate("=", header.length));
}

void printInfo(const dchar[] label,
               bool valueEquality,
               bool addressEquality) {
```

```
        writefln("%55s%9s%9s",
                 label, valueEquality, addressEquality);
}

void main() {
    printHeader();

    int number1 = 12;
    int number2 = 12;
    printInfo("variables with equal values (value type)",
              number1 == number2,
              &number1 == &number2);

    int number3 = 3;
    printInfo("variables with different values (value type)",
              number1 == number3,
              &number1 == &number3);

    int[] slice = [ 4 ];
    foreach (i, ref element; slice) {
        printInfo("foreach with 'ref' variable",
                  element == slice[i],
                  &element == &slice[i]);
    }

    foreach (i, element; slice) {
        printInfo("foreach without 'ref' variable",
                  element == slice[i],
                  &element == &slice[i]);
    }

    outParameter(moduleVariable);
    refParameter(moduleVariable);
    inParameter(moduleVariable);

    int[] longSlice = [ 5, 6, 7 ];
    int[] slice1 = longSlice;
    int[] slice2 = slice1;
    printInfo("slices providing access to same elements",
              slice1 == slice2,
              &slice1 == &slice2);

    int[] slice3 = slice1[0 .. $ - 1];
    printInfo("slices providing access to different elements",
              slice1 == slice3,
              &slice1 == &slice3);

    auto variable1 = new MyClass;
    auto variable2 = variable1;
    printInfo(
        "MyClass variables to same object (reference type)",
        variable1 == variable2,
        &variable1 == &variable2);

    auto variable3 = new MyClass;
    printInfo(
        "MyClass variables to different objects (reference type)",
        variable1 == variable3,
        &variable1 == &variable3);
}

void outParameter(out int parameter) {
    printInfo("function with 'out' parameter",
              parameter == moduleVariable,
              &parameter == &moduleVariable);
}

void refParameter(ref int parameter) {
    printInfo("function with 'ref' parameter",
              parameter == moduleVariable,
              &parameter == &moduleVariable);
}
```

```
void inParameter(in int parameter) {
    printInfo("function with 'in' parameter",
              parameter == moduleVariable,
              &parameter == &moduleVariable);
}
```

Notes:

- The program makes use of a module variable when comparing different types of function parameters. Module variables are defined at module level, outside of all of the functions. They are globally accessible to all of the code in the module.
- The replicate() function of the std.array module takes an array (the "=" string above) and repeats it the specified number of times.

34.6 Summary

- Variables of value types have their own values and adresses.
- Reference variables do not have their own values nor addresses. They are aliases of existing variables.
- Variables of reference types have their own addresses but the values that they reference do not belong to them.
- With reference types, assignment does not change value, it changes which value is being accessed.
- Variables of reference types may be null.

This chapter covers various kinds of function parameters.

Some of the concepts of this chapter have already appeared earlier in the book. For example, the ref keyword that we saw in the foreach Loop chapter (page 121) was making *actual elements* available in foreach loops as opposed to *copies* of those elements.

Additionally, we covered the const and immutable keywords and the differences between value types and reference types in previous chapters.

We have written functions that produced results by making use of their parameters. For example, the following function uses its parameters in a calculation:

```
double weightedAverage(double quizGrade, double finalGrade) {
    return quizGrade * 0.4 + finalGrade * 0.6;
}
```

That function calculates the average grade by taking 40% of the quiz grade and 60% of the final grade. Here is how it may be used:

```
int quizGrade = 76;
int finalGrade = 80;

writefln("Weighted average: %2.0f",
         weightedAverage(quizGrade, finalGrade));
```

35.1 Parameters are always copied

In the code above, the two variables are passed as arguments to weightedAverage(). The function *uses* its parameters. This fact may give the false impression that the function uses the actual variables that have been passed as arguments. In reality, what the function uses are *copies* of those variables.

This distinction is important because modifying a parameter changes only the copy. This can be seen in the following function that is trying to modify its parameter (i.e. making a side effect). Let's assume that the following function is written for reducing the energy of a game character:

```
void reduceEnergy(double energy) {
    energy /= 4;
}
```

Here is a program that tests reduceEnergy():

```
import std.stdio;

void reduceEnergy(double energy) {
    energy /= 4;
}

void main() {
    double energy = 100;

    reduceEnergy(energy);
    writeln("New energy: ", energy);
}
```

The output:

```
New energy: 100        ← Not changed
```

Although `reduceEnergy()` drops the value of its parameter to a quarter of its original value, the variable `energy` in `main()` does not change. The reason for this is that the `energy` variable in `main()` and the `energy` parameter of `reduceEnergy()` are separate; the parameter is a copy of the variable in `main()`.

To observe this more closely, let's insert some `writeln()` expressions:

```d
import std.stdio;

void reduceEnergy(double energy) {
    writeln("Entered the function    : ", energy);
    energy /= 4;
    writeln("Leaving the function    : ", energy);
}

void main() {
    double energy = 100;

    writeln("Calling the function    : ", energy);
    reduceEnergy(energy);
    writeln("Returned from the function: ", energy);
}
```

The output:

```
Calling the function    : 100
Entered the function    : 100
Leaving the function    : 25   ← the parameter changes,
Returned from the function: 100   ← the variable remains the same
```

35.2 Referenced variables are not copied

Even parameters of reference types like slices, associative arrays, and class variables are copied to functions. However, the original variables that are referenced (i.e. elements of slices and associative arrays, and class objects) are not copied. Effectively, such variables are passed to functions as *references*: the parameter becomes another reference to the original object. It means that a modification made through the reference modifies the original object as well.

Being slices of characters, this applies to strings as well:

```d
import std.stdio;

void makeFirstLetterDot(dchar[] str) {
    str[0] = '.';
}

void main() {
    dchar[] str = "abc"d.dup;
    makeFirstLetterDot(str);
    writeln(str);
}
```

The change made to the first element of the parameter affects the actual element in `main()`:

```
.bc
```

However, the original slice and associative array variables are still passed by copy. This may have surprising and seemingly unpredictable results unless the parameters are qualified as `ref` themselves.

Surprising reference semantics of slices

As we saw in the Slices and Other Array Features chapter (page 65), adding elements to a slice *may* terminate element sharing. Obviously, once sharing ends, a slice parameter like str above would not be a reference to the elements of the passed-in original variable anymore.

For example, the element that is appended by the following function will not be seen by the caller:

```d
import std.stdio;

void appendZero(int[] arr) {
    arr ~= 0;
    writefln("Inside appendZero()        : %s", arr);
}

void main() {
    auto arr = [ 1, 2 ];
    appendZero(arr);
    writefln("After appendZero() returns: %s", arr);
}
```

The element is appended only to the function parameter, not to the original slice:

```
Inside appendZero()        : [1, 2, 0]
After appendZero() returns: [1, 2]     ← No 0
```

If the new elements need to be appended to the original slice, then the slice must be passed as ref:

```d
void appendZero(ref int[] arr) {
    // ...
}
```

The ref qualifier will be explained below.

Surprising reference semantics of associative arrays

Associative arrays that are passed as function parameters may cause surprises as well because associative arrays start their lives as null, not empty.

In this context, null means an uninitialized associative array. Associative arrays are initialized automatically when their first key-value pair is added. As a consequence, if a function adds an element to a null associative array, then that element cannot be seen in the original variable because although the parameter is initialized, the original variable remains null:

```d
import std.stdio;

void appendElement(int[string] aa) {
    aa["red"] = 100;
    writefln("Inside appendElement()        : %s", aa);
}

void main() {
    int[string] aa;     // ← null to begin with
    appendElement(aa);
    writefln("After appendElement() returns: %s", aa);
}
```

The original variable does not have the added element:

```
Inside appendElement()        : ["red":100]
After appendElement() returns: []     ← Still null
```

On the other hand, if the associative array were not null to begin with, then the added element would be seen by the caller as well:

```d
    int[string] aa;
    aa["blue"] = 10;   // ← Not null before the call
    appendElement(aa);
```

This time the added element is seen by the caller:

```
Inside appendElement()        : ["red":100, "blue":10]
After appendElement() returns: ["red":100, "blue":10]
```

For that reason, it may be better to pass the associative array as a `ref` parameter, which will be explained below.

35.3 Parameter qualifiers

Parameters are passed to functions according to the general rules described above:

- Value types are copied, after which the original variable and the copy are independent.
- Reference types are copied as well but by nature of reference types, both the original reference and the parameter provide access to the same variable.

Those are the default rules that are applied when parameter definitions have no qualifiers. The following qualifiers change the way parameters are passed and what operations are allowed on them.

in

By default, `in` parameters are the same as `const` parameters. They cannot be modified:

```
void foo(in int value) {
    value = 1;    // ← compilation ERROR
}
```

However, when the `-preview=in` compiler command line switch is used, then `in` parameters become more useful to express the *intent* of "this parameter is used only as input by this function":

```
$ dmd -preview=in deneme.d
```

`-preview=in` changes the meaning of `in` parameters and allows the compiler to choose more appropriate methods when passing arguments for `in` parameters:

- The meaning of `in` changes to mean `const scope` (see below for `scope`)
- Unlike `ref` parameters, even *rvalues* can be passed as `in` parameters (see below for `ref` and the next chapter for rvalues)
- Types that would cause a side effect when copied (e.g. when the copy constructor is defined) or types that cannot be copied (e.g. copy constructor is disabled) are passed by reference

I recommend `in` parameters over `const` parameters regardless of whether the `-preview=in` command line switch is used or not.

out

We know that functions return what they produce as their return values. The fact that there is only one return value is sometimes limiting as some functions may need to produce more than one result. (**Note:** *It is possible to return more than one result by defining the return type as a* Tuple *or a* struct*. We will see these features in later chapters.*)

The `out` keyword makes it possible for functions to return results through their parameters. When `out` parameters are modified within the function, those modifications affect the original variable that has been passed to the function. In a sense, the assigned value goes *out* of the function through the out parameter.

Let's have a look at a function that divides two numbers and produces both the quotient and the remainder. The return value is used for the quotient and the remainder is *returned* through the out parameter:

```d
import std.stdio;

int divide(int dividend, int divisor, out int remainder) {
    remainder = dividend % divisor;
    return dividend / divisor;
}

void main() {
    int remainder;
    int result = divide(7, 3, remainder);

    writeln("result: ", result, ", remainder: ", remainder);
}
```

Modifying the remainder parameter of the function modifies the remainder variable in main() (their names need not be the same):

```
result: 2, remainder: 1
```

Regardless of their values at the call site, out parameters are first assigned to the .init value of their types automatically:

```d
import std.stdio;

void foo(out int parameter) {
    writeln("After entering the function     : ", parameter);
}

void main() {
    int variable = 100;

    writeln("Before calling the function     : ", variable);
    foo(variable);
    writeln("After returning from the function: ", variable);
}
```

Even though there is no explicit assignment to the parameter in the function, the value of the parameter automatically becomes the initial value of int, affecting the variable in main():

```
Before calling the function     : 100
After entering the function     : 0   ← the value of int.init
After returning from the function: 0
```

As this demonstrates, out parameters cannot pass values into functions; they are strictly for passing values out of functions.

We will see in later chapters that returning Tuple or struct types are better alternatives to out parameters.

const

I recommend in parameters over const parameters.

As we saw earlier, const guarantees that the parameter will not be modified inside the function. It is helpful for the programmers to know that certain variables will not be changed by a function. const also makes functions more useful by allowing const, immutable, and *mutable* variables to be passed through that parameter:

```
import std.stdio;

dchar lastLetter(const dchar[] str) {
    return str[$ - 1];
}

void main() {
    writeln(lastLetter("constant"));
}
```

immutable

As we saw earlier, `immutable` makes functions require that certain variables must be immutable. Because of such a requirement, the following function can only be called with strings with `immutable` elements (e.g. string literals):

```
import std.stdio;

dchar[] mix(immutable dchar[] first,
            immutable dchar[] second) {
    dchar[] result;
    int i;

    for (i = 0; (i < first.length) && (i < second.length); ++i) {
        result ~= first[i];
        result ~= second[i];
    }

    result ~= first[i..$];
    result ~= second[i..$];

    return result;
}

void main() {
    writeln(mix("HELLO", "world"));
}
```

Since it forces a requirement on the parameter, `immutable` parameters should be used only when immutability is required. Otherwise, in general `const` is more useful because it accepts `immutable`, `const`, and *mutable* variables.

ref

This keyword allows passing a variable by reference even though it would normally be passed as a copy (i.e. by value).

Rvalues (see the next chapter) cannot be passed to functions as `ref` parameters.

For the `reduceEnergy()` function that we saw earlier to modify the original variable, it must take its parameter as `ref`:

```
import std.stdio;

void reduceEnergy(ref double energy) {
    energy /= 4;
}

void main() {
    double energy = 100;

    reduceEnergy(energy);
    writeln("New energy: ", energy);
}
```

This time, the modification that is made to the parameter changes the original variable in `main()`:

```
New energy: 25
```

As can be seen, ref parameters can be used both as input and output. ref parameters can also be thought of as aliases of the original variables. The function parameter energy above is an alias of the variable energy in main().

Similar to out parameters, ref parameters allow functions to have side effects as well. In fact, reduceEnergy() does not return a value; it only causes a side effect through its single parameter.

The programming style called *functional programming* favors return values over side effects, so much so that some functional programming languages do not allow side effects at all. This is because functions that produce results *purely* through their return values are easier to understand, implement, and maintain.

The same function can be written in a functional programming style by returning the result, instead of causing a side effect. The parts of the program that changed are highlighted:

```d
import std.stdio;

double reducedEnergy(double energy) {
    return energy / 4;
}

void main() {
    double energy = 100;

    energy = reducedEnergy(energy);
    writeln("New energy: ", energy);
}
```

Note the change in the name of the function as well. Now it is a noun as opposed to a verb.

auto ref

This qualifier can only be used with templates (page 399). As we will see in the next chapter, an auto ref parameter takes *lvalues* by reference and *rvalues* by copy.

inout

Despite its name consisting of in and out, this keyword does not mean *input and output*; we have already seen that input and output is achieved by the ref keyword.

inout carries the *mutability* of the parameter to the return type. If the parameter is const, immutable, or *mutable*; then the return value is also const, immutable, or *mutable*; respectively.

To see how inout helps in programs, let's look at a function that returns a slice to the *inner* elements of its parameter:

```d
import std.stdio;

int[] inner(int[] slice) {
    if (slice.length) {
        --slice.length;             // trim from the end

        if (slice.length) {
            slice = slice[1 .. $];  // trim from the beginning
        }
    }

    return slice;
}

void main() {
    int[] numbers = [ 5, 6, 7, 8, 9 ];
```

```
    writeln(inner(numbers));
```

```
[6, 7, 8]
```

According to what we have established so far in the book, in order for the function to be more useful, its parameter should be const(int)[] because the elements are not being modified inside the function. (Note that there is no harm in modifying the parameter slice itself, as it is a copy of the original variable.)

However, defining the function that way would cause a compilation error:

```
int[] inner(const(int)[] slice) {
    // ...
    return slice;    // ← compilation ERROR
}
```

The compilation error indicates that a slice of const(int) cannot be returned as a slice of *mutable* int:

```
Error: cannot implicitly convert expression (slice) of type
const(int)[] to int[]
```

One may think that specifying the return type as const(int)[] would be the solution:

```
const(int)[] inner(const(int)[] slice) {
    // ...
    return slice;    // now compiles
}
```

Although the code now compiles, it brings a limitation: even when the function is called with a slice of *mutable* elements, this time the returned slice ends up consisting of const elements. To see how limiting this would be, let's look at the following code, which tries to modify the inner elements of a slice:

```
    int[] numbers = [ 5, 6, 7, 8, 9 ];
    int[] middle = inner(numbers);    // ← compilation ERROR
    middle[] *= 10;
```

The returned slice of type const(int)[] cannot be assigned to a slice of type int[], resulting in an error:

```
Error: cannot implicitly convert expression (inner(numbers))
of type const(int)[] to int[]
```

However, since we started with a slice of mutable elements, this limitation is artificial and unfortunate. inout solves this mutability problem between parameters and return values. It is specified on both the parameter and the return type and carries the mutability of the former to the latter:

```
inout(int)[] inner(inout(int)[] slice) {
    // ...
    return slice;
}
```

With that change, the same function can now be called with const, immutable, and *mutable* slices:

```
    {
        int[] numbers = [ 5, 6, 7, 8, 9 ];
```

```
    // The return type is a slice of mutable elements
    int[] middle = inner(numbers);
    middle[] *= 10;
    writeln(middle);
}
{
    immutable int[] numbers = [ 10, 11, 12 ];
    // The return type is a slice of immutable elements
    immutable int[] middle = inner(numbers);
    writeln(middle);
}
{
    const int[] numbers = [ 13, 14, 15, 16 ];
    // The return type is a slice of const elements
    const int[] middle = inner(numbers);
    writeln(middle);
}
```

lazy

It is natural to expect that arguments are evaluated *before* entering functions that use those arguments. For example, the function add() below is called with the return values of two other functions:

```
result = add(anAmount(), anotherAmount());
```

In order for add() to be called, first anAmount() and anotherAmount() must be called. Otherwise, the values that add() needs would not be available.

Evaluating arguments before calling a function is called *eager evaluation*.

However, depending on certain conditions, some parameters may not get a chance to be used in the function at all. In such cases, evaluating the arguments eagerly would be wasteful.

A classic example of this situation is a *logging* function that outputs a message only if the importance of the message is above a certain configuration setting:

```
enum Level { low, medium, high }

void log(Level level, string message) {
    if (level >= interestedLevel) {
        writeln(message);
    }
}
```

For example, if the user is interested only in the messages that are Level.high, a message with Level.medium would not be printed. However, the argument would still be evaluated before calling the function. For example, the entire format() expression below including the getConnectionState() call that it makes would be wasted if the message is never printed:

```
    if (failedToConnect) {
        log(Level.medium,
            format("Failure. The connection state is '%s'.",
                getConnectionState()));
    }
```

The lazy keyword specifies that an expression that is passed as a parameter will be evaluated only if and when needed:

```
void log(Level level, lazy string message) {
    // ... the body of the function is the same as before ...
}
```

This time, the expression would be evaluated only if the `message` parameter is used.

One thing to be careful about is that a `lazy` parameter is evaluated *every time* that parameter is used in the function.

For example, because the `lazy` parameter of the following function is used three times in the function, the expression that provides its value is evaluated three times:

```
import std.stdio;

int valueOfArgument() {
    writeln("Calculating...");
    return 1;
}

void functionWithLazyParameter(lazy int value) {
    int result = value + value + value;
    writeln(result);
}

void main() {
    functionWithLazyParameter(valueOfArgument());
}
```

The output:

```
Calculating
Calculating
Calculating
3
```

scope

This keyword specifies that a parameter will not be used beyond the scope of the function. As of this writing, `scope` is effective only if the function is defined as `@safe` (page 547) and if `-dip1000` compiler switch is used. DIP is short for *D Improvement Proposal*. DIP 1000 is experimental as of this writing; so it may not work as expected in all cases.

```
$ dmd -dip1000 deneme.d
```

```
int[] globalSlice;

@safe int[] foo(scope int[] parameter) {
    globalSlice = parameter;    // ← compilation ERROR
    return parameter;           // ← compilation ERROR
}

void main() {
    int[] slice = [ 10, 20 ];
    int[] result = foo(slice);
}
```

The function above violates the promise of `scope` in two places: It assigns the parameter to a global variable, and it returns it. Both those actions would make it possible for the parameter to be accessed after the function finishes.

shared

This keyword requires that the parameter is shareable between threads of execution:

```
void foo(shared int[] i) {
    // ...
}
```

```
void main() {
    int[] numbers = [ 10, 20 ];
    foo(numbers);     // ← compilation ERROR
}
```

The program above cannot be compiled because the argument is not shared. The following is the necessary change to make it compile:

```
    shared int[] numbers = [ 10, 20 ];
    foo(numbers);     // now compiles
```

We will see the shared keyword later in the Data Sharing Concurrency chapter (page 640).

return

Sometimes it is useful for a function to return one of its ref parameters directly. For example, the following pick() function picks and returns one of its parameters randomly so that the caller can mutate the lucky one directly:

```
import std.stdio;
import std.random;

ref int pick(ref int lhs, ref int rhs) {
    return uniform(0, 2) ? lhs : rhs;     // ← compilation ERROR
}

void main() {
    int a;
    int b;

    pick(a, b) = 42;

    writefln("a: %s, b: %s", a, b);
}
```

As a result, either a or b inside main() is assigned the value 42:

```
a: 42, b: 0
```

```
a: 0, b: 42
```

Unfortunately, one of the arguments of pick() may have a shorter lifetime than the returned reference. For example, the following foo() function calls pick() with two local variables, effectively itself returning a reference to one of them:

```
import std.random;

ref int pick(ref int lhs, ref int rhs) {
    return uniform(0, 2) ? lhs : rhs;     // ← compilation ERROR
}

ref int foo() {
    int a;
    int b;

    return pick(a, b);     // ← BUG: returning invalid reference
}

void main() {
    foo() = 42;            // ← BUG: writing to invalid memory
}
```

Since the lifetimes of both a and b end upon leaving foo(), the assignment in main() cannot be made to a valid variable. This results in *undefined behavior*.

The term *undefined behavior* describes situations where the behavior of the program is not defined by the programming language specification. Nothing can be said about the behavior of a program that contains undefined behavior. (In practice though, for the program above, the value 42 would most likely be written to a memory location that used to be occupied by either a or b, potentially currently a part of an unrelated variable, effectively corrupting the value of that unrelated variable.)

The return keyword can be applied to a parameter to prevent such bugs. It specifies that a parameter must be a reference to a variable with a longer lifetime than the returned reference:

```d
import std.random;

ref int pick(return ref int lhs, return ref int rhs) {
    return uniform(0, 2) ? lhs : rhs;
}

ref int foo() {
    int a;
    int b;

    return pick(a, b);    // ← compilation ERROR
}

void main() {
    foo() = 42;
}
```

This time the compiler sees that the arguments to pick() have a shorter lifetime than the reference that foo() is attempting to return:

```
Error: escaping reference to local variable a
Error: escaping reference to local variable b
```

This feature is called *sealed references*.

Note: *Although it is conceivable that the compiler could inspect pick() and detect the bug even without the return keyword, it cannot do so in general because the bodies of some functions may not be available to the compiler during every compilation.*

35.4 Summary

- A *parameter* is what the function takes from its caller to accomplish its task.
- An *argument* is an expression (e.g. a variable) that is passed to a function as a parameter.
- Every argument is passed by copy by default. (Note that for reference types, it is the reference that is copied, not the original variable.)
- in specifies that the parameter is used only for data input. Prefer in over const.
- out specifies that the parameter is used only for data output.
- ref specifies that the parameter is used for data input and data output.
- auto ref is used in templates only. It specifies that if the argument is an lvalue, then a reference to it is passed; if the argument is an rvalue, then it is passed by copy.
- const guarantees that the parameter is not modified inside the function. (Remember that const is transitive: any data reached through a const variable is const as well.) Prefer in over const.

- `immutable` requires the argument to be `immutable`.
- `inout` appears both at the parameter and the return type, and transfers the *mutability* of the parameter to the return type.
- `lazy` is used to make a parameter be evaluated when (and every time) it is actually used.
- `scope` guarantees that no reference to the parameter will be leaked from the function.
- `shared` requires the parameter to be `shared`.
- `return` on a parameter requires the parameter to live longer than the returned reference.

35.5 Exercise

The following program is trying to swap the values of two arguments:

```d
import std.stdio;

void swap(int first, int second) {
    int temp = first;
    first = second;
    second = temp;
}

void main() {
    int a = 1;
    int b = 2;

    swap(a, b);

    writeln(a, ' ', b);
}
```

However, the program does not have any effect on a or b:

```
1 2                 ← not swapped
```

Fix the function so that the values of a and b are swapped.

The solution is on page 712.

36 Lvalues and Rvalues

The value of every expression is classified as either an lvalue or an rvalue. A simple way of differentiating the two is thinking of lvalues as actual variables (including elements of arrays and associative arrays), and rvalues as temporary results of expressions (including literals).

As a demonstration, the first `writeln()` expression below uses only lvalues and the other one uses only rvalues:

```d
import std.stdio;

void main() {
    int i;
    immutable(int) imm;
    auto arr = [ 1 ];
    auto aa = [ 10 : "ten" ];

    /* All of the following arguments are lvalues. */

    writeln(i,          // mutable variable
            imm,        // immutable variable
            arr,        // array
            arr[0],     // array element
            aa[10]);    // associative array element
                        // etc.

    enum message = "hello";

    /* All of the following arguments are rvalues. */

    writeln(42,             // a literal
            message,        // a manifest constant
            i + 1,          // a temporary value
            calculate(i));  // return value of a function
                            // etc.
}

int calculate(int i) {
    return i * 2;
}
```

36.1 Limitations of rvalues

Compared to lvalues, rvalues have the following three limitations.

Rvalues don't have memory addresses

An lvalue has a memory location to which we can refer, while an rvalue does not.

For example, it is not possible to take the address of the rvalue expression `a + b` in the following program:

```d
import std.stdio;

void main() {
    int a;
    int b;

    readf(" %s", &a);        // ← compiles
    readf(" %s", &(a + b));  // ← compilation ERROR
}
```

```
Error: a + b is not an lvalue
```

Rvalues cannot be assigned new values

If mutable, an lvalue can be assigned a new value, while an rvalue cannot be:

```
    a = 1;          // ← compiles
    (a + b) = 2;    // ← compilation ERROR
```

```
Error: a + b is not an lvalue
```

Rvalues cannot be passed to functions by reference

An lvalue can be passed to a function that takes a parameter by reference, while an rvalue cannot be:

```
void incrementByTen(ref int value) {
    value += 10;
}

// ...

    incrementByTen(a);        // ← compiles
    incrementByTen(a + b);    // ← compilation ERROR
```

```
Error: function deneme.incrementByTen (ref int value)
is not callable using argument types (int)
```

The main reason for this limitation is the fact that a function taking a `ref` parameter can hold on to that reference for later use, at a time when the rvalue would not be available.

Different from languages like C++, in D an rvalue cannot be passed to a function even if that function does *not* modify the argument:

```
void print(ref const(int) value) {
    writeln(value);
}

// ...

    print(a);        // ← compiles
    print(a + b);    // ← compilation ERROR
```

```
Error: function deneme.print (ref const(int) value)
is not callable using argument types (int)
```

36.2 Using auto ref parameters to accept both lvalues and rvalues

As it was mentioned in the previous chapter, `auto ref` parameters of function templates (page 399) can take both lvalues and rvalues.

When the argument is an lvalue, `auto ref` means *by reference*. On the other hand, since rvalues cannot be passed to functions by reference, when the argument is an rvalue, it means *by copy*. For the compiler to generate code differently for these two distinct cases, the function must be a template.

We will see templates in a later chapter. For now, please accept that the highlighted empty parentheses below make the following definition a *function template*.

```
void incrementByTen()(auto ref int value) {
    /* WARNING: The parameter may be a copy if the argument is
     * an rvalue. This means that the following modification
     * may not be observable by the caller. */

    value += 10;
}

void main() {
    int a;
```

```
    int b;

    incrementByTen(a);        // ← lvalue; passed by reference
    incrementByTen(a + b);    // ← rvalue; copied
}
```

It is possible to determine whether the parameter is an lvalue or an rvalue by using __traits(isRef) with static if:

```
void incrementByTen()(auto ref int value) {
    static if (__traits(isRef, value)) {
        // 'value' is passed by reference
    } else {
        // 'value' is copied
    }
}
```

We will see static if and __traits later in the Conditional Compilation chapter (page 460).

36.3 Terminology

The names "lvalue" and "rvalue" do not represent the characteristics of these two kinds of values accurately. The initial letters *l* and *r* come from *left* and *right*, referring to the left- and the right-hand side expressions of the assignment operator:

- Assuming that it is mutable, an lvalue can be the left-hand expression of an assignment operation.
- An rvalue cannot be the left-hand expression of an assignment operation.

The terms "left value" and "right value" are confusing because in general both lvalues and rvalues can be on either side of an assignment operation:

```
    // rvalue 'a + b' on the left, lvalue 'a' on the right:
    array[a + b] = a;
```

37 Lazy Operators

Lazy evaluation is the delaying of the execution of expressions until the results of those expressions are needed. Lazy evaluation is among the fundamental features of some programming languages.

Naturally, this delaying may make programs run faster if the results end up not being needed.

A concept that is similar to lazy evaluation is the short-circuit behavior of the following operators:

- `||` (*or*) operator: The second expression is evaluated only if the first expression is `false`.

```
if (anExpression() || mayNotBeEvaluated()) {
    // ...
}
```

If the result of `anExpression()` is `true` then the result of the `||` expression is necessarily `true`. Since we no longer need to evaluate the second expression to determine the result of the `||` expression the second expression is not evaluated.

- `&&` (*and*) operator: The second expression is evaluated only if the first expression is `true`.

```
if (anExpression() && mayNotBeEvaluated()) {
    // ...
}
```

If the result of `anExpression()` is `false` then the result of the `&&` expression is necessarily `false`, so the second expression is not evaluated.

- `?:` (*ternary*) operator: Either the first or the second expression is evaluated, depending on whether the condition is `true` or `false`, respectively.

```
int i = condition() ? eitherThis() : orThis();
```

The laziness of these operators matters not only to performance. Sometimes, evaluating one of the expressions can be an error.

For example, the *is the first letter an A* condition check below would be an error when the string is empty:

```
dstring s;
// ...
if (s[0] == 'A') {
    // ...
}
```

In order to access the first element of s, we must first ensure that the string does have such an element. For that reason, the following condition check moves that potentially erroneous logical expression to the right-hand side of the `&&` operator, to ensure that it will be evaluated only when it is safe to do so:

```
if ((s.length >= 1) && (s[0] == 'A')) {
    // ...
}
```

Lazy evaluations can be achieved by using function pointers, delegates (page 475), and ranges (page 569) as well. We will see these in later chapters.

We have seen that main() is a function. Program execution starts with main() and branches off to other functions from there. The definition of main() that we have used so far has been the following:

```d
void main() {
    // ...
}
```

According to that definition main() does not take any parameters and does not return a value. In reality, in most systems every program necessarily returns a value to its environment when it ends, which is called an exit status or return code. Because of this, although it is possible to specify the return type of main() as void, it will actually return a value to the operating system or launch environment.

38.1 The return value of main()

Programs are always started by an entity in a particular environment. The entity that starts the program may be the shell where the user types the name of the program and presses the Enter key, a development environment where the programmer clicks the [Run] button, and so on.

In D and several other programming languages, the program communicates its exit status to its environment by the return value of main().

The exact meaning of return codes depend on the application and the system. In almost all systems a return value of zero means a successful completion, while other values generally mean some type of failure. There are exceptions to this, though. For instance, in OpenVMS even values indicate failure, while odd values indicate success. Still, in most systems the values in the range [0, 125] can be used safely, with values 1 to 125 having a meaning specific to that program.

For example, the common Unix program ls, which is used for listing contents of directories, returns 0 for success, 1 for minor errors and 2 for serious ones.

In many environments, the return value of the program that has been executed most recently in the terminal can be seen through the $? environment variable. For example, when we ask ls to list a file that does not exist, its nonzero return value can be observed with $? as seen below.

Note: *In the command line interactions below, the lines that start with # indicate the lines that the user types. If you want to try the same commands, you must enter the contents of those lines except for the # character. Also, the commands below start a program named* deneme; *replace that name with the name of your test program.*

Additionally, although the following examples show interactions in a Linux terminal, they would be similar but not exactly the same in terminals of other operating systems.

```
# ls a_file_that_does_not_exist
ls: cannot access a_file_that_does_not_exist: No such file
or directory
# echo $?
2          ← the return value of ls
```

main() always returns a value

Some of the programs that we have written so far threw exceptions when they could not continue with their tasks. As much as we have seen so far, when an exception is thrown, the program ends with an object.Exception error message.

When that happens, even if main() has been defined as returning void, a nonzero status code is automatically returned to the program's environment. Let's see this in action in the following simple program that terminates with an exception:

```
void main() {
    throw new Exception("There has been an error.");
}
```

Although the return type is specified as void, the return value is nonzero:

```
# ./deneme
object.Exception: There has been an error.
...
# echo $?
1
```

Similarly, void main() functions that terminate successfully also automatically return zero as their return values. Let's see this with the following program that terminates *successfully*:

```
import std.stdio;

void main() {
    writeln("Done!");
}
```

The program returns zero:

```
# ./deneme
Done!
# echo $?
0
```

Specifying the return value
To choose a specific return code we return a value from main() in the same way as we would from any other function. The return type must be specified as int and the value must be returned by the return statement:

```
import std.stdio;

int main() {
    int number;
    write("Please enter a number between 3 and 6: ");
    readf(" %s", &number);

    if ((number < 3) || (number > 6)) {
        stderr.writefln("ERROR: %s is not valid!", number);
        return 111;
    }

    writefln("Thank you for %s.", number);

    return 0;
}
```

When the entered number is within the valid range, the return value of the program is zero:

```
# ./deneme
Please enter a number between 3 and 6: 5
Thank you for 5.
```

```
# echo $?
0
```

When the number is outside of the valid range, the return value of the program is 111:

```
# ./deneme
Please enter a number between 3 and 6: 10
ERROR: 10 is not valid!
# echo $?
111
```

The value of 111 in the above program is arbitrary; normally 1 is suitable as the failure code.

38.2 Standard error stream `stderr`

The program above uses the stream `stderr`. That stream is the third of the standard streams. It is used for writing error messages:

- `stdin`: standard input stream
- `stdout`: standard output stream
- `stderr`: standard error stream

When a program is started in a terminal, normally the messages that are written to `stdout` and `stderr` both appear on the terminal window. When needed, it is possible to redirect these outputs individually. This subject is outside of the focus of this chapter and the details may vary for each shell program.

38.3 Parameters of `main()`

It is common for programs to take parameters from the environment that started them. For example, we have already passed a file name as a command line option to `ls` above. There are two command line options in the following line:

```
# ls -l deneme
-rwxr-xr-x 1 acehreli users 460668 Nov  6 20:38 deneme
```

The set of command line parameters and their meanings are defined entirely by the program. Every program documents its usage, including what every parameter means.

The arguments that are used when starting a D program are passed to that program's `main()` as a slice of `strings`. Defining `main()` as taking a parameter of type `string[]` is sufficient to have access to program arguments. The name of this parameter is commonly abbreviated as `args`. The following program prints all of the arguments with which it is started:

```
import std.stdio;

void main(string[] args) {
    foreach (i, arg; args) {
        writefln("Argument %-3s: %s", i, arg);
    }
}
```

Let's start the program with arbitrary arguments:

```
# ./deneme some arguments on the command line 42 --an-option
Argument 0   : ./deneme
Argument 1   : some
Argument 2   : arguments
Argument 3   : on
```

```
Argument 4  : the
Argument 5  : command
Argument 6  : line
Argument 7  : 42
Argument 8  : --an-option
```

In almost all systems, the first argument is the name of the program, in the way it has been entered by the user. The other arguments appear in the order they were entered.

It is completely up to the program how it makes use of the arguments. The following program prints its two arguments in reverse order:

```
import std.stdio;

int main(string[] args) {
    if (args.length != 3) {
        stderr.writefln("ERROR! Correct usage:\n" ~
                        "  %s word1 word2", args[0]);
        return 1;
    }

    writeln(args[2], ' ', args[1]);

    return 0;
}
```

The program also shows its correct usage if you don't enter exactly two words:

```
# ./deneme
ERROR! Correct usage:
  ./deneme word1 word2
# ./deneme world hello
hello world
```

38.4 Command line options and the `std.getopt` module

That is all there is to know about the parameters and the return value of `main()`. However, parsing the arguments is a repetitive task. The `std.getopt` module is designed to help with parsing the command line options of programs.

Some parameters like "world" and "hello" above are purely data for the program to use. Other kinds of parameters are called *command line options*, and are used to change the behaviors of programs. An example of a command line option is the -l option that has been passed to `ls` above.

Command line options make programs more useful by removing the need for a human user to interact with the program to have it behave in a certain way. With command line options, programs can be started from script programs and their behaviors can be specified through command line options.

Although the syntax and meanings of command line arguments of every program is specific to that program, their format is somewhat standard. For example, in POSIX, command line options start with - - followed by the name of the option, and values come after = characters:

```
# ./deneme --an-option=17
```

The `std.getopt` module simplifies parsing such options. It has more capabilities than what is covered in this section.

Let's design a program that prints random numbers. Let's take the minimum, maximum, and total number of these numbers as program arguments. Let's require the following syntax to get these values from the command line:

```
# ./deneme --count=7 --minimum=10 --maximum=15
```

The getopt() function parses and assigns those values to variables. Similarly to readf(), the addresses of variables must be specified by the & operator:

```d
import std.stdio;
import std.getopt;
import std.random;

void main(string[] args) {
    int count;
    int minimum;
    int maximum;

    getopt(args,
            "count", &count,
            "minimum", &minimum,
            "maximum", &maximum);

    foreach (i; 0 .. count) {
        write(uniform(minimum, maximum + 1), ' ');
    }

    writeln();
}
```

```
# ./deneme --count=7 --minimum=10 --maximum=15
11 11 13 11 14 15 10
```

Many command line options of most programs have a shorter syntax as well. For example, -c may have the same meaning as --count. Such alternative syntax for each option is specified in getopt() after a | character. There may be more than one shortcut for each option:

```d
getopt(args,
        "count|c", &count,
        "minimum|n", &minimum,
        "maximum|x", &maximum);
```

It is common to use a single dash for the short versions and the = character is usually either omitted or substituted by a space:

```
# ./deneme -c7 -n10 -x15
11 13 10 15 14 15 14
# ./deneme -c 7 -n 10 -x 15
11 13 10 15 14 15 14
```

getopt() converts the arguments from string to the type of each variable. For example, since count above is an int, getopt() converts the value specified for the --count argument to an int. When needed, such conversions may also be performed explicitly by to.

So far we have used std.conv.to only when converting to string. to can, in fact, convert from any type to any type, as long as that conversion is possible. For example, the following program takes advantage of to when converting its argument to size_t:

```d
import std.stdio;
import std.conv;

void main(string[] args) {
    // The default count is 10
    size_t count = 10;

    if (args.length > 1) {
        // There is an argument
        count = to!size_t(args[1]);
    }
```

```
    foreach (i; 0 .. count) {
        write(i * 2, ' ');
    }

    writeln();
}
```

The program produces 10 numbers when no argument is specified:

```
# ./deneme
0 2 4 6 8 10 12 14 16 18
# ./deneme 3
0 2 4
```

38.5 Environment variables

The environment that a program is started in generally provides some variables that the program can make use of. The environment variables can be accessed through the associative array interface of std.process.environment. For example, the following program prints the PATH environment variable:

```
import std.stdio;
import std.process;

void main() {
    writeln(environment["PATH"]);
}
```

The output:

```
# ./deneme
/usr/local/bin:/usr/bin
```

std.process.environment provides access to the environment variables through the associative array syntax. However, environment itself is not an associative array. When needed, the environment variables can be converted to an associative array by using toAA():

```
    string[string] envVars = environment.toAA();
```

38.6 Starting other programs

Programs may start other programs and become the *environment* for those programs. A function that enables this is executeShell, from the std.process module.

executeShell executes its parameter as if the command was typed at the terminal. It then returns both the return code and the output of that command as a *tuple*. Tuples are array-like structures, which we will see later in the Tuples chapter (page 513):

```
import std.stdio;
import std.process;

void main() {
    const result = executeShell("ls -l deneme");
    const returnCode = result[0];
    const output = result[1];

    writefln("ls returned %s.", returnCode);
    writefln("Its output:\n%s", output);
}
```

The output:

```
# ./deneme
ls returned 0.
Its output:
-rwxrwxr-x. 1 acehreli acehreli 1359178 Apr 21 15:01 deneme
```

38.7 Summary

- Even when it is defined with a return type of void, main() automatically returns zero for success and nonzero for failure.
- stderr is suitable to print error messages.
- main can take parameters as string[].
- std.getopt helps with parsing command line options.
- std.process helps with accessing environment variables and starting other programs.

38.8 Exercises

1. Write a calculator program that takes an operator and two operands as command line arguments. Have the program support the following usage:

   ```
   # ./deneme 3.4 x 7.8
   26.52
   ```

   Note: *Because the * character has a special meaning on most terminals (more accurately, on most shells), I have used x instead. You may still use * as long as it is escaped as | *.*

2. Write a program that asks the user which program to start, starts that program, and prints its output.

   The solutions are on page 713.

39 Exceptions

Unexpected situations are parts of programs: user mistakes, programming errors, changes in the program environment, etc. Programs must be written in ways to avoid producing incorrect results when faced with such *exceptional* conditions.

Some of these conditions may be severe enough to stop the execution of the program. For example, a required piece of information may be missing or invalid, or a device may not be functioning correctly. The exception handling mechanism of D helps with stopping program execution when necessary, and to recover from the unexpected situations when possible.

As an example of a severe condition, we can think of passing an unknown operator to a function that knows only the four arithmetic operators, as we have seen in the exercises of the previous chapter:

```d
    switch (operator) {

    case "+":
        writeln(first + second);
        break;

    case "-":
        writeln(first - second);
        break;

    case "x":
        writeln(first * second);
        break;

    case "/":
        writeln(first / second);
        break;

    default:
        throw new Exception(format("Invalid operator: %s", operator));
    }
```

The `switch` statement above does not know what to do with operators that are not listed on the `case` statements; so throws an exception.

There are many examples of thrown exceptions in Phobos. For example, `to!int`, which can be used to convert a string representation of an integer to an `int` value throws an exception when that representation is not valid:

```d
import std.conv;

void main() {
    const int value = to!int("hello");
}
```

The program terminates with an exception that is thrown by `to!int`:

```
std.conv.ConvException@std/conv.d(38): std.conv(1157): Can't
convert value `hello' of type const(char)[] to type int
```

`std.conv.ConvException` at the beginning of the message is the type of the thrown exception object. We can tell from the name that the type is `ConvException` that is defined in the `std.conv` module.

39.1 The throw statement to throw exceptions

We've seen the `throw` statement both in the examples above and in the previous chapters.

throw throws an *exception object* and this terminates the current operation of the program. The expressions and statements that are written after the throw statement are not executed. This behavior is according to the nature of exceptions: they must be thrown when the program cannot continue with its current task.

Conversely, if the program could continue then the situation would not warrant throwing an exception. In such cases the function would find a way and continue.

The exception types Exception and Error

Only the types that are inherited from the Throwable class can be thrown. Throwable is almost never used directly in programs. The types that are actually thrown are types that are inherited from Exception or Error, which themselves are the types that are inherited from Throwable. For example, all of the exceptions that Phobos throws are inherited from either Exception or Error.

Error represents unrecoverable conditions and is not recommended to be *caught*. For that reason, most of the exceptions that a program throws are the types that are inherited from Exception. (**Note:** *Inheritance is a topic related to classes. We will see classes in a later chapter.*)

Exception objects are constructed with a string value that represents an error message. You may find it easy to create this message with the format() function from the std.string module:

```
import std.stdio;
import std.random;
import std.string;

int[] randomDiceValues(int count) {
    if (count < 0) {
        throw new Exception(
            format("Invalid dice count: %s", count));
    }

    int[] values;

    foreach (i; 0 .. count) {
        values ~= uniform(1, 7);
    }

    return values;
}

void main() {
    writeln(randomDiceValues(-5));
}
```

```
object.Exception...: Invalid dice count: -5
```

In most cases, instead of creating an exception object explicitly by new and throwing it explicitly by throw, the enforce() function is called. For example, the equivalent of the error check above is the following enforce() call:

```
enforce(count >= 0, format("Invalid dice count: %s", count));
```

We will see the differences between enforce() and assert() in a later chapter.

Thrown exception terminates all scopes

We have seen that the program execution starts from the main function and branches into other functions from there. This layered execution of going deeper into functions and eventually returning from them can be seen as the branches of a tree.

For example, main() may call a function named makeOmelet, which in turn may call another function named prepareAll, which in turn may call another function named prepareEggs, etc. Assuming that the arrows indicate function calls, the branching of such a program can be shown as in the following function call tree:

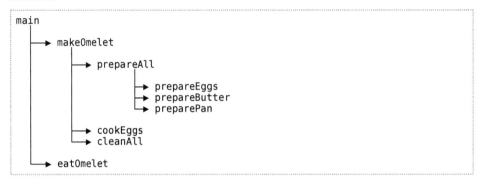

The following program demonstrates the branching above by using different levels of indentation in its output. The program doesn't do anything useful other than producing an output suitable to our purposes:

```d
import std.stdio;

void indent(int level) {
    foreach (i; 0 .. level * 2) {
        write(' ');
    }
}

void entering(string functionName, int level) {
    indent(level);
    writeln("▶ ", functionName, "'s first line");
}

void exiting(string functionName, int level) {
    indent(level);
    writeln("◁ ", functionName, "'s last line");
}

void main() {
    entering("main", 0);
    makeOmelet();
    eatOmelet();
    exiting("main", 0);
}

void makeOmelet() {
    entering("makeOmelet", 1);
    prepareAll();
    cookEggs();
    cleanAll();
    exiting("makeOmelet", 1);
}

void eatOmelet() {
    entering("eatOmelet", 1);
    exiting("eatOmelet", 1);
}

void prepareAll() {
    entering("prepareAll", 2);
    prepareEggs();
    prepareButter();
```

```
    preparePan();
    exiting("prepareAll", 2);
}

void cookEggs() {
    entering("cookEggs", 2);
    exiting("cookEggs", 2);
}

void cleanAll() {
    entering("cleanAll", 2);
    exiting("cleanAll", 2);
}

void prepareEggs() {
    entering("prepareEggs", 3);
    exiting("prepareEggs", 3);
}

void prepareButter() {
    entering("prepareButter", 3);
    exiting("prepareButter", 3);
}

void preparePan() {
    entering("preparePan", 3);
    exiting("preparePan", 3);
}
```

The program produces the following output:

```
▶ main, first line
  ▶ makeOmelet, first line
    ▶ prepareAll, first line
      ▶ prepareEggs, first line
      ◁ prepareEggs, last line
      ▶ prepareButter, first line
      ◁ prepareButter, last line
      ▶ preparePan, first line
      ◁ preparePan, last line
    ◁ prepareAll, last line
    ▶ cookEggs, first line
    ◁ cookEggs, last line
    ▶ cleanAll, first line
    ◁ cleanAll, last line
  ◁ makeOmelet, last line
  ▶ eatOmelet, first line
  ◁ eatOmelet, last line
◁ main, last line
```

The functions entering and exiting are used to indicate the first and last lines of functions with the help of the ▶ and ◁ characters. The program starts with the first line of main(), branches down to other functions, and finally ends with the last line of main.

Let's modify the prepareEggs function to take the number of eggs as a parameter. Since certain values of this parameter would be an error, let's have this function throw an exception when the number of eggs is less than one:

```
import std.string;

// ...

void prepareEggs(int count) {
    entering("prepareEggs", 3);

    if (count < 1) {
        throw new Exception(
            format("Cannot take %s eggs from the fridge", count));
    }
```

```
        exiting("prepareEggs", 3);
}
```

In order to be able to compile the program, we must modify other lines of the program to be compatible with this change. The number of eggs to take out of the fridge can be handed down from function to function, starting with main(). The parts of the program that need to change are the following. The invalid value of -8 is intentional to show how the output of the program will be different from the previous output when an exception is thrown:

```
// ...

void main() {
    entering("main", 0);
    makeOmelet(-8);
    eatOmelet();
    exiting("main", 0);
}

void makeOmelet(int eggCount) {
    entering("makeOmelet", 1);
    prepareAll(eggCount);
    cookEggs();
    cleanAll();
    exiting("makeOmelet", 1);
}

// ...

void prepareAll(int eggCount) {
    entering("prepareAll", 2);
    prepareEggs(eggCount);
    prepareButter();
    preparePan();
    exiting("prepareAll", 2);
}

// ...
```

When we start the program now, we see that the lines that used to be printed after the point where the exception is thrown are missing:

```
▶ main, first line
  ▶ makeOmelet, first line
    ▶ prepareAll, first line
      ▶ prepareEggs, first line
object.Exception: Cannot take -8 eggs from the fridge
```

When the exception is thrown, the program execution exits the prepareEggs, prepareAll, makeOmelet and main() functions in that order, from the bottom level to the top level. No additional steps are executed as the program exits these functions.

The rationale for such a drastic termination is that a failure in a lower level function would mean that the higher level functions that needed its successful completion should also be considered as failed.

The exception object that is thrown from a lower level function is transferred to the higher level functions one level at a time and causes the program to finally exit the main() function. The path that the exception takes can be shown as the highlighted path in the following tree:

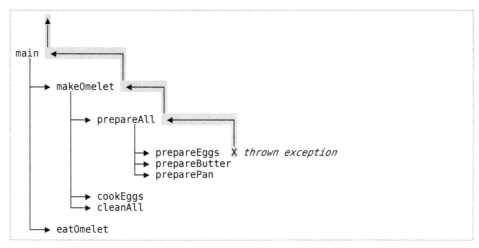

The point of the exception mechanism is precisely this behavior of exiting all of the layers of function calls right away.

Sometimes it makes sense to *catch* the thrown exception to find a way to continue the execution of the program. I will introduce the catch keyword below.

When to use throw

Use throw in situations when it is not possible to continue. For example, a function that reads the number of students from a file may throw an exception if this information is not available or incorrect.

On the other hand, if the problem is caused by some user action like entering invalid data, it may make more sense to validate the data instead of throwing an exception. Displaying an error message and asking the user to re-enter the data is more appropriate in many cases.

39.2 The try-catch statement to catch exceptions

As we've seen above, a thrown exception causes the program execution to exit all functions and this finally terminates the whole program.

The exception object can be caught by a try-catch statement at any point on its path as it exits the functions. The try-catch statement models the phrase "*try* to do something, and *catch* exceptions that may be thrown." Here is the syntax of try-catch:

```
try {
    // the code block that is being executed, where an
    // exception may be thrown

} catch (an_exception_type) {
    // expressions to execute if an exception of this
    // type is caught

} catch (another_exception_type) {
    // expressions to execute if an exception of this
    // other type is caught

// ... more catch blocks as appropriate ...

} finally {
    // expressions to execute regardless of whether an
    // exception is thrown
}
```

Let's start with the following program that does not use a try-catch statement at this state. The program reads the value of a die from a file and prints it to the standard output:

```d
import std.stdio;

int readDieFromFile() {
    auto file = File("the_file_that_contains_the_value", "r");

    int die;
    file.readf(" %s", &die);

    return die;
}

void main() {
    const int die = readDieFromFile();

    writeln("Die value: ", die);
}
```

Note that the readDieFromFile function is written in a way that ignores error conditions, expecting that the file and the value that it contains are available. In other words, the function is dealing only with its own task instead of paying attention to error conditions. This is a benefit of exceptions: many functions can be written in ways that focus on their actual tasks, rather than focusing on error conditions.

Let's start the program when the_file_that_contains_the_value is missing:

```
std.exception.ErrnoException@std/stdio.d(286): Cannot open
file `the_file_that_contains_the_value' in mode `r' (No such
file or directory)
```

An exception of type ErrnoException is thrown and the program terminates without printing "Die value: ".

Let's add an intermediate function to the program that calls readDieFromFile from within a try block and let's have main() call this new function:

```d
import std.stdio;
import std.exception;

int readDieFromFile() {
    auto file = File("the_file_that_contains_the_value", "r");

    int die;
    file.readf(" %s", &die);

    return die;
}

int tryReadingFromFile() {
    int die;

    try {
        die = readDieFromFile();

    } catch (std.exception.ErrnoException exc) {
        writeln("(Could not read from file; assuming 1)");
        die = 1;
    }

    return die;
}

void main() {
    const int die = tryReadingFromFile();
```

```
    writeln("Die value: ", die);
}
```

When we start the program again when `the_file_that_contains_the_value` is still missing, this time the program does not terminate with an exception:

```
(Could not read from file; assuming 1)
Die value: 1
```

The new program *tries* executing `readDieFromFile` in a `try` block. If that block executes successfully, the function ends normally with the `return die;` statement. If the execution of the `try` block ends with the specified `std.exception.ErrnoException`, then the program execution enters the `catch` block.

The following is a summary of events when the program is started when the file is missing:

- like in the previous program, a `std.exception.ErrnoException` object is thrown (by `File()`, not by our code),
- this exception is caught by `catch`,
- the value of 1 is assumed during the normal execution of the `catch` block,
- and the program continues its normal operations.

`catch` is to catch thrown exceptions to find a way to continue executing the program.

As another example, let's go back to the omelet program and add a `try-catch` statement to its `main()` function:

```
void main() {
    entering("main", 0);

    try {
        makeOmelet(-8);
        eatOmelet();

    } catch (Exception exc) {
        write("Failed to eat omelet: ");
        writeln('"', exc.msg, '"');
        writeln("Will eat at neighbor's...");
    }

    exiting("main", 0);
}
```

(**Note:** *The* .*msg property will be explained below.*)

That `try` block contains two lines of code. Any exception thrown from either of those lines would be caught by the `catch` block.

```
▶ main, first line
  ▶ makeOmelet, first line
    ▶ prepareAll, first line
      ▶ prepareEggs, first line
Failed to eat omelet: "Cannot take -8 eggs from the fridge"
Will eat at neighbor's...
◁ main, last line
```

As can be seen from the output, the program doesn't terminate because of the thrown exception anymore. It recovers from the error condition and continues executing normally till the end of the `main()` function.

catch blocks are considered sequentially

The type Exception, which we have used so far in the examples is a general exception type. This type merely specifies that an error occurred in the program. It also contains a message that can explain the error further, but it does not contain information about the *type* of the error.

ConvException and ErrnoException that we have seen earlier in this chapter are more specific exception types: the former is about a conversion error, and the latter is about a system error. Like many other exception types in Phobos and as their names suggest, ConvException and ErrnoException are both inherited from the Exception class.

Exception and its sibling Error are further inherited from Throwable, the most general exception type.

Although possible, it is not recommended to catch objects of type Error and objects of types that are inherited from Error. Since it is more general than Error, it is not recommended to catch Throwable either. What should normally be caught are the types that are under the Exception hierarchy, including Exception itself.

```
          Throwable  (not recommended to catch)
              ↗   ↖
   Exception       Error  (not recommended to catch)
      ↗   ↖         ↗   ↖
   ...     ...    ...     ...
```

Note: *I will explain the hierarchy representations later in the Inheritance chapter (page 328). The tree above indicates that Throwable is the most general and Exception and Error are more specific.*

It is possible to catch exception objects of a particular type. For example, it is possible to catch an ErrnoException object specifically to detect and handle a system error.

Exceptions are caught only if they match a type that is specified in a catch block. For example, a catch block that is trying to catch a SpecialExceptionType would not catch an ErrnoException.

The type of the exception object that is thrown during the execution of a try block is matched to the types that are specified by the catch blocks, in the order in which the catch blocks are written. If the type of the object matches the type of the catch block, then the exception is considered to be caught by that catch block, and the code that is within that block is executed. Once a match is found, the remaining catch blocks are ignored.

Because the catch blocks are matched in order from the first to the last, the catch blocks must be ordered from the most specific exception types to the most general exception types. Accordingly, and if it makes sense to catch that type of exceptions, the Exception type must be specified at the last catch block.

For example, a try-catch statement that is trying to catch several specific types of exceptions about student records must order the catch blocks from the most specific to the most general as in the following code:

```
try {
    // operations about student records that may throw ...

} catch (StudentIdDigitException exc) {

    // an exception that is specifically about errors with
    // the digits of student ids
```

```
    } catch (StudentIdException exc) {

        // a more general exception about student ids but not
        // necessarily about their digits

    } catch (StudentRecordException exc) {

        // even more general exception about student records

    } catch (Exception exc) {

        // the most general exception that may not be related
        // to student records

    }
```

The finally block

finally is an optional block of the try-catch statement. It includes expressions that should be executed regardless of whether an exception is thrown or not.

To see how finally works, let's look at a program that throws an exception 50% of the time:

```
import std.stdio;
import std.random;

void throwsHalfTheTime() {
    if (uniform(0, 2) == 1) {
        throw new Exception("the error message");
    }
}

void foo() {
    writeln("the first line of foo()");

    try {
        writeln("the first line of the try block");
        throwsHalfTheTime();
        writeln("the last line of the try block");

    // ... there may be one or more catch blocks here ...

    } finally {
        writeln("the body of the finally block");
    }

    writeln("the last line of foo()");
}

void main() {
    foo();
}
```

The output of the program is the following when the function does not throw:

```
the first line of foo()
the first line of the try block
the last line of the try block
the body of the finally block
the last line of foo()
```

The output of the program is the following when the function does throw:

```
the first line of foo()
the first line of the try block
the body of the finally block
object.Exception@deneme.d: the error message
```

As can be seen, although "the last line of the try block" and "the last line of foo()" are not printed, the content of the `finally` block is still executed when an exception is thrown.

When to use the `try-catch` statement

The `try-catch` statement is useful to catch exceptions to do something special about them.

For that reason, the `try-catch` statement should be used only when there is something special to be done. Do not catch exceptions otherwise and leave them to higher level functions that may want to catch them.

39.3 Exception properties

The information that is automatically printed on the output when the program terminates due to an exception is available as properties of exception objects as well. These properties are provided by the `Throwable` interface:

- `.file`: The source file where the exception was thrown from
- `.line`: The line number where the exception was thrown from
- `.msg`: The error message
- `.info`: The state of the program stack when the exception was thrown
- `.next`: The next collateral exception

We saw that `finally` blocks are executed when leaving scopes due to exceptions as well. (As we will see in later chapters, the same is true for `scope` statements and *destructors* as well.)

Naturally, such code blocks can throw exceptions as well. Exceptions that are thrown when leaving scopes due to an already thrown exception are called *collateral exceptions*. Both the main exception and the collateral exceptions are elements of a *linked list* data structure, where every exception object is accessible through the `.next` property of the previous exception object. The value of the `.next` property of the last exception is `null`. (We will see `null` in a later chapter.)

There are three exceptions that are thrown in the example below: The main exception that is thrown in `foo()` and the two collateral exceptions that are thrown in the `finally` blocks of `foo()` and `bar()`. The program accesses the collateral exceptions through the `.next` properties.

Some of the concepts that are used in this program will be explained in later chapters. For example, the continuation condition of the `for` loop that consists solely of exc means *as long as exc is not null*.

```
import std.stdio;

void foo() {
    try {
        throw new Exception("Exception thrown in foo");

    } finally {
        throw new Exception(
            "Exception thrown in foo's finally block");
    }
}

void bar() {
    try {
        foo();

    } finally {
        throw new Exception(
```

```
                "Exception thrown in bar's finally block");
    }
}

void main() {
    try {
        bar();

    } catch (Exception caughtException) {

        for (Throwable exc = caughtException;
             exc;      // ← Meaning: as long as exc is not 'null'
             exc = exc.next) {

            writefln("error message: %s", exc.msg);
            writefln("source file  : %s", exc.file);
            writefln("source line  : %s", exc.line);
            writeln();
        }
    }
}
```

The output:

```
error message: Exception thrown in foo
source file  : deneme.d
source line  : 6

error message: Exception thrown in foo's finally block
source file  : deneme.d
source line  : 9

error message: Exception thrown in bar's finally block
source file  : deneme.d
source line  : 20
```

39.4 Kinds of errors

We have seen how useful the exception mechanism is. It enables both the lower and higher level operations to be aborted right away, instead of the program continuing with incorrect or missing data, or behaving in any other incorrect way.

This does not mean that every error condition warrants throwing an exception. There may be better things to do depending on the kinds of errors.

User errors

Some of the errors are caused by the user. As we have seen above, the user may have entered a string like "hello" even though the program has been expecting a number. It may be more appropriate to display an error message and ask the user to enter appropriate data again.

Even so, it may be fine to accept and use the data directly without validating the data up front; as long as the code that uses the data would throw anyway. What is important is to be able to notify the user why the data is not suitable.

For example, let's look at a program that takes a file name from the user. There are at least two ways of dealing with potentially invalid file names:

- **Validating the data before use**: We can determine whether the file with the given name exists by calling exists() of the std.file module:

```
    if (exists(fileName)) {
        // yes, the file exists

    } else {
        // no, the file doesn't exist
    }
```

This gives us the chance to be able to open the data only if it exists. Unfortunately, it is still possible that the file cannot be opened even if exists() returns true, if for example another process on the system deletes or renames the file before this program actually opens it.

For that reason, the following method may be more useful.

- **Using the data without first validating it**: We can assume that the data is valid and start using it right away, because File would throw an exception if the file cannot be opened anyway.

```d
import std.stdio;
import std.exception;
import std.string;

void useTheFile(string fileName) {
    auto file = File(fileName, "r");
    // ...
}

string read_string(string prompt) {
    write(prompt, ": ");
    return strip(readln());
}

void main() {
    bool is_fileUsed = false;

    while (!is_fileUsed) {
        try {
            useTheFile(
                read_string("Please enter a file name"));

            /* If we are at this line, it means that
             * useTheFile() function has been completed
             * successfully. This indicates that the file
             * name was valid.
             *
             * We can now set the value of the loop flag to
             * terminate the while loop. */
            is_fileUsed = true;
            writeln("The file has been used successfully");

        } catch (std.exception.ErrnoException exc) {
            stderr.writeln("This file could not be opened");
        }
    }
}
```

Programmer errors

Some errors are caused by programmer mistakes. For example, the programmer may think that a function that has just been written will always be called with a value greater than or equal to zero, and this may be true according to the design of the program. The function having still been called with a value less than zero would indicate either a mistake in the design of the program or in the implementation of that design. Both of these can be thought of as programming errors.

It is more appropriate to use assert instead of the exception mechanism for errors that are caused by programmer mistakes. (**Note:** *We will cover* assert *in a later chapter (page 208).*)

```d
void processMenuSelection(int selection) {
    assert(selection >= 0);
    // ...
}
```

```
void main() {
    processMenuSelection(-1);
}
```

The program terminates with an `assert` failure:

```
core.exception.AssertError@deneme.d(2): Assertion failure
```

`assert` validates program state and prints the file name and line number of the validation if it fails. The message above indicates that the assertion at line 2 of deneme.d has failed.

Unexpected situations

For unexpected situations that are outside of the two general cases above, it is still appropriate to throw exceptions. If the program cannot continue its execution, there is nothing else to do but to throw.

It is up to the higher layer functions that call this function to decide what to do with thrown exceptions. They may catch the exceptions that we throw to remedy the situation.

39.5 Summary

- When faced with a user error either warn the user right away or ensure that an exception is thrown; the exception may be thrown anyway by another function when using incorrect data, or you may throw directly.

- Use `assert` to validate program logic and implementation. (***Note:*** *assert will be explained in a later chapter.*)

- When in doubt, throw an exception with `throw` or `enforce()`. (***Note:*** *enforce() will be explained in a later chapter.*)

- Catch exceptions if and only if you can do something useful about that exception. Otherwise, do not encapsulate code with a `try-catch` statement; instead, leave the exceptions to higher layers of the code that may do something about them.

- Order the `catch` blocks from the most specific to the most general.

- Put the expressions that must always be executed when leaving a scope, in `finally` blocks.

As we have seen in the previous chapter, expressions that must always be executed are written in the finally block, and expressions that must be executed when there are error conditions are written in catch blocks.

We can make the following observations about the use of these blocks:

- catch and finally cannot be used without a try block.
- Some of the variables that these blocks need may not be accessible within these blocks:

```d
void foo(ref int r) {
    try {
        int addend = 42;

        r += addend;
        mayThrow();

    } catch (Exception exc) {
        r -= addend;            // ← compilation ERROR
    }
}
```

That function first modifies the reference parameter and then reverts this modification when an exception is thrown. Unfortunately, addend is accessible only in the try block, where it is defined. (**Note:** *This is related to name scopes, as well as object lifetimes, which will be explained in a later chapter. (page 228))*

- Writing all of potentially unrelated expressions in the single finally block at the bottom separates those expressions from the actual code that they are related to.

The scope statements have similar functionality to the catch and finally scopes but they are better in many respects. Like finally, the three different scope statements are about executing expressions when leaving scopes:

- scope(exit): the expression is always executed when exiting the scope, regardless of whether successfully or due to an exception
- scope(success): the expression is executed only if the scope is being exited successfully
- scope(failure): the expression is executed only if the scope is being exited due to an exception

Although these statements are closely related to exceptions, they can be used without a try-catch block.

As an example, let's write the function above with a scope(failure) statement:

```d
void foo(ref int r) {
    int addend = 42;

    r += addend;
    scope(failure) r -= addend;

    mayThrow();
}
```

The scope(failure) statement above ensures that the r -= addend expression will be executed if the function's scope is exited due to an exception. A benefit of scope(failure) is the fact that the expression that reverts another expression is written close to it.

scope statements can be specified as blocks as well:

```
scope(exit) {
    // ... expressions ...
}
```

Here is another function that tests all three of these statements:

```
void test() {
    scope(exit) writeln("when exiting 1");

    scope(success) {
        writeln("if successful 1");
        writeln("if successful 2");
    }

    scope(failure) writeln("if thrown 1");
    scope(exit) writeln("when exiting 2");
    scope(failure) writeln("if thrown 2");

    throwsHalfTheTime();
}
```

If no exception is thrown, the output of the function includes only the scope(exit) and scope(success) expressions:

```
when exiting 2
if successful 1
if successful 2
when exiting 1
```

If an exception is thrown, the output includes the scope(exit) and scope(failure) expressions:

```
if thrown 2
when exiting 2
if thrown 1
when exiting 1
object.Exception@...: the error message
```

As seen in the outputs, the blocks of the scope statements are executed in reverse order. This is because later code may depend on previous variables. Executing the scope statements in reverse order enables undoing side effects of earlier expressions in a consistent order.

In the previous two chapters we have seen how exceptions and scope statements are used toward program correctness. assert is another powerful tool to achieve the same goal by ensuring that certain assumptions that the program is based on are valid.

It may sometimes be difficult to decide whether to throw an exception or to call assert. I will use assert in all of the examples below without much justification. I will explain the differences later in the chapter.

Although not always obvious, programs are full of assumptions. For example, the following function is written under the assumption that both age parameters are greater than or equal to zero:

```
double averageAge(double first, double second) {
    return (first + second) / 2;
}
```

Although it may be invalid for the program to ever have an age value that is negative, the function would still produce an average, which may be used in the program unnoticed, resulting in the program's continuing with incorrect data.

As another example, the following function assumes that it will always be called with two commands: "sing" or "dance":

```
void applyCommand(string command) {
    if (command == "sing") {
        robotSing();

    } else {
        robotDance();
    }
}
```

Because of that assumption, the robotDance() function would be called for every command other than "sing", valid or invalid.

When such assumptions are kept only in the programmer's mind, the program may end up working incorrectly. assert statements check assumptions and terminate programs immediately when they are not valid.

41.1 Syntax
assert can be used in two ways:

```
assert(logical_expression);
assert(logical_expression, message);
```

The logical expression represents an assumption about the program. assert evaluates that expression to validate that assumption. If the value of the logical expression is true then the assumption is considered to be valid. Otherwise the assumption is invalid and an AssertError is thrown.

As its name suggests, this exception is inherited from Error, and as you may remember from the Exceptions chapter (page 192), exceptions that are inherited from Error must never be caught. It is important for the program to be terminated right away instead of continuing under invalid assumptions.

The two implicit assumptions of averageAge() above may be spelled out by two assert calls as in the following function:

```
double averageAge(double first, double second) {
    assert(first >= 0);
```

```
    assert(second >= 0);

    return (first + second) / 2;
}

void main() {
    auto result = averageAge(-1, 10);
}
```

Those `assert` checks carry the meaning "assuming that both of the ages are greater than or equal to zero". It can also be thought of as meaning "this function can work correctly only if both of the ages are greater than or equal to zero".

Each `assert` checks its assumption and terminates the program with an `AssertError` when it is not valid:

```
core.exception.AssertError@deneme(2): Assertion failure
```

The part after the @ character in the message indicates the source file and the line number of the `assert` check that failed. According to the output above, the `assert` that failed is on line 2 of file deneme.d.

The other syntax of `assert` allows printing a custom message when the `assert` check fails:

```
    assert(first >= 0, "Age cannot be negative.");
```

The output:

```
core.exception.AssertError@deneme.d(2): Age cannot be negative.
```

Sometimes it is thought to be impossible for the program to ever enter a code path. In such cases it is common to use the literal `false` as the logical expression to fail an `assert` check. For example, to indicate that `applyCommand()` function is never expected to be called with a command other than "sing" and "dance", and to guard against such a possibility, an `assert(false)` can be inserted into the *impossible* branch:

```
void applyCommand(string command) {
    if (command == "sing") {
        robotSing();

    } else if (command == "dance") {
        robotDance();

    } else {
        assert(false);
    }
}
```

The function is guaranteed to work with the only two commands that it knows about. (***Note:*** *An alternative choice here would be to use a* `final switch` *statement (page 127).*)

41.2 static assert

Since `assert` checks are for correct execution of programs, they are applied when the program is actually running. There can be other checks that are about the structure of the program, which can be applied even at compile time.

`static assert` is the counterpart of `assert` that is applied at compile time. The advantage is that it does not allow even compiling a program that would have otherwise run incorrectly. A natural requirement is that it must be possible to evaluate the logical expression at compile time.

For example, assuming that the title of a menu will be printed on an output device that has limited width, the following `static assert` ensures that it will never be wider than that limit:

```
enum dstring menuTitle = "Command Menu";
static assert(menuTitle.length <= 16);
```

Note that the string is defined as enum so that its length can be evaluated at compile time.

Let's assume that a programmer changes that title to make it more descriptive:

```
enum dstring menuTitle = "Directional Commands Menu";
static assert(menuTitle.length <= 16);
```

The `static assert` check prevents compiling the program:

```
Error: static assert  (25u <= 16u) is false
```

This would remind the programmer of the limitation of the output device.

`static assert` is even more useful when used in templates. We will see templates in later chapters.

41.3 assert even if *absolutely true*

I emphasize "absolutely true" because assumptions about the program are never expected to be false anyway. A large set of program errors are caused by assumptions that are thought to be absolutely true.

For that reason, take advantage of `assert` checks even if they feel unnecessary. Let's look at the following function that returns the days of months in a given year:

```
int[] monthDays(int year) {
    int[] days = [
        31, februaryDays(year),
        31, 30, 31, 30, 31, 31, 30, 31, 30, 31
    ];

    assert((sum(days) == 365) ||
           (sum(days) == 366));

    return days;
}
```

That `assert` check may be seen as unnecessary because the function would naturally return either 365 or 366. However, those checks are guarding against potential mistakes even in the `februaryDays()` function. For example, the program would be terminated if `februaryDays()` returned 30.

Another seemingly unnecessary check can ensure that the length of the slice would always be 12:

```
assert(days.length == 12);
```

That way, deleting or adding elements to the slice unintentionally would also be caught. Such checks are important tools toward program correctness.

`assert` is also the fundamental tool that is used in *unit testing* and *contract programming*, both of which will be covered in later chapters.

41.4 No value nor side effect

We have seen that expressions produce values or make side effects. `assert` checks do not have values nor *should* they have any side effects.

The D language requires that the evaluation of the logical expression must not have any side effect. assert must remain as a passive observer of program state.

41.5 Disabling assert checks

Since assert is about program correctness, they can be seen as unnecessary once the program has been tested sufficiently. Further, since assert checks produce no values nor they have side effects, removing them from the program should not make any difference.

The compiler switch -release causes the assert checks to be ignored as if they have never been included in the program:

```
$ dmd deneme.d -release
```

This would allow programs to run faster by not evaluating potentially slow logical expressions of the assert checks.

As an exception, the assert checks that have the literal false (or 0) as the logical expression are not disabled even when the program is compiled with -release. This is because assert(false) is for ensuring that a block of code is never reached, and that should be prevented even for the -release compilations.

41.6 enforce for throwing exceptions

Not every unexpected situation is an indication of a program error. Programs may also experience unexpected inputs and unexpected environmental state. For example, the data that is entered by the user should not be validated by an assert check because invalid data has nothing to do with the correctness of the program itself. In such cases it is appropriate to throw exceptions like we have been doing in previous programs.

std.exception.enforce is a convenient way of throwing exceptions. For example, let's assume that an exception must be thrown when a specific condition is not met:

```
if (count < 3) {
    throw new Exception("Must be at least 3.");
}
```

enforce() is a wrapper around the condition check and the throw statement. The following is the equivalent of the previous code:

```
import std.exception;
// ...
    enforce(count >= 3, "Must be at least 3.");
```

Note how the logical expression is negated compared to the if statement. It now spells out what is being *enforced*.

41.7 How to use

assert is for catching programmer errors. The conditions that assert guards against in the monthDays() function and the menuTitle variable above are all about programmer mistakes.

Sometimes it is difficult to decide whether to rely on an assert check or to throw an exception. The decision should be based on whether the unexpected situation is due to a problem with how the program has been coded.

Otherwise, the program must throw an exception when it is not possible to accomplish a task. enforce() is expressive and convenient when throwing exceptions.

Another point to consider is whether the unexpected situation can be remedied in some way. If the program can not do anything special, even by simply printing an error message about the problem with some input data, then it is appropriate to throw an exception. That way, callers of the code that threw the exception can catch it to do something special to recover from the error condition.

41.8 Exercises

1. The following program includes a number of assert checks. Compile and run the program to discover its bugs that are revealed by those assert checks.

    The program takes a start time and a duration from the user and calculates the end time by adding the duration to the start time:

    ```
    10 hours and 8 minutes after 06:09 is 16:17.
    ```

    Note that this problem can be written in a much cleaner way by defining struct types. We will refer to this program in later chapters.

    ```
    import std.stdio;
    import std.string;
    import std.exception;

    /* Reads the time as hour and minute after printing a
     * message. */
    void readTime(string message,
                  out int hour,
                  out int minute) {
        write(message, "? (HH:MM) ");

        readf(" %s:%s", &hour, &minute);

        enforce((hour >= 0) && (hour <= 23) &&
                (minute >= 0) && (minute <= 59),
                "Invalid time!");
    }

    /* Returns the time in string format. */
    string timeToString(int hour, int minute) {
        assert((hour >= 0) && (hour <= 23));
        assert((minute >= 0) && (minute <= 59));

        return format("%02s:%02s", hour, minute);
    }

    /* Adds duration to start time and returns the result as the
     * third pair of parameters. */
    void addDuration(int startHour, int startMinute,
                     int durationHour, int durationMinute,
                     out int resultHour, out int resultMinute) {
        resultHour = startHour + durationHour;
        resultMinute = startMinute + durationMinute;

        if (resultMinute > 59) {
            ++resultHour;
        }
    }

    void main() {
        int startHour;
        int startMinute;
        readTime("Start time", startMinute, startHour);

        int durationHour;
        int durationMinute;
        readTime("Duration", durationHour, durationMinute);

        int endHour;
        int endMinute;
    ```

```
    addDuration(startHour, startMinute,
                durationHour, durationMinute,
                endHour, endMinute);

    writefln("%s hours and %s minutes after %s is %s.",
             durationHour, durationMinute,
             timeToString(startHour, startMinute),
             timeToString(endHour, endMinute));
}
```

Run the program and enter 06:09 as the start time and 1:2 as the duration. Observe that the program terminates normally.

Note: *You may notice a problem with the output. Ignore that problem for now as you will discover it by the help of* assert *checks soon.*

2. This time enter 06:09 and 15:2. Observe that the program is terminated by an AssertError. Go to the line of the program that is indicated in the assert message and see which one of the assert checks have failed. It may take a while to discover the cause of this particular failure.

3. Enter 06:09 and 20:0 and observe that the same assert check still fails and fix that bug as well.

4. Modify the program to print the times in 12-hour format with an "am" or "pm" indicator.

The solutions are on page 713.

42 Unit Testing

As it should be known by most people, any device that runs some piece of computer program contains software bugs. Software bugs plague computer devices from the simplest to the most complex. Debugging and fixing software bugs is among the less favorable daily activities of a programmer.

42.1 Causes of bugs

There are many reasons why software bugs occur. The following is an incomplete list roughly from the design stage of a program through the actual coding of it:

- The requirements and the specifications of the program may not be clear. What the program should actually do may not be known at the design stage.
- The programmer may misunderstand some of the requirements of the program.
- The programming language may not be expressive enough. Considering that there are confusions even between native speakers of human languages, the unnatural syntax and rules of a programming language may be cause of mistakes.
- Certain assumptions of the programmer may be incorrect. For example, the programmer may be assuming that 3.14 would be precise enough to represent π.
- The programmer may have incorrect information on a topic or none at all. For example, the programmer may not know that using a floating point variable in a particular logical expression would not be reliable.
- The program may encounter an unforeseen situation. For example, one of the files of a directory may be deleted or renamed while the program is using the files of that directory in a `foreach` loop.
- The programmer may make silly mistakes. For example, the name of a variable may be mistyped and accidentally matched the name of another variable.
- etc.

Unfortunately, there is still no software development methodology that ensures that a program will always work correctly. This is still a hot software engineering topic where promising solutions emerge every decade or so.

42.2 Discovering the bugs

Software bugs are discovered at various stages of the lifetime of the program by various types of tools and people. The following is a partial list of when a bug may be discovered, from the earliest to the latest:

- When writing the program
    - By the programmer
    - By another programmer during *pair programming*
    - By the compiler through compiler messages
    - By unit tests as a part of building the program
- When reviewing the code

- By tools that analyze the code at compile time
- By other programmers during *code reviews*

- When running the program

  - By tools that analyze the execution of the program at run time (e.g. by valgrind)
  - During QA testing, either by the failure of `assert` checks or by the observed behavior of the program
  - By the *beta* users before the release of the program
  - By the end users after the release of the program

Detecting bugs as early as possible reduces loss of money, time, and in some cases human lives. Additionally, identifying the causes of bugs that have been discovered by the end users are harder than identifying the causes of bugs that are discovered early, during development.

42.3 Unit testing for catching bugs

Since programs are written by programmers and D is a compiled language, the programmers and the compiler will always be there to discover bugs. Those two aside, the earliest and partly for that reason the most effective way of catching bugs is unit testing.

Unit testing is an indispensable part of modern programming. It is the most effective method of reducing coding errors. According to some development methodologies, code that is not guarded by unit tests is buggy code.

Unfortunately, the opposite is not true: Unit tests do not guarantee that the code is free of bugs. Although they are very effective, they can only reduce the risk of bugs.

Unit testing also enables refactoring the code (i.e. making improvements to it) with ease and confidence. Otherwise, it is common to accidentally break some of the existing functionality of a program when adding new features to it. Bugs of this type are called *regressions*. Without unit testing, regressions are sometimes discovered as late as during the QA testing of future releases, or worse, by the end users.

Risk of regressions discourage programmers from refactoring the code, sometimes preventing them from performing the simplest of improvements like correcting the name of a variable. This in turn causes *code rot*, a condition where the code becomes more and more unmaintainable. For example, although some lines of code would better be moved to a newly defined function in order to be called from more than one place, fear of regressions make programmers copy and paste the existing lines to other places instead, leading to the problem of *code duplication*.

Phrases like "if it isn't broken, don't fix it" are related to fear of regressions. Although they seem to be conveying wisdom, such guidelines cause the code to rot slowly and become an untouchable mess.

Modern programming rejects such "wisdom". To the contrary, to prevent it from becoming a source of bugs, the code is supposed to be "refactored mercilessly". The most powerful tool of this modern approach is unit testing.

Unit testing involves testing the smallest units of code independently. When units of code are tested independently, it is less likely that there are bugs in higher-level code that use those units. When the parts work correctly, it is more likely that the whole will work correctly as well.

Unit tests are provided as library solutions in other languages (e.g. JUnit, CppUnit, Unittest++, etc.) In D, unit testing is a core feature of the language. It is debatable whether a library solution or a language feature is better for unit testing. Because D does not provide some of the features that are commonly found in unit testing libraries, it may be worthwhile to consider library solutions as well.

The unit testing features of D are as simple as inserting `assert` checks into `unittest` blocks.

42.4 Activating the unit tests

Unit tests are not a part of the actual execution of the program. They should be activated only during program development when explicitly requested.

The dmd compiler switch that activates unit tests is `-unittest`.

Assuming that the program is written in a single source file named deneme.d, its unit tests can be activated by the following command:

```
$ dmd deneme.d -w -unittest
```

When a program that is built by the `-unittest` switch is started, its unit test blocks are executed first. Only if all of the unit tests pass then the program execution continues with `main()`.

42.5 `unittest` blocks

The lines of code that involve unit tests are written inside `unittest` blocks. These blocks do not have any significance for the program other than containing the unit tests:

```
unittest {
    /* ... the tests and the code that support them ... */
}
```

Although `unittest` blocks can appear anywhere, it is convenient to define them right after the code that they test.

As an example, let's test a function that returns the ordinal form of the specified number as in "1st", "2nd", etc. A `unittest` block of this function can simply contain `assert` statements that compare the return values of the function to the expected values. The following function is being tested with the four distinct expected outcomes of the function:

```
string ordinal(size_t number) {
    // ...
}

unittest {
    assert(ordinal(1) == "1st");
    assert(ordinal(2) == "2nd");
    assert(ordinal(3) == "3rd");
    assert(ordinal(10) == "10th");
}
```

The four tests above test that the function works correctly at least for the values of 1, 2, 3, and 10 by making four separate calls to the function and comparing the returned values to the expected ones.

Although unit tests are based on `assert` checks, `unittest` blocks can contain any D code. This allows for preparations before actually starting the tests or any other supporting code that the tests may need. For example, the following block first defines a variable to reduce code duplication:

```
dstring toFront(dstring str, dchar letter) {
    // ...
}

unittest {
    immutable str = "hello"d;

    assert(toFront(str, 'h') == "hello");
    assert(toFront(str, 'o') == "ohell");
    assert(toFront(str, 'l') == "llheo");
}
```

The three `assert` checks above test that `toFront()` works according to its specification.

As these examples show, unit tests are also useful as examples of how particular functions should be called. Usually it is easy to get an idea on what a function does just by reading its unit tests.

42.6 Testing for exceptions

It is common to test some code for exception types that it should or should not throw under certain conditions. The `std.exception` module contains two functions that help with testing for exceptions:

- `assertThrown`: Ensures that a specific exception type is thrown from an expression
- `assertNotThrown`: Ensures that a specific exception type is *not* thrown from an expression

For example, a function that requires that both of its slice parameters have equal lengths and that it works with empty slices can be tested as in the following tests:

```
import std.exception;

int[] average(int[] a, int[] b) {
    // ...
}

unittest {
    /* Must throw for uneven slices */
    assertThrown(average([1], [1, 2]));

    /* Must not throw for empty slices */
    assertNotThrown(average([], []));
}
```

Normally, `assertThrown` ensures that some type of exception is thrown without regard to the actual type of that exception. When needed, it can test against a specific exception type as well. Likewise, `assertNotThrown` ensures that no exception is thrown whatsoever but it can be instructed to test that a specific exception type is not thrown. The specific exception types are specified as template parameters to these functions:

```
    /* Must throw UnequalLengths for uneven slices */
    assertThrown!UnequalLengths(average([1], [1, 2]));

    /* Must not throw RangeError for empty slices (it may
     * throw other types of exceptions) */
    assertNotThrown!RangeError(average([], []));
```

We will see templates in a later chapter (page 399).

The main purpose of these functions is to make code more succinct and more readable. For example, the following `assertThrown` line is the equivalent of the lengthy code below it:

```
    assertThrown(average([1], [1, 2]));

// ...

    /* The equivalent of the line above */
    {
        auto isThrown = false;

        try {
            average([1], [1, 2]);

        } catch (Exception exc) {
            isThrown = true;
        }

        assert(isThrown);
    }
```

42.7 Test driven development

Test driven development (TDD) is a software development methodology that prescribes writing unit tests before implementing functionality. In TDD, the focus is on unit testing. Coding is a secondary activity that makes the tests pass.

In accordance to TDD, the `ordinal()` function above can first be implemented intentionally incorrectly:

```
import std.string;

string ordinal(size_t number) {
    return "";     // ← intentionally wrong
}

unittest {
    assert(ordinal(1) == "1st");
    assert(ordinal(2) == "2nd");
    assert(ordinal(3) == "3rd");
    assert(ordinal(10) == "10th");
}

void main() {
}
```

Although the function is obviously wrong, the next step would be to run the unit tests to see that the tests do indeed catch problems with the function:

```
$ dmd deneme.d -w -unittest
$ ./deneme
core.exception.AssertError@deneme(10): unittest failure
```

The function should be implemented only *after* seeing the failure, and only to make the tests pass. Here is just one implementation that passes the tests:

```
import std.string;

string ordinal(size_t number) {
    string suffix;

    switch (number) {
    case  1: suffix = "st"; break;
    case  2: suffix = "nd"; break;
    case  3: suffix = "rd"; break;
    default: suffix = "th"; break;
```

```
        }

        return format("%s%s", number, suffix);
    }

    unittest {
        assert(ordinal(1)  == "1st");
        assert(ordinal(2)  == "2nd");
        assert(ordinal(3)  == "3rd");
        assert(ordinal(10) == "10th");
    }

    void main() {
    }
```

Since the implementation above does pass the unit tests, there is reason to trust that the ordinal() function is correct. Under the assurance that the tests bring, the implementation of the function can be changed in many ways with confidence.

Unit tests before bug fixes

Unit tests are not a panacea; there will always be bugs. If a bug is discovered when actually running the program, it can be seen as an indication that the unit tests have been incomplete. For that reason, it is better to *first* write a unit test that reproduces the bug and only *then* to fix the bug to pass the new test.

Let's have a look at the following function that returns the spelling of the ordinal form of a number specified as a dstring:

```
import std.exception;
import std.string;

dstring ordinalSpelled(dstring number) {
    enforce(number.length, "number cannot be empty");

    dstring[dstring] exceptions = [
        "one": "first", "two" : "second", "three" : "third",
        "five" : "fifth", "eight": "eighth", "nine" : "ninth",
        "twelve" : "twelfth"
    ];

    dstring result;

    if (number in exceptions) {
        result = exceptions[number];

    } else {
        result = number ~ "th";
    }

    return result;
}

unittest {
    assert(ordinalSpelled("one") == "first");
    assert(ordinalSpelled("two") == "second");
    assert(ordinalSpelled("three") == "third");
    assert(ordinalSpelled("ten") == "tenth");
}

void main() {
}
```

The function takes care of exceptional spellings and even includes a unit test for that. Still, the function has a bug yet to be discovered:

```
import std.stdio;
```

```
void main() {
    writefln("He came the %s in the race.",
             ordinalSpelled("twenty"));
}
```

The spelling error in the output of the program is due to a bug in
ordinalSpelled(), which its unit tests fail to catch:

```
He came the twentyth in the race.
```

Although it is easy to see that the function does not produce the correct spelling
for numbers that end with the letter y, TDD prescribes that first a unit test must
be written to reproduce the bug before actually fixing it:

```
unittest {
// ...
    assert(ordinalSpelled("twenty") == "twentieth");
}
```

With that improvement to the tests, now the bug in the function is being caught
during development:

```
core.exception.AssertError@deneme(3274338): unittest failure
```

The function should be fixed only then:

```
dstring ordinalSpelled(dstring number) {
// ...
    if (number in exceptions) {
        result = exceptions[number];

    } else {
        if (number[$-1] == 'y') {
            result = number[0..$-1] ~ "ieth";

        } else {
            result = number ~ "th";
        }
    }

    return result;
}
```

42.8 Exercise

Implement toFront() according to TDD. Start with the intentionally incomplete
implementation below. Observe that the unit tests fail and provide an
implementation that passes the tests.

```
dstring toFront(dstring str, dchar letter) {
    dstring result;
    return result;
}

unittest {
    immutable str = "hello"d;

    assert(toFront(str, 'h') == "hello");
    assert(toFront(str, 'o') == "ohell");
    assert(toFront(str, 'l') == "llheo");
}

void main() {
}
```

The solution is on page 715.

43 Contract Programming

Contract programming is a software design approach that treats parts of software as individual entities that provide services to each other. This approach realizes that software can work according to its specification as long as the provider and the consumer of the service both obey a *contract*.

D's contract programming features involve functions as the units of software services. Like in unit testing, contract programming is also based on `assert` checks.

Contract programming in D is implemented by three types of code blocks:

- Function `in` blocks
- Function `out` blocks
- Struct and class `invariant` blocks

We will see `invariant` blocks and *contract inheritance* in a later chapter (page 393) after covering structs and classes.

43.1 in blocks for preconditions

Correct execution of functions usually depend on whether the values of their parameters are valid. For example, a square root function may require that its parameter cannot be negative. A function that deals with dates may require that the number of the month must be between 1 and 12. Such requirements of a function are called its *preconditions*.

We have already seen such condition checks in the `assert` and `enforce` chapter (page 208). Conditions on parameter values can be enforced by `assert` checks within function definitions:

```
string timeToString(int hour, int minute) {
    assert((hour >= 0) && (hour <= 23));
    assert((minute >= 0) && (minute <= 59));

    return format("%02s:%02s", hour, minute);
}
```

In contract programming, the same checks are written inside the `in` blocks of functions. When an `in` or `out` block is used, the actual body of the function must be specified as a do block:

```
import std.stdio;
import std.string;

string timeToString(int hour, int minute)
in {
    assert((hour >= 0) && (hour <= 23));
    assert((minute >= 0) && (minute <= 59));

} do {
    return format("%02s:%02s", hour, minute);
}

void main() {
    writeln(timeToString(12, 34));
}
```

Note: *In earlier versions of D, the body keyword was used for this purpose instead of do.*

A benefit of an `in` block is that all of the preconditions can be kept together and separate from the actual body of the function. This way, the function body would be free of `assert` checks about the preconditions. As needed, it is still possible and advisable to have other `assert` checks inside the function body as unrelated checks that guard against potential programming errors in the function body.

The code that is inside the `in` block is executed automatically every time the function is called. The actual execution of the function starts only if all of the `assert` checks inside the `in` block pass. This prevents executing the function with invalid preconditions and as a consequence, avoids producing incorrect results.

An `assert` check that fails inside the `in` block indicates that the contract has been violated by the caller.

43.2 out blocks for postconditions

The other side of the contract involves guarantees that the function provides. Such guarantees are called the function's *postconditions*. An example of a function with a postcondition would be a function that returns the number of days in February: The function can guarantee that the returned value would always be either 28 or 29.

The postconditions are checked inside the `out` blocks of functions.

Because the value that a function returns by the `return` statement need not be defined as a variable inside the function, there is usually no name to refer to the return value. This can be seen as a problem because the `assert` checks inside the `out` block cannot refer to the returned variable by name.

D solves this problem by providing a way of naming the return value right after the `out` keyword. That name represents the very value that the function is in the process of returning:

```d
int daysInFebruary(int year)
out (result) {
    assert((result == 28) || (result == 29));

} do {
    return isLeapYear(year) ? 29 : 28;
}
```

Although `result` is a reasonable name for the returned value, other valid names may also be used.

Some functions do not have return values or the return value need not be checked. In that case the `out` block does not specify a name:

```d
out {
    // ...
}
```

Similar to `in` blocks, the `out` blocks are executed automatically after the body of the function is executed.

An `assert` check that fails inside the `out` block indicates that the contract has been violated by the function.

As it has been obvious, `in` and `out` blocks are optional. Considering the `unittest` blocks as well, which are also optional, D functions may consist of up to four blocks of code:

- `in`: Optional
- `out`: Optional
- `do`: Mandatory but the `do` keyword may be skipped if no `in` or `out` block is defined.

- `unittest`: Optional and technically not a part of a function's definition but commonly defined right after the function.

Here is an example that uses all of these blocks:

```d
import std.stdio;

/* Distributes the sum between two variables.
 *
 * Distributes to the first variable first, but never gives
 * more than 7 to it. The rest of the sum is distributed to
 * the second variable. */
void distribute(int sum, out int first, out int second)
in {
    assert(sum >= 0, "sum cannot be negative");

} out {
    assert(sum == (first + second));

} do {
    first = (sum >= 7) ? 7 : sum;
    second = sum - first;
}

unittest {
    int first;
    int second;

    // Both must be 0 if the sum is 0
    distribute(0, first, second);
    assert(first == 0);
    assert(second == 0);

    // If the sum is less than 7, then all of it must be given
    // to first
    distribute(3, first, second);
    assert(first == 3);
    assert(second == 0);

    // Testing a boundary condition
    distribute(7, first, second);
    assert(first == 7);
    assert(second == 0);

    // If the sum is more than 7, then the first must get 7
    // and the rest must be given to second
    distribute(8, first, second);
    assert(first == 7);
    assert(second == 1);

    // A random large value
    distribute(1_000_007, first, second);
    assert(first == 7);
    assert(second == 1_000_000);
}

void main() {
    int first;
    int second;

    distribute(123, first, second);
    writeln("first: ", first, " second: ", second);
}
```

The program can be compiled and run on the terminal by the following commands:

```
$ dmd deneme.d -w -unittest
$ ./deneme
first: 7 second: 116
```

Although the actual work of the function consists of only two lines, there are a total of 19 nontrivial lines that support its functionality. It may be argued that so much extra code is too much for such a short function. However, bugs are never intentional. The programmer always writes code that is *expected to work correctly*, which commonly ends up containing various types of bugs.

When expectations are laid out explicitly by unit tests and contracts, functions that are initially correct have a greater chance of staying correct. I recommend that you take full advantage of any feature that improves program correctness. Both unit tests and contracts are effective tools toward that goal. They help reduce time spent for debugging, effectively increasing time spent for actually writing code.

43.3 Expression-based contracts
Although in and out blocks are useful for allowing any D code, precondition and postcondition checks are usually not more than simple assert expressions. As a convenience in such cases, there is a shorter expression-based contract syntax. Let's consider the following function:

```d
int func(int a, int b)
in {
    assert(a >= 7, "a cannot be less than 7");
    assert(b < 10);

} out (result) {
    assert(result > 1000);

} do {
    // ...
}
```

The expression-based contract obviates curly brackets, explicit assert calls, and the do keyword:

```d
int func(int a, int b)
in (a >= 7, "a cannot be less than 7")
in (b < 10)
out (result; result > 1000) {
    // ...
}
```

Note how the return value of the function is named before a semicolon in the out contract. When there is no return value or when the out contract does not refer to the return value, the semicolon must still be present:

```d
out (; /* ... */)
```

43.4 Disabling contract programming
Contrary to unit testing, contract programming features are enabled by default. The -release compiler switch disables contract programming:

```
$ dmd deneme.d -w -release
```

When the program is compiled with the -release switch, the contents of in, out, and invariant blocks are ignored.

43.5 in blocks versus enforce checks
We have seen in the assert and enforce chapter (page 208) that sometimes it is difficult to decide whether to use assert or enforce checks. Similarly, sometimes

it is difficult to decide whether to use assert checks within in blocks versus enforce checks within function bodies.

The fact that it is possible to disable contract programming is an indication that contract programming is for protecting against programmer errors. For that reason, the decision here should be based on the same guidelines that we saw in the assert and enforce chapter (page 208):

- If the check is guarding against a coding error, then it should be in the in block. For example, if the function is called only from other parts of the program, likely to help with achieving a functionality of it, then the parameter values are entirely the responsibility of the programmer. For that reason, the preconditions of such a function should be checked in its in block.
- If the function cannot achieve some task for any other reason, including invalid parameter values, then it must throw an exception, conveniently by enforce.

    To see an example of this, let's define a function that returns a slice of the middle of another slice. Let's assume that this function is for the consumption of the users of the module, as opposed to being an internal function used by the module itself. Since the users of this module can call this function by various and potentially invalid parameter values, it would be appropriate to check the parameter values every time the function is called. It would be insufficient to only check them at program development time, after which contracts can be disabled by -release.

    For that reason, the following function validates its parameters by calling enforce in the function body instead of an assert check in the in block:

```
import std.exception;

inout(int)[] middle(inout(int)[] originalSlice, size_t width)
out (result) {
    assert(result.length == width);

} do {
    enforce(originalSlice.length >= width);

    immutable start = (originalSlice.length - width) / 2;
    immutable end = start + width;

    return originalSlice[start .. end];
}

unittest {
    auto slice = [1, 2, 3, 4, 5];

    assert(middle(slice, 3) == [2, 3, 4]);
    assert(middle(slice, 2) == [2, 3]);
    assert(middle(slice, 5) == slice);
}

void main() {
}
```

There isn't a similar problem with the out blocks. Since the return value of every function is the responsibility of the programmer, postconditions must always be checked in the out blocks. The function above follows this guideline.

- Another criterion to consider when deciding between in blocks versus enforce is to consider whether the condition is recoverable. If it is recoverable by the higher layers of code, then it may be more appropriate to throw an exception, conveniently by `enforce`.

43.6 Exercise

Write a program that increases the total points of two football (soccer) teams according to the result of a game.

The first two parameters of this function are the goals that each team has scored. The other two parameters are the points of each team before the game. This function should adjust the points of the teams according to the goals that they have scored. As a reminder, the winner takes 3 points and the loser takes no point. In the event of a draw, both teams get 1 point each.

Additionally, the function should indicate which team has been the winner: 1 if the first team has won, 2 if the second team has won, and 0 if the game has ended in a draw.

Start with the following program and fill in the four blocks of the function appropriately. Do not remove the `assert` checks in `main()`; they demonstrate how this function is expected to work.

```
int addPoints(int goals1, int goals2,
              ref int points1, ref int points2)
in {
    // ...

} out (result) {
    // ...

} do {
    int winner;

    // ...

    return winner;
}

unittest {
    // ...
}

void main() {
    int points1 = 10;
    int points2 = 7;
    int winner;

    winner = addPoints(3, 1, points1, points2);
    assert(points1 == 13);
    assert(points2 == 7);
    assert(winner == 1);

    winner = addPoints(2, 2, points1, points2);
    assert(points1 == 14);
    assert(points2 == 8);
    assert(winner == 0);
}
```

Although I chose to return an `int`, it would be better to return an enum value from this function:

```
enum GameResult {
    draw, firstWon, secondWon
}

GameResult addPoints(int goals1, int goals2,
                     ref int points1, ref int points2)
// ...
```

The solution is on page 717.

44 Lifetimes and Fundamental Operations

We will soon cover structs, the basic feature that allows the programmer to define application-specific types. Structs are for combining fundamental types and other structs together to define higher-level types that behave according to special needs of programs. After structs, we will learn about classes, which are the basis of the object oriented programming features of D.

Before getting to structs and classes, it will be better to talk about some important concepts first. These concepts will help understand structs and classes and some of their differences.

We have been calling any piece of data that represented a concept in a program a *variable*. In a few places we have referred to struct and class variables specifically as *objects*. I will continue calling both of these concepts variables in this chapter.

Although this chapter includes only fundamental types, slices, and associative arrays; these concepts apply to user-defined types as well.

44.1 Lifetime of a variable

The time between when a variable is defined and when it is *finalized* is the lifetime of that variable. Although it is the case for many types, *becoming unavailable* and *being finalized* need not be at the same time.

You would remember from the Name Scope chapter (page 90) how variables become unavailable. In simple cases, exiting the scope where a variable was defined would render that variable unavailable.

Let's consider the following example as a reminder:

```
void speedTest() {
    int speed;              // Single variable ...

    foreach (i; 0 .. 10) {
        speed = 100 + i;    // ... takes 10 different values.
        // ...
    }
} // ← 'speed' is unavailable beyond this point.
```

The lifetime of the speed variable in that code ends upon exiting the speedTest() function. There is a single variable in the code above, which takes ten different values from 100 to 109.

When it comes to variable lifetimes, the following code is very different compared to the previous one:

```
void speedTest() {
    foreach (i; 0 .. 10) {
        int speed = 100 + i; // Ten separate variables.
        // ...
    } // ← Lifetime of each variable ends here.
}
```

There are ten separate variables in that code, each taking a single value. Upon every iteration of the loop, a new variable starts its life, which eventually ends at the end of each iteration.

44.2 Lifetime of a parameter

The lifetime of a parameter depends on its qualifiers:

ref: The parameter is just an alias of the actual variable that is specified when calling the function. ref parameters do not affect the lifetimes of actual variables.

in: For *value types*, the lifetime of the parameter starts upon entering the function and ends upon exiting it. For *reference types*, the lifetime of the parameter is the same as with ref.

out: Same with ref, the parameter is just an alias of the actual variable that is specified when calling the function. The only difference is that the variable is set to its .init value automatically upon entering the function.

lazy: The life of the parameter starts when the parameter is actually used and ends right then.

The following example uses these four types of parameters and explains their lifetimes in program comments:

```
void main() {
    int main_in;      /* The value of main_in is copied to the
                       * parameter. */

    int main_ref;     /* main_ref is passed to the function as
                       * itself. */

    int main_out;     /* main_out is passed to the function as
                       * itself. Its value is set to int.init
                       * upon entering the function. */

    foo(main_in, main_ref, main_out, aCalculation());
}

void foo(
    in int p_in,      /* The lifetime of p_in starts upon
                       * entering the function and ends upon
                       * exiting the function. */

    ref int p_ref,    /* p_ref is an alias of main_ref. */

    out int p_out,    /* p_out is an alias of main_out. Its
                       * value is set to int.init upon
                       * entering the function. */

    lazy int p_lazy) { /* The lifetime of p_lazy starts when
                        * it is used and ends when its use
                        * ends. Its value is calculated by
                        * calling aCalculation() every time
                        * p_lazy is used in the function. */
    // ...
}

int aCalculation() {
    int result;
    // ...
    return result;
}
```

44.3 Fundamental operations

Regardless of its type, there are three fundamental operations throughout the lifetime of a variable:

- **Initialization**: The start of its life.
- **Finalization**: The end of its life.
- **Assignment**: Changing its value as a whole.

To be considered an object, it must first be initialized. There may be final operations for some types. The value of a variable may change during its lifetime.

Initialization

Every variable must be initialized before being used. Initialization involves two steps:

1. **Reserving space for the variable**: This space is where the value of the variable is stored in memory.
2. **Construction**: Setting the first value of the variable on that space (or the first values of the members of structs and classes).

Every variable lives in a place in memory that is reserved for it. Some of the code that the compiler generates is about reserving space for each variable.

Let's consider the following variable:

```d
int speed = 123;
```

As we have seen in the Value Types and Reference Types chapter (page 159), we can imagine this variable living on some part of the memory:

The memory location that a variable is placed at is called its address. In a sense, the variable lives at that address. When the value of a variable is changed, the new value is stored at the same place:

```d
++speed;
```

The new value would be at the same place where the old value has been:

```
|   | 124 |   |
```

Construction is necessary to prepare variables for use. Since a variable cannot be used reliably before being constructed, it is performed by the compiler automatically.

Variables can be constructed in three ways:

- **By their default value**: when the programmer does not specify a value explicitly
- **By copying**: when the variable is constructed as a copy of another variable of the same type
- **By a specific value**: when the programmer specifies a value explicitly

When a value is not specified, the value of the variable would be the *default* value of its type, i.e. its .init value.

```d
int speed;
```

The value of speed above is int.init, which happens to be zero. Naturally, a variable that is constructed by its default value may have other values during its lifetime (unless it is immutable).

```d
File file;
```

With the definition above, the variable `file` is a `File` object that is not yet associated with an actual file on the file system. It is not usable until it is modified to be associated with a file.

Variables are sometimes constructed as a copy of another variable:

```
int speed = otherSpeed;
```

`speed` above is constructed by the value of `otherSpeed`.

As we will see in later chapters, this operation has a different meaning for class variables:

```
auto classVariable = otherClassVariable;
```

Although `classVariable` starts its life as a copy of `otherClassVariable`, there is a fundamental difference with classes: Although `speed` and `otherSpeed` are distinct values, `classVariable` and `otherClassVariable` both provide access to the same value. This is the fundamental difference between value types and reference types.

Finally, variables can be constructed by the value of an expression of a compatible type:

```
int speed = someCalculation();
```

`speed` above would be constructed by the return value of `someCalculation()`.

Finalization

Finalizing is the final operations that are executed for a variable and reclaiming its memory:

1. **Destruction**: The final operations that must be executed for the variable.
2. **Reclaiming the variable's memory**: Reclaiming the piece of memory that the variable has been living on.

For simple fundamental types, there are no final operations to execute. For example, the value of a variable of type `int` is not set back to zero. For such variables there is only reclaiming their memory, so that it will be used for other variables later.

On the other hand, some types of variables require special operations during finalization. For example, a `File` object would need to write the characters that are still in its output buffer to disk and notify the file system that it no longer uses the file. These operations are the destruction of a `File` object.

Final operations of arrays are at a little higher-level: Before finalizing the array, first its elements are destructed. If the elements are of a simple fundamental type like `int`, then there are no special final operations for them. If the elements are of a struct or a class type that needs finalization, then those operations are executed for each element.

Associative arrays are similar to arrays. Additionally, the keys may also be finalized if they are of a type that needs destruction.

The garbage collector: D is a *garbage-collected* language. In such languages finalizing an object need not be initiated explicitly by the programmer. When a variable's lifetime ends, its finalization is automatically handled by the garbage collector. We will cover the garbage collector and special memory management in a later chapter (page 667).

Variables can be finalized in two ways:

- **When the lifetime ends**: Finalization happens at the end of the variable's life.
- **Some time in the future**: Finalization happens at an indeterminate time in the future by the garbage collector.

Which of the two ways a variable will be finalized depends primarily on its type. Some types like arrays, associative arrays and classes are normally destructed by the garbage collector some time in the future.

Assignment

The other fundamental operation that a variable experiences during its lifetime is assignment.

For simple fundamental types assignment is merely changing the value of the variable. As we have seen above on the memory representation, an int variable would start having the value 124 instead of 123. However, more generally, assignment consists of two steps, which are not necessarily executed in the following order:

- **Destructing the old value**
- **Constructing the new value**

These two steps are not important for simple fundamental types that don't need destruction. For types that need destruction, it is important to remember that assignment is a combination of the two steps above.

45 The null Value and the is Operator

We saw in earlier chapters that a variable of a reference type needs not reference a particular object:

```
MyClass referencesAnObject = new MyClass;

MyClass variable;    // does not reference an object
```

Being a reference type, `variable` above does have an identity but it does not reference any object yet. Such an object can be imagined to have a place in memory as in the following picture:

```
    variable
   _____
  |  null   |
  |_____|
```

A reference that does not reference any value is `null`. We will expand on this below.

Such a variable is in an almost useless state. Since there is no `MyClass` object that it references, it cannot be used in a context where an actual `MyClass` object is needed:

```
import std.stdio;

class MyClass {
    int member;
}

void use(MyClass variable) {
    writeln(variable.member);    // ← BUG
}

void main() {
    MyClass variable;
    use(variable);
}
```

As there is no object that is referenced by the parameter that `use()` receives, attempting to access a member of a non-existing object results in a program crash:

```
$ ./deneme
Segmentation fault
```

"Segmentation fault" is an indication that the program has been terminated by the operating system because of attempting to access an illegal memory address.

45.1 The null value

The special value `null` can be printed just like any other value.

```
    writeln(null);
```

The output:

```
null
```

A `null` variable can be used only in two contexts:

1. Assigning an object to it

```
    variable = new MyClass;  // now references an object
```

The assignment above makes `variable` provide access to the newly
constructed object. From that point on, `variable` can be used for any valid
operation of the `MyClass` type.

2. Determining whether it is `null`
   However, because the `==` operator needs actual objects to compare, the
   expression below cannot be compiled:

```
    if (variable == null)     // ← compilation ERROR
```

For that reason, whether a variable is `null` must be determined by the `is`
operator.

45.2 The `is` operator

This operator answers the question "does have the null value?":

```
    if (variable is null) {
        // Does not reference any object
    }
```

`is` can be used with other types of variables as well. In the following use, it
compares the `values` of two integers:

```
    if (speed is newSpeed) {
        // Their values are equal

    } else {
        // Their values are different
    }
```

When used with slices, it determines whether the two slices reference the same
set of elements:

```
    if (slice is slice2) {
        // They provide access to the same elements
    }
```

45.3 The `!is` operator

`!is` is the opposite of `is`. It produces `true` when the values are different:

```
    if (speed !is newSpeed) {
        // Their values are different
    }
```

45.4 Assigning the `null` value

Assigning the `null` value to a variable of a reference type makes that variable
stop referencing its current object.

If that assignment happens to be terminating the very last reference to the
actual object, then the actual object becomes a candidate for finalization by the
garbage collector. After all, not being referenced by any variable means that the
object is not being used in the program at all.

Let's look at the example from an earlier chapter (page 159) where two variables
were referencing the same object:

```
    auto variable = new MyClass;
    auto variable2 = variable;
```

The following is a representation of the state of the memory after executing that code:

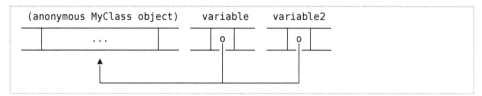

Assigning the null value to one of these variables breaks its relationship with the object:

```
variable = null;
```

At this point there is only variable2 that references the MyClass object:

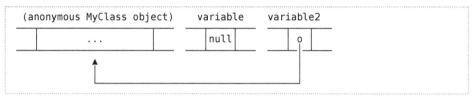

Assigning null to the last reference would make the MyClass object unreachable:

```
variable2 = null;
```

Such unreachable objects are finalized by the garbage collector at some time in the future. From the point of view of the program, the object does not exist:

We had discussed ways of emptying an associative array in the exercises section of the Associative Arrays chapter (page 117). We now know a fourth method: Assigning null to an associative array variable will break the relationship of that variable with the elements:

```
string[int] names;
// ...
names = null;    // Not providing access to any element
```

Similar to the MyClass examples, if names has been the last reference to the elements of the associative array, those elements would be finalized by the garbage collector.

Slices can be assigned null as well:

```
int[] slice = otherSlice[ 10 .. 20 ];
// ...
slice = null;    // Not providing access to any element
```

45.5 Summary

- null is the value indicating that a variable does not provide access to any value
- References that have the null value can only be used in two operations: assigning a value to them and determining whether they are null or not

- Since the == operator may have to access an actual object, determining whether a variable is null must be performed by the is operator
- !is is the opposite of is
- Assigning null to a variable makes that variable provide access to nothing
- Objects that are not referenced by any variable are finalized by the garbage collector

Variables must be compatible with the expressions that they take part in. As it has probably been obvious from the programs that we have seen so far, D is a *statically typed language*, meaning that the compatibility of types is validated at compile time.

All of the expressions that we have written so far always had compatible types because otherwise the code would be rejected by the compiler. The following is an example of code that has incompatible types:

```
char[] slice;
writeln(slice + 5);    // ← compilation ERROR
```

The compiler rejects the code due to the incompatible types `char[]` and `int` for the addition operation:

```
Error: incompatible types for ((slice) + (5)): 'char[]' and 'int'
```

Type incompatibility does not mean that the types are different; different types can indeed be used in expressions safely. For example, an `int` variable can safely be used in place of a `double` value:

```
double sum = 1.25;
int increment = 3;
sum += increment;
```

Even though `sum` and `increment` are of different types, the code above is valid because incrementing a `double` variable by an `int` value is legal.

46.1 Automatic type conversions

Automatic type conversions are also called *implicit type conversions*.

Although `double` and `int` are compatible types in the expression above, the addition operation must still be evaluated as a specific type at the microprocessor level. As you would remember from the Floating Point Types chapter (page 42), the 64-bit type `double` is *wider* (or *larger*) than the 32-bit type `int`. Additionally, any value that fits in an `int` also fits in a `double`.

When the compiler encounters an expression that involves mismatched types, it first converts the parts of the expressions to a common type and then evaluates the overall expression. The automatic conversions that are performed by the compiler are in the direction that avoids data loss. For example, `double` can hold any value that `int` can hold but the opposite is not true. The += operation above can work because any `int` value can safely be converted to `double`.

The value that has been generated automatically as a result of a conversion is always an anonymous (and often temporary) variable. The original value does not change. For example, the automatic conversion during += above does not change the type of `increment`; it is always an `int`. Rather, a temporary value of type `double` is constructed with the value of `increment`. The conversion that takes place in the background is equivalent to the following code:

```
{
    double an_anonymous_double_value = increment;
    sum += an_anonymous_double_value;
}
```

The compiler converts the int value to a temporary double value and uses that value in the operation. In this example, the temporary variable lives only during the += operation.

Automatic conversions are not limited to arithmetic operations. There are other cases where types are converted to other types automatically. As long as the conversions are valid, the compiler takes advantage of type conversions to be able to use values in expressions. For example, a byte value can be passed for an int parameter:

```d
void func(int number) {
    // ...
}

void main() {
    byte smallValue = 7;
    func(smallValue);    // automatic type conversion
}
```

In the code above, first a temporary int value is constructed and the function is called with that value.

Integer promotions

Values of types that are on the left-hand side of the following table never take part in arithmetic expressions as their actual types. Each type is first promoted to the type that is on the right-hand side of the table.

From	To
bool	int
byte	int
ubyte	int
short	int
ushort	int
char	int
wchar	int
dchar	uint

Integer promotions are applied to enum values as well.

The reasons for integer promotions are both historical (where the rules come from C) and the fact that the natural arithmetic type for the microprocessor is int. For example, although the following two variables are both ubyte, the addition operation is performed only after both of the values are individually promoted to int:

```d
ubyte a = 1;
ubyte b = 2;
writeln(typeof(a + b).stringof);  // the addition is not in ubyte
```

The output:

```
int
```

Note that the types of the variables a and b do not change; only their values are temporarily promoted to int for the duration of the addition operation.

Arithmetic conversions

There are other conversion rules that are applied for arithmetic operations. In general, automatic arithmetic conversions are applied in the safe direction: from the *narrower* type to the *wider* type. Although this rule is easy to remember and is correct in most cases, automatic conversion rules are very complicated and in the case of signed-to-unsigned conversions, carry some risk of bugs.

The arithmetic conversion rules are the following:

1. If one of the values is `real`, then the other value is converted to `real`
2. Else, if one of the values is `double`, then the other value is converted to `double`
3. Else, if one of the values is `float`, then the other value is converted to `float`
4. Else, first *integer promotions* are applied according to the table above, and then the following rules are followed:

    1. If both types are the same, then no more steps needed
    2. If both types are signed or both types are unsigned, then the narrower value is converted to the wider type
    3. If the signed type is wider than the unsigned type, then the unsigned value is converted to the signed type
    4. Otherwise the signed type is converted to the unsigned type

Unfortunately, the last rule above can cause subtle bugs:

```
int     a = 0;
int     b = 1;
size_t c = 0;
writeln(a - b + c);   // Surprising result!
```

Surprisingly, the output is not -1, but `size_t.max`:

```
18446744073709551615
```

Although one would expect (0 - 1 + 0) to be calculated as -1, according to the rules above, the type of the entire expression is `size_t`, not int; and since `size_t` cannot hold negative values, the result overflows and becomes `size_t.max`.

Slice conversions

As a convenience, fixed-length arrays can automatically be converted to slices when calling a function:

```
import std.stdio;

void foo() {
    int[2] array = [ 1, 2 ];
    bar(array);    // Passes fixed-length array as a slice
}

void bar(int[] slice) {
    writeln(slice);
}

void main() {
    foo();
}
```

`bar()` receives a slice to all elements of the fixed-length array and prints it:

```
[1, 2]
```

Warning: A *local* fixed-length array must not be passed as a slice if the function stores the slice for later use. For example, the following program has a bug because the slice that `bar()` stores would not be valid after `foo()` exits:

```
import std.stdio;

void foo() {
    int[2] array = [ 1, 2 ];
```

```
    bar(array);     // Passes fixed-length array as a slice
} // ← NOTE: 'array' is not valid beyond this point

int[] sliceForLaterUse;

void bar(int[] slice) {
    // Saves a slice that is about to become invalid
    sliceForLaterUse = slice;
    writefln("Inside bar : %s", sliceForLaterUse);
}

void main() {
    foo();

    /* BUG: Accesses memory that is not array elements anymore */
    writefln("Inside main: %s", sliceForLaterUse);
}
```

The result of such a bug is undefined behavior. A sample execution can prove that the memory that used to be the elements of array has already been reused for other purposes:

```
Inside bar : [1, 2]          ← actual elements
Inside main: [4396640, 0]    ← a manifestation of undefined behavior
```

const conversions

As we have seen earlier in the Function Parameters chapter (page 168), reference types can automatically be converted to the const of the same type. Conversion to const is safe because the width of the type does not change and const is a promise to not modify the variable:

```
char[] parenthesized(const char[] text) {
    return "{" ~ text ~ "}";
}

void main() {
    char[] greeting;
    greeting ~= "hello world";
    parenthesized(greeting);
}
```

The mutable greeting above is automatically converted to a const char[] as it is passed to parenthesized().

As we have also seen earlier, the opposite conversion is not automatic. A const reference is not automatically converted to a mutable reference:

```
char[] parenthesized(const char[] text) {
    char[] argument = text;   // ← compilation ERROR
// ...
}
```

Note that this topic is only about references; since variables of value types are copied, it is not possible to affect the original through the copy anyway:

```
    const int totalCorners = 4;
    int theCopy = totalCorners;      // compiles (value type)
```

The conversion from const to mutable above is legal because the copy is not a reference to the original.

immutable conversions

Because immutable specifies that a variable can never change, neither conversion from immutable nor to immutable are automatic:

```
string a = "hello";    // immutable characters
char[] b = a;          // ← compilation ERROR
string c = b;          // ← compilation ERROR
```

As with `const` conversions above, this topic is also only about reference types. Since variables of value types are copied anyway, conversions to and from `immutable` are valid:

```
immutable a = 10;
int b = a;             // compiles (value type)
```

enum conversions

As we have seen in the enum chapter (page 132), enum is for defining *named constants*:

```
enum Suit { spades, hearts, diamonds, clubs }
```

Remember that since no values are specified explicitly above, the values of the enum members start with zero and are automatically incremented by one. Accordingly, the value of `Suit.clubs` is 3.

enum values are atomically converted to integral types. For example, the value of `Suit.hearts` is taken to be 1 in the following calculation and the result becomes 11:

```
int result = 10 + Suit.hearts;
assert(result == 11);
```

The opposite conversion is not automatic: Integer values are not automatically converted to corresponding enum values. For example, the `suit` variable below might be expected to become `Suit.diamonds`, but the code cannot be compiled:

```
Suit suit = 2;    // ← compilation ERROR
```

As we will see below, conversions from integers to enum values are still possible but they must be explicit.

bool conversions

Although `bool` is the natural type of logical expressions, as it has only two values, it can be seen as a 1-bit integer and does behave like one in some cases. `false` and `true` are automatically converted to 0 and 1, respectively:

```
int a = false;
assert(a == 0);

int b = true;
assert(b == 1);
```

Regarding *literal values*, the opposite conversion is automatic only for two special literal values: 0 and 1 are converted automatically to `false` and `true`, respectively:

```
bool a = 0;
assert(!a);      // false

bool b = 1;
assert(b);       // true
```

Other literal values cannot be converted to `bool` automatically:

```
bool b = 2;    // ← compilation ERROR
```

Some statements make use of logical expressions: if, while, etc. For the logical expressions of such statements, not only bool but most other types can be used as well. The value zero is automatically converted to false and the nonzero values are automatically converted to true.

```
int i;
// ...

if (i) {    // ← int value is being used as a logical expression
    // ... 'i' is not zero

} else {
    // ... 'i' is zero
}
```

Similarly, null references are automatically converted to false and non-null references are automatically converted to true. This makes it easy to ensure that a reference is non-null before actually using it:

```
int[] a;
// ...

if (a) {    // ← automatic bool conversion
    // ... not null; 'a' can be used ...

} else {
    // ... null; 'a' cannot be used ...
}
```

46.2 Explicit type conversions

As we have seen above, there are cases where automatic conversions are not available:

- Conversions from wider types to narrower types
- Conversions from const to mutable
- immutable conversions
- Conversions from integers to enum values
- etc.

If such a conversion is known to be safe, the programmer can explicitly ask for a type conversion by one of the following methods:

- Construction syntax
- std.conv.to function
- std.exception.assumeUnique function
- cast operator

Construction syntax

The struct and class construction syntax is available for other types as well:

```
DestinationType(value)
```

For example, the following *conversion* makes a double value from an int value, presumably to preserve the fractional part of the division operation:

```
int i;
// ...
const result = double(i) / 2;
```

to() for most conversions

The to() function, which we have already used mostly to convert values to string, can actually be used for many other types. Its complete syntax is the following:

```
to!(DestinationType)(value)
```

Being a template, to() can take advantage of the shortcut template parameter notation: When the destination type consists only of a single token (generally, *a single word*), it can be called without the first pair of parentheses:

```
to!DestinationType(value)
```

The following program is trying to convert a double value to short and a string value to int:

```
void main() {
    double d = -1.75;

    short s = d;      // ← compilation ERROR
    int i = "42";     // ← compilation ERROR
}
```

Since not every double value can be represented as a short and not every string can be represented as an int, those conversions are not automatic. When it is known by the programmer that the conversions are in fact safe or that the potential consequences are acceptable, then the types can be converted by to():

```
import std.conv;

void main() {
    double d = -1.75;

    short s = to!short(d);
    assert(s == -1);

    int i = to!int("42");
    assert(i == 42);
}
```

Note that because short cannot carry fractional values, the converted value is -1.
    to() is safe: It throws an exception when a conversion is not possible.

assumeUnique() for fast immutable conversions

to() can perform immutable conversions as well:

```
    int[] slice = [ 10, 20, 30 ];
    auto immutableSlice = to!(immutable int[])(slice);
```

In order to guarantee that the elements of immutableSlice will never change, it cannot share the same elements with slice. For that reason, to() creates an additional slice with immutable elements above. Otherwise, modifications to the elements of slice would cause the elements of immutableSlice change as well. This behavior is the same with the .idup property of arrays.

We can see that the elements of immutableSlice are indeed copies of the elements of slice by looking at the addresses of their first elements:

```
    assert(&(slice[0]) != &(immutableSlice[0]));
```

Sometimes this copy is unnecessary and may slow the speed of the program noticeably in certain cases. As an example of this, let's look at the following function that takes an `immutable` slice:

```d
void calculate(immutable int[] coordinates) {
    // ...
}

void main() {
    int[] numbers;
    numbers ~= 10;
    // ... various other modifications ...
    numbers[0] = 42;

    calculate(numbers);    // ← compilation ERROR
}
```

The program above cannot be compiled because the caller is not passing an `immutable` argument to `calculate()`. As we have seen above, an `immutable` slice can be created by `to()`:

```d
import std.conv;
// ...
    auto immutableNumbers = to!(immutable int[])(numbers);
    calculate(immutableNumbers);    // ← now compiles
```

However, if `numbers` is needed only to produce this argument and will never be used after the function is called, copying its elements to `immutableNumbers` would be unnecessary. `assumeUnique()` makes the elements of a slice `immutable` without copying:

```d
import std.exception;
// ...
    auto immutableNumbers = assumeUnique(numbers);
    calculate(immutableNumbers);
    assert(numbers is null);    // the original slice becomes null
```

`assumeUnique()` returns a new slice that provides `immutable` access to the existing elements. It also makes the original slice `null` to prevent the elements from accidentally being modified through it.

The cast operator

Both `to()` and `assumeUnique()` make use of the conversion operator `cast`, which is available to the programmer as well.

The `cast` operator takes the destination type in parentheses:

```d
cast(DestinationType)value
```

`cast` is powerful even for conversions that `to()` cannot safely perform. For example, `to()` fails for the following conversions at runtime:

```d
    Suit suit = to!Suit(7);    // ← throws exception
    bool b = to!bool(2);       // ← throws exception
```

```
std.conv.ConvException@phobos/std/conv.d(1778): Value (7)
does not match any member value of enum 'Suit'
```

Sometimes only the programmer can know whether an integer value corresponds to a valid enum value or that it makes sense to treat an integer value as a bool. The `cast` operator can be used when the conversion is known to be correct according the program's logic:

```
// Probably incorrect but possible:
Suit suit = cast(Suit)7;

bool b = cast(bool)2;
assert(b);
```

cast is the only option when converting to and from pointer types:

```
void * v;
// ...
int * p = cast(int*)v;
```

Although rare, some C library interfaces make it necessary to store a pointer value as a non-pointer type. If it is guaranteed that the conversion will preserve the actual value, cast can convert between pointer and non-pointer types as well:

```
size_t savedPointerValue = cast(size_t)p;
// ...
int * p2 = cast(int*)savedPointerValue;
```

46.3 Summary

- Automatic type conversions are mostly in the safe direction: From the narrower type to the wider type and from mutable to const.
- However, conversions to unsigned types may have surprising effects because unsigned types cannot have negative values.
- enum types can automatically be converted to integer values but the opposite conversion is not automatic.
- false and true are automatically converted to 0 and 1 respectively. Similarly, zero values are automatically converted to false and nonzero values are automatically converted to true.
- null references are automatically converted to false and non-null references are automatically converted to true.
- The construction syntax can be used for explicit conversions.
- to() covers most of the explicit conversions.
- assumeUnique() converts to immutable without copying.
- The cast operator is the most powerful conversion tool.

47 Structs

As has been mentioned several times earlier in the book, fundamental types are not suitable to represent higher-level concepts. For example, although a value of type int is suitable to represent the hour of day, two int variables would be more suitable together to represent a point in time: one for the hour and the other for the minute.

Structs are the feature that allow defining new types by combining already existing other types. The new type is defined by the struct keyword. By this definition, structs are *user defined types*. Most of the content of this chapter is directly applicable to classes as well. Especially the concept of *combining existing types to define a new type* is exactly the same for them.

This chapter covers only the basic features of structs. We will see more of structs in the following chapters:

- Member Functions (page 269)
- const ref Parameters and const Member Functions (page 275)
- Constructor and Other Special Functions (page 279)
- Operator Overloading (page 298)
- Encapsulation and Protection Attributes (page 379)
- Properties (page 388)
- Contract Programming for Structs and Classes (page 393)
- foreach with Structs and Classes (page 491)

To understand how useful structs are, let's take a look at the addDuration() function that we had defined earlier in the assert and enforce chapter (page 208). The following definition is from the exercise solution of that chapter:

```
void addDuration(int startHour, int startMinute,
                 int durationHour, int durationMinute,
                 out int resultHour, out int resultMinute) {
    resultHour = startHour + durationHour;
    resultMinute = startMinute + durationMinute;
    resultHour += resultMinute / 60;

    resultMinute %= 60;
    resultHour %= 24;
}
```

Note: *I will ignore the in, out, and unittest blocks in this chapter to keep the code samples short.*

Although the function above clearly takes six parameters, when the three pairs of parameters are considered, it is conceptually taking only three bits of information for the starting time, the duration, and the result.

47.1 Definition

The struct keyword defines a new type by combining variables that are related in some way:

```
struct TimeOfDay {
    int hour;
    int minute;
}
```

The code above defines a new type named `TimeOfDay`, which consists of two variables named `hour` and `minute`. That definition allows the new `TimeOfDay` type to be used in the program just like any other type. The following code demonstrates how similar its use is to an `int`'s:

```
int number;            // a variable
number = otherNumber;  // taking the value of otherNumber

TimeOfDay time;        // an object
time = otherTime;      // taking the value of otherTime
```

The syntax of `struct` definition is the following:

```
struct TypeName {
    // ... member variables and functions ...
}
```

We will see member functions in later chapters.

The variables that a struct combines are called its *members*. According to this definition, `TimeOfDay` has two members: `hour` and `minute`.

`struct` defines a type, not a variable

There is an important distinction here: Especially after the Name Scope (page 90) and Lifetimes and Fundamental Operations (page 228) chapters, the curly brackets of `struct` definitions may give the wrong impression that the struct members start and end their lives inside that scope. This is not true.

Member definitions are not variable definitions:

```
struct TimeOfDay {
    int hour;     // ← Not a variable; will become a part of
                  //    a struct variable used in the program.

    int minute;   // ← Not a variable; will become a part of
                  //    a struct variable used in the program.
}
```

The definition of a `struct` determines the types and the names of the members that the objects of that `struct` will have. Those member variables will be constructed as parts of `TimeOfDay` objects that take part in the program:

```
TimeOfDay bedTime;     // This object contains its own hour
                       // and minute member variables.

TimeOfDay wakeUpTime;  // This object contains its own hour
                       // and minute member variables as
                       // well. The member variables of
                       // this object are not related to
                       // the member variables of the
                       // previous object.
```

Variables of `struct` and `class` types are called *objects*.

Coding convenience

Being able to combine the concepts of hour and minute together as a new type is a great convenience. For example, the function above can be rewritten in a more meaningful way by taking three `TimeOfDay` parameters instead of the existing six `int` parameters:

```
void addDuration(TimeOfDay start,
                 TimeOfDay duration,
                 out TimeOfDay result) {
    // ...
}
```

Note: *It is not normal to add two variables that represent two points in time. For example, it is meaningless to add the lunch time 12:00 to the breakfast time 7:30. It would make more sense to define another type, appropriately called* Duration, *and to add objects of that type to* TimeOfDay *objects. Despite this design flaw, I will continue using only* TimeOfDay *objects in this chapter and introduce* Duration *in a later chapter.*

As you remember, functions return up-to a single value. That has precisely been the reason why the earlier definition of addDuration() was taking two out parameters: It could not return the hour and minute information as a single value.

Structs remove this limitation as well: Since multiple values can be combined as a single struct type, functions can return an object of such a struct, effectively returning multiple values at once. addDuration() can now be defined as returning its result:

```
TimeOfDay addDuration(TimeOfDay start,
                      TimeOfDay duration) {
    // ...
}
```

As a consequence, addDuration() now becomes a function that produces a value, as opposed to being a function that has side effects. As you would remember from the Functions chapter (page 136), producing results is preferred over having side effects.

Structs can be members of other structs. For example, the following struct has two TimeOfDay members:

```
struct Meeting {
    string     topic;
    size_t     attendanceCount;
    TimeOfDay start;
    TimeOfDay end;
}
```

Meeting can in turn be a member of another struct. Assuming that there is also the Meal struct:

```
struct DailyPlan {
    Meeting projectMeeting;
    Meal    lunch;
    Meeting budgetMeeting;
}
```

47.2 Accessing the members

Struct members are used like any other variable. The only difference is that the actual struct variable and a *dot* must be specified before the name of the member:

```
    start.hour = 10;
```

The line above assigns the value 10 to the hour member of the start object.

Let's rewrite the addDuration() function with what we have seen so far:

```
TimeOfDay addDuration(TimeOfDay start,
                      TimeOfDay duration) {
    TimeOfDay result;

    result.minute = start.minute + duration.minute;
    result.hour = start.hour + duration.hour;
    result.hour += result.minute / 60;
```

```
    result.minute %= 60;
    result.hour %= 24;

    return result;
}
```

Notice that the names of the variables are now much shorter in this version of the function: `start`, `duration`, and `result`. Additionally, instead of using complex names like `startHour`, it is possible to access struct members through their respective struct variables as in `start.hour`.

Here is a code that uses the new `addDuration()` function. Given the start time and the duration, the following code calculates when a class period at a school would end:

```
void main() {
    TimeOfDay periodStart;
    periodStart.hour = 8;
    periodStart.minute = 30;

    TimeOfDay periodDuration;
    periodDuration.hour = 1;
    periodDuration.minute = 15;

    immutable periodEnd = addDuration(periodStart,
                                      periodDuration);

    writefln("Period end: %s:%s",
             periodEnd.hour, periodEnd.minute);
}
```

The output:

```
Period end: 9:45
```

The `main()` above has been written only by what we have seen so far. We will make this code even shorter and cleaner soon.

47.3 Construction

The first three lines of `main()` are about constructing the `periodStart` object and the next three lines are about constructing the `periodDuration` object. In each three lines of code first an object is being defined and then its hour and minute values are being set.

In order for a variable to be used in a safe way, that variable must first be constructed in a consistent state. Because construction is so common, there is a special construction syntax for struct objects:

```
    TimeOfDay periodStart = TimeOfDay(8, 30);
    TimeOfDay periodDuration = TimeOfDay(1, 15);
```

The values are automatically assigned to the members in the order that they are specified: Because `hour` is defined first in the `struct`, the value 8 is assigned to `periodStart.hour` and 30 is assigned to `periodStart.minute`.

As we have seen in the Type Conversions chapter (page 237), the construction syntax can be used for other types as well:

```
    auto u = ubyte(42);    // u is a ubyte
    auto i = int(u);       // i is an int
```

Constructing objects as `immutable`

Being able to construct the object by specifying the values of its members at once makes it possible to define objects as `immutable`:

```
immutable periodStart = TimeOfDay(8, 30);
immutable periodDuration = TimeOfDay(1, 15);
```

Otherwise it would not be possible to mark an object first as `immutable` and then modify its members:

```
immutable TimeOfDay periodStart;
periodStart.hour = 8;      // ← compilation ERROR
periodStart.minute = 30;   // ← compilation ERROR
```

Trailing members need not be specified

There may be fewer values specified than the number of members. In that case, the remaining members are initialized by the `.init` values of their respective types.

The following program constructs `Test` objects each time with one less constructor parameter. The `assert` checks indicate that the unspecified members are initialized automatically by their `.init` values. (The reason for needing to call `isNaN()` is explained after the program):

```
import std.math;

struct Test {
    char   c;
    int    i;
    double d;
}

void main() {
    // The initial values of all of the members are specified
    auto t1 = Test('a', 1, 2.3);
    assert(t1.c == 'a');
    assert(t1.i == 1);
    assert(t1.d == 2.3);

    // Last one is missing
    auto t2 = Test('a', 1);
    assert(t2.c == 'a');
    assert(t2.i == 1);
    assert(isNaN(t2.d));

    // Last two are missing
    auto t3 = Test('a');
    assert(t3.c == 'a');
    assert(t3.i == int.init);
    assert(isNaN(t3.d));

    // No initial value specified
    auto t4 = Test();
    assert(t4.c == char.init);
    assert(t4.i == int.init);
    assert(isNaN(t4.d));

    // The same as above
    Test t5;
    assert(t5.c == char.init);
    assert(t5.i == int.init);
    assert(isNaN(t5.d));
}
```

As you would remember from the Floating Point Types chapter (page 42), the initial value of `double` is `double.nan`. Since the `.nan` value is *unordered*, it is meaningless to use it in equality comparisons. That is why calling `std.math.isNaN` is the correct way of determining whether a value equals to `.nan`.

Specifying default values for members

It is important that member variables are automatically initialized with known initial values. This prevents the program from continuing with indeterminate values. However, the `.init` value of their respective types may not be suitable for every type. For example, `char.init` is not even a valid value.

The initial values of the members of a struct can be specified when the struct is defined. This is useful for example to initialize floating point members by `0.0`, instead of the mostly-unusable `.nan`.

The default values are specified by the assignment syntax as the members are defined:

```d
struct Test {
    char   c = 'A';
    int    i = 11;
    double d = 0.25;
}
```

Please note that the syntax above is not really assignment. The code above merely determines the default values that will be used when objects of that struct are actually constructed later in the program.

For example, the following `Test` object is being constructed without any specific values:

```d
Test t;  // no value is specified for the members
writefln("%s,%s,%s", t.c, t.i, t.d);
```

All of the members are initialized by their default values:

```
A,11,0.25
```

Constructing by the {} syntax

Struct objects can also be constructed by the following syntax:

```d
TimeOfDay periodStart = { 8, 30 };
```

Similar to the earlier syntax, the specified values are assigned to the members in the order that they are specified. The trailing members get their default values.

This syntax is inherited from the C programming language:

```d
auto periodStart = TimeOfDay(8, 30);   // ← regular
TimeOfDay periodEnd = { 9, 30 };       // ← C-style
```

This syntax allows *designated initializers*. Designated initializers are for specifying the member that an initialization value is associated with. It is even possible to initialize members in a different order than they are defined in the `struct`:

```d
TimeOfDay t = { minute: 42, hour: 7 };
```

47.4 Copying and assignment

Structs are value types. As has been described in the Value Types and Reference Types chapter (page 159), this means that every `struct` object has its own value. Objects get their own values when constructed, and their values change when they are assigned new values.

```
    auto yourLunchTime = TimeOfDay(12, 0);
    auto myLunchTime = yourLunchTime;

    // Only my lunch time becomes 12:05:
    myLunchTime.minute += 5;

    // ... your lunch time is still the same:
    assert(yourLunchTime.minute == 0);
```

During a copy, all of the members of the source object are automatically copied to the corresponding members of the destination object. Similarly, assignment involves assigning each member of the source to the corresponding member of the destination.

Struct members that are of reference types need extra attention.

Careful with members that are of reference types!

As you remember, copying or assigning variables of reference types does not change any value, it changes what object is being referenced. As a result, copying or assigning generates one more reference to the right-hand side object. The relevance of this for struct members is that, the members of two separate struct objects would start providing access to the same value.

To see an example of this, let's have a look at a struct where one of the members is a reference type. This struct is used for keeping the student number and the grades of a student:

```
struct Student {
    int number;
    int[] grades;
}
```

The following code constructs a second Student object by copying an existing one:

```
    // Constructing the first object:
    auto student1 = Student(1, [ 70, 90, 85 ]);

    // Constructing the second student as a copy of the first
    // one and then changing its number:
    auto student2 = student1;
    student2.number = 2;

    // WARNING: The grades are now being shared by the two objects!

    // Changing the grades of the first student ...
    student1.grades[0] += 5;

    // ... affects the second student as well:
    writeln(student2.grades[0]);
```

When student2 is constructed, its members get the values of the members of student1. Since int is a value type, the second object gets its own number value.

The two Student objects also have individual grades members as well. However, since slices are reference types, the actual elements that the two slices share are the same. Consequently, a change made through one of the slices is seen through the other slice.

The output of the code indicates that the grade of the second student has been increased as well:

```
75
```

For that reason, a better approach might be to construct the second object by the copies of the grades of the first one:

```
    // The second Student is being constructed by the copies
    // of the grades of the first one:
    auto student2 = Student(2, student1.grades.dup);

    // Changing the grades of the first student ...
    student1.grades[0] += 5;

    // ... does not affect the grades of the second student:
    writeln(student2.grades[0]);
```

Since the grades have been copied by .dup, this time the grades of the second student are not affected:

```
70
```

Note: It is possible to have even the reference members copied automatically. We will see how this is done later when covering struct member functions.

47.5 Struct literals
Similar to being able to use integer literal values like 10 in expressions without needing to define a variable, struct objects can be used as literals as well.

Struct literals are constructed by the object construction syntax.

```
    TimeOfDay(8, 30) // ← struct literal value
```

Let's first rewrite the main() function above with what we have learned since its last version. The variables are constructed by the construction syntax and are immutable this time:

```
void main() {
    immutable periodStart = TimeOfDay(8, 30);
    immutable periodDuration = TimeOfDay(1, 15);

    immutable periodEnd = addDuration(periodStart,
                                      periodDuration);

    writefln("Period end: %s:%s",
             periodEnd.hour, periodEnd.minute);
}
```

Note that periodStart and periodDuration need not be defined as named variables in the code above. Those are in fact temporary variables in this simple program, which are used only for calculating the periodEnd variable. They could be passed to addDuration() as literal values instead:

```
void main() {
    immutable periodEnd = addDuration(TimeOfDay(8, 30),
                                      TimeOfDay(1, 15));

    writefln("Period end: %s:%s",
             periodEnd.hour, periodEnd.minute);
}
```

47.6 static members
Although objects mostly need individual copies of the struct's members, sometimes it makes sense for the objects of a particular struct type to share some variables. This may be necessary to maintain e.g. a general information about that struct type.

As an example, let's imagine a type that assigns a separate identifier for every object that is constructed of that type:

```d
struct Point {
    // The identifier of each object
    size_t id;

    int line;
    int column;
}
```

In order to be able to assign different ids to each object, a separate variable is needed to keep the next available id. It would be incremented every time a new object is created. Assume that nextId is to be defined elsewhere and to be available in the following function:

```d
Point makePoint(int line, int column) {
    size_t id = nextId;
    ++nextId;

    return Point(id, line, column);
}
```

A decision must be made regarding where the common nextId variable is to be defined. static members are useful in such cases.

Such common information is defined as a static member of the struct. Contrary to the regular members, there is a single variable of each static member for each thread. (Note that most programs consist of a single thread that starts executing the main() function.) That single variable is shared by all of the objects of that struct in that thread:

```d
import std.stdio;

struct Point {
    // The identifier of each object
    size_t id;

    int line;
    int column;

    // The id of the next object to construct
    static size_t nextId;
}

Point makePoint(int line, int column) {
    size_t id = Point.nextId;
    ++Point.nextId;

    return Point(id, line, column);
}

void main() {
    auto top = makePoint(7, 0);
    auto middle = makePoint(8, 0);
    auto bottom =  makePoint(9, 0);

    writeln(top.id);
    writeln(middle.id);
    writeln(bottom.id);
}
```

As nextId is incremented at each object construction, each object gets a unique id:

```
0
1
2
```

Since static members are owned by the entire type, there need not be an object to access them. As we have seen above, such objects can be accessed by the name of the type, as well as by the name of any object of that struct:

```
    ++Point.nextId;
    ++bottom.nextId;    // would be the same as above
```

When a variable is needed not *one per thread* but *one per program*, then those variables must be defined as shared static. We will see the shared keyword in a later chapter.

static this() for initialization and static ~this() for finalization

Instead of explicitly assigning an initial value to nextId above, we relied on its default initial value, zero. We could have used any other value:

```
    static size_t nextId = 1000;
```

However, such initialization is possible only when the initial value is known at compile time. Further, some special code may have to be executed before a struct can be used in a thread. Such code is written in static this() scopes.

For example, the following code reads the initial value from a file if that file exists:

```
import std.file;

struct Point {
// ...

    enum nextIdFile = "Point_next_id_file";

    static this() {
        if (exists(nextIdFile)) {
            auto file = File(nextIdFile, "r");
            file.readf(" %s", &nextId);
        }
    }
}
```

The contents of static this() blocks are automatically executed once per thread before the struct type is ever used in that thread. Code that should be executed only once for the entire program (e.g. initializing shared and immutable variables) must be defined in shared static this() and shared static ~this() blocks, which will be covered in the Data Sharing Concurrency chapter (page 640).

Similarly, static ~this() is for the final operations of a thread and shared static ~this() is for the final operations of the entire program.

The following example complements the previous static this() by writing the value of nextId to the same file, effectively persisting the object ids over consecutive executions of the program:

```
struct Point {
// ...

    static ~this() {
        auto file = File(nextIdFile, "w");
        file.writeln(nextId);
    }
}
```

The program would now initialize nextId from where it was left off. For example, the following would be the output of the program's second execution:

```
3
4
5
```

47.7 Exercises

1. Design a struct named `Card` to represent a playing card.

   This struct can have two members for the suit and the value. It may make sense to use an `enum` to represent the suit, or you can simply use the characters ♠, ♡, ◇, and ♣.

   An `int` or a `dchar` value can be used for the card value. If you decide to use an `int`, the values 1, 11, 12, and 13 may represent the cards that do not have numbers (ace, jack, queen, and king).

   There are other design choices to make. For example, the card values can be represented by an `enum` type as well.

   The way objects of this struct will be constructed will depend on the choice of the types of its members. For example, if both members are dchar, then `Card` objects can be constructed like this:

   ```
       auto card = Card('♠', '2');
   ```

2. Define a function named `printCard()`, which takes a `Card` object as a parameter and simply prints it:

   ```
   struct Card {
       // ... please define the struct ...
   }

   void printCard(Card card) {
       // ... please define the function body ...
   }

   void main() {
       auto card = Card(/* ... */);
       printCard(card);
   }
   ```

   For example, the function can print the 2 of clubs as:

   ```
   ♠2
   ```

   The implementation of that function may depend on the choice of the types of the members.

3. Define a function named `newDeck()` and have it return 52 cards of a deck as a `Card` slice:

   ```
   Card[] newDeck()
   out (result) {
       assert(result.length == 52);

   } do {
       // ... please define the function body ...
   }
   ```

   It should be possible to call `newDeck()` as in the following code:

   ```
       Card[] deck = newDeck();

       foreach (card; deck) {
           printCard(card);
           write(' ');
       }
   ```

```
    writeln();
```

The output should be similar to the following with 52 distinct cards:

```
♠2 ♠3 ♠4 ♠5 ♠6 ♠7 ♠8 ♠9 ♠0 ♠J ♠Q ♠K ♠A ♡2 ♡3 ♡4
♡5 ♡6 ♡7 ♡8 ♡9 ♡0 ♡J ♡Q ♡K ♡A ◇2 ◇3 ◇4 ◇5 ◇6 ◇7
◇8 ◇9 ◇0 ◇J ◇Q ◇K ◇A ♣2 ♣3 ♣4 ♣5 ♣6 ♣7 ♣8 ♣9 ♣0
♣J ♣Q ♣K ♣A
```

4. Write a function that shuffles the deck. One way is to pick two cards at random by std.random.uniform, to swap those two cards, and to repeat this process a sufficient number of times. The function should take the number of repetition as a parameter:

```
void shuffle(Card[] deck, int repetition) {
    // ... please define the function body ...
}
```

Here is how it should be used:

```
    Card[] deck = newDeck();
    shuffle(deck, 1);

    foreach (card; deck) {
        printCard(card);
        write(' ');
    }

    writeln();
```

The function should swap cards repetition number of times. For example, when called by 1, the output should be similar to the following:

```
♠2 ♠3 ♠4 ♠5 ♠6 ♠7 ♠8 ♠9 ♠0 ♠J ♠Q ♠K ♠A ♡2 ♡3 ♡4
♡5 ♡6 ♡7 ♡8 ♣4 ♡0 ♡J ♡Q ♡K ♡A ◇2 ◇3 ◇4 ◇5 ◇6 ◇7
◇8 ◇9 ◇0 ◇J ◇Q ◇K ◇A ♣2 ♣3 ♡9 ♣5 ♣6 ♣7 ♣8 ♣9 ♣0
♣J ♣Q ♣K ♣A
```

A higher value for repetition should result in a more shuffled deck:

```
    shuffled(deck, 100);
```

The output:

```
♠4 ♣7 ◇9 ◇6 ♡2 ♠6 ♣6 ◇A ♠5 ◇8 ◇3 ♡Q ◇J ♣K ♣8 ♣4
♡J ♣Q ♠Q ♠9 ◇0 ♡A ♠A ♡9 ♠7 ♡3 ◇K ◇2 ♡0 ♠J ◇7 ♡7
♠8 ♡4 ♣J ◇4 ♣0 ♡6 ◇5 ♡5 ♡K ♠3 ◇Q ♠2 ♠5 ♣2 ♡8 ♣A
♠K ♣9 ♠0 ♣3
```

Note: *A much better way of shuffling the deck is explained in the solutions.*

The solutions are on page 718.

This chapter covers two D features that bring flexibility on parameters when calling functions:

- Default arguments
- Variadic functions

48.1 Default arguments

A convenience with function parameters is the ability to specify default values for them. This is similar to the default initial values of struct members.

Some of the parameters of some functions are called mostly by the same values. To see an example of this, let's consider a function that prints the elements of an associative array of type `string[string]`. Let's assume that the function takes the separator characters as parameters as well:

```d
import std.algorithm;

// ...

void printAA(string title,
             string[string] aa,
             string keySeparator,
             string elementSeparator) {
    writeln("-- ", title, " --");

    auto keys = sort(aa.keys);

    // Don't print element separator before the first element
    if (keys.length != 0) {
        auto key = keys[0];
        write(key, keySeparator, aa[key]);
        keys = keys[1..$];    // Remove the first element
    }

    // Print element separator before the remaining elements
    foreach (key; keys) {
        write(elementSeparator);
        write(key, keySeparator, aa[key]);
    }

    writeln();
}
```

That function is being called below with `":"` as the key separator and `", "` as the element separator:

```d
void main() {
    string[string] dictionary = [
        "blue":"mavi", "red":"kırmızı", "gray":"gri" ];

    printAA("Color Dictionary", dictionary, ":", ", ");
}
```

The output:

```
-- Color Dictionary --
blue:mavi, gray:gri, red:kırmızı
```

If the separators are almost always going to be those two, they can be defined with default values:

```d
void printAA(string title,
             string[string] aa,
```

```
            string keySeparator = ": ",
            string elementSeparator = ", ") {
    // ...
}
```

Parameters with default values need not be specified when the function is called:

```
    printAA("Color Dictionary",
            dictionary);  /* ← No separator specified. Both
                           *     parameters will get their
                           *     default values. */
```

The parameter values can still be specified when needed, and not necessarily all of them:

```
    printAA("Color Dictionary", dictionary, "=");
```

The output:

```
-- Color Dictionary --
blue=mavi, gray=gri, red=kırmızı
```

The following call specifies both of the parameters:

```
    printAA("Color Dictionary", dictionary, "=", "\n");
```

The output:

```
-- Color Dictionary --
blue=mavi
gray=gri
red=kırmızı
```

Default values can only be defined for the parameters that are at the end of the parameter list.

Special keywords as default arguments

The following special keywords act like compile-time literals having values corresponding to where they appear in code:

- __MODULE__ : Name of the module as string
- __FILE__ : Name of the source file as string
- __FILE_FULL_PATH__ : Name of the source file including its full path as string
- __LINE__ : Line number as int
- __FUNCTION__ : Name of the function as string
- __PRETTY_FUNCTION__ : Full signature of the function as string

Although they can be useful anywhere in code, they work differently when used as default arguments. When they are used in regular code, their values refer to where they appear in code:

```
import std.stdio;

void func(int parameter) {
    writeln("Inside function %s at file %s, line %s.",
            __FUNCTION__, __FILE__, __LINE__);    // ← line 5
}

void main() {
    func(42);
}
```

The reported line 5 is inside the function:

```
Inside function deneme.func at file deneme.d, line 5.
```

However, sometimes it is more interesting to determine the line where a function is called from, not where the definition of the function is. When these special keywords are provided as default arguments, their values refer to where the function is called from:

```
import std.stdio;

void func(int parameter,
          string functionName = __FUNCTION__,
          string file = __FILE__,
          int line = __LINE__) {
    writeln("Called from function %s at file %s, line %s.",
            functionName, file, line);
}

void main() {
    func(42);    // ← line 12
}
```

This time the special keywords refer to main(), the caller of the function:

```
Called from function deneme.main at file deneme.d, line 12.
```

In addition to the above, there are also the following *special tokens* that take values depending on the compiler and the time of day:

- __DATE__: Date of compilation as string
- __TIME__: Time of compilation as string
- __TIMESTAMP__: Date and time of compilation as string
- __VENDOR__: Compiler vendor as string (e.g. "Digital Mars D")
- __VERSION__: Compiler version as long (e.g. the value 2081L for version 2.081)

48.2 Variadic functions

Despite appearances, default parameter values do not change the number of parameters that a function receives. For example, even though some parameters may be assigned their default values, printAA() always takes four parameters and uses them according to its implementation.

On the other hand, variadic functions can be called with unspecified number of arguments. We have already been taking advantage of this feature with functions like writeln(). writeln() can be called with any number of arguments:

```
    writeln(
        "hello", 7, "world", 9.8 /*, and any number of other
         *  arguments as needed */);
```

There are four ways of defining variadic functions in D:

- The feature that works only for functions that are marked as extern(C). This feature defines the hidden _argptr variable that is used for accessing the parameters. This book does not cover this feature partly because it is unsafe.
- The feature that works with regular D functions, which also uses the hidden _argptr variable, as well as the _arguments variable, the latter being of type TypeInfo[]. This book does not cover this feature as well both because it relies on *pointers*, which have not been covered yet, and because this feature can be used in unsafe ways as well.

- A safe feature with the limitation that the unspecified number of parameters must all be of the same type. This is the feature that is covered in this section.
- Unspecified number of template parameters. This feature will be explained later in the templates chapters.

The parameters of variadic functions are passed to the function as a slice. Variadic functions are defined with a single parameter of a specific type of slice followed immediately by the . . . characters:

```
double sum(double[] numbers...) {
    double result = 0.0;

    foreach (number; numbers) {
        result += number;
    }

    return result;
}
```

That definition makes sum() a variadic function, meaning that it is able to receive any number of arguments as long as they are double or any other type that can implicitly be convertible to double:

```
    writeln(sum(1.1, 2.2, 3.3));
```

The single slice parameter and the . . . characters represent all of the arguments. For example, the slice would have five elements if the function were called with five double values.

In fact, the variable number of parameters can also be passed as a single slice:

```
    writeln(sum([ 1.1, 2.2, 3.3 ]));    // same as above
```

Variadic functions can also have required parameters, which must be defined first in the parameter list. For example, the following function prints an unspecified number of parameters within parentheses. Although the function leaves the number of the elements flexible, it requires that the parentheses are always specified:

```
char[] parenthesize(
    string opening,   // ← The first two parameters must be
    string closing,   //   specified when the function is called
    string[] words...) { // ← Need not be specified
    char[] result;

    foreach (word; words) {
        result ~= opening;
        result ~= word;
        result ~= closing;
    }

    return result;
}
```

The first two parameters are mandatory:

```
    parenthesize("{");    // ← compilation ERROR
```

As long as the mandatory parameters are specified, the rest are optional:

```
    writeln(parenthesize("{", "}", "apple", "pear", "banana"));
```

The output:

```
{apple}{pear}{banana}
```

Variadic function arguments have a short lifetime

The slice argument that is automatically generated for a variadic parameter points at a temporary array that has a short lifetime. This fact does not matter if the function uses the arguments only during its execution. However, it would be a bug if the function kept a slice to those elements for later use:

```d
int[] numbersForLaterUse;

void foo(int[] numbers...) {
    numbersForLaterUse = numbers;    // ← BUG
}

struct S {
    string[] namesForLaterUse;

    void foo(string[] names...) {
        namesForLaterUse = names;    // ← BUG
    }
}

void bar() {
    foo(1, 10, 100);   /* The temporary array [ 1, 10, 100 ] is
                        * not valid beyond this point. */

    auto s = S();
    s.foo("hello", "world");   /* The temporary array
                                * [ "hello", "world" ] is not
                                * valid beyond this point. */

    // ...
}

void main() {
    bar();
}
```

Both the free-standing function `foo()` and the member function `S.foo()` are in error because they store slices to automatically-generated temporary arrays that live on the program stack. Those arrays are valid only during the execution of the variadic functions.

For that reason, if a function needs to store a slice to the elements of a variadic parameter, it must first take a copy of those elements:

```d
void foo(int[] numbers...) {
    numbersForLaterUse = numbers.dup;    // ← correct
}

// ...

    void foo(string[] names...) {
        namesForLaterUse = names.dup;    // ← correct
    }
```

However, since variadic functions can also be called with slices of proper arrays, copying the elements would be unnecessary in those cases.

A solution that is both correct and efficient is to define two functions having the same name, one taking a variadic parameter and the other taking a proper slice. If the caller passes variable number of arguments, then the variadic version of the function is called; and if the caller passes a proper slice, then the version that takes a proper slice is called:

```
int[] numbersForLaterUse;

void foo(int[] numbers...) {
    /* Since this is the variadic version of foo(), we must
     * first take a copy of the elements before storing a
     * slice to them. */
    numbersForLaterUse = numbers.dup;
}

void foo(int[] numbers) {
    /* Since this is the non-variadic version of foo(), we can
     * store the slice as is. */
    numbersForLaterUse = numbers;
}

struct S {
    string[] namesForLaterUse;

    void foo(string[] names...) {
        /* Since this is the variadic version of S.foo(), we
         * must first take a copy of the elements before
         * storing a slice to them. */
        namesForLaterUse = names.dup;
    }

    void foo(string[] names) {
        /* Since this is the non-variadic version of S.foo(),
         * we can store the slice as is. */
        namesForLaterUse = names;
    }
}

void bar() {
    // This call is dispatched to the variadic function.
    foo(1, 10, 100);

    // This call is dispatched to the proper slice function.
    foo([ 2, 20, 200 ]);

    auto s = S();

    // This call is dispatched to the variadic function.
    s.foo("hello", "world");

    // This call is dispatched to the proper slice function.
    s.foo([ "hi", "moon" ]);

    // ...
}

void main() {
    bar();
}
```

Defining multiple functions with the same name but with different parameters is called *function overloading*, which is the subject of the next chapter.

48.3 Exercise

Assume that the following enum is already defined:

```
enum Operation { add, subtract, multiply, divide }
```

Also assume that there is a struct that represents the calculation of an operation and its two operands:

```
struct Calculation {
    Operation op;
    double first;
    double second;
}
```

For example, the object `Calculation(Operation.divide, 7.7, 8.8)` would represent the division of 7.7 by 8.8.

Design a function that receives an unspecified number of these `struct` objects, calculates the result of each `Calculation`, and then returns all of the results as a slice of type `double[]`.

For example, it should be possible to call the function as in the following code:

```
void main() {
    writeln(
        calculate(Calculation(Operation.add, 1.1, 2.2),
                  Calculation(Operation.subtract, 3.3, 4.4),
                  Calculation(Operation.multiply, 5.5, 6.6),
                  Calculation(Operation.divide, 7.7, 8.8)));
}
```

The output of the code should be similar to the following:

```
[3.3, -1.1, 36.3, 0.875]
```

The solution is on page 721.

49 Function Overloading

Defining more than one function having the same name is *function overloading*. In order to be able to differentiate these functions, their parameters must be different.

The following code has multiple overloads of the `info()` function, each taking a different type of parameter:

```d
import std.stdio;

void info(double number) {
    writeln("Floating point: ", number);
}

void info(int number) {
    writeln("Integer     : ", number);
}

void info(string str) {
    writeln("String      : ", str);
}

void main() {
    info(1.2);
    info(3);
    info("hello");
}
```

Although all of the functions are named `info()`, the compiler picks the one that matches the argument that is used when making the call. For example, because the literal `1.2` is of type `double`, the `info()` function that takes a `double` gets called for it.

The choice of which function to call is made at compile time, which may not always be easy or clear. For example, because `int` can implicitly be converted to both `double` and `real`, the compiler cannot decide which of the functions to call in the following program:

```d
real sevenTimes(real value) {
    return 7 * value;
}

double sevenTimes(double value) {
    return 7 * value;
}

void main() {
    int value = 5;
    auto result = sevenTimes(value);    // ← compilation ERROR
}
```

Note: It is usually unnecessary to write separate functions when the function bodies are exactly the same. We will see later in the Templates chapter (page 399) how a single definition can be used for multiple types.

However, if there is another function overload that takes a `long` parameter, then the ambiguity would be resolved because `long` is a *better match* for `int` than `double` or `real`:

```d
long sevenTimes(long value) {
    return 7 * value;
}

// ...
```

```
    auto result = sevenTimes(value);     // now compiles
```

49.1 Overload resolution

The compiler picks the overload that is the *best match* for the arguments. This is called overload resolution.

Although overload resolution is simple and intuitive in most cases, it is sometimes complicated. The following are the rules of overload resolution. They are being presented in a simplified way in this book.

There are four states of match, listed from the worst to the best:

- mismatch
- match through automatic type conversion
- match through `const` qualification
- exact match

The compiler considers all of the overloads of a function during overload resolution. It first determines the match state of every parameter for every overload. For each overload, the least match state among the parameters is taken to be the match state of that overload.

After all of the match states of the overloads are determined, then the overload with the best match is selected. If there are more than one overload that has the best match, then more complicated resolution rules are applied. I will not get into more details of these rules in this book. If your program is in a situation where it depends on complicated overload resolution rules, it may be an indication that it is time to change the design of the program. Another option is to take advantage of other features of D, like templates. An even simpler but not always desirable approach would be to abandon function overloading altogether by naming functions differently for each type e.g. like `sevenTimes_real()` and `sevenTimes_double()`.

49.2 Function overloading for user-defined types

Function overloading is useful with structs and classes as well. Additionally, overload resolution ambiguities are much less frequent with user-defined types. Let's overload the `info()` function above for some of the types that we have defined in the Structs chapter (page 246):

```
struct TimeOfDay {
    int hour;
    int minute;
}

void info(TimeOfDay time) {
    writef("%02s:%02s", time.hour, time.minute);
}
```

That overload enables `TimeOfDay` objects to be used with `info()`. As a result, variables of user-defined types can be printed in exactly the same way as fundamental types:

```
    auto breakfastTime = TimeOfDay(7, 0);
    info(breakfastTime);
```

The `TimeOfDay` objects would be matched with that overload of `info()`:

```
07:00
```

The following is an overload of info() for the Meeting type:

```
struct Meeting {
    string    topic;
    size_t    attendanceCount;
    TimeOfDay start;
    TimeOfDay end;
}

void info(Meeting meeting) {
    info(meeting.start);
    write('-');
    info(meeting.end);

    writef(" \"%s\" meeting with %s attendees",
            meeting.topic,
            meeting.attendanceCount);
}
```

Note that this overload makes use of the already-defined overload for TimeOfDay. Meeting objects can now be printed in exactly the same way as fundamental types as well:

```
auto bikeRideMeeting = Meeting("Bike Ride", 3,
                                TimeOfDay(9, 0),
                                TimeOfDay(9, 10));
info(bikeRideMeeting);
```

The output:

```
09:00-09:10 "Bike Ride" meeting with 3 attendees
```

49.3 Limitations
Although the info() function overloads above are a great convenience, this method has some limitations:

- info() always prints to stdout. It would be more useful if it could print to any File. One way of achieving this is to pass the output stream as a parameter as well e.g. for the TimeOfDay type:

  ```
  void info(File file, TimeOfDay time) {
      file.writef("%02s:%02s", time.hour, time.minute);
  }
  ```

  That would enable printing TimeOfDay objects to any file, including stdout:

  ```
  info(stdout, breakfastTime);

  auto file = File("a_file", "w");
  info(file, breakfastTime);
  ```

  Note: *The special objects stdin, stdout, and stderr are of type File.*

- More importantly, info() does not solve the more general problem of producing the string representation of variables. For example, it does not help with passing objects of user-defined types to writeln():

  ```
  writeln(breakfastTime);  // Not useful: prints in generic format
  ```

  The code above prints the object in a generic format that includes the name of the type and the values of its members, not in a way that would be useful in the program:

  ```
  TimeOfDay(7, 0)
  ```

It would be much more useful if there were a function that converted TimeOfDay objects to string in their special format as in "12:34". We will see how to define string representations of struct objects in the next chapter.

49.4 Exercise

Overload the info() function for the following structs as well:

```
struct Meal {
    TimeOfDay time;
    string    address;
}

struct DailyPlan {
    Meeting amMeeting;
    Meal    lunch;
    Meeting pmMeeting;
}
```

Since Meal has only the start time, add an hour and a half to determine its end time. You can use the addDuration() function that we have defined earlier in the structs chapter:

```
TimeOfDay addDuration(TimeOfDay start,
                      TimeOfDay duration) {
    TimeOfDay result;

    result.minute = start.minute + duration.minute;
    result.hour = start.hour + duration.hour;
    result.hour += result.minute / 60;

    result.minute %= 60;
    result.hour %= 24;

    return result;
}
```

Once the end times of Meal objects are calculated by addDuration(), DailyPlan objects should be printed as in the following output:

```
10:30-11:45 "Bike Ride" meeting with 4 attendees
12:30-14:00 Meal, Address: İstanbul
15:30-17:30 "Budget" meeting with 8 attendees
```

The solution is on page 722.

Although this chapter focuses only on structs, most of the information in this chapter is applicable to classes as well.

In this chapter we will cover member functions of structs and define the special `toString()` member function that is used for representing objects in the `string` format.

When a struct or class is defined, usually a number of functions are also defined alongside with it. We have seen examples of such functions in the earlier chapters: `addDuration()` and an overload of `info()` have been written specifically to be used with the `TimeOfDay` type. In a sense, these two functions define the *interface* of `TimeOfDay`.

The first parameter of both `addDuration()` and `info()` has been the `TimeOfDay` object that each function would be operating on. Additionally, just like all of the other functions that we have seen so far, both of the functions have been defined at the *module level*, outside of any other scope.

The concept of a set of functions determining the interface of a struct is very common. For that reason, functions that are closely related to a type can be defined within the body of that type.

50.1 Defining member functions

Functions that are defined within the curly brackets of a `struct` are called *member functions*:

```
struct SomeStruct {
    void member_function(/* the parameters of the function */) {
        // ... the definition of the function ...
    }

    // ... the other members of the struct ...
}
```

Member functions are accessed the same way as member variables, separated from the name of the object by a dot:

```
object.member_function(arguments);
```

We have used member functions before when specifying `stdin` and `stdout` explicitly during input and output operations:

```
stdin.readf(" %s", &number);
stdout.writeln(number);
```

The `readf()` and `writeln()` above are member function calls, operating on the objects `stdin` and `stdout`, respectively.

Let's define `info()` as a member function. Its previous definition has been the following:

```
void info(TimeOfDay time) {
    writef("%02s:%02s", time.hour, time.minute);
}
```

Making `info()` a member function is not as simple as moving its definition inside the struct. The function must be modified in two ways:

```
struct TimeOfDay {
    int hour;
```

```
    int minute;

    void info() {      // (1)
        writef("%02s:%02s", hour, minute);      // (2)
    }
}
```

1. The member function does not take the object explicitly as a parameter.
2. For that reason, it refers to the member variables simply as `hour` and `minute`.

This is because member functions are always called on an existing object. The object is implicitly available to the member function:

```
    auto time = TimeOfDay(10, 30);
    time.info();
```

The `info()` member function is being called on the `time` object above. The members `hour` and `minute` that are referred to within the function definition correspond to the members of the `time` object, specifically `time.hour` and `time.minute`.

The member function call above is almost the equivalent of the following regular function call:

```
    time.info();      // member function
    info(time);       // regular function (the previous definition)
```

Whenever a member function is called on an object, the members of the object are implicitly accessible by the function:

```
    auto morning = TimeOfDay(10, 0);
    auto evening = TimeOfDay(22, 0);

    morning.info();
    write('-');
    evening.info();
    writeln();
```

When called on `morning`, the `hour` and `minute` that are used inside the member function refer to `morning.hour` and `morning.minute`. Similarly, when called on `evening`, they refer to `evening.hour` and `evening.minute`:

```
10:00-22:00
```

toString() for string representations

We have discussed the limitations of the `info()` function in the previous chapter. There is at least one more inconvenience with it: Although it prints the time in human-readable format, printing the `'-'` character and terminating the line still needs to be done explicitly by the programmer.

However, it would be more convenient if `TimeOfDay` objects could be used as easy as fundamental types as in the following code:

```
    writefln("%s-%s", morning, evening);
```

In addition to reducing four lines of code to one, it would also allow printing objects to any stream:

```
    auto file = File("time_information", "w");
    file.writefln("%s-%s", morning, evening);
```

The `toString()` member function of user-defined types is treated specially: It is called automatically to produce the `string` representations of objects. `toString()` must return the `string` representation of the object.

Without getting into more detail, let's first see how the `toString()` function is defined:

```
import std.stdio;

struct TimeOfDay {
    int hour;
    int minute;

    string toString() {
        return "todo";
    }
}

void main() {
    auto morning = TimeOfDay(10, 0);
    auto evening = TimeOfDay(22, 0);

    writefln("%s-%s", morning, evening);
}
```

`toString()` does not produce anything meaningful yet, but the output shows that it has been called by `writefln()` twice for the two object:

```
todo-todo
```

Also note that `info()` is not needed anymore. `toString()` is replacing its functionality.

The simplest implementation of `toString()` would be to call `format()` of the `std.string` module. `format()` works in the same way as the formatted output functions like `writef()`. The only difference is that instead of printing variables, it returns the formatted result in `string` format.

`toString()` can simply return the result of `format()` directly:

```
import std.string;
// ...
struct TimeOfDay {
// ...
    string toString() {
        return format("%02s:%02s", hour, minute);
    }
}
```

Note that `toString()` returns the representation of only *this* object. The rest of the output is handled by `writefln()`: It calls the `toString()` member function for the two objects separately, prints the `'-'` character in between, and finally terminates the line:

```
10:00-22:00
```

The definition of `toString()` that is explained above does not take any parameters; it simply produces a `string` and returns it. An alternative definition of `toString()` takes a `delegate` parameter. We will see that definition later in the Function Pointers, Delegates, and Lambdas chapter (page 475).

Example: `increment()` member function

Let's define a member function that adds a duration to `TimeOfDay` objects.

Before doing that, let's first correct a design flaw that we have been living with. We have seen in the Structs chapter (page 246) that adding two TimeOfDay objects in addDuration() is not a meaningful operation:

```
TimeOfDay addDuration(TimeOfDay start,
                      TimeOfDay duration) {  // meaningless
    // ...
}
```

What is natural to add to a point in time is *duration*. For example, adding the travel duration to the departure time would result in the arrival time.

On the other hand, subtracting two points in time is a natural operation, in which case the result would be a *duration*.

The following program defines a Duration struct with minute-precision, and an addDuration() function that uses it:

```
struct Duration {
    int minute;
}

TimeOfDay addDuration(TimeOfDay start,
                      Duration duration) {
    // Begin with a copy of start
    TimeOfDay result = start;

    // Add the duration to it
    result.minute += duration.minute;

    // Take care of overflows
    result.hour += result.minute / 60;
    result.minute %= 60;
    result.hour %= 24;

    return result;
}

unittest {
    // A trivial test
    assert(addDuration(TimeOfDay(10, 30), Duration(10))
           == TimeOfDay(10, 40));

    // A time at midnight
    assert(addDuration(TimeOfDay(23, 9), Duration(51))
           == TimeOfDay(0, 0));

    // A time in the next day
    assert(addDuration(TimeOfDay(17, 45), Duration(8 * 60))
           == TimeOfDay(1, 45));
}
```

Let's redefine a similar function this time as a member function. addDuration() has been producing a new object as its result. Let's define an increment() member function that will directly modify *this* object instead:

```
struct Duration {
    int minute;
}

struct TimeOfDay {
    int hour;
    int minute;

    string toString() {
        return format("%02s:%02s", hour, minute);
    }

    void increment(Duration duration) {
        minute += duration.minute;
```

```
            hour += minute / 60;
            minute %= 60;
            hour %= 24;
        }

    unittest {
            auto time = TimeOfDay(10, 30);

            // A trivial test
            time.increment(Duration(10));
            assert(time == TimeOfDay(10, 40));

            // 15 hours later must be in the next day
            time.increment(Duration(15 * 60));
            assert(time == TimeOfDay(1, 40));

            // 22 hours 20 minutes later must be midnight
            time.increment(Duration(22 * 60 + 20));
            assert(time == TimeOfDay(0, 0));
        }
}
```

increment() increments the value of the object by the specified amount of duration. In a later chapter we will see how the *operator overloading* feature of D will make it possible to add a duration by the += operator syntax:

```
    time += Duration(10);    // to be explained in a later chapter
```

Also note that unittest blocks can be written inside struct definitions as well, mostly for testing member functions. It is still possible to move such unittest blocks outside of the body of the struct:

```
struct TimeOfDay {
    // ... struct definition ...
}

unittest {
    // ... struct tests ...
}
```

50.2 Exercises

1. Add a decrement() member function to TimeOfDay, which should reduce the time by the specified amount of duration. Similar to increment(), it should *overflow* to the previous day when there is not enough time in the current day. For example, subtracting 10 minutes from 00:05 should result in 23:55.

    In other words, implement decrement() to pass the following unit tests:

```
struct TimeOfDay {
    // ...

    void decrement(Duration duration) {
        // ... please implement this function ...
    }

    unittest {
        auto time = TimeOfDay(10, 30);

        // A trivial test
        time.decrement(Duration(12));
        assert(time == TimeOfDay(10, 18));

        // 3 days and 11 hours earlier
        time.decrement(Duration(3 * 24 * 60 + 11 * 60));
        assert(time == TimeOfDay(23, 18));
```

```
                // 23 hours and 18 minutes earlier must be midnight
                time.decrement(Duration(23 * 60 + 18));
                assert(time == TimeOfDay(0, 0));

                // 1 minute earlier
                time.decrement(Duration(1));
                assert(time == TimeOfDay(23, 59));
        }
}
```

2. Convert Meeting, Meal, and DailyPlan overloads of info() to toString()
    member functions as well. (See the exercise solutions of the Function
    Overloading chapter (page 722) for their info() overloads.)

    You will notice that in addition to making their respective structs more
    convenient, the implementations of the toString() member functions will
    all consist of single lines.

The solutions are on page 724.

This chapter is about how parameters and member functions are marked as `const` so that they can be used with `immutable` variables as well. As we have already covered `const` parameters in earlier chapters, some information in this chapter will be a review of some of the features that you already know.

Although the examples in this chapter use only structs, `const` member functions apply to classes as well.

51.1 `immutable` objects

We have already seen that it is not possible to modify `immutable` variables:

```
immutable readingTime = TimeOfDay(15, 0);
```

`readingTime` cannot be modified:

```
readingTime = TimeOfDay(16, 0);    // ← compilation ERROR
readingTime.minute += 10;          // ← compilation ERROR
```

The compiler does not allow modifying `immutable` objects in any way.

51.2 `ref` parameters that are not `const`

We have seen this concept earlier in the Function Parameters chapter (page 168). Parameters that are marked as `ref` can freely be modified by the function. For that reason, even if the function does not actually modify the parameter, the compiler does not allow passing `immutable` objects as that parameter:

```
/* Although not being modified by the function, 'duration'
 * is not marked as 'const' */
int totalSeconds(ref Duration duration) {
    return 60 * duration.minute;
}
// ...
    immutable warmUpTime = Duration(3);
    totalSeconds(warmUpTime);    // ← compilation ERROR
```

The compiler does not allow passing the `immutable warmUpTime` to `totalSeconds` because that function does not guarantee that the parameter will not be modified.

51.3 `const ref` parameters

`const ref` means that the parameter is not modified by the function:

```
int totalSeconds(const ref Duration duration) {
    return 60 * duration.minute;
}
// ...
    immutable warmUpTime = Duration(3);
    totalSeconds(warmUpTime);    // ← now compiles
```

Such functions can receive `immutable` objects as parameters because the immutability of the object is enforced by the compiler:

```
int totalSeconds(const ref Duration duration) {
    duration.minute = 7;    // ← compilation ERROR
// ...
}
```

An alternative to `const ref` is `in ref`. As we will see in a later chapter (page 168), `in` means that the parameter is used only as input to the function, disallowing any modification to it.

```
int totalSeconds(in ref Duration duration) {
    // ...
}
```

51.4 Non-const member functions

As we have seen with the `TimeOfDay.increment` member function, objects can be modified through member functions as well. `increment()` modifies the members of the object that it is called on:

```
struct TimeOfDay {
// ...
    void increment(Duration duration) {
        minute += duration.minute;

        hour += minute / 60;
        minute %= 60;
        hour %= 24;
    }
// ...
}
// ...
    auto start = TimeOfDay(5, 30);
    start.increment(Duration(30));          // 'start' gets modified
```

51.5 const member functions

Some member functions do not make any modifications to the object that they are called on. An example of such a function is `toString()`:

```
struct TimeOfDay {
// ...
    string toString() {
        return format("%02s:%02s", hour, minute);
    }
// ...
}
```

Since the whole purpose of `toString()` is to represent the object in string format anyway, it should not modify the object.

The fact that a member function does not modify the object is declared by the `const` keyword after the parameter list:

```
struct TimeOfDay {
// ...
    string toString() const {
        return format("%02s:%02s", hour, minute);
    }
}
```

That `const` guarantees that the object itself is not going to be modified by the member function. As a consequence, `toString()` member function is allowed to be called even on `immutable` objects. Otherwise, the struct's `toString()` would not be called:

```
struct TimeOfDay {
// ...
    // Inferior design: Not marked as 'const'
    string toString() {
        return format("%02s:%02s", hour, minute);
    }
```

```
}
// ...
    immutable start = TimeOfDay(5, 30);
    writeln(start);    // TimeOfDay.toString() is not called!
```

The output is not the expected 05:30, indicating that a generic function gets called instead of TimeOfDay.toString:

```
immutable(TimeOfDay)(5, 30)
```

Further, calling toString() on an immutable object explicitly would cause a compilation error:

```
    auto s = start.toString(); // ← compilation ERROR
```

Accordingly, the toString() functions that we have defined in the previous chapter have all been designed incorrectly; they should have been marked as const.

Note: *The const keyword can be specified before the definition of the function as well:*

```
    // The same as above
    const string toString() {
        return format("%02s:%02s", hour, minute);
    }
```

Since this version may give the incorrect impression that the const is a part of the return type, I recommend that you specify it after the parameter list.

51.6 inout member functions

As we have seen in the Function Parameters chapter (page 168), inout transfers the mutability of a parameter to the return type.

Similarly, an inout member function transfers the mutability of the *object* to the function's return type:

```
import std.stdio;

struct Container {
    int[] elements;

    inout(int)[] firstPart(size_t n) inout {
        return elements[0 .. n];
    }
}

void main() {
    {
        // An immutable container
        auto container = immutable(Container)([ 1, 2, 3 ]);
        auto slice = container.firstPart(2);
        writeln(typeof(slice).stringof);
    }
    {
        // A const container
        auto container = const(Container)([ 1, 2, 3 ]);
        auto slice = container.firstPart(2);
        writeln(typeof(slice).stringof);
    }
    {
        // A mutable container
        auto container = Container([ 1, 2, 3 ]);
        auto slice = container.firstPart(2);
        writeln(typeof(slice).stringof);
    }
}
```

The three slices that are returned by the three objects of different mutability are consistent with the objects that returned them:

```
immutable(int)[]
const(int)[]
int[]
```

Because it must be called on `const` and `immutable` objects as well, an `inout` member function is compiled as if it were `const`.

51.7 How to use

- To give the guarantee that a parameter is not modified by the function, mark that parameter as `in`, `const`, or `const ref`.
- Mark member functions that do not modify the object as `const`:

```
struct TimeOfDay {
// ...
    string toString() const {
        return format("%02s:%02s", hour, minute);
    }
}
```

This would make the struct (or class) more useful by removing an unnecessary limitation. The examples in the rest of the book will observe this guideline.

52 Constructor and Other Special Functions

Although this chapter focuses only on structs, the topics that are covered here apply mostly to classes as well. The differences will be explained in later chapters.

Four member functions of structs are special because they define the fundamental operations of that type:

- `this()` for construction
- `~this()` for destruction
- `this(ref const(S))` for copy construction
  (S is just an example there, representing the type of the struct.)
- `opAssign()` for assignment

In addition, there is a legacy function, which is not recommended for newly written code:

- `this(this)` for postblit

These fundamental operations are handled automatically for structs. But it is possible to define them manually to provide different implementations when needed.

52.1 Constructor

The responsibility of the constructor is to prepare an object for use by assigning appropriate values to its members.

We have already used constructors in previous chapters. When the name of a type is used like a function, it is actually the constructor that gets called. We can see this on the right-hand side of the following line:

```d
auto busArrival = TimeOfDay(8, 30);
```

Similarly, a *class* object is being constructed on the right hand side of the following line:

```d
auto variable = new SomeClass();
```

The arguments that are specified within parentheses correspond to the constructor parameters. For example, the values 8 and 30 above are passed to the `TimeOfDay` constructor as its parameters.

In addition to different object construction syntaxes that we have seen so far; `const`, `immutable`, and `shared` objects can be constructed with the *type constructor* syntax as well (e.g. as `immutable(S)(2)`). (We will see the `shared` keyword in a later chapter (page 640).)

For example, although all three variables below are `immutable`, the construction of variable a is semantically different from the constructions of variables b and c:

```d
/* More familiar syntax; immutable variable of a mutable
 * type: */
immutable a = S(1);

/* Type constructor syntax; a variable of an immutable
 * type: */
auto b = immutable(S)(2);
```

```
/* Same meaning as 'b' */
immutable c = immutable(S)(3);
```

Constructor syntax

Different from other functions, constructors do not have return values. The name of the constructor is always this:

```
struct SomeStruct {
    // ...

    this(/* constructor parameters */) {
        // ... operations that prepare the object for use ...
    }
}
```

The constructor parameters include information that is needed to make a useful and consistent object.

Compiler-generated automatic constructor

All of the structs that we have seen so far have been taking advantage of a constructor that has been generated automatically by the compiler. The automatic constructor assigns the parameter values to the members in the order that they are specified.

As you will remember from the Structs chapter (page 246), the initial values for the trailing members need not be specified. The members that are not specified get initialized by the .init value of their respective types. The .init values of a member could be provided during the definition of that member after the = operator:

```
struct Test {
    int member = 42;
}
```

Also considering the *default parameter values* feature from the Variable Number of Parameters chapter (page 258), we can imagine that the automatic constructor for the following struct would be the equivalent of the following this():

```
struct Test {
    char   c;
    int    i;
    double d;

    /* The equivalent of the compiler-generated automatic
     * constructor (Note: This is only for demonstration; the
     * following constructor would not actually be called
     * when default-constructing the object as Test().) */
    this(in char   c_parameter = char.init,
         in int    i_parameter = int.init,
         in double d_parameter = double.init) {
        c = c_parameter;
        i = i_parameter;
        d = d_parameter;
    }
}
```

For most structs, the compiler-generated constructor is sufficient: Providing appropriate values for each member is all that is needed for objects to be constructed.

Accessing the members by `this`.

To avoid mixing the parameters with the members, the parameter names above had _parameter appended to their names. There would be compilation errors without doing that:

```
struct Test {
    char   c;
    int    i;
    double d;

    this(in char   c = char.init,
         in int    i = int.init,
         in double d = double.init) {
        // An attempt to assign an 'in' parameter to itself!
        c = c;    // ← compilation ERROR
        i = i;
        d = d;
    }
}
```

The reason is; c alone would mean the parameter, not the member, and as the parameters above are defined as in, they cannot be modified:

```
Error: variable deneme.Test.this.c cannot modify const
```

A solution is to prepend the member names with `this..` Inside member functions, `this` means "this object", making `this.c` mean "the c member of this object":

```
    this(in char   c = char.init,
         in int    i = int.init,
         in double d = double.init) {
        this.c = c;
        this.i = i;
        this.d = d;
    }
```

Now c alone means the parameter and `this.c` means the member, and the code compiles and works as expected: The member c gets initialized by the value of the parameter c.

User-defined constructors

I have described the behavior of the compiler-generated constructor. Since that constructor is suitable for most cases, there is no need to define a constructor by hand.

Still, there are cases where constructing an object involves more complicated operations than assigning values to each member in order. As an example, let's consider Duration from the earlier chapters:

```
struct Duration {
    int minute;
}
```

The compiler-generated constructor is sufficient for this single-member struct:

```
    time.decrement(Duration(12));
```

Since that constructor takes the duration in minutes, the programmers would sometimes need to make calculations:

```
    // 23 hours and 18 minutes earlier
    time.decrement(Duration(23 * 60 + 18));
```

```
    // 22 hours and 20 minutes later
    time.increment(Duration(22 * 60 + 20));
```

To eliminate the need for these calculations, we can design a `Duration` constructor that takes two parameters and makes the calculation automatically:

```
struct Duration {
    int minute;

    this(int hour, int minute) {
        this.minute = hour * 60 + minute;
    }
}
```

Since hour and minute are now separate parameters, the users simply provide their values without needing to make the calculation themselves:

```
    // 23 hours and 18 minutes earlier
    time.decrement(Duration(23, 18));

    // 22 hours and 20 minutes later
    time.increment(Duration(22, 20));
```

First assignment to a member is construction

When setting values of members in a constructor, the first assignment to each member is treated specially: Instead of assigning a new value over the `.init` value of that member, the first assignment actually constructs that member. Further assignments to that member are treated regularly as assignment operations.

This special behavior is necessary so that `immutable` and `const` members can in fact be constructed with values known only at run time. Otherwise, they could never be set to desired values as assignment is disallowed for `immutable` and `const` variables.

The following program demonstrates how assigment operation is allowed only once for an `immutable` member:

```
struct S {
    int m;
    immutable int i;

    this(int m, int i) {
        this.m = m;      // ← construction
        this.m = 42;     // ← assignment (possible for mutable member)

        this.i = i;      // ← construction
        this.i = i;      // ← compilation ERROR
    }
}

void main() {
    auto s = S(1, 2);
}
```

User-defined constructor disables compiler-generated constructor

A constructor that is defined by the programmer makes some uses of the compiler-generated constructor invalid: Objects cannot be constructed by *default parameter values* anymore. For example, trying to construct `Duration` by a single parameter is a compilation error:

```
    time.decrement(Duration(12));    // ← compilation ERROR
```

The compilation error is due to the fact that the programmer's constructor does not take a single parameter and the compiler-generated constructor is disabled.

One solution is to *overload* the constructor by providing another constructor that takes just one parameter:

```
struct Duration {
    int minute;

    this(int hour, int minute) {
        this.minute = hour * 60 + minute;
    }

    this(int minute) {
        this.minute = minute;
    }
}
```

A user-defined constructor disables constructing objects by the { } syntax as well:

```
    Duration duration = { 5 };    // ← compilation ERROR
```

Initializing without providing any parameter is still valid:

```
    auto d = Duration();    // compiles
```

The reason is, in D, the .init value of every type must be known at compile time. The value of d above is equal to the initial value of Duration:

```
    assert(d == Duration.init);
```

static opCall instead of the default constructor

Because the initial value of every type must be known at compile time, it is impossible to define the default constructor explicitly.

Let's consider the following constructor that tries to print some information every time an object of that type is constructed:

```
struct Test {
    this() {    // ← compilation ERROR
        writeln("A Test object is being constructed.");
    }
}
```

The compiler output:

```
Error: constructor deneme.Deneme.this default constructor for
structs only allowed with @disable and no body
```

Note: *We will see in later chapters that it is possible to define the default constructor for classes.*

As a workaround, a parameterless static opCall() can be used for constructing objects without providing any parameters. Note that this has no effect on the .init value of the type.

For this to work, static opCall() must construct and return an object of that struct type:

```
import std.stdio;

struct Test {
    static Test opCall() {
        writeln("A Test object is being constructed.");
        Test test;
```

```
        return test;
    }
}

void main() {
    auto test = Test();
}
```

The Test() call in main() executes static opCall():

```
A Test object is being constructed.
```

Note that it is not possible to type Test() inside static opCall(). That syntax would execute static opCall() again and cause an infinite recursion:

```
    static Test opCall() {
        writeln("A Test object is being constructed.");
        return Test();    // ← Calls 'static opCall()' again
    }
```

The output:

```
A Test object is being constructed.
A Test object is being constructed.
A Test object is being constructed.
...      ← repeats the same message
```

Calling other constructors

Constructors can call other constructors to avoid code duplication. Although Duration is too simple to demonstrate how useful this feature is, the following single-parameter constructor takes advantage of the two-parameter constructor:

```
    this(int hour, int minute) {
        this.minute = hour * 60 + minute;
    }

    this(int minute) {
        this(0, minute);    // calls the other constructor
    }
```

The constructor that only takes the minute value calls the other constructor by passing 0 as the value of hour.

Warning: *There is a design flaw in the Duration constructors above because the intention is not clear when the objects are constructed by a single parameter.*

```
    // 10 hours or 10 minutes?
    auto travelDuration = Duration(10);
```

Although it is possible to determine by reading the documentation or the code of the struct that the parameter actually means "10 minutes," it is an inconsistency as the first parameter of the two-parameter constructor is *hours*.

Such design mistakes are causes of bugs and must be avoided.

Constructor qualifiers

Normally, the same constructor is used for *mutable*, const, immutable, and shared objects:

```
import std.stdio;

struct S {
    this(int i) {
        writeln("Constructing an object");
    }
}
```

```
void main() {
    auto m = S(1);
    const c = S(2);
    immutable i = S(3);
    shared s = S(4);
}
```

Semantically, the objects that are constructed on the right-hand sides of those expressions are all mutable; only the variables have different type qualifiers. The same constructor is used for all of them:

```
Constructing an object
Constructing an object
Constructing an object
Constructing an object
```

Depending on the qualifier of the resulting object, sometimes some members may need to be initialized differently or need not be initialized at all. For example, since no member of an immutable object can be mutated throughout the lifetime of that object, leaving its mutable members uninitialized can improve program performance.

Qualified constructors can be defined differently for objects with different qualifiers:

```
import std.stdio;

struct S {
    this(int i) {
        writeln("Constructing an object");
    }

    this(int i) const {
        writeln("Constructing a const object");
    }

    this(int i) immutable {
        writeln("Constructing an immutable object");
    }

    // We will see the 'shared' keyword in a later chapter.
    this(int i) shared {
        writeln("Constructing a shared object");
    }
}

void main() {
    auto m = S(1);
    const c = S(2);
    immutable i = S(3);
    shared s = S(4);
}
```

However, as indicated above, as the right-hand side expressions are all semantically mutable, those objects are still constructed with the *mutable* object contructor:

```
Constructing an object
Constructing an object     ← NOT the const constructor
Constructing an object     ← NOT the immutable constructor
Constructing an object     ← NOT the shared constructor
```

To take advantage of qualified constructors, one must use the *type constructor* syntax. (The term *type constructor* should not be confused with object constructors; type constructor is related to types, not objects.) This syntax *makes* a different type by combining a qualifier with an existing type. For example, `immutable(S)` is a qualified type made from `immutable` and `S`:

```
auto m = S(1);
auto c = const(S)(2);
auto i = immutable(S)(3);
auto s = shared(S)(4);
```

This time, the objects that are in the right-hand expressions are different: *mutable*, `const`, `immutable`, and `shared`, respectively. As a result, each object is constructed with its matching constructor:

```
Constructing an object
Constructing a const object
Constructing an immutable object
Constructing a shared object
```

As expected, since all of the variables above are defined with the `auto` keyword, they are correctly inferred to be *mutable*, `const`, `immutable`, and `shared`, respectively.

Immutability of constructor parameters

In the Immutability chapter (page 147) we have seen that it is not easy to decide whether parameters of reference types should be defined as `const` or `immutable`. Although the same considerations apply for constructor parameters as well, `immutable` is usually a better choice for constructor parameters.

The reason is, it is common to assign the parameters to members to be used at a later time. When a parameter is not `immutable`, there is no guarantee that the original variable will not change by the time the member gets used.

Let's consider a constructor that takes a file name as a parameter. The file name will be used later on when writing student grades. According to the guidelines in the Immutability chapter (page 147), to be more useful, let's assume that the constructor parameter is defined as `const char[]`:

```
import std.stdio;

struct Student {
    const char[] fileName;
    int[] grades;

    this(const char[] fileName) {
        this.fileName = fileName;
    }

    void save() {
        auto file = File(fileName.idup, "w");
        file.writeln("The grades of the student:");
        file.writeln(grades);
    }

    // ...
}

void main() {
    char[] fileName;
    fileName ~= "student_grades";

    auto student = Student(fileName);

    // ...

    /* Assume the fileName variable is modified later on
     * perhaps unintentionally (all of its characters are
     * being set to 'A' here): */
    fileName[] = 'A';
```

```
    // ...

    /* The grades would be written to the wrong file: */
    student.save();
}
```

The program above saves the grades of the student under a file name that consists of A characters, not to `"student_grades"`. For that reason, sometimes it is more suitable to define constructor parameters and members of reference types as `immutable`. We know that this is easy for strings by using aliases like `string`. The following code shows the parts of the struct that would need to be modified:

```
struct Student {
    string fileName;
    // ...
    this(string fileName) {
        // ...
    }
    // ...
}
```

Now the users of the struct must provide `immutable` strings and as a result the confusion about the name of the file would be prevented.

Type conversions through single-parameter constructors

Single-parameter constructors can be thought of as providing a sort of type conversion: They produce an object of the particular struct type starting from a constructor parameter. For example, the following constructor produces a `Student` object from a `string`:

```
struct Student {
    string name;

    this(string name) {
        this.name = name;
    }
}
```

`to()` and `cast` observe this behavior as a *conversion* as well. To see examples of this, let's consider the following `salute()` function. Sending a `string` parameter when it expects a `Student` would naturally cause a compilation error:

```
void salute(Student student) {
    writeln("Hello ", student.name);
}
// ...
    salute("Jane");     // ← compilation ERROR
```

On the other hand, all of the following lines ensure that a `Student` object is constructed before calling the function:

```
import std.conv;
// ...
    salute(Student("Jane"));
    salute(to!Student("Jean"));
    salute(cast(Student)"Jim");
```

`to` and `cast` take advantage of the single-parameter constructor by constructing a temporary `Student` object and calling `salute()` with that object.

52.2 Destructor

The destructor includes the operations that must be executed when the lifetime of an object ends.

The compiler-generated automatic destructor executes the destructors of all of the members in order. For that reason, as it is with the constructor, there is no need to define a destructor for most structs.

However, sometimes some special operations may need to be executed when an object's lifetime ends. For example, an operating system resource that the object owns may need to be returned to the system; a member function of another object may need to be called; a server running somewhere on the network may need to be notified that a connection to it is about to be terminated; etc.

The name of the destructor is ~this and just like constructors, it has no return type.

Destructor is executed automatically

The destructor is executed as soon as the lifetime of the struct object ends. (This is not the case for objects that are constructed with the new keyword.)

As we have seen in the Lifetimes and Fundamental Operations chapter, (page 228) the lifetime of an object ends when leaving the scope that it is defined in. The following are times when the lifetime of a struct ends:

- When leaving the scope of the object either normally or due to a thrown exception:

```
    if (aCondition) {
        auto duration = Duration(7);
        // ...

    } // ← The destructor is executed for 'duration'
      //    at this point
```

- Anonymous objects are destroyed at the end of the whole expression that they are constructed in:

```
    time.increment(Duration(5)); // ← The Duration(5) object
                                 //    gets destroyed at the end
                                 //    of the whole expression.
```

- All of the struct members of a struct object get destroyed when the outer object is destroyed.

Destructor example

Let's design a type for generating simple XML documents. XML elements are defined by angle brackets. They contain data and other XML elements. XML elements can have attributes as well; we will ignore them here.

Our aim will be to ensure that an element that has been *opened* by a <name> tag will always be *closed* by a matching </name> tag:

```
    <class1>     ← opening the outer XML element
      <grade>    ← opening the inner XML element
        57       ← the data
      </grade>   ← closing the inner element
    </class1>    ← closing the outer element
```

A struct that can produce the output above can be designed by two members that store the tag for the XML element and the indentation to use when printing it:

```
struct XmlElement {
    string name;
    string indentation;
}
```

If the responsibilities of opening and closing the XML element are given to the constructor and the destructor, respectively, the desired output can be produced by managing the lifetimes of XmlElement objects. For example, the constructor can print <tag> and the destructor can print </tag>.

The following definition of the constructor produces the opening tag:

```
    this(string name, int level) {
        this.name = name;
        this.indentation = indentationString(level);

        writeln(indentation, '<', name, '>');
    }
```

indentationString() is the following function:

```
import std.array;
// ...
string indentationString(int level) {
    return replicate(" ", level * 2);
}
```

The function calls replicate() from the std.array module, which makes and returns a new string made up of the specified value repeated the specified number of times.

The destructor can be defined similar to the constructor to produce the closing tag:

```
    ~this() {
        writeln(indentation, "</", name, '>');
    }
```

Here is a test code to demonstrate the effects of the automatic constructor and destructor calls:

```
import std.conv;
import std.random;
import std.array;

string indentationString(int level) {
    return replicate(" ", level * 2);
}

struct XmlElement {
    string name;
    string indentation;

    this(string name, int level) {
        this.name = name;
        this.indentation = indentationString(level);

        writeln(indentation, '<', name, '>');
    }

    ~this() {
        writeln(indentation, "</", name, '>');
    }
}

void main() {
    immutable classes = XmlElement("classes", 0);
```

```
    foreach (classId; 0 .. 2) {
        immutable classTag = "class" ~ to!string(classId);
        immutable classElement = XmlElement(classTag, 1);

        foreach (i; 0 .. 3) {
            immutable gradeElement = XmlElement("grade", 2);
            immutable randomGrade = uniform(50, 101);

            writeln(indentationString(3), randomGrade);
        }
    }
}
```

Note that the XmlElement objects are created in three separate scopes in the
program above. The opening and closing tags of the XML elements in the output
are produced solely by the constructor and the destructor of XmlElement.

```
<classes>
  <class0>
    <grade>
      72
    </grade>
    <grade>
      97
    </grade>
    <grade>
      90
    </grade>
  </class0>
  <class1>
    <grade>
      77
    </grade>
    <grade>
      87
    </grade>
    <grade>
      56
    </grade>
  </class1>
</classes>
```

The <classes> element is produced by the classes variable. Because that
variable is constructed first in main(), the output contains the output of its
construction first. Since it is also the variable that is destroyed last, upon leaving
main(), the output contains the output of the destructor call for its destruction
last.

52.3 Copy constructor
Copy construction is creating a new object as a copy of an existing one.
    Assuming S is a struct type, the following are the cases when objects are copied:

- Passing an object to a function that takes by value:

```
void foo(S s) {     // The caller's argument is copied as the parameter
    // ...
}
```

- Returning an object from a function by value:

```
S foo() {
    S result;
    // ...
    return result;     // The return value is copied to the caller's context
}
```

Note: *In practice, that copy is elided if the compiler applies "named return value optimization" (NRVO).*

- Copying objects explicitly

    There may be a confusion in this case because the assignment operator is used for copying. For example, the second line in the following code is *copy construction* of the newly created object a from existingObject. The auto keyword there is the indication that a new object is being defined (and being constructed).

```
auto existingObject = S();
auto a = existingObject;       // copy construction
     a = existingObject;       // assignment
     a = a;                    // assignment
     a = S();                  // assignment
```

In contrast, all of the lines following the copy construction line are *assignments* because a already exists as an object on those lines.

By default, copying is automatically handled by the compiler by copying corresponding members of the objects one after the other. Let's assume the following struct definition and the variable a that is copied from existingObject:

```
struct S {
    int i;
    double d;
}

// ...

    auto existingObject = S();
    auto a = existingObject;    // copy construction
```

The automatic copy constructor executes the following steps:

1. Copy a.i from existingObject.i
2. Copy a.d from existingObject.d

An example where the automatic behavior is not suitable is the Student type defined in the Structs chapter (page 246), which had a problem about copying objects of that type:

```
struct Student {
    int number;
    int[] grades;
}
```

Being a slice, the grades member of that struct is a reference type. The consequence of copying a Student object is that the grades members of both the original and the copy provide access to the same actual array elements of type int. As a result, the effect of modifying a grade through one of those objects is seen through the other object as well:

```
auto student1 = Student(1, [ 70, 90, 85 ]);

auto student2 = student1;    // copy construction
student2.number = 2;

student1.grades[0] += 5;     // this changes the grade of the
                             // second student as well:
assert(student2.grades[0] == 75);
```

To avoid such a confusion, the elements of the grades member of the second object must be separate and belong only to that object. Such special copy behavior is implemented in the copy constructor.

Being a constructor, the name of the copy constructor is this as well and it does not have a return type. Its parameter type must be the same type as the struct and must be defined as ref. Since the source object of a copy should not be modified, it is appropriate to mark the parameter as const (or inout). Complementing the this keyword, it is convenient to name the parameter as that to signify "this object is being copied from that object":

```d
struct Student {
    int number;
    int[] grades;

    this(ref const(Student) that) {
        this.number = that.number;
        this.grades = that.grades.dup;
    }
}
```

That copy constructor copies the members one by one, especially making sure the elements of grades are copied with .dup. As a result, the new object gets its own copy of the array elements.

Note: *As described in the "First assignment to a member is construction" section above, those assignment operations are actually copy constructions of the members.*

Making modifications through the first object does not affect the second object anymore:

```d
student1.grades[0] += 5;
assert(student2.grades[0] == 70);
```

Although it may make the code less readable, instead of repeating the type of the struct e.g. as Student as in the code above, the parameter type may generically be written as typeof(this) for all structs:

```d
this(ref const(typeof(this)) that) {
    // ...
}
```

52.4 Postblit

Postblit is a legacy feature of D, which is discouraged. Newly written code should use copy constructors instead. Postblit is still accepted for backward compatibility but is incompatible with the copy constructor: If the postblit is defined for a type, the copy constructor is disabled.

The legacy way of copying objects in D involves two steps:

1. Copying the members of the existing object to the new object bit-by-bit. This step is called *blit*, short for *block transfer*.
2. Making further adjustments to the new object. This step is called *postblit*.

The name of the postblit is this as well and it does not have a return type. To separate it from the other constructors, its parameter list contains the keyword this:

```d
this(this) {
    // ...
}
```

The main difference from the copy constructor is that the members of the existing object are already copied (blitted) to the members of the new object by the time the postblit starts executing. Further, there is no that object to speak of because the postblit is executed on the new object, using only its members. For that reason, all that is needed (and is possible) is to make adjustments to the new object.

The postblit function for the Student struct could be written as the following:

```d
struct Student {
    int number;
    int[] grades;

    this(this) {
        // 'number' and 'grades' are already copied at this
        //  point. We just need to make copies of the elements:
        grades = grades.dup;
    }
}
```

52.5 Assignment operator

Assigment is giving a new value to an existing object:

```d
returnTripDuration = tripDuration;   // assignment
```

Assignment is more complicated from the other special operations because it is actually a combination of two operations:

- Destroying the left-hand side object
- Copying the right-hand side object to the left-hand side object

However, applying those two steps in that order is risky because the original object would be destroyed before knowing that copying will succeed. Otherwise, an exception that is thrown during the copy operation can leave the left-hand side object in an inconsistent state: fully destroyed but not completely copied.

For that reason, the compiler-generated assignment operator acts safely by applying the following steps:

1. Copy the right-hand side object to a temporary object
   This is the actual copying half of the assignment operation. Since there is no change to the left-hand side object yet, it will remain intact if an exception is thrown during this copy operation.
2. Destroy the left-hand side object
   This is the other half of the assignment operation.
3. Transfer the temporary object to the left-hand side object
   No postblit nor a destructor is executed during or after this step. As a result, the left-hand side object becomes the equivalent of the temporary object.

After the steps above, the temporary object disappears and only the right-hand side object and its copy (i.e. the left-hand side object) remain.

Although the compiler-generated assignment operator is suitable in most cases, it can be defined by the programmer. When you do that, consider potential exceptions and write the assignment operator in a way that works even at the presence of thrown exceptions.

The syntax of the assignment operator is the following:

- The name of the function is opAssign.

- The type of the parameter is the same as the struct type. (Like the copy constructor, it may be ref const(typeof(this)) as well.) This parameter is often named as rhs, short for *right-hand side*. (As in the copy constructor, that is an appropriate name as well.)
- The return type is the same as the struct type.
- The function is exited by return this.

As an example, let's consider a simple Duration struct where the assignment operator prints a message:

```d
struct Duration {
    int minute;

    Duration opAssign(Duration rhs) {
        writefln("minute is being changed from %s to %s",
                 this.minute, rhs.minute);

        this.minute = rhs.minute;

        return this;
    }
}
// ...
    auto duration = Duration(100);
    duration = Duration(200);          // assignment
```

The output:

```
minute is being changed from 100 to 200
```

Assigning from other types

Sometimes it is convenient to assign values of types that are different from the type of the struct. For example, instead of requiring a Duration object on the right-hand side, it may be useful to assign from an integer:

```d
    duration = 300;
```

This is possible by defining another assignment operator that takes an int parameter:

```d
struct Duration {
    int minute;

    Duration opAssign(Duration rhs) {
        writefln("minute is being changed from %s to %s",
                 this.minute, rhs.minute);

        this.minute = rhs.minute;

        return this;
    }

    Duration opAssign(int minute) {
        writefln("minute is being replaced by an int");

        this.minute = minute;

        return this;
    }
}
// ...
    duration = Duration(200);
    duration = 300;
```

The output:

```
minute is being changed from 100 to 200
minute is being replaced by an int
```

Note: Although convenient, assigning different types to each other may cause confusions or bugs.

52.6 Disabling member functions

Functions that are declared as @disable cannot be used.

When there are no sensible default values for the members of a type, its default constructor can be disabled. For example, it may be incorrect for the following type to have an empty file name:

```
struct Archive {
    string fileName;
}
```

Unfortunately, the compiler-generated default constructor would initialize fileName as empty:

```
    auto archive = Archive();    // ← fileName member is empty
```

The default constructor can explicitly be disabled by declaring it as @disable so that objects must be constructed by one of the other constructors. There is no need to provide a body for a disabled function:

```
struct Archive {
    string fileName;

    @disable this();            // ← cannot be called

    this(string fileName) {     // ← can be called
        // ...
    }
}

// ...

    auto archive = Archive();    // ← compilation ERROR
```

This time the compiler does not allow calling this():

```
Error: constructor deneme.Archive.this is not callable because
it is annotated with @disable
```

Objects of Archive must be constructed either with one of the other constructors or explicitly with its .init value:

```
    auto a = Archive("records");    // ← compiles
    auto b = Archive.init;          // ← compiles
```

The copy costructor, the postblit function, and the assignment operator can be disabled as well:

```
struct Archive {
// ...

    // Disables the copy constructor
    @disable this(ref const(typeof(this)));

    // Disables the postblit
    @disable this(this);

    // Disables the assignment operator
    @disable typeof(this) opAssign(ref const(typeof(this)));
```

```
}
// ...

    auto a = Archive("records");
    auto b = a;                    // ← compilation ERROR
    b = a;                         // ← compilation ERROR
```

Disabling the copy constructor and the postblit can help in the cases where destructors execute operations that should be performed only once. Copying the objects of such types might cause bugs as the destructor would be executed for multiple copies.

For example, the following destructor intends to write a final "Finishing" message to a file that it uses for logging:

```
import std.stdio;
import std.datetime;

struct Logger {
    File file;

    this(File file) {
        this.file = file;
        log("Started");
    }

    ~this() {
        log("Finishing");     // ← Intended to be the last message
    }

    void log(string message) {
        file.writefln("%s %s", Clock.currTime(), message);
    }
}

void main() {
    auto logger = Logger(stdout);

    logger.log("Working inside main");
    logger.log("Calling foo");
    foo(logger);
    logger.log("Back to main");
}

void foo(Logger logger) {
    logger.log("Working inside foo");
}
```

The output of the program shows that the program does not work as intended because *the final message* appears more than once:

```
2022-Jan-03 22:21:24.3143894 Started
2022-Jan-03 22:21:24.3144467 Working inside main
2022-Jan-03 22:21:24.3144628 Calling foo
2022-Jan-03 22:21:24.3144767 Working inside foo
2022-Jan-03 22:21:24.3144906 Finishing
2022-Jan-03 22:21:24.3145035 Back to main
2022-Jan-03 22:21:24.3145155 Finishing
```

The problem is caused because more than one Logger object is constructed and the destructor is executed for each of them. The object that causes the unintended early "Finishing" message is the parameter of foo, which is copied because it is *by-value*.

The simplest solution in such cases is to disable copying and assignment altogether:

```
struct Logger {
    @disable this(this);
    @disable this(ref const(typeof(this)));
    @disable Logger opAssign(ref const(typeof(this)));

    // ...
}
```

As `Logger` cannot be copied anymore, `foo` must be changed to take its parameter *by reference*:

```
void foo(ref Logger logger) {
    // ...
}
```

52.7 Summary

- Constructor (`this`) is for preparing objects for use. The compiler-generated default constructor is sufficient in most cases.
- The behavior of the default constructor may not be changed in structs; `static opCall` can be used instead.
- Single-parameter constructors can be used during type conversions by `to` and `cast`.
- Destructor (`~this`) is for the operations that must be executed when the lifetimes of objects end.
- Copy constructor (`this(ref const(typeof(this)))`) is for defining how an object is copied from an existing one.
- Postblit (`this(this)`) is discouraged in new code; it is for adjustments to the object after the members are copied automatically.
- Assigment operator (`opAssign`) is for changing values of existing objects.
- Member functions can be disabled with `@disable`.

The topics covered in this chapter apply mostly for classes as well. The biggest difference is that the behavior of assignment operation opAssign() cannot be overloaded for classes.

Operator overloading involves many concepts, some of which will be covered later in the book (templates, auto ref, etc.). For that reason, you may find this chapter to be harder to follow than the previous ones.

Operator overloading enables defining how user-defined types behave when used with operators. In this context, the term *overload* means providing the definition of an operator for a specific type.

We have seen how to define structs and their member functions in previous chapters. As an example, we have defined the increment() member function to be able to add Duration objects to TimeOfDay objects. Here are the two structs from previous chapters, with only the parts that are relevant to this chapter:

```
struct Duration {
    int minute;
}

struct TimeOfDay {
    int hour;
    int minute;

    void increment(Duration duration) {
        minute += duration.minute;

        hour += minute / 60;
        minute %= 60;
        hour %= 24;
    }
}

void main() {
    auto lunchTime = TimeOfDay(12, 0);
    lunchTime.increment(Duration(10));
}
```

A benefit of member functions is being able to define operations of a type alongside the member variables of that type.

Despite their advantages, member functions can be seen as being limited compared to operations on fundamental types. After all, fundamental types can readily be used with operators:

```
    int weight = 50;
    weight += 10;                    // by an operator
```

According to what we have seen so far, similar operations can only be achieved by member functions for user-defined types:

```
    auto lunchTime = TimeOfDay(12, 0);
    lunchTime.increment(Duration(10));  // by a member function
```

Operator overloading enables using structs and classes with operators as well. For example, assuming that the += operator is defined for TimeOfDay, the operation above can be written in exactly the same way as with fundamental types:

```
    lunchTime += Duration(10);       // by an operator
                                     // (even for a struct)
```

Before getting to the details of operator overloading, let's first see how the line above would be enabled for `TimeOfDay`. What is needed is to redefine the `increment()` member function under the special name `opOpAssign(string op)` and also to specify that this definition is for the + character. As it will be explained below, this definition actually corresponds to the += operator.

The definition of this member function does not look like the ones that we have seen so far. That is because `opOpAssign` is actually a *function template*. Since we will see templates in much later chapters, I will have to ask you to accept the operator overloading syntax as is for now:

```
struct TimeOfDay {
// ...
    ref TimeOfDay opOpAssign(string op)(Duration duration) // (1)
            if (op == "+") {                               // (2)

        minute += duration.minute;
        hour += minute / 60;
        minute %= 60;
        hour %= 24;

        return this;
    }
}
```

The template definition consists of two parts:

1. `opOpAssign(string op)`: This part must be written as is and should be accepted as the *name* of the function. We will see below that there are other member functions in addition to `opOpAssign`.

2. `if (op == "+")`: `opOpAssign` is used for more than one operator overload. `"+"` specifies that this is the operator overload that corresponds to the + character. This syntax is a *template constraint*, which will also be covered in later chapters.

Also note that this time the return type is different from the return type of the `increment()` member function: It is not `void` anymore. We will discuss the return types of operators later below.

Behind the scenes, the compiler replaces the uses of the += operator with calls to the `opOpAssign!"+"` member function:

```
lunchTime += Duration(10);

// The following line is the equivalent of the previous one
lunchTime.opOpAssign!"+"(Duration(10));
```

The `!"+"` part that is after `opOpAssign` specifies that this call is for the definition of the operator for the + character. We will cover this template syntax in later chapters as well.

Note that the operator definition that corresponds to += is defined by `"+"`, not by `"+="`. The `Assign` in the name of `opOpAssign()` already implies that this name is for an assignment operator.

Being able to define the behaviors of operators brings a responsibility: The programmer must observe expectations. As an extreme example, the previous operator could have been defined to decrement the time value instead of incrementing it. However, people who read the code would still expect the value to be incremented by the += operator.

To some extent, the return types of operators can also be chosen freely. Still, general expectations must be observed for the return types as well.

Keep in mind that operators that behave unnaturally would cause confusion and bugs.

53.1 Overloadable operators

There are different kinds of operators that can be overloaded.

Unary operators

An operator that takes a single operand is called a unary operator:

```
++weight;
```

++ is a unary operator because it works on a single variable.

Unary operators are defined by member functions named opUnary. opUnary does not take any parameters because it uses only the object that the operator is being executed on.

The overloadable unary operators and the corresponding operator strings are the following:

Operator	Description	Operator String
-object	negative of (numeric complement of)	"-"
+object	the same value as (or, a copy of)	"+"
~object	bitwise negation	"~"
*object	access to what it points to	"*"
++object	increment	"++"
--object	decrement	"--"

For example, the ++ operator for Duration can be defined like this:

```
struct Duration {
    int minute;

    ref Duration opUnary(string op)()
            if (op == "++") {
        ++minute;
        return this;
    }
}
```

Note that the return type of the operator is marked as ref here as well. This will be explained later below.

Duration objects can now be incremented by ++:

```
auto duration = Duration(20);
++duration;
```

The post-increment and post-decrement operators cannot be overloaded. The object++ and object-- uses are handled by the compiler automatically by saving the previous value of the object. For example, the compiler applies the equivalent of the following code for post-increment:

```
/* The previous value is copied by the compiler
 * automatically: */
Duration __previousValue__ = duration;

/* The ++ operator is called: */
++duration;

/* Then __previousValue__ is used as the value of the
 * post-increment operation. */
```

Unlike some other languages, the copy inside post-increment has no cost in D if the value of the post-increment expression is not actually used. This is because the compiler replaces such post-increment expressions with their pre-increment counterparts:

```
/* The value of the expression is not used below. The
 * only effect of the expression is incrementing 'i'. */
i++;
```

Because the *previous value* of i is not actually used above, the compiler replaces the expression with the following one:

```
/* The expression that is actually used by the compiler: */
++i;
```

Additionally, if an opBinary overload supports the duration += 1 usage, then opUnary need not be overloaded for ++duration and duration++. Instead, the compiler uses the duration += 1 expression behind the scenes. Similarly, the duration -= 1 overload covers the uses of --duration and duration-- as well.

Binary operators

An operator that takes two operands is called a binary operator:

```
totalWeight = boxWeight + chocolateWeight;
```

The line above has two separate binary operators: the + operator, which adds the values of the two operands that are on its two sides, and the = operator that assigns the value of its right-hand operand to its left-hand operand.

The rightmost column below describes the category of each operator. The ones marked as "=" assign to the left-hand side object.

Operator	Description	Function name	Function name for right-hand side	Category
+	add	opBinary	opBinaryRight	arithmetic
-	subtract	opBinary	opBinaryRight	arithmetic
*	multiply	opBinary	opBinaryRight	arithmetic
/	divide	opBinary	opBinaryRight	arithmetic
%	remainder of	opBinary	opBinaryRight	arithmetic
^^	to the power of	opBinary	opBinaryRight	arithmetic
&	bitwise *and*	opBinary	opBinaryRight	bitwise
|	bitwise *or*	opBinary	opBinaryRight	bitwise
^	bitwise *xor*	opBinary	opBinaryRight	bitwise
<<	left-shift	opBinary	opBinaryRight	bitwise
>>	right-shift	opBinary	opBinaryRight	bitwise
>>>	unsigned right-shift	opBinary	opBinaryRight	bitwise
~	concatenate	opBinary	opBinaryRight	
in	whether contained in	opBinary	opBinaryRight	
==	whether equal to	opEquals	-	logical
!=	whether not equal to	opEquals	-	logical
<	whether before	opCmp	-	sorting
<=	whether not after	opCmp	-	sorting
>	whether after	opCmp	-	sorting
>=	whether not before	opCmp	-	sorting
=	assign	opAssign	-	=
+=	increment by	opOpAssign	-	=
-=	decrement by	opOpAssign	-	=
*=	multiply and assign	opOpAssign	-	=
/=	divide and assign	opOpAssign	-	=
%=	assign the remainder of	opOpAssign	-	=
^^=	assign the power of	opOpAssign	-	=
&=	assign the result of &	opOpAssign	-	=

`|=`	assign the result of `|`	`opOpAssign`		-	=
`^=`	assign the result of `^`	`opOpAssign`		-	=
`<<=`	assign the result of `<<`	`opOpAssign`		-	=
`>>=`	assign the result of `>>`	`opOpAssign`		-	=
`>>>=`	assign the result of `>>>`	`opOpAssign`		-	=
`~=`	append	`opOpAssign`		-	=

`opBinaryRight` is for when the object can appear on the right-hand side of the operator. Let's assume a binary operator that we shall call *op* appears in the program:

```
x op y
```

In order to determine what member function to call, the compiler considers the following two options:

```
// the definition for x being on the left:
x.opBinary!"op"(y);

// the definition for y being on the right:
y.opBinaryRight!"op"(x);
```

The compiler picks the option that is a better match than the other.

`opBinaryRight` is useful when defining arithmetic types that would normally work on both sides of an operator like e.g. `int` does:

```
auto x = MyInt(42);
x + 1;    // calls opBinary!"+"
1 + x;    // calls opBinaryRight!"+"
```

Another common use of `opBinaryRight` is the `in` operator. It usually makes more sense to define `opBinaryRight` for the object that appears on the right-hand side of `in`. We will see an example of this below.

The parameter name `rhs` that appears in the following definitions is short for *right-hand side*. It denotes the operand that appears on the right-hand side of the operator:

```
x op y
```

For the expression above, the `rhs` parameter would represent the variable `y`.

53.2 Element indexing and slicing operators

The following operators enable using a type as a collection of elements:

Description	Function Name	Sample Usage
element access	`opIndex`	`collection[i]`
assignment to element	`opIndexAssign`	`collection[i] = 7`
unary operation on element	`opIndexUnary`	`++collection[i]`
operation with assignment on element	`opIndexOpAssign`	`collection[i] *= 2`
number of elements	`opDollar`	`collection[$ - 1]`
slice of all elements	`opSlice`	`collection[]`
slice of some elements	`opSlice(size_t, size_t)`	`collection[i..j]`

We will cover those operators later below.

The following operator functions are from the earlier versions of D. They are discouraged:

Description	Function Name	Sample Usage
unary operation on all elements	`opSliceUnary` (discouraged)	`++collection[]`
unary operation on some elements	`opSliceUnary` (discouraged)	`++collection[i..j]`

assignment to all elements	opSliceAssign (discouraged)	collection[] = 42
assignment to some elements	opSliceAssign (discouraged)	collection[i..j] = 7
operation with assignment on all elements	opSliceOpAssign (discouraged)	collection[] *= 2
operation with assignment on some elements	opSliceOpAssign (discouraged)	collection[i..j] *= 2

Other operators

The following operators can be overloaded as well:

Description	Function Name	Sample Usage
function call	opCall	object(42)
type conversion	opCast	to!int(object)
dispatch for non-existent function	opDispatch	object.nonExistent()

These operators will be explained below under their own sections.

53.3 Defining more than one operator at the same time

To keep the code samples short, we have used only the ++, +, and += operators above. It is conceivable that when one operator is overloaded for a type, many others would also need to be overloaded. For example, the - - and -= operators are also defined for the following Duration:

```d
struct Duration {
    int minute;

    ref Duration opUnary(string op)()
            if (op == "++") {
        ++minute;
        return this;
    }

    ref Duration opUnary(string op)()
            if (op == "--") {
        --minute;
        return this;
    }

    ref Duration opOpAssign(string op)(int amount)
            if (op == "+") {
        minute += amount;
        return this;
    }

    ref Duration opOpAssign(string op)(int amount)
            if (op == "-") {
        minute -= amount;
        return this;
    }
}

unittest {
    auto duration = Duration(10);

    ++duration;
    assert(duration.minute == 11);

    --duration;
    assert(duration.minute == 10);

    duration += 5;
    assert(duration.minute == 15);

    duration -= 3;
    assert(duration.minute == 12);
}
```

```
void main() {
}
```

The operator overloads above have code duplications. The only differences between the similar functions are highlighted. Such code duplications can be reduced and sometimes avoided altogether by *string mixins*. We will see the mixin keyword in a later chapter as well. I would like to show briefly how this keyword helps with operator overloading.

mixin inserts the specified string as source code right where the mixin statement appears in code. The following struct is the equivalent of the one above:

```
struct Duration {
    int minute;

    ref Duration opUnary(string op)()
            if ((op == "++") || (op == "--")) {
        mixin (op ~ "minute;");
        return this;
    }

    ref Duration opOpAssign(string op)(int amount)
            if ((op == "+") || (op == "-")) {
        mixin ("minute " ~ op ~ "= amount;");
        return this;
    }
}
```

If the Duration objects also need to be multiplied and divided by an amount, all that is needed is to add two more conditions to the template constraint:

```
struct Duration {
// ...

    ref Duration opOpAssign(string op)(int amount)
        if ((op == "+") || (op == "-") ||
            (op == "*") || (op == "/")) {
        mixin ("minute " ~ op ~ "= amount;");
        return this;
    }
}

unittest {
    auto duration = Duration(12);

    duration *= 4;
    assert(duration.minute == 48);

    duration /= 2;
    assert(duration.minute == 24);
}
```

In fact, the template constraints are optional:

```
    ref Duration opOpAssign(string op)(int amount)
            /* no constraint */ {
        mixin ("minute " ~ op ~ "= amount;");
        return this;
    }
```

53.4 Return types of operators

When overloading an operator, it is advisable to observe the return type of the same operator on fundamental types. This would help with making sense of code and reducing confusions.

None of the operators on fundamental types return `void`. This fact should be obvious for some operators. For example, the result of adding two `int` values as `a + b` is `int`:

```
int a = 1;
int b = 2;
int c = a + b;   // c gets initialized by the return value
                 // of the + operator
```

The return values of some other operators may not be so obvious. For example, even operators like ++i have values:

```
int i = 1;
writeln(++i);    // prints 2
```

The ++ operator not only increments i, it also produces the new value of i. Further, the value that is produced by ++ is not just the new value of i, rather *the variable i itself.* We can see this fact by printing the address of the result of that expression:

```
int i = 1;
writeln("The address of i                 : ", &i);
writeln("The address of the result of ++i: ", &(++i));
```

The output contains identical addresses:

```
The address of i                 : 7FFF39BFEE78
The address of the result of ++i: 7FFF39BFEE78
```

I recommend that you observe the following guidelines when overloading operators for your own types:

- **Operators that modify the object**
  With the exception of `opAssign`, it is recommended that the operators that modify the object return the object itself. This guideline has been observed above with the `TimeOfDay.opOpAssign!"+"` and `Duration.opUnary!"++"`.
  The following two steps achieve returning the object itself:

  1. The return type is the type of the struct, marked by the `ref` keyword to mean *reference*.
  2. The function is exited by `return this` to mean *return this object*.

  The operators that modify the object are `opUnary!"++"`, `opUnary!"--"`, and all of the `opOpAssign` overloads.

- **Logical operators**
  `opEquals` that represents both `==` and `!=` must return `bool`. Although the `in` operator normally returns *the contained object*, it can simply return `bool` as well.

- **Sort operators**
  `opCmp` that represents `<`, `<=`, `>`, and `>=` must return `int`.

- **Operators that make a new object**
  Some operators must make and return a new object:

  - Unary operators `-`, `+`, and `~`; and the binary operator `~`.
  - Arithmetic operators `+`, `-`, `*`, `/`, `%`, and `^^`.
  - Bitwise operators `&`, `|`, `^`, `<<`, `>>`, and `>>>`.

○ As has been seen in the previous chapter, opAssign returns a copy of this object by return this.

Note: *As an optimization, sometimes it makes more sense for opAssign to return const ref for large structs. I will not apply this optimization in this book.*

As an example of an operator that makes a new object, let's define the opBinary!"+" overload for Duration. This operator should add two Duration objects to make and return a new one:

```
struct Duration {
    int minute;

    Duration opBinary(string op)(Duration rhs) const
            if (op == "+") {
        return Duration(minute + rhs.minute);  // new object
    }
}
```

That definition enables adding Duration objects by the + operator:

```
auto travelDuration = Duration(10);
auto returnDuration = Duration(11);
Duration totalDuration;
// ...
totalDuration = travelDuration + returnDuration;
```

The compiler replaces that expression with the following member function call on the travelDuration object:

```
// the equivalent of the expression above:
totalDuration =
    travelDuration.opBinary!"+"(returnDuration);
```

* opDollar

Since it returns the number of elements of the container, the most suitable type for opDollar is size_t. However, the return type can be other types as well (e.g. int).

* **Unconstrained operators**

The return types of some of the operators depend entirely on the design of the user-defined type: The unary *, opCall, opCast, opDispatch, opSlice, and all opIndex varieties.

53.5 opEquals() for equality comparisons

This member function defines the behaviors of the == and the != operators.

The return type of opEquals is bool.

For structs, the parameter of opEquals can be defined as in. However, for speed efficiency opEquals can be defined as a template that takes auto ref const (also note the empty template parentheses below):

```
bool opEquals()(auto ref const TimeOfDay rhs) const {
    // ...
}
```

As we have seen in the Lvalues and Rvalues chapter (page 181), auto ref allows lvalues to be passed by reference and rvalues by copy. However, since rvalues are not copied, rather moved, the signature above is efficient for both lvalues and rvalues.

To reduce confusion, `opEquals` and `opCmp` must work consistently. For two objects that `opEquals` returns `true`, `opCmp` must return zero.

Once `opEquals()` is defined for equality, the compiler uses its opposite for inequality:

```
x == y;
// the equivalent of the previous expression:
x.opEquals(y);

x != y;
// the equivalent of the previous expression:
!(x.opEquals(y));
```

Normally, it is not necessary to define `opEquals()` for structs. The compiler generates it for structs automatically. The automatically-generated `opEquals` compares all of the members individually.

Sometimes the equality of two objects must be defined differently from this automatic behavior. For example, some of the members may not be significant in this comparison, or the equality may depend on a more complex logic.

Just as an example, let's define `opEquals()` in a way that disregards the minute information altogether:

```
struct TimeOfDay {
    int hour;
    int minute;

    bool opEquals(TimeOfDay rhs) const {
        return hour == rhs.hour;
    }
}
// ...
    assert(TimeOfDay(20, 10) == TimeOfDay(20, 59));
```

Since the equality comparison considers the values of only the `hour` members, 20:10 and 20:59 end up being equal. (This is just an example; it should be clear that such an equality comparison would cause confusions.)

53.6 opCmp() for sorting

Sort operators determine the sort orders of objects. All of the ordering operators `<`, `<=`, `>`, and `>=` are covered by the `opCmp()` member function.

For structs, the parameter of `opCmp` can be defined as `in`. However, as with `opEquals`, it is more efficient to define `opCmp` as a template that takes `auto ref const`:

```
int opCmp()(auto ref const TimeOfDay rhs) const {
    // ...
}
```

To reduce confusion, `opEquals` and `opCmp` must work consistently. For two objects that `opEquals` returns `true`, `opCmp` must return zero.

Let's assume that one of these four operators is used as in the following code:

```
if (x op y) {  // ← op is one of <, <=, >, or >=
```

The compiler converts that expression to the following logical expression and uses the result of the new logical expression:

```
if (x.opCmp(y) op 0) {
```

Let's consider the `<=` operator:

```
    if (x <= y) {
```

The compiler generates the following code behind the scenes:

```
    if (x.opCmp(y) <= 0) {
```

For the user-defined opCmp() to work correctly, this member function must return a result according to the following rules:

- *A negative value* if the left-hand object is considered to be before the right-hand object
- *A positive value* if the left-hand object is considered to be after the right-hand object
- *Zero* if the objects are considered to have the same sort order

To be able to support those values, the return type of opCmp() must be int, not bool.

The following is a way of ordering TimeOfDay objects by first comparing the values of the hour members, and then comparing the values of the minute members (only if the hour members are equal):

```
    int opCmp(TimeOfDay rhs) const {
        /* Note: Subtraction is a bug here if the result can
         * overflow. (See the following warning in text.) */

        return (hour == rhs.hour
                  ? minute - rhs.minute
                  : hour - rhs.hour);
    }
```

That definition returns the difference between the minute values when the hour members are the same, and the difference between the hour members otherwise. The return value would be a *negative value* when the *left-hand* object comes before in chronological order, a *positive value* if the *right-hand* object is before, and *zero* when they represent exactly the same time of day.

Warning: Using subtraction for the implementation of opCmp is a bug if valid values of a member can cause overflow. For example, the two objects below would be sorted incorrectly as the object with value -2 is calculated to be *greater* than the one with value int.max:

```
struct S {
    int i;

    int opCmp(S rhs) const {
        return i - rhs.i;          // ← BUG
    }
}

void main() {
    assert(S(-2) > S(int.max));    // ← wrong sort order
}
```

On the other hand, subtraction is acceptable for TimeOfDay because none of the valid values of the members of that struct can cause overflow in subtraction.

You can use std.algorithm.cmp for comparing slices (including all string types and ranges). cmp() compares slices lexicographically and produces a negative value, zero, or positive value depending on their order. That result can directly be used as the return value of opCmp:

```
import std.algorithm;

struct S {
    string name;

    int opCmp(S rhs) const {
        return cmp(name, rhs.name);
    }
}
```

Once opCmp() is defined, this type can be used with sorting algorithms like
std.algorithm.sort as well. As sort() works on the elements, it is the opCmp()
operator that gets called behind the scenes to determine their order. The
following program constructs 10 objects with random values and sorts them with
sort():

```
import std.random;
import std.stdio;
import std.string;
import std.algorithm;

struct TimeOfDay {
    int hour;
    int minute;

    int opCmp(TimeOfDay rhs) const {
        return (hour == rhs.hour
                ? minute - rhs.minute
                : hour - rhs.hour);
    }

    string toString() const {
        return format("%02s:%02s", hour, minute);
    }
}

void main() {
    TimeOfDay[] times;

    foreach (i; 0 .. 10) {
        times ~= TimeOfDay(uniform(0, 24), uniform(0, 60));
    }

    sort(times);

    writeln(times);
}
```

As expected, the elements are sorted from the earliest time to the latest time:

```
[03:40, 04:10, 09:06, 10:03, 10:09, 11:04, 13:42, 16:40, 18:03, 21:08]
```

53.7 opCall() to call objects as functions

The parentheses around the parameter list when calling functions are operators
as well. We have already seen how static opCall() makes it possible to use the
name of the *type* as a function. static opCall() allows creating objects with
default values at run time.

Non-static opCall() on the other hand allows using the *objects* of user-defined
types as functions:

```
    Foo foo;
    foo();
```

The object foo above is being called like a function.

As an example, let's consider a `struct` that represents a linear equation. This `struct` will be used for calculating the *y* values of the following linear equation for specific *x* values:

```
y = ax + b
```

The following `opCall()` simply calculates and returns the value of *y* according to that equation:

```d
struct LinearEquation {
    double a;
    double b;

    double opCall(double x) const {
        return a * x + b;
    }
}
```

With that definition, each object of `LinearEquation` represents a linear equation for specific *a* and *b* values. Such an object can be used as a function that calculates the *y* values:

```d
LinearEquation equation = { 1.2, 3.4 };
// the object is being used like a function:
double y = equation(5.6);
```

Note: *Defining opCall() for a struct disables the compiler-generated automatic constructor. That is why the { } syntax is used above instead of the recommended LinearEquation(1.2, 3.4). When the latter syntax is desired, a static opCall() that takes two double parameters must also be defined.*

equation above represents the $y = 1.2x + 3.4$ linear equation. Using that object as a function executes the `opCall()` member function.

This feature can be useful to define and store the *a* and *b* values in an object once and to use that object multiple times later on. The following code uses such an object in a loop:

```d
LinearEquation equation = { 0.01, 0.4 };

for (double x = 0.0; x <= 1.0; x += 0.125) {
    writefln("%f: %f", x, equation(x));
}
```

That object represents the $y = 0.01x + 0.4$ equation. It is being used for calculating the results for *x* values in the range from 0.0 to 1.0.

53.8 Indexing operators

`opIndex`, `opIndexAssign`, `opIndexUnary`, `opIndexOpAssign`, and `opDollar` make it possible to use indexing operators on user-defined types similar to arrays as in `object[index]`.

Unlike arrays, these operators support multi-dimensional indexing as well. Multiple index values are specified as a comma-separated list inside the square brackets (e.g. `object[index0, index1]`). In the following examples we will use these operators only with a single dimension and cover their multi-dimensional uses in the More Templates chapter (page 520).

The deque variable in the following examples is an object of `struct` `DoubleEndedQueue`, which we will define below; and e is a variable of type `int`.

`opIndex` is for element access. The index that is specified inside the brackets becomes the parameter of the operator function:

```
e = deque[3];                    // the element at index 3
e = deque.opIndex(3);            // the equivalent of the above
```

`opIndexAssign` is for assigning to an element. The first parameter is the value that is being assigned and the second parameter is the index of the element:

```
deque[5] = 55;                   // assign 55 to the element at index 5
deque.opIndexAssign(55, 5);      // the equivalent of the above
```

`opIndexUnary` is similar to `opUnary`. The difference is that the operation is applied to the element at the specified index:

```
++deque[4];                      // increment the element at index 4
deque.opIndexUnary!"++"(4);      // the equivalent of the above
```

`opIndexOpAssign` is similar to `opOpAssign`. The difference is that the operation is applied to an element:

```
deque[6] += 66;                      // add 66 to the element at index 6
deque.opIndexOpAssign!"+"(66, 6);// the equivalent of the above
```

`opDollar` defines the $ character that is used during indexing and slicing. It is for returning the number of elements in the container:

```
e = deque[$ - 1];                     // the last element
e = deque[deque.opDollar() - 1]; // the equivalent of the above
```

Indexing operators example

Double-ended queue is a data structure that is similar to arrays but it provides efficient insertion at the head of the collection as well. (In contrast, inserting at the head of an array is a relatively slow operation as it requires moving the existing elements to a newly created array.)

One way of implementing a double-ended queue is to use two arrays in the background but to use the first one in reverse. The element that is conceptually inserted at the head of the queue is actually appended to the *head* array. As a result, this operation is as efficient as appending to the end.

The following `struct` implements a double-ended queue that overloads the operators that we have seen in this section:

```
import std.stdio;
import std.string;
import std.conv;

struct DoubleEndedQueue // Also known as Deque
{
private:

    /* The elements are represented as the chaining of the two
     * member slices. However, 'head' is indexed in reverse so
     * that the first element of the entire collection is
     * head[$-1], the second one is head[$-2], etc.:
     *
     * head[$-1], head[$-2], ... head[0], tail[0], ... tail[$-1]
     */
    int[] head;    // the first group of elements
    int[] tail;    // the second group of elements

    /* Determines the actual slice that the specified element
     * resides in and returns it as a reference. */
    ref inout(int) elementAt(size_t index) inout {
        return (index < head.length
                ? head[$ - 1 - index]
                : tail[index - head.length]);
```

```
    }
public:

    string toString() const {
        string result;

        foreach_reverse (element; head) {
            result ~= format("%s ", to!string(element));
        }

        foreach (element; tail) {
            result ~= format("%s ", to!string(element));
        }

        return result;
    }

    /* Note: As we will see in the next chapter, the following
     * is a simpler and more efficient implementation of
     * toString(): */
    version (none) {
        void toString(void delegate(const(char)[]) sink) const {
            import std.format;
            import std.range;

            formattedWrite(
                sink, "%(%s %)", chain(head.retro, tail));
        }
    }

    /* Adds a new element to the head of the collection. */
    void insertAtHead(int value) {
        head ~= value;
    }

    /* Adds a new element to the tail of the collection.
     *
     * Sample: deque ~= value
     */
    ref DoubleEndedQueue opOpAssign(string op)(int value)
            if (op == "~") {
        tail ~= value;
        return this;
    }

    /* Returns the specified element.
     *
     * Sample: deque[index]
     */
    inout(int) opIndex(size_t index) inout {
        return elementAt(index);
    }

    /* Applies a unary operation to the specified element.
     *
     * Sample: ++deque[index]
     */
    int opIndexUnary(string op)(size_t index) {
        mixin ("return " ~ op ~ "elementAt(index);");
    }

    /* Assigns a value to the specified element.
     *
     * Sample: deque[index] = value
     */
    int opIndexAssign(int value, size_t index) {
        return elementAt(index) = value;
    }

    /* Uses the specified element and a value in a binary
     * operation and assigns the result back to the same
     * element.
```

```
     *
     * Sample: deque[index] += value
     */
    int opIndexOpAssign(string op)(int value, size_t index) {
        mixin ("return elementAt(index) " ~ op ~ "= value;");
    }

    /* Defines the $ character, which is the length of the
     * collection.
     *
     * Sample: deque[$ - 1]
     */
    size_t opDollar() const {
        return head.length + tail.length;
    }
}

void main() {
    auto deque = DoubleEndedQueue();

    foreach (i; 0 .. 10) {
        if (i % 2) {
            deque.insertAtHead(i);

        } else {
            deque ~= i;
        }
    }

    writefln("Element at index 3: %s",
             deque[3]);        // accessing an element
    ++deque[4];                // incrementing an element
    deque[5] = 55;             // assigning to an element
    deque[6] += 66;            // adding to an element

    (deque ~= 100) ~= 200;

    writeln(deque);
}
```

According to the guidelines above, the return type of opOpAssign is ref so that the ~= operator can be chained on the same collection:

```
    (deque ~= 100) ~= 200;
```

As a result, both 100 and 200 get appended to the same collection:

```
Element at index 3: 3
9 7 5 3 2 55 68 4 6 8 100 200
```

53.9 Slicing operators

opSlice allows slicing the objects of user-defined types with the [] operator.

In addition to this operator, there are also opSliceUnary, opSliceAssign, and opSliceOpAssign but they are discouraged.

D supports multi-dimensional slicing. We will see a multi-dimensional example later in the More Templates chapter (page 520). Although the methods described in that chapter can be used for a single dimension as well, they do not match the indexing operators that are defined above and they involve templates which we have not covered yet. For that reason, we will see the non-templated use of opSlice in this chapter, which works only with a single dimension. (This use of opSlice is discouraged as well.)

opSlice has two distinct forms:

- The square brackets can be empty as in deque[] to mean *all elements*.

- The square brackets can contain a number range as in deque[begin..end] to mean *the elements in the specified range.*

The slicing operators are relatively more complex than other operators because they involve two distinct concepts: *container* and *range*. We will see these concepts in more detail in later chapters.

In single-dimensional slicing which does not use templates, opSlice returns an object that represents a specific range of elements of the container. The object that opSlice returns is responsible for defining the operations that are applied on that range elements. For example, behind the scenes the following expression is executed by first calling opSlice to obtain a range object and then applying opOpAssign!"*" on that object:

```
deque[] *= 10;      // multiply all elements by 10

// The equivalent of the above:
{
    auto range = deque.opSlice();
    range.opOpAssign!"*"(10);
}
```

Accordingly, the opSlice operators of DoubleEndedQueue return a special Range object so that the operations are applied to it:

```
import std.exception;

struct DoubleEndedQueue {
// ...

    /* Returns a range that represents all of the elements.
     * ('Range' struct is defined below.)
     *
     * Sample: deque[]
     */
    inout(Range) opSlice() inout {
        return inout(Range)(head[], tail[]);
    }

    /* Returns a range that represents some of the elements.
     *
     * Sample: deque[begin .. end]
     */
    inout(Range) opSlice(size_t begin, size_t end) inout {
        enforce(end <= opDollar());
        enforce(begin <= end);

        /* Determine what parts of 'head' and 'tail'
         * correspond to the specified range: */

        if (begin < head.length) {
            if (end < head.length) {
                /* The range is completely inside 'head'. */
                return inout(Range)(
                    head[$ - end .. $ - begin],
                    []);

            } else {
                /* Some part of the range is inside 'head' and
                 * the rest is inside 'tail'. */
                return inout(Range)(
                    head[0 .. $ - begin],
                    tail[0 .. end - head.length]);
            }

        } else {
            /* The range is completely inside 'tail'. */
            return inout(Range)(
```

```
                    [],
                    tail[begin - head.length .. end - head.length]);
            }
        }

    /* Represents a range of elements of the collection. This
     * struct is responsible for defining the opUnary,
     * opAssign, and opOpAssign operators. */
    struct Range {
        int[] headRange;    // elements that are in 'head'
        int[] tailRange;    // elements that are in 'tail'

        /* Applies the unary operation to the elements of the
         * range. */
        Range opUnary(string op)() {
            mixin (op ~ "headRange[];");
            mixin (op ~ "tailRange[];");
            return this;
        }

        /* Assigns the specified value to each element of the
         * range. */
        Range opAssign(int value) {
            headRange[] = value;
            tailRange[] = value;
            return this;
        }

        /* Uses each element and a value in a binary operation
         * and assigns the result back to that element. */
        Range opOpAssign(string op)(int value) {
            mixin ("headRange[] " ~ op ~ "= value;");
            mixin ("tailRange[] " ~ op ~ "= value;");
            return this;
        }
    }
}

void main() {
    auto deque = DoubleEndedQueue();

    foreach (i; 0 .. 10) {
        if (i % 2) {
            deque.insertAtHead(i);

        } else {
            deque ~= i;
        }
    }

    writeln(deque);
    deque[] *= 10;
    deque[3 .. 7] = -1;
    writeln(deque);
}
```

The output:

```
9 7 5 3 1 0 2 4 6 8
90 70 50 -1 -1 -1 -1 40 60 80
```

53.10 opCast for type conversions

opCast defines explicit type conversions. It can be overloaded separately for each target type. As you would remember from the earlier chapters, explicit type conversions are performed by the to function and the cast operator.

opCast is a template as well, but it has a different format: The target type is specified by the (T : target_type) syntax:

```
    target_type opCast(T : target_type)() {
        // ...
    }
```

This syntax will become clear later after the templates chapter as well.

Let's change the definition of Duration so that it now has two members: hours and minutes. The operator that converts objects of this type to double can be defined as in the following code:

```
import std.stdio;
import std.conv;

struct Duration {
    int hour;
    int minute;

    double opCast(T : double)() const {
        return hour + (to!double(minute) / 60);
    }
}

void main() {
    auto duration = Duration(2, 30);
    double d = to!double(duration);
    // (could be 'cast(double)duration' as well)

    writeln(d);
}
```

The compiler replaces the type conversion call above with the following one:

```
    double d = duration.opCast!double();
```

The double conversion function above produces 2.5 for two hours and thirty minutes:

```
2.5
```

Although opCast is for explicit type conversions, its bool specialization is called automatically when the variable is used in a logical expression:

```
struct Duration {
// ...

    bool opCast(T : bool)() const {
        return (hour != 0) || (minute != 0);
    }
}
// ...

    if (duration) {                 // compiles
        // ...
    }

    while (duration) {              // compiles
        // ...
    }

    auto r = duration ? 1 : 2;     // compiles
```

Still, the bool specialization of opCast is not for all implicit bool conversions:

```
void foo(bool b) {
    // ...
}
// ...
```

```
    foo(duration);              // ← compilation ERROR
    bool b = duration;          // ← compilation ERROR
```

```
Error: cannot implicitly convert expression (duration) of type Duration to
bool
Error: function deneme.foo (bool b) is not callable using argument types
(Duration)
```

53.11 Catch-all operator opDispatch

opDispatch gets called whenever a *missing* member of an object is accessed. All attempts to access non-existent members are dispatched to this function.

The name of the missing member becomes the template parameter value of opDispatch.

The following code demonstrates a simple definition:

```
import std.stdio;

struct Foo {
    void opDispatch(string name, T)(T parameter) {
        writefln("Foo.opDispatch - name: %s, value: %s",
                 name, parameter);
    }
}

void main() {
    Foo foo;
    foo.aNonExistentFunction(42);
    foo.anotherNonExistentFunction(100);
}
```

There are no compiler errors for the calls to non-existent members. Instead, all of those calls are dispatched to opDispatch. The first template parameter is the name of the member. The parameter values that are used when calling the function appear as the parameters of opDispatch:

```
Foo.opDispatch - name: aNonExistentFunction, value: 42
Foo.opDispatch - name: anotherNonExistentFunction, value: 100
```

The name template parameter can be used inside the function to make decisions on how the call to that specific non-existent function should be handled:

```
    switch (name) {
        // ...
    }
```

53.12 Inclusion query by opBinaryRight!"in"

This operator allows defining the behavior of the in operator for user-defined types. in is commonly used with associative arrays to determine whether a value for a specific key exists in the array.

Different from other operators, this operator is normally overloaded for the case where the object appears on the right-hand side:

```
        if (time in lunchBreak) {
```

The compiler would use opBinaryRight behind the scenes:

```
        // the equivalent of the above:
        if (lunchBreak.opBinaryRight!"in"(time)) {
```

There is also `!in` to determine whether a value for a specific key *does not* exist in the array:

```
if (a !in b) {
```

`!in` cannot be overloaded because the compiler uses the negative of the result of the `in` operator instead:

```
if (!(a in b)) {    // the equivalent of the above
```

Example of the `in` operator

The following program defines a `TimeSpan` type in addition to `Duration` and `TimeOfDay`. The `in` operator that is defined for `TimeSpan` determines whether a moment in time is within that time span.

To keep the code short, the following program defines only the necessary member functions.

Note how the `TimeOfDay` object is used seamlessly in the `for` loop. That loop is a demonstration of how useful operator overloading can be.

```d
import std.stdio;
import std.string;

struct Duration {
    int minute;
}

struct TimeOfDay {
    int hour;
    int minute;

    ref TimeOfDay opOpAssign(string op)(Duration duration)
            if (op == "+") {
        minute += duration.minute;

        hour += minute / 60;
        minute %= 60;
        hour %= 24;

        return this;
    }

    int opCmp(TimeOfDay rhs) const {
        return (hour == rhs.hour
                ? minute - rhs.minute
                : hour - rhs.hour);
    }

    string toString() const {
        return format("%02s:%02s", hour, minute);
    }
}

struct TimeSpan {
    TimeOfDay begin;
    TimeOfDay end;     // end is outside of the span

    bool opBinaryRight(string op)(TimeOfDay time) const
            if (op == "in") {
        return (time >= begin) && (time < end);
    }
}

void main() {
    auto lunchBreak = TimeSpan(TimeOfDay(12, 00),
                               TimeOfDay(13, 00));

    for (auto time = TimeOfDay(11, 30);
```

```
        time < TimeOfDay(13, 30);
        time += Duration(15)) {

    if (time in lunchBreak) {
        writeln(time, " is during the lunch break");

    } else {
        writeln(time, " is outside of the lunch break");
    }
  }
}
```

The output:

```
11:30 is outside of the lunch break
11:45 is outside of the lunch break
12:00 is during the lunch break
12:15 is during the lunch break
12:30 is during the lunch break
12:45 is during the lunch break
13:00 is outside of the lunch break
13:15 is outside of the lunch break
```

53.13 Exercise

Define a fraction type that stores its numerator and denominator as members of type `long`. Such a type may be useful because it does not lose value like `float`, `double`, and `real` do due to their precisions. For example, although the result of multiplying a `double` value of 1.0/3 by 3 is *not* 1.0, multiplying a `Fraction` object that represents the fraction 1/3 by 3 would be exactly 1:

```
struct Fraction {
    long num;   // numerator
    long den;   // denominator

    /* As a convenience, the constructor uses the default
     * value of 1 for the denominator. */
    this(long num, long den = 1) {
        enforce(den != 0, "The denominator cannot be zero");

        this.num = num;
        this.den = den;

        /* Ensuring that the denominator is always positive
         * will simplify the definitions of some of the
         * operator functions. */
        if (this.den < 0) {
            this.num = -this.num;
            this.den = -this.den;
        }
    }

    /* ... you define the operator overloads ... */
}
```

Define operators as needed for this type to make it a convenient type as close to fundamental types as possible. Ensure that the definition of the type passes all of the following unit tests. The unit tests ensure the following behaviors:

- An exception must be thrown when constructing an object with zero denominator. (This is already taken care of by the `enforce` expression above.)
- Producing the negative of the value: For example, the negative of 1/3 should be -1/3 and negative of -2/5 should be 2/5.
- Incrementing and decrementing the value by ++ and - -.

- Support for four arithmetic operations: Both modifying the value of an object by +=, -=, *=, and /=; and producing the result of using two objects with the +, -, *, and / operators. (Similar to the constructor, dividing by zero should be prevented.)

  As a reminder, here are the formulas of arithmetic operations that involve two fractions a/b and c/d:

  - Addition: a/b + c/d = (a*d + c*b)/(b*d)
  - Subtraction: a/b - c/d = (a*d - c*b)/(b*d)
  - Multiplication: a/b * c/d = (a*c)/(b*d)
  - Division: (a/b) / (c/d) = (a*d)/(b*c)

- The actual (and necessarily lossful) value of the object can be converted to `double`.

- Sort order and equality comparisons are performed by the actual values of the fractions, not by the values of the numerators and denominators. For example, the fractions 1/3 and 20/60 must be considered to be equal.

```d
unittest {
    /* Must throw when denominator is zero. */
    assertThrown(Fraction(42, 0));

    /* Let's start with 1/3. */
    auto a = Fraction(1, 3);

    /* -1/3 */
    assert(-a == Fraction(-1, 3));

    /* 1/3 + 1 == 4/3 */
    ++a;
    assert(a == Fraction(4, 3));

    /* 4/3 - 1 == 1/3 */
    --a;
    assert(a == Fraction(1, 3));

    /* 1/3 + 2/3 == 3/3 */
    a += Fraction(2, 3);
    assert(a == Fraction(1));

    /* 3/3 - 2/3 == 1/3 */
    a -= Fraction(2, 3);
    assert(a == Fraction(1, 3));

    /* 1/3 * 8 == 8/3 */
    a *= Fraction(8);
    assert(a == Fraction(8, 3));

    /* 8/3 / 16/9 == 3/2 */
    a /= Fraction(16, 9);
    assert(a == Fraction(3, 2));

    /* Must produce the equivalent value in type 'double'.
     *
     * Note that although double cannot represent every value
     * precisely, 1.5 is an exception. That is why this test
     * is being applied at this point. */
    assert(to!double(a) == 1.5);

    /* 1.5 + 2.5 == 4 */
    assert(a + Fraction(5, 2) == Fraction(4, 1));

    /* 1.5 - 0.75 == 0.75 */
    assert(a - Fraction(3, 4) == Fraction(3, 4));

    /* 1.5 * 10 == 15 */
```

```
    assert(a * Fraction(10) == Fraction(15, 1));

    /* 1.5 / 4 == 3/8 */
    assert(a / Fraction(4) == Fraction(3, 8));

    /* Must throw when dividing by zero. */
    assertThrown(Fraction(42, 1) / Fraction(0));

    /* The one with lower numerator is before. */
    assert(Fraction(3, 5) < Fraction(4, 5));

    /* The one with larger denominator is before. */
    assert(Fraction(3, 9) < Fraction(3, 8));
    assert(Fraction(1, 1_000) > Fraction(1, 10_000));

    /* The one with lower value is before. */
    assert(Fraction(10, 100) < Fraction(1, 2));

    /* The one with negative value is before. */
    assert(Fraction(-1, 2) < Fraction(0));
    assert(Fraction(1, -2) < Fraction(0));

    /* The ones with equal values must be both <= and >=. */
    assert(Fraction(-1, -2) <= Fraction(1, 2));
    assert(Fraction(1, 2) <= Fraction(-1, -2));
    assert(Fraction(3, 7) <= Fraction(9, 21));
    assert(Fraction(3, 7) >= Fraction(9, 21));

    /* The ones with equal values must be equal. */
    assert(Fraction(1, 3) == Fraction(20, 60));

    /* The ones with equal values with sign must be equal. */
    assert(Fraction(-1, 2) == Fraction(1, -2));
    assert(Fraction(1, 2) == Fraction(-1, -2));
}
```

The solution is on page 726.

Similar to structs, class is a feature for defining new types. By this definition, classes are *user defined types*. Different from structs, classes provide the *object oriented programming* (OOP) paradigm in D. The major aspects of OOP are the following:

- **Encapsulation:** Controlling access to members (*Encapsulation is available for structs as well but it has not been mentioned until this chapter.*)
- **Inheritance:** Acquiring members of another type
- **Polymorphism:** Being able to use a more special type in place of a more general type

Encapsulation is achieved by *protection attributes*, which we will see in a later chapter (page 379). Inheritance is for acquiring *implementations* of other types. Polymorphism (page 328) is for abstracting parts of programs from each other and is achieved by class *interfaces*.

This chapter will introduce classes at a high level, underlining the fact that they are reference types. Classes will be explained in more detail in later chapters.

54.1 Comparing with structs

In general, classes are very similar to structs. Most of the features that we have seen for structs in the following chapters apply to classes as well:

- Structs (page 246)
- Member Functions (page 269)
- const ref Parameters and const Member Functions (page 275)
- Constructor and Other Special Functions (page 279)
- Operator Overloading (page 298)

However, there are important differences between classes and structs.

Classes are reference types

The biggest difference from structs is that structs are *value types* and classes are *reference types*. The other differences outlined below are mostly due to this fact.

Class variables may be null

As it has been mentioned briefly in The null Value and the is Operator chapter (page 233), class variables can be null. In other words, class variables may not be providing access to any object. Class variables do not have values themselves; the actual class objects must be constructed by the new keyword.

As you would also remember, comparing a reference to null by the == or the != operator is an error. Instead, the comparison must be done by the is or the !is operator, accordingly:

```
MyClass referencesAnObject = new MyClass;
assert(referencesAnObject !is null);

MyClass variable;   // does not reference an object
assert(variable is null);
```

The reason is that, the == operator may need to consult the values of the members of the objects and that attempting to access the members through a potentially `null` variable would cause a memory access error. For that reason, class variables must always be compared by the `is` and `!is` operators.

Class variables versus class objects

Class variable and class object are separate concepts.

Class objects are constructed by the `new` keyword; they do not have names. The actual concept that a class type represents in a program is provided by a class object. For example, assuming that a `Student` class represents students by their names and grades, such information would be stored by the members of `Student` *objects*. Partly because they are anonymous, it is not possible to access class objects directly.

A class variable on the other hand is a language feature for accessing class objects. Although it may seem syntactically that operations are being performed on a class *variable*, the operations are actually dispatched to a class *object*.

Let's consider the following code that we saw previously in the Value Types and Reference Types chapter (page 159):

```d
auto variable1 = new MyClass;
auto variable2 = variable1;
```

The `new` keyword constructs an anonymous class object. `variable1` and `variable2` above merely provide access to that anonymous object:

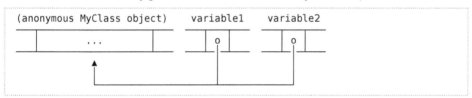

Copying

Copying affects only the variables, not the object.

Because classes are reference types, defining a new class variable as a copy of another makes two variables that provide access to the same object. The actual object is not copied.

The postblit function `this(this)` is not available for classes.

```d
auto variable2 = variable1;
```

In the code above, `variable2` is being initialized by `variable1`. The two variables start providing access to the same object.

When the actual object needs to be copied, the class must have a member function for that purpose. To be compatible with arrays, this function may be named `dup()`. This function must create and return a new class object. Let's see this on a class that has various types of members:

```d
class Foo {
    S       o;   // assume S is a struct type
    char[]  s;
    int     i;

// ...

    this(S o, const char[] s, int i) {
        this.o = o;
        this.s = s.dup;
        this.i = i;
    }
```

```
    Foo dup() const {
        return new Foo(o, s, i);
    }
}
```

The dup() member function makes a new object by taking advantage of the constructor of Foo and returns the new object. Note that the constructor copies the s member explicitly by the .dup property of arrays. Being value types, o and i are copied automatically.

The following code makes use of dup() to create a new object:

```
    auto var1 = new Foo(S(1.5), "hello", 42);
    auto var2 = var1.dup();
```

As a result, the objects that are associated with var1 and var2 are different.

Similarly, an immutable copy of an object can be provided by a member function appropriately named idup(). In this case, the constructor must be defined as pure as well. We will cover the pure keyword in a later chapter (page 547).

```
class Foo {
// ...
    this(S o, const char[] s, int i) pure {
        // ...

    }
    immutable(Foo) idup() const {
        return new immutable(Foo)(o, s, i);
    }
}

// ...

    immutable(Foo) imm = var1.idup();
```

Assignment

Just like copying, assignment affects only the variables.

Assigning to a class variable disassociates that variable from its current object and associates it with a new object.

If there is no other class variable that still provides access to the object that has been disassociated from, then that object is going to be destroyed some time in the future by the garbage collector.

```
    auto variable1 = new MyClass();
    auto variable2 = new MyClass();
    variable1 = variable2;
```

The assignment above makes variable1 leave its object and start providing access to variable2's object. Since there is no other variable for variable1's original object, that object will be destroyed by the garbage collector.

The behavior of assignment cannot be changed for classes. In other words, opAssign cannot be overloaded for them.

Definition

Classes are defined by the class keyword instead of the struct keyword:

```
class ChessPiece {
    // ...
}
```

Construction

As with structs, the name of the constructor is `this`. Unlike structs, class objects cannot be constructed by the `{ }` syntax.

```
class ChessPiece {
    dchar shape;

    this(dchar shape) {
        this.shape = shape;
    }
}
```

Unlike structs, there is no automatic object construction where the constructor parameters are assigned to members sequentially:

```
class ChessPiece {
    dchar shape;
    size_t value;
}

void main() {
    auto king = new ChessPiece('♔', 100);  // ← compilation ERROR
}
```

```
Error: no constructor for ChessPiece
```

For that syntax to work, a constructor must be defined explicitly by the programmer.

Destruction

As with structs, the name of the destructor is `~this`:

```
    ~this() {
        // ...
    }
```

However, different from structs, class destructors are not executed at the time when the lifetime of a class object ends. As we have seen above, the destructor is executed some time in the future during a garbage collection cycle. (By this distinction, class destructors should have more accurately been called *finalizers*).

As we will see later in the Memory Management chapter (page 667), class destructors must observe the following rules:

- A class destructor must not access a member that is managed by the garbage collector. This is because garbage collectors are not required to guarantee that the object and its members are finalized in any specific order. All members may have already been finalized when the destructor is executing.
- A class destructor must not allocate new memory that is managed by the garbage collector. This is because garbage collectors are not required to guarantee that they can allocate new objects during a garbage collection cycle.

Violating these rules is undefined behavior. It is easy to see an example of such a problem simply by trying to allocate an object in a class destructor:

```
class C {
    ~this() {
        auto c = new C();   // ← WRONG: Allocates explicitly
        //                          in a class destructor
    }
}
```

```
void main() {
    auto c = new C();
}
```

The program is terminated with an exception:

```
core.exception.InvalidMemoryOperationError@(0)
```

It is equally wrong to allocate new memory *indirectly* from the garbage collector in a destructor. For example, memory used for the elements of a dynamic array is allocated by the garbage collector as well. Using an array in a way that would require allocating a new memory block for the elements is undefined behavior as well:

```
    ~this() {
        auto arr = [ 1 ];    // ← WRONG: Allocates indirectly
                             //           in a class destructor
    }
```

```
core.exception.InvalidMemoryOperationError@(0)
```

Member access
Same as structs, the members are accessed by the *dot* operator:

```
    auto king = new ChessPiece('♔');
    writeln(king.shape);
```

Although the syntax makes it look as if a member of the *variable* is being accessed, it is actually the member of the *object*. Class variables do not have members, the class objects do. The king variable does not have a shape member, the anonymous object does.

Note: *It is usually not proper to access members directly as in the code above. When that exact syntax is desired, properties should be preferred, which will be explained in a later chapter (page 388).*

Operator overloading
Other than the fact that opAssign cannot be overloaded for classes, operator overloading is the same as structs. For classes, the meaning of opAssign is always *associating a class variable with a class object*.

Member functions
Although member functions are defined and used the same way as structs, there is an important difference: Class member functions can be and by-default are *overridable*. We will see this concept later in the Inheritance chapter (page 328).

As overridable member functions have a runtime performance cost, without going into more detail, I recommend that you define all class functions that do not need to be overridden with the final keyword. You can apply this guideline blindly unless there are compilation errors:

```
class C {
    final int func() {    // ← Recommended
        // ...
    }
}
```

Another difference from structs is that some member functions are automatically inherited from the Object class. We will see in the next chapter (page 328) how the definition of toString can be changed by the override keyword.

The is and !is operators

These operators operate on class variables.

is specifies whether two class variables provide access to the same class object. It returns true if the object is the same and false otherwise. !is is the opposite of is.

```
    auto myKing = new ChessPiece('♚');
    auto yourKing = new ChessPiece('♚');
    assert(myKing !is yourKing);
```

Since the objects of myKing and yourKing variables are different, the !is operator returns true. Even though the two objects are constructed by the same character '♚', they are still two separate objects.

When the variables provide access to the same object, is returns true:

```
    auto myKing2 = myKing;
    assert(myKing2 is myKing);
```

Both of the variables above provide access to the same object.

54.2 Summary

- Classes and structs share common features but have big differences.
- Classes are reference types. The new keyword constructs an anonymous *class object* and returns a *class variable*.
- Class variables that are not associated with any object are null. Checking against null must be done by is or !is, not by == or !=.
- The act of copying associates an additional variable with an object. In order to copy class objects, the type must have a special function likely named dup().
- Assignment associates a variable with an object. This behavior cannot be changed.

Inheritance is defining a more specialized type based on an existing more general base type. The specialized type acquires the members of the base type and as a result can be substituted in place of the base type.

Inheritance is available for classes, not structs. The class that inherits another class is called the *subclass*, and the class that gets inherited is called the *superclass*, also called the *base class*.

There are two types of inheritance in D. We will cover *implementation inheritance* in this chapter and leave *interface inheritance* to a later chapter.

When defining a subclass, the superclass is specified after a colon character:

```d
class SubClass : SuperClass {
    // ...
}
```

To see an example of this, let's assume that there is already the following class that represents a clock:

```d
class Clock {
    int hour;
    int minute;
    int second;

    void adjust(int hour, int minute, int second = 0) {
        this.hour = hour;
        this.minute = minute;
        this.second = second;
    }
}
```

Apparently, the members of that class do not need special values during construction; so there is no constructor. Instead, the members are set by the adjust() member function:

```d
auto deskClock = new Clock;
deskClock.adjust(20, 30);
writefln(
    "%02s:%02s:%02s",
    deskClock.hour, deskClock.minute, deskClock.second);
```

Note: *It would be more useful to produce the time string by a toString() function. It will be added later when explaining the override keyword below.*

The output:

```
20:30:00
```

With only that much functionality, Clock could be a struct as well, and depending on the needs of the program, that could be sufficient.

However, being a class makes it possible to inherit from Clock.

To see an example of inheritance, let's consider an AlarmClock that not only includes all of the functionality of Clock, but also provides a way of setting the alarm. Let's first define this type without regard to Clock. If we did that, we would have to include the same three members of Clock and the same adjust() function that adjusted them. AlarmClock would also have other members for its additional functionality:

```d
class AlarmClock {
    int hour;
    int minute;
```

```
    int second;
    int alarmHour;
    int alarmMinute;

    void adjust(int hour, int minute, int second = 0) {
        this.hour = hour;
        this.minute = minute;
        this.second = second;
    }

    void adjustAlarm(int hour, int minute) {
        alarmHour = hour;
        alarmMinute = minute;
    }
}
```

The members that appear exactly in `Clock` are highlighted. As can be seen, defining `Clock` and `AlarmClock` separately results in code duplication.

Inheritance is helpful in such cases. Inheriting `AlarmClock` from `Clock` simplifies the new class and reduces code duplication:

```
class AlarmClock : Clock {
    int alarmHour;
    int alarmMinute;

    void adjustAlarm(int hour, int minute) {
        alarmHour = hour;
        alarmMinute = minute;
    }
}
```

The new definition of `AlarmClock` is the equivalent of the previous one. The highlighted part of the new definition corresponds to the highlighted parts of the old definition.

Because `AlarmClock` inherits the members of `Clock`, it can be used just like a `Clock`:

```
    auto bedSideClock = new AlarmClock;
    bedSideClock.adjust(20, 30);
    bedSideClock.adjustAlarm(7, 0);
```

The members that are inherited from the superclass can be accessed as if they were the members of the subclass:

```
    writefln("%02s:%02s:%02s ♪%02s:%02s",
            bedSideClock.hour,
            bedSideClock.minute,
            bedSideClock.second,
            bedSideClock.alarmHour,
            bedSideClock.alarmMinute);
```

The output:

```
20:30:00 ♪07:00
```

Note: An *AlarmClock.toString* function would be more useful in this case. It will be defined later below.

The inheritance used in this example is *implementation inheritance*.

If we imagine the memory as a ribbon going from top to bottom, the placement of the members of `AlarmClock` in memory can be pictured as in the following illustration:

The illustration above is just to give an idea on how the members of the superclass and the subclass may be combined together. The actual layout of the members depends on the implementation details of the compiler in use. For example, the part that is marked as *other data* typically includes the pointer to the *virtual function table* (vtbl) of that particular class type. The details of the object layout are outside the scope of this book.

55.1 Warning: Inherit only if "is a"

We have seen that implementation inheritance is about acquiring members. Consider this kind of inheritance only if the subtype can be thought of being a kind of the supertype as in the phrase "alarm clock *is a* clock."

"Is a" is not the only relationship between types; a more common relationship is the "has a" relationship. For example, let's assume that we want to add the concept of a Battery to the Clock class. It would not be appropriate to add Battery to Clock by inheritance because the statement "clock is a battery" is not true:

```d
class Clock : Battery {      // ← WRONG DESIGN
    // ...
}
```

A clock is not a battery; it *has a* battery. When there is such a relationship of containment, the type that is contained must be defined as a member of the type that contains it:

```d
class Clock {
    Battery battery;         // ← Correct design
    // ...
}
```

55.2 Inheritance from at most one class

Classes can only inherit from a single base class (which itself can potentially inherit from another single class). In other words, multiple inheritance is not supported in D.

For example, assuming that there is also a SoundEmitter class, and even though "alarm clock is a sound emitting object" is also true, it is not possible to inherit AlarmClock both from Clock and SoundEmitter:

```d
class SoundEmitter {
    // ...
}

class AlarmClock : Clock, SoundEmitter {      // ← compilation ERROR
    // ...
}
```

On the other hand, there is no limit to the number of *interfaces* that a class can inherit from. We will see the interface keyword in a later chapter.

Additionally, there is no limit to how deep the inheritance hierarchy can go:

```
class MusicalInstrument {
    // ...
}

class StringInstrument : MusicalInstrument {
    // ...
}

class Violin : StringInstrument {
    // ...
}
```

The inheritance hierarchy above defines a relationship from the more general to the more specific: musical instrument, string instrument, and violin.

55.3 Hierarchy charts

Types that are related by the "is a" relationship form a *class hierarchy*.

According to OOP conventions, class hierarchies are represented by superclasses being on the top and the subclasses being at the bottom. The inheritance relationships are indicated by arrows pointing from the subclasses to the superclasses.

For example, the following can be a hierarchy of musical instruments:

```
              MusicalInstrument
                 ↗        ↖
    StringInstrument   WindInstrument
         ↗   ↖            ↗    ↖
     Violin  Guitar   Flute   Recorder
```

55.4 Accessing superclass members

The super keyword allows referring to members that are inherited from the superclass.

```
class AlarmClock : Clock {
    // ...

    void foo() {
        super.minute = 10; // The inherited 'minute' member
        minute = 10;       // Same thing if there is no ambiguity
    }
}
```

The super keyword is not always necessary; minute alone has the same meaning in the code above. The super keyword is needed when both the superclass and the subclass have members under the same names. We will see this below when we will need to write super.reset() and super.toString().

If multiple classes in an inheritance tree define a symbol with the same name, one can use the specific name of the class in the inheritance tree to disambiguate between the symbols:

```
class Device {
    string manufacturer;
}

class Clock : Device {
    string manufacturer;
}

class AlarmClock : Clock {
    // ...
```

```
    void foo() {
        Device.manufacturer = "Sunny Horology, Inc.";
        Clock.manufacturer = "Better Watches, Ltd.";
    }
}
```

55.5 Constructing superclass members

The other use of the super keyword is to call the constructor of the superclass. This is similar to calling the overloaded constructors of the current class: this when calling constructors of the current class and super when calling constructors of the superclass.

It is not required to call the superclass constructor explicitly. If the constructor of the subclass makes an explicit call to any overload of super, then that constructor is executed by that call. Otherwise, and if the superclass has a default constructor, it is executed automatically before entering the body of the subclass.

We have not defined constructors for the Clock and AlarmClock classes yet. For that reason, the members of both of those classes are initialized by the .init values of their respective types, which is 0 for int.

Let's assume that Clock has the following constructor:

```
class Clock {
    this(int hour, int minute, int second) {
        this.hour = hour;
        this.minute = minute;
        this.second = second;
    }

    // ...
}
```

That constructor must be used when constructing Clock objects:

```
    auto clock = new Clock(17, 15, 0);
```

Naturally, the programmers who use the Clock type directly would have to use that syntax. However, when constructing an AlarmClock object, they cannot construct its Clock part separately. Besides, the users of AlarmClock need not even know that it inherits from Clock.

A user of AlarmClock should simply construct an AlarmClock object and use it in the program without needing to pay attention to its Clock heritage:

```
    auto bedSideClock = new AlarmClock(/* ... */);
    // ... use as an AlarmClock ...
```

For that reason, constructing the superclass part is the responsibility of the subclass. The subclass calls the constructor of the superclass with the super() syntax:

```
class AlarmClock : Clock {
    this(int hour, int minute, int second,  // for Clock's members
         int alarmHour, int alarmMinute) {   // for AlarmClock's members
        super(hour, minute, second);
        this.alarmHour = alarmHour;
        this.alarmMinute = alarmMinute;
    }

    // ...
}
```

The constructor of `AlarmClock` takes arguments for both its own members and the members of its superclass. It then uses part of those arguments to construct its superclass part.

55.6 Overriding the definitions of member functions

One of the benefits of inheritance is being able to redefine the member functions of the superclass in the subclass. This is called *overriding*: The existing definition of the member function of the superclass is overridden by the subclass with the `override` keyword.

Overridable functions are called *virtual functions*. Virtual functions are implemented by the compiler through *virtual function pointer tables* (vtbl) and *vtbl pointers*. The details of this mechanism are outside the scope of this book. However, it must be known by every system programmer that virtual function calls are more expensive than regular function calls. Every non-private `class` member function in D is virtual by default. For that reason, when a superclass function does not need to be overridden at all, it should be defined as `final` so that it is not virtual. We will see the `final` keyword later in the Interfaces chapter (page 354).

Let's assume that `Clock` has a member function that is used for resetting its members all to zero:

```
class Clock {
    void reset() {
        hour = 0;
        minute = 0;
        second = 0;
    }

    // ...
}
```

That function is inherited by `AlarmClock` and can be called on an `AlarmClock` object:

```
auto bedSideClock = new AlarmClock(20, 30, 0, 7, 0);
// ...
bedSideClock.reset();
```

However, necessarily ignorant of the members of `AlarmClock`, `Clock.reset` can only reset its own members. For that reason, to reset the members of the subclass as well, `reset()` must be overridden:

```
class AlarmClock : Clock {
    override void reset() {
        super.reset();
        alarmHour = 0;
        alarmMinute = 0;
    }

    // ...
}
```

The subclass resets only its own members and dispatches the rest of the task to `Clock` by the `super.reset()` call. Note that writing just `reset()` would not work as it would call the `reset()` function of `AlarmClock` itself. Calling `reset()` from within itself would cause an infinite recursion.

The reason that I have delayed the definition of `toString()` until this point is that it must be defined by the `override` keyword for classes. As we will see in the next chapter, every class is automatically inherited from a superclass called Object and Object already defines a toString() member function.

For that reason, the toString() member function for classes must be defined by using the override keyword:

```d
import std.string;

class Clock {
    override string toString() const {
        return format("%02s:%02s:%02s", hour, minute, second);
    }

    // ...
}

class AlarmClock : Clock {
    override string toString() const {
        return format("%s ♪%02s:%02s", super.toString(),
                      alarmHour, alarmMinute);
    }

    // ...
}
```

Note that AlarmClock is again dispatching some of the task to Clock by the super.toString() call.

Those two overrides of toString() allow converting AlarmClock objects to strings:

```d
void main() {
    auto deskClock = new AlarmClock(10, 15, 0, 6, 45);
    writeln(deskClock);
}
```

The output:

```
10:15:00 ♪06:45
```

55.7 Using the subclass in place of the superclass

Since the superclass is more *general* and the subclass is more *specialized*, objects of a subclass can be used in places where an object of the superclass type is required. This is called *polymorphism*.

The concepts of general and specialized types can be seen in statements like "this type is of that type": "alarm clock is a clock", "student is a person", "cat is an animal", etc. Accordingly, an alarm clock can be used where a clock is needed, a student can be used where a person is needed, and a cat can be used where an animal is needed.

When a subclass object is being used as a superclass object, it does not lose its own specialized type. This is similar to the examples in real life: Using an alarm clock simply as a clock does not change the fact that it is an alarm clock; it would still behave like an alarm clock.

Let's assume that a function takes a Clock object as parameter, which it resets at some point during its execution:

```d
void use(Clock clock) {
    // ...
    clock.reset();
    // ...
}
```

Polymorphism makes it possible to send an AlarmClock to such a function:

```
    auto deskClock = new AlarmClock(10, 15, 0, 6, 45);
    writeln("Before: ", deskClock);
    use(deskClock);
    writeln("After : ", deskClock);
```

This is in accordance with the relationship "alarm clock is a clock." As a result, the members of the deskClock object get reset:

```
Before: 10:15:00 ♪06:45
After : 00:00:00 ♪00:00
```

The important observation here is that not only the members of Clock but also the members of AlarmClock have been reset.

Although use() calls reset() on a Clock object, since the actual object is an AlarmClock, the function that gets called is AlarmClock.reset. According to its definition above, AlarmClock.reset resets the members of both Clock and AlarmClock.

In other words, although use() uses the object as a Clock, the actual object may be an inherited type that behaves in its own special way.

Let's add another class to the Clock hierarchy. The reset() function of this type sets its members to random values:

```
import std.random;

class BrokenClock : Clock {
    this() {
        super(0, 0, 0);
    }

    override void reset() {
        hour = uniform(0, 24);
        minute = uniform(0, 60);
        second = uniform(0, 60);
    }
}
```

When an object of BrokenClock is sent to use(), then the special reset() function of BrokenClock would be called. Again, although it is passed as a Clock, the actual object is still a BrokenClock:

```
    auto shelfClock = new BrokenClock;
    use(shelfClock);
    writeln(shelfClock);
```

The output shows random time values as a result of resetting a BrokenClock:

```
22:46:37
```

55.8 Inheritance is transitive

Polymorphism is not just limited to two classes. Subclasses of subclasses can also be used in place of any superclass in the hierarchy.

Let's consider the MusicalInstrument hierarchy:

```
class MusicalInstrument {
    // ...
}

class StringInstrument : MusicalInstrument {
    // ...
}

class Violin : StringInstrument {
```

```
    // ...
}
```

The inheritances above builds the following relationships: "string instrument is a musical instrument" and "violin is a string instrument." Therefore, it is also true that "violin is a musical instrument." Consequently, a `Violin` object can be used in place of a `MusicalInstrument`.

Assuming that all of the supporting code below has also been defined:

```
void playInTune(MusicalInstrument instrument,
                MusicalPiece piece) {
    instrument.tune();
    instrument.play(piece);
}

// ...

auto myViolin = new Violin;
playInTune(myViolin, improvisation);
```

Although `playInTune()` expects a `MusicalInstrument`, it is being called with a `Violin` due to the relationship "violin is a musical instrument."

Inheritance can be as deep as needed.

55.9 Abstract member functions and abstract classes

Sometimes there are member functions that are natural to appear in a class interface even though that class cannot provide its definition. When there is no *concrete* definition of a member function, that function is an *abstract* member function. A class that has at least one abstract member function is an abstract class.

For example, the `ChessPiece` superclass in a hierarchy may have an `isValid()` member function that determines whether a given move is valid for that chess piece. Since validity of a move depends on the actual type of the chess piece, the `ChessPiece` general class cannot make this decision itself. The valid moves can only be known by the subclasses like Pawn, King, etc.

The `abstract` keyword specifies that the inherited class must implement such a method itself:

```
class ChessPiece {
    abstract bool isValid(Square from, Square to);
}
```

It is not possible to construct objects of abstract classes:

```
    auto piece = new ChessPiece;    // ← compilation ERROR
```

The subclass would have to override and implement all the abstract functions in order to make the class non-abstract and therefore constructible:

```
class Pawn : ChessPiece {
    override bool isValid(Square from, Square to) {
        // ... the implementation of isValid for pawn ...
        return decision;
    }
}
```

It is now possible to construct objects of Pawn:

```
    auto piece = new Pawn;                    // compiles
```

Note that an abstract function may have an implementation of its own, but it would still require the subclass to provide its own implementation of such a function. For example, the ChessPiece'es implementation may provide some useful checks of its own:

```
class ChessPiece {
    abstract bool isValid(Square from, Square to) {
        // We require the 'to' position to be different than
        // the 'from' position
        return from != to;
    }
}

class Pawn : ChessPiece {
    override bool isValid(Square from, Square to) {
        // First verify if it is a valid move for any ChessPiece
        if (!super.isValid(from, to)) {
            return false;
        }

        // ... then check if it is valid for the Pawn ...

        return decision;
    }
}
```

The ChessPiece class is still abstract even though isValid() was already implemented, but the Pawn class is non-abstract and can be instantiated.

55.10 Example

Let's consider a class hierarchy that represents railway vehicles:

```
            RailwayVehicle
          /       |       \
  Locomotive    Train    RailwayCar { load()?, unload()? }
                          /    \
                 PassengerCar    FreightCar
```

The functions that RailwayCar will declare as abstract are indicated by question marks.

Since my goal is only to present a class hierarchy and point out some of its design decisions, I will not fully implement these classes. Instead of doing actual work, they will simply print messages.

The most general class of the hierarchy above is RailwayVehicle. In this program, it will only know how to move itself:

```
class RailwayVehicle {
    void advance(size_t kilometers) {
        writefln("The vehicle is advancing %s kilometers",
                 kilometers);
    }
}
```

A class that inherits from RailwayVehicle is Locomotive, which does not have any special members yet:

```
class Locomotive : RailwayVehicle {
}
```

We will add a special makeSound() member function to Locomotive later during one of the exercises.

RailwayCar is a RailwayVehicle as well. However, if the hierarchy supports different types of railway cars, then certain behaviors like loading and unloading must be done according to their exact types. For that reason, `RailwayCar` can only declare these two functions as abstract:

```
class RailwayCar : RailwayVehicle {
    abstract void load();
    abstract void unload();
}
```

Loading and unloading a passenger car is as simple as opening the doors of the car, while loading and unloading a freight car may involve porters and winches. The following subclasses provide definitions for the abstract functions of `RailwayCar`:

```
class PassengerCar : RailwayCar {
    override void load() {
        writeln("The passengers are getting on");
    }

    override void unload() {
        writeln("The passengers are getting off");
    }
}
class FreightCar : RailwayCar {
    override void load() {
        writeln("The crates are being loaded");
    }

    override void unload() {
        writeln("The crates are being unloaded");
    }
}
```

Being an abstract class does not preclude the use of `RailwayCar` in the program. Objects of `RailwayCar` can not be constructed but `RailwayCar` can be used as an interface. As the subclasses define the two relationships "passenger car is a railway car" and "freight car is a railway car", the objects of `PassengerCar` and `FreightCar` can be used in places of `RailwayCar`. This will be seen in the `Train` class below.

The class that represents a train can consist of a locomotive and an array of railwaycars:

```
class Train : RailwayVehicle {
    Locomotive locomotive;
    RailwayCar[] cars;

    // ...
}
```

I would like to repeat an important point: Although both `Locomotive` and `RailwayCar` inherit from `RailwayVehicle`, it would not be correct to inherit `Train` from either of them. Inheritance models the "is a" relationship and a train is neither a locomotive nor a passenger car. A train consists of them.

If we require that every train must have a locomotive, the `Train` constructor must ensure that it takes a valid `Locomotive` object. Similarly, if the railway cars are optional, they can be added by a member function:

```
import std.exception;
// ...

class Train : RailwayVehicle {
    // ...
```

```
    this(Locomotive locomotive) {
        enforce(locomotive !is null,
                "Locomotive cannot be null");
        this.locomotive = locomotive;
    }

    void addCar(RailwayCar[] cars...) {
        this.cars ~= cars;
    }

    // ...
}
```

Note that addCar() can validate the RailwayCar objects as well. I am ignoring that validation here.

We can imagine that the departures and arrivals of trains should also be supported:

```
class Train : RailwayVehicle {
    // ...

    void departStation(string station) {
        foreach (car; cars) {
            car.load();
        }

        writefln("Departing from %s station", station);
    }

    void arriveStation(string station) {
        writefln("Arriving at %s station", station);

        foreach (car; cars) {
            car.unload();
        }
    }
}
```

The following main() is making use of the RailwayVehicle hierarchy:

```
import std.stdio;

// ...

void main() {
    auto locomotive = new Locomotive;
    auto train = new Train(locomotive);

    train.addCar(new PassengerCar, new FreightCar);

    train.departStation("Ankara");
    train.advance(500);
    train.arriveStation("Haydarpaşa");
}
```

The Train class is being used by functions that are provided by two separate interfaces:

1. When the advance() function is called, the Train object is being used as a RailwayVehicle because that function is declared by RailwayVehicle.
2. When the departStation() and arriveStation() functions are called, train is being used as a Train because those functions are declared by Train.

The arrows indicate that load() and unload() functions work according to the actual type of RailwayCar:

```
The passengers are getting on       ←
The crates are being loaded          ←
Departing from Ankara station
The vehicle is advancing 500 kilometers
Arriving at Haydarpaşa station
The passengers are getting off       ←
The crates are being unloaded        ←
```

55.11 Summary

- Inheritance is used for the "is a" relationship.
- Every class can inherit from up to one class.
- super has two uses: Calling the constructor of the superclass and accessing the members of the superclass.
- override is for redefining member functions of the superclass specially for the subclass.
- abstract requires that a member function must be overridden.

55.12 Exercises

1. Let's modify RailwayVehicle. In addition to reporting the distance that it advances, let's have it also make sounds. To keep the output short, let's print the sounds per 100 kilometers:

```
class RailwayVehicle {
    void advance(size_t kilometers) {
        writefln("The vehicle is advancing %s kilometers",
                 kilometers);

        foreach (i; 0 .. kilometers / 100) {
            writefln("  %s", makeSound());
        }
    }

    // ...
}
```

However, makeSound() cannot be defined by RailwayVehicle because vehicles may have different sounds:

- "choo choo" for Locomotive
- "clack clack" for RailwayCar

Note: *Leave Train.makeSound to the next exercise.*

Because it must be overridden, makeSound() must be declared as abstract by the superclass:

```
class RailwayVehicle {
    // ...

    abstract string makeSound();
}
```

Implement makeSound() for the subclasses and try the code with the following main():

```
void main() {
    auto railwayCar1 = new PassengerCar;
    railwayCar1.advance(100);

    auto railwayCar2 = new FreightCar;
```

```
        railwayCar2.advance(200);

        auto locomotive = new Locomotive;
        locomotive.advance(300);
}
```

Make the program produce the following output:

```
The vehicle is advancing 100 kilometers
    clack clack
The vehicle is advancing 200 kilometers
    clack clack
    clack clack
The vehicle is advancing 300 kilometers
    choo choo
    choo choo
    choo choo
```

Note that there is no requirement that the sounds of PassengerCar and FreightCar be different. They can share the same implemention from RailwayCar.

2. Think about how makeSound() can be implemented for Train. One idea is that Train.makeSound may return a string that consists of the sounds of the members of Train.

The solutions are on page 730.

Classes that do not explicitly inherit any class, automatically inherit the `Object` class.

By that definition, the topmost class in any class hierarchy inherits `Object`:

```
// ": Object" is not written; it is automatic
class MusicalInstrument : Object {
    // ...
}

// Inherits Object indirectly
class StringInstrument : MusicalInstrument {
    // ...
}
```

Since the topmost class inherits `Object`, every class indirectly inherits `Object` as well. In that sense, every class "is an" `Object`.

Every class inherits the following member functions of `Object`:

- `toString`: The `string` representation of the object.
- `opEquals`: Equality comparison with another object.
- `opCmp`: Sort order comparison with another object.
- `toHash`: Associative array hash value.

The last three of these functions emphasize the values of objects. They also make a class eligible for being the key type of associative arrays.

Because these functions are inherited, their redefinitions for the subclasses require the `override` keyword.

Note: *Object defines other members as well. This chapter will include only those four member functions of it.*

56.1 typeid and TypeInfo

`Object` is defined in the `object` module[1] (which is not a part of the `std` package). The `object` module defines `TypeInfo` as well, a class that provides information about types. Every type has a distinct `TypeInfo` object. The `typeid` *expression* provides access to the `TypeInfo` object that is associated with a particular type. As we will see later below, the `TypeInfo` class can be used for determining whether two types are the same, as well as for accessing special functions of a type (`toHash`, `postblit`, etc.).

`TypeInfo` is always about the actual run-time type. For example, although both `Violin` and `Guitar` below inherit `StringInstrument` directly and `MusicalInstrument` indirectly, the `TypeInfo` instances of `Violin` and `Guitar` are different. They are exactly for `Violin` and `Guitar` types, respectively:

```
class MusicalInstrument {
}

class StringInstrument : MusicalInstrument {
}

class Violin : StringInstrument {
}

class Guitar : StringInstrument {
```

---

1. http://dlang.org/phobos/object.html

```
}

void main() {
    TypeInfo v = typeid(Violin);
    TypeInfo g = typeid(Guitar);
    assert(v != g);      // ← the two types are not the same
}
```

The typeid expressions above are being used with *types* like Violin itself. typeid can take an *expression* as well, in which case it returns the TypeInfo object for the run-time type of that expression. For example, the following function takes two parameters of different but related types:

```
import std.stdio;

// ...

void foo(MusicalInstrument m, StringInstrument s) {
    const isSame = (typeid(m) == typeid(s));

    writefln("The types of the arguments are %s.",
             isSame ? "the same" : "different");
}

// ...

    auto a = new Violin();
    auto b = new Violin();
    foo(a, b);
```

Since both arguments to foo() are two Violin objects for that particular call, foo() determines that their types are the same:

```
The types of the arguments are the same.
```

Unlike .sizeof and typeof, which never execute their expressions, typeid always executes the expression that it receives:

```
import std.stdio;

int foo(string when) {
    writefln("Called during '%s'.", when);
    return 0;
}

void main() {
    const s = foo("sizeof").sizeof;        // foo() is not called
    alias T = typeof(foo("typeof"));       // foo() is not called
    auto ti = typeid(foo("typeid"));       // foo() is called
}
```

The output indicates that only the expression of typeid is executed:

```
Called during 'typeid'.
```

The reason for this difference is because actual run-time types of expressions may not be known until those expressions are executed. For example, the exact return type of the following function would be either Violin or Guitar depending on the value of function argument i:

```
MusicalInstrument foo(int i) {
    return (i % 2) ? new Violin() : new Guitar();
}
```

There are various subclasses of TypeInfo for various kinds of types like arrays, structs, classes, etc. Of these, TypeInfo_Class can be particularly useful. For example, the name of the run-time type of an object can be obtained through its `TypeInfo_Class.name` property as a `string`. You can access the `TypeInfo_Class` instance of an object by its `.classinfo` property:

```
TypeInfo_Class info = a.classinfo;
string runtimeTypeName = info.name;
```

56.2 toString

Same with structs, `toString` enables using class objects as strings:

```
auto clock = new Clock(20, 30, 0);
writeln(clock);          // Calls clock.toString()
```

The inherited `toString()` is usually not useful; it produces just the name of the type:

```
deneme.Clock
```

The part before the name of the type is the name of the module. The output above indicates that `Clock` has been defined in the deneme module.

As we have seen in the previous chapter, this function is almost always overridden to produce a more meaningful `string` representation:

```
import std.string;

class Clock {
    override string toString() const {
        return format("%02s:%02s:%02s", hour, minute, second);
    }

    // ...
}

class AlarmClock : Clock {
    override string toString() const {
        return format("%s ♪%02s:%02s", super.toString(),
                      alarmHour, alarmMinute);
    }

    // ...
}

// ...

    auto bedSideClock = new AlarmClock(20, 30, 0, 7, 0);
    writeln(bedSideClock);
```

The output:

```
20:30:00 ♪07:00
```

56.3 opEquals

As we have seen in the Operator Overloading chapter (page 298), this member function is about the behavior of the `==` operator (and the `!=` operator indirectly). The return value of the operator must be `true` if the objects are considered to be equal and `false` otherwise.

Warning: The definition of this function must be consistent with `opCmp()`; for two objects that `opEquals()` returns `true`, `opCmp()` must return zero.

Contrary to structs, the compiler does not call `a.opEquals(b)` right away when it sees the expression `a == b`. When two class objects are compared by the `==` operator, a four-step algorithm is executed:

```
bool opEquals(Object a, Object b) {
    if (a is b) return true;                         // (1)
    if (a is null || b is null) return false;        // (2)
    if (typeid(a) == typeid(b)) return a.opEquals(b); // (3)
    return a.opEquals(b) && b.opEquals(a);           // (4)
}
```

1. If the two variables provide access to the same object (or they are both null), then they are equal.
2. Following from the previous check, if only one is null then they are not equal.
3. If both of the objects are of the same type, then a.opEquals(b) is called to determine the equality.
4. Otherwise, for the two objects to be considered equal, opEquals must have been defined for both of their types and a.opEquals(b) and b.opEquals(a) must agree that the objects are equal.

Accordingly, if opEquals() is not provided for a class type, then the values of the objects are not considered; rather, equality is determined by checking whether the two class variables provide access to the same object:

```
    auto variable0 = new Clock(6, 7, 8);
    auto variable1 = new Clock(6, 7, 8);

    assert(variable0 != variable1); // They are not equal
                                    // because the objects are
                                    // different
```

Even though the two objects are constructed by the same arguments above, the variables are not equal because they are not associated with the same object.

On the other hand, because the following two variables provide access to the same object, they are *equal*:

```
    auto partner0 = new Clock(9, 10, 11);
    auto partner1 = partner0;

    assert(partner0 == partner1);   // They are equal because
                                    // the object is the same
```

Sometimes it makes more sense to compare objects by their values instead of their identities. For example, it is conceivable that variable0 and variable1 above compare equal because their values are the same.

Different from structs, the type of the parameter of opEquals for classes is Object:

```
class Clock {
    override bool opEquals(Object o) const {
        // ...
    }

    // ...
}
```

As you will see below, the parameter is almost never used directly. For that reason, it should be acceptable to name it simply as o. Most of the time the first thing to do with that parameter is to use it in a type conversion.

The parameter of opEquals is the object that appears on the right-hand side of the == operator:

```
    variable0 == variable1;    // o represents variable1
```

Since the purpose of opEquals() is to compare two objects of this class type, the first thing to do is to convert o to a variable of the same type of this class. Since it would not be appropriate to modify the right-hand side object in an equality comparison, it is also proper to convert the type as const:

```d
override bool opEquals(Object o) const {
    auto rhs = cast(const Clock)o;

    // ...
}
```

As you would remember, rhs is a common abbreviation for *right-hand side*. Also, std.conv.to can be used for the conversion as well:

```d
import std.conv;
// ...
    auto rhs = to!(const Clock)(o);
```

If the original object on the right-hand side can be converted to Clock, then rhs becomes a non-null class variable. Otherwise, rhs is set to null, indicating that the objects are not of the same type.

According to the design of a program, it may make sense to compare objects of two incompatible types. I will assume here that for the comparison to be valid, rhs must not be null; so, the first logical expression in the following return statement checks that it is not null. Otherwise, it would be an error to try to access the members of rhs:

```d
class Clock {
    int hour;
    int minute;
    int second;

    override bool opEquals(Object o) const {
        auto rhs = cast(const Clock)o;

        return (rhs &&
                (hour == rhs.hour) &&
                (minute == rhs.minute) &&
                (second == rhs.second));
    }

    // ...
}
```

With that definition, Clock objects can now be compared by their values:

```d
    auto variable0 = new Clock(6, 7, 8);
    auto variable1 = new Clock(6, 7, 8);

    assert(variable0 == variable1); // Now they are equal
                                    // because their values
                                    // are equal
```

When defining opEquals it is important to remember the members of the superclass. For example, when comparing objects of AlarmClock it would make sense to also consider the inherited members:

```d
class AlarmClock : Clock {
    int alarmHour;
    int alarmMinute;

    override bool opEquals(Object o) const {
        auto rhs = cast(const AlarmClock)o;
```

```
        return (rhs &&
                (alarmHour == rhs.alarmHour) &&
                (alarmMinute == rhs.alarmMinute) &&
                super.opEquals(o));
    }

    // ...
}
```

That expression could be written as super == o as well. However, that would initiate the four-step algorithm again and as a result, the code might be a little slower.

56.4 opCmp

This operator is used when sorting class objects. opCmp is the function that gets called behind the scenes for the <, <=, >, and >=.

This operator must return a negative value when the left-hand object is before, a positive value when the left-hand object is after, and zero when both objects have the same sorting order.

Warning: The definition of this function must be consistent with opEquals(); for two objects that opEquals() returns true, opCmp() must return zero.

Unlike toString and opEquals, there is no default implementation of this function in Object. If the implementation is not available, comparing objects for sort order causes an exception to be thrown:

```
    auto variable0 = new Clock(6, 7, 8);
    auto variable1 = new Clock(6, 7, 8);

    assert(variable0 <= variable1);      // ← Causes exception
```

```
object.Exception: need opCmp for class deneme.Clock
```

It is up to the design of the program what happens when the left-hand and right-hand objects are of different types. One way is to take advantage of the order of types that is maintained by the compiler automatically. This is achieved by calling the opCmp function on the typeid values of the two types:

```
class Clock {
    int hour;
    int minute;
    int second;

    override int opCmp(Object o) const {
        /* Taking advantage of the automatically-maintained
         * order of the types. */
        if (typeid(this) != typeid(o)) {
            return typeid(this).opCmp(typeid(o));
        }

        auto rhs = cast(const Clock)o;
        /* No need to check whether rhs is null, because it is
         * known at this line that it has the same type as o. */

        if (hour != rhs.hour) {
            return hour - rhs.hour;

        } else if (minute != rhs.minute) {
            return minute - rhs.minute;

        } else {
            return second - rhs.second;
        }
    }
```

```
        // ...
}
```

The definition above first checks whether the types of the two objects are the same. If not, it uses the ordering of the types themselves. Otherwise, it compares the objects by the values of their hour, minute, and second members.

A chain of ternary operators may also be used:

```
    override int opCmp(Object o) const {
        if (typeid(this) != typeid(o)) {
            return typeid(this).opCmp(typeid(o));
        }

        auto rhs = cast(const Clock)o;

        return (hour != rhs.hour
                    ? hour - rhs.hour
                    : (minute != rhs.minute
                        ? minute - rhs.minute
                        : second - rhs.second));
    }
```

If important, the comparison of the members of the superclass must also be considered. The following AlarmClock.opCmp is calling Clock.opCmp first:

```
class AlarmClock : Clock {
    override int opCmp(Object o) const {
        auto rhs = cast(const AlarmClock)o;

        const int superResult = super.opCmp(o);

        if (superResult != 0) {
            return superResult;

        } else if (alarmHour != rhs.alarmHour) {
            return alarmHour - rhs.alarmHour;

        } else {
            return alarmMinute - rhs.alarmMinute;
        }
    }

    // ...
}
```

Above, if the superclass comparison returns a nonzero value then that result is used because the sort order of the objects is already determined by that value.

AlarmClock objects can now be compared for their sort orders:

```
    auto ac0 = new AlarmClock(8, 0, 0, 6, 30);
    auto ac1 = new AlarmClock(8, 0, 0, 6, 31);

    assert(ac0 < ac1);
```

opCmp is used by other language features and libraries as well. For example, the sort() function takes advantage of opCmp when sorting elements.

opCmp for string members

When some of the members are strings, they can be compared explicitly to return a negative, positive, or zero value:

```
import std.exception;

class Student {
    string name;
```

```
    override int opCmp(Object o) const {
        auto rhs = cast(Student)o;
        enforce(rhs);

        if (name < rhs.name) {
            return -1;

        } else if (name > rhs.name) {
            return 1;

        } else {
            return 0;
        }
    }

    // ...
}
```

Instead, the existing `std.algorithm.cmp` function can be used, which happens to be faster as well:

```
import std.algorithm;

class Student {
    string name;

    override int opCmp(Object o) const {
        auto rhs = cast(Student)o;
        enforce(rhs);

        return cmp(name, rhs.name);
    }

    // ...
}
```

Also note that `Student` does not support comparing incompatible types by enforcing that the conversion from `Object` to `Student` is possible.

56.5 toHash

This function allows objects of a class type to be used as associative array *keys*. It does not affect the cases where the type is used as associative array *values*. If this function is defined, `opEquals` must be defined as well.

Hash table indexes

Associative arrays are a hash table implementation. Hash table is a very fast data structure when it comes to searching elements in the table. (*Note: Like most other things in software, this speed comes at a cost: Hash tables must keep elements in an unordered way, and they may be taking up space that is more than exactly necessary.*)

The high speed of hash tables comes from the fact that they first produce integer values for keys. These integers are called *hash values*. The hash values are then used for indexing into an internal array that is maintained by the table.

A benefit of this method is that any type that can produce unique integer values for its objects can be used as the key type of associative arrays. `toHash` is the function that returns the hash value for an object.

Even `Clock` objects can be used as associative array key values:

```
    string[Clock] timeTags;
    timeTags[new Clock(12, 0, 0)] = "Noon";
```

The default definition of `toHash` that is inherited from `Clock` produces different hash values for different objects without regard to their values. This is similar to how the default behavior of opEquals considers different objects as being not equal.

The code above compiles and runs even when there is no special definition of toHash for Clock. However, its default behavior is almost never what is desired. To see that default behavior, let's try to access an element by an object that is different from the one that has been used when inserting the element. Although the new Clock object below has the same value as the Clock object that has been used when inserting into the associative array above, the value cannot be found:

```
if (new Clock(12, 0, 0) in timeTags) {
    writeln("Exists");

} else {
    writeln("Missing");
}
```

According to the in operator, there is no element in the table that corresponds to the value Clock(12, 0, 0):

```
Missing
```

The reason for this surprising behavior is that the key object that has been used when inserting the element is not the same as the key object that has been used when accessing the element.

Selecting members for toHash
Although the hash value is calculated from the members of an object, not every member is suitable for this task.

The candidates are the members that distinguish objects from each other. For example, the members name and lastName of a Student class would be suitable if those members can be used for identifying objects of that type.

On the other hand, a grades array of a Student class would not be suitable both because many objects may have the same array and also it is likely that the grades array may change over time.

Calculating hash values
The choice of hash values has a direct effect on the performance of associative arrays. Furthermore, a hash calculation that is effective on one type of data may not be as effective on another type of data. As *hash algorithms* are beyond the scope of this book, I will give just one guideline here: In general, it is better to produce different hash values for objects that are considered to have different values. However, it is not an error if two objects with different values produce the same index value; it is merely undesirable for performance reasons.

It is conceivable that all of the members of Clock are significant to distinguish its objects from each other. For that reason, the hash values can be calculated from the values of its three members. *The number of seconds since midnight* would be effective hash values for objects that represent different points in time:

```
class Clock {
    int hour;
    int minute;
    int second;

    override size_t toHash() const {
        /* Because there are 3600 seconds in an hour and 60
         * seconds in a minute: */
        return (3600 * hour) + (60 * minute) + second;
    }
```

```
    // ...
}
```

Whenever `Clock` is used as the key type of associative arrays, that special definition of `toHash` would be used. As a result, even though the two key objects of `Clock(12, 0, 0)` above are distinct, they would now produce the same hash value.

The new output:

```
Exists
```

Similar to the other member functions, the superclass may need to be considered as well. For example, `AlarmClock.toHash` can take advantage of `Clock.toHash` during its index calculation:

```
class AlarmClock : Clock {
    int alarmHour;
    int alarmMinute;

    override size t toHash() const {
        return super.toHash() + alarmHour + alarmMinute;
    }

    // ...
}
```

Note: *Take the calculation above just as an example. In general, adding integer values is not an effective way of generating hash values.*

There are existing efficient algorithms for calculating hash values for variables of floating point, array, and struct types. These algorithms are available to the programmer as well.

What needs to be done is to call `getHash()` on the `typeid` of each member. The syntax of this method is the same for floating point, array, and struct types.

For example, hash values of a `Student` type can be calculated from its name member as in the following code:

```
class Student {
    string name;

    override size_t toHash() const {
        return typeid(name).getHash(&name);
    }

    // ...
}
```

Hash values for structs

Since structs are value types, hash values for their objects are calculated automatically by an efficient algorithm. That algorithm takes all of the members of the object into consideration.

When there is a specific reason like needing to exclude certain members from the hash calculation, `toHash()` can be overridden for structs as well.

56.6 Exercises

1. Start with the following class, which represents colored points:

```
enum Color { blue, green, red }

class Point {
    int x;
```

```
    int y;
    Color color;

    this(int x, int y, Color color) {
        this.x = x;
        this.y = y;
        this.color = color;
    }
}
```

Implement opEquals for this class in a way that ignores colors. When implemented in that way, the following assert check should pass:

```
// Different colors
auto bluePoint = new Point(1, 2, Color.blue);
auto greenPoint = new Point(1, 2, Color.green);

// They are still equal
assert(bluePoint == greenPoint);
```

2. Implement opCmp by considering first x then y. The following assert checks should pass:

```
auto redPoint1 = new Point(-1, 10, Color.red);
auto redPoint2 = new Point(-2, 10, Color.red);
auto redPoint3 = new Point(-2,  7, Color.red);

assert(redPoint1 < bluePoint);
assert(redPoint3 < redPoint2);

/* Even though blue is before green in enum Color,
 * because color is being ignored, bluePoint must not be
 * before greenPoint. */
assert(!(bluePoint < greenPoint));
```

Like the Student class above, you can implement opCmp by excluding incompatible types by the help of enforce.

3. Consider the following class that combines three Point objects in an array:

```
class TriangularArea {
    Point[3] points;

    this(Point one, Point two, Point three) {
        points = [ one, two, three ];
    }
}
```

Implement toHash for that class. Again, the following assert checks should pass:

```
/* area1 and area2 are constructed by distinct points that
 * happen to have the same values. (Remember that
 * bluePoint and greenPoint should be considered equal.) */
auto area1 = new TriangularArea(bluePoint, greenPoint, redPoint1);
auto area2 = new TriangularArea(greenPoint, bluePoint, redPoint1);

// The areas should be equal
assert(area1 == area2);

// An associative array
double[TriangularArea] areas;

// A value is being entered by area1
areas[area1] = 1.25;

// The value is being accessed by area2
assert(area2 in areas);
assert(areas[area2] == 1.25);
```

Remember that opEquals must also be defined when toHash is defined.

The solutions are on page 732.

57 Interfaces

The `interface` keyword is for defining interfaces in class hierarchies. `interface` is very similar to `class` with the following restrictions:

- The member functions that it declares (but not implements) are abstract even without the `abstract` keyword.
- The member functions that it implements must be `static` or `final`. (`static` and `final` member functions are explained below.)
- Its member variables must be `static`.
- Interfaces can inherit only interfaces.

Despite these restrictions, there is no limit on the number of `interface`s that a class can inherit from. (In contrast, a class can inherit from up to one `class`.)

57.1 Definition

Interfaces are defined by the `interface` keyword, the same way as classes:

```
interface SoundEmitter {
    // ...
}
```

An `interface` is for declaring member functions that are implicitly abstract:

```
interface SoundEmitter {
    string emitSound();    // Declared (not implemented)
}
```

Classes that inherit from that interface would have to provide the implementations of the abstract functions of the interface.

Interface function declarations can have `in` and `out` contract blocks:

```
interface I {
    int func(int i)
    in {
        /* Strictest requirements that the callers of this
         * function must meet. (Derived interfaces and classes
         * can loosen these requirements.) */

    } out {    // (optionally with (result) parameter)
        /* Exit guarantees that the implementations of this
         * function must give. (Derived interfaces and classes
         * can give additional guarantees.) */
    }
}
```

We will see examples of contract inheritance later in the Contract Programming for Structs and Classes chapter (page 393).

57.2 Inheriting from an `interface`

The `interface` inheritance syntax is the same as `class` inheritance:

```
class Violin : SoundEmitter {
    string emitSound() {
        return "♩♪♫";
    }
}

class Bell : SoundEmitter {
    string emitSound() {
        return "ding";
```

```
    }
}
```

Interfaces support polymorphism: Functions that take interface parameters can use those parameters without needing to know the actual types of objects. For example, the following function that takes a parameter of SoundEmitter calls emitSound() on that parameter without needing to know the actual type of the object:

```
void useSoundEmittingObject(SoundEmitter object) {
    // ... some operations ...
    writeln(object.emitSound());
    // ... more operations ...
}
```

Just like with classes, that function can be called with any type of object that inherits from the SoundEmitter interface:

```
    useSoundEmittingObject(new Violin);
    useSoundEmittingObject(new Bell);
```

The special emitSound() function for each object would get called and the outputs of Violin.emitSound and Bell.emitSound would be printed:

```
♪♪
ding
```

57.3 Inheriting from more than one `interface`

A class can be inherited from up to one class. There is no limit on the number of interfaces to inherit from.

Let's consider the following interface that represents communication devices:

```
interface CommunicationDevice {
    void talk(string message);
    string listen();
}
```

If a Phone class needs to be used both as a sound emitter and a communication device, it can inherit both of those interfaces:

```
class Phone : SoundEmitter, CommunicationDevice {
    // ...
}
```

That definition represents both of these relationships: "phone is a sound emitter" and "phone is a communication device."

In order to construct objects of this class, Phone must implement the abstract functions of both of the interfaces:

```
class Phone : SoundEmitter, CommunicationDevice {
    string emitSound() {           // for SoundEmitter
        return "rrring";
    }

    void talk(string message) {    // for CommunicationDevice
        // ... put the message on the line ...
    }

    string listen() {              // for CommunicationDevice
        string soundOnTheLine;
        // ... get the message from the line ...
        return soundOnTheLine;
```

```
        }
}
```

A class can inherit from any number of interfaces as it makes sense according to the design of the program.

57.4 Inheriting from `interface` and `class`

Classes can still inherit from up to one `class` as well:

```
class Clock {
    // ... clock implementation ...
}

class AlarmClock : Clock, SoundEmitter {
    string emitSound() {
        return "beep";
    }
}
```

`AlarmClock` inherits the members of `Clock`. Additionally, it also provides the `emitSound()` function that the `SoundEmitter` interface requires.

57.5 Inheriting `interface` from `interface`

An interface that is inherited from another interface effectively increases the number of functions that the subclasses must implement:

```
interface MusicalInstrument : SoundEmitter {
    void adjustTuning();
}
```

According to the definition above, in order to be a `MusicalInstrument`, both the `emitSound()` function that `SoundEmitter` requires and the `adjustTuning()` function that `MusicalInstrument` requires must be implemented.

For example, if `Violin` inherits from `MusicalInstrument` instead of `SoundEmitter`, it must now also implement `adjustTuning()`:

```
class Violin : MusicalInstrument {
    string emitSound() {      // for SoundEmitter
        return "♩♪♪";
    }

    void adjustTuning() {     // for MusicalInstrument
        // ... special tuning of the violin ...
    }
}
```

57.6 `static` member functions

I have delayed explaining `static` member functions until this chapter to keep the earlier chapters shorter. `static` member functions are available for structs, classes, and interfaces.

Regular member functions are always called on an object. The member variables that are referenced inside the member function are the members of a particular object:

```
struct Foo {
    int i;

    void modify(int value) {
        i = value;
    }
}
```

```
void main() {
    auto object0 = Foo();
    auto object1 = Foo();

    object0.modify(10);    // object0.i changes
    object1.modify(10);    // object1.i changes
}
```

The members can also be referenced by this:

```
void modify(int value) {
    this.i = value;    // equivalent of the previous one
}
```

A static member function does not operate on an object; there is no object that the this keyword would refer to, so this is not valid inside a static function. For that reason, none of the regular member variables are available inside static member functions:

```
struct Foo {
    int i;

    static void commonFunction(int value) {
        i = value;          // ← compilation ERROR
        this.i = value;     // ← compilation ERROR
    }
}
```

static member functions can use only the static member variables.

Let's redesign the Point struct that we have seen earlier in the Structs chapter (page 246), this time with a static member function. In the following code, every Point object gets a unique id, which is determined by a static member function:

```
import std.stdio;

struct Point {
    size_t id;    // Object id
    int line;
    int column;

    // The id to be used for the next object
    static size_t nextId;

    this(int line, int column) {
        this.line = line;
        this.column = column;
        this.id = makeNewId();
    }

    static size_t makeNewId() {
        immutable newId = nextId;
        ++nextId;
        return newId;
    }
}

void main() {
    auto top = Point(7, 0);
    auto middle = Point(8, 0);
    auto bottom =  Point(9, 0);

    writeln(top.id);
    writeln(middle.id);
    writeln(bottom.id);
}
```

The static makeNewId() function can use the common variable nextId. As a result, every object gets a unique id:

```
0
1
2
```

Although the example above contains a `struct`, `static` member functions are available for classes and interfaces as well.

57.7 `final` member functions

I have delayed explaining `final` member functions until this chapter to keep the earlier chapters shorter. `final` member functions are relevant only for classes and interfaces because structs do not support inheritance.

`final` specifies that a member function cannot be redefined by a subclass. In a sense, the implementation that this `class` or `interface` provides is the *final* implementation of that function. An example of a case where this feature is useful is where the general steps of an algorithm are defined by an interface and the finer details are left to subclasses.

Let's see an example of this with a Game interface. The general steps of playing a game is being determined by the `play()` function of the following `interface`:

```
interface Game {
    final void play() {
        string name = gameName();
        writefln("Starting %s", name);

        introducePlayers();
        prepare();
        begin();
        end();

        writefln("Ending %s", name);
    }

    string gameName();
    void introducePlayers();
    void prepare();
    void begin();
    void end();
}
```

It is not possible for subclasses to modify the definition of the `play()` member function. The subclasses can (and must) provide the definitions of the five abstract member functions that are declared by the interface. By doing so, the subclasses complete the missing steps of the algorithm:

```
import std.stdio;
import std.string;
import std.random;
import std.conv;

class DiceSummingGame : Game {
    string player;
    size_t count;
    size_t sum;

    string gameName() {
        return "Dice Summing Game";
    }

    void introducePlayers() {
        write("What is your name? ");
        player = strip(readln());
    }

    void prepare() {
        write("How many times to throw the dice? ");
```

```
            readf(" %s", &count);
            sum = 0;
        }

        void begin() {
            foreach (i; 0 .. count) {
                immutable dice = uniform(1, 7);
                writefln("%s: %s", i, dice);
                sum += dice;
            }
        }

        void end() {
            writefln("Player: %s, Dice sum: %s, Average: %s",
                     player, sum, to!double(sum) / count);
        }
    }

    void useGame(Game game) {
        game.play();
    }

    void main() {
        useGame(new DiceSummingGame());
    }
```

Although the example above contains an `interface`, `final` member functions are available for classes as well.

57.8 How to use

`interface` is a commonly used feature. There is one or more `interface` at the top of almost every class hierarchy. A kind of hierarchy that is commonly encountered in programs involves a single `interface` and a number of classes that implement that interface:

```
            MusicalInstrument
               (interface)
           /    |    \    \
      Violin  Guitar  Flute  ...
```

Although there are more complicated hierarchies in practice, the simple hierarchy above solves many problems.

It is also common to move common implementation details of class hierarchies to intermediate classes. The subclasses inherit from these intermediate classes. The `StringInstrument` and `WindInstrument` classes below can contain the common members of their respective subclasses:

```
              MusicalInstrument
                 (interface)
              /              \
   StringInstrument        WindInstrument
   /    |    \             /    |    \
Violin  Viola   ...    Flute  Clarinet  ...
```

The subclasses would implement their respective special definitions of member functions.

57.9 Abstraction

Interfaces help make parts of programs independent from each other. This is called *abstraction*. For example, a program that deals with musical instruments can be written primarily by using the `MusicalInstrument` interface, without ever specifying the actual types of the musical instruments.

A Musician class can contain a `MusicalInstrument` without ever knowing the actual type of the instrument:

```
class Musician {
    MusicalInstrument instrument;
    // ...
}
```

Different types of musical instruments can be combined in a collection without regard to the actual types of these instruments:

```
    MusicalInstrument[] orchestraInstruments;
```

Most of the functions of the program can be written only by using this interface:

```
bool needsTuning(MusicalInstrument instrument) {
    bool result;
    // ...
    return result;
}

void playInTune(MusicalInstrument instrument) {
    if (needsTuning(instrument)) {
        instrument.adjustTuning();
    }

    writeln(instrument.emitSound());
}
```

Abstracting away parts of a program from each other allows making changes in one part of the program without needing to modify the other parts. When implementations of certain parts of the program are *behind* a particular interface, the code that uses only that interface does not get affected.

57.10 Example

The following program defines the `SoundEmitter`, `MusicalInstrument`, and `CommunicationDevice` interfaces:

```
import std.stdio;

/* This interface requires emitSound(). */
interface SoundEmitter {
    string emitSound();
}

/* This class needs to implement only emitSound(). */
class Bell : SoundEmitter {
    string emitSound() {
        return "ding";
    }
}

/* This interface additionally requires adjustTuning(). */
interface MusicalInstrument : SoundEmitter {
    void adjustTuning();
}

/* This class needs to implement both emitSound() and
 * adjustTuning(). */
class Violin : MusicalInstrument {
    string emitSound() {
        return "♩♪♪";
    }

    void adjustTuning() {
        // ... tuning of the violin ...
    }
```

```
}

/* This interface requires talk() and listen(). */
interface CommunicationDevice {
    void talk(string message);
    string listen();
}

/* This class needs to implement emitSound(), talk(), and
 * listen(). */
class Phone : SoundEmitter, CommunicationDevice {
    string emitSound() {
        return "rrring";
    }

    void talk(string message) {
        // ... put the message on the line ...
    }

    string listen() {
        string soundOnTheLine;
        // ... get the message from the line ...
        return soundOnTheLine;
    }
}

class Clock {
    // ... the implementation of Clock ...
}

/* This class needs to implement only emitSound(). */
class AlarmClock : Clock, SoundEmitter {
    string emitSound() {
        return "beep";
    }

    // ... the implementation of AlarmClock ...
}

void main() {
    SoundEmitter[] devices;

    devices ~= new Bell;
    devices ~= new Violin;
    devices ~= new Phone;
    devices ~= new AlarmClock;

    foreach (device; devices) {
        writeln(device.emitSound());
    }
}
```

Because devices is a SoundEmitter slice, it can contain objects of any type that inherits from SoundEmitter (i.e. types that have an "is a" relationship with SoundEmitter). As a result, the output of the program consists of different sounds that are emitted by the different types of objects:

```
ding
♪♪♪
rrring
beep
```

57.11 Summary

- interface is similar to a class that consists only of abstract functions. interface can have static member variables and static or final member functions.

- For a class to be constructible, it must have implementations for all member functions of all interfaces that it inherits from.
- It is possible to inherit from unlimited number of `interfaces`.
- A common hierarchy consists of a single `interface` and a number of subclasses that implement that interface.

We have seen the lifetimes of objects in the Lifetimes and Fundamental Operations chapter (page 228).

In later chapters, we have seen that the objects are prepared for use in the constructor, which is called `this()`; and the final operations of objects are applied in the destructor, which is called `~this()`.

For structs and other value types, the destructor is executed at the time when the lifetime of an object ends. For classes and other reference types, it is executed by the garbage collector some time in the future. The important distinction is that the destructor of a class object is not executed when its lifetime ends.

System resources are commonly returned back to the system in destructors. For example, `std.stdio.File` returns the file resource back to the operating system in its destructor. As it is not certain when the destructor of a class object will be called, the system resources that it holds may not be returned until too late when other objects cannot get a hold of the same resource.

58.1 An example of calling destructors late

Let's define a class to see the effects of executing class destructors late. The following constructor increments a `static` counter, and the destructor decrements it. As you remember, there is only one of each `static` member, which is shared by all of the objects of a type. Such a counter would indicate the number of objects that are yet to be destroyed.

```
class LifetimeObserved {
    int[] array;          // ← Belongs to each object

    static size_t counter; // ← Shared by all objects

    this() {
        /* We are using a relatively large array to make each
         * object consume a large amount of memory. Hopefully
         * this will make the garbage collector call object
         * destructors more frequently to open up space for
         * more objects. */
        array.length = 30_000;

        /* Increment the counter for this object that is being
         * constructed. */
        ++counter;
    }

    ~this() {
        /* Decrement the counter for this object that is being
         * destroyed. */
        --counter;
    }
}
```

The following program constructs objects of that class inside a loop:

```
import std.stdio;

void main() {
    foreach (i; 0 .. 20) {
        auto variable = new LifetimeObserved;  // ← start
        write(LifetimeObserved.counter, ' ');
    } // ← end

    writeln();
}
```

The lifetime of each `LifetimeObserved` object is in fact very short: Its life starts when it is constructed by the new keyword and ends at the closing curly bracket of the `foreach` loop. Each object then becomes the responsibility of the garbage collector. The `start` and `end` comments indicate the start and end of the lifetimes.

Even though there is up to one object alive at a given time, the value of the counter indicates that the destructor is not executed when the lifetime ends:

```
1 2 3 4 5 6 7 8 2 3 4 5 6 7 8 2 3 4 5 6
```

According to that output, the memory sweep algorithm of the garbage collector has delayed executing the destructor for up to 8 objects. (*Note: The output may be different depending on the garbage collection algorithm, available memory, and other factors.*)

58.2 `destroy()` to execute the destructor

`destroy()` executes the destructor for an object:

```d
void main() {
    foreach (i; 0 .. 20) {
        auto variable = new LifetimeObserved;
        write(LifetimeObserved.counter, ' ');
        destroy(variable);
    }

    writeln();
}
```

Like before, the value of `LifetimeObserved.counter` is incremented by the constructor as a result of new, and becomes 1. This time, right after it gets printed, `destroy()` executes the destructor for the object and the value of the counter is decremented again down to zero. For that reason, this time its value is always 1:

```
1 1 1 1 1 1 1 1 1 1 1 1 1 1 1 1 1 1 1 1
```

Once destroyed, the object should be considered to be in an invalid state and must not be used anymore:

```d
    destroy(variable);
    // ...
    // Warning: Using a potentially invalid object
    writeln(variable.array);
```

Although `destroy()` is primarily for reference types, it can also be called on `struct` objects to destroy them before the end of their normal lifetimes.

58.3 When to use

As has been seen in the previous example, `destroy()` is used when resources need to be released at a specific time without relying on the garbage collector.

58.4 Example

We had designed an `XmlElement` struct in the Constructor and Other Special Functions chapter (page 279). That struct was being used for printing XML elements in the format `<tag>value</tag>`. Printing the closing tag has been the responsibility of the destructor:

```d
struct XmlElement {
    // ...

    ~this() {
```

```
            writeln(indentation, "</", name, '>');
        }
}
```

The following output was produced by a program that used that struct. This time, I am replacing the word "class" with "course" to avoid confusing it with the `class` keyword:

```
<courses>
  <course0>
    <grade>
      72
    </grade>        ← The closing tags appear on correct lines
    <grade>
      97
    </grade>        ←
    <grade>
      90
    </grade>        ←
  </course0>        ←
  <course1>
    <grade>
      77
    </grade>        ←
    <grade>
      87
    </grade>        ←
    <grade>
      56
    </grade>        ←
  </course1>        ←
</courses>          ←
```

The previous output happens to be correct because `XmlElement` is a `struct`. The desired output is achieved simply by placing the objects in appropriate scopes:

```
void main() {
    const courses = XmlElement("courses", 0);

    foreach (courseId; 0 .. 2) {
        const courseTag = "course" ~ to!string(courseId);
        const courseElement = XmlElement(courseTag, 1);

        foreach (i; 0 .. 3) {
            const gradeElement = XmlElement("grade", 2);
            const randomGrade = uniform(50, 101);

            writeln(indentationString(3), randomGrade);

        } // ← gradeElement is destroyed

    } // ← courseElement is destroyed

} // ← courses is destroyed
```

The destructor prints the closing tags as the objects gets destroyed.

To see how classes behave differently, let's convert `XmlElement` to a class:

```
import std.stdio;
import std.array;
import std.random;
import std.conv;

string indentationString(int level) {
    return replicate(" ", level * 2);
}

class XmlElement {
    string name;
    string indentation;
```

```
    this(string name, int level) {
        this.name = name;
        this.indentation = indentationString(level);

        writeln(indentation, '<', name, '>');
    }

    ~this() {
        writeln(indentation, "</", name, '>');
    }
}

void main() {
    const courses = new XmlElement("courses", 0);

    foreach (courseId; 0 .. 2) {
        const courseTag = "course" ~ to!string(courseId);
        const courseElement = new XmlElement(courseTag, 1);

        foreach (i; 0 .. 3) {
            const gradeElement = new XmlElement("grade", 2);
            const randomGrade = uniform(50, 101);

            writeln(indentationString(3), randomGrade);
        }
    }
}
```

As the responsibility of calling the destructors are now left to the garbage collector, the program does not produce the desired output:

```
<courses>
  <course0>
    <grade>
      57
    <grade>
      98
    <grade>
      87
  <course1>
    <grade>
      84
    <grade>
      60
    <grade>
      99
    </grade>     ← The closing tags appear at the end
    </grade>     ←
    </grade>     ←
  </course1>     ←
    </grade>     ←
    </grade>     ←
    </grade>     ←
  </course0>     ←
</courses>       ←
```

The destructor is still executed for every object but this time at the end when the program is exiting. (*Note: The garbage collector does not guarantee that the destructor will be called for every object. In reality, it is possible that there are no closing tags printed at all.*)

destroy() ensures that the destructor is called at desired points in the program:

```
void main() {
    const courses = new XmlElement("courses", 0);

    foreach (courseId; 0 .. 2) {
        const courseTag = "course" ~ to!string(courseId);
        const courseElement = new XmlElement(courseTag, 1);
```

```
    foreach (i; 0 .. 3) {
        const gradeElement = new XmlElement("grade", 2);
        const randomGrade = uniform(50, 101);

        writeln(indentationString(3), randomGrade);

        destroy(gradeElement);
    }

    destroy(courseElement);
}

destroy(courses);
}
```

With those changes, the output of the code now matches the output of the code that use structs:

```
<courses>
  <course0>
    <grade>
      66
    </grade>      ← The closing tags appear on correct lines
    <grade>
      75
    </grade>      ←
    <grade>
      68
    </grade>      ←
  </course0>      ←
  <course1>
    <grade>
      73
    </grade>      ←
    <grade>
      62
    </grade>      ←
    <grade>
      100
    </grade>      ←
  </course1>      ←
</courses>        ←
```

58.5 scoped() to call the destructor automatically

The program above has a weakness: The scopes may be exited before the destroy() lines are executed, commonly by thrown exceptions. If the destroy() lines must be executed even when exceptions are thrown, a solution is to take advantage of scope() and other features that we saw in the Exceptions chapter (page 192).

Another solution is to construct class objects by std.typecons.scoped instead of by the new keyword. scoped() wraps the class object inside a struct and the destructor of that struct object destroys the class object when itself goes out of scope.

The effect of scoped() is to make class objects behave similar to struct objects regarding lifetimes.

With the following changes, the program produces the expected output as before:

```
import std.typecons;
// ...
void main() {
    const courses = scoped!XmlElement("courses", 0);

    foreach (courseId; 0 .. 2) {
```

```
            const courseTag = "course" ~ to!string(courseId);
            const courseElement = scoped!XmlElement(courseTag, 1);

            foreach (i; 0 .. 3) {
                const gradeElement = scoped!XmlElement("grade", 2);
                const randomGrade = uniform(50, 101);

                writeln(indentationString(3), randomGrade);
            }
        }
    }
}
```

Note that there are no destroy() lines anymore.

scoped() is a function that returns a special struct object encapsulating the actual class object. The returned object acts as a proxy to the encapsulated one. (In fact, the type of courses above is Scoped, not XmlElement.)

When the destructor of the struct object is called automatically as its lifetime ends, it calls destroy() on the class object that it encapsulates. (This is an application of the *Resource Acquisition Is Initialization* (RAII) idiom. scoped() achieves this by the help of templates (page 399) and alias this (page 424), both of which we will see in later chapters.)

It is desirable for a proxy object to be used as conveniently as possible. In fact, the object that scoped() returns can be used exactly like the actual class type. For example, the member functions of the actual type can be called on it:

```
import std.typecons;

class C {
    void foo() {
    }
}

void main() {
    auto p = scoped!C();
    p.foo();    // Proxy object p is being used as type C
}
```

However, that convenience comes with a price: The proxy object may hand out a reference to the actual object right before destroying it. This can happen when the actual class type is specified explicitly on the left hand-side:

```
C c = scoped!C();    // ← BUG
c.foo();             // ← Accesses a destroyed object
```

In that definition, c is not the proxy object; rather, as defined by the programmer, a class variable referencing the encapsulated object. Unfortunately, the proxy object that is constructed on the right-hand side gets terminated at the end of the expression that constructs it. As a result, using c in the program would be an error, likely causing a runtime error:

```
Segmentation fault
```

For that reason, do not define scoped() variables by the actual type:

```
C         a = scoped!C();    // ← BUG
auto      b = scoped!C();    // ← correct
const     c = scoped!C();    // ← correct
immutable d = scoped!C();    // ← correct
```

58.6 Summary

- destroy() is for executing the destructor of a class object explicitly.

- Objects that are constructed by `scoped()` are destroyed upon leaving their respective scopes.
- It is a bug to define `scoped()` variables by the actual type.

The building blocks of D programs (and libraries) are modules.

D modules are based on a simple concept: Every source file is a module. Accordingly, the single files that we have been writing our programs in have all been individual modules.

By default, the name of a module is the same as its filename without the .d extension. When explicitly specified, the name of the module is defined by the `module` keyword, which must appear as the first non-comment line in the source file.

For example, assuming that the name of a source file is "cat.d", the name of the module would be specified by the `module` keyword:

```d
module cat;

class Cat {
    // ...
}
```

The `module` line is optional if the module is not part of any package (see below). When not specified, it is the same as the file name without the .d extension.

static this() and static ~this()

`static this()` and `static ~this()` at module scope are similar to their `struct` and `class` counterparts:

```d
module cat;

static this() {
    // ... the initial operations of the module ...
}

static ~this() {
    // ... the final operations of the module ...
}
```

Code that are in these scopes are executed once for each thread. (Note that most programs consist of a single thread that starts executing the `main()` function.) Code that should be executed only once for the entire program (e.g. initializing `shared` and `immutable` variables) must be defined in `shared static this()` and `shared static ~this()` blocks, which will be covered in the Data Sharing Concurrency chapter (page 640).

File and module names

D supports Unicode in source code and module names. However, the Unicode support of file systems vary. For example, although most Linux file systems support Unicode, the file names in Windows file systems may not distinguish between lower and upper case letters. Additionally, most file systems limit the characters that can be used in file and directory names.

For portability reasons, I recommend that you use only lower case ASCII letters in file names. For example, "resume.d" would be a suitable file name for a class named Résumé.

Accordingly, the name of the module would consist of ASCII letters as well:

```d
module resume;   // Module name consisting of ASCII letters

class Résumé {   // Program code consisting of Unicode characters
```

```
    // ...
}
```

59.1 Packages

A combination of related modules are called a *package*. D packages are a simple concept as well: The source files that are inside the same directory are considered to belong to the same package. The name of the directory becomes the name of the package, which must also be specified as the first parts of module names.

For example, if "cat.d" and "dog.d" are inside the directory "animal", then specifying the directory name along with the module name makes them be a part of the same package:

```
module animal.cat;

class Cat {
    // ...
}
```

Similarly, for the dog module:

```
module animal.dog;

class Dog {
    // ...
}
```

For modules that are parts of packages, the module line is not optional and the whole module name including the package name must be specified.

Since package names correspond to directory names, the package names of modules that are deeper than one directory level must reflect that hierarchy. For example, if the "animal" directory included a "vertebrate" directory, the name of a module inside that directory would include vertebrate as well:

```
module animal.vertebrate.cat;
```

The directory hierarchies can be arbitrarily complex depending on the needs of the program. Relatively short programs usually have all of their source files in a single directory.

59.2 Importing modules

The import keyword, which we have been using in almost every program so far, is for introducing a module to the current module:

```
import std.stdio;
```

The module name may contain the package name as well. For example, the std. part above indicates that stdio is a module that is a part of the std package.

The animal.cat and animal.dog modules would be imported similarly. Let's assume that the following code is inside a file named "deneme.d":

```
module deneme;          // the name of this module

import animal.cat;      // a module that it uses
import animal.dog;      // another module that it uses

void main() {
    auto cat = new Cat();
    auto dog = new Dog();
}
```

Note: *As described below, for the program to be built correctly, those module files must also be provided to the linker.*

More than one module can be imported at the same time:

```
import animal.cat, animal.dog;
```

Selective imports

Instead of importing a module as a whole with all of its names, it is possible to import just specific names from it.

```
import std.stdio : writeln;

// ...

    writefln("Hello %s.", name);    // ← compilation ERROR
```

The code above cannot be compiled because only `writeln` is imported, not `writefln`.

Selective imports are considered to be better than importing an entire module because it reduces the chance of *name collisions*. As we will see in an example below, a name collision can occur when the same name appears in more than one imported module.

Selective imports may reduce compilation times as well because the compiler needs to compile only the parts of a module that are actually imported. On the other hand, selective imports require more work as every imported name must be specified separately on the `import` line.

This book does not take advantage of selective imports mostly for brevity.

Local imports

So far we have always imported all of the required modules at the tops of programs:

```
import std.stdio;     // ← at the top
import std.string;    // ← at the top

// ... the rest of the module ...
```

Instead, modules can be imported at any other line of the source code. For example, the two functions of the following program import the modules that they need in their own scopes:

```
string makeGreeting(string name) {
    import std.string;

    string greeting = format("Hello %s", name);
    return greeting;
}

void interactWithUser() {
    import std.stdio;

    write("Please enter your name: ");
    string name = readln();
    writeln(makeGreeting(name));
}

void main() {
    interactWithUser();
}
```

Local imports are recommended over global imports because instead of importing every module unconditionally at the top, the compiler can import only the ones that are in the scopes that are actually used. If the compiler knows that the program never calls a function, it can ignore the import directives inside that function.

Additionally, a locally imported module is accessible only inside that local scope, further reducing the risk of name collisions.

We will later see in the Mixins chapter (page 560) that local imports are in fact required for *template mixins*.

The examples throughout this book do not take advantage of local imports mostly because local imports were added to D after the start of writing this book.

Locations of modules

The compiler finds the module files by converting the package and module names directly to directory and file names.

For example, the previous two modules would be located as "animal/cat.d" and "animal/dog.d", respectively (or "animal\cat.d" and "animal\dog.d", depending on the file system). Considering the main source file as well, the program above consists of three files.

Long and short module names

The names that are used in the program may be spelled out with the module and package names:

```
auto cat0 = Cat();
auto cat1 = animal.cat.Cat();   // same as above
```

The long names are normally not needed but sometimes there are name conflicts. For example, when referring to a name that appears in more than one module, the compiler cannot decide which one is meant.

The following program is spelling out the long names to distinguish between two separate Jaguar structs that are defined in two separate modules: animal and car:

```
import animal.jaguar;
import car.jaguar;

// ...

    auto conflicted =  Jaguar();              // ← compilation ERROR

    auto myAnimal = animal.jaguar.Jaguar(); // ← compiles
    auto myCar    =    car.jaguar.Jaguar(); // ← compiles
```

Renamed imports

It is possible to rename imported modules either for convenience or to resolve name conflicts:

```
import carnivore = animal.jaguar;
import vehicle = car.jaguar;

// ...

    auto myAnimal = carnivore.Jaguar();       // ← compiles
    auto myCar    = vehicle.Jaguar();         // ← compiles
```

Instead of renaming the entire import, it is possible to rename individual imported symbols.

For example, when the following code is compiled with the -w compiler switch, the compiler would warn that sort() *function* should be preferred instead of .sort *property*:

```
import std.stdio;
import std.algorithm;

// ...

    auto arr = [ 2, 10, 1, 5 ];
    arr.sort;    // ← compilation WARNING
    writeln(arr);
```

```
Warning: use std.algorithm.sort instead of .sort property
```

Note: *The* arr.sort *expression above is the equivalent of* sort(arr) *but it is written in the UFCS syntax, which we will see in a later chapter (page 385).*

One solution in this case is to import std.algorithm.sort by renaming it. The new name algSort below means the sort() *function* and the compiler warning is eliminated:

```
import std.stdio;
import std.algorithm : algSort = sort;

void main() {
    auto arr = [ 2, 10, 1, 5 ];
    arr.algSort;
    writeln(arr);
}
```

Importing a package as a module
Sometimes multiple modules of a package may need to be imported together. For example, whenever one module from the animal package is imported, all of the other modules may need to be imported as well: animal.cat, animal.dog, animal.horse, etc.

In such cases it is possible to import some or all of the modules of a package by importing the package as if it were a module:

```
import animal;    // ← entire package imported as a module
```

It is achieved by a special configuration file in the package directory, which must always be named as package.d. That special file includes the module directive for the package and imports the modules of the package *publicly*:

```
// The contents of the file animal/package.d:
module animal;

public import animal.cat;
public import animal.dog;
public import animal.horse;
// ... same for the other modules ...
```

Importing a module publicly makes that module available to the users of the importing module as well. As a result, when the users import just the animal module (which actually is a package), they get access to animal.cat and all the other modules as well.

Deprecating features
Modules evolve over time and get released under new version numbers. Going forward from a particular version, the authors of the module may decide to *deprecate* some of its features. Deprecating a feature means that newly written programs should not rely on that feature anymore; using a deprecated feature is disapproved. Deprecated features may even be removed from the module in the future.

There can be many reasons why a feature is deprecated. For example, the new version of the module may include a better alternative, the feature may have been moved to another module, the name of the feature may have changed to be consistent with the rest of the module, etc.

The deprecation of a feature is made official by defining it with the `deprecated` attribute, optionally with a custom message. For example, the following deprecation message communicates to its user that the name of the function has been changed:

```
deprecated("Please use doSomething() instead.")
void do_something() {
    // ...
}
```

By specifying one of the following compiler switches, the user of the module can determine how the compiler should react when a deprecated feature is used:

- `-d`: Using deprecated features should be allowed
- `-dw`: Using deprecated features should produce compilation warnings
- `-de`: Using deprecated features should produce compilation errors

For example, calling the deprecated feature in a program and compiling it with -de would fail compilation:

```
    do_something();
```

```
$ dmd deneme.d -de
deneme.d: Deprecation: function deneme.do_something is
deprecated - Please use doSomething() instead.
```

The name of a deprecated feature is usually defined as an `alias` of the new name:

```
deprecated("Please use doSomething() instead.")
alias do_something = doSomething;

void doSomething() {
    // ...
}
```

We will see the `alias` keyword in a later chapter (page 418).

Adding module definitions to the program
The `import` keyword is not sufficient to make modules become parts of the program. It simply makes available the features of a module inside the current module. That much is needed only to *compile* the code.

It is not possible to build the previous program only by the main source file, "deneme.d":

```
$ dmd deneme.d -w -de
deneme.o: In function `_Dmain':
deneme.d: undefined reference to `_D6animal3cat3Cat7__ClassZ'
deneme.d: undefined reference to `_D6animal3dog3Dog7__ClassZ'
collect2: ld returned 1 exit status
```

Those error messages are generated by the *linker*. Although they are not user-friendly messages, they indicate that some definitions that are needed by the program are missing.

The actual build of the program is the responsibility of the linker, which gets called automatically by the compiler behind the scenes. The compiler passes the modules that it has just compiled to the linker, and the linker combines those modules (and libraries) to produce the executable program.

For that reason, all of the modules that make up the program must be provided to the linker. For the program above to be built, "animal/cat.d" and "animal/dog.d" must also be specified on the compilation line:

```
$ dmd deneme.d animal/cat.d animal/dog.d -w -de
```

Instead of having to mention the modules individually every time on the command line, they can be combined as libraries.

59.3 Libraries

A collection of compiled modules is called a library. Libraries are not programs themselves; they do not have the main() function. Libraries contain compiled definitions of functions, structs, classes, and other features of modules, which are to be linked later by the linker to produce the program.

dmd's -lib command line option is for making libraries. The following command makes a library that contains the "cat.d" and the "dog.d" modules. The name of the library is specified with the -of switch:

```
$ dmd animal/cat.d animal/dog.d -lib -ofanimal -w -de
```

The actual name of the library file depends on the platform. For example, the extension of library files is .a under Linux systems: animal.a.

Once that library is built, It is not necessary to specify the "animal/cat.d" and "animal/dog.d" modules individually anymore. The library file is sufficient:

```
$ dmd deneme.d animal.a -w -de
```

The command above replaces the following one:

```
$ dmd deneme.d animal/cat.d animal/dog.d -w -de
```

As an exception, the D standard library Phobos need not be specified on the command line. That library is automatically included behind the scenes. Otherwise, it could be specified similar to the following line:

```
$ dmd deneme.d animal.a /usr/lib64/libphobos2.a -w -de
```

Note: *The name and location of the Phobos library may be different on different systems.*

Using libraries of other languages

D can use libraries that are written in some other compiled languages like C and C++. However, because different languages use different *linkages*, such libraries are available to D code only through their *D bindings*.

Linkage is the set of rules that determines the accessibility of entities in a library as well as how the names (symbols) of those entities are represented in compiled code. The names in compiled code are different from the names that the programmer writes in source code: The compiled names are *name-mangled* according to the rules of a particular language or compiler.

For example, according to C linkage, the C function name foo would be *mangled* with a leading underscore as _foo in compiled code. Name-mangling is more complex in languages like C++ and D because these languages allow using the same name for different entities in different modules, structs, classes, etc. as well as for overloads of functions. A D function named foo in source code has to be mangled in a way that would differentiate it from all other foo names that can exist in a program. Although the exact mangled names are usually not important to the programmer, the core.demangle module can be used to mangle and demangle symbols:

```
module deneme;

import std.stdio;
import core.demangle;

void foo() {
}

void main() {
    writeln(mangle!(typeof(foo))("deneme.foo"));
}
```

Note: *mangle() is a function template, the syntax of which is unfamiliar at this point in the book. We will see templates later in the Templates chapter (page 399).*

A function that has the same type as foo above and is named as deneme.foo, has the following mangled name in compiled code:

```
_D6deneme3fooFZv
```

Name mangling is the reason why linker error messages cannot include user-friendly names. For example, a symbol in an error message above was _D6animal3cat3Cat7__ClassZ instead of animal.cat.Cat.

The extern() attribute specifies the linkage of entities. The valid linkage types that can be used with extern() are C, C++, D, Objective-C, Pascal, System, and Windows. For example, when a D code needs to make a call to a function that is defined in a C library, that function must be declared as having C linkage:

```
// Declaring that 'foo' has C linkage (e.g. it may be defined
// in a C library):
extern(C) void foo();

void main() {
    foo();   // this call would be compiled as a call to '_foo'
}
```

In the case of C++ linkage, the namespace that a name is defined in is specified as the second argument to the extern() attribute. For example, according to the following declaration, bar() is the declaration of the function a::b::c::bar() defined in a C++ library (note that D code uses dots instead of colons):

```
// Declaring that 'bar' is defined inside namespace a::b::c
// and that it has C++ linkage:
extern(C++, a.b.c) void bar();

void main() {
    bar();           // a call to a::b::c::bar()
    a.b.c.bar();     // same as above
}
```

A file that contains such D declarations of the features of an external library is called a *D binding* of that library. Fortunately, in most cases programmers do not need to write them from scratch as D bindings for many popular non-D libraries are available through the Deimos project[1].

When used without a linkage type, the extern attribute has a different meaning: It specifies that the storage for a variable is the responsibility of an

---

1. https://github.com/D-Programming-Deimos/

external library; the D compiler should not reserve space for it in this module. Having different meanings, extern and extern() can be used together:

```d
// Declaring that the storage for 'g_variable' is already
// defined in a C library:
extern(C) extern int g_variable;
```

If the extern attribute were not specified above, while having C linkage, g_variable would be a variable of this D module.

All of the structs and classes that we have defined so far have all been accessible from the *outside*.

Let's consider the following struct:

```
enum Gender { female, male }

struct Student {
    string name;
    Gender gender;
}
```

The members of that struct is freely accessible to the rest of the program:

```
    auto student = Student("Tim", Gender.male);
    writefln("%s is a %s student.", student.name, student.gender);
```

Such freedom is a convenience in programs. For example, the previous line has been useful to produce the following output:

```
Tim is a male student.
```

However, this freedom is also a liability. As an example, let's assume that perhaps by mistake, the name of a student object gets modified in the program:

```
    student.name = "Anna";
```

That assignment may put the object in an invalid state:

```
Anna is a male student.
```

As another example, let's consider a School class. Let's assume that this class has two member variables that store the numbers of the male and female students separately:

```
class School {
    Student[] students;
    size_t femaleCount;
    size_t maleCount;

    void add(Student student) {
        students ~= student;

        final switch (student.gender) {

        case Gender.female:
            ++femaleCount;
            break;

        case Gender.male:
            ++maleCount;
            break;
        }
    }

    override string toString() const {
        return format("%s female, %s male; total %s students",
                      femaleCount, maleCount, students.length);
    }
}
```

The add() member function adds students while ensuring that the counts are always correct:

```
    auto school = new School;
    school.add(Student("Lindsey", Gender.female));
    school.add(Student("Mark", Gender.male));
    writeln(school);
```

The program produces the following consistent output:

```
1 female, 1 male; total 2 students
```

However, being able to access the members of School freely would not guarantee that this consistency would always be maintained. Let's consider adding a new element to the students member, this time directly:

```
    school.students ~= Student("Nancy", Gender.female);
```

Because the new student has been added to the array directly, without going through the add() member function, the School object is now in an inconsistent state:

```
1 female, 1 male; total 3 students
```

60.1 Encapsulation

Encapsulation is a programming concept of restricting access to members to avoid problems similar to the one above.

Another benefit of encapsulation is to eliminate the need to know the implementation details of types. In a sense, encapsulation allows presenting a type as a black box that is used only through its interface.

Additionally, preventing users from accessing the members directly allows changing the members of a class freely in the future. As long as the functions that define the interface of a class is kept the same, its implementation can be changed freely.

Encapsulation is not for restricting access to sensitive data like a credit card number or a password, and it cannot be used for that purpose. Encapsulation is a development tool: It allows using and coding types easily and safely.

60.2 Protection attributes

Protection attributes limit access to members of structs, classes, and modules. There are two ways of specifying protection attributes:

- At struct or class level to specify the protection of every struct or class member individually.
- At module level to specify the protection of every feature of a module individually: class, struct, function, enum, etc.

Protection attributes can be specified by the following keywords. The default attribute is public.

- public: Specifies accessibility by any part of the program without any restriction.

    An example of this is stdout. Merely importing std.stdio makes stdout available to every module that imported it.
- private: Specifies restricted accessibility.

    private class members and module members can only be accessed by the module that defines that member.

Additionally, `private` member functions cannot be overridden by subclasses.

- `package`: Specifies package-level accessibility.

   A feature that is marked as `package` can be accessed by all of the code that is a part of the same package. The `package` attribute involves only the inner-most package.

   For example, a `package` definition that is inside the `animal.vertebrate.cat` module can be accessed by any other module of the `vertebrate` package.

   Similar to the `private` attribute, `package` member functions cannot be overridden by subclasses.

- `protected`: Specifies accessibility by derived classes.

   This attribute extends the `private` attribute: A `protected` member can be accessed not only by the module that defines it, but also by the classes that inherit from the class that defines that `protected` member.

Additionally, the `export` attribute specifies accessibility from the outside of the program.

60.3 Definition

Protection attributes can be specified in three ways.

When written in front of a single definition, it specifies the protection attribute of that definition only. This is similar to the Java programming language:

```
private int foo;

private void bar() {
    // ...
}
```

When specified by a colon, it specifies the protection attributes of all of the following definitions until the next specification of a protection attribute. This is similar to the C++ programming language:

```
private:
    // ...
    // ... all of the definitions here are private ...
    // ...

protected:
    // ...
    // ... all of the definitions here are protected ...
    // ...
```

When specified for a block, the protection attribute is for all of the definitions that are inside that block:

```
private {
    // ...
    // ... all of the definitions here are private ...
    // ...
}
```

60.4 Module imports are private by default

A module that is imported by `import` is private to the module that imports it. It would not be visible to other modules that import it indirectly. For example, if a `school` module imports `std.stdio`, modules that import `school` cannot automatically use the `std.stdio` module.

Let's assume that the school module starts by the following lines:

```
module school.school;

import std.stdio;     // imported for this module's own use...

// ...
```

The following program cannot be compiled because writeln is not visible to it:

```
import school.school;

void main() {
    writeln("hello");    // ← compilation ERROR
}
```

std.stdio must be imported by that module as well:

```
import school.school;
import std.stdio;

void main() {
    writeln("hello");    // now compiles
}
```

Sometimes it is desired that a module presents other modules indirectly. For example, it would make sense for a school module to automatically import a student module for its users. This is achieved by marking the import as public:

```
module school.school;

public import school.student;

// ...
```

With that definition, modules that import school can use the definitions that are inside the student module without needing to import it:

```
import school.school;

void main() {
    auto student = Student("Tim", Gender.male);

    // ...
}
```

Although the program above imports only the school module, the student.Student struct is also available to it.

60.5 When to use encapsulation

Encapsulation avoids problems similar to the one we have seen in the introduction section of this chapter. It is an invaluable tool to ensure that objects are always in consistent states. Encapsulation helps preserve struct and class *invariants* by protecting members from direct modifications by the users of the type.

Encapsulation provides freedom of implementation by abstracting implementations away from user code. Otherwise, if users had direct access to for example School.students, it would be hard to modify the design of the class by changing that array e.g. to an associative array, because this would affect all user code that has been accessing that member.

Encapsulation is one of the most powerful benefits of object oriented programming.

60.6 Example

Let's define the `Student` struct and the `School` class by taking advantage of encapsulation and let's use them in a short test program.

This example program will consist of three files. As you remember from the previous chapter, being parts of the `school` package, two of these files will be under the "school" directory:

- "school/student.d": The `student` module that defines the `Student` struct
- "school/school.d": The `school` module that defines the `School` class
- "deneme.d": A short test program

Here is the "school/student.d" file:

```
module school.student;

import std.string;
import std.conv;

enum Gender { female, male }

struct Student {
    package string name;
    package Gender gender;

    string toString() const {
        return format("%s is a %s student.",
                      name, to!string(gender));
    }
}
```

The members of this struct are marked as `package` to enable access only to modules of the same package. We will soon see that `School` will be accessing these members directly. (Note that even this should be considered as violating the principle of encapsulation. Still, let's stick with the `package` attribute in this example program.)

The following is the "school/school.d" module that makes use of the previous one:

```
module school.school;

public import school.student;             // 1

import std.string;

class School {
private:                                  // 2

    Student[] students;
    size_t femaleCount;
    size_t maleCount;

public:                                   // 3

    void add(Student student) {
        students ~= student;

        final switch (student.gender) {   // 4a

        case Gender.female:
            ++femaleCount;
            break;

        case Gender.male:
            ++maleCount;
            break;
```

```
        }
    }

    override string toString() const {
        string result = format(
            "%s female, %s male; total %s students",
            femaleCount, maleCount, students.length);

        foreach (i, student; students) {
            result ~= (i == 0) ? ": " : ", ";
            result ~= student.name;              // 4b
        }

        return result;
    }
}
```

1. `school.student` is being imported publicly so that the users of `school.school` will not need to import that module explicitly. In a sense, the `student` module is made available by the `school` module.

2. All of the member variables of `School` are marked as private. This is important to help protect the consistency of the member variables of this class.

3. For this class to be useful, it must present some member functions. `add()` and `toString()` are made available to the users of this class.

4. As the two member variables of `Student` have been marked as package, being a part of the same package, `School` can access those variables.

Finally, the following is a test program that uses those types:

```
import std.stdio;
import school.school;

void main() {
    auto student = Student("Tim", Gender.male);
    writeln(student);

    auto school = new School;

    school.add(Student("Lindsey", Gender.female));
    school.add(Student("Mark", Gender.male));
    school.add(Student("Nancy", Gender.female));

    writeln(school);
}
```

This program can use `Student` and `School` only through their public interfaces. It cannot access the member variables of those types. As a result, the objects would always be consistent:

```
Tim is a male student.
2 female, 1 male; total 3 students: Lindsey, Mark, Nancy
```

Note that the program interacts with `School` only by its `add()` and `toString()` functions. As long as the interfaces of these functions are kept the same, changes in their implementations would not affect the program above.

61 Universal Function Call Syntax (UFCS)

UFCS is a feature that is applied by the compiler automatically. It enables the member function syntax even for regular functions. It can be explained simply by comparing two expressions:

```
variable.foo(arguments)
```

When the compiler encounters an expression such as the one above, if there is no member function named foo that can be called on variable with the provided arguments, then the compiler also tries to compile the following expression:

```
foo(variable, arguments)
```

If this new expression can indeed be compiled, then the compiler simply accepts that one. As a result, although foo() evidently has been a regular function, it gets accepted to be used by the member function syntax.

Note: UFCS considers only functions that are defined at module scope; for example, nested functions (page 500) cannot be called with the UFCS syntax.

We know that functions that are closely related to a type are defined as member functions of that type. This is especially important for encapsulation as only the member functions of a type (and that type's module) can access its private members.

Let's consider a Car class which maintains the amount of fuel:

```
class Car {
    enum economy = 12.5;        // kilometers per liter (average)
    private double fuelAmount;   // liters

    this(double fuelAmount) {
        this.fuelAmount = fuelAmount;
    }

    double fuel() const {
        return fuelAmount;
    }

    // ...
}
```

Although member functions are very useful and sometimes necessary, not every function that operates on a type should be a member function. Some operations on a type are too specific to a certain application to be member functions. For example, a function that determines whether a car can travel a specific distance may more appropriately be defined as a regular function:

```
bool canTravel(Car car, double distance) {
    return (car.fuel() * car.economy) >= distance;
}
```

This naturally brings a discrepancy in calling functions that are related to a type: objects appear at different places in these two syntaxes:

```
void main() {
    auto car = new Car(5);

    auto remainingFuel = car.fuel();  // Member function syntax

    if (canTravel(car, 100)) {        // Regular function syntax
        // ...
```

```
    }
}
```

UFCS removes this discrepancy by allowing regular functions to be called by the member function syntax:

```
    if (car.canTravel(100)) {  // Regular function, called by the
                               // member function syntax
        // ...
    }
```

This feature is available for fundamental types as well, including literals:

```
int half(int value) {
    return value / 2;
}

void main() {
    assert(42.half() == 21);
}
```

As we will see in the next chapter, when there are no arguments to pass to a function, that function can be called without parentheses. When that feature is used as well, the expression above gets even shorter. All three of the following statements are equivalent:

```
    result = half(value);
    result = value.half();
    result = value.half;
```

UFCS is especially useful when function calls are *chained*. Let's see this on a group of functions that operate on int slices:

```
// Returns the result of dividing all of the elements by
// 'divisor'
int[] divide(int[] slice, int divisor) {
    int[] result;
    result.reserve(slice.length);

    foreach (value; slice) {
        result ~= value / divisor;
    }

    return result;
}

// Returns the result of multiplying all of the elements by
// 'multiplier'
int[] multiply(int[] slice, int multiplier) {
    int[] result;
    result.reserve(slice.length);

    foreach (value; slice) {
        result ~= value * multiplier;
    }

    return result;
}

// Filters out elements that have odd values
int[] evens(int[] slice) {
    int[] result;
    result.reserve(slice.length);

    foreach (value; slice) {
        if (!(value % 2)) {
            result ~= value;
        }
```

```
    }

    return result;
}
```

When written by the regular syntax, without taking advantage of UFCS, an expression that chains three calls to these functions can be written as in the following program:

```
import std.stdio;

// ...

void main() {
    auto values = [ 1, 2, 3, 4, 5 ];
    writeln(evens(divide(multiply(values, 10), 3)));
}
```

The values are first multiplied by 10, then divided by 3, and finally only the even numbers are used:

```
[6, 10, 16]
```

A problem with the expression above is that although the pair of `multiply` and 10 are related and the pair of `divide` and 3 are related, parts of each pair end up written away from each other. UFCS eliminates this issue and enables a more natural syntax that reflects the actual order of operations:

```
    writeln(values.multiply(10).divide(3).evens);
```

Some programmers take advantage of UFCS even for calls like `writeln()`:

```
    values.multiply(10).divide(3).evens.writeln;
```

As an aside, the entire program above could have been written in a much simpler way by `map()` and `filter()`:

```
import std.stdio;
import std.algorithm;

void main() {
    auto values = [ 1, 2, 3, 4, 5 ];

    writeln(values
            .map!(a => a * 10)
            .map!(a => a / 3)
            .filter!(a => !(a % 2)));
}
```

The program above takes advantage of templates (page 399), ranges (page 569), and lambda functions (page 475), all of which will be explained in later chapters.

62 Properties

Properties allow using member functions like member variables.

We are familiar with this feature from slices. The `length` property of a slice returns the number of elements of that slice:

```
int[] slice = [ 7, 8, 9 ];
assert(slice.length == 3);
```

Looking merely at that usage, one might think that `.length` is implemented as a member variable:

```
struct SliceImplementation {
    int length;

    // ...
}
```

However, the other functionality of this property proves that it cannot be a member variable: Assigning a new value to the `.length` property actually changes the length of the slice, sometimes by adding new elements to the underlying array:

```
slice.length = 5;      // The slice now has 5 elements
assert(slice.length == 5);
```

Note: The `.length` property of fixed-length arrays cannot be modified.

The assignment to `.length` above involves more complicated operations than a simple value change: Determining whether the array has capacity for the new length, allocating more memory if not, and moving the existing elements to the new place; and finally initializing each additional element by `.init`.

Evidently, the assignment to `.length` operates like a function.

Properties are member functions that are used like member variables.

62.1 Calling functions without parentheses

As has been mentioned in the previous chapter, when there is no argument to pass, functions can be called without parentheses:

```
writeln();
writeln;       // Same as the previous line
```

This feature is closely related to properties because properties are used almost always without parentheses.

62.2 Property functions that return values

As a simple example, let's consider a rectangle struct that consists of two members:

```
struct Rectangle {
    double width;
    double height;
}
```

Let's assume that a third property of this type becomes a requirement, which should provide the area of the rectangle:

```
auto garden = Rectangle(10, 20);
writeln(garden.area);
```

One way of achieving that requirement is to define a third member:

```
struct Rectangle {
    double width;
    double height;
    double area;
}
```

A flaw in that design is that the object may easily become inconsistent: Although rectangles must always have the invariant of "width * height == area", this consistency may be broken if the members are allowed to be modified freely and independently.

As an extreme example, objects may even begin their lives in inconsistent states:

```
    // Inconsistent object: The area is not 10 * 20 == 200.
    auto garden = Rectangle(10, 20, 1111);
```

A better way would be to represent the concept of area as a property. Instead of defining an additional member, the value of that member is calculated by a function named area, the same as the concept that it represents:

```
struct Rectangle {
    double width;
    double height;

    double area() const {
        return width * height;
    }
}
```

Note: *As you would remember from the* const ref *Parameters and* const *Member Functions chapter (page 275), the* const *specifier on the function declaration ensures that the object is not modified by this function.*

That property function enables the struct to be used as if it has a third member variable:

```
    auto garden = Rectangle(10, 20);
    writeln("The area of the garden: ", garden.area);
```

As the value of the area property is calculated by multiplying the width and the height of the rectangle, this time it would always be consistent:

```
The area of the garden: 200
```

62.3 Property functions that are used in assignment

Similar to the length property of slices, the properties of user-defined types can be used in assignment operations as well:

```
    garden.area = 50;
```

For that assignment to actually change the area of the rectangle, the two members of the struct must be modified accordingly. To enable this functionality, we can assume that the rectangle is *flexible* so that to maintain the invariant of "width * height == area", the sides of the rectangle can be changed.

The function that enables such an assignment syntax is also named as area. The value that is used on the right-hand side of the assignment becomes the only parameter of this function.

The following additional definition of `area()` enables using that property in assignment operations and effectively modifying the area of `Rectangle` objects:

```
import std.stdio;
import std.math;

struct Rectangle {
    double width;
    double height;

    double area() const {
        return width * height;
    }

    void area(double newArea) {
        auto scale = sqrt(newArea / area);

        width *= scale;
        height *= scale;
    }
}

void main() {
    auto garden = Rectangle(10, 20);
    writeln("The area of the garden: ", garden.area);

    garden.area = 50;

    writefln("New state: %s x %s = %s",
             garden.width, garden.height, garden.area);
}
```

The new function takes advantage of the `sqrt` function from the `std.math` module, which returns the square root of the specified value. When both of the width and the height of the rectangle are scaled by the square root of the ratio, then the area would equal the desired value.

As a result, assigning the quarter of its current value to `area` ends up halving both sides of the rectangle:

```
The area of the garden: 200
New state: 5 x 10 = 50
```

62.4 Properties are not absolutely necessary

We have seen above how `Rectangle` can be used as if it has a third member variable. However, regular member functions could also be used instead of properties:

```
import std.stdio;
import std.math;

struct Rectangle {
    double width;
    double height;

    double area() const {
        return width * height;
    }

    void setArea(double newArea) {
        auto scale = sqrt(newArea / area);

        width *= scale;
        height *= scale;
    }
}

void main() {
```

```
    auto garden = Rectangle(10, 20);
    writeln("The area of the garden: ", garden.area());

    garden.setArea(50);

    writefln("New state: %s x %s = %s",
             garden.width, garden.height, garden.area());
}
```

Further, as we have seen in the Function Overloading chapter (page 265), these two functions could even have the same names:

```
    double area() const {
        // ...
    }

    void area(double newArea) {
        // ...
    }
```

62.5 When to use

It may not be easy to chose between regular member functions and properties. Sometimes regular member functions feel more natural and sometimes properties.

However, as we have seen in the Encapsulation and Protection Attributes chapter (page 379), it is important to restrict direct access to member variables. Allowing user code to freely modify member variables always ends up causing issues with code maintenance. For that reason, member variables better be encapsulated either by regular member functions or by property functions.

Leaving members like width and height open to public access is acceptable only for very simple types. Almost always a better design is to use property functions:

```
struct Rectangle {
private:

    double width_;
    double height_;

public:

    double area() const {
        return width * height;
    }

    void area(double newArea) {
        auto scale = sqrt(newArea / area);

        width_ *= scale;
        height_ *= scale;
    }

    double width() const {
        return width_;
    }

    double height() const {
        return height_;
    }
}
```

Note how the members are made private so that they can only be accessed by corresponding property functions.

Also note that to avoid confusing their names with the member functions, the names of the member variables are appended by the _ character. *Decorating* the names of member variables is a common practice in object oriented programming.

That definition of `Rectangle` still presents `width` and `height` as if they are member variable:

```
auto garden = Rectangle(10, 20);
writefln("width: %s, height: %s",
         garden.width, garden.height);
```

When there is no property function that modifies a member variable, then that member is effectively read-only from the outside:

```
garden.width = 100;     // ← compilation ERROR
```

This is important for controlled modifications of members. The member variables can only be modified by the `Rectangle` type itself to ensure the consistency of its objects.

When it later makes sense that a member variable should be allowed to be modified from the outside, then it is simply a matter of defining another property function for that member.

@property

Property functions may be defined with the `@property` attribute as well. However, as a best practice, the use of this attribute is discouraged.

```
import std.stdio;

struct Foo {
    @property int a() const {
        return 42;
    }

    int b() const {      // ← Defined without @property
        return 42;
    }
}

void main() {
    auto f = Foo();

    writeln(typeof(f.a).stringof);
    writeln(typeof(f.b).stringof);
}
```

The only effect of the `@property` attribute is when determining the type of an expression that could syntactically be a property function call. As seen in the output below, the types of the expressions `f.a` and `f.b` are different:

```
int           ← The type of the expression f.a (the return type)
const int()   ← The type of the member function Foo.b
```

63 Contract Programming for Structs and Classes

Contract programming is very effective in reducing coding errors. We have seen two of the contract programming features earlier in the Contract Programming chapter (page 221): The `in` and `out` blocks ensure input and output contracts of functions.

Note: *It is very important that you consider the guidelines under the "`in` blocks versus `enforce` checks" section of that chapter. The examples in this chapter are based on the assumption that problems with object and parameter consistencies are due to programmer errors. Otherwise, you should use `enforce` checks inside function bodies.*

As a reminder, let's write a function that calculates the area of a triangle by Heron's formula. We will soon move the `in` and `out` blocks of this function to the constructor of a struct.

For this calculation to work correctly, the length of every side of the triangle must be greater than zero. Additionally, since it is impossible to have a triangle where one of the sides is greater than the sum of the other two, that condition must also be checked.

Once these input conditions are satisfied, the area of the triangle would be greater than zero. The following function ensures that all of these requirements are satisfied:

```d
private import std.math;

double triangleArea(double a, double b, double c)
in {
    // Every side must be greated than zero
    assert(a > 0);
    assert(b > 0);
    assert(c > 0);

    // Every side must be less than the sum of the other two
    assert(a < (b + c));
    assert(b < (a + c));
    assert(c < (a + b));

} out (result) {
    assert(result > 0);

} do {
    immutable halfPerimeter = (a + b + c) / 2;

    return sqrt(halfPerimeter
                * (halfPerimeter - a)
                * (halfPerimeter - b)
                * (halfPerimeter - c));
}
```

63.1 Preconditions and postconditions for member functions

The `in` and `out` blocks can be used with member functions as well.

Let's convert the function above to a member function of a `Triangle` struct:

```d
import std.stdio;
import std.math;

struct Triangle {
private:

    double a;
    double b;
    double c;

public:
```

```
    double area() const
    out (result) {
        assert(result > 0);

    } do {
        immutable halfPerimeter = (a + b + c) / 2;

        return sqrt(halfPerimeter
                        * (halfPerimeter - a)
                        * (halfPerimeter - b)
                        * (halfPerimeter - c));
    }
}

void main() {
    auto threeFourFive = Triangle(3, 4, 5);
    writeln(threeFourFive.area);
}
```

As the sides of the triangle are now member variables, the function does not take parameters anymore. That is why this function does not have an in block. Instead, it assumes that the members already have consistent values.

The consistency of objects can be ensured by the following features.

63.2 Preconditions and postconditions for object consistency

The member function above is written under the assumption that the members of the object already have consistent values. One way of ensuring that assumption is to define an in block for the constructor so that the objects are guaranteed to start their lives in consistent states:

```
struct Triangle {
// ...

    this(double a, double b, double c)
    in {
        // Every side must be greated than zero
        assert(a > 0);
        assert(b > 0);
        assert(c > 0);

        // Every side must be less than the sum of the other two
        assert(a < (b + c));
        assert(b < (a + c));
        assert(c < (a + b));

    } do {
        this.a = a;
        this.b = b;
        this.c = c;
    }

// ...
}
```

This prevents creating invalid Triangle objects at run time:

```
    auto negativeSide = Triangle(-1, 1, 1);
    auto sideTooLong = Triangle(1, 1, 10);
```

The in block of the constructor would prevent such invalid objects:

```
core.exception.AssertError@deneme.d: Assertion failure
```

Although an out block has not been defined for the constructor above, it is possible to define one to ensure the consistency of members right after construction.

63.3 `invariant()` blocks for object consistency

The `in` and `out` blocks of constructors guarantee that the objects start their lives in consistent states and the `in` and `out` blocks of member functions guarantee that those functions themselves work correctly.

However, these checks are not suitable for guaranteeing that the objects are always in consistent states. Repeating the `out` blocks for every member function would be excessive and error-prone.

The conditions that define the consistency and validity of an object are called the *invariants* of that object. For example, if there is a one-to-one correspondence between the orders and the invoices of a customer class, then an invariant of that class would be that the lengths of the order and invoice arrays would be equal. When that condition is not satisfied for any object, then the object would be in an inconsistent state.

As an example of an invariant, let's consider the `School` class from the Encapsulation and Protection Attributes chapter (page 379):

```
class School {
private:

    Student[] students;
    size_t femaleCount;
    size_t maleCount;

// ...
}
```

The objects of that class are consistent only if an invariant that involves its three members are satisfied. The length of the student array must be equal to the sum of the female and male students:

```
    assert(students.length == (femaleCount + maleCount));
```

If that condition is ever false, then there must be a bug in the implementation of this class.

`invariant()` blocks are for guaranteeing the invariants of user-defined types. `invariant()` blocks are defined inside the body of a `struct` or a `class`. They contain `assert` checks similar to `in` and `out` blocks:

```
class School {
private:

    Student[] students;
    size_t femaleCount;
    size_t maleCount;

    invariant() {
        assert(students.length == (femaleCount + maleCount));
    }

// ...
}
```

As needed, there can be more than one `invariant()` block in a user-defined type.

The `invariant()` blocks are executed automatically at the following times:

- After the execution of the constructor: This guarantees that every object starts its life in a consistent state.
- Before the execution of the destructor: This guarantees that the destructor will be executed on a consistent object.

- Before and after the execution of a `public` member function: This guarantees that the member functions do not invalidate the consistency of objects.

    Note: *export functions are the same as public functions in this regard. (Very briefly, export functions are functions that are exported on dynamic library interfaces.)*

If an `assert` check inside an `invariant()` block fails, an `AssertError` is thrown. This ensures that the program does not continue executing with invalid objects.

As with `in` and `out` blocks, the checks inside `invariant()` blocks can be disabled by the `-release` command line option:

```
$ dmd deneme.d -w -release
```

63.4 Contract inheritance

Interface and class member functions can have `in` and `out` blocks as well. This allows an `interface` or a `class` to define preconditions for its derived types to depend on, as well as to define postconditions for its users to depend on. Derived types can define further `in` and `out` blocks for the overrides of those member functions. Overridden `in` blocks can loosen preconditions and overridden `out` blocks can offer more guarantees.

User code is commonly *abstracted away* from the derived types, written in a way to satisfy the preconditions of the topmost type in a hierarchy. The user code does not even know about the derived types. Since user code would be written for the contracts of an interface, it would not be acceptable for a derived type to put stricter preconditions on an overridden member function. However, the preconditions of a derived type can be more permissive than the preconditions of its superclass.

Upon entering a function, the `in` blocks are executed automatically from the topmost type to the bottom-most type in the hierarchy . If *any* `in` block succeeds without any `assert` failure, then the preconditions are considered to be fulfilled.

Similarly, derived types can define `out` blocks as well. Since postconditions are about guarantees that a function provides, the member functions of the derived type must observe the postconditions of its ancestors as well. On the other hand, it can provide additional guarantees.

Upon exiting a function, the `out` blocks are executed automatically from the topmost type to the bottom-most type. The function is considered to have fullfilled its postconditions only if *all* of the `out` blocks succeed.

The following artificial program demonstrates these features on an `interface` and a `class`. The `class` requires less from its callers while providing more guarantees:

```d
interface Iface {
    int[] func(int[] a, int[] b)
    in {
        writeln("Iface.func.in");

        /* This interface member function requires that the
         * lengths of the two parameters are equal. */
        assert(a.length == b.length);

    } out (result) {
        writeln("Iface.func.out");

        /* This interface member function guarantees that the
         * result will have even number of elements.
         * (Note that an empty slice is considered to have
         * even number of elements.) */
```

```
            assert((result.length % 2) == 0);
    }
}
class Class : Iface {
    int[] func(int[] a, int[] b)
    in {
        writeln("Class.func.in");

        /* This class member function loosens the ancestor's
         * preconditions by allowing parameters with unequal
         * lengths as long as at least one of them is empty. */
        assert((a.length == b.length) ||
               (a.length == 0) ||
               (b.length == 0));

    } out (result) {
        writeln("Class.func.out");

        /* This class member function provides additional
         * guarantees: The result will not be empty and that
         * the first and the last elements will be equal. */
        assert((result.length != 0) &&
               (result[0] == result[$ - 1]));

    } do {
        writeln("Class.func.do");

        /* This is just an artificial implementation to
         * demonstrate how the 'in' and 'out' blocks are
         * executed. */

        int[] result;

        if (a.length == 0) {
            a = b;
        }

        if (b.length == 0) {
            b = a;
        }

        foreach (i; 0 .. a.length) {
            result ~= a[i];
            result ~= b[i];
        }

        result[0] = result[$ - 1] = 42;

        return result;
    }
}

import std.stdio;

void main() {
    auto c = new Class();

    /* Although the following call fails Iface's precondition,
     * it is accepted because it fulfills Class' precondition. */
    writeln(c.func([1, 2, 3], []));
}
```

The in block of Class is executed only because the parameters fail to satisfy the preconditions of Iface:

```
Iface.func.in
Class.func.in   ← would not be executed if Iface.func.in succeeded
Class.func.do
Iface.func.out
Class.func.out
[42, 1, 2, 2, 3, 42]
```

63.5 Summary

- `in` and `out` blocks are useful in constructors as well. They ensure that objects are constructed in valid states.
- `invariant()` blocks ensure that objects remain in valid states throughout their lifetimes.
- Derived types can define `in` blocks for overridden member functions. Preconditions of a derived type should not be stricter than the preconditions of its superclasses. (*Note that not defining an* `in` *block means "no precondition at all", which may not be the intent of the programmer.*)
- Derived types can define `out` blocks for overridden member functions. In addition to its own, a derived member function must observe the postconditions of its superclasses as well.

Templates are the feature that allows describing the code as a pattern, for the compiler to generate program code automatically. Parts of the source code may be left to the compiler to be filled in until that part is actually used in the program.

Templates are very useful especially in libraries because they enable writing generic algorithms and data structures, instead of tying them to specific types.

Compared to the template supports in other languages, D's templates are very powerful and extensive. I will not get into all of the details of templates in this chapter. I will cover only function, struct, and class templates and only *type* template parameters. We will see more about templates in the More Templates chapter (page 520). For a complete reference on D templates, see Philippe Sigaud's *D Templates: A Tutorial*[1].

To see the benefits of templates let's start with a function that prints values in parentheses:

```
void printInParens(int value) {
    writefln("(%s)", value);
}
```

Because the parameter is specified as int, that function can only be used with values of type int, or values that can automatically be converted to int. For example, the compiler would not allow calling it with a floating point type.

Let's assume that the requirements of a program changes and that other types need to be printed in parentheses as well. One of the solutions for this would be to take advantage of function overloading and provide overloads of the function for all of the types that the function is used with:

```
// The function that already exists
void printInParens(int value) {
    writefln("(%s)", value);
}

// Overloading the function for 'double'
void printInParens(double value) {
    writefln("(%s)", value);
}
```

This solution does not scale well because this time the function cannot be used with e.g. real or any user-defined type. Although it is possible to overload the function for other types, the cost of doing this may be prohibitive.

An important observation here is that regardless of the type of the parameter, the contents of the overloads would all be *generically* the same: a single writefln() expression.

Such genericity is common in algorithms and data structures. For example, the binary search algorithm is independent of the type of the elements: It is about the specific steps and operations of the search. Similarly, the linked list data structure is independent of the type of the elements: Linked list is merely about *how* the elements are stored in the container, regardless of their type.

Templates are useful in such situations: Once a piece of code is described as a template, the compiler generates overloads of the same code automatically according to the actual uses of that code in the program.

---

1. https://github.com/PhilippeSigaud/D-templates-tutorial

As I have mentioned above, in this chapter I will cover only function, struct, and class templates, and *type* template parameters.

64.1 Function templates

Defining a function as a template is leaving one or more of the types that it uses as unspecified, to be deduced later by the compiler.

The types that are being left unspecified are defined within the template parameter list, which comes between the name of the function and the function parameter list. For that reason, function templates have two parameter lists: the template parameter list and the function parameter list:

```
void printInParens(T)(T value) {
    writefln("(%s)", value);
}
```

The T within the template parameter list above means that T can be any type. Although T is an arbitrary name, it is an acronym for "type" and is very common in templates.

Since T represents any type, the templated definition of printInParens() above is sufficient to use it with almost every type, including the user-defined ones:

```
import std.stdio;

void printInParens(T)(T value) {
    writefln("(%s)", value);
}

void main() {
    printInParens(42);           // with int
    printInParens(1.2);          // with double

    auto myValue = MyStruct();
    printInParens(myValue);      // with MyStruct
}

struct MyStruct {
    string toString() const {
        return "hello";
    }
}
```

The compiler considers all of the uses of printInParens() in the program and generates code to support all those uses. The program is then compiled as if the function has been overloaded explicitly for int, double, and MyStruct:

```
/* Note: These functions are not part of the source
 *       code. They are the equivalents of the functions that
 *       the compiler would automatically generate. */

void printInParens(int value) {
    writefln("(%s)", value);
}

void printInParens(double value) {
    writefln("(%s)", value);
}

void printInParens(MyStruct value) {
    writefln("(%s)", value);
}
```

The output of the program is produced by those different *instantiations* of the function template:

```
(42)
(1.2)
(hello)
```

Each template parameter can determine more than one function parameter. For example, both the two function parameters and the return type of the following function template are determined by its single template parameter:

```
/* Returns a copy of 'slice' except the elements that are
 * equal to 'value'. */
T[] removed(T)(const(T)[] slice, T value) {
    T[] result;

    foreach (element; slice) {
        if (element != value) {
            result ~= element;
        }
    }

    return result;
}
```

64.2 More than one template parameter

Let's change the function template to take the parentheses characters as well:

```
void printInParens(T)(T value, char opening, char closing) {
    writeln(opening, value, closing);
}
```

Now we can call the same function with different sets of parentheses:

```
    printInParens(42, '<', '>');
```

Although being able to specify the parentheses makes the function more usable, specifying the type of the parentheses as char makes it less flexible because it is not possible to call the function with characters of type wchar or dchar:

```
    printInParens(42, '→', '←');        // ← compilation ERROR
```

```
Error: template deneme.printInParens(T) cannot deduce
template function from argument types !()(int,wchar,wchar)
```

One solution would be to specify the type of the parentheses as dchar but this would still be insufficient as this time the function could not be called e.g. with string or user-defined types.

Another solution is to leave the type of the parentheses to the compiler as well. Defining an additional template parameter instead of the specific char is sufficient:

```
void printInParens(T, ParensType)(T value,
                                  ParensType opening,
                                  ParensType closing) {
    writeln(opening, value, closing);
}
```

The meaning of the new template parameter is similar to T's: ParensType can be any type.

It is now possible to use many different types of parentheses. The following are with wchar and string:

```
    printInParens(42, '→', '←');
    printInParens(1.2, "-=", "=-");
```

```
→42←
-=1.2=-
```

The flexibility of `printInParens()` has been increased, as it now works correctly for any combination of T and ParensType as long as those types are printable with `writeln()`.

64.3 Type deduction

The compiler's deciding on what type to use for a template parameter is called *type deduction*.

Continuing from the last example above, the compiler decides on the following types according to the two uses of the function template:

- `int` and `wchar` when 42 is printed
- `double` and `string` when 1.2 is printed

The compiler can deduce types only from the types of the parameter values that are passed to function templates. Although the compiler can usually deduce the types without any ambiguity, there are times when the types must be specified explicitly by the programmer.

64.4 Explicit type specification

Sometimes it is not possible for the compiler to deduce the template parameters. A situation that this can happen is when the types do not appear in the function parameter list. When template parameters are not related to function parameters, the compiler cannot deduce the template parameter types.

To see an example of this, let's design a function that asks a question to the user, reads a value as a response, and returns that value. Additionally, let's make this a function template so that it can be used to read any type of response:

```
T getResponse(T)(string question) {
    writef("%s (%s): ", question, T.stringof);

    T response;
    readf(" %s", &response);

    return response;
}
```

That function template would be very useful in programs to read different types of values from the input. For example, to read some user information, we can imagine calling it as in the following line:

```
getResponse("What is your age?");
```

Unfortunately, that call does not give the compiler any clue as to what the template parameter T should be. What is known is that the question is passed to the function as a `string`, but the type of the return value cannot be deduced:

```
Error: template deneme.getResponse(T) cannot deduce template
function from argument types !()(string)
```

In such cases, the template parameters must be specified explicitly by the programmer. Template parameters are specified in parentheses after an exclamation mark:

```
getResponse!(int)("What is your age?");
```

The code above can now be accepted by the compiler and the function template is compiled as T being an alias of int within the definition of the template.

When there is only one template parameter specified, the parentheses around it are optional:

```
getResponse!int("What is your age?");    // same as above
```

You may recognize that syntax from to!string, which we have been using in earlier programs. to() is a function template, which takes the target type of the conversion as a template parameter. Since it has only one template parameter that needs to be specified, it is commonly written as to!string instead of to!(string).

64.5 Template instantiation

Automatic generation of code for a specific set of template parameter values is called an *instantiation* of that template for that specific set of parameter values. For example, to!string and to!int are two different instantiations of the to function template.

As I will mention again in a separate section below, distinct instantiations of templates produce distinct and incompatible types.

64.6 Template specializations

Although the getResponse() function template can in theory be used for any template type, the code that the compiler generates may not be suitable for every type. Let's assume that we have the following type that represents points on a two dimensional space:

```
struct Point {
    int x;
    int y;
}
```

Although the instantiation of getResponse() for the Point type itself would be fine, the generated readf() call for Point cannot be compiled. This is because the standard library function readf() does not know how to read a Point object. The two lines that actually read the response would look like the following in the Point instantiation of the getResponse() function template:

```
Point response;
readf(" %s", &response);    // ← compilation ERROR
```

One way of reading a Point object would be to read the values of the x and y members separately and then to *construct* a Point object from those values.

Providing a special definition of a template for a specific template parameter value is called a *template specialization*. The specialization is defined by the type name after a : character in the template parameter list. A Point specialization of the getResponse() function template can be defined as in the following code:

```
// The general definition of the function template (same as before)
T getResponse(T)(string question) {
    writef("%s (%s): ", question, T.stringof);

    T response;
    readf(" %s", &response);

    return response;
}
```

```
// The specialization of the function template for Point
T getResponse(T : Point)(string question) {
    writefln("%s (Point)", question);

    auto x = getResponse!int("  x");
    auto y = getResponse!int("  y");

    return Point(x, y);
}
```

Note that the specialization takes advantage of the general definition of getResponse() to read two int values to be used as the values of the x and y members.

Instead of instantiating the template itself, now the compiler uses the specialization above whenever getResponse() is called for the Point type:

```
    auto center = getResponse!Point("Where is the center?");
```

Assuming that the user enters 11 and 22:

```
Where is the center? (Point)
  x (int): 11
  y (int): 22
```

The getResponse!int() calls are directed to the general definition of the template and the getResponse!Point() calls are directed to the Point specialization of it.

As another example, let's consider using the same template with string. As you would remember from the Strings chapter (page 75), readf() would read all of the characters from the input as part of a single string until the end of the input. For that reason, the default definition of getResponse() would not be useful when reading string responses:

```
    // Reads the entire input, not only the name!
    auto name = getResponse!string("What is your name?");
```

We can provide a template specialization for string as well. The following specialization reads just the *line* instead:

```
T getResponse(T : string)(string question) {
    writef("%s (string): ", question);

    // Read and ignore whitespace characters which have
    // presumably been left over from the previous user input
    string response;
    do {
        response = strip(readln());
    } while (response.length == 0);

    return response;
}
```

64.7 Struct and class templates

The Point struct may be seen as having a limitation: Because its two members are defined specifically as int, it cannot represent fractional coordinate values. This limitation can be removed if the Point struct is defined as a template.

Let's first add a member function that returns the distance to another Point object:

```
import std.math;

// ...
```

```
struct Point {
    int x;
    int y;

    int distanceTo(Point that) const {
        immutable real xDistance = x - that.x;
        immutable real yDistance = y - that.y;

        immutable distance = sqrt((xDistance * xDistance) +
                                  (yDistance * yDistance));

        return cast(int)distance;
    }
}
```

That definition of `Point` is suitable when the required precision is relatively low: It can calculate the distance between two points at kilometer precision, e.g. between the center and branch offices of an organization:

```
auto center = getResponse!Point("Where is the center?");
auto branch = getResponse!Point("Where is the branch?");

writeln("Distance: ", center.distanceTo(branch));
```

Unfortunately, `Point` is inadequate at higher precisions than `int` can provide.

Structs and classes can be defined as templates as well, by specifying a template parameter list after their names. For example, `Point` can be defined as a struct template by providing a template parameter and replacing the `int`s by that parameter:

```
struct Point(T) {
    T x;
    T y;

    T distanceTo(Point that) const {
        immutable real xDistance = x - that.x;
        immutable real yDistance = y - that.y;

        immutable distance = sqrt((xDistance * xDistance) +
                                  (yDistance * yDistance));

        return cast(T)distance;
    }
}
```

Since structs and classes are not functions, they cannot be called with parameters. This makes it impossible for the compiler to deduce their template parameters. The template parameter list must always be specified for struct and class templates:

```
auto center = Point!int(0, 0);
auto branch = Point!int(100, 100);

writeln("Distance: ", center.distanceTo(branch));
```

The definitions above make the compiler generate code for the `int` instantiation of the `Point` template, which is the equivalent of its earlier non-template definition. However, now it can be used with any type. For example, when more precision is needed, with `double`:

```
auto point1 = Point!double(1.2, 3.4);
auto point2 = Point!double(5.6, 7.8);

writeln(point1.distanceTo(point2));
```

Although the template itself has been defined independently of any specific type, its single definition makes it possible to represent points of various precisions.

Simply converting `Point` to a template would cause compilation errors in code that has already been written according to its non-template definition. For example, now the `Point` specialization of `getResponse()` cannot be compiled:

```
T getResponse(T : Point)(string question) {  // ← compilation ERROR
    writefln("%s (Point)", question);

    auto x = getResponse!int("  x");
    auto y = getResponse!int("  y");

    return Point(x, y);
}
```

The reason for the compilation error is that `Point` itself is not a type anymore: `Point` is now a *struct template*. Only instantiations of that template would be considered as types. The following changes are required to correctly specialize `getResponse()` for any instantiation of `Point`:

```
Point!T getResponse(T : Point!T)(string question) {  // 2, 1
    writefln("%s (Point!%s)", question, T.stringof); // 5

    auto x = getResponse!T("  x");                    // 3a
    auto y = getResponse!T("  y");                    // 3b

    return Point!T(x, y);                             // 4
}
```

1. In order for this template specialization to support all instantiations of `Point`, the template parameter list must mention `Point!T`. This simply means that the `getResponse()` specialization is for `Point!T`, regardless of T. This specialization would match `Point!int`, `Point!double`, etc.
2. Similarly, to return the correct type as the response, the return type must be specified as `Point!T` as well.
3. Since the types of `x` and `y` members of `Point!T` are now T, as opposed to `int`, the members must be read by calling `getResponse!T()`, not `getResponse!int()`, as the latter would be correct only for `Point!int`.
4. Similar to items 1 and 2, the type of the return value is `Point!T`.
5. To print the name of the type accurately for every type, as in `Point!int`, `Point!double`, etc., `T.stringof` is used.

64.8 Default template parameters

Sometimes it is cumbersome to provide template parameter types every time a template is used, especially when that type is almost always a particular type. For example, `getResponse()` may almost always be called for the `int` type in the program, and only in a few places for the `double` type.

It is possible to specify default types for template parameters, which are assumed when the types are not explicitly provided. Default parameter types are specified after the = character:

```
T getResponse(T = int)(string question) {
    // ...
}

// ...

    auto age = getResponse("What is your age?");
```

As no type has been specified when calling getResponse() above, T becomes the default type int and the call ends up being the equivalent of getResponse!int().

Default template parameters can be specified for struct and class templates as well, but in their case the template parameter list must always be written even when empty:

```d
struct Point(T = int) {
    // ...
}

// ...

    Point!() center;
```

Similar to default function parameter values as we have seen in the Variable Number of Parameters chapter (page 258), default template parameters can be specified for all of the template parameters or for the *last* ones:

```d
void myTemplate(T0, T1 = int, T2 = char)() {
    // ...
}
```

The last two template parameters of that function may be left unspecified but the first one is required:

```d
    myTemplate!string();
```

In that usage, the second and third parameters are int and char, respectively.

64.9 Every template instantiation yields a distinct type

Every instantiation of a template for a given set of types is considered to be a distinct type. For example, Point!int and Point!double are separate types:

```d
Point!int point3 = Point!double(0.25, 0.75); // ←  compilation ERROR
```

Those different types cannot be used in the assignment operation above:

```
Error: cannot implicitly convert expression (Point(0.25,0.75))
of type Point!(double) to Point!(int)
```

64.10 A compile-time feature

Templates are entirely a compile-time feature. The instances of templates are generated by the compiler at compile time.

64.11 Class template example: stack data structure

Struct and class templates are commonly used in the implementations of data structures. Let's design a stack container that will be able to contain any type.

Stack is one of the simplest data structures. It represents a container where elements are placed conceptually on top of each other as would be in a stack of papers. New elements go on top, and only the topmost element is accessed. When an element is removed, it is always the topmost one.

If we also define a property that returns the total number of elements in the stack, all of the operations of this data structure would be the following:

- Add element (push())
- Remove element (pop())
- Access the topmost element (.top)

- Report the number of elements (`.length`)

An array can be used to store the elements such that the last element of the array would be representing the topmost element of the stack. Finally, it can be defined as a class template to be able to contain elements of any type:

```
class Stack(T) {
private:

    T[] elements;

public:

    void push(T element) {
        elements ~= element;
    }

    void pop() {
        --elements.length;
    }

    T top() const {
        return elements[$ - 1];
    }

    size_t length() const {
        return elements.length;
    }
}
```

Here is a `unittest` block for this class that uses its `int` instantiation:

```
unittest {
    auto stack = new Stack!int;

    // The newly added element must appear on top
    stack.push(42);
    assert(stack.top == 42);
    assert(stack.length == 1);

    // .top and .length should not affect the elements
    assert(stack.top == 42);
    assert(stack.length == 1);

    // The newly added element must appear on top
    stack.push(100);
    assert(stack.top == 100);
    assert(stack.length == 2);

    // Removing the last element must expose the previous one
    stack.pop();
    assert(stack.top == 42);
    assert(stack.length == 1);

    // The stack must become empty when the last element is
    // removed
    stack.pop();
    assert(stack.length == 0);
}
```

To take advantage of this class template, let's try using it this time with a user-defined type. As an example, here is a modified version of `Point`:

```
struct Point(T) {
    T x;
    T y;

    string toString() const {
        return format("(%s,%s)", x, y);
```

```
    }
}
```

A `Stack` that contains elements of type `Point!double` can be defined as follows:

```
auto points = new Stack!(Point!double);
```

Here is a test program that first adds ten elements to this stack and then removes them one by one:

```d
import std.string;
import std.stdio;
import std.random;

struct Point(T) {
    T x;
    T y;

    string toString() const {
        return format("(%s,%s)", x, y);
    }
}

// Returns a random value between -0.50 and 0.50.
double random_double()
out (result) {
    assert((result >= -0.50) && (result < 0.50));

} do {
    return (double(uniform(0, 100)) - 50) / 100;
}

// Returns a Stack that contains 'count' number of random
// Point!double elements.
Stack!(Point!double) randomPoints(size_t count)
out (result) {
    assert(result.length == count);

} do {
    auto points = new Stack!(Point!double);

    foreach (i; 0 .. count) {
        immutable point = Point!double(random_double(),
                                       random_double());
        writeln("adding   : ", point);
        points.push(point);
    }

    return points;
}

void main() {
    auto stackedPoints = randomPoints(10);

    while (stackedPoints.length) {
        writeln("removing: ", stackedPoints.top);
        stackedPoints.pop();
    }
}
```

As the output of the program shows, the elements are removed in the reverse order as they have been added:

```
adding   : (-0.02,-0.01)
adding   : (0.17,-0.5)
adding   : (0.12,0.23)
adding   : (-0.05,-0.47)
adding   : (-0.19,-0.11)
adding   : (0.42,-0.32)
adding   : (0.48,-0.49)
```

```
adding   : (0.35,0.38)
adding   : (-0.2,-0.32)
adding   : (0.34,0.27)
removing: (0.34,0.27)
removing: (-0.2,-0.32)
removing: (0.35,0.38)
removing: (0.48,-0.49)
removing: (0.42,-0.32)
removing: (-0.19,-0.11)
removing: (-0.05,-0.47)
removing: (0.12,0.23)
removing: (0.17,-0.5)
removing: (-0.02,-0.01)
```

64.12 Function template example: binary search algorithm

Binary search is the fastest algorithm to search for an element among the elements of an already sorted array. It is a very simple algorithm: The element in the middle is considered; if that element is the one that has been sought, then the search is over. If not, then the algorithm is repeated on the elements that are either on the left-hand side or on the right-hand side of the middle element, depending on whether the sought element is greater or less than the middle element.

Algorithms that repeat themselves on a smaller range of the initial elements are recursive. Let's write the binary search algorithm recursively by calling itself.

Before converting it to a template, let's first write this function to support only arrays of int. We can easily convert it to a template later, by adding a template parameter list and replacing appropriate ints in its definition by Ts. Here is a binary search algorithm that works on arrays of int:

```d
/* This function returns the index of the value if it exists
 * in the array, size_t.max otherwise. */
size_t binarySearch(const int[] values, int value) {
    // The value is not in the array if the array is empty.
    if (values.length == 0) {
        return size_t.max;
    }

    immutable midPoint = values.length / 2;

    if (value == values[midPoint]) {
        // Found.
        return midPoint;

    } else if (value < values[midPoint]) {
        // The value can only be in the left-hand side; let's
        // search in a slice that represents that half.
        return binarySearch(values[0 .. midPoint], value);

    } else {
        // The value can only be in the right-hand side; let's
        // search in the right-hand side.
        auto index =
            binarySearch(values[midPoint + 1 .. $], value);

        if (index != size_t.max) {
            // Adjust the index; it is 0-based in the
            // right-hand side slice.
            index += midPoint + 1;
        }

        return index;
    }

    assert(false, "We should have never gotten to this line");
}
```

The function above implements this simple algorithm in four steps:

- If the array is empty, return `size_t.max` to indicate that the value has not been found.
- If the element at the mid-point is equal to the sought value, then return the index of that element.
- If the value is less than the element at the mid-point, then repeat the same algorithm on the left-hand side.
- Else, repeat the same algorithm on the right-hand side.

Here is a unittest block that tests the function:

```d
unittest {
    auto array = [ 1, 2, 3, 5 ];
    assert(binarySearch(array, 0) == size_t.max);
    assert(binarySearch(array, 1) == 0);
    assert(binarySearch(array, 4) == size_t.max);
    assert(binarySearch(array, 5) == 3);
    assert(binarySearch(array, 6) == size_t.max);
}
```

Now that the function has been implemented and tested for `int`, we can convert it to a template. `int` appears only in two places in the definition of the template:

```d
size_t binarySearch(const int[] values, int value) {
    // ... int does not appear here ...
}
```

The `int`s that appear in the parameter list are the types of the elements and the value. Specifying those as template parameters is sufficient to make this algorithm a template and to be usable with other types as well:

```d
size_t binarySearch(T)(const T[] values, T value) {
    // ...
}
```

That function template can be used with any type that matches the operations that are applied to that type in the template. In `binarySearch()`, the elements are used only with comparison operators `==` and `<`:

```d
    if (value == values[midPoint]) {
        // ...

    } else if (value < values[midPoint]) {

        // ...
```

For that reason, `Point` is not ready to be used with `binarySearch()` yet:

```d
import std.string;

struct Point(T) {
    T x;
    T y;

    string toString() const {
        return format("(%s,%s)", x, y);
    }
}

void main() {
    Point!int[] points;

    foreach (i; 0 .. 15) {
```

```
        points ~= Point!int(i, i);
    }

    assert(binarySearch(points, Point!int(10, 10)) == 10);
}
```

The program above would cause a compilation error:

```
Error: need member function opCmp() for struct
const(Point!(int)) to compare
```

According to the error message, opCmp() needs to be defined for Point. opCmp() has been covered in the Operator Overloading chapter (page 298):

```
struct Point(T) {
// ...

    int opCmp(const ref Point that) const {
        return (x == that.x
                ? y - that.y
                : x - that.x);
    }
}
```

64.13 Summary

We will see other features of templates in a later chapter (page 520). The following are what we have covered in this chapter:

- Templates define the code as a pattern, for the compiler to generate instances of it according to the actual uses in the program.
- Templates are a compile-time feature.
- Specifying template parameter lists is sufficient to make function, struct, and class definitions templates.

```
void functionTemplate(T)(T functionParameter) {
    // ...
}

class ClassTemplate(T) {
    // ...
}
```

- Template arguments can be specified explicitly after an exclamation mark. The parentheses are not necessary when there is only one token inside the parentheses.

```
auto object1 = new ClassTemplate!(double);
auto object2 = new ClassTemplate!double;     // same thing
```

- Every template instantiation yields a distinct type.

```
assert(typeid(ClassTemplate!int) !=
       typeid(ClassTemplate!uint));
```

- Template arguments can only be deduced for function templates.

```
functionTemplate(42);  // functionTemplate!int is deduced
```

- Templates can be specialized for the type that is after the : character.

```
class ClassTemplate(T : dchar) {
    // ...
}
```

- Default template arguments are specified after the = character.

```
void functionTemplate(T = long)(T functionParameter) {
    // ...
}
```

65 Pragmas

Pragmas are a way of interacting with the compiler. They can be for providing special information to the compiler as well as getting information from it. Although they are useful in non-templated code as well, `pragma(msg)` can be helpful when debugging templates.

Every compiler vendor is free to introduce their special `pragma` directives in addition to the following mandatory ones:

65.1 pragma(msg)

Prints a message to `stderr` during compilation. No message is printed during the execution of the compiled program.

For example, the following `pragma(msg)` is being used for exposing the types of template parameters, presumably during debugging:

```
import std.string;

void func(A, B)(A a, B b) {
    pragma(msg, format("Called with types '%s' and '%s'",
                       A.stringof, B.stringof));
    // ...
}

void main() {
    func(42, 1.5);
    func("hello", 'a');
}
```

```
Called with types 'int' and 'double'
Called with types 'string' and 'char'
```

65.2 pragma(lib)

Instructs the compiler to link the program with a particular library. This is the easiest way of linking the program with a library that is already installed on the system.

For example, the following program would be linked with the `curl` library without needing to mention the library on the command line:

```
import std.stdio;
import std.net.curl;

pragma(lib, "curl");

void main() {
    // Get this chapter
    writeln(get("ddili.org/ders/d.en/pragma.html"));
}
```

65.3 pragma(inline)

Specifies whether a function should be *inlined* or not.

Every function call has some performance cost. Function calls involve passing arguments to the function, returning its return value to the caller, and handling some bookkeeping information to remember where the function was called from so that the execution can continue after the function returns.

This cost is usually insignificant compared to the cost of actual work that the caller and the callee perform. However, in some cases just the act of calling a certain function can have a measurable effect on the program's performance.

This can happen especially when the function body is relatively fast and when it is called from a short loop that repeats many times.

The following program calls a small function from a loop and increments a counter when the returned value satisfies a condition:

```d
import std.stdio;
import std.datetime.stopwatch;

// A function with a fast body:
ubyte compute(ubyte i) {
    return cast(ubyte)(i * 42);
}

void main() {
    size_t counter = 0;

    StopWatch sw;
    sw.start();

    // A short loop that repeats many times:
    foreach (i; 0 .. 100_000_000) {
        const number = cast(ubyte)i;

        if (compute(number) == number) {
            ++counter;
        }
    }

    sw.stop();

    writefln("%s milliseconds", sw.peek.total!"msecs");
}
```

The code takes advantage of `std.datetime.stopwatch.StopWatch` to measure the time it takes executing the entire loop:

```
674 milliseconds
```

The `-inline` compiler switch instructs the compiler to perform a compiler optimization called *function inlining*:

```
$ dmd deneme.d -w -inline
```

When a function is inlined, its body is injected into code right where it is called from; no actual function call happens. The following is the equivalent code that the compiler would compile after inlining:

```d
    // An equivalent of the loop when compute() is inlined:
    foreach (i; 0 .. 100_000_000) {
        const number = cast(ubyte)i;

        const result = cast(ubyte)(number * 42);
        if (result == number) {
            ++counter;
        }
    }
```

On the platform that I tested that program, eliminating the function call reduced the execution time by about 40%:

```
407 milliseconds
```

Although function inlining looks like a big gain, it cannot be applied for every function call because otherwise inlined bodies of functions would make code too large to fit in the CPU's *instruction cache*. Unfortunately, this can make the code even slower. For that reason, the decision of which function calls to inline is usually left to the compiler.

However, there may be cases where it is beneficial to help the compiler with this decision. The `inline` pragma instructs the compiler in its inlining decisions:

- `pragma(inline, false)`: Instructs the compiler to never inline certain functions even when the `-inline` compiler switch is specified.
- `pragma(inline, true)`: Instructs the compiler to definitely inline certain functions when the `-inline` compiler switch is specified. This causes a compilation error if the compiler cannot inline such a function. (The exact behavior of this pragma may be different on your compiler.)
- `pragma(inline)`: Sets the inlining behavior back to the setting on the compiler command line: whether `-inline` is specified or not.

These pragmas can affect the function that they appear in, as well as they can be used with a scope or colon to affect more than one function:

```
pragma(inline, false) {
    // Functions defined in this scope should not be inlined
    // ...
}

int foo() {
    pragma(inline, true);  // This function should be inlined
    // ...
}

pragma(inline, true):
// Functions defined in this section should be inlined
// ...

pragma(inline):
// Functions defined in this section should be inlined or not
// depending on the -inline compiler switch
// ...
```

Another compiler switch that can make programs run faster is `-O`, which instructs the compiler to perform more optimization algorithms. However, faster program speeds come at the expense of slower compilation speeds because these algorithms take significant amounts of time.

65.4 pragma(`startaddress`)

Specifies the start address of the program. Since the start address is normally assigned by the D runtime environment, it is very unlikely that you will ever use this pragma.

65.5 pragma(`mangle`)

Specifies that a symbol should be *name mangled* differently from the default name mangling method. Name mangling is about how the linker identifies functions and their callers. This pragma is useful when D code needs to call a library function that happens to be a D keyword.

For example, if a C library had a function named `override`, because `override` happens to be a keyword in D, the only way of calling it from D would be through a different name. However, that different name must still be mangled as the actual function name in the library for the linker to be able to identify it:

```
/* If a C library had a function named 'override', it could
 * only be called from D through a name like 'c_override',
```

```
  * mangled as the actual function name: */
pragma(mangle, "override")
extern(C) string c_override(string);

void main() {
    /* D code calls the function as c_override() but the
     * linker would find it by its correct C library name
     * 'override': */
    auto s = c_override("hello");
}
```

66.1 alias

The alias keyword assigns aliases to existing names. alias is different from and unrelated to alias this.

Shortening a long name

As we have encountered in the previous chapter, some names may become too long to be convenient. Let's consider the following function from that chapter:

```
Stack!(Point!double) randomPoints(size_t count) {
    auto points = new Stack!(Point!double);
    // ...
}
```

Having to type Stack!(Point!double) explicitly in multiple places in the program has a number of drawbacks:

- Longer names can make the code harder to read.
- It is unnecessary to be reminded at every point that the type is the Stack data structure that contains objects of the double instantiations of the Point struct template.
- If the requirements of the program change and e.g. double needs to be changed to real, this change must be carried out in multiple places.

These drawbacks can be eliminated by giving a new name to Stack!(Point!double):

```
alias Points = Stack!(Point!double);

// ...

Points randomPoints(size_t count) {
    auto points = new Points;
    // ...
}
```

It may make sense to go further and define two aliases, one taking advantage of the other:

```
alias PrecisePoint = Point!double;
alias Points = Stack!PrecisePoint;
```

The syntax of alias is the following:

```
    alias new_name = existing_name;
```

After that definition, the new name and the existing name become synonymous: They mean the same thing in the program.

You may encounter the older syntax of this feature in some programs:

```
    // Use of old syntax is discouraged:
    alias existing_name new_name;
```

alias is also useful when shortening names which otherwise need to be spelled out along with their module names. Let's assume that the name Queen appears in two separate modules: chess and palace. When both modules are imported, typing merely Queen would cause a compilation error:

```
import chess;
import palace;

// ...

    Queen person;              // ← compilation ERROR
```

The compiler cannot decide which Queen has been meant:

```
Error: chess.Queen at chess.d(1) conflicts with
palace.Queen at palace.d(1)
```

A convenient way of resolving this conflict is to assign aliases to one or more of the names:

```
import palace;

alias PalaceQueen = palace.Queen;

void main() {
    PalaceQueen person;
    // ...
    PalaceQueen anotherPerson;
}
```

alias works with other names as well. The following code gives a new name to a variable:

```
    int variableWithALongName = 42;

    alias var = variableWithALongName;
    var = 43;

    assert(variableWithALongName == 43);
```

Design flexibility

For flexibility, even fundamental types like int can have aliases:

```
alias CustomerNumber = int;
alias CompanyName = string;
// ...

struct Customer {
    CustomerNumber number;
    CompanyName company;
    // ...
}
```

If the users of this struct always type CustomerNumber and CompanyName instead of int and string, then the design can be changed in the future to some extent, without affecting user code.

This helps with the readability of code as well. Having the type of a variable as CustomerNumber conveys more information about the meaning of that variable than int.

Sometimes such type aliases are defined inside structs and classes and become parts of the interfaces of those types. The following class has a weight property:

```
class Box {
private:

    double weight_;

public:

    double weight() const {
```

```
        return weight_;
    }
    // ...
}
```

Because the member variable and the property of that class is defined as double, the users would have to use double as well:

```
double totalWeight = 0;

foreach (box; boxes) {
    totalWeight += box.weight;
}
```

Let's compare it to another design where the type of weight is defined as an alias:

```
class Box {
private:

    Weight weight_;

public:

    alias Weight = double;

    Weight weight() const {
        return weight_;
    }
    // ...
}
```

Now the user code would normally use Weight as well:

```
Box.Weight totalWeight = 0;

foreach (box; boxes) {
    totalWeight += box.weight;
}
```

With this design, changing the actual type of Weight in the future would not affect user code. (That is, if the new type supports the += operator as well.)

Revealing hidden names of superclasses

When the same name appears both in the superclass and in the subclass, the matching names that are in the superclass are hidden. Even a single name in the subclass is sufficient to hide all of the names of the superclass that match that name:

```
class Super {
    void foo(int x) {
        // ...
    }
}

class Sub : Super {
    void foo() {
        // ...
    }
}

void main() {
    auto object = new Sub;
    object.foo(42);         // ← compilation ERROR
}
```

Since the argument is 42, an `int` value, one might expect that the `Super.foo` function that takes an `int` would be called for that use. However, even though their parameter lists are different, `Sub.foo` *hides* `Super.foo` and causes a compilation error. The compiler disregards `Super.foo` altogether and reports that `Sub.foo` cannot be called by an `int`:

```
Error: function deneme.Sub.foo () is not callable
using argument types (int)
```

Note that this is not the same as overriding a function of the superclass. For that, the function signatures would be the same and the function would be overridden by the `override` keyword. (The `override` keyword has been explained in the Inheritance chapter (page 328).)

Here, not overriding, but a language feature called *name hiding* is in effect. If there were not name hiding, functions that happen to have the same name `foo` that are added to or removed from these classes might silently change the function that would get called. Name hiding prevents such surprises. It is a feature of other OOP languages as well.

`alias` can reveal the hidden names when desired:

```
class Super {
    void foo(int x) {
        // ...
    }
}

class Sub : Super {
    void foo() {
        // ...
    }

    alias foo = Super.foo;
}
```

The `alias` above brings the `foo` names from the superclass into the subclass interface. As a result, the code now compiles and `Super.foo` gets called.

When it is more appropriate, it is possible to bring the names under a different name as well:

```
class Super {
    void foo(int x) {
        // ...
    }
}

class Sub : Super {
    void foo() {
        // ...
    }

    alias generalFoo = Super.foo;
}

// ...

void main() {
    auto object = new Sub;
    object.generalFoo(42);
}
```

Name hiding affects member variables as well. `alias` can bring those names to the subclass interface as well:

```
class Super {
    int city;
}

class Sub : Super {
    string city() const {
        return "Kayseri";
    }
}
```

Regardless of one being a member variable and the other a member function, the name `city` of the subclass hides the name `city` of the superclass:

```
void main() {
    auto object = new Sub;
    object.city = 42;      // ← compilation ERROR
}
```

Similarly, the names of the member variables of the superclass can be brought to the subclass interface by `alias`, possibly under a different name:

```
class Super {
    int city;
}

class Sub : Super {
    string city() const {
        return "Kayseri";
    }

    alias cityCode = Super.city;
}

void main() {
    auto object = new Sub;
    object.cityCode = 42;
}
```

66.2 with

`with` is for removing repeated references to an object or symbol. It takes an expression or a symbol in parentheses and uses that expression or symbol when looking up other symbols that are used inside the scope of `with`:

```
struct S {
    int i;
    int j;
}

void main() {
    auto s = S();

    with (s) {
        i = 1;     // means s.i
        j = 2;     // means s.j
    }
}
```

It is possible to create a temporary object inside the parentheses. In that case, the temporary object becomes an lvalue (page 181), lifetime of which ends upon leaving the scope:

```
    with (S()) {
        i = 1;     // the i member of the temporary object
        j = 2;     // the j member of the temporary object
    }
```

As we will see later in the Pointers chapter (page 425), it is possible to construct the temporary object with the new keyword, in which case its lifetime can be extended beyond the scope.

with is especially useful with case sections for removing repeated references to e.g. an enum type:

```d
enum Color { red, orange }

// ...

    final switch (c) with (Color) {

    case red:       // means Color.red
        // ...

    case orange:    // means Color.orange
        // ...
    }
```

66.3 Summary

- alias assigns aliases to existing names.
- with removes repeated references to the same object or symbol.

67 alias this

We have seen the individual meanings of the `alias` and the `this` keywords in previous chapters. These two keywords have a completely different meaning when used together as `alias this`.

`alias this` enables *automatic type conversions* (also known as *implicit type conversions*) of user-defined types. As we have seen in the Operator Overloading chapter (page 298), another way of providing type conversions for a type is by defining `opCast` for that type. The difference is that, while `opCast` is for explicit type conversions, `alias this` is for automatic type conversions.

The keywords `alias` and `this` are written separately where the name of a member variable or a member function is specified between them:

```
alias member_variable_or_member_function this;
```

`alias this` enables the specific conversion from the user-defined type to the type of that member. The value of the member becomes the resulting value of the conversion.

The following `Fraction` example uses `alias this` with a *member function*. The `TeachingAssistant` example that is further below will use it with *member variables*.

Since the return type of `value()` below is `double`, the following `alias this` enables automatic conversion of `Fraction` objects to `double` values:

```d
import std.stdio;

struct Fraction {
    long numerator;
    long denominator;

    double value() const {
        return double(numerator) / denominator;
    }

    alias value this;

    // ...
}

double calculate(double lhs, double rhs) {
    return 2 * lhs + rhs;
}

void main() {
    auto fraction = Fraction(1, 4);     // meaning 1/4
    writeln(calculate(fraction, 0.75));
}
```

`value()` gets called automatically to produce a `double` value when `Fraction` objects appear in places where a `double` value is expected. That is why the variable `fraction` can be passed to `calculate()` as an argument. `value()` returns 0.25 as the value of 1/4 and the program prints the result of 2 * 0.25 + 0.75:

```
1.25
```

68 Pointers

Pointers are variables that provide access to other variables. The value of a pointer is the address of the variable that it provides access to.

Pointers can point at any type of variable, object, and even other pointers. In this chapter, I will refer to all of these simply as *variables*.

Pointers are low level features of microprocessors. They are an important part of system programming.

The syntax and semantics of pointers in D are inherited directly from C. Although pointers are notoriously the most difficult feature of C to comprehend, they should not be as difficult in D. This is because other features of D that are semantically close to pointers are more useful in situations where pointers would have to be used in other languages. When the ideas behind pointers are already understood from those other features of D, pointers should be easier to grasp.

The short examples throughout the most of this chapter are decidedly simple. The programs at the end of the chapter will be more realistic.

The names like ptr (short for "pointer") that I have used in these examples should not be considered as useful names in general. As always, names must be chosen to be more meaningful and explanatory in actual programs.

68.1 The concept of a reference

Although we have encountered references many times in the previous chapters, let's summarize this concept one more time.

The ref variables in foreach loops

As we have seen in the foreach Loop chapter (page 121), normally the loop variables are *copies* of elements:

```d
import std.stdio;

void main() {
    int[] numbers = [ 1, 11, 111 ];

    foreach (number; numbers) {
        number = 0;      // ← the copy changes, not the element
    }

    writeln("After the loop: ", numbers);
}
```

The number that gets assigned 0 each time is a copy of one of the elements of the array. Modifying that copy does not modify the element:

```
After the loop: [1, 11, 111]
```

When the actual elements need to be modified, the foreach variable must be defined as ref:

```d
    foreach (ref number; numbers) {
        number = 0;      // ← the actual element changes
    }
```

This time number is a reference to an actual element in the array:

```
After the loop: [0, 0, 0]
```

ref function parameters

As we have seen in the Function Parameters chapter (page 168), the parameters of *value types* are normally copies of the arguments:

```
import std.stdio;

void addHalf(double value) {
    value += 0.5;          // ← Does not affect 'value' in main
}

void main() {
    double value = 1.5;

    addHalf(value);

    writeln("The value after calling the function: ", value);
}
```

Because the function parameter is not defined as ref, the assignment inside the function affects only the local variable there. The variable in main() is not affected:

```
The value after calling the function: 1.5
```

The ref keyword would make the function parameter a reference to the argument:

```
void addHalf(ref double value) {
    value += 0.5;
}
```

This time the variable in main() gets modified:

```
The value after calling the function: 2
```

Reference types

Some types are reference types. Variables of such types provide access to separate variables:

- Class variables
- Slices
- Associative arrays

We have seen this distinction in the Value Types and Reference Types chapter (page 159). The following example demonstrates reference types by two class variables:

```
import std.stdio;

class Pen {
    double ink;

    this() {
        ink = 15;
    }

    void use(double amount) {
        ink -= amount;
    }
}

void main() {
    auto pen = new Pen;
    auto otherPen = pen;  // ← Now both variables provide
```

```
                        //   access to the same object

    writefln("Before: %s %s", pen.ink, otherPen.ink);

    pen.use(1);          // ← the same object is used
    otherPen.use(2);     // ← the same object is used

    writefln("After : %s %s", pen.ink, otherPen.ink);
}
```

Because classes are reference types, the class variables pen and otherPen provide access to the same Pen object. As a result, using either of those class variables affects the same object:

```
Before: 15 15
After : 12 12
```

That single object and the two class variables would be laid out in memory similar to the following figure:

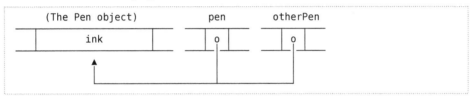

References *point at* actual variables as pen and otherPen do above.

Programming languages implement the reference and pointer concepts by special registers of the microprocessor, which are specifically for *pointing at* memory locations.

Behind the scenes, D's higher-level concepts (class variables, slices, associative arrays, etc.) are all implemented by pointers. As these higher-level features are already efficient and convenient, pointers are rarely needed in D programming. Still, it is important for D programmers to understand pointers well.

68.2 Syntax

The pointer syntax of D is mostly the same as in C. Although this can be seen as an advantage, the peculiarities of C's pointer syntax are necessarily inherited by D as well. For example, the different meanings of the * character may be confusing.

With the exception of void pointers, every pointer is associated with a certain type and can point at only variables of that specific type. For example, an int pointer can only point at variables of type int.

The pointer definition syntax consists of the associated type and a * character:

```
type_to_point_at * name_of_the_pointer_variable;
```

Accordingly, a pointer variable that would be pointing at int variables would be defined like this:

```
int * myPointer;
```

The * character in that syntax may be pronounced as "pointer". So, the type of myPointer above is an "int pointer". The spaces before and after the * character are optional. The following syntaxes are common as well:

```
int* myPointer;
int *myPointer;
```

When it is specifically a pointer type that is being mentioned as in "int pointer", it is common to write the type without any spaces as in `int*`.

68.3 Pointer value and the address-of operator &

Being variables themselves pointers have values as well. The default value of a pointer is the special value `null`, which means that the pointer is not *pointing at* any variable yet (i.e. does not provide access to any variable).

To make a pointer provide access to a variable, the value of the pointer must be set to the address of that variable. The pointer starts pointing at the variable that is at that specific address. From now on, I will call that variable *the pointee*.

The & operator which we have used many times before with `readf` has also been briefly mentioned in the Value Types and Reference Types chapter (page 159). This operator produces the address of the variable that is written after it. Its value can be used when initializing a pointer:

```
int myVariable = 180;
int * myPointer = &myVariable;
```

Initializing `myPointer` by the address of `myVariable` makes `myPointer` point at `myVariable`.

The value of the pointer is the same as the address of `myVariable`:

```
writeln("The address of myVariable: ", &myVariable);
writeln("The value of myPointer    : ", myPointer);
```

```
The address of myVariable: 7FFF2CE73F10
The value of myPointer    : 7FFF2CE73F10
```

Note: *The address value is likely to be different every time the program is started.*

The following figure is a representation of these two variables in memory:

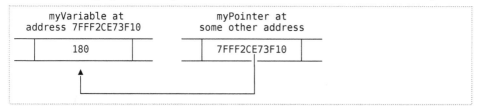

The value of `myPointer` is the address of `myVariable`, conceptually *pointing at* the variable that is at that location.

Since pointers are variables as well, the & operator can produce the address of the pointer as well:

```
writeln("The address of myPointer : ", &myPointer);
```

```
The address of myPointer : 7FFF2CE73F18
```

Since the difference between the two addresses above is 8, remembering that an `int` takes up 4 bytes, we can deduce that `myVariable` and `myPointer` are 4 bytes apart in memory.

After removing the arrow that represented the concept of *pointing at*, we can picture the contents of memory around these addresses like this:

7FFF2CE73F10	7FFF2CE73F14	7FFF2CE73F18	
⋮	⋮	⋮	⋮
180	(unused)	7FFF2CE73F10	

The names of variables, functions, classes, etc. and keywords are not parts of programs of compiled languages like D. The variables that have been defined by the programmer in the source code are converted to bytes that occupy memory or registers of the microprocessor.

Note: *The names (a.k.a. symbols) may actually be included in programs to help with debugging but those names do not affect the operation of the program.*

68.4 The access operator *

We have seen above that the * character which normally represents multiplication is also used when defining pointers. A difficulty with the syntax of pointers is that the same character has a third meaning: It is also used when accessing the pointee through the pointer.

When it is written before the name of a pointer, it means *the variable that the pointer is pointing at* (i.e. the pointee):

```
writeln("The value that it is pointing at: ", *myPointer);
```

```
The value that it is pointing at: 180
```

68.5 The . (dot) operator to access a member of the pointee

If you know pointers from C, this operator is the same as the -> operator in that language.

We have seen above that the * operator is used for accessing the pointee. That is sufficiently useful for pointers of fundamental types like int*: The value of a fundamental type is accessed simply by writing *myPointer.

However, when the pointee is a struct or a class object, the same syntax becomes inconvenient. To see why, let's consider the following struct:

```
struct Coordinate {
    int x;
    int y;

    string toString() const {
        return format("(%s,%s)", x, y);
    }
}
```

The following code defines an object and a pointer of that type:

```
auto center = Coordinate(0, 0);
Coordinate * ptr = &center;    // pointer definition
writeln(*ptr);                 // object access
```

That syntax is convenient when accessing the value of the entire Coordinate object:

```
(0,0)
```

However, the code becomes complicated when accessing a member of an object through a pointer and the * operator:

```
// Adjust the x coordinate
(*ptr).x += 10;
```

That expression modifies the value of the x member of the center object. The left-hand side of that expression can be explained by the following steps:

- ptr: The pointer that points at center
- *ptr: Accessing the object (i.e. center itself)
- (*ptr): Parentheses so that the . (dot) operator is applied to the object, not to the pointer
- (*ptr).x: The x member of the object that ptr is pointing at

To reduce the complexity of pointer syntax in D, the . (dot) operator is transferred to the pointee and provides access to the member of the object. (The exceptions to this rule are at the end of this section.)

So, the previous expression is normally written as:

```
ptr.x += 10;
```

Since the pointer itself does not have a member named x, .x is applied to the pointee and the x member of center gets modified:

```
(10,0)
```

Note that this is the same as the use of the . (dot) operator with classes. When the . (dot) operator is applied to a class *variable*, it provides access to a member of the class *object*:

```
class ClassType {
    int member;
}

// ...

    // Variable on the left, object on the right
    ClassType variable = new ClassType;

    // Applied to the variable but accesses the member of
    // the object
    variable.member = 42;
```

As you remember from the Classes chapter (page 322), the class object is constructed by the new keyword on the right-hand side. variable is a class variable that provides access to it.

Realizing that it is the same with pointers is an indication that class variables and pointers are implemented similarly by the compiler.

There is an exception to this rule both for class variables and for pointers. Type properties like .sizeof are applied to the type of the pointer, not to the type of the pointee:

```
char c;
char * p = &c;

writeln(p.sizeof);   // size of the pointer, not the pointee
```

.sizeof produces the size of p, which is a char*, not the size of c, which is a char. On a 64-bit system pointers are 8-byte long:

```
8
```

68.6 Modifying the value of a pointer

The values of pointers can be incremented or decremented and they can be used in addition and subtraction:

```
++ptr;
--ptr;
ptr += 2;
ptr -= 2;
writeln(ptr + 3);
writeln(ptr - 3);
```

Different from their arithmetic counterparts, these operations do not modify the actual value by the specified amount. Rather, the value of the pointer gets modified so that it now points at the variable that is a certain number of variables beyond the current one. The amount of the increment or the decrement specifies *how many variables away* should the pointer now point at.

For example, incrementing the value of a pointer makes it point at the next variable:

```
++ptr;   // Starts pointing at a variable that is next in
         // memory from the old variable
```

For that to work correctly, the actual value of the pointer must be incremented by the size of the variable. For example, because the size of int is 4, incrementing a pointer of type int* changes its value by 4. The programmer need not pay attention to this detail; the pointer value is modified by the correct amount automatically.

Warning: It is undefined behavior to point at a location that is not a valid byte that belongs to the program. Even if it is not actually used to access any variable there, it is invalid for a pointer to point at a nonexistent variable. (The only exception to this rule is that it is valid to point at the imaginary element one past the end of an array. This will be explained later below.)

For example, it is invalid to increment a pointer that points at myVariable, because myVariable is defined as a single int:

```
++myPointer;        // ← undefined behavior
```

Undefined behavior means that it cannot be known what the behavior of the program will be after that operation. There may be systems where the program crashes after incrementing that pointer. However, on most modern systems the pointer is likely to point at the unused memory location that has been shown as being between myVariable and myPointer in the previous figure.

For that reason, the value of a pointer must be incremented or decremented only if there is a valid object at the new location. (As we will see below, pointing at the element one past the end of an array is valid as well). Arrays (and slices) have that property: The elements of an array are side by side in memory.

A pointer that is pointing at an element of a slice can be incremented safely as long as it is not used to access an element beyond the end of the slice. Incrementing such a pointer by the ++ operator makes it point at the next element:

```
import std.stdio;
import std.string;
import std.conv;

enum Color { red, yellow, blue }
```

```
struct Crayon {
    Color color;
    double length;

    string toString() const {
        return format("%scm %s crayon", length, color);
    }
}

void main() {
    writefln("Crayon objects are %s bytes each.", Crayon.sizeof);

    Crayon[] crayons = [ Crayon(Color.red, 11),
                         Crayon(Color.yellow, 12),
                         Crayon(Color.blue, 13) ];

    Crayon * ptr = &crayons[0];                       // (1)

    for (int i = 0; i != crayons.length; ++i) {
        writeln("Pointer value: ", ptr);              // (2)

        writeln("Crayon: ", *ptr);                    // (3)
        ++ptr;                                        // (4)
    }
}
```

1. Definition: The pointer is initialized by the address of the first element.
2. Using its value: The value of the pointer is the address of the element that it is pointing at.
3. Accessing the element that is being pointed at.
4. Pointing at the next element.

The output:

```
Crayon objects are 16 bytes each.
Pointer value: 7F37AC9E6FC0
Crayon: 11cm red crayon
Pointer value: 7F37AC9E6FD0
Crayon: 12cm yellow crayon
Pointer value: 7F37AC9E6FE0
Crayon: 13cm blue crayon
```

Note that the loop above is iterated a total of `crayons.length` times so that the pointer is always used for accessing a valid element.

68.7 Pointers are risky

The compiler and the D runtime environment cannot guarantee that the pointers are always used correctly. It is the programmer's responsibility to ensure that a pointer is either `null` or points at a valid memory location (at a variable, at an element of an array, etc.).

For that reason, it is always better to consider higher-level features of D before thinking about using pointers.

68.8 The element one past the end of an array

It is valid to point at the imaginary element one past the end of an array.

This is a useful idiom that is similar to number ranges. When defining a slice with a number range, the second index is one past the elements of the slice:

```
int[] values = [ 0, 1, 2, 3 ];
writeln(values[1 .. 3]);    // 1 and 2 included, 3 excluded
```

This idiom can be used with pointers as well. It is a common function design in C and C++ where a function parameter points at the first element and another one points at the element after the last element:

```d
import std.stdio;

void tenTimes(int * begin, int * end) {
    while (begin != end) {
        *begin *= 10;
        ++begin;
    }
}

void main() {
    int[] values = [ 0, 1, 2, 3 ];

    // The address of the second element:
    int * begin = &values[1];

    // The address of two elements beyond that one
    tenTimes(begin, begin + 2);

    writeln(values);
}
```

The value begin + 2 means two elements after the one that begin is pointing at (i.e. the element at index 3).

The tenTimes() function takes two pointer parameters. It uses the element that the first one is pointing at but it never accesses the element that the second one is pointing at. As a result, only the elements at indexes 1 and 2 get modified:

```
[0, 10, 20, 3]
```

Such functions can be implemented by a for loop as well:

```d
    for ( ; begin != end; ++begin) {
        *begin *= 10;
    }
```

Two pointers that define a range can also be used with foreach loops:

```d
    foreach (ptr; begin .. end) {
        *ptr *= 10;
    }
```

For these methods to be applicable to *all of the elements* of a slice, the second pointer must necessarily point after the last element:

```d
    // The second pointer is pointing at the imaginary element
    // past the end of the array:
    tenTimes(begin, begin + values.length);
```

That is the reason why it is legal to point at the imaginary element one beyond the last element of an array.

68.9 Using pointers with the array indexing operator [ ]

Although it is not absolutely necessary in D, pointers can directly be used for accessing the elements of an array by an index value:

```d
    double[] floats = [ 0.0, 1.1, 2.2, 3.3, 4.4 ];

    double * ptr = &floats[2];

    *ptr = -100;      // direct access to what it points at
    ptr[1] = -200;    // access by indexing
```

```
    writeln(floats);
```

The output:

```
[0, 1.1, -100, -200, 4.4]
```

In that syntax, the element that the pointer is pointing at is thought of being the first element of an imaginary slice. The [ ] operator provides access to the specified element of that slice. The ptr above initially points at the element at index 2 of the original floats slice. ptr[1] is a reference to the element 1 of the imaginary slice that starts at ptr (i.e. index 3 of the original slice).

Although this behavior may seem complicated, there is a very simple conversion behind that syntax. Behind the scenes, the compiler converts the pointer[index] syntax to the *(pointer + index) expression:

```
    ptr[1] = -200;        // slice syntax
    *(ptr + 1) = -200;    // the equivalent of the previous line
```

As I have mentioned earlier, the compiler may not guarantee that this expression refers to a valid element. D's slices provide a much safer alternative and should be considered instead:

```
    double[] slice = floats[2 .. 4];
    slice[0] = -100;
    slice[1] = -200;
```

Normally, index values are checked for slices at run time:

```
    slice[2] = -300;   // Runtime error: accessing outside of the slice
```

Because the slice above does not have an element at index 2, an exception would be thrown at run time (unless the program has been compiled with the -release compiler switch):

```
core.exception.RangeError@deneme(8391): Range violation
```

68.10 Producing a slice from a pointer

Pointers are not as safe or as useful as slices because although they can be used with the slice indexing operator, they are not aware of the valid range of elements.

However, when the number of valid elements is known, a pointer can be used to construct a slice.

Let's assume that the makeObjects() function below is inside a C library. Let's assume that makeObjects makes specified number of Struct objects and returns a pointer to the first one of those objects:

```
    Struct * ptr = makeObjects(10);
```

The syntax that produces a slice from a pointer is the following:

```
    /* ... */ slice = pointer[0 .. count];
```

Accordingly, a slice to the 10 objects that are returned by makeObjects() can be constructed by the following code:

```
    Struct[] slice = ptr[0 .. 10];
```

After that definition, `slice` is ready to be used safely in the program just like any other slice:

```
    writeln(slice[1]);    // prints the second element
```

68.11 void* can point at any type

Although it is almost never needed in D, C's special pointer type `void*` is available in D as well. `void*` can point at any type:

```
    int number = 42;
    double otherNumber = 1.25;
    void * canPointAtAnything;

    canPointAtAnything = &number;
    canPointAtAnything = &otherNumber;
```

The `void*` above is able to point at variables of two different types: `int` and `double`.

void* pointers are limited in functionality. As a consequence of their flexibility, they cannot provide access to the pointee. When the actual type is unknown, its size is not known either:

```
    *canPointAtAnything = 43;    // ← compilation ERROR
```

Instead, its value must first be converted to a pointer of the correct type:

```
    int number = 42;                                // (1)
    void * canPointAtAnything = &number;            // (2)

    // ...

    int * intPointer = cast(int*)canPointAtAnything;  // (3)
    *intPointer = 43;                                 // (4)
```

1. The actual variable
2. Storing the address of the variable in a `void*`
3. Assigning that address to a pointer of the correct type
4. Modifying the variable through the new pointer

It is possible to increment or decrement values of `void*` pointers, in which case their values are modified as if they are pointers of 1-byte types like `ubyte`:

```
    ++canPointAtAnything;    // incremented by 1
```

void* is sometimes needed when interacting with libraries that are written in C. Since C does not have higher level features like interfaces, classes, templates, etc. C libraries must rely on the `void*` type.

68.12 Using pointers in logical expressions

Pointers can automatically be converted to `bool`. Pointers that have the value `null` produce `false` and the others produce `true`. In other words, pointers that do not point at any variable are `false`.

Let's consider a function that prints objects to the standard output. Let's design this function so that it also provides the number of bytes that it has just output. However, let's have it produce this information only when specifically requested.

It is possible to make this behavior optional by checking whether the value of a pointer is `null` or not:

```
void print(Crayon crayon, size_t * numberOfBytes) {
    immutable info = format("Crayon: %s", crayon);
    writeln(info);

    if (numberOfBytes) {
        *numberOfBytes = info.length;
    }
}
```

When the caller does not need this special information, they can pass `null` as the argument:

```
print(Crayon(Color.yellow, 7), null);
```

When the number of bytes is indeed important, then a non-`null` pointer value must be passed:

```
size_t numberOfBytes;
print(Crayon(Color.blue, 8), &numberOfBytes);
writefln("%s bytes written to the output", numberOfBytes);
```

Note that this is just an example. Otherwise, it would be better for a function like `print()` to return the number of bytes unconditionally:

```
size_t print(Crayon crayon) {
    immutable info = format("Crayon: %s", crayon);
    writeln(info);

    return info.length;
}
```

68.13 new returns a pointer for some types

new, which we have been using only for constructing class objects can be used with other types as well: structs, arrays, and fundamental types. The variables that are constructed by new are called dynamic variables.

new first allocates space from the memory for the variable and then constructs the variable in that space. The variable itself does not have a symbolic name in the compiled program; it would be accessed through the reference that is returned by new.

The reference that new returns is a different kind depending on the type of the variable:

- For class objects, it is a *class variable*:

```
Class classVariable = new Class;
```

- For struct objects and variables of fundamental types, it is a *pointer*:

```
Struct * structPointer = new Struct;
int * intPointer = new int;
```

- For arrays, it is a *slice*:

```
int[] slice = new int[100];
```

This distinction is usually not obvious when the type is not spelled-out on the left-hand side:

```
auto classVariable = new Class;
auto structPointer = new Struct;
```

```
    auto intPointer = new int;
    auto slice = new int[100];
```

The following program prints the return type of new for different kinds of variables:

```
import std.stdio;

struct Struct {
}

class Class {
}

void main() {
    writeln(typeof(new int    ).stringof);
    writeln(typeof(new int[5]).stringof);
    writeln(typeof(new Struct).stringof);
    writeln(typeof(new Class ).stringof);
}
```

new returns pointers for structs and fundamental types:

```
int*
int[]
Struct*
Class
```

When new is used for constructing a dynamic variable of a value type (page 159), then the lifetime of that variable is extended as long as there is still a reference (e.g. a pointer) to that object in the program. (This is the default situation for reference types.)

68.14 The .ptr property of arrays

The .ptr property of arrays and slices is the address of the first element. The type of this value is a pointer to the type of the elements:

```
    int[] numbers = [ 7, 12 ];

    int * addressOfFirstElement = numbers.ptr;
    writeln("First element: ", *addressOfFirstElement);
```

This property is useful especially when interacting with C libraries. Some C functions take the address of the first of a number of consecutive elements in memory.

Remembering that strings are also arrays, the .ptr property can be used with strings as well. However, note that the first element of a string need not be the first *letter* of the string; rather, the first Unicode code unit of that letter. As an example, the letter é is stored as two code units in a char string.

When accessed through the .ptr property, the code units of strings can be accessed individually. We will see this in the examples section below.

68.15 The in operator of associative arrays

Actually, we have used pointers earlier in the Associative Arrays chapter (page 117). In that chapter, I had intentionally not mentioned the exact type of the in operator and had used it only in logical expressions:

```
    if ("purple" in colorCodes) {
        // there is an element for key "purple"

    } else {
```

```
        // no element for key "purple"
    }
```

In fact, the `in` operator returns the address of the element if there is an element for the specified key; otherwise, it returns `null`. The `if` statement above actually relies on the automatic conversion of the pointer value to `bool`.

When the return value of `in` is stored in a pointer, the element can be accessed efficiently through that pointer:

```
import std.stdio;

void main() {
    string[int] numbers =
        [ 0 : "zero", 1 : "one", 2 : "two", 3 : "three" ];

    int number = 2;
    auto element = number in numbers;          // (1)

    if (element) {                             // (2)
        writeln("I know: %s.", *element);      // (3)

    } else {
        writeln("I don't know the spelling of %s.", number);
    }
}
```

The pointer variable `element` is initialized by the value of the `in` operator (1) and its value is used in a logical expression (2). The value of the element is accessed through that pointer (3) only if the pointer is not `null`.

The actual type of `element` above is a pointer to the same type of the elements (i.e. values) of the associative array. Since the elements of `numbers` above are of type `string`, `in` returns a `string*`. Accordingly, the type could have been spelled out explicitly:

```
    string * element = number in numbers;
```

68.16 When to use pointers

Pointers are rare in D. As we have seen in the Reading from the Standard Input chapter (page 15), `readf` can in fact be used without explicit pointers.

When required by libraries

Pointers can appear on C and C++ library bindings. For example, the following function from the GtkD library takes a pointer:

```
    GdkGeometry geometry;
    // ... set the members of 'geometry' ...

    window.setGeometryHints(/* ... */, &geometry, /* ... */);
```

When referencing variables of value types

Pointers can be used for referring to local variables. The following program counts the outcomes of flipping a coin. It takes advantage of a pointer when referring to one of two local variables:

```
import std.stdio;
import std.random;

void main() {
    size_t headsCount = 0;
    size_t tailsCount = 0;
```

```
    foreach (i; 0 .. 100) {
        size_t * theCounter = (uniform(0, 2) == 1)
                                ? &headsCount
                                : &tailsCount;
        ++(*theCounter);
    }

    writefln("heads: %s  tails: %s", headsCount, tailsCount);
}
```

Obviously, there are other ways of achieving the same goal. For example, using the ternary operator in a different way:

```
    uniform(0, 2) ? ++headsCount : ++tailsCount;
```

By using an if statement:

```
    if (uniform(0, 2)) {
        ++headsCount;

    } else {
        ++tailsCount;
    }
```

As member variables of data structures

Pointers are essential when implementing many data structures.

Unlike the elements of an array being next to each other in memory, elements of many other data structures are apart. Such data structures are based on the concept of their elements *pointing at* other elements.

For example, each node of a linked list *points at* the next node. Similarly, each node of a binary tree *points at* the left and right branches under that node. Pointers are encountered in most other data structures as well.

Although it is possible to take advantage of D's reference types, pointers may be more natural and efficient in some cases.

We will see examples of pointer members below.

When accessing memory directly

Being low-level microprocessor features, pointers provide byte-level access to memory locations. Note that such locations must still belong to valid variables. It is undefined behavior to attempt to access a random memory location.

68.17 Examples

A simple linked list

The elements of linked lists are stored in *nodes*. The concept of a linked list is based on each node pointing at the node that comes after it. The last node has no other node to point at, so it is set to null:

The figure above may be misleading: In reality, the nodes are not side-by-side in memory. Each node does point to the next node but the next node may be at a completely different location.

The following struct can be used for representing the nodes of such a linked list of ints:

```
struct Node {
    int element;
    Node * next;

    // ...
}
```

Note: *Because it contains a reference to the same type as itself, Node is a recursive type.*

The entire list can be represented by a single pointer that points at the first node, which is commonly called *the head*:

```
struct List {
    Node * head;

    // ...
}
```

To keep the example short, let's define just one function that adds an element to the head of the list:

```
struct List {
    Node * head;

    void insertAtHead(int element) {
        head = new Node(element, head);
    }

    // ...
}
```

The line inside insertAtHead() keeps the nodes *linked* by adding a new node to the head of the list. (A function that adds to the end of the list would be more natural and more useful. We will see that function later in one of the problems.)

The right-hand side expression of that line constructs a Node object. When this new object is constructed, its next member is initialized by the current head of the list. When the head member of the list is assigned to this newly linked node, the new element ends up being the first element.

The following program tests these two structs:

```
import std.stdio;
import std.conv;
import std.string;

struct Node {
    int element;
    Node * next;

    string toString() const {
        string result = to!string(element);

        if (next) {
            result ~= " -> " ~ to!string(*next);
        }

        return result;
    }
}

struct List {
    Node * head;

    void insertAtHead(int element) {
        head = new Node(element, head);
    }

    string toString() const {
        return format("(%s)", head ? to!string(*head) : "");
```

```
    }
}

void main() {
    List numbers;

    writeln("before: ", numbers);

    foreach (number; 0 .. 10) {
        numbers.insertAtHead(number);
    }

    writeln("after : ", numbers);
}
```

The output:

```
before: ()
after : (9 -> 8 -> 7 -> 6 -> 5 -> 4 -> 3 -> 2 -> 1 -> 0)
```

Observing the contents of memory by ubyte*

The data stored at each memory address is a byte. Every variable is constructed on a piece of memory that consists of as many bytes as the size of the type of that variable.

A suitable pointer type to observe the content of a memory location is ubyte*. Once the address of a variable is assigned to a ubyte pointer, then all of the bytes of that variable can be observed by incrementing the pointer.

Let's consider the following integer that is initialized by the hexadecimal notation so that it will be easy to understand how its bytes are placed in memory:

```
    int variable = 0x01_02_03_04;
```

A pointer that points at that variable can be defined like this:

```
    int * address = &variable;
```

The value of that pointer can be assigned to a ubyte pointer by the cast operator:

```
    ubyte * bytePointer = cast(ubyte*)address;
```

Such a pointer allows accessing the four bytes of the int variable individually:

```
    writeln(bytePointer[0]);
    writeln(bytePointer[1]);
    writeln(bytePointer[2]);
    writeln(bytePointer[3]);
```

If your microprocessor is *little-endian* like mine, you should see the bytes of the value 0x01_02_03_04 in reverse:

```
4
3
2
1
```

Let's use that idea in a function that will be useful when observing the bytes of all types of variables:

```
import std.stdio;

void printBytes(T)(ref T variable) {
    const ubyte * begin = cast(ubyte*)&variable;    // (1)

    writefln("type    : %s", T.stringof);
```

```
        writefln("value   : %s", variable);
        writefln("address: %s", begin);                  // (2)
        writef  ("bytes   : ");

        writefln("%(%02x %)", begin[0 .. T.sizeof]);      // (3)

        writeln();
}
```

1. Assigning the address of the variable to a ubyte pointer.

2. Printing the value of the pointer.

3. Obtaining the size of the type by .sizeof and printing the bytes of the variable. (Note how a slice is produced from the begin pointer and then that slice is printed directly by writefln().)

Another way of printing the bytes would be to apply the * operator individually:

```
        foreach (bytePointer; begin .. begin + T.sizeof) {
            writef("%02x ", *bytePointer);
        }
```

The value of bytePointer would change from begin to begin + T.sizeof to visit all of the bytes of the variable. Note that the value begin + T.sizeof is outside of the range and is never accessed.

The following program calls printBytes() with various types of variables:

```
struct Struct {
    int first;
    int second;
}

class Class {
    int i;
    int j;
    int k;

    this(int i, int j, int k) {
        this.i = i;
        this.j = j;
        this.k = k;
    }
}

void main() {
    int integerVariable = 0x11223344;
    printBytes(integerVariable);

    double doubleVariable = double.nan;
    printBytes(doubleVariable);

    string slice = "a bright and charming façade";
    printBytes(slice);

    int[3] array = [ 1, 2, 3 ];
    printBytes(array);

    auto structObject = Struct(0xaa, 0xbb);
    printBytes(structObject);

    auto classVariable = new Class(1, 2, 3);
    printBytes(classVariable);
}
```

The output of the program is informative:

```
type    : int
value   : 287454020
```

442

```
address: 7FFF19A83FB0
bytes  : 44 33 22 11                                    ← (1)

type   : double
value  : nan
address: 7FFF19A83FB8
bytes  : 00 00 00 00 00 00 f8 7f                        ← (2)

type   : string
value  : a bright and charming façade
address: 7FFF19A83FC0
bytes  : 1d 00 00 00 00 00 00 00 e0 68 48 00 00 00 00 00
                                                        ← (3)
type   : int[3LU]
value  : [1, 2, 3]
address: 7FFF19A83FD0
bytes  : 01 00 00 00 02 00 00 00 03 00 00 00            ← (1)

type   : Struct
value  : Struct(170, 187)
address: 7FFF19A83FE8
bytes  : aa 00 00 00 bb 00 00 00                        ← (1)

type   : Class
value  : deneme.Class
address: 7FFF19A83FF0
bytes  : 80 df 79 d5 97 7f 00 00                        ← (4)
```

Observations:

1. Although in reverse order on little-endian systems, the bytes of some of the types are as one would expect: The bytes are laid out in memory side by side for ints, fixed-length arrays (int[3]), and struct objects.

2. Considering that the bytes of the special value of double.nan are also in reverse order in memory, we can see that it is represented by the special bit pattern 0x7ff8000000000000.

3. string is reported to be consisting of 16 bytes but it is impossible to fit the letters "a bright and charming façade" into so few bytes. This is due to the fact that behind the scenes string is actually implemented as a struct. Prefixing its name by __ to stress the fact that it is an internal type used by the compiler, that struct is similar to the following one:

```
struct __string {
    size_t length;
    char * ptr;     // the actual characters
}
```

The evidence of this fact is hidden in the bytes that are printed for string above. Note that because ç is made up of two UTF-8 code units, the 28 letters of the string "a bright and charming façade" consists of a total of 29 bytes. The value 0x000000000000001d, the first 8 of the bytes of the string in the output above, is also 29. This is a strong indicator that strings are indeed laid out in memory as in the struct above.

4. Similarly, it is not possible to fit the three int members of the class object in 8 bytes. The output above hints at the possibility that behind the scenes a class variable is implemented as a single pointer that points at the actual class object:

```
struct __Class_VariableType {
    __Class_ActualObjecType * object;
}
```

Let's now consider a more flexible function. Instead of printing the bytes of a variable, let's define a function that prints specified number of bytes at a specified location:

```d
import std.stdio;
import std.ascii;

void printMemory(T)(T * location, size_t length) {
    const ubyte * begin = cast(ubyte*)location;

    foreach (address; begin .. begin + length) {
        char c = (isPrintable(*address) ? *address : '.');

        writefln("%s:  %02x  %s", address, *address, c);
    }
}
```

Since some of the UTF-8 code units may correspond to control characters of the terminal and disrupt its output, we print only the printable characters by first checking them individually by std.ascii.isPrintable(). The non-printable characters are printed as a dot.

We can use that function to print the UTF-8 code units of a string through its .ptr property:

```d
import std.stdio;

void main() {
    string s = "a bright and charming façade";
    printMemory(s.ptr, s.length);
}
```

As seen in the output, the letter ç consists of two bytes:

```
47B4F0:   61   a
47B4F1:   20
47B4F2:   62   b
47B4F3:   72   r
47B4F4:   69   i
47B4F5:   67   g
47B4F6:   68   h
47B4F7:   74   t
47B4F8:   20
47B4F9:   61   a
47B4FA:   6e   n
47B4FB:   64   d
47B4FC:   20
47B4FD:   63   c
47B4FE:   68   h
47B4FF:   61   a
47B500:   72   r
47B501:   6d   m
47B502:   69   i
47B503:   6e   n
47B504:   67   g
47B505:   20
47B506:   66   f
47B507:   61   a
47B508:   c3   .
47B509:   a7   .
47B50A:   61   a
47B50B:   64   d
47B50C:   65   e
```

444

68.18 Exercises

1. Fix the following function so that the values of the arguments that are passed
    to it are swapped. For this exercise, do not specify the parameters as ref but
    take them as pointers:

```
void swap(int lhs, int rhs) {
    int temp = lhs;
    lhs = rhs;
    rhs = temp;
}

void main() {
    int i = 1;
    int j = 2;

    swap(i, j);

    // Their values should be swapped
    assert(i == 2);
    assert(j == 1);
}
```

When you start the program you will notice that the assert checks currently
fail.

2. Convert the linked list that we have defined above to a template so that it can
    be used for storing elements of any type.

3. It is more natural to add elements to the end of a linked list. Modify List so
    that it is possible to add elements to the end as well.

    For this exercise, an additional pointer member variable that points at the
    last element will be useful.

The solutions are on page 733.

This chapter covers operations on bits, the smallest data units. Bit operations are among the most fundamental features of microprocessors.

System programmers must understand bit operations at least to use *flag* parameters correctly.

69.1 Representation of data at the lowest level

Programming languages are abstractions. A user type like Student defined in a programming language is not directly related to the internals of the computer. Programming languages are tools that help humans use the hardware without needing to know the details of the hardware.

Although it is usually not necessary to deal with the hardware directly, it is helpful to understand how data is represented at hardware level.

Transistor

The processing abilities of modern electronic devices are mostly based on the electronic element called *the transistor*. A significant ability of the transistor is that it can be controlled by other parts of the electronic circuit that the transistor is a part of. In a way, it allows the electronic circuit be aware of itself and be able to change its own state.

Bit

The smallest unit of information is a bit. A bit can be represented by any two-state system (e.g. by a special arrangement of a few transistors of an electronic circuit). A bit can have one of two values: 0 or 1. In the computer's memory, the information that is stored in a bit persists until a new value is stored or until the energy source is disconnected.

Computers do not provide direct access to bits. One reason is that doing so would complicate the design of the computer and as a consequence make the computer more expensive. Another reason is that there are not many concepts that can be represented by a single bit.

Byte

A byte is a combination of 8 bits. The smallest unit of information that can be addressed uniquely is a byte. Computers read from or write to memory at least one byte at a time.

For that reason, although it carries one bit of information (false or true), even bool must be implemented as one byte:

```
    writefln("%s is %s byte(s)", bool.stringof, bool.sizeof);
```

```
bool is 1 byte(s)
```

Register

Data that are being operated on in a microprocessor are stored in registers. Registers provide very limited but very fast operations.

The size of the registers depend on the architecture of the microprocessor. For example, 32-bit microprocessors commonly have 4-byte registers and 64-bit microprocessors commonly have 8-byte registers. The size of the registers determine how much information the microprocessor can process efficiently at a time and how many memory addresses that it can support.

Every task that is achieved by a programming language ends up being executed by one or more registers of the microprocessor.

69.2 Binary number system

The decimal number system which is used in daily life consists of 10 numerals: 0123456789. In contrast, the binary number system which is used by computer hardware consists of 2 numerals: 0 and 1. This is a direct consequence of a bit consisting of two values. If bits had three values then the computers would use a number system based on three numerals.

The digits of the decimal system are named incrementally as *ones*, *tens*, *hundreds*, *thousands*, etc. For example, the number 1023 can be expanded as in the following way:

```
1023 == 1 count of thousand, no hundred, 2 counts of ten, and 3 counts of one
```

Naturally, moving one digit to the left multiplies the value of that digit by 10: 1, 10, 100, 1000, etc.

When the same rules are applied to a system that has two numerals, we arrive at the binary number system. The digits are named incrementally as *ones*, *twos*, *fours*, *eights*, etc. In other words, moving one digit to the left would multiply the value of that digit by 2: 1, 2, 4, 8, etc. For example, the *binary* number 1011 can be expanded as in the following way:

```
1011 == 1 count of eight, no four, 1 count of two, and 1 count of one
```

To make it easy to refer to digits, they are numbered from the rightmost digit to the leftmost digit, starting by 0. The following table lists the values of all of the digits of a 32-bit unsigned number in the binary system:

Digit	Value
31	2,147,483,648
30	1,073,741,824
29	536,870,912
28	268,435,456
27	134,217,728
26	67,108,864
25	33,554,432
24	16,777,216
23	8,388,608
22	4,194,304
21	2,097,152
20	1,048,576
19	524,288
18	262,144
17	131,072
16	65,536
15	32,768
14	16,384
13	8,192
12	4,096
11	2,048
10	1,024
9	512
8	256
7	128
6	64
5	32
4	16
3	8

2	4
1	2
0	1

The bits that have higher values are called the *upper* bits and the bits that have lower values are called the *lower* bits.

Remembering from the Literals chapter (page 99) that binary literals are specified by the 0b prefix, the following program demonstrates how the value of a literal would correspond to the rows of the previous table:

```
import std.stdio;

void main() {
    //                  1073741824                  4 1
    //                      ↓                        ↓ ↓
    int number = 0b_01000000_00000000_00000000_00000101;
    writeln(number);
}
```

The output:

```
1073741829
```

Note that the literal consists of only three nonzero bits. The value that is printed is the sum of the values that correspond to those bits from the previous table: 1073741824 + 4 + 1 == 1073741829.

The *sign* bit of signed integer types

The uppermost bit of a signed type determines whether the value is positive or negative:

```
int number = 0b_10000000_00000000_00000000_00000000;
writeln(number);
```

```
-2147483648
```

However, the uppermost bit is not entirely separate from the value. For example, as evidenced above, the fact that all of the other bits of the number being 0 does not mean that the value is -0. (In fact, -0 is not a valid value for integers.) I will not get into more detail in this chapter other than noting that this is due to the *twos complement* representation, which is used by D as well.

What is important here is that 2,147,483,648; the highest value in the previous table, is only for unsigned integer types. The same experiment with uint would print that exact value:

```
uint number = 0b_10000000_00000000_00000000_00000000;
writeln(number);
```

```
2147483648
```

Partly for that reason, unless there is a reason not to, bit operations must always be executed on unsigned types: ubyte, ushort, uint, and ulong.

69.3 Hexadecimal number system

As can be seen in the literals above, consisting only of 0s and 1s, the binary system may not be readable especially when the numbers are large. For that reason, the more readable hexadecimal system has been widely adopted especially in computer technologies.

The hexadecimal system has 16 numerals. Since alphabets do not have more than 10 numerals, this system borrows 6 letters from the Latin alphabet and uses them along with regular numerals: 0123456789abcdef. The numerals a, b, c, d, e, and f have the values 10, 11, 12, 13, 14, and 15, respectively. The letters ABCDEF can be used as well.

Similar to other number systems, the value of every digit is 16 times the value of the digit on its right-hand side: 1, 16, 256, 4096, etc. For example, the values of all of the digits of an 8-digit unsigned hexadecimal number are the following:

Digit	Value
7	268,435,456
6	16,777,216
5	1,048,576
4	65,536
3	4,096
2	256
1	16
0	1

Remembering that hexadecimal literals are specified by the 0x prefix, we can see how the values of the digits contribute to the overall value of a number:

```
//              1048576 4096 1
//                 ↓     ↓   ↓
uint number = 0x_0030_a00f;
writeln(number);
```

```
3186703
```

The value that is printed is by the contributions of all of the nonzero digits: 3 count of 1048576, a count of 4096, and f count of 1. Remembering that a represents 10 and f represents 15, the value is 3145728 + 40960 + 15 == 3186703.

It is straightforward to convert between binary and hexadecimal numbers. In order to convert a hexadecimal number to binary, the digits of the hexadecimal number are converted to their binary representations individually. The corresponding representations in the three number systems are as in the following table:

Hexadecimal	Binary	Decimal
0	0000	0
1	0001	1
2	0010	2
3	0011	3
4	0100	4
5	0101	5
6	0110	6
7	0111	7
8	1000	8
9	1001	9
a	1010	10
b	1011	11
c	1100	12
d	1101	13
e	1110	14
f	1111	15

For example, the hexadecimal number 0x0030a00f can be written in the binary form by converting its digits individually according to the previous table:

```
// hexadecimal:    0    0    3    0    a    0    0    f
uint binary = 0b_0000_0000_0011_0000_1010_0000_0000_1111;
```

Converting from binary to hexadecimal is the reverse: The digits of the binary number are converted to their hexadecimal representations four digits at a time. For example, here is how to write in hexadecimal the same binary value that we have used earlier:

```
// binary:           0100 0000 0000 0000 0000 0000 0000 0101
uint hexadecimal = 0x___4____0____0____0____0____0____0____5;
```

69.4 Bit operations

After going over how values are represented by bits and how numbers are represented in binary and hexadecimal, we can now see operations that change values at bit-level.

Because there is no direct access to individual bits, even though these operations are at bit-level, they affect at least 8 bits at a time. For example, for a variable of type `ubyte`, a bit operation would be applied to all of the 8 bits of that variable.

As the uppermost bit is the sign bit for signed types, I will ignore signed types and use only `uint` in the examples below. You can repeat these operations with `ubyte`, `ushort`, and `ulong`; as well as `byte`, `short`, `int`, and `long` as long as you remember the special meaning of the uppermost bit.

Let's first define a function which will be useful later when examining how bit operators work. This function will print a value in binary, hexadecimal, and decimal systems:

```
import std.stdio;

void print(uint number) {
    writefln("  %032b %08x %10s", number, number, number);
}

void main() {
    print(123456789);
}
```

Here is the same value printed in the binary, hexadecimal, and decimal number systems:

```
  00000111010110111100110100010101 075bcd15  123456789
```

Complement operator: ~

Not to be confused with the binary ~ operator that is used for array concatenation, this is the unary ~ operator.

This operator converts each bit of a value to its opposite: The bits that are 0 become 1, and the bits that are 1 become 0.

```
    uint value = 123456789;
    print(value);
    writeln("~ --------------------------------");
    print(~value);
```

The effect is obvious in the binary representation. Every bit has been reversed (under the dashed line):

```
  00000111010110111100110100010101 075bcd15  123456789
~ --------------------------------
  11111000101001000011001011101010 f8a432ea 4171510506
```

Here is the summary of how the unary ~ operator works:

```
~0 → 1
~1 → 0
```

And operator: &

& is a binary operator, written between two expressions. The microprocessor considers two corresponding bits of the two expressions separately from all of the other bits: Bits 31, 30, 29, etc. of the expressions are evaluated separately. The value of each resultant bit is 1 if both of the corresponding bits of the expressions are 1; 0 otherwise.

```
    uint lhs = 123456789;
    uint rhs = 987654321;

    print(lhs);
    print(rhs);
    writeln("& -------------------------------");
    print(lhs & rhs);
```

The following output contains first the left-hand side expression (lhs) and then the right-hand side expression (rhs). The result of the & operation is under the dashed line:

```
  00000111010110111100110100010101 075bcd15  123456789
  00111010110111100110100010110001 3ade68b1  987654321
& --------------------------------
  00000010001011010010100000010001 025a4811   39471121
```

Note that the bits of the result that have the value 1 are the ones where the corresponding bits of the expressions are both 1.

This operator is called the *and* operator because it produces 1 when both the left-hand side *and* the right-hand side bits are 1. Among the four possible combinations of 0 and 1 values, only the one where both of the values are 1 produces 1:

```
0 & 0 → 0
0 & 1 → 0
1 & 0 → 0
1 & 1 → 1
```

Observations:

- When one of the bits is 0, regardless of the other bit the result is always 0. Accordingly, "*anding* a bit by 0" means to clear that bit.
- When one of the bits is 1, the result is the value of the other bit; *anding* by 1 has no effect.

Or operator: |

| is a binary operator, written between two expressions. The microprocessor considers two corresponding bits of the two expressions separately from all of the other bits. The value of each resultant bit is 0 if both of the corresponding bits of the expressions are 0; 1 otherwise.

```
    uint lhs = 123456789;
    uint rhs = 987654321;

    print(lhs);
    print(rhs);
    writeln("| -------------------------------");
    print(lhs | rhs);
```

```
000001110101101111001101000010101 075bcd15   123456789
001110101101111001101000010110001 3ade68b1   987654321
| --------------------------------
001111111101111111101101101101101  3fdfedb5  1071639989
```

Note that the bits of the result that have the value 0 are the ones where the corresponding bits of the expressions are both 0. When the corresponding bit in the left-hand side or in the right-hand side is 1, then the result is 1:

```
0 | 0 → 0
0 | 1 → 1
1 | 0 → 1
1 | 1 → 1
```

Observations:

- When one of the bits is 1, regardless of the other bit the result is always 1. Accordingly, "*orring* a bit by 1" means to set it.
- When one of the bits is 0, the result is the value of the other bit; *orring* by 0 has no effect.

Xor operator: ^

Xor is the short for *exclusive or*. This is a binary operator as well. It produces 1 if the corresponding bits of the two expressions are different:

```
uint lhs = 123456789;
uint rhs = 987654321;

print(lhs);
print(rhs);
writeln("^ -------------------------------");
print(lhs ^ rhs);
```

```
000001110101101111001101000010101 075bcd15   123456789
001110101101111001101000010110001 3ade68b1   987654321
^ --------------------------------
001111011000010110100101101001000100 3d85a5a4 1032168868
```

Note that the bits of the result that have the value 1 are the ones where the corresponding bits of the expressions are different from each other.

```
0 ^ 0 → 0
0 ^ 1 → 1
1 ^ 0 → 1
1 ^ 1 → 0
```

Observation:

- "*Xorring* a bit" with itself means to clear that bit.

Regardless of its value, *xorring* a variable with itself always produces 0:

```
uint value = 123456789;

print(value ^ value);
```

```
00000000000000000000000000000000 00000000        0
```

Right-shift operator: >>

This operator shifts the bits of an expression by the specified number of bits to the right. The rightmost bits, which do not have room to shift into, get *dropped* from the value. For unsigned types, the leftmost bits are filled with zeros.

The following example produces a result by shifting a value by two bits to the right:

```
uint value = 123456789;
print(value);
print(value >> 2);
```

In the following output, I highlighted both the bits that are going to be lost due to dropping off from the right-hand side and the leftmost bits that get the value 0:

```
00000111010110111100110100010101 075bcd15 123456789
00000001110101101111001101000101 01d6f345  30864197
```

Note that the bits that are not highlighted have been shifted two bit positions to the right.

The new bits that enter from the left-hand side are 0 only for unsigned types. For signed types, the value of the leftmost bits are determined by a process called *sign extension*. Sign extension preserves the value of the sign bit of the original expression. The value of that bit is used for all of the bits that *enter* from the left.

Let's see this effect on a value of a signed type where the sign bit is 1 (i.e. the value is negative):

```
int value = 0x80010300;
print(value);
print(value >> 3);
```

Because the leftmost bit of the original value is 1, all of the new bits of the result are 1 as well:

```
10000000000000010000000100000000 80010300 2147549952
11110000000000000010000000100000 f0002060 4026540128
```

When the leftmost bit is 0, then all new bits are 0:

```
int value = 0x40010300;
print(value);
print(value >> 3);
```

```
01000000000000010000000100000000 40010300 1073808128
00001000000000000010000000100000 08002060  134226016
```

Unsigned right-shift operator: >>>

This operator works similarly to the regular right-shift operator. The difference is that the new leftmost bits are always 0 regardless of the type of the expression and the value of the leftmost bit:

```
int value = 0x80010300;
print(value);
print(value >>> 3);
```

```
10000000000000010000000100000000 80010300 2147549952
00010000000000000010000000100000 10002060  268443744
```

Left-shift operator: <<

This operator works as the reverse of the right-shift operator. The bits are shifted to the left:

```
uint value = 123456789;
print(value);
print(value << 4);
```

The bits on the left-hand side are lost and the new bits on the right-hand side are 0:

```
00000111010110111100110100010101 075bcd15  123456789
01110101101111001101000101010000 75bcd150 1975308624
```

Operators with assignment

All of the binary operators above have assignment counterparts: &=, |=, ^=, >>=, >>>=, and <<=. Similar to the operators that we saw in the Integers and Arithmetic Operations chapter (page 31), these operators assign the result back to the left-hand operand.

Let's see this on the &= operator:

```
value = value & 123;
value &= 123;            // the same as above
```

69.5 Semantics

Merely understanding how these operators work at bit-level may not be sufficient to see how they are useful in programs. The following sections describe common ways that these operators are used in.

| is a union set

The | operator produces the union of the 1 bits in the two expressions.

As an extreme example, let's consider two values that both have alternating bits set to 1. The union of these values would produce a result where all of the bits are 1:

```
uint lhs = 0xaaaaaaaa;
uint rhs = 0x55555555;

print(lhs);
print(rhs);
writeln("| ------------------------------");
print(lhs | rhs);
```

```
10101010101010101010101010101010 aaaaaaaa 2863311530
01010101010101010101010101010101 55555555 1431655765
| ------------------------------
11111111111111111111111111111111 ffffffff 4294967295
```

& is an intersection set

The & operator produces the intersection of the 1 bits in the two expressions.

As an extreme example, let's consider the last two values again. Since none of the 1 bits of the previous two expressions match the ones in the other expression, all of the bits of the result are 0:

```
uint lhs = 0xaaaaaaaa;
uint rhs = 0x55555555;

print(lhs);
print(rhs);
writeln("& ------------------------------");
print(lhs & rhs);
```

```
10101010101010101010101010101010 aaaaaaaa 2863311530
01010101010101010101010101010101 55555555 1431655765
& ------------------------------
00000000000000000000000000000000 00000000          0
```

| = sets selected bits to 1

To understand how this works, it helps to see one of the expressions as the *actual* expression and the other expression as a *selector* for the bits to set to 1:

```
    uint expression = 0x00ff00ff;
    uint bitsToSet = 0x10001000;

    write("before    :"); print(expression);
    write("to set to 1:"); print(bitsToSet);

    expression |= bitsToSet;
    write("after      :"); print(expression);
```

The before and after values of the bits that are affected are highlighted:

```
before     :  00000000111111110000000011111111 00ff00ff   16711935
to set to 1:  00010000000000000001000000000000 10001000  268439552
after      :  00010000111111110001000011111111 10ff10ff  285151487
```

In a sense, `bitsToSet` determines which bits to set to 1. The other bits are not affected.

&= clears selected bits

One of the expressions can be seen as the *actual* expression and the other expression can be seen as a *selector* for the bits to clear (to set to 0):

```
    uint expression = 0x00ff00ff;
    uint bitsToClear = 0xfffefffef;

    write("before      :"); print(expression);
    write("bits to clear:"); print(bitsToClear);

    expression &= bitsToClear;
    write("after        :"); print(expression);
```

The before and after values of the bits that are affected are highlighted:

```
before      :  00000000111111110000000011111111 00ff00ff   16711935
bits to clear: 11111111111011111111111111101111 ffefffef 4293918703
after       :  00000000111011110000000011101111 00ef00ef   15663343
```

In a sense, `bitsToClear` determines which bits to set to 0. The other bits are not affected.

& determines whether a bit is 1 or not

If one of the expressions has only one bit set to 1, then it can be used to query whether the corresponding bit of the other expression is 1:

```
    uint expression = 123456789;
    uint bitToQuery = 0x00010000;

    print(expression);
    print(bitToQuery);
    writeln(expression & bitToQuery ? "yes, 1" : "not 1");
```

The bit that is being *queried* is highlighted:

```
  00000111010110111100110100010101 075bcd15  123456789
  00000000000000010000000000000000 00010000      65536
yes, 1
```

Let's query another bit of the same expression by this time having another bit of `bitToQuery` set to 1:

```
    uint bitToQuery = 0x00001000;
```

```
00000111010110111100110100010101 075bcd15   123456789
00000000000000000001000000000000 00001000        4096
not 1
```

When the query expression has more than one bit set to 1, then the query would determine whether *any* of the corresponding bits in the other expression are 1.

Right-shifting by one is the equivalent of dividing by two

Shifting all of the bits of a value by one position to the right produces half of the original value. The reason for this can be seen in the digit-value table above: In that table, every bit has half the value of the bit that is on its left.

Shifting a value to the right multiple bits at a time means dividing by 2 for that many times. For example, right-shifting by 3 bits would divide a value by 8:

```
    uint value = 8000;

    writeln(value >> 3);
```

```
1000
```

According to how the *twos complement* system works, right-shifting has the same effect on signed values:

```
    int value = -8000;

    writeln(value >> 3);
```

```
-1000
```

Left-shifting by one is the equivalent of multiplying by two

Because each bit is two times the value of the bit on its right, shifting a value one bit to the left means multiplying that value by two:

```
    uint value = 10;

    writeln(value << 5);
```

Multiplying by 2 a total of 5 times is the same as multiplying by 32:

```
320
```

69.6 Common uses

Flags

Flags are single-bit independent data that are kept together in the same variable. As they are only one bit wide each, they are suitable for representing binary concepts like enabled/disabled, valid/invalid, etc.

Such one-bit concepts are sometimes encountered in D modules that are based on C libraries.

Flags are usually defined as non-overlapping values of an enum type.

As an example, let's consider a car racing game where the realism of the game is configurable:

- The fuel consumption is realistic or not.
- Collisions can damage the cars or not.
- Tires can deteriorate by use or not.
- Skid marks are left on the road surface or not.

These configuration options can be specified at run time by the following enum values:

```d
enum Realism {
    fuelUse     = 1 << 0,
    bodyDamage  = 1 << 1,
    tireUse     = 1 << 2,
    skidMarks   = 1 << 3
}
```

Note that all of those values consist of single bits that do not conflict with each other. Each value is determined by left-shifting 1 by a different number of bits. The corresponding bit representations are the following:

```
fuelUse    : 0001
bodyDamage : 0010
tireUse    : 0100
skidMarks  : 1000
```

Since their 1 bits do not match others', these values can be combined by the | operator to be kept in the same variable. For example, the two configuration options that are related to tires can be combined as in the following code:

```d
    Realism flags = Realism.tireUse | Realism.skidMarks;
    writefln("%b", flags);
```

The bits of these two flags would be side-by-side in the variable flags:

```
1100
```

Later, these flags can be queried by the & operator:

```d
    if (flags & Realism.fuelUse) {
        // ... code related to fuel consumption ...
    }

    if (flags & Realism.tireUse) {
        // ... code related to tire consumption ...
    }
```

The & operator produces 1 only if the specified flag is set in flags.

Also note that the result is usable in the if condition due to automatic conversion of the nonzero value to true. The conditional expression is false when the result of & is 0 and true otherwise. As a result, the corresponding code block is executed only if the flag is enabled.

Masking

In some libraries and some protocols an integer value may carry more than one piece of information. For example, the upper 3 bits of a 32-bit value may have a certain meaning, while the lower 29 bits may have another meaning. These separate parts of data can be extracted from the variable by masking.

The four octets of an IPv4 address are an example of this concept. The octets are the individual values that make up the common dotted representation of an IPv4 address. They are all kept in a single 32-bit value. For example, the IPv4 address 192.168.1.2 is the 32-bit value 0xc0a80102:

```
c0 == 12 * 16 + 0 = 192
a8 == 10 * 16 + 8 = 168
01 ==  0 * 16 + 1 =   1
02 ==  0 * 16 + 2 =   2
```

A mask consists of a number of 1 bits that would *cover* the specific part of a variable. *"And"ing* the value by the mask extracts the part of the variable that is covered by that mask. For example, the mask value of 0x000000ff would cover the lower 8 bits of a value:

```
uint value = 123456789;
uint mask  = 0x000000ff;

write("value :"); print(value);
write("mask   :"); print(mask);
write("result:"); print(value & mask);
```

The bits that are covered by the mask are highlighted. All of the other bits are cleared:

```
value  :  00000111010110111100110100010101 075bcd15   123456789
mask   :  00000000000000000000000011111111 000000ff         255
result:   00000000000000000000000000010101 00000015          21
```

Let's apply the same method to the 0xc0a80102 IPv4 address with a mask that would cover the uppermost 8 bits:

```
uint value = 0xc0a80102;
uint mask  = 0xff000000;

write("value :"); print(value);
write("mask   :"); print(mask);
write("result:"); print(value & mask);
```

This mask covers the uppermost 8 bits of the value:

```
value  :  11000000101010000000000100000010 c0a80102 3232235778
mask   :  11111111000000000000000000000000 ff000000 4278190080
result:   11000000000000000000000000000000 c0000000 3221225472
```

However, note that the printed result is not the expected 192 but 3221225472. That is because the masked value must also be shifted all the way to the right-hand side. Shifting the value 24 bit positions to the right would produce the value that those 8 bits represent:

```
uint value = 0xc0a80102;
uint mask  = 0xff000000;

write("value :"); print(value);
write("mask   :"); print(mask);
write("result:"); print((value & mask) >> 24);
```

```
value  :  11000000101010000000000100000010 c0a80102 3232235778
mask   :  11111111000000000000000000000000 ff000000 4278190080
result:   00000000000000000000000011000000 000000c0        192
```

69.7 Exercises

1. Write a function that returns an IPv4 address in its dotted form:

```
string dotted(uint address) {
    // ...
}

unittest {
    assert(dotted(0xc0a80102) == "192.168.1.2");
}
```

2. Write a function that converts four octet values to the corresponding 32-bit IPv4 address:

```
uint ipAddress(ubyte octet3,     // most significant octet
               ubyte octet2,
               ubyte octet1,
               ubyte octet0) {  // least significant octet
    // ...
}

unittest {
    assert(ipAddress(192, 168, 1, 2) == 0xc0a80102);
}
```

3. Write a function that can be used for making a mask. It should start with the specified bit and have the specified width:

```
uint mask(int lowestBit, int width) {
    // ...
}

unittest {
    assert(mask(2, 5) ==
           0b_0000_0000_0000_0000_0000_0000_0111_1100);
    //                                            ↑
    //                                   lowest bit is 2,
    //                                   and the mask is 5-bit wide
}
```

The solutions are on page 736.

Conditional compilation is for compiling parts of programs in special ways depending on certain compile time conditions. Sometimes, entire sections of a program may need to be taken out and not compiled at all.

Conditional compilation involves condition checks that are evaluable at compile time. Runtime conditional statements like `if`, `for`, `while` are not conditional compilation features.

We have already encountered some features in the previous chapters, which can be seen as conditional compilation:

- `unittest` blocks are compiled and run only if the `-unittest` compiler switch is enabled.
- The contract programming blocks `in`, `out`, and `invariant` are activated only if the `-release` compiler switch is *not* enabled.

Unit tests and contracts are about program correctness; whether they are included in the program should not change the behavior of the program.

The following are the features of D that are specifically for conditional compilation:

- debug
- version
- static if
- is expression
- __traits

We will see the `is` expression in the next chapter.

70.1 debug

debug is useful during program development. The expressions and statements that are marked as debug are compiled into the program only when the `-debug` compiler switch is enabled:

```d
debug a_conditionally_compiled_expression;

debug {
    // ... conditionally compiled code ...

} else {
    // ... code that is compiled otherwise ...
}
```

The `else` clause is optional.

Both the single expression and the code block above are compiled only when the `-debug` compiler switch is enabled.

We have been adding statements into the programs, which printed messages like "adding", "subtracting", etc. to the output. Such messages (aka *logs* and *log messages*) are helpful in finding errors by visualizing the steps that are taken by the program.

Remember the `binarySearch()` function from the Templates chapter (page 399). The following version of the function is intentionally incorrect:

```d
import std.stdio;
```

```
// WARNING! This algorithm is wrong
size_t binarySearch(const int[] values, int value) {
    if (values.length == 0) {
        return size_t.max;
    }

    immutable midPoint = values.length / 2;

    if (value == values[midPoint]) {
        return midPoint;

    } else if (value < values[midPoint]) {
        return binarySearch(values[0 .. midPoint], value);

    } else {
        return binarySearch(values[midPoint + 1 .. $], value);
    }
}

void main() {
    auto numbers = [ -100, 0, 1, 2, 7, 10, 42, 365, 1000 ];

    auto index = binarySearch(numbers, 42);
    writeln("Index: ", index);
}
```

Although the index of 42 is 6, the program incorrectly reports 1:

```
Index: 1
```

One way of locating the bug in the program is to insert lines that would print messages to the output:

```
size_t binarySearch(const int[] values, int value) {
    writefln("searching %s among %s", value, values);

    if (values.length == 0) {
        writefln("%s not found", value);
        return size_t.max;
    }

    immutable midPoint = values.length / 2;

    writefln("considering index %s", midPoint);

    if (value == values[midPoint]) {
        writefln("found %s at index %s", value, midPoint);
        return midPoint;

    } else if (value < values[midPoint]) {
        writefln("must be in the first half");
        return binarySearch(values[0 .. midPoint], value);

    } else {
        writefln("must be in the second half");
        return binarySearch(values[midPoint + 1 .. $], value);
    }
}
```

The output of the program now includes steps that the program takes:

```
searching 42 among [-100, 0, 1, 2, 7, 10, 42, 365, 1000]
considering index 4
must be in the second half
searching 42 among [10, 42, 365, 1000]
considering index 2
must be in the first half
searching 42 among [10, 42]
considering index 1
found 42 at index 1
Index: 1
```

Let's assume that the previous output does indeed help the programmer locate the bug. It is obvious that the writefln() expressions are not needed anymore once the bug has been located and fixed. However, removing those lines can also be seen as wasteful, because they might be useful again in the future.

Instead of being removed altogether, the lines can be marked as debug instead:

```
debug writefln("%s not found", value);
```

Such lines are included in the program only when the -debug compiler switch is enabled:

```
$ dmd deneme.d -ofdeneme -w -debug
```

debug(*tag*)

If there are many debug keywords in the program, possibly in unrelated parts, the output may become too crowded. To avoid that, the debug statements can be given names (tags) to be included in the program selectively:

```
debug(binarySearch) writefln("%s not found", value);
```

The tagged debug statements are enabled by the -debug=*tag* compiler switch:

```
$ dmd deneme.d -ofdeneme -w -debug=binarySearch
```

debug blocks can have tags as well:

```
debug(binarySearch) {
    // ...
}
```

It is possible to enable more than one debug tag at a time:

```
$ dmd deneme.d -w -debug=binarySearch -debug=stackContainer
```

In that case both the binarySearch and the stackContainer debug statements and blocks would be included.

debug(*level*)

Sometimes it is more useful to associate debug statements by numerical levels. Increasing levels can provide more detailed information:

```
debug import std.stdio;

void myFunction(string fileName, int[] values) {
    debug(1) writeln("entered myFunction");

    debug(2) {
        writeln("the arguments:");
        writeln("  file name: ", fileName);

        foreach (i, value; values) {
            writefln("  %4s: %s", i, value);
        }
    }

    // ... the implementation of the function ...
}

void main() {
    myFunction("deneme.txt", [ 10, 4, 100 ]);
}
```

The debug expressions and blocks that are lower than or equal to the specified level would be compiled:

```
$ dmd deneme.d -w -debug=1
$ ./deneme
entered myFunction
```

The following compilation would provide more information:

```
$ dmd deneme.d -w -debug=2
$ ./deneme
entered myFunction
the arguments:
  file name: deneme.txt
    0: 10
    1: 4
    2: 100
```

70.2 version(*tag*) and version(*level*)

version is similar to debug and is used in the same way:

```
    version(testRelease) /* ... an expression ... */;

    version(schoolRelease) {
        /* ... expressions that are related to the version of
        *     this program that is presumably shipped to schools ... */

    } else {
        // ... code compiled otherwise ...
    }

    version(1) aVariable = 5;

    version(2) {
        // ... a feature of version 2 ...
    }
```

The else clause is optional.

Although version works essentially the same as debug, having separate keywords helps distinguish their unrelated uses.

As with debug, more than one version can be enabled:

```
$ dmd deneme.d -w -version=record -version=precise_calculation
```

There are many predefined version tags, the complete list of which is available at the Conditional Compilation specification[1]. The following short list is just a sampling:

Predefined version tags

The compiler	DigitalMars GNU LDC SDC
The operating system	Windows Win32 Win64 linux OSX Posix FreeBSD OpenBSD NetBSD DragonFlyBSD BSD Solaris AIX Haiku SkyOS SysV3 SysV4 Hurd
CPU endianness	LittleEndian BigEndian
Enabled compiler switches	D_Coverage D_Ddoc D_InlineAsm_X86 D_InlineAsm_X86_64 D_LP64 D_PIC D_X32 D_HardFloat D_SoftFloat D_SIMD D_Version2 D_NoBoundsChecks unittest assert
CPU architecture	X86 X86_64
Platform	Android Cygwin MinGW ARM ARM_Thumb ARM_Soft ARM_SoftFP ARM_HardFP ARM64 PPC PPC_SoftFP PPC_HardFP PPC64 IA64 MIPS MIPS32 MIPS64 MIPS_O32 MIPS_N32 MIPS_O64 MIPS_N64 MIPS_EABI MIPS_NoFloat MIPS_SoftFloat MIPS_HardFloat SPARC SPARC_V8Plus SPARC_SoftFP SPARC_HardFP SPARC64 S390 S390X HPPA HPPA64 SH SH64 Alpha Alpha_SoftFP Alpha_HardFP
...	...

---

1. http://dlang.org/version.html

In addition, there are the following two special version tags:

- none: This tag is never defined; it is useful for disabling code blocks.
- all: This tag is always defined; it is useful for enabling code blocks.

As an example of how predefined version tags are used, the following is an excerpt (formatted differently here) from the std.ascii module, which is for determining the newline character sequence for the system (static assert will be explained later below):

```d
version(Windows) {
    immutable newline = "\r\n";

} else version(Posix) {
    immutable newline = "\n";

} else {
    static assert(0, "Unsupported OS");
}
```

70.3 Assigning identifiers to debug and version

Similar to variables, debug and version can be assigned identifiers. Unlike variables, this assignment does not change any value, it activates the specified identifier *as well*.

```d
import std.stdio;

debug(everything) {
    debug = binarySearch;
    debug = stackContainer;
    version = testRelease;
    version = schoolRelease;
}

void main() {
    debug(binarySearch) writeln("binarySearch is active");
    debug(stackContainer) writeln("stackContainer is active");

    version(testRelease) writeln("testRelease is active");
    version(schoolRelease) writeln("schoolRelease is active");
}
```

The assignments inside the debug(everything) block above activates all of the specified identifiers:

```
$ dmd deneme.d -w -debug=everything
$ ./deneme
binarySearch is active
stackContainer is active
testRelease is active
schoolRelease is active
```

70.4 static if

static if is the compile time equivalent of the if statement.

Just like the if statement, static if takes a logical expression and evaluates it. Unlike the if statement, static if is not about execution flow; rather, it determines whether a piece of code should be included in the program or not.

The logical expression must be evaluable at compile time. If the logical expression evaluates to true, the code inside the static if gets compiled. If the condition is false, the code is not included in the program as if it has never been written. The logical expressions commonly take advantage of the is expression and __traits.

static if can appear at module scope or inside definitions of struct, class, template, etc. Optionally, there may be else clauses as well.

Let's use static if with a simple template, making use of the is expression. We will see other examples of static if in the next chapter:

```d
import std.stdio;

struct MyType(T) {
    static if (is (T == float)) {
        alias ResultType = double;

    } else static if (is (T == double)) {
        alias ResultType = real;

    } else {
        static assert(false, T.stringof ~ " is not supported");
    }

    ResultType doWork() {
        writefln("The return type for %s is %s.",
                 T.stringof, ResultType.stringof);
        ResultType result;
        // ...
        return result;
    }
}

void main() {
    auto f = MyType!float();
    f.doWork();

    auto d = MyType!double();
    d.doWork();
}
```

According to the code, MyType can be used only with two types: float or double. The return type of doWork() is chosen depending on whether the template is instantiated for float or double:

```
The return type for float is double.
The return type for double is real.
```

Note that one must write else static if when chaining static if clauses. Otherwise, writing else if would result in inserting that if conditional into the code, which would naturally be executed at run time.

70.5 static assert

Although it is not a conditional compilation feature, I have decided to introduce static assert here.

static assert is the compile time equivalent of assert. If the conditional expression is false, the compilation gets aborted due to that assertion failure.

Similar to static if, static assert can appear in any scope in the program.

We have seen an example of static assert in the program above: There, compilation gets aborted if T is any type other than float or double:

```d
    auto i = MyType!int();
```

The compilation is aborted with the message that was given to static assert:

```
Error: static assert  "int is not supported"
```

As another example, let's assume that a specific algorithm can work only with types that are a multiple of a certain size. Such a condition can be ensured at compile time by a static assert:

```
T myAlgorithm(T)(T value) {
    /* This algorithm requires that the size of type T is a
     * multiple of 4. */
    static assert((T.sizeof % 4) == 0);

    // ...
}
```

If the function was called with a char, the compilation would be aborted with the following error message:

```
Error: static assert  (1LU == 0LU) is false
```

Such a test prevents the function from working with an incompatible type, potentially producing incorrect results.

static assert can be used with any logical expression that is evaluable at compile time.

70.6 Type traits

The __traits keyword and the std.traits module provide information about types and expressions at compile time.

Some information that is collected by the compiler is made available to the program by __traits. Its syntax includes a traits *keyword* and *parameters* that are relevant to that keyword:

```
__traits(keyword, parameters)
```

keyword specifies the information that is being queried. The *parameters* are either types or expressions, meanings of which are determined by each particular keyword.

The information that can be gathered by __traits is especially useful in templates. For example, the isArithmetic keyword can determine whether a particular template parameter T is an arithmetic type:

```
    static if (__traits(isArithmetic, T)) {
        // ... an arithmetic type ...

    } else {
        // ... not an arithmetic type ...
    }
```

Similarly, the std.traits module provides information at compile time through its templates. For example, std.traits.isSomeChar returns true if its template parameter is a character type:

```
import std.traits;

// ...

    static if (isSomeChar!T) {
        // ... char, wchar, or dchar ...

    } else {
        // ... not a character type ...
    }
```

Please refer to the __traits documentation[1] and the std.traits documentation[2] for more information.

---

1. http://dlang.org/traits.html
2. http://dlang.org/phobos/std_traits.html

70.7 Summary

- Code that is defined as debug is included to the program only if the -debug compiler switch is used.
- Code that is defined as version is included to the program only if a corresponding -version compiler switch is used.
- static if is similar to an if statement that is executed at compile time. It introduces code to the program depending on certain compile-time conditions.
- static assert validates assumptions about code at compile time.
- __traits and std.traits provide information about types at compile time.

71 is Expression

The is *expression* is not related to the is *operator* that we saw in The null Value and the is Operator chapter (page 233), neither syntactically nor semantically:

```
a is b              // is operator, which we have seen before

is (/* ... */)     // is expression
```

The is expression is evaluated at compile time. It produces an int value, either 0 or 1 depending on the expression specified in parentheses. Although the expression that it takes is not a logical expression, the is expression itself is used as a compile time logical expression. It is especially useful in static if conditionals and template constraints.

The condition that it takes is always about types, which must be written in one of several syntaxes.

71.1 is (*T*)

Determines whether T is valid as a type.

It is difficult to come up with examples for this use at this point. We will take advantage of it in later chapters with template parameters.

```
static if (is (int)) {
    writeln("valid");

} else {
    writeln("invalid");
}
```

int above is a valid type:

```
valid
```

As another example, because void is not valid as the key type of an associative array, the else block would be enabled below:

```
static if (is (string[void])) {
    writeln("valid");

} else {
    writeln("invalid");
}
```

The output:

```
invalid
```

71.2 is (*T Alias*)

Works in the same way as the previous syntax. Additionally, defines Alias as an alias of T:

```
static if (is (int NewAlias)) {
    writeln("valid");
    NewAlias var = 42; // int and NewAlias are the same

} else {
    writeln("invalid");
}
```

Such aliases are useful especially in more complex is expressions as we will see below.

71.3 is (*T : OtherT*)

Determines whether T can automatically be converted to OtherT.

It is used for detecting automatic type conversions which we have seen in the Type Conversions chapter (page 237), as well as relationships like "this type is of that type", which we have seen in the Inheritance chapter (page 328).

```d
import std.stdio;

interface Clock {
    void tellTime();
}

class AlarmClock : Clock {
    override void tellTime() {
        writeln("10:00");
    }
}

void myFunction(T)(T parameter) {
    static if (is (T : Clock)) {
        // If we are here then T can be used as a Clock
        writeln("This is a Clock; we can tell the time");
        parameter.tellTime();

    } else {
        writeln("This is not a Clock");
    }
}

void main() {
    auto var = new AlarmClock;
    myFunction(var);
    myFunction(42);
}
```

When the myFunction() template is instantiated for a type that can be used like a Clock, then the tellTime() member function is called on its parameter. Otherwise, the else clause gets compiled:

```
This is a Clock; we can tell the time    ← for AlarmClock
10:00                                     ← for AlarmClock
This is not a Clock                       ← for int
```

71.4 is (*T Alias : OtherT*)

Works in the same way as the previous syntax. Additionally, defines Alias as an alias of T.

71.5 is (*T == Specifier*)

Determines whether T *is the same type* as Specifier or whether T *matches that specifier*.

Whether the same type

When we change the previous example to use == instead of :, the condition would not be satisfied for AlarmClock:

```d
    static if (is (T == Clock)) {
        writeln("This is a Clock; we can tell the time");
        parameter.tellTime();

    } else {
        writeln("This is not a Clock");
    }
```

Although `AlarmClock` *is a* `Clock`, it is not exactly the same type as `Clock`. For that reason, now the condition is invalid for both `AlarmClock` and `int`:

```
This is not a Clock
This is not a Clock
```

Whether matches the same specifier

When `Specifier` is one of the following keywords, this use of `is` determines whether the type matches that specifier (we will see some of these keywords in later chapters):

- `struct`
- `union`
- `class`
- `interface`
- `enum`
- `function`
- `delegate`
- `const`
- `immutable`
- `shared`

```
void myFunction(T)(T parameter) {
    static if (is (T == class)) {
        writeln("This is a class type");

    } else static if (is (T == enum)) {
        writeln("This is an enum type");

    } else static if (is (T == const)) {
        writeln("This is a const type");

    } else {
        writeln("This is some other type");
    }
}
```

Function templates can take advantage of such information to behave differently depending on the type that the template is instantiated with. The following code demonstrates how different blocks of the template above get compiled for different types:

```
    auto var = new AlarmClock;
    myFunction(var);

    // (enum WeekDays will be defined below for another example)
    myFunction(WeekDays.Monday);

    const double number = 1.2;
    myFunction(number);

    myFunction(42);
```

The output:

```
This is a class type
This is an enum type
This is a const type
This is some other type
```

71.6 is (*T identifier* == *Specifier*)

Works in the same way as the previous syntax. identifier is either an alias of the type; or some other information depending on Specifier:

Specifier	The meaning of identifier
struct	alias of the type that satisfied the condition
union	alias of the type that satisfied the condition
class	alias of the type that satisfied the condition
interface	alias of the type that satisfied the condition
super	a *tuple* consisting of the base classes and the interfaces
enum	the actual implementation type of the enum
function	a *tuple* consisting of the function parameters
delegate	the type of the delegate
return	the return type of the regular function, the delegate, or the function pointer
__parameters	a *tuple* consisting of the parameters of the regular function, the delegate, or the function pointer
const	alias of the type that satisfied the condition
immutable	alias of the type that satisfied the condition
shared	alias of the type that satisfied the condition

Let's first define various types before experimenting with this syntax:

```d
struct Point {
    // ...
}

interface Clock {
    // ...
}

class AlarmClock : Clock {
    // ...
}

enum WeekDays {
    Monday, Tuesday, Wednesday, Thursday, Friday,
    Saturday, Sunday
}

char foo(double d, int i, Clock c) {
    return 'a';
}
```

The following function template uses different specifiers with this syntax of the is expression:

```d
void myFunction(T)(T parameter) {
    static if (is (T LocalAlias == struct)) {
        writefln("\n--- struct ---");
        // LocalAlias is the same as T. 'parameter' is the
        // struct object that has been passed to this
        // function.

        writefln("Constructing a new %s object by copying it.",
                LocalAlias.stringof);
        LocalAlias theCopy = parameter;
    }

    static if (is (T baseTypes == super)) {
        writeln("\n--- super ---");
        // The 'baseTypes' tuple contains all of the base
        // types of T. 'parameter' is the class variable that
        // has been passed to this function.

        writefln("class %s has %s base types.",
                T.stringof, baseTypes.length);
```

```
        writeln("All of the bases: ", baseTypes.stringof);
        writeln("The topmost base: ", baseTypes[0].stringof);
    }

    static if (is (T ImplT == enum)) {
        writeln("\n--- enum ---");
        // 'ImplT' is the actual implementation type of this
        //  enum type. 'parameter' is the enum value that has
        //  been passed to this function.

        writefln("The implementation type of enum %s is %s",
                 T.stringof, ImplT.stringof);
    }

    static if (is (T ReturnT == return)) {
        writeln("\n--- return ---");
        // 'ReturnT' is the return type of the function
        // pointer that has been passed to this function.

        writefln("This is a function with a return type of %s:",
                 ReturnT.stringof);
        writeln("    ", T.stringof);
        write("calling it... ");

        // Note: Function pointers can be called like
        // functions
        ReturnT result = parameter(1.5, 42, new AlarmClock);
        writefln("and the result is '%s'", result);
    }
}
```

Let's now call that function template with various types that we have defined above:

```
// Calling with a struct object
myFunction(Point());

// Calling with a class reference
myFunction(new AlarmClock);

// Calling with an enum value
myFunction(WeekDays.Monday);

// Calling with a function pointer
myFunction(&foo);
```

The output:

```
--- struct ---
Constructing a new Point object by copying it.

--- super ---
class AlarmClock has 2 base types.
All of the bases: (Object, Clock)
The topmost base: Object

--- enum ---
The implementation type of enum WeekDays is int

--- return ---
This is a function with a return type of char:
    char function(double d, int i, Clock c)
calling it... and the result is 'a'
```

71.7 is (/* ... */ *Specifier*, *TemplateParamList*)

There are four different syntaxes of the is expression that uses a template parameter list:

- is (*T* : *Specifier*, *TemplateParamList*)

- is (*T == Specifier, TemplateParamList*)
- is (*T identifier : Specifier, TemplateParamList*)
- is (*T identifier == Specifier, TemplateParamList*)

These syntaxes allow for more complex cases.

identifier, Specifier, :, and == all have the same meanings as described above.

TemplateParamList is both a part of the condition that needs to be satisfied and a facility to define additional aliases if the condition is indeed satisfied. It works in the same way as template type deduction.

As a simple example, let's assume that an is expression needs to match associative arrays that have keys of type string:

```
static if (is (T == Value[Key],    // (1)
               Value,              // (2)
               Key : string)) {    // (3)
```

That condition can be explained in three parts where the last two are parts of the TemplateParamList:

1. If T matches the syntax of Value[Key]
2. If Value is a type
3. If Key is string (remember template specialization syntax (page 399))

Having Value[Key] as the Specifier requires that T is an associative array. Leaving Value *as is* means that it can be any type. Additionally, the key type of the associative array must be string. As a result, the previous is expression means "if T is an associative array where the key type is string."

The following program tests that is expression with four different types:

```
import std.stdio;

void myFunction(T)(T parameter) {
    writefln("\n--- Called with %s ---", T.stringof);

    static if (is (T == Value[Key],
                   Value,
                   Key : string)) {

        writeln("Yes, the condition has been satisfied.");

        writeln("The value type: ", Value.stringof);
        writeln("The key type   : ", Key.stringof);

    } else {
        writeln("No, the condition has not been satisfied.");
    }
}

void main() {
    int number;
    myFunction(number);

    int[string] intTable;
    myFunction(intTable);

    double[string] doubleTable;
    myFunction(doubleTable);

    dchar[long] dcharTable;
    myFunction(dcharTable);
}
```

The condition is satisfied only if the key type is string:

```
--- Called with int ---
No, the condition has not been satisfied.

--- Called with int[string] ---
Yes, the condition has been satisfied.
The value type: int
The key type  : string

--- Called with double[string] ---
Yes, the condition has been satisfied.
The value type: double
The key type  : string

--- Called with dchar[long] ---
No, the condition has not been satisfied.
```

Function pointers are for storing addresses of functions in order to execute those functions at a later time. Function pointers are similar to their counterparts in the C programming language.

Delegates store both a function pointer and the context to execute that function pointer in. The stored context can either be the scope that the function execution will take place or a `struct` or `class` object.

Delegates enable *closures* as well, a concept that is supported by most functional programming languages.

72.1 Function pointers

We have seen in the previous chapter that it is possible to take addresses of functions with the & operator. In one of those examples, we passed such an address to a function template.

Taking advantage of the fact that template type parameters can match any type, let's pass a function pointer to a template to observe its type by printing its `.stringof` property:

```d
import std.stdio;

int myFunction(char c, double d) {
    return 42;
}

void main() {
    myTemplate(&myFunction);    // Taking the function's address and
                                // passing it as a parameter
}

void myTemplate(T)(T parameter) {
    writeln("type : ", T.stringof);
    writeln("value: ", parameter);
}
```

The output of the program reveals the type and the address of `myFunction()`:

```
type : int function(char c, double d)
value: 406948
```

Member function pointers

The address of a member function can be taken either on a type or on an object of a type, with different results:

```d
struct MyStruct {
    void func() {
    }
}

void main() {
    auto o = MyStruct();

    auto f = &MyStruct.func;    // on a type
    auto d = &o.func;           // on an object

    static assert(is (typeof(f) == void function()));
    static assert(is (typeof(d) == void delegate()));
}
```

As the two `static assert` lines above indicate, f is a `function` and d is a `delegate`. We will see later below that d can be called directly but f needs an object to be called on.

Definition

Similar to regular pointers, each function pointer type can point exactly to a particular type of function; the parameter list and the return type of the function pointer and the function must match. Function pointers are defined by the `function` keyword between the return type and the parameter list of that particular type:

```
return_type function(parameters) ptr;
```

The names of the parameters (c and d in the output above) are optional. Because `myFunction()` takes a `char` and a `double` and returns an `int`, the type of a function pointer that can point at `myFunction()` must be defined accordingly:

```
int function(char, double) ptr = &myFunction;
```

The line above defines `ptr` as a function pointer taking two parameters (`char` and `double`) and returning `int`. Its value is the address of `myFunction()`.

Function pointer syntax is relatively harder to read; it is common to make code more readable by an `alias`:

```
alias CalculationFunc = int function(char, double);
```

That alias makes the code easier to read:

```
CalculationFunc ptr = &myFunction;
```

As with any type, `auto` can be used as well:

```
auto ptr = &myFunction;
```

Calling a function pointer

Function pointers can be called exactly like functions:

```
int result = ptr('a', 5.67);
assert(result == 42);
```

The call `ptr('a', 5.67)` above is the equivalent of calling the actual function by `myFunction('a', 5.67)`.

When to use

Because function pointers store what function to call and they are called exactly like the functions that they point at, function pointers effectively store the behavior of the program for later.

There are many other features of D that are about program behavior. For example, the appropriate function to call to calculate the wages of an `Employee` can be determined by the value of an enum member:

```
final switch (employee.type) {

case EmployeeType.fullTime:
    fullTimeEmployeeWages();
    break;

case EmployeeType.hourly:
    hourlyEmployeeWages();
    break;
}
```

Unfortunately, that method is relatively harder to maintain because it obviously has to support all known employee types. If a new type of employee is added to the program, then all such `switch` statements must be located so that a new `case` clause is added for the new employee type.

A more common alternative of implementing behavior differences is polymorphism. An `Employee` interface can be defined and different wage calculations can be handled by different implementations of that interface:

```
interface Employee {
    double wages();
}

class FullTimeEmployee : Employee {
    double wages() {
        double result;
        // ...
        return result;
    }
}

class HourlyEmployee : Employee {
    double wages() {
        double result;
        // ...
        return result;
    }
}

// ...

    double result = employee.wages();
```

Function pointers are yet another alternative for implementing different behavior. They are more common in programming languages that do not support object oriented programming.

Function pointer as a parameter

Let's design a function that takes an array and returns another array. This function will filter out elements with values less than or equal to zero, and multiply the others by ten:

```
int[] filterAndConvert(const int[] numbers) {
    int[] result;

    foreach (e; numbers) {
        if (e > 0) {                        // filtering,
            immutable newNumber = e * 10;   // and conversion
            result ~= newNumber;
        }
    }

    return result;
}
```

The following program demonstrates its behavior with randomly generated values:

```
import std.stdio;
import std.random;

void main() {
    int[] numbers;

    // Random numbers
    foreach (i; 0 .. 10) {
        numbers ~= uniform(0, 10) - 5;
```

```
    }

    writeln("input : ", numbers);
    writeln("output: ", filterAndConvert(numbers));
}
```

The output contains numbers that are ten times the original numbers, which were greater than zero to begin with. The original numbers that have been selected are highlighted:

```
input : [-2, 2, -2, 3, -2, 2, -1, -4, 0, 0]
output: [20, 30, 20]
```

filterAndConvert() is for a very specific task: It always selects numbers that are greater than zero and always multiplies them by ten. It could be more useful if the behaviors of filtering and conversion were parameterized.

Noting that filtering is a form of conversion as well (from int to bool), filterAndConvert() performs two conversions:

- number > 0, which produces bool by considering an int value.
- number * 10, which produces int from an int value.

Let's define convenient aliases for function pointers that would match the two conversions above:

```
alias Predicate = bool function(int);    // makes bool from int
alias Convertor = int function(int);      // makes int from int
```

Predicate is the type of functions that take int and return bool, and Convertor is the type of functions that take int and return int.

If we provide such function pointers as parameters, we can have filterAndConvert() use those function pointers during its work:

```
int[] filterAndConvert(const int[] numbers,
                       Predicate predicate,
                       Convertor convertor) {
    int[] result;

    foreach (number; numbers) {
        if (predicate(number)) {
            immutable newNumber = convertor(number);
            result ~= newNumber;
        }
    }

    return result;
}
```

filterAndConvert() is now an algorithm that is independent of the actual filtering and conversion operations. When desired, its earlier behavior can be achieved by the following two simple functions:

```
bool isGreaterThanZero(int number) {
    return number > 0;
}

int tenTimes(int number) {
    return number * 10;
}

// ...

    writeln("output: ", filterAndConvert(numbers,
```

```
                                    &isGreaterThanZero,
                                    &tenTimes));
```

This design allows calling `filterAndConvert()` with any filtering and conversion behaviors. For example, the following two functions would make `filterAndConvert()` produce *the negatives of the even numbers*:

```
bool isEven(int number) {
    return (number % 2) == 0;
}

int negativeOf(int number) {
    return -number;
}

// ...

    writeln("output: ", filterAndConvert(numbers,
                                &isEven,
                                &negativeOf));
```

The output:

```
input : [3, -3, 2, 1, -5, 1, 2, 3, 4, -4]
output: [-2, -2, -4, 4]
```

As seen in these examples, sometimes such functions are so trivial that defining them as proper functions with name, return type, parameter list, and curly brackets is unnecessarily wordy.

As we will see below, the => syntax of anonymous functions makes the code more concise and more readable. The following line has anonymous functions that are the equivalents of `isEven()` and `negativeOf()`, without proper function definitions:

```
    writeln("output: ", filterAndConvert(numbers,
                            number => (number % 2) == 0,
                            number => -number));
```

Function pointer as a member

Function pointers can be stored as members of structs and classes as well. To see this, let's design a `class` that takes the predicate and convertor as constructor parameters in order to use them later on:

```
class NumberHandler {
    Predicate predicate;
    Convertor convertor;

    this(Predicate predicate, Convertor convertor) {
        this.predicate = predicate;
        this.convertor = convertor;
    }

    int[] handle(const int[] numbers) {
        int[] result;

        foreach (number; numbers) {
            if (predicate(number)) {
                immutable newNumber = convertor(number);
                result ~= newNumber;
            }
        }

        return result;
    }
}
```

An object of that type can be used similarly to `filterAndConvert()`:

```
auto handler = new NumberHandler(&isEven, &negativeOf);
writeln("result: ", handler.handle(numbers));
```

72.2 Anonymous functions

The code can be more readable and concise when short functions are defined without proper function definitions.

Anonymous functions, which are also knows as *function literals* or *lambdas*, allow defining functions inside of expressions. Anonymous functions can be used at any point where a function pointer can be used.

We will get to their shorter => syntax later below. Let's first see their full syntax, which is usually too wordy especially when it appears inside of other expressions:

```
function return_type(parameters) { /* operations */ }
```

For example, an object of `NumberHandler` that produces *7 times the numbers that are greater than 2* can be constructed by anonymous functions as in the following code:

```
new NumberHandler(function bool(int number) { return number > 2; },
                  function int(int number) { return number * 7; });
```

Two advantages of the code above is that the functions are not defined as proper functions and that their implementations are visible right where the `NumberHandler` object is constructed.

Note that the anonymous function syntax is very similar to regular function syntax. Although this consistency has benefits, the full syntax of anonymous functions makes code too wordy.

For that reason, there are various shorter ways of defining anonymous functions.

Shorter syntax

When the return type can be deduced from the `return` statement inside the anonymous function, then the return type need not be specified (The place where the return type would normally appear is highlighted by code comments.):

```
new NumberHandler(function /**/(int number) { return number > 2; },
                  function /**/(int number) { return number * 7; });
```

Further, when the anonymous function does not take parameters, its parameter list need not be provided. Let's consider a function that takes a function pointer that takes *nothing* and returns `double`:

```
void foo(double function() func) {
    // ...
}
```

Anonymous functions that are passed to that function need not have the empty parameter list. Therefore, all three of the following anonymous function syntaxes are equivalent:

```
foo(function double() { return 42.42; });
foo(function () { return 42.42; });
foo(function { return 42.42; });
```

The first one is written in the full syntax. The second one omits the return type, taking advantage of the return type deduction. The third one omits the unnecessary parameter list.

Even further, the keyword `function` need not be provided either. In that case it is left to the compiler to determine whether it is an anonymous function or an anonymous delegate. Unless it uses a variable from one of the enclosing scopes, it is a function:

```
foo({ return 42.42; });
```

Most anonymous functions can be defined even shorter by the *lambda syntax.*

Lambda syntax instead of a single `return` statement

In most cases even the shortest syntax above is unnecessarily cluttered. The curly brackets that are just inside the function parameter list make the code harder to read and a `return` statement as well as its semicolon inside a function argument looks out of place.

Let's start with the full syntax of an anonymous function that has a single `return` statement:

```
function return_type(parameters) { return expression; }
```

We have already seen that the `function` keyword is not necessary and the return type can be deduced:

```
(parameters) { return expression; }
```

The equivalent of that definition is the following => syntax, where the => characters replace the curly brackets, the `return` keyword, and the semicolon:

```
(parameters) => expression
```

The meaning of that syntax can be spelled out as "given those parameters, produce this expression (value)".

Further, when there is a single parameter, the parentheses around the parameter list can be omitted as well:

```
single_parameter => expression
```

On the other hand, to avoid grammar ambiguities, the parameter list must still be written as empty parentheses when there is no parameter at all:

```
() => expression
```

Programmers who know lambdas from other languages may make a mistake of using curly brackets after the => characters, which can be valid D syntax with a different meaning:

```
// A lambda that returns 'a + 1'
auto l0 = (int a) => a + 1

// A lambda that returns a parameter-less lambda that
// returns 'a + 1'
auto l1 = (int a) => { return a + 1; }

assert(l0(42) == 43);
assert(l1(42)() == 43);    // Executing what l1 returns
```

Let's use the lambda syntax in a predicate passed to `std.algorithm.filter`. `filter()` takes a predicate as its template parameter and a range as its function parameter. It applies the predicate to each element of the range and returns the ones that satisfy the predicate. One of several ways of specifying the predicate is the lambda syntax.

(*Note: We will see ranges in a later chapter. At this point, it should be sufficient to know that D slices are ranges.*)

The following lambda is a predicate that matches elements that are greater than 10:

```d
import std.stdio;
import std.algorithm;

void main() {
    int[] numbers = [ 20, 1, 10, 300, -2 ];
    writeln(numbers.filter!(number => number > 10));
}
```

The output contains only the elements that satisfy the predicate:

```
[20, 300]
```

For comparison, let's write the same lambda in the longest syntax. The curly brackets that define the body of the anonymous function are highlighted:

```d
    writeln(numbers.filter!(function bool(int number) {
                    return number > 10;
                }));
```

As another example, this time let's define an anonymous function that takes two parameters. The following algorithm takes two slices and passes their corresponding elements one by one to a `function` that itself takes two parameters. It then collects and returns the results as another slice:

```d
import std.exception;

int[] binaryAlgorithm(int function(int, int) func,
                      const int[] slice1,
                      const int[] slice2) {
    enforce(slice1.length == slice2.length);

    int[] results;

    foreach (i; 0 .. slice1.length) {
        results ~= func(slice1[i], slice2[i]);
    }

    return results;
}
```

Since the `function` parameter above takes two parameters, lambdas that can be passed to `binaryAlgorithm()` must take two parameters as well:

```d
import std.stdio;

void main() {
    writeln(binaryAlgorithm((a, b) => (a * 10) + b,
                            [ 1, 2, 3 ],
                            [ 4, 5, 6 ]));
}
```

The output contains ten times the elements of the first array plus the elements of the second array (e.g. 14 is 10 * 1 + 4):

```
[14, 25, 36]
```

72.3 Delegates

A delegate is a combination of a function pointer and the context that it should be executed in. Delegates also support *closures* in D. Closures are a feature supported by many functional programming languages.

As we have seen in the Lifetimes and Fundamental Operations chapter (page 228), the lifetime of a variable ends upon leaving the scope that it is defined in:

```
{
    int increment = 10;
    // ...
} // ← the life of 'increment' ends here
```

That is why the address of such a local variable cannot be returned from a function.

Let's imagine that `increment` is a local variable of a function that itself returns a `function`. Let's make it so that the returned lambda happens to use that local variable:

```
alias Calculator = int function(int);

Calculator makeCalculator() {
    int increment = 10;
    return value => increment + value;    // ← compilation ERROR
}
```

That code is in error because the returned lambda makes use of a local variable that is about to go out of scope. If the code were allowed to compile, the lambda would be trying to access `increment`, whose life has already ended.

For that code to be compiled and work correctly, the lifetime of `increment` must at least be as long as the lifetime of the lambda that uses it. Delegates extend the lifetime of the context of a lambda so that the local state that the function uses remains valid.

`delegate` syntax is similar to `function` syntax, the only difference being the keyword. That change is sufficient to make the previous code compile:

```
alias Calculator = int delegate(int);

Calculator makeCalculator() {
    int increment = 10;
    return value => increment + value;
}
```

Having been used by a delegate, the local variable `increment` will now live as long as that delegate lives. The variable is available to the delegate just as any other variable would be, mutable as needed. We will see examples of this in the next chapter when using delegates with `opApply()` member functions.

The following is a test of the delegate above:

```
auto calculator = makeCalculator();
writeln("The result of the calculation: ", calculator(3));
```

Note that `makeCalculator()` returns an anonymous delegate. The code above assigns that delegate to the variable `calculator` and then calls it by `calculator(3)`. Since the delegate is implemented to return the sum of its parameter and the variable `increment`, the code outputs the sum of 3 and 10:

```
The result of the calculation: 13
```

Shorter syntax

As we have already used in the previous example, delegates can take advantage of the shorter syntaxes as well. When neither function nor delegate is specified, the type of the lambda is decided by the compiler, depending on whether the lambda accesses local state. If so, then it is a delegate.

The following example has a delegate that does not take any parameters:

```
int[] delimitedNumbers(int count, int delegate() numberGenerator) {
    int[] result = [ -1 ];
    result.reserve(count + 2);

    foreach (i; 0 .. count) {
        result ~= numberGenerator();
    }

    result ~= -1;

    return result;
}
```

The function delimitedNumbers() generates a slice where the first and last elements are -1. It takes two parameters that specify the other elements that come between those first and last elements.

Let's call that function with a trivial delegate that always returns the same value. Remember that when there is no parameter, the parameter list of a lambda must be specified as empty:

```
    writeln(delimitedNumbers(3, () => 42));
```

The output:

```
-1 42 42 42 -1
```

Let's call delimitedNumbers() this time with a delegate that makes use of a local variable:

```
    int lastNumber;
    writeln(delimitedNumbers(
                15, () => lastNumber += uniform(0, 3)));

    writeln("Last number: ", lastNumber);
```

Although that delegate produces a random value, since the value is added to the last one, none of the generated values is less than its predecessor:

```
-1 0 2 3 4 6 6 8 9 9 9 10 12 14 15 17 -1
Last number: 17
```

An object and a member function as a delegate

We have seen that a delegate is nothing but a function pointer and the context that it is to be executed in. Instead of those two, a delegate can also be composed of a member function and an existing object that that member function is to be called on.

The syntax that defines such a delegate from an object is the following:

```
    &object.member_function
```

Let's first observe that such a syntax indeed defines a delegate by printing its string representation:

```d
import std.stdio;

struct Location {
    long x;
    long y;

    void moveHorizontally(long step) { x += step; }
    void moveVertically(long step)   { y += step; }
}

void main() {
    auto location = Location();
    writeln(typeof(&location.moveHorizontally).stringof);
}
```

According to the output, the type of moveHorizontally() called on location is indeed a delegate:

```
void delegate(long step)
```

Note that the & syntax is only for constructing the delegate. The delegate will be called later by the function call syntax:

```d
    // The definition of the delegate variable:
    auto directionFunction = &location.moveHorizontally;

    // Calling the delegate by the function call syntax:
    directionFunction(3);

    writeln(location);
```

Since the delegate combines the location object and the moveHorizontally() member function, calling the delegate is the equivalent of calling moveHorizontally() on location. The output indicates that the object has indeed moved 3 steps horizontally:

```
Location(3, 0)
```

Function pointers, lambdas, and delegates are expressions. They can be used in places where a value of their type is expected. For example, a slice of delegate objects is initialized below from delegates constructed from an object and its various member functions. The delegate elements of the slice are later called just like functions:

```d
    auto location = Location();

    void delegate(long)[] movements =
        [ &location.moveHorizontally,
          &location.moveVertically,
          &location.moveHorizontally ];

    foreach (movement; movements) {
        movement(1);
    }

    writeln(location);
```

According to the elements of the slice, the location has been changed twice horizontally and once vertically:

```
Location(2, 1)
```

Delegate properties

The function and context pointers of a delegate can be accessed through its
`.funcptr` and `.ptr` properties, respectively:

```d
struct MyStruct {
    void func() {
    }
}

void main() {
    auto o = MyStruct();

    auto d = &o.func;

    assert(d.funcptr == &MyStruct.func);
    assert(d.ptr == &o);
}
```

It is possible to make a `delegate` from scratch by setting those properties
explicitly:

```d
struct MyStruct {
    int i;

    void func() {
        import std.stdio;
        writeln(i);
    }
}

void main() {
    auto o = MyStruct(42);

    void delegate() d;
    assert(d is null);      // null to begin with

    d.funcptr = &MyStruct.func;
    d.ptr = &o;

    d();
}
```

Calling the delegate above as `d()` is the equivalent of the expression `o.func()` (i.e.
calling `MyStruct.func` on `o`):

```
42
```

Lazy parameters are delegates

We saw the `lazy` keyword in the Function Parameters chapter (page 168):

```d
void log(Level level, lazy string message) {
    if (level >= interestedLevel) {
        writeln(message);
    }
}
// ...

    if (failedToConnect) {
        log(Level.medium,
            format("Failure. The connection state is '%s'.",
                getConnectionState()));
    }
```

Because `message` is a `lazy` parameter above, the entire `format` expression
(including the `getConnectionState()` call that it makes) would be evaluated if
and when that parameter is used inside `log()`.

Behind the scenes, lazy parameters are in fact delegates and the arguments that are passed to lazy parameters are delegate objects that are created automatically by the compiler. The code below is the equivalent of the one above:

```d
void log(Level level, string delegate() lazyMessage) {  // (1)
    if (level >= interestedLevel) {
        writefln("%s", lazyMessage());                    // (2)
    }
}

// ...

    if (failedToConnect) {
        log(Level.medium,
            delegate string() {                           // (3)
                return format(
                    "Failure. The connection state is '%s'.",
                    getConnectionState());
            });
    }
```

1. The `lazy` parameter is not a `string` but a delegate that returns a `string`.
2. The delegate is called to get its return value.
3. The entire expression is wrapped inside a delegate and returned from it.

Lazy variadic functions

When a function needs a variable number of lazy parameters, it is necessarily impossible to specify those *unknown number of* parameters as `lazy`.

The solution is to use variadic `delegate` parameters. Such parameters can receive any number of expressions that are the same as the *return type* of those delegates. The delegates cannot take parameters:

```d
import std.stdio;

void foo(double delegate()[] args...) {
    foreach (arg; args) {
        writeln(arg());      // Calling each delegate
    }
}

void main() {
    foo(1.5, () => 2.5);     // 'double' passed as delegate
}
```

Note how both a `double` expression and a lambda are matched to the variadic parameter. The `double` expression is automatically wrapped inside a delegate and the function prints the values of all its *effectively-lazy* parameters:

```
1.5
2.5
```

A limitation of this method is that all parameters must be the same type (`double` above). We will see later in the More Templates chapter (page 520) how to take advantage of *tuple template parameters* to remove that limitation.

72.4 `toString()` with a delegate parameter

We have defined many `toString()` functions up to this point in the book to represent objects as strings. Those `toString()` definitions all returned a `string` without taking any parameters. As noted by the comment lines below, structs and classes took advantage of `toString()` functions of their respective members by simply passing those members to `format()`:

```d
import std.stdio;
import std.string;

struct Point {
    int x;
    int y;

    string toString() const {
        return format("(%s,%s)", x, y);
    }
}

struct Color {
    ubyte r;
    ubyte g;
    ubyte b;

    string toString() const {
        return format("RGB:%s,%s,%s", r, g, b);
    }
}

struct ColoredPoint {
    Color color;
    Point point;

    string toString() const {
        /* Taking advantage of Color.toString and
         * Point.toString: */
        return format("{%s;%s}", color, point);
    }
}

struct Polygon {
    ColoredPoint[] points;

    string toString() const {
        /* Taking advantage of ColoredPoint.toString: */
        return format("%s", points);
    }
}

void main() {
    auto polygon = Polygon(
        [ ColoredPoint(Color(10, 10, 10), Point(1, 1)),
          ColoredPoint(Color(20, 20, 20), Point(2, 2)),
          ColoredPoint(Color(30, 30, 30), Point(3, 3)) ]);

    writeln(polygon);
}
```

In order for `polygon` to be sent to the output as a `string` on the last line of the program, all of the `toString()` functions of `Polygon`, `ColoredPoint`, `Color`, and `Point` are called indirectly, creating a total of 10 strings in the process. Note that the strings that are constructed and returned by the lower-level functions are used only once by the respective higher-level function that called them.

However, although a total of 10 strings get constructed, only the very last one is printed to the output:

```
[{RGB:10,10,10;(1,1)}, {RGB:20,20,20;(2,2)}, {RGB:30,30,30;(3,3)}]
```

However practical, this method may degrade the performance of the program because of the many `string` objects that are constructed and promptly thrown away.

An overload of `toString()` avoids this performance issue by taking a `delegate` parameter:

```d
void toString(void delegate(const(char)[]) sink) const;
```

As seen in its declaration, this overload of toString() does not return a string. Instead, the characters that are going to be printed are passed to its delegate parameter. It is the responsibility of the delegate to append those characters to the single string that is going to be printed to the output.

All the programmer needs to do differently is to call std.format.formattedWrite instead of std.string.format and pass the delegate parameter as its first parameter (in UFCS below). Also note that the following calls are providing the format strings as template arguments to take advantage of formattedWrite's compile-time format string checks.

```
import std.stdio;
import std.format;

struct Point {
    int x;
    int y;

    void toString(void delegate(const(char)[]) sink) const {
        sink.formattedWrite!"(%s,%s)"(x, y);
    }
}

struct Color {
    ubyte r;
    ubyte g;
    ubyte b;

    void toString(void delegate(const(char)[]) sink) const {
        sink.formattedWrite!"RGB:%s,%s,%s"(r, g, b);
    }
}

struct ColoredPoint {
    Color color;
    Point point;

    void toString(void delegate(const(char)[]) sink) const {
        sink.formattedWrite!"{%s;%s}"(color, point);
    }
}

struct Polygon {
    ColoredPoint[] points;

    void toString(void delegate(const(char)[]) sink) const {
        sink.formattedWrite!"%s"(points);
    }
}

void main() {
    auto polygon = Polygon(
        [ ColoredPoint(Color(10, 10, 10), Point(1, 1)),
          ColoredPoint(Color(20, 20, 20), Point(2, 2)),
          ColoredPoint(Color(30, 30, 30), Point(3, 3)) ]);

    writeln(polygon);
}
```

The advantage of this program is that, even though there are still a total of 10 calls made to various toString() functions, those calls collectively produce a single string, not 10.

72.5 Summary

- The function keyword is for defining function pointers to be called later just like a function.

- The `delegate` keyword is for defining delegates. A delegate is the pair of a function pointer and the context that that function pointer to be executed in.
- A `delegate` can be created from an object and a member function by the syntax `&object.member_function`.
- A delegate can be constructed explicitly by setting its `.funcptr` and `.ptr` properties.
- Anonymous functions and anonymous delegates (lambdas) can be used in places of function pointers and delegates in expressions.
- There are several syntaxes for lambdas, the shortest of which is for when the equivalent consists only of a single `return` statement:
  `parameter => expression`.
- A more efficient overload of `toString()` takes a `delegate`.

As you remember from the foreach Loop chapter (page 121), both how foreach works and the types and numbers of loop variables that it supports depend on the kind of collection: For slices, foreach provides access to elements with or without a counter; for associative arrays, to values with or without keys; for number ranges, to the individual values. For library types, foreach behaves in a way that is specific to that type; e.g. for File, it provides the lines of a file.

It is possible to define the behavior of foreach for user-defined types as well. There are two methods of providing this support:

- Defining *range member functions*, which allows using the user-defined type with other range algorithms as well
- Defining one or more opApply member functions

Of the two methods, opApply has priority: If it is defined, the compiler uses opApply, otherwise it considers the range member functions. However, in most cases range member functions are sufficient, easier, and more useful.

foreach need not be supported for every type. Iterating over an object makes sense only if that object defines the concept of *a collection*.

For example, it may not be clear what elements should foreach provide when iterating over a class that represents a student, so the class better not support foreach at all. On the other hand, a design may require that Student is a collection of grades and foreach may provide individual grades of the student.

It depends on the design of the program what types should provide this support and how.

73.1 foreach support by range member functions

We know that foreach is very similar to for, except that it is more useful and safer than for. Consider the following loop:

```
foreach (element; myObject) {
    // ... expressions ...
}
```

Behind the scenes, the compiler rewrites that foreach loop as a for loop, roughly an equivalent of the following one:

```
for ( ; /* while not done */; /* skip the front element */) {

    auto element = /* the front element */;

    // ... expressions ...
}
```

User-defined types that need to support foreach can provide three member functions that correspond to the three sections of the previous code: determining whether the loop is over, skipping the front element, and providing access to the front element.

Those three member functions must be named as empty, popFront, and front, respectively. The code that is generated by the compiler calls those functions:

```
for ( ; !myObject.empty(); myObject.popFront()) {

    auto element = myObject.front();
```

```
    // ... expressions ...
}
```

These three functions must work according to the following expectations:

- .empty() must return true if the loop is over, false otherwise
- .popFront() must move to the next element (in other words, skip the front element)
- .front() must return the front element

Any type that defines those member functions can be used with foreach.

Example

Let's define a struct that produces numbers within a certain range. In order to be consistent with D's number ranges and slice indexes, let's have the last number be outside of the valid numbers. Under these requirements, the following struct would work exactly like D's number ranges:

```
struct NumberRange {
    int begin;
    int end;

    invariant() {
        // There is a bug if begin is greater than end
        assert(begin <= end);
    }

    bool empty() const {
        // The range is consumed when begin equals end
        return begin == end;
    }

    void popFront() {
        // Skipping the first element is achieved by
        // incrementing the beginning of the range
        ++begin;
    }

    int front() const {
        // The front element is the one at the beginning
        return begin;
    }
}
```

Note: *The safety of that implementation depends solely on a single* invariant *block. Additional checks could be added to* front *and* popFront *to ensure that those functions are never called when the range is empty.*

Objects of that struct can be used with foreach:

```
foreach (element; NumberRange(3, 7)) {
    write(element, ' ');
}
```

foreach uses those three functions behind the scenes and iterates until empty() returns true:

```
3 4 5 6
```

std.range.retro to iterate in reverse

The std.range module contains many range algorithms. retro is one of those algorithms, which iterates a range in reverse order. It requires two additional range member functions:

- `.popBack()` must move to the element that is one before the end (skips the last element)
- `.back()` must return the last element

However, although not directly related to reverse iteration, for retro to consider those functions at all, there must be one more function defined:

- `.save()` must return a copy of this object

We will learn more about these member functions later in the Ranges chapter (page 569).

These three additional member functions can trivially be defined for NumberRange:

```d
struct NumberRange {
// ...

    void popBack() {
        // Skipping the last element is achieved by
        // decrementing the end of the range.
        --end;
    }

    int back() const {
        // As the 'end' value is outside of the range, the
        // last element is one less than that
        return end - 1;
    }

    NumberRange save() const {
        // Returning a copy of this struct object
        return this;
    }
}
```

Objects of this type can now be used with retro:

```d
import std.range;

// ...

    foreach (element; NumberRange(3, 7).retro) {
        write(element, ' ');
    }
```

The output of the program is now in reverse:

```
6 5 4 3
```

73.2 foreach support by opApply and opApplyReverse member functions

Everything that is said about opApply in this section is valid for opApplyReverse as well. opApplyReverse is for defining the behaviors of objects in the foreach_reverse loops.

The member functions above allow using objects as ranges. That method is more suitable when there is only one sensible way of iterating over a range. For example, it would be easy to provide access to individual students of a Students type.

On the other hand, sometimes it makes more sense to iterate over the same object in different ways. We know this from associative arrays where it is possible to access either only to the values or to both the keys and the values:

```
    string[string] dictionary;    // from English to Turkish

    // ...

    foreach (inTurkish; dictionary) {
        // ... only values ...
    }

    foreach (inEnglish, inTurkish; dictionary) {
        // ... keys and values ...
    }
```

opApply allows using user-defined types with foreach in various and sometimes more complex ways. Before learning how to define opApply, we must first understand how it is called automatically by foreach.

The program execution alternates between the expressions inside the foreach block and the expressions inside the opApply() function. First the opApply() member function gets called, and then opApply makes an explicit call to the foreach block. They alternate in that way until the loop eventually terminates. This process is based on a *convention*, which I will explain soon.

Let's first observe the structure of the foreach loop one more time:

```
// The loop that is written by the programmer:

    foreach (/* loop variables */; myObject) {
        // ... expressions inside the foreach block ...
    }
```

If there is an opApply() member function that matches the loop variables, then the foreach block becomes a delegate, which is then passed to opApply().

Accordingly, the loop above is converted to the following code behind the scenes. The curly brackets that define the body of the delegate are highlighted:

```
// The code that the compiler generates behind the scenes:

    myObject.opApply(delegate int(/* loop variables */) {
        // ... expressions inside the foreach block ...
        return hasBeenTerminated;
    });
```

In other words, the foreach loop is replaced by a delegate that is passed to opApply(). Before showing an example, here are the requirements and expectations of this convention that opApply() must observe:

1. The body of the foreach loop becomes the body of the delegate. opApply must call this delegate for each iteration.
2. The loop variables become the parameters of the delegate. opApply() must define these parameters as ref. (The variables may be defined without the ref keyword as well but doing that would prevent iterating over the elements *by reference* (page 159).)
3. The return type of the delegate is int. Accordingly, the compiler injects a return statement at the end of the delegate, which determines whether the loop has been terminated (by a break or a return statement): If the return value is zero, the iteration must continue, otherwise it must terminate.
4. The actual iteration happens inside opApply().
5. opApply() must return the same value that is returned by the delegate.

The following is a definition of `NumberRange` that is implemented according to that convention:

```d
struct NumberRange {
    int begin;
    int end;
                           //     (2)         (1)
    int opApply(int delegate(ref int) operations) const {
        int result = 0;

        for (int number = begin; number != end; ++number) { // (4)
            result = operations(number);   // (1)

            if (result) {
                break;                        // (3)
            }
        }

        return result;                        // (5)
    }
}
```

This definition of `NumberRange` can be used with `foreach` in exactly the same way as before:

```d
foreach (element; NumberRange(3, 7)) {
    write(element, ' ');
}
```

The output is the same as the one produced by range member functions:

```
3 4 5 6
```

Overloading opApply to iterate in different ways

It is possible to iterate over the same object in different ways by defining overloads of `opApply()` that take different types of delegates. The compiler calls the overload that matches the particular set of loop variables.

As an example, let's make it possible to iterate over `NumberRange` by two loop variables as well:

```d
foreach (first, second; NumberRange(0, 15)) {
    writef("%s,%s ", first, second);
}
```

Note how it is similar to the way associative arrays are iterated over by both keys and values.

For this example, let's require that when a `NumberRange` object is iterated by two variables, it should provide two consecutive values and that it arbitrarily increases the values by 5. So, the loop above should produce the following output:

```
0,1 5,6 10,11
```

This is achieved by an additional definition of `opApply()` that takes a delegate that takes two parameters. `opApply()` must call that delegate with two values:

```d
int opApply(int delegate(ref int, ref int) dg) const {
    int result = 0;

    for (int i = begin; (i + 1) < end; i += 5) {
        int first = i;
        int second = i + 1;

        result = dg(first, second);
```

```
        if (result) {
            break;
        }
    }

    return result;
}
```

When there are two loop variables, this overload of opApply() gets called.

There may be as many overloads of opApply() as needed.

It is possible and sometimes necessary to give hints to the compiler on what overload to choose. This is done by specifying types of the loop variables explicitly.

For example, let's assume that there is a School type that supports iterating over the teachers and the students separately:

```
class School {
    int opApply(int delegate(ref Student) dg) const {
        // ...
    }

    int opApply(int delegate(ref Teacher) dg) const {
        // ...
    }
}
```

To indicate the desired overload, the loop variable must be specified:

```
    foreach (Student student; school) {
        // ...
    }

    foreach (Teacher teacher; school) {
        // ...
    }
```

73.3 Loop counter

The convenient loop counter of slices is not automatic for other types. Loop counter can be achieved for user-defined types in different ways depending on whether the foreach support is provided by range member functions or by opApply overloads.

Loop counter with range functions

If foreach support is provided by range member functions, then a loop counter can be achieved simply by enumerate from the std.range module:

```
import std.range;

// ...

    foreach (i, element; NumberRange(42, 47).enumerate) {
        writefln("%s: %s", i, element);
    }
```

enumerate is a range that produces consecutive numbers starting by default from 0. enumerate pairs each number with the elements of the range that it is applied on. As a result, the numbers that enumerate generates and the elements of the actual range (NumberRange in this case) appear in lockstep as loop variables:

```
0: 42
1: 43
2: 44
```

```
3: 45
4: 46
```

Loop counter with opApply

On the other hand, if `foreach` support is provided by `opApply()`, then the loop counter must be defined as a separate parameter of the delegate, suitably as type `size_t`. Let's see this on a `struct` that represents a colored polygon.

As we have already seen above, an `opApply()` that provides access to the points of this polygon can be implemented *without* a counter as in the following code:

```
import std.stdio;

enum Color { blue, green, red }

struct Point {
    int x;
    int y;
}

struct Polygon {
    Color color;
    Point[] points;

    int opApply(int delegate(ref const(Point)) dg) const {
        int result = 0;

        foreach (point; points) {
            result = dg(point);

            if (result) {
                break;
            }
        }

        return result;
    }
}

void main() {
    auto polygon = Polygon(Color.blue,
                           [ Point(0, 0), Point(1, 1) ] );

    foreach (point; polygon) {
        writeln(point);
    }
}
```

Note that `opApply()` itself is implemented by a `foreach` loop. As a result, the `foreach` inside `main()` ends up making indirect use of a `foreach` over the `points` member.

Also note that the type of the delegate parameter is `ref const(Point)`. This means that this definition of `opApply()` does not allow modifying the `Point` elements of the polygon. In order to allow user code to modify the elements, both the `opApply()` function itself and the delegate parameter must be defined without the `const` specifier.

The output:

```
const(Point)(0, 0)
const(Point)(1, 1)
```

Naturally, trying to use this definition of `Polygon` with a loop counter would cause a compilation error:

```
foreach (i, point; polygon) {     // ← compilation ERROR
    writefln("%s: %s", i, point);
}
```

The compilation error:

```
Error: cannot uniquely infer foreach argument types
```

For that to work, another opApply() overload that supports a counter must be defined:

```
int opApply(int delegate(ref size_t,
                         ref const(Point)) dg) const {
    int result = 0;

    foreach (i, point; points) {
        result = dg(i, point);

        if (result) {
            break;
        }
    }

    return result;
}
```

This time the foreach variables are matched to the new opApply() overload and the program prints the desired output:

```
0: const(Point)(0, 0)
1: const(Point)(1, 1)
```

Note that this implementation of opApply() takes advantage of the automatic counter over the points member. (*Although the delegate variable is defined as* ref size_t, *the* foreach *loop inside* main() *cannot modify the counter variable over* points).

When needed, the loop counter can be defined and incremented explicitly as well. For example, because the following opApply() is implemented by a while statement it must define a separate variable for the counter:

```
int opApply(int delegate(ref size_t,
                         ref const(Point)) dg) const {
    int result = 0;
    bool isDone = false;

    size_t counter = 0;
    while (!isDone) {
        // ...

        result = dg(counter, nextElement);

        if (result) {
            break;
        }

        ++counter;
    }

    return result;
}
```

73.4 Warning: The collection must not mutate during the iteration

Regardless of whether the iteration support is provided by the range member functions or by opApply() functions, the collection itself must not mutate. New elements must not be added to the container and the existing elements must not be removed. (Mutating the existing elements is allowed.)

Doing otherwise is undefined behavior.

73.5 Exercises

1. Design a struct that works similarly to NumberRange, which also supports specifying the step size. The step size can be the third member:

   ```
   foreach (element; NumberRange(0, 10, 2)) {
       write(element, ' ');
   }
   ```

   The expected output of the code above is every second number from 0 to 10:

   ```
   0 2 4 6 8
   ```

2. Implement the School class that was mentioned in the text in a way that it provides access to students or teachers depending on the foreach variable.

   The solutions are on page 737.

Up to this point, we have been defining functions, structs, and classes in the outermost scopes (i.e. the module scope). They can be defined in inner scopes as well. Defining them in inner scopes helps with encapsulation by narrowing the visibility of their symbols, as well as creating *closures* that we saw in the Function Pointers, Delegates, and Lambdas chapter (page 475).

As an example, the following `outerFunc()` function contains definitions of a nested function, a nested `struct`, and a nested `class`:

```
void outerFunc(int parameter) {
    int local;

    void nestedFunc() {
        local = parameter * 2;
    }

    struct NestedStruct {
        void memberFunc() {
            local /= parameter;
        }
    }

    class NestedClass {
        void memberFunc() {
            local += parameter;
        }
    }

    // Using the nested definitions inside this scope:

    nestedFunc();

    auto s = NestedStruct();
    s.memberFunc();

    auto c = new NestedClass();
    c.memberFunc();
}
void main() {
    outerFunc(42);
}
```

Like any other variable, nested definitions can access symbols that are defined in their outer scopes. For example, all three of the nested definitions above are able to use the variables named `parameter` and `local`.

As usual, the names of the nested definitions are valid only in the scopes that they are defined in. For example, `nestedFunc()`, `NestedStruct`, and `NestedClass` are not accessible from `main()`:

```
void main() {
    auto a = NestedStruct();                // ← compilation ERROR
    auto b = outerFunc.NestedStruct();      // ← compilation ERROR
}
```

Although their names cannot be accessed, nested definitions can still be used in other scopes. For example, many Phobos algorithms handle their tasks by nested structs that are defined inside Phobos functions.

To see an example of this, let's design a function that consumes a slice from both ends in alternating order:

```
import std.stdio;
import std.array;
```

```d
auto alternatingEnds(T)(T[] slice) {
    bool isFromFront = true;

    struct EndAlternatingRange {
        bool empty() const {
            return slice.empty;
        }

        T front() const {
            return isFromFront ? slice.front : slice.back;
        }

        void popFront() {
            if (isFromFront) {
                slice.popFront();
                isFromFront = false;

            } else {
                slice.popBack();
                isFromFront = true;
            }
        }
    }

    return EndAlternatingRange();
}

void main() {
    auto a = alternatingEnds([ 1, 2, 3, 4, 5 ]);
    writeln(a);
}
```

Even though the nested `struct` cannot be named inside `main()`, it is still usable:

```
[1, 5, 2, 4, 3]
```

Note: *Because their names cannot be mentioned outside of their scopes, such types are called Voldemort types due to analogy to a Harry Potter character.*

Note that the nested `struct` that `alternatingEnds()` returns does not have any member variables. That `struct` handles its task using merely the function parameter `slice` and the local function variable `isFromFront`. The fact that the returned object can safely use those variables even after leaving the context that it was created in is due to a *closure* that has been created automatically. We have seen closures in the Function Pointers, Delegates, and Lambdas chapter (page 475).

`static` when a closure is not needed

Since they keep their contexts alive, nested definitions are more expensive than their regular counterparts. Additionally, as they must include a *context pointer* to determine the context that they are associated with, objects of nested definitions occupy more space as well. For example, although the following two structs have exactly the same member variables, their sizes are different:

```d
import std.stdio;

struct ModuleStruct {
    int i;

    void memberFunc() {
    }
}

void moduleFunc() {
    struct NestedStruct {
        int i;
```

```
        void memberFunc() {
        }
    }

    writefln("OuterStruct: %s bytes, NestedStruct: %s bytes.",
             ModuleStruct.sizeof, NestedStruct.sizeof);
}
void main() {
    moduleFunc();
}
```

The sizes of the two structs may be different on other environments:

```
OuterStruct: 4 bytes, NestedStruct: 16 bytes.
```

However, some nested definitions are merely for keeping them as local as possible, with no need to access variables from the outer contexts. In such cases, the associated cost would be unnecessary. The `static` keyword removes the context pointer from nested definitions, making them equivalents of their module counterparts. As a result, `static` nested definitions cannot access their outer contexts:

```
void outerFunc(int parameter) {
    static class NestedClass {
        int i;

        this() {
            i = parameter;    // ← compilation ERROR
        }
    }
}
```

The context pointer of a nested `class` object is available as a `void*` through its `.outer` property. For example, because they are defined in the same scope, the context pointers of the following two objects are equal:

```
void foo() {
    class C {
    }

    auto a = new C();
    auto b = new C();

    assert(a.outer is b.outer);
}
```

As we will see below, for *classes nested inside classes*, the type of the context pointer is the type of the outer class, not `void*`.

Classes nested inside classes

When a `class` is nested inside another one, the context that the nested object is associated with is the outer object itself.

Such nested classes are constructed by the `this.new` syntax. When necessary, the outer object of a nested object can be accessed by `this.outer`:

```
class OuterClass {
    int outerMember;

    class NestedClass {
        int func() {
            /* A nested class can access members of the outer
             * class. */
            return outerMember * 2;
```

```
        }

        OuterClass context() {
            /* A nested class can access its outer object
             * (i.e. its context) by '.outer'. */
            return this.outer;
        }
    }

    NestedClass algorithm() {
        /* An outer class can construct a nested object by
         * '.new'. */
        return this.new NestedClass();
    }
}

void main() {
    auto outerObject = new OuterClass();

    /* A member function of an outer class is returning a
     * nested object: */
    auto nestedObject = outerObject.algorithm();

    /* The nested object gets used in the program: */
    nestedObject.func();

    /* Naturally, the context of nestedObject is the same as
     * outerObject: */
    assert(nestedObject.context() is outerObject);
}
```

Instead of this.new and this.outer, .new and .outer can be used on existing objects as well:

```
    auto var = new OuterClass();
    auto nestedObject = var.new OuterClass.NestedClass();
    auto var2 = nestedObject.outer;
```

74.1 Summary

- Functions, structs, and classes that are defined in inner scopes can access those scopes as their contexts.
- Nested definitions keep their contexts alive to form closures.
- Nested definitions are more costly than their module counterparts. When a nested definition does not need to access its context, this cost can be avoided by the static keyword.
- Classes can be nested inside other classes. The context of such a nested object is the outer object itself. Nested class objects are constructed by this.new or variable.new and their contexts are available by this.outer or variable.outer.

Unions, a low-level feature inherited from the C programming language, allow more than one member to share the same memory area.

Unions are very similar to structs with the following main differences:

- Unions are defined by the union keyword.
- The members of a union are not independent; they share the same memory area.

Just like structs, unions can have member functions as well.

The examples below will produce different results depending on whether they are compiled on a 32-bit or a 64-bit environment. To avoid getting confusing results, please use the -m32 compiler switch when compiling the examples in this chapter. Otherwise, your results may be different than mine due to *alignment*, which we will see in a later chapter.

Naturally, struct objects are as large as necessary to accommodate all of their members:

```
// Note: Please compile with the -m32 compiler switch
struct S {
    int i;
    double d;
}

// ...

    writeln(S.sizeof);
```

Since int is 4 bytes long and double is 8 bytes long, the size of that struct is the sum of their sizes:

```
12
```

In contrast, the size of a union with the same members is only as large as its largest member:

```
union U {
    int i;
    double d;
}

// ...

    writeln(U.sizeof);
```

The 4-byte int and the 8-byte double share the same area. As a result, the size of the entire union is the same as its largest member:

```
8
```

Unions are not a memory-saving feature. It is impossible to fit multiple data into the same memory location. The purpose of a union is to use the same area for different type of data at different times. Only one of the members can be used reliably at one time. However, although doing so may not be portable to different platforms, union members can be used for accessing fragments of other members.

One of the examples below takes advantage of typeid to disallow access to members other than the one that is currently valid.

The following diagram shows how the 8 bytes of the `union` above are shared by its members:

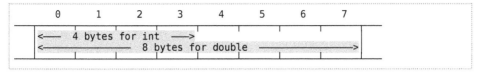

Either all of the 8 bytes are used for the `double` member, or only the first 4 bytes are used for the `int` member and the other 4 bytes are unused.

Unions can have as many members as needed. All of the members would share the same memory location.

The fact that the same memory location is used for all of the members can have surprising effects. For example, let's initialize a `union` object by its `int` member and then access its `double` member:

```d
auto u = U(42);     // initializing the int member
writeln(u.d);       // accessing the double member
```

Initializing the `int` member by the value 42 sets just the first 4 bytes, and this affects the `double` member in an unpredictable way:

```
2.07508e-322
```

Depending on the endianness of the microprocessor, the 4 bytes may be arranged in memory as 0|0|0|42, 42|0|0|0, or in some other order. For that reason, the value of the `double` member may appear differently on different platforms.

75.1 Anonymous unions

Anonymous unions specify what members of a user-defined type share the same area:

```d
struct S {
    int first;

    union {
        int second;
        int third;
    }
}

// ...

    writeln(S.sizeof);
```

The last two members of S share the same area. So, the size of the `struct` is a total of two `int`s: 4 bytes needed for `first` and another 4 bytes to be shared by `second` and `third`:

```
8
```

75.2 Dissecting other members

Unions can be used for accessing individual bytes of variables of other types. For example, they make it easy to access the 4 bytes of an IPv4 address individually.

The 32-bit value of the IPv4 address and a fixed-length array can be defined as the two members of a `union`:

```d
union IpAddress {
    uint value;
```

```
    ubyte[4] bytes;
}
```

The members of that union would share the same memory area as in the following figure:

```
        0              1            2            3

        <——— 32 bits of the IPv4 address ———>
      bytes[0]  |  bytes[1]  |  bytes[2]  |  bytes[3]
```

For example, when an object of this union is initialized by 0xc0a80102 (the value that corresponds to the dotted form 192.168.1.2), the elements of the bytes array would automatically have the values of the four octets:

```
import std.stdio;

void main() {
    auto address = IpAddress(0xc0a80102);
    writeln(address.bytes);
}
```

When run on a little-endian system, the octets would appear in reverse of their dotted form:

```
[2, 1, 168, 192]
```

The reverse order of the octets is another example of how accessing different members of a union may produce unpredictable results. This is because the behavior of a union is guaranteed only if that union is used through just one of its members. There are no guarantees on the values of the members other than the one that the union has been initialized with.

Although it is not directly related to this chapter, bswap from the core.bitop module is useful in dealing with endianness issues. bswap returns its parameter after swapping its bytes. Also taking advantage of the endian value from the std.system module, the octets of the previous IPv4 address can be printed in the expected order after swapping its bytes:

```
import std.system;
import core.bitop;

// ...

    if (endian == Endian.littleEndian) {
        address.value = bswap(address.value);
    }
```

The output:

```
[192, 168, 1, 2]
```

Please take the IpAddress type as a simple example; in general, it would be better to consider a dedicated networking module for non-trivial programs.

75.3 Examples

Communication protocol

In some protocols like TCP/IP, the meanings of certain parts of a protocol packet depend on a specific value inside the same packet. Usually, it is a field in the header of the packet that determines the meanings of successive bytes. Unions can be used for representing such protocol packets.

The following design represents a protocol packet that has two kinds:

```d
struct Host {
    // ...
}

struct ProtocolA {
    // ...
}

struct ProtocolB {
    // ...
}

enum ProtocolType { A, B }

struct NetworkPacket {
    Host source;
    Host destination;
    ProtocolType type;

    union {
        ProtocolA aParts;
        ProtocolB bParts;
    }

    ubyte[] payload;
}
```

The struct above can make use of the type member to determine whether aParts or bParts of the union to be used.

Discriminated union

Discriminated union is a data structure that brings type safety over a regular union. Unlike a union, it does not allow accessing the members other than the one that is currently valid.

The following is a simple discriminated union type that supports only two types: int and double. In addition to a union to store the data, it maintains a TypeInfo (page 342) member to know which one of the two union members is valid.

```d
import std.stdio;
import std.exception;

struct Discriminated {
private:

    TypeInfo validType_;

    union {
        int i_;
        double d_;
    }

public:

    this(int value) {
        // This is a call to the property function below:
        i = value;
    }

    // Setter for 'int' data
    void i(int value) {
        i_ = value;
        validType_ = typeid(int);
    }

    // Getter for 'int' data
    int i() const {
```

```
        enforce(validType_ == typeid(int),
                "The data is not an 'int'.");
        return i_;
    }

    this(double value) {
        // This is a call to the property function below:
        d = value;
    }

    // Setter for 'double' data
    void d(double value) {
        d_ = value;
        validType_ = typeid(double);
    }

    // Getter for 'double' data
    double d() const {
        enforce(validType_ == typeid(double),
                "The data is not a 'double'." );
        return d_;
    }

    // Identifies the type of the valid data
    const(TypeInfo) type() const {
        return validType_;
    }
}

unittest {
    // Let's start with 'int' data
    auto var = Discriminated(42);

    // The type should be reported as 'int'
    assert(var.type == typeid(int));

    // 'int' getter should work
    assert(var.i == 42);

    // 'double' getter should fail
    assertThrown(var.d);

    // Let's replace 'int' with 'double' data
    var.d = 1.5;

    // The type should be reported as 'double'
    assert(var.type == typeid(double));

    // Now 'double' getter should work ...
    assert(var.d == 1.5);

    // ... and 'int' getter should fail
    assertThrown(var.i);
}
```

This is just an example. You should consider using Algebraic and Variant from the std.variant module in your programs. Additionally, this code could take advantage of other features of D like templates (page 399) and mixins (page 560) to reduce code duplication.

Regardless of the data that is being stored, there is only one Discriminated type. (An alternative template solution could take the data type as a template parameter, in which case each instantiation of the template would be a distinct type.) For that reason, it is possible to have an array of Discriminated objects, effectively enabling a collection where elements can be of different types. However, the user must still know the valid member before accessing it. For example, the following function determines the actual type of the valid data with the type property of Discriminated:

```
void main() {
    Discriminated[] arr = [ Discriminated(1),
                            Discriminated(2.5) ];

    foreach (value; arr) {
        if (value.type == typeid(int)) {
            writeln("Working with an 'int'  : ", value.i);

        } else if (value.type == typeid(double))  {
            writeln("Working with a 'double': ", value.d);

        } else {
            assert(0);
        }
    }
}
```

```
Working with an 'int'  : 1
Working with a 'double': 2.5
```

Labels are names given to lines of code in order to direct program flow to those lines later on.

A label consists of a name and the : character:

```
end:    // ← a label
```

That label gives the name *end* to the line that it is defined on.

Note: *In reality, a label can appear between statements on the same line to name the exact spot that it appears at, but this is not a common practice:*

```
anExpression(); end: anotherExpression();
```

76.1 goto

goto directs program flow to the specified label:

```
void foo(bool condition) {
    writeln("first");

    if (condition) {
        goto end;
    }

    writeln("second");

end:

    writeln("third");
}
```

When condition is true, the program flow *goes to* label end, effectively skipping the line that prints "second":

```
first
third
```

goto works the same way as in the C and C++ programming languages. Being notorious for making it hard to understand the intent and flow of code, goto is discouraged even in those languages. Statements like if, while, for etc. should be used instead.

For example, the previous code can be written without goto in a more *structured* way:

```
void foo(bool condition) {
    writeln("first");

    if (!condition) {
        writeln("second");
    }

    writeln("third");
}
```

However, there are two acceptable uses of goto in C, none of which is necessary in D.

Finalization area

One of the valid uses of goto in C is going to the finalization area where the cleanup operations of a function are performed (e.g. giving resources back, undoing certain operations, etc.):

```
// --- C code ---

int foo() {
    // ...

    if (error) {
        goto finally;
    }

    // ...

finally:
    // ... cleanup operations ...

    return error;
}
```

This use of goto is not necessary in D because there are other ways of managing resources: the garbage collector, destructors, the catch and finally blocks, scope() statements, etc.

Note: *This use of goto is not necessary in C++ either.*

continue and break for outer loops
The other valid use of goto in C is about outer loops.

Since continue and break affect only the inner loop, one way of continuing or breaking out of the outer loop is by goto statements:

```
// --- C code ---

    while (condition) {

        while (otherCondition) {

            // affects the inner loop
            continue;

            // affects the inner loop
            break;

            // works like 'continue' for the outer loop
            goto continueOuter;

            // works like 'break' for the outer loop
            goto breakOuter;
        }
    continueOuter:
        ;
    }
breakOuter:
```

The same technique can be used for outer switch statements as well.

This use of goto is not needed in D because D has loop labels, which we will see below.

Note: *This use of goto can be encountered in C++ as well.*

The problem of skipping constructors
The constructor is called on an object exactly where that object is defined. This is mainly because the information that is needed to construct an object is usually not available until that point. Also, there is no need to construct an object if that object is not going to be used in the program at all.

When goto skips a line that an object is constructed on, the program can be using an object that has not been prepared yet:

```
    if (condition) {
        goto aLabel;      // skips the constructor
    }

    auto s = S(42);       // constructs the object properly

aLabel:

    s.bar();              // BUG: 's' may not be ready for use
```

The compiler prevents this bug:

```
Error: goto skips declaration of variable deneme.main.s
```

76.2 Loop labels

Loops can have labels and goto statements can refer to those labels:

```
outerLoop:
    while (condition) {

        while (otherCondition) {

            // affects the inner loop
            continue;

            // affects the inner loop
            break;

            // continues the outer loop
            continue outerLoop;

            // breaks the outer loop
            break outerLoop;
        }
    }
```

switch statements can have labels as well. An inner break statement can refer to an outer switch to break out of the outer switch statement.

76.3 goto in case sections

We have already seen the use of goto in case sections in the switch and case chapter (page 127):

- goto case causes the execution to continue to the next case.
- goto default causes the execution to continue to the default section.
- goto case *expression* causes the execution to continue to the case that matches that expression.

76.4 Summary

- Some of the uses of goto are not necessary in D.
- break and continue can specify labels to affect outer loops and switch statements.
- goto inside case sections can make the program flow jump to other case and default sections.

77 Tuples

Tuples are for combining multiple values to be used as a single object. They are implemented as a library feature by the `Tuple` template from the `std.typecons` module.

Tuple makes use of `AliasSeq` from the `std.meta` module for some of its operations.

This chapter covers only the more common operations of tuples. For more information on tuples and templates see Philippe Sigaud's *D Templates: A Tutorial*[1].

77.1 Tuple and tuple()

Tuples are usually constructed by the convenience function `tuple()`:

```d
import std.stdio;
import std.typecons;

void main() {
    auto t = tuple(42, "hello");
    writeln(t);
}
```

The `tuple` call above constructs an object that consists of the `int` value 42 and the `string` value "hello". The output of the program includes the type of the tuple object and its members:

```
Tuple!(int, string)(42, "hello")
```

The tuple type above is the equivalent of the following pseudo `struct` definition and likely have been implemented in exactly the same way:

```d
// The equivalent of Tuple!(int, string)
struct __Tuple_int_string {
    int __member_0;
    string __member_1;
}
```

The members of a tuple are normally accessed by their index values. That syntax suggests that tuples can be seen as arrays consisting of different types of elements:

```d
    writeln(t[0]);
    writeln(t[1]);
```

The output:

```
42
hello
```

Member properties

It is possible to access the members by properties if the tuple is constructed directly by the `Tuple` template instead of the `tuple()` function. The type and the name of each member are specified as two consecutive template parameters:

```d
    auto t = Tuple!(int, "number",
                    string, "message")(42, "hello");
```

The definition above allows accessing the members by `.number` and `.message` properties as well:

---

1. https://github.com/PhilippeSigaud/D-templates-tutorial

```
    writeln("by index 0 : ", t[0]);
    writeln("by .number : ", t.number);
    writeln("by index 1 : ", t[1]);
    writeln("by .message: ", t.message);
```

The output:

```
by index 0 : 42
by .number : 42
by index 1 : hello
by .message: hello
```

Expanding the members as a list of values

Tuple members can be expanded as a list of values that can be used e.g. as an argument list when calling a function. The members can be expanded either by the .expand property or by slicing:

```
import std.stdio;
import std.typecons;

void foo(int i, string s, double d, char c) {
    // ...
}

void bar(int i, double d, char c) {
    // ...
}

void main() {
    auto t = tuple(1, "2", 3.3, '4');

    // Both of the following lines are equivalents of
    // foo(1, "2", 3.3, '4'):
    foo(t.expand);
    foo(t[]);

    // The equivalent of bar(1, 3.3, '4'):
    bar(t[0], t[$-2..$]);
}
```

The tuple above consists of four values of int, string, double, and char. Since those types match the parameter list of foo(), an expansion of its members can be used as arguments to foo(). When calling bar(), a matching argument list is made up of the first member and the last two members of the tuple.

As long as the members are compatible to be elements of the same array, the expansion of a tuple can be used as the element values of an array literal as well:

```
import std.stdio;
import std.typecons;

void main() {
    auto t = tuple(1, 2, 3);
    auto a = [ t.expand, t[] ];
    writeln(a);
}
```

The array literal above is initialized by expanding the same tuple twice:

```
[1, 2, 3, 1, 2, 3]
```

Compile-time foreach

Because their values can be expanded, tuples can be used with the foreach statement as well:

```
    auto t = tuple(42, "hello", 1.5);

    foreach (i, member; t) {
        writefln("%s: %s", i, member);
    }
```

The output:

```
0: 42
1: hello
2: 1.5
```

The foreach statement above may give a false impression: It may be thought of being a loop that gets executed at run time. That is not the case. Rather, a foreach statement that operates on the members of a tuple is an *unrolling* of the loop body for each member. The foreach statement above is the equivalent of the following code:

```
    {
        enum size_t i = 0;
        int member = t[i];
        writefln("%s: %s", i, member);
    }
    {
        enum size_t i = 1;
        string member = t[i];
        writefln("%s: %s", i, member);
    }
    {
        enum size_t i = 2;
        double member = t[i];
        writefln("%s: %s", i, member);
    }
```

The reason for the unrolling is the fact that when the tuple members are of different types, the foreach body has to be compiled differently for each type.

We will see static foreach, a more powerful loop unrolling feature, in a later chapter (page 602).

Returning multiple values from functions

Tuples can be a simple solution to the limitation of functions having to return a single value. An example of this is std.algorithm.findSplit. findSplit() searches for a range inside another range and produces a result consisting of three pieces: the part before the found range, the found range, and the part after the found range:

```
import std.algorithm;

// ...

    auto entireRange = "hello";
    auto searched = "ll";

    auto result = findSplit(entireRange, searched);

    writeln("before: ", result[0]);
    writeln("found : ", result[1]);
    writeln("after : ", result[2]);
```

The output:

```
before: he
found : ll
after : o
```

Another option for returning multiple values from a function is to return a `struct` object:

```
struct Result {
    // ...
}

Result foo() {
    // ...
}
```

77.2 AliasSeq

`AliasSeq` is defined in the `std.meta` module. It is used for representing a concept that is normally used by the compiler but otherwise not available to the programmer as an entity: A comma-separated list of values, types, and symbols (i.e. `alias` template arguments). The following are three examples of such lists:

- Function argument list
- Template argument list
- Array literal element list

The following three lines of code are examples of those lists in the same order:

```
foo(1, "hello", 2.5);          // function arguments
auto o = Bar!(char, long)();   // template arguments
auto a = [ 1, 2, 3, 4 ];       // array literal elements
```

Tuple takes advantage of `AliasSeq` when expanding its members.

The name `AliasSeq` comes from "alias sequence" and it can contain types, values, and symbols. (`AliasSeq` and `std.meta` used to be called `TypeTuple` and `std.typetuple`, respectively.)

This chapter includes `AliasSeq` examples that consist only of types or only of values. Examples of its use with both types and values will appear in the next chapter. `AliasSeq` is especially useful with variadic templates, which we will see in the next chapter as well.

AliasSeq consisting of values

The values that an `AliasSeq` represents are specified as its template arguments.

Let's imagine a function that takes three parameters:

```
import std.stdio;

void foo(int i, string s, double d) {
    writefln("foo is called with %s, %s, and %s.", i, s, d);
}
```

That function would normally be called with three arguments:

```
foo(1, "hello", 2.5);
```

`AliasSeq` can combine those arguments as a single entity and can automatically be expanded when calling functions:

```
import std.meta;

// ...

    alias arguments = AliasSeq!(1, "hello", 2.5);
    foo(arguments);
```

Although it looks like the function is now being called with a single argument, the `foo()` call above is the equivalent of the previous one. As a result, both calls produce the same output:

```
foo is called with 1, hello, and 2.5.
```

Also note that `arguments` is not defined as a variable, e.g. with `auto`. Rather, it is an `alias` of a specific `AliasSeq` instance. Although it is possible to define variables of `AliasSeq`s as well, the examples in this chapter will use them only as aliases.

As we have seen above with `Tuple`, when the values are compatible to be elements of the same array, an `AliasSeq` can be used to initialize an array literal as well:

```
alias elements = AliasSeq!(1, 2, 3, 4);
auto arr = [ elements ];
assert(arr == [ 1, 2, 3, 4 ]);
```

Indexing and slicing

Same with `Tuple`, the members of an `AliasSeq` can be accessed by indexes and slices:

```
alias arguments = AliasSeq!(1, "hello", 2.5);
assert(arguments[0] == 1);
assert(arguments[1] == "hello");
assert(arguments[2] == 2.5);
```

Let's assume there is a function with parameters matching the last two members of the `AliasSeq` above. That function can be called with a slice of just the last two members of the `AliasSeq`:

```
void bar(string s, double d) {
    // ...
}

// ...

    bar(arguments[$-2 .. $]);
```

AliasSeq consisting of types

Members of an `AliasSeq` can consist of types. In other words, not a specific value of a specific type but a type like `int` itself. An `AliasSeq` consisting of types can represent template arguments.

Let's use an `AliasSeq` with a `struct` template that has two parameters. The first parameter of this template determines the element type of a member array and the second parameter determines the return value of a member function:

```
import std.conv;

struct S(ElementT, ResultT) {
    ElementT[] arr;

    ResultT length() {
        return to!ResultT(arr.length);
    }
}

void main() {
    auto s = S!(double, int)([ 1, 2, 3 ]);
    auto l = s.length();
}
```

In the code above, we see that the template is instantiated with (double, int). An AliasSeq can represent the same argument list as well:

```
import std.meta;

// ...

    alias Types = AliasSeq!(double, int);
    auto s = S!Types([ 1, 2, 3 ]);
```

Although it appears to be a single template argument, Types gets expanded automatically and the template instantiation becomes S!(double, int) as before.

AliasSeq is especially useful in *variadic templates*. We will see examples of this in the next chapter.

foreach with AliasSeq

Same with Tuple, the foreach statement operating on an AliasSeq is not a run time loop. Rather, it is the unrolling of the loop body for each member.

Let's see an example of this with a unit test written for the S struct that was defined above. The following code tests S for element types int, long, and float (ResultT is always size_t in this example):

```
unittest {
    alias Types = AliasSeq!(int, long, float);

    foreach (Type; Types) {
        auto s = S!(Type, size_t)([ Type.init, Type.init ]);
        assert(s.length() == 2);
    }
}
```

The foreach variable Type corresponds to int, long, and float, in that order. As a result, the foreach statement gets compiled as the equivalent of the code below:

```
    {
        auto s = S!(int, size_t)([ int.init, int.init ]);
        assert(s.length() == 2);
    }
    {
        auto s = S!(long, size_t)([ long.init, long.init ]);
        assert(s.length() == 2);
    }
    {
        auto s = S!(float, size_t)([ float.init, float.init ]);
        assert(s.length() == 2);
    }
```

77.3 .tupleof property

.tupleof represents the members of a type or an object. When applied to a user-defined type, .tupleof provides access to the definitions of the members of that type:

```
import std.stdio;

struct S {
    int number;
    string message;
    double value;
}

void main() {
    foreach (i, MemberType; typeof(S.tupleof)) {
        writefln("Member %s:", i);
```

```
        writefln("  type: %s", MemberType.stringof);

        string name = S.tupleof[i].stringof;
        writefln("  name: %s", name);
    }
}
```

`S.tupleof` appears in two places in the program. First, the types of the elements are obtained by applying `typeof` to `.tupleof` so that each type appears as the `MemberType` variable. Second, the name of the member is obtained by `S.tupleof[i].stringof`.

```
Member 0:
  type: int
  name: number
Member 1:
  type: string
  name: message
Member 2:
  type: double
  name: value
```

`.tupleof` can be applied to an object as well. In that case, it produces a tuple consisting of the values of the members of the object:

```
    auto object = S(42, "hello", 1.5);

    foreach (i, member; object.tupleof) {
        writefln("Member %s:", i);
        writefln("  type : %s", typeof(member).stringof);
        writefln("  value: %s", member);
    }
```

The `foreach` variable `member` represents each member of the object:

```
Member 0:
  type : int
  value: 42
Member 1:
  type : string
  value: hello
Member 2:
  type : double
  value: 1.5
```

Here, an important point to make is that the tuple that `.tupleof` returns consists of the members of the object themselves, not their copies. In other words, the tuple members are references to the actual object members.

77.4 Summary

- `tuple()` combines different types of values similar to a `struct` object.
- Explicit use of `Tuple` allows accessing the members by properties.
- The members can be expanded as a value list by `.expand` or by slicing.
- `foreach` with a tuple is not a run time loop; rather, it is a loop unrolling.
- `AliasSeq` represents concepts like function argument list, template argument list, array literal element list, etc.
- `AliasSeq` can consist of values and types.
- Tuples support indexing and slicing.
- `.tupleof` provides information about the members of types and objects.

78 More Templates

We have seen the power and convenience of templates in the Templates chapter (page 399). A single templated definition of an algorithm or a data structure is sufficient to use that definition for multiple types.

That chapter covered only the most common uses of templates: function, struct, and class templates and their uses with *type* template parameters. In this chapter we will see templates in more detail. Before going further, I recommend that you review at least the summary section of that chapter.

78.1 The shortcut syntax

In addition to being powerful, D templates are easy to define and use and they are very readable. Defining a function, struct, or class template is as simple as providing a template parameter list:

```
T twice(T)(T value) {
    return 2 * value;
}

class Fraction(T) {
    T numerator;
    T denominator;

    // ...
}
```

Template definitions like the ones above are taking advantage of D's shortcut template syntax.

In their full syntax, templates are defined by the template keyword. The equivalents of the two template definitions above are the following:

```
template twice(T) {
    T twice(T value) {
        return 2 * value;
    }
}

template Fraction(T) {
    class Fraction {
        T numerator;
        T denominator;

        // ...
    }
}
```

Although most templates are defined by the shortcut syntax, the compiler always uses the full syntax. We can imagine the compiler applying the following steps to convert a shortcut syntax to its full form behind the scenes:

1. Wrap the definition with a template block.
2. Give the same name to that block.
3. Move the template parameter list to the template block.

The full syntax that is arrived after those steps is called an *eponymous template*, which the programmer can define explicitly as well. We will see eponymous templates later below.

Template name space

It is possible to have more than one definition inside a template block. The following template contains both a function and a struct definition:

```
template MyTemplate(T) {
    T foo(T value) {
        return value / 3;
    }

    struct S {
        T member;
    }
}
```

Instantiating the template for a specific type instantiates all of the definitions inside the block. The following code instantiates the template for int and double:

```
auto result = MyTemplate!int.foo(42);
writeln(result);

auto s = MyTemplate!double.S(5.6);
writeln(s.member);
```

A specific instantiation of a template introduces a *name space*. The definitions that are inside an instantiation can be used by that name. However, if these names are too long, it is always possible to use aliases as we have seen in the alias chapter (page 418):

```
alias MyStruct = MyTemplate!dchar.S;

// ...

auto o = MyStruct('a');
writeln(o.member);
```

Eponymous templates

Eponymous templates are template blocks that contain a definition that has the same name as that block. In fact, each shortcut template syntax is the shortcut of an eponymous template.

As an example, assume that a program needs to qualify types that are larger than 20 bytes as *too large*. Such a qualification can be achieved by a constant bool value inside a template block:

```
template isTooLarge(T) {
    enum isTooLarge = T.sizeof > 20;
}
```

Note how the names of both the template block and its only definition are the same. This eponymous template is used by the shortcut syntax instead of the whole isTooLarge!int.isTooLarge:

```
writeln(isTooLarge!int);
```

The highlighted part above is the same as the bool value inside the block. Since the size of int is less than 20, the output of the code would be false.

That eponymous template can be defined by the shortcut syntax as well:

```
enum isTooLarge(T) = T.sizeof > 20;
```

A common use of eponymous templates is defining type aliases depending on certain conditions. For example, the following eponymous template picks the larger of two types by setting an alias to it:

```
template LargerOf(A, B) {
    static if (A.sizeof < B.sizeof) {
        alias LargerOf = B;

    } else {
        alias LargerOf = A;
    }
}
```

Since `long` is larger than `int` (8 bytes versus 4 bytes), `LargerOf!(int, long)` would be the same as the type `long`. Such templates are especially useful in other templates where the two types are template parameters themselves (or depend on template parameters):

```
// ...

/* The return type of this function is the larger of its two
 * template parameters: Either type A or type B. */
auto calculate(A, B)(A a, B b) {
    LargerOf!(A, B) result;
    // ...
    return result;
}

void main() {
    auto f = calculate(1, 2L);
    static assert(is (typeof(f) == long));
}
```

78.2 Kinds of templates

Function, class, and struct templates

We have already covered function, `class`, and `struct` templates in the Templates chapter (page 399) and we have seen many examples of them since then.

Member function templates

`struct` and `class` member functions can be templates as well. For example, the following `put()` member function template would work with any parameter type as long as that type is compatible with the operations inside the template (for this specific template, it should be convertible to `string`):

```
class Sink {
    string content;

    void put(T)(auto ref const T value) {
        import std.conv;
        content ~= value.to!string;
    }
}
```

However, as templates can have potentially infinite number of instantiations, they cannot be virtual functions (page 328) because the compiler cannot know which specific instantiations of a template to include in the interface. (Accordingly, the `abstract` keyword cannot be used either.)

For example, although the presence of the `put()` template in the following subclass may give the impression that it is overriding a function, it actually hides the `put` name of the superclass (see *name hiding* in the alias chapter (page 418)):

```
class Sink {
    string content;

    void put(T)(auto ref const T value) {
        import std.conv;
        content ~= value.to!string;
    }
}

class SpecialSink : Sink {
    /* The following template definition does not override
     * the template instances of the superclass; it hides
     * those names. */
    void put(T)(auto ref const T value) {
        import std.string;
        super.put(format("{%s}", value));
    }
}

void fillSink(Sink sink) {
    /* The following function calls are not virtual. Because
     * parameter 'sink' is of type 'Sink', the calls will
     * always be dispatched to Sink's 'put' template
     * instances. */

    sink.put(42);
    sink.put("hello");
}

void main() {
    auto sink = new SpecialSink();
    fillSink(sink);

    import std.stdio;
    writeln(sink.content);
}
```

As a result, although the object actually is a `SpecialSink`, both of the calls inside `fillSink()` are dispatched to `Sink` and the content does not contain the curly brackets that `SpecialSink.put()` inserts:

```
42hello    ← Sink's behavior, not SpecialSink's
```

Union templates

Union templates are similar to struct templates. The shortcut syntax is available for them as well.

As an example, let's design a more general version of the `IpAdress` union that we saw in the Unions chapter (page 504). There, the value of the IPv4 address was kept as a `uint` member in that earlier version of `IpAdress`, and the element type of the segment array was `ubyte`:

```
union IpAddress {
    uint value;
    ubyte[4] bytes;
}
```

The `bytes` array provided easy access to the four segments of the IPv4 address.

The same concept can be implemented in a more general way as the following union template:

```
union SegmentedValue(ActualT, SegmentT) {
    ActualT value;
    SegmentT[/* number of segments */] segments;
}
```

That template would allow specifying the types of the value and its segments freely.

The number of segments that are needed depends on the types of the actual value and the segments. Since an IPv4 address has four `ubyte` segments, that value was hard-coded as 4 in the earlier definition of `IpAddress`. For the `SegmentedValue` template, the number of segments must be computed at compile time when the template is instantiated for the two specific types.

The following eponymous template takes advantage of the `.sizeof` properties of the two types to calculate the number of segments needed:

```
template segmentCount(ActualT, SegmentT) {
    enum segmentCount = ((ActualT.sizeof + (SegmentT.sizeof - 1))
                         / SegmentT.sizeof);
}
```

The shortcut syntax may be more readable:

```
enum segmentCount(ActualT, SegmentT) =
    ((ActualT.sizeof + (SegmentT.sizeof - 1))
     / SegmentT.sizeof);
```

Note: *The expression SegmentT.sizeof - 1 is for when the sizes of the types cannot be divided evenly. For example, when the actual type is 5 bytes and the segment type is 2 bytes, even though a total of 3 segments are needed, the result of the integer division 5/2 would incorrectly be 2.*

The definition of the union template is now complete:

```
union SegmentedValue(ActualT, SegmentT) {
    ActualT value;
    SegmentT[segmentCount!(ActualT, SegmentT)] segments;
}
```

Instantiation of the template for `uint` and `ubyte` would be the equivalent of the earlier definition of `IpAddress`:

```
import std.stdio;

void main() {
    auto address = SegmentedValue!(uint, ubyte)(0xc0a80102);

    foreach (octet; address.segments) {
        write(octet, ' ');
    }
}
```

The output of the program is the same as the one in the Unions chapter (page 504):

```
2 1 168 192
```

To demonstrate the flexibility of this template, let's imagine that it is required to access the parts of the IPv4 address as two `ushort` values. It would be as easy as providing `ushort` as the segment type:

```
    auto address = SegmentedValue!(uint, ushort)(0xc0a80102);
```

Although unusual for an IPv4 address, the output of the program would consist of two `ushort` segment values:

```
258 49320
```

Interface templates

Interface templates provide flexibility on the types that are used on an interface (as well as values such as sizes of fixed-length arrays and other features of an interface).

Let's define an interface for colored objects where the type of the color is determined by a template parameter:

```
interface ColoredObject(ColorT) {
    void paint(ColorT color);
}
```

That interface template requires that its subtypes must define the `paint()` function but it leaves the type of the color flexible.

A class that represents a frame on a web page may choose to use a color type that is represented by its red, green, and blue components:

```
struct RGB {
    ubyte red;
    ubyte green;
    ubyte blue;
}

class PageFrame : ColoredObject!RGB {
    void paint(RGB color) {
        // ...
    }
}
```

On the other hand, a class that uses the frequency of light can choose a completely different type to represent color:

```
alias Frequency = double;

class Bulb : ColoredObject!Frequency {
    void paint(Frequency color) {
        // ...
    }
}
```

However, as explained in the Templates chapter (page 399), "every template instantiation yields a distinct type". Accordingly, the interfaces `ColoredObject!RGB` and `ColoredObject!Frequency` are unrelated interfaces, and `PageFrame` and `Bulb` are unrelated classes.

78.3 Kinds of template parameters

The template parameters that we have seen so far have all been *type* parameters. So far, parameters like T and ColorT all represented types. For example, T meant int, double, Student, etc. depending on the instantiation of the template.

There are other kinds of template parameters: value, this, alias, and tuple.

Type template parameters

This section is only for completeness. All of the templates that we have seen so far had type parameters.

Value template parameters

Value template parameters allow flexibility on certain values used in the template implementation.

Since templates are a compile-time feature, the values for the value template parameters must be known at compile time; values that must be calculated at run time cannot be used.

To see the advantage of value template parameters, let's start with a set of structs representing geometric shapes:

```d
struct Triangle {
    Point[3] corners;
    // ...
}

struct Rectangle {
    Point[4] corners;
    // ...
}

struct Pentagon {
    Point[5] corners;
    // ...
}
```

Let's assume that other member variables and member functions of those types are exactly the same and that the only difference is the *value* that determines the number of corners.

Value template parameters help in such cases. The following struct template is sufficient to represent all of the types above and more:

```d
struct Polygon(size_t N) {
    Point[N] corners;
    // ...
}
```

The only template parameter of that struct template is a value named N of type size_t. The value N can be used as a compile-time constant anywhere inside the template.

That template is flexible enough to represent shapes of any sides:

```d
    auto centagon = Polygon!100();
```

The following aliases correspond to the earlier struct definitions:

```d
alias Triangle = Polygon!3;
alias Rectangle = Polygon!4;
alias Pentagon = Polygon!5;

// ...

    auto triangle = Triangle();
    auto rectangle = Rectangle();
    auto pentagon = Pentagon();
```

The type of the *value* template parameter above was size_t. As long as the value can be known at compile time, a value template parameter can be of any type: a fundamental type, a struct type, an array, a string, etc.

```d
struct S {
    int i;
}

// Value template parameter of struct S
void foo(S s)() {
    // ...
}

void main() {
    foo!(S(42))();    // Instantiating with literal S(42)
}
```

The following example uses a `string` template parameter to represent an XML tag to produce a simple XML output:

- First the tag between the < > characters: `<tag>`
- Then the value
- Finally the tag between the </ > characters: `</tag>`

For example, an XML tag representing *location 42* would be printed as `<location>42</location>`.

```d
import std.string;

class XmlElement(string tag) {
    double value;

    this(double value) {
        this.value = value;
    }

    override string toString() const {
        return format("<%s>%s</%s>", tag, value, tag);
    }
}
```

Note that the template parameter is not about a type that is used in the implementation of the template, rather it is about a `string` *value*. That value can be used anywhere inside the template as a `string`.

The XML elements that a program needs can be defined as aliases as in the following code:

```d
alias Location = XmlElement!"location";
alias Temperature = XmlElement!"temperature";
alias Weight = XmlElement!"weight";

void main() {
    Object[] elements;

    elements ~= new Location(1);
    elements ~= new Temperature(23);
    elements ~= new Weight(78);

    writeln(elements);
}
```

The output:

```
[<location>1</location>, <temperature>23</temperature>, <weight>78</weight>]
```

Value template parameters can have default values as well. For example, the following struct template represents points in a multi-dimensional space where the default number of dimensions is 3:

```d
struct Point(T, size_t dimension = 3) {
    T[dimension] coordinates;
}
```

That template can be used without specifying the `dimension` template parameter:

```d
    Point!double center;    // a point in 3-dimensional space
```

The number of dimensions can still be specified when needed:

```d
    Point!(int, 2) point;   // a point on a surface
```

We have seen in the Variable Number of Parameters chapter (page 258) how *special keywords* work differently depending on whether they appear inside code or as default function arguments.

Similarly, when used as default template arguments, the special keywords refer to where the template is instantiated at, not where the keywords appear:

```d
import std.stdio;

void func(T,
          string functionName = __FUNCTION__,
          string file = __FILE__,
          size_t line = __LINE__)(T parameter) {
    writefln("Instantiated at function %s at file %s, line %s.",
             functionName, file, line);
}

void main() {
    func(42);    // ← line 12
}
```

Although the special keywords appear in the definition of the template, their values refer to `main()`, where the template is instantiated at:

```
Instantiated at function deneme.main at file deneme.d, line 12.
```

We will use __FUNCTION__ below in a multi-dimensional operator overloading example.

this template parameters for member functions

Member functions can be templates as well. Their template parameters have the same meanings as other templates.

However, unlike other templates, member function template parameters can also be *this parameters*. In that case, the identifier that comes after the `this` keyword represents the exact type of the `this` reference of the object. (*this reference* means the object itself, as is commonly written in constructors as `this.member = value`.)

```d
struct MyStruct(T) {
    void foo(this OwnType)() const {
        writeln("Type of this object: ", OwnType.stringof);
    }
}
```

The `OwnType` template parameter is the actual type of the object that the member function is called on:

```d
    auto m = MyStruct!int();
    auto c = const(MyStruct!int)();
    auto i = immutable(MyStruct!int)();

    m.foo();
    c.foo();
    i.foo();
```

The output:

```
Type of this object: MyStruct!int
Type of this object: const(MyStruct!int)
Type of this object: immutable(MyStruct!int)
```

As you can see, the type includes the corresponding type of T as well as the type qualifiers like `const` and `immutable`.

The struct (or class) need not be a template. this template parameters can appear on member function templates of non-templated types as well.

this template parameters can be useful in *template mixins* as well, which we will see two chapters later.

alias template parameters

alias template parameters can correspond to any symbol or expression that is used in the program. The only constraint on such a template argument is that the argument must be compatible with its use inside the template.

filter() and map() use alias template parameters to determine the operations that they execute.

Let's see a simple example on a struct template that is for modifying an existing variable. The struct template takes the variable as an alias parameter:

```
struct MyStruct(alias variable) {
    void set(int value) {
        variable = value;
    }
}
```

The member function simply assigns its parameter to the variable that the struct template is instantiated with. That variable must be specified during the instantiation of the template:

```
    int x = 1;
    int y = 2;

    auto object = MyStruct!x();
    object.set(10);
    writeln("x: ", x, ", y: ", y);
```

In that instantiation, the variable template parameter corresponds to the variable x:

```
x: 10, y: 2
```

Conversely, MyStruct!y instantiation of the template would associate variable with y.

Let's now have an alias parameter that represents a callable entity, similar to filter() and map():

```
void caller(alias func)() {
    write("calling: ");
    func();
}
```

As seen by the () parentheses, caller() uses its template parameter as a function. Additionally, since the parentheses are empty, it must be legal to call the function without specifying any arguments.

Let's have the following two functions that match that description. They can both represent func because they can be called as func() in the template:

```
void foo() {
    writeln("foo called.");
}

void bar() {
    writeln("bar called.");
}
```

Those functions can be used as the alias parameter of caller():

```
    caller!foo();
    caller!bar();
```

The output:

```
calling: foo called.
calling: bar called.
```

As long as it matches the way it is used in the template, any symbol can be used as an `alias` parameter. As a counter example, using an `int` variable with `caller()` would cause a compilation error:

```
    int variable;
    caller!variable();    // ← compilation ERROR
```

The compilation error indicates that the variable does not match its use in the template:

```
Error: function expected before (), not variable of type int
```

Although the mistake is with the `caller!variable` instantiation, the compilation error necessarily points at `func()` inside the `caller()` template because from the point of view of the compiler the error is with trying to call `variable` as a function. One way of dealing with this issue is to use *template constraints*, which we will see below.

If the variable supports the function call syntax perhaps because it has an `opCall()` overload or it is a function literal, it would still work with the `caller()` template. The following example demonstrates both of those cases:

```
class C {
    void opCall() {
        writeln("C.opCall called.");
    }
}

// ...

    auto o = new C();
    caller!o();

    caller!({ writeln("Function literal called."); })();
```

The output:

```
calling: C.opCall called.
calling: Function literal called.
```

`alias` parameters can be specialized as well. However, they have a different specialization syntax. The specialized type must be specified between the `alias` keyword and the name of the parameter:

```
import std.stdio;

void foo(alias variable)() {
    writefln("The general definition is using '%s' of type %s.",
             variable.stringof, typeof(variable).stringof);
}

void foo(alias int i)() {
    writefln("The int specialization is using '%s'.",
             i.stringof);
}

void foo(alias double d)() {
    writefln("The double specialization is using '%s'.",
```

```
            d.stringof);
}

void main() {
    string name;
    foo!name();

    int count;
    foo!count();

    double length;
    foo!length();
}
```

Also note that `alias` parameters make the names of the actual variables available inside the template:

```
The general definition is using 'name' of type string.
The int specialization is using 'count'.
The double specialization is using 'length'.
```

Tuple template parameters

We have seen in the Variable Number of Parameters chapter (page 258) that variadic functions can take any number and any type of parameters. For example, `writeln()` can be called with any number of parameters of any type.

Templates can be variadic as well. A template parameter that consists of a name followed by `...` allows any number and kind of parameters at that parameter's position. Such parameters appear as a tuple inside the template, which can be used like an `AliasSeq`.

Let's see an example of this with a template that simply prints information about every template argument that it is instantiated with:

```
void info(T...)(T args) {
    // ...
}
```

The template parameter `T...` makes `info` a *variadic template*. Both `T` and `args` are tuples:

- `T` represents the types of the arguments.
- `args` represents the arguments themselves.

The following example instantiates that function template with three values of three different types:

```
import std.stdio;

// ...

void main() {
    info(1, "abc", 2.3);
}
```

The following implementation simply prints information about the arguments by iterating over them in a `foreach` loop:

```
void info(T...)(T args) {
    // 'args' is being used like a tuple:
    foreach (i, arg; args) {
        writefln("%s: %s argument %s",
                 i, typeof(arg).stringof, arg);
    }
}
```

Note: *As seen in the previous chapter, since the arguments are a tuple, the* `foreach` *statement above is a* compile-time `foreach`.

The output:

```
0: int argument 1
1: string argument abc
2: double argument 2.3
```

Note that instead of obtaining the type of each argument by `typeof(arg)`, we could have used `T[i]` as well.

We know that template arguments can be deduced for function templates. That's why the compiler deduces the types as `int`, `string`, and `double` in the previous program.

However, it is also possible to specify template parameters explicitly. For example, `std.conv.to` takes the destination type as an explicit template parameter:

```
to!string(42);
```

When template parameters are explicitly specified, they can be a mixture of value, type, and other kinds. That flexibility makes it necessary to be able to determine whether each template parameter is a type or not, so that the body of the template can be coded accordingly. That is achieved by treating the arguments as an `AliasSeq`.

Let's see an example of this in a function template that produces `struct` definitions as source code in text form. Let's have this function return the produced source code as `string`. This function can first take the name of the `struct` followed by the types and names of the members specified as pairs:

```
import std.stdio;

void main() {
    writeln(structDefinition!("Student",
                              string, "name",
                              int,    "id",
                              int[],  "grades")());
}
```

That `structDefinition` instantiation is expected to produce the following `string`:

```
struct Student {
    string name;
    int id;
    int[] grades;
}
```

Note: *Functions that produce source code are used with the* `mixin` *keyword, which we will see in a later chapter (page 560).*

The following is an implementation that produces the desired output. Note how the function template makes use of the `is` expression. Remember that the expression `is (arg)` produces `true` when `arg` is a valid type:

```
import std.string;

string structDefinition(string name, Members...)() {
    /* Ensure that members are specified as pairs: first the
     * type then the name. */
    static assert((Members.length % 2) == 0,
                  "Members must be specified as pairs.");
```

```d
    /* The first part of the struct definition. */
    string result = "struct " ~ name ~ "\n{\n";

    foreach (i, arg; Members) {
        static if (i % 2) {
            /* The odd numbered arguments should be the names
             * of members. Instead of dealing with the names
             * here, we use them as Members[i+1] in the 'else'
             * clause below.
             *
             * Let's at least ensure that the member name is
             * specified as a string. */
            static assert(is (typeof(arg) == string),
                          "Member name " ~ arg.stringof ~
                          " is not a string.");

        } else {
            /* In this case 'arg' is the type of the
             * member. Ensure that it is indeed a type. */
            static assert(is (arg),
                          arg.stringof ~ " is not a type.");

            /* Produce the member definition from its type and
             * its name.
             *
             * Note: We could have written 'arg' below instead
             * of Members[i]. */
            result ~= format("    %s %s;\n",
                             Members[i].stringof, Members[i+1]);
        }
    }

    /* The closing bracket of the struct definition. */
    result ~= "}";

    return result;
}

import std.stdio;

void main() {
    writeln(structDefinition!("Student",
                              string, "name",
                              int, "id",
                              int[], "grades")());
}
```

78.4 `typeof(this)`, `typeof(super)`, and `typeof(return)`

In some cases, the generic nature of templates makes it difficult to know or spell out certain types in the template code. The following three special `typeof` varieties are useful in such cases. Although they are introduced in this chapter, they work in non-templated code as well.

- `typeof(this)` generates the type of the `this` reference. It works in any `struct` or `class`, even outside of member functions:

```d
struct List(T) {
    // The type of 'next' is List!int when T is int
    typeof(this) *next;
    // ...
}
```

- `typeof(super)` generates the base type of a `class` (i.e. the type of `super`).

```d
class ListImpl(T) {
    // ...
}

class List(T) : ListImpl!T {
```

```
    // The type of 'next' is ListImpl!int when T is int
    typeof(super) *next;
    // ...
}
```

- `typeof(return)` generates the return type of a function, inside that function.

  For example, instead of defining the `calculate()` function above as an `auto` function, we can be more explicit by replacing `auto` with `LargerOf!(A, B)` in its definition. (Being more explicit would have the added benefit of obviating at least some part of its function comment.)

```
LargerOf!(A, B) calculate(A, B)(A a, B b) {
    // ...
}
```

`typeof(return)` prevents having to repeat the return type inside the function body:

```
LargerOf!(A, B) calculate(A, B)(A a, B b) {
    typeof(return) result;    // The type is either A or B
    // ...
    return result;
}
```

78.5 Template specializations

We have seen template specializations in the Templates chapter (page 399). Like type parameters, other kinds of template parameters can be specialized as well. The following is the general definition of a template and its specialization for 0:

```
void foo(int value)() {
    // ... general definition ...
}

void foo(int value : 0)() {
    // ... special definition for zero ...
}
```

We will take advantage of template specializations in the *meta programming* section below.

78.6 Meta programming

As they are about code generation, templates are among the higher level features of D. A template is indeed code that generates code. Writing code that generates code is called *meta programming*.

Due to templates being compile-time features, some operations that are normally executed at runtime can be moved to compile time as template instantiations.

(**Note:** *Compile time function execution* (CTFE) *is another feature that achieves the same goal. We will see CTFE in a later chapter.*)

Executing templates at compile time is commonly based on recursive template instantiations.

To see an example of this, let's first consider a regular function that calculates the sum of numbers from 0 to a specific value. For example, when its argument is 4, this fuction should return the result of 0+1+2+3+4:

```
int sum(int last) {
    int result = 0;

    foreach (value; 0 .. last + 1) {
```

```
        result += value;
    }

    return result;
}
```

That is an iterative implementation of the function. The same function can be implemented by recursion as well:

```
int sum(int last) {
    return (last == 0
            ? last
            : last + sum(last - 1));
}
```

The recursive function returns the sum of the last value and the previous sum. As you can see, the function terminates the recursion by treating the value 0 specially.

Functions are normally run-time features. As usual, sum() can be executed at run time:

```
    writeln(sum(4));
```

When the result is needed at compile time, one way of achieving the same calculation is by defining a function template. In this case, the parameter must be a template parameter, not a function parameter:

```
// WARNING: This code is incorrect.
int sum(int last)() {
    return (last == 0
            ? last
            : last + sum!(last - 1)());
}
```

That function template instantiates itself by `last - 1` and tries to calculate the sum again by recursion. However, that code is incorrect.

As the ternary operator would be compiled to be executed at run time, there is no condition check that terminates the recursion at compile time:

```
    writeln(sum!4());       // ←  compilation ERROR
```

The compiler detects that the template instances would recurse infinitely and stops at an arbitrary number of recursions:

```
Error: template instance deneme.sum!(-296) recursive expansion
```

Considering the difference between the template argument 4 and -296, the compiler restricts template expansion at 300 by default.

In meta programming, recursion is terminated by a template specialization. The following specialization for 0 produces the expected result:

```
// The general definition
int sum(int last)() {
    return last + sum!(last - 1)();
}

// The special definition for zero
int sum(int last : 0)() {
    return 0;
}
```

The following is a program that tests sum():

```
import std.stdio;

void main() {
    writeln(sum!4());
}
```

Now the program compiles successfully and produces the result of 4+3+2+1+0:

```
10
```

An important point to make here is that the function sum!4() is executed entirely at compile time. The compiled code is the equivalent of calling writeln() with literal 10:

```
    writeln(10);         // the equivalent of writeln(sum!4())
```

As a result, the compiled code is as fast and simple as can be. Although the value 10 is still calculated as the result of 4+3+2+1+0, the entire calculation happens at compile time.

The previous example demonstrates one of the benefits of meta programming: moving operations from run time to compile time. CTFE obviates some of the idioms of meta programming in D.

78.7 Compile-time polymorphism

In object oriented programming (OOP), polymorphism is achieved by inheritance. For example, if a function takes an interface, it accepts objects of any class that inherits that interface.

Let's recall an earlier example from a previous chapter:

```
import std.stdio;

interface SoundEmitter {
    string emitSound();
}

class Violin : SoundEmitter {
    string emitSound() {
        return "♩♪♪";
    }
}

class Bell : SoundEmitter {
    string emitSound() {
        return "ding";
    }
}

void useSoundEmittingObject(SoundEmitter object) {
    // ... some operations ...
    writeln(object.emitSound());
    // ... more operations ...
}

void main() {
    useSoundEmittingObject(new Violin);
    useSoundEmittingObject(new Bell);
}
```

useSoundEmittingObject() is benefiting from polymorphism. It takes a SoundEmitter so that it can be used with any type that is derived from that interface.

Since *working with any type* is inherent to templates, they can be seen as providing a kind of polymorphism as well. Being a compile-time feature, the polymorphism that templates provide is called *compile-time polymorphism*. Conversely, OOP's polymorphism is called *run-time polymorphism*.

In reality, neither kind of polymorphism allows being used with *any type* because the types must satisfy certain requirements.

Run-time polymorphism requires that the type implements a certain interface.

Compile-time polymorphism requires that the type is compatible with how it is used by the template. As long as the code compiles, the template argument can be used with that template. (**Note:** *Optionally, the argument must satisfy template constraints as well. We will see template constraints later below.*)

For example, if useSoundEmittingObject() were implemented as a function template instead of a function, it could be used with any type that supported the object.emitSound() call:

```
void useSoundEmittingObject(T)(T object) {
    // ... some operations ...
    writeln(object.emitSound());
    // ... more operations ...
}

class Car {
    string emitSound() {
        return "honk honk";
    }
}

// ...

    useSoundEmittingObject(new Violin);
    useSoundEmittingObject(new Bell);
    useSoundEmittingObject(new Car);
```

Note that although Car has no inheritance relationship with any other type, the code compiles successfully, and the emitSound() member function of each type gets called.

Compile-time polymorphism is also known as *duck typing*, a humorous term, emphasizing behavior over actual type.

78.8 Code bloat

The code generated by the compiler is different for every different argument of a type parameter, of a value parameter, etc.

The reason for that can be seen by considering int and double as type template arguments. Each type would have to be processed by different kinds of CPU registers. For that reason, the same template needs to be compiled differently for different template arguments. In other words, the compiler needs to generate different code for each instantiation of a template.

For example, if useSoundEmittingObject() were implemented as a template, it would be compiled as many times as the number of different instantiations of it.

Because it results in larger program size, this effect is called *code bloat*. Although this is not a problem in most programs, it is an effect of templates that must be known.

Conversely, non-templated version of useSoundEmittingObject() would not have any code repetition. The compiler would compile that function just once and execute the same code for all types of the SoundEmitter interface. In run-time polymorphism, having the same code behave differently for different types is achieved by function pointers on the background. Although function pointers have a small cost at run time, that cost is not significant in most programs.

Since both code bloat and run-time polymorphism have effects on program performance, it cannot be known beforehand whether run-time polymorphism or compile-time polymorphism would be a better approach for a specific program.

78.9 Template constraints

The fact that templates can be instantiated with any argument yet not every argument is compatible with every template brings an inconvenience. If a template argument is not compatible with a particular template, the incompatibility is necessarily detected during the compilation of the template code for that argument. As a result, the compilation error points at a line inside the template implementation.

Let's see this by using `useSoundEmittingObject()` with a type that does not support the `object.emitSound()` call:

```
class Cup {
    // ... does not have emitSound() ...
}

// ...

    useSoundEmittingObject(new Cup);   // ← incompatible type
```

Although arguably the error is with the code that uses the template with an incompatible type, the compilation error points at a line inside the template:

```
void useSoundEmittingObject(T)(T object) {
    // ... some operations ...
    writeln(object.emitSound());    // ← compilation ERROR
    // ... more operations ...
}
```

An undesired consequence is that when the template is a part of a third-party library module, the compilation error would appear to be a problem with the library itself.

Note that this issue does not exist for interfaces: A function that takes an interface can only be called with a type that implements that interface. Attempting to call such a function with any other type is a compilation error at the caller.

Template constraints are for disallowing incorrect instantiations of templates. They are defined as logical expressions of an `if` condition right before the template body:

```
void foo(T)()
        if (/* ... constraints ... */) {
    // ...
}
```

A template definition is considered by the compiler only if its constraints evaluate to `true` for a specific instantiation of the template. Otherwise, the template definition is ignored for that use.

Since templates are a compile-time feature, template constraints must be evaluable at compile time. The `is` expression that we saw in the `is` Expression chapter (page 468) is commonly used in template constraints. We will use the `is` expression in the following examples as well.

Tuple parameter of single element

Sometimes the single parameter of a template needs to be one of type, value, or
alias kinds. That can be achieved by a tuple parameter of length one:

```d
template myTemplate(T...)
        if (T.length == 1) {
    static if (is (T[0])) {
        // The single parameter is a type
        enum bool myTemplate = /* ... */;

    } else {
        // The single parameter is some other kind
        enum bool myTemplate = /* ... */;
    }
}
```

Some of the templates of the std.traits module take advantage of this idiom.
We will see std.traits in a later chapter.

Named constraints

Sometimes the constraints are complex, making it hard to understand the
requirements of template parameters. This complexity can be handled by an
idiom that effectively gives names to constraints. This idiom combines four
features of D: anonymous functions, typeof, the is expression, and eponymous
templates.

Let's see this on a function template that has a type parameter. The template
uses its function parameter in specific ways:

```d
void use(T)(T object) {
    // ...
    object.prepare();
    // ...
    object.fly(42);
    // ...
    object.land();
    // ...
}
```

As is obvious from the implementation of the template, the types that this
function can work with must support three specific function calls on the object:
prepare(), fly(42), and land().

One way of specifying a template constraint for that type is by the is and
typeof expressions for each function call inside the template:

```d
void use(T)(T object)
        if (is (typeof(object.prepare())) &&
            is (typeof(object.fly(1))) &&
            is (typeof(object.land())))) {
    // ...
}
```

I will explain that syntax below. For now, accept the whole construct of
is (typeof(object.prepare())) to mean *whether the type supports the*
.prepare() call.

Although such constraints achieve the desired goal, sometimes they are too
complex to be readable. Instead, it is possible to give a more descriptive name to
the whole constraint:

```d
void use(T)(T object)
        if (canFlyAndLand!T) {
    // ...
}
```

That constraint is more readable because it is now more clear that the template is designed to work with types that *can fly and land.*

Such constraints are achieved by an idiom that is implemented similar to the following eponymous template:

```
template canFlyAndLand(T) {
    enum canFlyAndLand = is (typeof(
    {
        T object;
        object.prepare();  // should be preparable for flight
        object.fly(1);     // should be flyable for a certain distance
        object.land();     // should be landable
    }()));
}
```

The D features that take part in that idiom and how they interact with each other are explained below:

```
template canFlyAndLand(T) {
    //          (6)          (5)   (4)
    enum canFlyAndLand = is (typeof(
    { // (1)
        T object;          // (2)
        object.prepare();
        object.fly(1);
        object.land();
    // (3)
    }()));
}
```

1. **Anonymous function:** We have seen anonymous functions in the Function Pointers, Delegates, and Lambdas chapter (page 475). The highlighted curly brackets above define an anonymous function.

2. **Function block:** The function block uses the type as it is supposed to be used in the actual template. First an object of that type is defined and then that object is used in specific ways. (This code never gets executed; see below.)

3. **Evaluation of the function:** The empty parentheses at the end of an anonymous function normally execute that function. However, since that call syntax is within a typeof, it is never executed.

4. **The typeof expression:** typeof produces the type of an expression.

   An important fact about typeof is that it never executes the expression. Rather, it produces the type of the expression *if* that expression would be executed:

   ```
   int i = 42;
   typeof(++i) j;    // same as 'int j;'

   assert(i == 42);  // ++i has not been executed
   ```

   As the previous assert proves, the expression ++i has not been executed. typeof has merely produced the type of that expression as int.

   If the expression that typeof receives is not valid, typeof produces no type at all (not even void). So, if the anonymous function inside canFlyAndLand can be compiled successfully for T, typeof produces a valid type. Otherwise, it produces no type at all.

5. **The is expression:** We have seen many different uses of the is expression in the is Expression chapter (page 468). The is (*Type*) syntax produces true if Type is valid:

```
    int i;
    writeln(is (typeof(i)));                  // true
    writeln(is (typeof(nonexistentSymbol)));  // false
```

Although the second `typeof` above receives a nonexistent symbol, the compiler does not emit a compilation error. Rather, the effect is that the `typeof` expression does not produce any type, so the `is` expression produces `false`:

```
true
false
```

6. **Eponymous template:** As described above, since the `canFlyAndLand` template contains a definition by the same name, the template instantiation is that definition itself.

In the end, `use()` gains a more descriptive constraint:

```
void use(T)(T object)
        if (canFlyAndLand!T) {
    // ...
}
```

Let's try to use that template with two types, one that satisfies the constraint and one that does not satisfy the constraint:

```
// A type that does match the template's operations
class ModelAirplane {
    void prepare() {
    }

    void fly(int distance) {
    }

    void land() {
    }
}

// A type that does not match the template's operations
class Pigeon {
    void fly(int distance) {
    }
}

// ...

    use(new ModelAirplane);    // ← compiles
    use(new Pigeon);           // ← compilation ERROR
```

Named or not, since the template has a constraint, the compilation error points at the line where the template is used rather than where it is implemented.

78.10 Using templates in multi-dimensional operator overloading

We have seen in the Operator Overloading chapter (page 298) that `opDollar`, `opIndex`, and `opSlice` are for element indexing and slicing. When overloaded for single-dimensional collections, these operators have the following responsibilities:

- `opDollar`: Returns the number of elements of the collection.
- `opSlice`: Returns an object that represents some or all of the elements of the collection.
- `opIndex`: Provides access to an element.

Those operator functions have templated versions as well, which have different responsibilities from the non-templated ones above. Note especially that in multi-dimensional operator overloading `opIndex` assumes the responsibility of `opSlice`.

- `opDollar` template: Returns the length of a specific dimension of the collection. The dimension is determined by the template parameter:

```d
size_t opDollar(size_t dimension)() const {
    // ...
}
```

- `opSlice` template: Returns the range information that specifies the range of elements (e.g. the begin and end values in `array[begin..end]`). The information can be returned as `Tuple!(size_t, size_t)` or an equivalent type. The dimension that the range specifies is determined by the template parameter:

```d
Tuple!(size_t, size_t) opSlice(size_t dimension)(size_t begin,
                                                  size_t end) {
    return tuple(begin, end);
}
```

- `opIndex` template: Returns a range object that represents a part of the collection. The range of elements are determined by the template parameters:

```d
Range opIndex(A...)(A arguments) {
    // ...
}
```

`opIndexAssign` and `opIndexOpAssign` have templated versions as well, which operate on a range of elements of the collection.

The user-defined types that define these operators can be used with the multi-dimensional indexing and slicing syntax:

```d
              // Assigns 42 to the elements specified by the
              // indexing and slicing arguments:
              m[a, b..c, $-1, d..e] = 42;
//               ↑   ↑     ↑    ↑
// dimensions:   0   1     2    3
```

Such expressions are first converted to the ones that call the operator functions. The conversions are performed by replacing the $ characters with calls to `opDollar!dimension()`, and the index ranges with calls to `opSlice!dimension(begin, end)`. The length and range information that is returned by those calls is in turn used as arguments when calling e.g. `opIndexAssign`. Accordingly, the expression above is executed as the following equivalent (the dimension values are highlighted):

```d
// The equivalent of the above:
m.opIndexAssign(
    42,                         // ← value to assign
    a,                          // ← argument for dimension 0
    m.opSlice!1(b, c),          // ← argument for dimension 1
    m.opDollar!2() - 1,         // ← argument for dimension 2
    m.opSlice!3(d, e));         // ← argument for dimension 3
```

Consequently, `opIndexAssign` determines the range of elements from the arguments.

Multi-dimensional operator overloading example

The following `Matrix` example demonstrates how these operators can be overloaded for a two-dimensional type.

Note that this code can be implemented in more efficient ways. For example, instead of constructing a *single-element sub-matrix* even when operating on a single element e.g. by `m[i, j]`, it could apply the operation directly on that element.

Additionally, the `writeln(__FUNCTION__)` expressions inside the functions have nothing to do with the behavior of the code. They merely help expose the functions that get called behind the scenes for different operator usages.

Also note that the correctness of dimension values are enforced by template constraints.

```d
import std.stdio;
import std.format;
import std.string;

/* Works as a two-dimensional int array. */
struct Matrix {
private:

    int[][] rows;

    /* Represents a range of rows or columns. */
    struct Range {
        size_t begin;
        size_t end;
    }

    /* Returns the sub-matrix that is specified by the row and
     * column ranges. */
    Matrix subMatrix(Range rowRange, Range columnRange) {
        writeln(__FUNCTION__);

        int[][] slices;

        foreach (row; rows[rowRange.begin .. rowRange.end]) {
            slices ~= row[columnRange.begin .. columnRange.end];
        }

        return Matrix(slices);
    }

public:

    this(size_t height, size_t width) {
        writeln(__FUNCTION__);

        rows = new int[][](height, width);
    }

    this(int[][] rows) {
        writeln(__FUNCTION__);

        this.rows = rows;
    }

    void toString(void delegate(const(char)[]) sink) const {
        sink.formattedWrite!"%(%(%5s %)\n%)"(rows);
    }

    /* Assigns the specified value to each element of the
     * matrix. */
    Matrix opAssign(int value) {
        writeln(__FUNCTION__);

        foreach (row; rows) {
            row[] = value;
```

```
        }

        return this;
    }

    /* Uses each element and a value in a binary operation
     * and assigns the result back to that element. */
    Matrix opOpAssign(string op)(int value) {
        writeln(__FUNCTION__);

        foreach (row; rows) {
            mixin ("row[] " ~ op ~ "= value;");
        }

        return this;
    }

    /* Returns the length of the specified dimension. */
    size_t opDollar(size_t dimension)() const
            if (dimension <= 1) {
        writeln(__FUNCTION__);

        static if (dimension == 0) {
            /* The length of dimension 0 is the length of the
             * 'rows' array. */
            return rows.length;

        } else {
            /* The length of dimension 1 is the lengths of the
             * elements of 'rows'. */
            return rows.length ? rows[0].length : 0;
        }
    }

    /* Returns an object that represents the range from
     * 'begin' to 'end'.
     *
     * Note: Although the 'dimension' template parameter is
     * not used here, that information can be useful for other
     * types. */
    Range opSlice(size_t dimension)(size_t begin, size_t end)
            if (dimension <= 1) {
        writeln(__FUNCTION__);

        return Range(begin, end);
    }

    /* Returns a sub-matrix that is defined by the
     * arguments. */
    Matrix opIndex(A...)(A arguments)
            if (A.length <= 2) {
        writeln(__FUNCTION__);

        /* We start with ranges that represent the entire
         * matrix so that the parameter-less use of opIndex
         * means "all of the elements". */
        Range[2] ranges = [ Range(0, opDollar!0),
                            Range(0, opDollar!1) ];

        foreach (dimension, a; arguments) {
            static if (is (typeof(a) == Range)) {
                /* This dimension is already specified as a
                 * range like 'matrix[begin..end]', which can
                 * be used as is. */
                ranges[dimension] = a;

            } else static if (is (typeof(a) : size_t)) {
                /* This dimension is specified as a single
                 * index value like 'matrix[i]', which we want
                 * to represent as a single-element range. */
                ranges[dimension] = Range(a, a + 1);

            } else {
```

```
                    /* We don't expect other types. */
                    static assert(
                        false, format("Invalid index type: %s",
                                      typeof(a).stringof));
            }
        }

        /* Return the sub-matrix that is specified by
         * 'arguments'. */
        return subMatrix(ranges[0], ranges[1]);
    }

    /* Assigns the specified value to each element of the
     * sub-matrix. */
    Matrix opIndexAssign(A...)(int value, A arguments)
            if (A.length <= 2) {
        writeln(__FUNCTION__);

        Matrix subMatrix = opIndex(arguments);
        return subMatrix = value;
    }

    /* Uses each element of the sub-matrix and a value in a
     * binary operation and assigns the result back to that
     * element. */
    Matrix opIndexOpAssign(string op, A...)(int value,
                                             A arguments)
            if (A.length <= 2) {
        writeln(__FUNCTION__);

        Matrix subMatrix = opIndex(arguments);
        mixin ("return subMatrix " ~ op ~ "= value;");
    }
}

/* Executes the expression that is specified as a string, and
 * prints the result as well as the new state of the
 * matrix. */
void execute(string expression)(Matrix m) {
    writefln("\n--- %s ---", expression);
    mixin ("auto result = " ~ expression ~ ";");
    writefln("result:\n%s", result);
    writefln("m:\n%s", m);
}

void main() {
    enum height = 10;
    enum width = 8;

    auto m = Matrix(height, width);

    int counter = 0;
    foreach (row; 0 .. height) {
        foreach (column; 0 .. width) {
            writefln("Initializing %s of %s",
                     counter + 1, height * width);

            m[row, column] = counter;
            ++counter;
        }
    }

    writeln(m);

    execute!("m[1, 1] = 42")(m);
    execute!("m[0, 1 .. $] = 43")(m);
    execute!("m[0 .. $, 3] = 44")(m);
    execute!("m[$-4 .. $-1, $-4 .. $-1] = 7")(m);

    execute!("m[1, 1] *= 2")(m);
    execute!("m[0, 1 .. $] *= 4")(m);
    execute!("m[0 .. $, 0] *= 10")(m);
    execute!("m[$-4 .. $-2, $-4 .. $-2] -= 666")(m);
```

```
        execute!("m[1, 1]")(m);
        execute!("m[2, 0 .. $]")(m);
        execute!("m[0 .. $, 2]")(m);
        execute!("m[0 .. $ / 2, 0 .. $ / 2]")(m);

        execute!("++m[1..3, 1..3]")(m);
        execute!("--m[2..5, 2..5]")(m);

        execute!("m[]")(m);
        execute!("m[] = 20")(m);
        execute!("m[] /= 4")(m);
        execute!("(m[] += 5) /= 10")(m);
}
```

78.11 Summary

The earlier template chapter had the following reminders:

- Templates define the code as a pattern, for the compiler to generate instances of it according to the actual uses in the program.
- Templates are a compile-time feature.
- Specifying template parameter lists is sufficient to make function, struct, and class definitions templates.
- Template arguments can be specified explicitly after an exclamation mark. The parentheses are not necessary when there is only one token inside the parentheses.
- Each template instantiation yields a different type.
- Template arguments can only be deduced for function templates.
- Templates can be specialized for the type that is after the : character.
- Default template arguments are specified after the = character.

This chapter added the following concepts:

- Templates can be defined by the full syntax or the shortcut syntax.
- The scope of the template is a name space.
- A template that contains a definition with the same name as the template is called an eponymous template. The template represents that definition.
- Templates can be of functions, classes, structs, unions, and interfaces, and every template body can contain any number of definitions.
- Template parameters can be of type, value, this, alias, and tuple kinds.
- typeof(this), typeof(super), and typeof(return) are useful in templates.
- Templates can be specialized for particular arguments.
- Meta programming is a way of executing operations at compile time.
- Templates enable *compile-time polymorphism*.
- Separate code generation for different instantiations can cause *code bloat*.
- Template constraints limit the uses of templates for specific template arguments. They help move compilation errors from the implementations of templates to where the templates are actually used incorrectly.
- It is more readable to give names to template constraints.
- The templated versions of opDollar, opSlice, opIndex, opIndexAssign, and opIndexOpAssign are for multi-dimensional indexing and slicing.

Functions have been covered in the following chapters so far in the book:

- Functions (page 136)
- Function Parameters (page 168)
- Function Overloading (page 265)
- Function Pointers, Delegates, and Lambdas (page 475)

This chapter will cover more features of functions.

79.1 Return type attributes

Functions can be marked as `auto`, `ref`, `inout`, and `auto ref`. These attributes are about return types of functions.

auto functions

The return types of `auto` functions need not be specified:

```d
auto add(int first, double second) {
    double result = first + second;
    return result;
}
```

The return type is deduced by the compiler from the `return` expression. Since the type of `result` is `double`, the return type of `add()` is `double`.

If there are more than one `return` statement, then the return type of the function is their *common type*. (We have seen common type in the Ternary Operator ?: chapter (page 96).) For example, because the common type of `int` and `double` is `double`, the return type of the following `auto` function is `double` as well:

```d
auto func(int i) {
    if (i < 0) {
        return i;       // returns 'int' here
    }

    return i * 1.5;     // returns 'double' here
}

void main() {
    // The return type of the function is 'double'
    auto result = func(42);
    static assert(is (typeof(result) == double));
}
```

ref functions

Normally, the expression that is returned from a function is copied to the caller's context. `ref` specifies that the expression should be returned by-reference instead.

For example, the following function returns the greater of its two parameters:

```d
int greater(int first, int second) {
    return (first > second) ? first : second;
}
```

Normally, both the parameters and the return value of that function are copied:

```d
import std.stdio;
```

```
void main() {
    int a = 1;
    int b = 2;
    int result = greater(a, b);
    result += 10;              // ← neither a nor b changes
    writefln("a: %s, b: %s, result: %s", a, b, result);
}
```

Because the return value of greater() is copied to result, adding to result affects only that variable; neither a nor b changes:

```
a: 1, b: 2, result: 12
```

ref parameters are passed by references instead of being copied. The same keyword has the same effect on return values:

```
ref int greater(ref int first, ref int second) {
    return (first > second) ? first : second;
}
```

This time, the returned reference would be an alias to one of the arguments and mutating the returned reference would modify either a or b:

```
    int a = 1;
    int b = 2;
    greater(a, b) += 10;       // ← either a or b changes
    writefln("a: %s, b: %s", a, b);
```

Note that the returned reference is incremented directly. As a result, the greater of the two arguments changes:

```
a: 1, b: 12
```

Local reference requires a pointer: An important point is that although the return type is marked as ref, a and b would still not change if the return value were assigned to a local variable:

```
    int result = greater(a, b);
    result += 10;                   // ← only result changes
```

Although greater() returns a reference to a or b, that reference gets copied to the local variable result, and again neither a nor b changes:

```
a: 1, b: 2, result: 12
```

For result be a reference to a or b, it has to be defined as a pointer:

```
    int * result = &greater(a, b);
    *result += 10;
    writefln("a: %s, b: %s, result: %s", a, b, *result);
```

This time result would be a reference to either a or b and the mutation through it would affect the actual variable:

```
a: 1, b: 12, result: 12
```

It is not possible to return a reference to a local variable: The ref return value is an alias to one of the arguments that start their lives even before the function is called. That means, regardless of whether a reference to a or b is returned, the returned reference refers to a variable that is still alive.

Conversely, it is not possible to return a reference to a variable that is not going to be alive upon leaving the function:

```
ref string parenthesized(string phrase) {
    string result = '(' ~ phrase ~ ')';
    return result;      // ← compilation ERROR
} // ← the lifetime of result ends here
```

The lifetime of local `result` ends upon leaving the function. For that reason, it is not possible to return a reference to that variable:

```
Error: escaping reference to local variable result
```

auto ref functions

`auto ref` helps with functions like `parenthesized()` above. Similar to `auto`, the return type of an `auto ref` function is deduced by the compiler. Additionally, if the returned expression can be a reference, that variable is returned by reference as opposed to being copied.

`parenthesized()` can be compiled if the return type is `auto ref`:

```
auto ref string parenthesized(string phrase) {
    string result = '(' ~ phrase ~ ')';
    return result;                  // ← compiles
}
```

The very first `return` statement of the function determines whether the function returns a copy or a reference.

`auto ref` is more useful in function templates where template parameters may be references or copies depending on context.

inout functions

The `inout` keyword appears for parameter and return types of functions. It works like a template for `const`, `immutable`, and *mutable*.

Let's rewrite the previous function as taking `string` (i.e. `immutable(char)[]`) and returning `string`:

```
string parenthesized(string phrase) {
    return '(' ~ phrase ~ ')';
}

// ...

    writeln(parenthesized("hello"));
```

As expected, the code works with that `string` argument:

```
(hello)
```

However, as it works only with `immutable` strings, the function can be seen as being less useful than it could have been:

```
    char[] m;     // has mutable elements
    m ~= "hello";
    writeln(parenthesized(m));    // ← compilation ERROR
```

```
Error: function deneme.parenthesized (string phrase)
is not callable using argument types (char[])
```

The same limitation applies to `const(char)[]` strings as well.

One solution for this usability issue is to overload the function for `const` and *mutable* strings:

```
char[] parenthesized(char[] phrase) {
    return '(' ~ phrase ~ ')';
```

```
}

const(char)[] parenthesized(const(char)[] phrase) {
    return '(' ~ phrase ~ ')';
}
```

That design would be less than ideal due to the obvious code duplications. Another solution would be to define the function as a template:

```
T parenthesized(T)(T phrase) {
    return '(' ~ phrase ~ ')';
}
```

Although that would work, this time it may be seen as being too flexible and potentially requiring template constraints.

inout is very similar to the template solution. The difference is that not the entire type but just the mutability attribute is deduced from the parameter:

```
inout(char)[] parenthesized(inout(char)[] phrase) {
    return '(' ~ phrase ~ ')';
}
```

inout transfers the deduced mutability attribute to the return type.

When the function is called with char[], it gets compiled as if inout is not specified at all. On the other hand, when called with immutable(char)[] or const(char)[], inout means immutable or const, respectively.

The following code demonstrates this by printing the type of the returned expression:

```
    char[] m;
    writeln(typeof(parenthesized(m)).stringof);

    const(char)[] c;
    writeln(typeof(parenthesized(c)).stringof);

    immutable(char)[] i;
    writeln(typeof(parenthesized(i)).stringof);
```

The output:

```
char[]
const(char)[]
string
```

79.2 Behavioral attributes

pure, nothrow, and @nogc are about function behaviors.

pure functions

As we have seen in the Functions chapter (page 136), functions can produce return values and side effects. When possible, return values should be preferred over side effects because functions that do not have side effects are easier to make sense of, which in turn helps with program correctness and maintainability.

A similar concept is the purity of a function. Purity is defined differently in D from most other programming languages: In D, a function that does not access *mutable* global or static state is pure. (Since input and output streams are considered as mutable global state, pure functions cannot perform input or output operations either.)

In other words, a function is pure if it produces its return value and side effects only by accessing its parameters, local variables, and *immutable* global state.

An important aspect of purity in D is that pure functions can mutate their parameters.

Additionally, the following operations that mutate the global state of the program are explicitly allowed in pure functions:

- Allocate memory with the new expression
- Terminate the program
- Access the floating point processing flags
- Throw exceptions

The pure keyword specifies that a function should behave according to those conditions and the compiler guarantees that it does so.

Naturally, since impure functions do not provide the same guarantees, a pure function cannot call impure functions.

The following program demonstrates some of the operations that a pure function can and cannot perform:

```d
import std.stdio;
import std.exception;

int mutableGlobal;
const int constGlobal;
immutable int immutableGlobal;

void impureFunction() {
}

int pureFunction(ref int i, int[] slice) pure {
    // Can throw exceptions:
    enforce(slice.length >= 1);

    // Can mutate its parameters:
    i = 42;
    slice[0] = 43;

    // Can access immutable global state:
    i = constGlobal;
    i = immutableGlobal;

    // Can use the new expression:
    auto p = new int;

    // Cannot access mutable global state:
    i = mutableGlobal;      // ← compilation ERROR

    // Cannot perform input and output operations:
    writeln(i);             // ← compilation ERROR

    static int mutableStatic;

    // Cannot access mutable static state:
    i = mutableStatic;      // ← compilation ERROR

    // Cannot call impure functions:
    impureFunction();       // ← compilation ERROR

    return 0;
}

void main() {
    int i;
    int[] slice = [ 1 ];
    pureFunction(i, slice);
}
```

Although they are allowed to, some pure functions do not mutate their parameters. Following from the rules of purity, the only observable effect of such a function would be its return value. Further, since the function cannot access any mutable global state, the return value would be the same for a given set of arguments, regardless of when and how many times the function is called during the execution of the program. This fact gives both the compiler and the programmer optimization opportunities. For example, instead of calling the function a second time for a given set of arguments, its return value from the first call can be cached and used instead of actually calling the function again.

Since the exact code that gets generated for a template instantiation depends on the actual template arguments, whether the generated code is pure depends on the arguments as well. For that reason, the purity of a template is inferred by the compiler from the generated code. (The pure keyword can still be specified by the programmer.) Similarly, the purity of an auto function is inferred.

As a simple example, since the following function template would be impure when N is zero, it would not be possible to call templ!0() from a pure function:

```d
import std.stdio;

// This template is impure when N is zero
void templ(size_t N)() {
    static if (N == 0) {
        // Prints when N is zero:
        writeln("zero");
    }
}

void foo() pure {
    templ!0();    // ← compilation ERROR
}

void main() {
    foo();
}
```

The compiler infers that the 0 instantiation of the template is impure and rejects calling it from the pure function foo():

```
Error: pure function 'deneme.foo' cannot call impure function
'deneme.templ!0.templ'
```

However, since the instantiation of the template for values other than zero is pure, the program can be compiled for such values:

```d
void foo() pure {
    templ!1();    // ← compiles
}
```

We have seen earlier above that input and output functions like writeln() cannot be used in pure functions because they access global state. Sometimes such limitations are too restrictive e.g. when needing to print a message temporarily during debugging. For that reason, the purity rules are relaxed for code that is marked as debug:

```d
import std.stdio;

debug size_t fooCounter;

void foo(int i) pure {
    debug ++fooCounter;

    if (i == 0) {
```

```
        debug writeln("i is zero");
        i = 42;
    }

    // ...
}

void main() {
    foreach (i; 0..100) {
        if ((i % 10) == 0) {
            foo(i);
        }
    }

    debug writefln("foo is called %s times", fooCounter);
}
```

The pure function above mutates the global state of the program by modifying a global variable and printing a message. Despite those impure operations, it still can be compiled because those operations are marked as debug.

Note: *Remember that those statements are included in the program only if the program is compiled with the -debug command line switch.*

Member functions can be marked as pure as well. Subclasses can override impure functions as pure but the reverse is not allowed:

```
interface Iface {
    void foo() pure;      // Subclasses must define foo as pure.

    void bar();           // Subclasses may define bar as pure.
}

class Class : Iface {
    void foo() pure {     // Required to be pure
        // ...
    }

    void bar() pure {     // pure although not required
        // ...
    }
}
```

Delegates and anonymous functions can be pure as well. Similar to templates, whether a function or delegate literal, or auto function is pure is inferred by the compiler:

```
import std.stdio;

void foo(int delegate(double) pure dg) {
    int i = dg(1.5);
}

void main() {
    foo(a => 42);                 // ← compiles

    foo((a) {                     // ← compilation ERROR
            writeln("hello");
            return 42;
        });
}
```

foo() above requires that its parameter be a pure delegate. The compiler infers that the lambda a => 42 is pure and allows it as an argument for foo(). However, since the other delegate is impure it cannot be passed to foo():

```
Error: function deneme.foo (int delegate(double) pure dg)
is not callable using argument types (void)
```

One benefit of `pure` functions is that their return values can be used to initialize `immutable` variables. Although the array produced by `makeNumbers()` below is mutable, it is not possible for its elements to be changed by any code outside of that function. For that reason, the initialization works.

```
int[] makeNumbers() pure {
    int[] result;
    result ~= 42;
    return result;
}

void main() {
    immutable array = makeNumbers();
}
```

nothrow functions

We saw the exception mechanism in the Exceptions chapter. (page 192)

It would be good practice for functions to document the types of exceptions that they may throw under specific error conditions. However, as a general rule, callers should assume that any function can throw any exception.

Sometimes it is more important to know that a function does not emit any exception at all. For example, some algorithms can take advantage of the fact that certain of their steps cannot be interrupted by an exception.

`nothrow` guarantees that a function does not emit any exception:

```
int add(int lhs, int rhs) nothrow {
    // ...
}
```

Note: *Remember that it is not recommended to catch Error nor its base class Throwable. What is meant here by "any exception" is "any exception that is defined under the Exception hierarchy." A nothrow function can still emit exceptions that are under the Error hierarchy, which represents irrecoverable error conditions that should preclude the program from continuing its execution.*

Such a function can neither throw an exception itself nor can call a function that may throw an exception:

```
int add(int lhs, int rhs) nothrow {
    writeln("adding");    // ← compilation ERROR
    return lhs + rhs;
}
```

The compiler rejects the code because `add()` violates the no-throw guarantee:

```
Error: function 'deneme.add' is nothrow yet may throw
```

This is because `writeln` is not (and cannot be) a `nothrow` function.

The compiler can infer that a function can never emit an exception. The following implementation of `add()` is `nothrow` because it is obvious to the compiler that the `try-catch` block prevents any exception from escaping the function:

```
int add(int lhs, int rhs) nothrow {
    int result;

    try {
        writeln("adding");    // ← compiles
        result = lhs + rhs;

    } catch (Exception error) {    // catches all exceptions
```

```
    // ...
    }

    return result;
}
```

As mentioned above, nothrow does not include exceptions that are under the Error hierarchy. For example, although accessing an element of an array with [] can throw RangeError, the following function can still be defined as nothrow:

```
int foo(int[] arr, size_t i) nothrow {
    return 10 * arr[i];
}
```

As with purity, the compiler automatically deduces whether a template, delegate, or anonymous function is nothrow.

@nogc functions

D is a garbage collected language. Many data structures and algorithms in most D programs take advantage of dynamic memory blocks that are managed by the garbage collector (GC). Such memory blocks are reclaimed again by the GC by an algorithm called *garbage collection*.

Some commonly used D operations take advantage of the GC as well. For example, elements of arrays live on dynamic memory blocks:

```
// A function that takes advantage of the GC indirectly
int[] append(int[] slice) {
    slice ~= 42;
    return slice;
}
```

If the slice does not have sufficient capacity, the ~= operator above allocates a new memory block from the GC.

Although the GC is a significant convenience for data structures and algorithms, memory allocation and garbage collection are costly operations that make the execution of some programs noticeably slow.

@nogc means that a function cannot use the GC directly or indirectly:

```
void foo() @nogc {
    // ...
}
```

The compiler guarantees that a @nogc function does not involve GC operations. For example, the following function cannot call append() above, which does not provide the @nogc guarantee:

```
void foo() @nogc {
    int[] slice;
    // ...
    append(slice);    // ← compilation ERROR
}
```

```
Error: @nogc function 'deneme.foo' cannot call non-@nogc function
'deneme.append'
```

79.3 Code safety attributes

@safe, @trusted, and @system are about the code safety that a function provides. As with purity, the compiler infers the safety level of templates, delegates, anonymous functions, and auto functions.

@safe functions

A class of programming errors involve *corrupting* data at unrelated locations in memory by writing at those locations unintentionally. Such errors are mostly due to mistakes made in using pointers and applying type casts.

@safe functions guarantee that they do not contain any operation that may corrupt memory. The compiler does not allow the following operations in @safe functions:

- Pointers cannot be converted to other pointer types other than void*.
- A non-pointer expression cannot be converted to a pointer value.
- Pointer values cannot be changed (no pointer *arithmetic*; however, assigning a pointer to another pointer of the same type is safe).
- Unions that have pointer or reference members cannot be used.
- Functions marked as @system cannot be called.
- Exceptions that are not descended from Exception cannot be caught.
- *Inline assembler* cannot be used.
- *Mutable* variables cannot be cast to immutable.
- immutable variables cannot be cast to *mutable*.
- Thread-local variables cannot be cast to shared.
- shared variables cannot be cast to thread-local.
- Addresses of function-local variables cannot be taken.
- __gshared variables cannot be accessed.

@trusted functions

Some functions may actually be safe but cannot be marked as @safe for various reasons. For example, a function may have to call a library written in C, where no language support exists for safety in that language.

Some other functions may actually perform operations that are not allowed in @safe code, but may be well tested and *trusted* to be correct.

@trusted is an attribute that communicates to the compiler that *although the function cannot be marked as @safe, consider it safe*. The compiler trusts the programmer and treats @trusted code as if it is safe. For example, it allows @safe code to call @trusted code.

@system functions

Any function that is not marked as @safe or @trusted is considered @system, which is the default safety attribute.

79.4 Compile time function execution (CTFE)

In many programming languages, computations that are performed at compile time are very limited. Such computations are usually as simple as calculating the length of a fixed-length array or simple arithmetic operations:

```
writeln(1 + 2);
```

The 1 + 2 expression above is compiled as if it has been written as 3; there is no computation at runtime.

D has CTFE, which allows any function to be executed at compile time as long as it is possible to do so.

Let's consider the following program that prints a menu to the output:

```
import std.stdio;
import std.string;
import std.range;

string menuLines(string[] choices) {
    string result;

    foreach (i, choice; choices) {
        result ~= format(" %s. %s\n", i + 1, choice);
    }

    return result;
}

string menu(string title,
            string[] choices,
            size_t width) {
    return format("%s\n%s\n%s",
                  title.center(width),
                  '='.repeat(width),     // horizontal line
                  menuLines(choices));
}

void main() {
    enum drinks =
        menu("Drinks",
             [ "Coffee", "Tea", "Hot chocolate" ], 20);

    writeln(drinks);
}
```

Although the same result can be achieved in different ways, the program above performs non-trivial operations to produce the following `string`:

```
        Drinks
====================
 1. Coffee
 2. Tea
 3. Hot chocolate
```

Remember that the initial value of enum constants like `drinks` must be known at compile time. That fact is sufficient for `menu()` to be executed at compile time. The value that it returns at compile time is used as the initial value of `drinks`. As a result, the program is compiled as if that value is written explicitly in the program:

```
    // The equivalent of the code above:
    enum drinks = "        Drinks      \n"
                  "====================\n"
                  " 1. Coffee\n"
                  " 2. Tea\n"
                  " 3. Hot chocolate\n";
```

For a function to be executed at compile time, it must appear in an expression that in fact is needed at compile time:

- Initializing a `static` variable
- Initializing an enum variable
- Calculating the length of a fixed-length array
- Calculating a template *value* argument

Clearly, it would not be possible to execute every function at compile time. For example, a function that accesses a global variable cannot be executed at compile time because the global variable does not start its life until run time. Similarly, since stdout is available only at run time, functions that print cannot be executed at compile time.

The __ctfe variable

It is a powerful aspect of CTFE that the same function is used for both compile time and run time depending on when its result is needed. Although the function need not be written in any special way for CTFE, some operations in the function may make sense only at compile time or run time. The special variable __ctfe can be used to differentiate the code that are only for compile time or only for run time. The value of this variable is true when the function is being executed for CTFE, false otherwise:

```d
import std.stdio;

size_t counter;

int foo() {
    if (!__ctfe) {
        // This code is for execution at run time
        ++counter;
    }

    return 42;
}

void main() {
    enum i = foo();
    auto j = foo();
    writefln("foo is called %s times.", counter);
}
```

As counter lives only at run time, it cannot be incremented at compile time. For that reason, the code above attempts to increment it only for run-time execution. Since the value of i is determined at compile time and the value of j is determined at run time, foo() is reported to have been called just once during the execution of the program:

```
foo is called 1 times.
```

79.5 Summary

- The return type of an auto function is deduced automatically.
- The return value of a ref function is a reference to an existing variable.
- The return value of an auto ref function is a reference if possible, a copy otherwise.
- inout carries the const, immutable, or *mutable* attribute of the parameter to the return type.
- A pure function cannot access *mutable* global or static state. The compiler infers the purity of templates, delegates, anonymous functions, and auto functions.
- nothrow functions cannot emit exceptions. The compiler infers whether a template, delegate, anonymous function, or auto function is no-throw.
- @nogc functions cannot involve GC operations.
- @safe functions cannot corrupt memory. The compiler infers the safety attributes of templates, delegates, anonymous functions, and auto functions.
- @trusted functions are indeed safe but cannot be specified as such; they are considered @safe both by the programmer and the compiler.

- `@system` functions can use every D feature. `@system` is the default safety attribute.
- Functions can be executed at compile time as well (CTFE). This can be differentiated by the value of the special variable `__ctfe`.

80 Mixins

Mixins are for *mixing in* generated code into the source code. The mixed-in code may be generated as a template instance or a `string`.

Code can be inserted into the program as a *string import* as well.

80.1 Template mixins

We have seen in the Templates (page 399) and More Templates (page 520) chapters that templates define code as a pattern, for the compiler to generate actual instances from that pattern. Templates can generate functions, structs, unions, classes, interfaces, and any other legal D code.

Template mixins insert instantiations of templates into the code by the `mixin` keyword:

```
mixin a_template!(template_parameters)
```

As we will see in the example below, the `mixin` keyword is used in the definitions of template mixins as well.

The instantiation of the template for the specific set of template parameters is inserted into the source code right where the `mixin` keyword appears.

For example, let's have a template that defines both an array of edges and a pair of functions that operate on those edges:

```
mixin template EdgeArrayFeature(T, size_t count) {
    T[count] edges;

    void setEdge(size_t index, T edge) {
        edges[index] = edge;
    }

    void printEdges() {
        writeln("The edges:");

        foreach (i, edge; edges) {
            writef("%s:%s ", i, edge);
        }

        writeln();
    }
}
```

That template leaves the type and number of array elements flexible. The instantiation of that template for `int` and 2 would be mixed in by the following syntax:

```
mixin EdgeArrayFeature!(int, 2);
```

For example, the `mixin` above can insert the two-element `int` array and the two functions that are generated by the template right inside a `struct` definition:

```
struct Line {
    mixin EdgeArrayFeature!(int, 2);
}
```

As a result, `Line` ends up defining a member array and two member functions:

```
import std.stdio;

void main() {
    auto line = Line();
    line.setEdge(0, 100);
```

```
        line.setEdge(1, 200);
        line.printEdges();
}
```

The output:

```
The edges:
0:100 1:200
```

Another instantiation of the same template can be used e.g. inside a function:

```
struct Point {
    int x;
    int y;
}

void main() {
    mixin EdgeArrayFeature!(Point, 5);

    setEdge(3, Point(3, 3));
    printEdges();
}
```

That `mixin` inserts an array and two local functions inside `main()`. The output:

```
The edges:
0:Point(0, 0) 1:Point(0, 0) 2:Point(0, 0) 3:Point(3, 3) 4:Point(0, 0)
```

Template mixins must use local imports

Mixing in template instantiations *as is* can cause problems about the modules that the template itself is making use of: Those modules may not be available at the `mixin` site.

Let's consider the following module named a. Naturally, it would have to import the `std.string` module that it is making use of:

```
module a;

import std.string;    // ← wrong place

mixin template A(T) {
    string a() {
        T[] array;
        // ...
        return format("%(%s, %)", array);
    }
}
```

However, if `std.string` is not imported at the actual `mixin` site, then the compiler would not be able to find the definition of `format()` at that point. Let's consider the following program that imports a and tries to mix in `A!int` from that module:

```
import a;

void main() {
    mixin A!int;    // ← compilation ERROR
}
```

```
Error: undefined identifier format
Error: mixin deneme.main.A!int error instantiating
```

For that reason, the modules that template mixins use must be imported in local scopes:

```
module a;

mixin template A(T) {
    string a() {
        import std.string;    // ← right place

        T[] array;
        // ...
        return format("%(%s, %)", array);
    }
}
```

As long as it is inside the template definition, the import directive above can be outside of the a() function as well.

Identifying the type that is mixing in

Sometimes a mixin may need to identify the actual type that is mixing it in. That information is available through *this template parameters* as we have seen in the More Templates chapter (page 520):

```
mixin template MyMixin(T) {
    void foo(this MixingType)() {
        import std.stdio;
        writefln("The actual type that is mixing in: %s",
                 MixingType.stringof);
    }
}

struct MyStruct {
    mixin MyMixin!(int);
}

void main() {
    auto a = MyStruct();
    a.foo();
}
```

The output of the program shows that the actual type is available inside the template as MyStruct:

```
The actual type that is mixing in: MyStruct
```

80.2 String mixins

Another powerful feature of D is being able to insert code as string as long as that string is known at compile time. The syntax of string mixins requires the use of parentheses:

```
    mixin (compile_time_generated_string)
```

For example, the *hello world* program can be written with a mixin as well:

```
import std.stdio;

void main() {
    mixin (`writeln("Hello, World!");`);
}
```

The string gets inserted as code and the program produces the following output:

```
Hello, World!
```

We can go further and insert all of the program as a string mixin:

```
mixin (
`import std.stdio; void main() { writeln("Hello, World!"); }`
);
```

Obviously, there is no need for mixins in these examples, as the strings could have been written as code as well.

The power of string mixins comes from the fact that the code can be generated at compile time. The following example takes advantage of CTFE to generate statements at compile time:

```
import std.stdio;

string printStatement(string message) {
    return `writeln("` ~ message ~ `");`;
}

void main() {
    mixin (printStatement("Hello, World!"));
    mixin (printStatement("Hi, World!"));
}
```

The output:

```
Hello, World!
Hi, World!
```

Note that the "writeln" expressions are not executed inside printStatement(). Rather, printStatement() generates code that includes writeln() expressions that are executed inside main(). The generated code is the equivalent of the following:

```
import std.stdio;

void main() {
    writeln("Hello, World!");
    writeln("Hi, World!");
}
```

Multiple mixin arguments
As long as they are all known at compile time, mixin can take multiple arguments and automatically concatenates their string representations:

```
mixin ("const a = ", int.sizeof, ";");
```

This can be more convenient compared to using e.g. a format expression:

```
mixin (format!"const a = %s;"(int.sizeof));  // Same as above
```

Debugging string mixins
Because generated code is not readily visible as a whole in source code, it can be difficult to identify causes of compilation errors with mixin expressions. To help with debugging string mixins, there is the dmd compiler switch -mixin, which writes all mixed-in code to a specified file.

Let's consider the following program that has a syntax error in code that is being mixed in. It is not obvious from the compiler error that the syntax error is the missing semicolon at the end of the definition of the struct member:

```
string makeStruct(string name, string member) {
  import std.format;
  return format!"struct %s {\n  int %s\n}"(name, member);
}
```

```
mixin (makeStruct("S", "m"));     // ←  compilation ERROR

void main() {
}
```

When compiled with the -mixin switch, the compilation error would point at a line inside the specified file (mixed_in_code in the example below):

```
$ dmd -mixin=mixed_in_code deneme.d
mixed_in_code(154): Error: semicolon expected, not }
```

Along with all other code that are mixed-in by the standard library, there would be the following code at the specified line inside file mixed_in_code:

```
[...]
// expansion at deneme.d(6)
struct S {
  int m
}          ← Line 154
```

Another option for debugging string mixins is pragma(msg) (page 414), which would print the generated code during compilation. This option is less practical because it requires replacing the mixin keyword with pragma(msg) temporarily for debugging:

```
pragma(msg, makeStruct("S", "m"));
```

80.3 Mixin name spaces

It is possible to avoid and resolve name ambiguities in template mixins.

For example, there are two i variables defined inside main() in the following program: one is defined explicitly in main and the other is mixed in. When a mixed-in name is the same as a name that is in the surrounding scope, then the name that is in the surrounding scope gets used:

```
import std.stdio;

template Templ() {
    int i;

    void print() {
        writeln(i);  // Always the 'i' that is defined in Templ
    }
}

void main() {
    int i;
    mixin Templ;

    i = 42;        // Sets the 'i' that is defined explicitly in main
    writeln(i);    // Prints the 'i' that is defined explicitly in main
    print();       // Prints the 'i' that is mixed in
}
```

As implied in the comments above, template mixins define a name space for their contents and the names that appear in the template code are first looked up in that name space. We can see this in the behavior of print():

```
42
0       ← printed by print()
```

The compiler cannot resolve name conflicts if the same name is defined by more than one template mixin. Let's see this in a short program that mixes in the same template instance twice:

```
template Templ() {
    int i;
}

void main() {
    mixin Templ;
    mixin Templ;

    i = 42;          // ← compilation ERROR
}
```

```
Error: deneme.main.Templ!().i at ... conflicts with
deneme.main.Templ!().i at ...
```

To prevent this, it is possible to assign name space identifiers for template mixins and refer to contained names by those identifiers:

```
    mixin Templ A;      // Defines A.i
    mixin Templ B;      // Defines B.i

    A.i = 42;           // ← not ambiguous anymore
```

String mixins do not have these name space features. However, it is trivial to use a string as a template mixin simply by passing it through a simple wrapper template.

Let's first see a similar name conflict with string mixins:

```
void main() {
    mixin ("int i;");
    mixin ("int i;");    // ← compilation ERROR

    i = 42;
}
```

```
Error: declaration deneme.main.i is already defined
```

One way of resolving this issue is to pass the string through the following trivial template that effectively converts a string mixin to a template mixin:

```
template Templatize(string str) {
    mixin (str);
}

void main() {
    mixin Templatize!("int i;") A;      // Defines A.i
    mixin Templatize!("int i;") B;      // Defines B.i

    A.i = 42;                           // ← not ambiguous anymore
}
```

80.4 String mixins in operator overloading

We have seen in the Operator Overloading chapter (page 298) how `mixin` expressions helped with the definitions of some of the operators.

In fact, the reason why most operator member functions are defined as templates is to make the operators available as `string` values so that they can be used for code generation. We have seen examples of this both in that chapter and its exercise solutions.

80.5 Mixed in destructors

It is possible to mix in multiple destructors to a user defined type. Those destructors are called in the reverse order of the `mixin` statements that added them. This feature allows mixing in different resources to a type, each introducing its own cleanup code.

```
import std.stdio;

mixin template Foo() {
    ~this() {
        writeln("Destructor mixed-in by Foo");
    }
}

mixin template Bar() {
    ~this() {
        writeln("Destructor mixed-in by Bar");
    }
}

struct S {
    ~this() {
        writeln("Actual destructor");
    }
    mixin Foo;
    mixin Bar;
}

void main() {
    auto s = S();
}
```

```
Destructor mixed-in by Bar
Destructor mixed-in by Foo
Actual destructor
```

Due to a bug as of this writing, the same behavior does not apply to other special functions like constructors. Additionally, a destructor mixed in by a string mixin does conflict with the existing destructor of the type.

80.6 Importing text files

It is possible to insert contents of text files into code at compile time. The contents are treated as string literals and can be used anywhere strings can be used. For example, they can be mixed in as code.

For example, let's assume there are two text files on the file system named file_one and file_two having the following contents.

- file_one:

```
Hello
```

- file_two:

```
s ~= ", World!";
import std.stdio;
writeln(s);
```

The two import directives in the following program would correspond to the contents of those files converted to string literals at compile time:

```
void main() {
    string s = import ("file_one");
    mixin (import ("file_two"));
}
```

Text file imports (a.k.a. string imports) require the -J compiler switch which tells the compiler where to find the text files. For example, if the two files are in the *current directory* (specified with . in Linux environments), the program can be compiled with the following command:

```
$ dmd -J. deneme.d
```

The output:

```
Hello, World!
```

Considering the file contents as string literals, the program is the equivalent of the following one:

```
void main() {
    string s = `Hello`;           // ← Content of file_one as string
    mixin (`s ~= ", World!";
import std.stdio;
writeln(s);`);                    // ← Content of file_two as string
}
```

Further, considering the mixed-in string as well, the program is the equivalent of the following one:

```
void main() {
    string s = `Hello`;
    s ~= ", World!";
    import std.stdio;
    writeln(s);
}
```

80.7 Example

(**Note:** *Specifying predicates as strings was used more commonly before the lambda syntax was added to D. Although string predicates as in this example are still used in Phobos, the => lambda syntax may be more suitable in most cases.*)

Let's consider the following function template that takes an array of numbers and returns another array that consists of the elements that satisfy a specific condition:

```
int[] filter(string predicate)(int[] numbers) {
    int[] result;

    foreach (number; numbers) {
        if (mixin (predicate)) {
            result ~= number;
        }
    }

    return result;
}
```

That function template takes the filtering condition as its template parameter and inserts that condition directly into an if statement as is.

For that condition to choose numbers that are e.g. less than 7, the if condition should look like the following code:

```
        if (number < 7) {
```

The users of filter() template can provide the condition as a string:

```
    int[] numbers = [ 1, 8, 6, -2, 10 ];
    int[] chosen = filter!"number < 7"(numbers);
```

Importantly, the name used in the template parameter must match the name of the variable used in the implementation of `filter()`. So, the template must document what that name should be and the users must use that name.

Phobos uses names consisting of single letters like a, b, n, etc.

81 Ranges

Ranges are an abstraction of element access. This abstraction enables the use of great number of algorithms over great number of container types. Ranges emphasize how container elements are accessed, as opposed to how the containers are implemented.

Ranges are a very simple concept that is based on whether a type defines certain sets of member functions. We have already seen this concept in the `foreach` with Structs and Classes chapter (page 491): any type that provides the member functions `empty`, `front`, and `popFront()` can be used with the `foreach` loop. The set of those three member functions is the requirement of the range type `InputRange`.

I will start introducing ranges with `InputRange`, the simplest of all the range types. The other ranges require more member functions over `InputRange`.

Before going further, I would like to provide the definitions of containers and algorithms.

Container (data structure): Container is a very useful concept that appears in almost every program. Variables are put together for a purpose and are used together as elements of a container. D's containers are its core features arrays and associative arrays, and special container types that are defined in the `std.container` module. Every container is implemented as a specific data structure. For example, associative arrays are a *hash table* implementation.

Every data structure stores its elements and provides access to them in ways that are special to that data structure. For example, in the array data structure the elements are stored side by side and accessed by an element index; in the linked list data structure the elements are stored in nodes and are accessed by going through those nodes one by one; in a sorted binary tree data structure, the nodes provide access to the preceding and successive elements through separate branches; etc.

In this chapter, I will use the terms *container* and *data structure* interchangeably.

Algorithm (function): Processing of data structures for specific purposes in specific ways is called an *algorithm*. For example, *linear search* is an algorithm that searches by iterating over a container from the beginning to the end; *binary search* is an algorithm that searches for an element by eliminating half of the candidates at every step; etc.

In this chapter, I will use the terms *algorithm* and *function* interchangeably.

For most of the samples below, I will use `int` as the element type and `int[]` as the container type. In reality, ranges are more powerful when used with templated containers and algorithms. In fact, most of the containers and algorithms that ranges tie together are all templates. I will leave examples of templated ranges to the next chapter (page 596).

81.1 History

A very successful library that abstracts algorithms and data structures from each other is the Standard Template Library (STL), which also appears as a part of the C++ standard library. STL provides this abstraction with the *iterator* concept, which is implemented by C++'s templates.

Although they are a very useful abstraction, iterators do have some weaknesses. D's ranges were designed to overcome these weaknesses.

Andrei Alexandrescu introduces ranges in his paper On Iteration[1] and demonstrates how they can be superior to iterators.

81.2 Ranges are an integral part of D

D's slices happen to be implementations of the most powerful range RandomAccessRange, and there are many range features in Phobos. It is essential to understand how ranges are used in Phobos.

Many Phobos algorithms return temporary range objects. For example, filter(), which chooses elements that are greater than 10 in the following code, actually returns a range object, not an array:

```d
import std.stdio;
import std.algorithm;

void main() {
    int[] values = [ 1, 20, 7, 11 ];
    writeln(values.filter!(value => value > 10));
}
```

writeln uses that range object lazily and accesses the elements as it needs them:

```
[20, 11]
```

That output may suggest that filter() returns an int[] but this is not the case. We can see this from the fact that the following assignment produces a compilation error:

```d
    int[] chosen = values.filter!(value => value > 10); // ← compilation ERROR
```

The error message contains the type of the range object:

```
Error: cannot implicitly convert expression (filter(values))
of type FilterResult!(__lambda2, int[]) to int[]
```

Note: *The type may be different in the version of Phobos that you are using.*

It is possible to convert that temporary object to an actual array, as we will see later in the chapter.

81.3 Traditional implementations of algorithms

In traditional implementations of algorithms, the algorithms know how the data structures that they operate on are implemented. For example, the following function that prints the elements of a linked list must know that the nodes of the linked list have members named element and next:

```d
struct Node {
    int element;
    Node * next;
}

void print(const(Node) * list) {
    for ( ; list; list = list.next) {
        write(' ', list.element);
    }
}
```

Similarly, a function that prints the elements of an array must know that arrays have a length property and their elements are accessed by the [] operator:

---

1. http://www.informit.com/articles/printerfriendly.aspx?p=1407357

```
void print(const int[] array) {
    for (int i = 0; i != array.length; ++i) {
        write(' ', array[i]);
    }
}
```

Note: *We know that* `foreach` *is more useful when iterating over arrays. As a demonstration of how traditional algorithms are tied to data structures, let's assume that the use of* `for` *is justified.*

Having algorithms tied to data structures makes it necessary to write them specially for each type. For example, the functions find(), sort(), swap(), etc. must be written separately for array, linked list, associative array, binary tree, heap, etc. As a result, N algorithms that support M data structures must be written NxM times. (Note: In reality, the count is less than NxM because not every algorithm can be applied to every data structure; for example, associative arrays cannot be sorted.)

Conversely, because ranges abstract algorithms away from data structures, implementing just N algorithms and M data structures would be sufficient. A newly implemented data structure can work with all of the existing algorithms that support the type of range that the new data structure provides, and a newly implemented algorithm can work with all of the existing data structures that support the range type that the new algorithm requires.

81.4 Phobos ranges

The ranges in this chapter are different from number ranges that are written in the form `begin..end`. We have seen how number ranges are used with the `foreach` loop and with slices:

```
foreach (value; 3..7) {        // number range,
                               // NOT a Phobos range

int[] slice = array[5..10];    // number range,
                               // NOT a Phobos range
```

When I write *range* in this chapter, I mean a Phobos range .

Ranges form a *range hierarchy*. At the bottom of this hierarchy is the simplest range `InputRange`. The other ranges bring more requirements on top of the range on which they are based. The following are all of the ranges with their requirements, sorted from the simplest to the more capable:

- `InputRange`: requires the `empty`, `front` and `popFront()` member functions
- `ForwardRange`: additionally requires the `save` member function
- `BidirectionalRange`: additionally requires the `back` and `popBack()` member functions
- `RandomAccessRange`: additionally requires the `[]` operator (and another property depending on whether the range is finite or infinite)

This hierarchy can be shown as in the following graph. `RandomAccessRange` has finite and infinite versions:

```
                    InputRange
                        ↑
                    ForwardRange
                   ↗          ↖
    BidirectionalRange     RandomAccessRange (infinite)
            ↑
 RandomAccessRange (finite)
```

The graph above is in the style of class hierarchies where the lowest level type is at the top.

Those ranges are about providing element access. There is one more range, which is about element *output*:

- `OutputRange`: requires support for the `put(range, element)` operation

These five range types are sufficient to abstract algorithms from data structures.

Iterating by shortening the range

Normally, iterating over the elements of a container does not change the container itself. For example, iterating over a slice with `foreach` or `for` does not affect the slice:

```
int[] slice = [ 10, 11, 12 ];

for (int i = 0; i != slice.length; ++i) {
    write(' ', slice[i]);
}

assert(slice.length == 3);   // ← the length doesn't change
```

Another way of iteration requires a different way of thinking: iteration can be achieved by shortening the range from the beginning. In this method, it is always the first element that is used for element access and the first element is *popped* from the beginning in order to get to the next element:

```
for ( ; slice.length; slice = slice[1..$]) {
    write(' ', slice[0]);     // ← always the first element
}
```

Iteration is achieved by removing the first element by the `slice = slice[1..$]` expression. The slice above is completely consumed by going through the following stages:

```
[ 10, 11, 12 ]
   [ 11, 12 ]
      [ 12 ]
         [ ]
```

The iteration concept of Phobos ranges is based on this new thinking of shortening the range from the beginning. (`BidirectionalRange` and finite `RandomAccessRange` types can be shortened from the end as well.)

Please note that the code above is just to demonstrate this type of iteration; it should not be considered normal to iterate as in that example.

Since losing elements just to iterate over a range would not be desired in most cases, a surrogate range may be consumed instead. The following code uses a separate slice to preserve the elements of the original one:

```
int[] slice = [ 10, 11, 12 ];
int[] surrogate = slice;

for ( ; surrogate.length; surrogate = surrogate[1..$]) {
    write(' ', surrogate[0]);
}

assert(surrogate.length == 0); // ← surrogate is consumed
assert(slice.length == 3);     // ← slice remains the same
```

This is the method employed by most of the Phobos range functions: they return special range objects to be consumed in order to preserve the original containers.

81.5 InputRange

This type of range models the type of iteration where elements are accessed in sequence as we have seen in the print() functions above. Most algorithms only require that elements are iterated in the forward direction without needing to look at elements that have already been iterated over. InputRange models the standard input streams of programs as well, where elements are removed from the stream as they are read.

For completeness, here are the three functions that InputRange requires:

- empty: specifies whether the range is empty; it must return true when the range is considered to be empty, and false otherwise
- front: provides access to the element at the beginning of the range
- popFront(): shortens the range from the beginning by removing the first element

Note: *I write* empty *and* front *without parentheses, as they can be seen as properties of the range; and* popFront() *with parentheses as it is a function with side effects.*

Here is how print() can be implemented by using these range functions:

```
void print(T)(T range) {
    for ( ; !range.empty; range.popFront()) {
        write(' ', range.front);
    }

    writeln();
}
```

Please also note that print() is now a function template to avoid limiting the range type arbitrarily. print() can now work with any type that provides the three InputRange functions.

InputRange example

Let's redesign the School type that we have seen before, this time as an InputRange. We can imagine School as a Student container so when designed as a range, it can be seen as a range of Students.

In order to keep the example short, let's disregard some important design aspects. Let's

- implement only the members that are related to this section
- design all types as structs
- ignore specifiers and qualifiers like private, public, and const
- not take advantage of contract programming and unit testing

```
import std.string;

struct Student {
    string name;
    int number;

    string toString() const {
        return format("%s(%s)", name, number);
    }
}

struct School {
    Student[] students;
}

void main() {
```

```
    auto school = School( [ Student("Ebru", 1),
                            Student("Derya", 2) ,
                            Student("Damla", 3) ] );
}
```

To make School be accepted as an InputRange, we must define the three
InputRange member functions.

For empty to return true when the range is empty, we can use the length of the
students array. When the length of that array is 0, the range is considered
empty:

```
struct School {
    // ...

    bool empty() const {
        return students.length == 0;
    }
}
```

For front to return the first element of the range, we can return the first element
of the array:

```
struct School {
    // ...

    ref Student front() {
        return students[0];
    }
}
```

Note: *I have used the ref keyword to be able to provide access to the actual element
instead of a copy of it. Otherwise the elements would be copied because Student is a
struct.*

For popFront() to shorten the range from the beginning, we can shorten the
students array from the beginning:

```
struct School {
    // ...

    void popFront() {
        students = students[1 .. $];
    }
}
```

Note: *As I have mentioned above, it is not normal to lose the original elements from the
container just to iterate over them. We will address this issue below by introducing a
special range type.*

These three functions are sufficient to make School to be used as an
InputRange. As an example, let's add the following line at the end of main()
above to have our new print() function template to use school as a range:

```
    print(school);
```

print() uses that object as an InputRange and prints its elements to the output:

```
Ebru(1) Derya(2) Damla(3)
```

We have achieved our goal of defining a user type as an InputRange; we have sent
it to an algorithm that operates on InputRange types. School is actually ready to
be used with algorithms of Phobos or any other library that work with
InputRange types. We will see examples of this below.

The `std.array` module to use slices as ranges

Merely importing the `std.array` module makes the most common container type conform to the most capable range type: slices can seamlessly be used as RandomAccessRange objects.

The `std.array` module provides the functions `empty`, `front`, `popFront()` and other range functions for slices. As a result, slices are ready to be used with any range function, for example with `print()`:

```d
import std.array;

// ...

    print([ 1, 2, 3, 4 ]);
```

It is not necessary to import `std.array` if the `std.range` module has already been imported.

Since it is not possible to remove elements from fixed-length arrays, `popFront()` cannot be defined for them. For that reason, fixed-length arrays cannot be used as ranges themselves:

```d
void print(T)(T range) {
    for ( ; !range.empty; range.popFront()) {  // ← compilation ERROR
        write(' ', range.front);
    }

    writeln();
}

void main() {
    int[4] array = [ 1, 2, 3, 4 ];
    print(array);
}
```

It would be better if the compilation error appeared on the line where `print()` is called. This is possible by adding a template constraint to `print()`. The following template constraint takes advantage of `isInputRange`, which we will see in the next chapter. By the help of the template constraint, now the compilation error is for the line where `print()` is called, not for a line where `print()` is defined:

```d
void print(T)(T range)
        if (isInputRange!T) {     // template constraint
    // ...
}
// ...
    print(array);     // ← compilation ERROR
```

The elements of a fixed-length array can still be accessed by range functions. What needs to be done is to use a slice of the whole array, not the array itself:

```d
    print(array[]);    // now compiles
```

Even though slices can be used as ranges, not every range type can be used as an array. When necessary, all of the elements can be copied one by one into an array. `std.array.array` is a helper function to simplify this task; `array()` iterates over InputRange ranges, copies the elements, and returns a new array:

```d
import std.array;

// ...

    // Note: Also taking advantage of UFCS
```

```
    auto copiesOfStudents = school.array;
    writeln(copiesOfStudents);
```

The output:

```
[Ebru(1), Derya(2), Damla(3)]
```

Also note the use of UFCS (page 385) in the code above. UFCS goes very well with range algorithms by making code naturally match the execution order of expressions.

Automatic decoding of strings as ranges of dchar

Being character arrays by definition, strings can also be used as ranges just by importing std.array. However, char and wchar strings cannot be used as RandomAccessRange.

std.array provides a special functionality with all types of strings: Iterating over strings becomes iterating over Unicode code points, not over UTF code units. As a result, strings appear as ranges of Unicode characters.

The following strings contain ç and é, which cannot be represented by a single char, and 𝔸 (mathematical double-struck capital A), which cannot be represented by a single wchar (note that these characters may not be displayed correctly in the environment that you are reading this chapter):

```
import std.array;

// ...

    print("abcçdeéA"c);
    print("abcçdeéA"w);
    print("abcçdeéA"d);
```

The output of the program is what we would normally expect from a *range of letters*:

```
a b c ç d e é 𝔸
a b c ç d e é 𝔸
a b c ç d e é 𝔸
```

As you can see, that output does not match what we saw in the Characters (page 57) and Strings (page 75) chapters. We have seen in those chapters that string is an alias to an array of immutable(char) and wstring is an alias to an array of immutable(wchar). Accordingly, one might expect to see UTF code units in the previous output instead of the properly decoded Unicode characters.

The reason why the characters are displayed correctly is because when used as ranges, string elements are automatically decoded. As we will see below, the decoded dchar values are not actual elements of the strings but rvalues (page 181).

As a reminder, let's consider the following function that treats the strings as arrays of code units:

```
void printElements(T)(T str) {
    for (int i = 0; i != str.length; ++i) {
        write(' ', str[i]);
    }

    writeln();
}

// ...

    printElements("abcçdeéA"c);
```

```
    printElements("abcçdeéA"w);
    printElements("abcçdeéA"d);
```

When the characters are accessed directly by indexing, the elements of the arrays are not decoded:

```
a b c 🔲 🔲 d e 🔲 🔲 🔲 🔲 🔲 🔲
a b c ç d e é 🔲🔲 🔲🔲
a b c ç d e é A
```

Automatic decoding is not always the desired behavior. For example, the following program that is trying to assign to the first element of a string cannot be compiled because the return value of .front is an rvalue:

```
import std.array;

void main() {
    char[] s = "hello".dup;
    s.front = 'H';              // ←  compilation ERROR
}
```

```
Error: front(s) is not an lvalue
```

When a range algorithm needs to modify the actual code units of a string (and when doing so does not invalidate the UTF encoding), then the string can be used as a range of ubyte elements by std.string.representation:

```
import std.array;
import std.string;

void main() {
    char[] s = "hello".dup;
    s.representation.front = 'H';   // compiles
    assert(s == "Hello");
}
```

representation presents the actual elements of char, wchar, and dchar strings as ranges of ubyte, ushort, and uint, respectively.

Ranges without actual elements

The elements of the School objects were actually stored in the students member slices. So, School.front returned a reference to an existing Student object.

One of the powers of ranges is the flexibility of not actually owning elements. front need not return an actual element of an actual container. The returned *element* can be calculated each time when popFront() is called, and can be used as the value that is returned by front.

We have already seen a range without actual elements above: Since char and wchar cannot represent all Unicode characters, the Unicode characters that appear as range elements cannot be actual elements of any char or wchar array. In the case of strings, front returns a dchar that is *constructed* from the corresponding UTF code units of arrays:

```
import std.array;

void main() {
    dchar letter = "é".front; // The dchar that is returned by
                              // front is constructed from the
                              // two chars that represent é
}
```

Although the element type of the array is char, the return type of front above is dchar. That dchar is not an element of the array but is an rvalue (page 181) decoded as a Unicode character from the elements of the array.

Similarly, some ranges do not own any elements but are used for providing access to elements of other ranges. This is a solution to the problem of losing elements while iterating over School objects above. In order to preserve the elements of the actual School objects, a special InputRange can be used.

To see how this is done, let's define a new struct named StudentRange and move all of the range member functions from School to this new struct. Note that School itself is not a range anymore:

```d
struct School {
    Student[] students;
}

struct StudentRange {
    Student[] students;

    this(School school) {
        this.students = school.students;
    }

    bool empty() const {
        return students.length == 0;
    }

    ref Student front() {
        return students[0];
    }

    void popFront() {
        students = students[1 .. $];
    }
}
```

The new range starts with a member slice that provides access to the students of School and consumes that member slice in popFront(). As a result, the actual slice in School is preserved:

```d
auto school = School( [ Student("Ebru", 1),
                        Student("Derya", 2) ,
                        Student("Damla", 3) ] );

print(StudentRange(school));

// The actual array is now preserved:
assert(school.students.length == 3);
```

Note: *Since all its work is dispatched to its member slice, StudentRange may not be seen as a good example of a range. In fact, assuming that students is an accessible member of School, the user code could have created a slice of School.students directly and could have used that slice as a range.*

Infinite ranges

Another benefit of not storing elements as actual members is the ability to create infinite ranges.

Making an infinite range is as simple as having empty always return false. Since it is constant, empty need not even be a function and can be defined as an enum value:

```d
    enum empty = false;                    // ← infinite range
```

Another option is to use an immutable static member:

```
    static immutable empty = false;        // same as above
```

As an example of this, let's design a range that represents the Fibonacci series. Despite having only two int members, the following range can be used as the infinite Fibonacci series:

```
struct FibonacciSeries
{
    int current = 0;
    int next = 1;

    enum empty = false;    // ← infinite range

    int front() const {
        return current;
    }

    void popFront() {
        const nextNext = current + next;
        current = next;
        next = nextNext;
    }
}
```

Note: *Although it is infinite, because the members are of type* int, *the elements of this Fibonacci series would be wrong beyond* int.max.

Since empty is always false for FibonacciSeries objects, the for loop in print() never terminates for them:

```
    print(FibonacciSeries());    // never terminates
```

An infinite range is useful when the range need not be consumed completely right away. We will see how to use only some of the elements of a FibonacciSeries below.

Functions that return ranges

Earlier, we have created a StudentRange object by explicitly writing StudentRange(school).

In most cases, a convenience function that returns the object of such a range is used instead. For example, a function with the whole purpose of returning a StudentRange would simplify the code:

```
StudentRange studentsOf(ref School school) {
    return StudentRange(school);
}

// ...

    // Note: Again, taking advantage of UFCS
    print(school.studentsOf);
```

This is a convenience over having to remember and spell out the names of range types explicitly, which can get quite complicated in practice.

We can see an example of this with the simple std.range.take function. take() is a function that provides access to a specified number of elements of a range, from the beginning. In reality, this functionality is not achieved by the take() function itself, but by a special range object that it returns. This fact need not be explicit when using take():

```
import std.range;

// ...
```

```
    auto school = School( [ Student("Ebru", 1),
                            Student("Derya", 2) ,
                            Student("Damla", 3) ] );

    print(school.studentsOf.take(2));
```

`take()` returns a temporary range object above, which provides access to the first 2 elements of `school`. In turn, `print()` uses that object and produces the following output:

```
  Ebru(1) Derya(2)
```

The operations above still don't make any changes to `school`; it still has 3 elements:

```
    print(school.studentsOf.take(2));
    assert(school.students.length == 3);
```

The specific types of the range objects that are returned by functions like `take()` are not important. These types may sometimes be exposed in error messages, or we can print them ourselves with the help of `typeof` and `stringof`:

```
    writeln(typeof(school.studentsOf.take(2)).stringof);
```

According to the output, `take()` returns an instance of a template named Take:

```
  Take!(StudentRange)
```

std.range and std.algorithm modules

A great benefit of defining our types as ranges is being able to use them not only with our own functions, but with Phobos and other libraries as well.

`std.range` includes a large number of range functions, structs, and classes. `std.algorithm` includes many algorithms that are commonly found also in the standard libraries of other languages.

To see an example of how our types can be used with standard modules, let's use `School` with the `std.algorithm.swapFront` algorithm. `swapFront()` swaps the front elements of two InputRange ranges. (It requires that the front elements of the two ranges are swappable. Arrays satisfy that condition.)

```
import std.algorithm;

// ...

    auto turkishSchool = School( [ Student("Ebru", 1),
                                   Student("Derya", 2) ,
                                   Student("Damla", 3) ] );

    auto americanSchool = School( [ Student("Mary", 10),
                                    Student("Jane", 20) ] );

    swapFront(turkishSchool.studentsOf,
              americanSchool.studentsOf);

    print(turkishSchool.studentsOf);
    print(americanSchool.studentsOf);
```

The first elements of the two schools are swapped:

```
  Mary(10) Derya(2) Damla(3)
  Ebru(1) Jane(20)
```

As another example, let's now look at the std.algorithm.filter algorithm. filter() returns a special range that filters out elements that do not satisfy a specific condition (a *predicate*). The operation of filtering out the elements only affects accessing the elements; the original range is preserved.

Predicates are expressions that must evaluate to true for the elements that are considered to satisfy a condition, and false for the elements that do not. There are a number of ways of specifying the predicate that filter() should use. As we have seen in earlier examples, one way is to use a lambda expression. The parameter a below represents each student:

```
school.studentsOf.filter!(a => a.number % 2)
```

The predicate above selects the elements of the range school.studentsOf that have odd numbers.

Like take(), filter() returns a special range object as well. That range object in turn can be passed to other range functions. For example, it can be passed to print():

```
print(school.studentsOf.filter!(a => a.number % 2));
```

That expression can be explained as *start with the range school.studentsOf, construct a range object that will filter out the elements of that initial range, and pass the new range object to print().*

The output consists of students with odd numbers:

```
Ebru(1) Damla(3)
```

As long as it returns true for the elements that satisfy the condition, the predicate can also be specified as a function:

```
import std.array;

// ...

    bool startsWithD(Student student) {
        return student.name.front == 'D';
    }

    print(school.studentsOf.filter!startsWithD);
```

The predicate function above returns true for students having names starting with the letter D, and false for the others.

Note: Using *student.name[0]* would have meant the first UTF-8 code unit, not the first letter. As I have mentioned above, *front* uses *name* as a range and always returns the first Unicode character.

This time the students whose names start with D are selected and printed:

```
Derya(2) Damla(3)
```

generate(), a convenience function template of the std.range module, makes it easy to present values returned from a function as the elements of an InputRange. It takes any callable entity (function pointer, delegate, etc.) and returns an InputRange object conceptually consisting of the values that are returned from that callable entity.

The returned range object is infinite. Every time the front property of that range object is accessed, the original callable entity is called to get a new *element* from it. The popFront() function of the range object does not perform any work.

For example, the following range object `diceThrower` can be used as an infinite range:

```
import std.stdio;
import std.range;
import std.random;

void main() {
    auto diceThrower = generate!(() => uniform(0, 6));
    writeln(diceThrower.take(10));
}
```

```
[1, 0, 3, 5, 5, 1, 5, 1, 0, 4]
```

Laziness

Another benefit of functions' returning range objects is that, those objects can be used lazily. Lazy ranges produce their elements one at a time and only when needed. This may be essential for execution speed and memory consumption. Indeed, the fact that infinite ranges can even exist is made possible by ranges being lazy.

Lazy ranges produce their elements one at a time and only when needed. We see an example of this with the `FibonacciSeries` range: The elements are calculated by `popFront()` only as they are needed. If `FibonacciSeries` were an eager range and tried to produce all of the elements up front, it could never end or find room for the elements that it produced.

Another problem of eager ranges is the fact that they would have to spend time and space for elements that would perhaps never going to be used.

Like most of the algorithms in Phobos, `take()` and `filter()` benefit from laziness. For example, we can pass `FibonacciSeries` to `take()` and have it generate a finite number of elements:

```
print(FibonacciSeries().take(10));
```

Although `FibonacciSeries` is infinite, the output contains only the first 10 numbers:

```
0 1 1 2 3 5 8 13 21 34
```

81.6 ForwardRange

`InputRange` models a range where elements are taken out of the range as they are iterated over.

Some ranges are capable of saving their states, as well as operating as an `InputRange`. For example, `FibonacciSeries` objects can save their states because these objects can freely be copied and the two copies continue their lives independently from each other.

`ForwardRange` provides the `save` member function, which is expected to return a copy of the range. The copy that `save` returns must operate independently from the range object that it was copied from: iterating over one copy must not affect the other copy.

Importing `std.array` automatically makes slices become `ForwardRange` ranges.

In order to implement `save` for `FibonacciSeries`, we can simply return a copy of the object:

```
struct FibonacciSeries {
    // ...
```

```
    FibonacciSeries save() const {
        return this;
    }
}
```

The returned copy is a separate range that would continue from the point where it was copied from.

We can demonstrate that the copied object is independent from the actual range with the following program. The algorithm `std.range.popFrontN()` in the following code removes a specified number of elements from the specified range:

```
import std.range;

// ...

void report(T)(const dchar[] title, const ref T range) {
    writefln("%40s: %s", title, range.take(5));
}

void main() {
    auto range = FibonacciSeries();
    report("Original range", range);

    range.popFrontN(2);
    report("After removing two elements", range);

    auto theCopy = range.save;
    report("The copy", theCopy);

    range.popFrontN(3);
    report("After removing three more elements", range);
    report("The copy", theCopy);
}
```

The output of the program shows that removing elements from the range does not affect its saved copy:

```
                      Original range: [0, 1, 1, 2, 3]
          After removing two elements: [1, 2, 3, 5, 8]
                            The copy: [1, 2, 3, 5, 8]
    After removing three more elements: [5, 8, 13, 21, 34]
                            The copy: [1, 2, 3, 5, 8]
```

Also note that the range is passed directly to `writefln` in `report()`. Like our `print()` function, the output functions of the `stdio` module can take InputRange objects. I will use `stdio`'s output functions from now on.

An algorithm that works with ForwardRange is `std.range.cycle`. `cycle()` iterates over the elements of a range repeatedly from the beginning to the end. In order to be able to start over from the beginning it must be able to save a copy of the initial state of the range, so it requires a ForwardRange.

Since `FibonacciSeries` is now a ForwardRange, we can try `cycle()` with a `FibonacciSeries` object; but in order to avoid having `cycle()` iterate over an infinite range, and as a result never find the end of it, we must first make a finite range by passing `FibonacciSeries` through `take()`:

```
    writeln(FibonacciSeries().take(5).cycle.take(20));
```

In order to make the resultant range finite as well, the range that is returned by `cycle` is also passed through `take()`. The output consists of *the first twenty elements of cycling through the first five elements of FibonacciSeries*.

```
[0, 1, 1, 2, 3, 0, 1, 1, 2, 3, 0, 1, 1, 2, 3, 0, 1, 1, 2, 3]
```

We could have defined intermediate variables as well. The following is an equivalent of the single-line code above:

```
    auto series               = FibonacciSeries();
    auto firstPart            = series.take(5);
    auto cycledThrough        = firstPart.cycle;
    auto firstPartOfCycledThrough = cycledThrough.take(20);

    writeln(firstPartOfCycledThrough);
```

I would like to point out the importance of laziness one more time: The first four lines above merely construct range objects that will eventually produce the elements. The numbers that are part of the result are calculated by `FibonacciSeries.popFront()` as needed.

Note: *Although we have started with FibonacciSeries as a ForwardRange, we have actually passed the result of FibonacciSeries().take(5) to cycle(). take() is adaptive: the range that it returns is a ForwardRange if its parameter is a ForwardRange. We will see how this is accomplished with isForwardRange in the next chapter.*

81.7 BidirectionalRange

`BidirectionalRange` provides two member functions over the member functions of `ForwardRange`. `back` is similar to `front`: it provides access to the last element of the range. `popBack()` is similar to `popFront()`: it removes the last element from the range.

Importing `std.array` automatically makes slices become `BidirectionalRange` ranges.

A good `BidirectionalRange` example is the `std.range.retro` function. `retro()` takes a `BidirectionalRange` and ties its `front` to `back`, and `popFront()` to `popBack()`. As a result, the original range is iterated over in reverse order:

```
    writeln([ 1, 2, 3 ].retro);
```

The output:

```
[3, 2, 1]
```

Let's define a range that behaves similarly to the special range that `retro()` returns. Although the following range has limited functionality, it shows how powerful ranges are:

```
import std.array;
import std.stdio;

struct Reversed {
    int[] range;

    this(int[] range) {
        this.range = range;
    }

    bool empty() const {
        return range.empty;
    }

    int front() const {
        return range.back;  // ← reverse
    }
```

```
    int back() const {
        return range.front;   // ← reverse
    }

    void popFront() {
        range.popBack();       // ← reverse
    }

    void popBack() {
        range.popFront();      // ← reverse
    }
}

void main() {
    writeln(Reversed([ 1, 2, 3]));
}
```

The output is the same as `retro()`:

```
[3, 2, 1]
```

81.8 RandomAccessRange

RandomAccessRange represents ranges that allow accessing elements by the [ ] operator. As we have seen in the Operator Overloading chapter (page 298), [ ] operator is defined by the opIndex() member function.

Importing std.array module makes slices become RandomAccessRange ranges only if possible. For example, since UTF-8 and UTF-16 encodings do not allow accessing Unicode characters by an index, char and wchar arrays cannot be used as RandomAccessRange ranges of Unicode characters. On the other hand, since the codes of the UTF-32 encoding correspond one-to-one to Unicode character codes, dchar arrays can be used as RandomAccessRange ranges of Unicode characters.

It is natural that every type would define the opIndex() member function according to its functionality. However, computer science has an expectation on its algorithmic complexity: random access must take *constant time*. Constant time access means that the time spent when accessing an element is independent of the number of elements in the container. Therefore, no matter how large the range is, element access should not depend on the length of the range.

In order to be considered a RandomAccessRange, *one* of the following conditions must also be satisfied:

* to be an infinite ForwardRange

or

* to be a BidirectionalRange that also provides the length property

Depending on the condition that is satisfied, the range is either infinite or finite.

Infinite RandomAccessRange

The following are all of the requirements of a RandomAccessRange that is based on an *infinite ForwardRange*:

* empty, front and popFront() that InputRange requires
* save that ForwardRange requires
* opIndex() that RandomAccessRange requires
* the value of empty to be known at compile time as false

We were able to define FibonacciSeries as a ForwardRange. However, opIndex() cannot be implemented to operate at constant time for FibonacciSeries because accessing an element requires accessing all of the previous elements first.

As an example where opIndex() can operate at constant time, let's define an infinite range that consists of squares of integers. Although the following range is infinite, accessing any one of its elements can happen at constant time:

```d
class SquaresRange {
    int first;

    this(int first = 0) {
        this.first = first;
    }

    enum empty = false;

    int front() const {
        return opIndex(0);
    }

    void popFront() {
        ++first;
    }

    SquaresRange save() const {
        return new SquaresRange(first);
    }

    int opIndex(size_t index) const {
        /* This function operates at constant time */
        immutable integerValue = first + cast(int)index;
        return integerValue * integerValue;
    }
}
```

Note: *It would make more sense to define SquaresRange as a struct.*

Although no space has been allocated for the elements of this range, the elements can be accessed by the [ ] operator:

```d
    auto squares = new SquaresRange();

    writeln(squares[5]);
    writeln(squares[10]);
```

The output contains the elements at indexes 5 and 10:

```
25
100
```

The element with index 0 should always represent the first element of the range. We can take advantage of popFrontN() when testing whether this really is the case:

```d
    squares.popFrontN(5);
    writeln(squares[0]);
```

The first 5 elements of the range are 0, 1, 4, 9 and 16; the squares of 0, 1, 2, 3 and 4. After removing those, the square of the next value becomes the first element of the range:

```
25
```

Being a RandomAccessRange (the most functional range), SquaresRange can also be used as other types of ranges. For example, as an InputRange when passing to filter():

```
bool are_lastTwoDigitsSame(int value) {
    /* Must have at least two digits */
    if (value < 10) {
        return false;
    }

    /* Last two digits must be divisible by 11 */
    immutable lastTwoDigits = value % 100;
    return (lastTwoDigits % 11) == 0;
}

writeln(squares.take(50).filter!are_lastTwoDigitsSame);
```

The output consists of elements among the first 50, where last two digits are the same:

```
[100, 144, 400, 900, 1444, 1600]
```

Finite RandomAccessRange

The following are all of the requirements of a RandomAccessRange that is based on a *finite BidirectionalRange*:

- empty, front and popFront() that InputRange requires
- save that ForwardRange requires
- back and popBack() that BidirectionalRange requires
- opIndex() that RandomAccessRange requires
- length, which provides the length of the range

As an example of a finite RandomAccessRange, let's define a range that works similarly to std.range.chain. chain() presents the elements of a number of separate ranges as if they are elements of a single larger range. Although chain() works with any type of element and any type of range, to keep the example short, let's implement a range that works only with int slices.

Let's name this range Together and expect the following behavior from it:

```
auto range = Together([ 1, 2, 3 ], [ 101, 102, 103]);
writeln(range[4]);
```

When constructed with the two separate arrays above, range should present all of those elements as a single range. For example, although neither array has an element at index 4, the element 102 should be the element that corresponds to index 4 of the collective range:

```
102
```

As expected, printing the entire range should contain all of the elements:

```
writeln(range);
```

The output:

```
[1, 2, 3, 101, 102, 103]
```

Together will operate lazily: the elements will not be copied to a new larger array; they will be accessed from the original slices.

We can take advantage of *variadic functions*, which were introduced in the Variable Number of Parameters chapter (page 258), to initialize the range by any number of original slices:

```
struct Together {
    const(int)[][] slices;

    this(const(int)[][] slices...) {
        this.slices = slices.dup;

        clearFront();
        clearBack();
    }
// ...
}
```

Note that the element type is const(int), indicating that this struct will not modify the elements of the ranges. However, the slices will necessarily be modified by popFront() to implement iteration.

The clearFront() and clearBack() calls that the constructor makes are to remove empty slices from the beginning and the end of the original slices. Such empty slices do not change the behavior of Together and removing them up front will simplify the implementation:

```
struct Together {
// ...

    private void clearFront() {
        while (!slices.empty && slices.front.empty) {
            slices.popFront();
        }
    }

    private void clearBack() {
        while (!slices.empty && slices.back.empty) {
            slices.popBack();
        }
    }
}
```

We will call those functions later from popFront() and popBack() as well.

Since clearFront() and clearBack() remove all of the empty slices from the beginning and the end, still having a slice would mean that the collective range is not yet empty. In other words, the range should be considered empty only if there is no slice left:

```
struct Together {
// ...

    bool empty() const {
        return slices.empty;
    }
}
```

The first element of the first slice is the first element of this Together range:

```
struct Together {
// ...

    int front() const {
        return slices.front.front;
    }
}
```

Removing the first element of the first slice removes the first element of this range as well. Since this operation may leave the first slice empty, we must call clearFront() to remove that empty slice and the ones that are after that one:

```d
struct Together {
// ...

    void popFront() {
        slices.front.popFront();
        clearFront();
    }
}
```

A copy of this range can be constructed from a copy of the slices member:

```d
struct Together {
// ...

    Together save() const {
        return Together(slices.dup);
    }
}
```

Please note that .dup copies only slices in this case, not the slice elements that it contains.

The operations at the end of the range are similar to the ones at the beginning:

```d
struct Together {
// ...

    int back() const {
        return slices.back.back;
    }

    void popBack() {
        slices.back.popBack();
        clearBack();
    }
}
```

The length of the range can be calculated as the sum of the lengths of the slices:

```d
struct Together {
// ...

    size_t length() const {
        size_t totalLength = 0;

        foreach (slice; slices) {
            totalLength += slice.length;
        }

        return totalLength;
    }
}
```

Alternatively, the length may be calculated with less code by taking advantage of std.algorithm.fold. fold() takes an operation as its template parameter and applies that operation to all elements of a range:

```d
import std.algorithm;

// ...

    size_t length() const {
        return slices.fold!((a, b) => a + b.length)(size_t.init);
    }
```

The a in the template parameter represents the current result (*the sum* in this case) and b represents the current element. The first function parameter is the range that contains the elements and the second function parameter is the initial value of the result (size_t.init is 0). (Note how slices is written before fold by taking advantage of UFCS (page 385).)

Note: *Further, instead of calculating the length every time when length is called, it may be measurably faster to maintain a member variable perhaps named length_, which always equals the correct length of the collective range. That member may be calculated once in the constructor and adjusted accordingly as elements are removed by popFront() and popBack().*

One way of returning the element that corresponds to a specific index is to look at every slice to determine whether the element would be among the elements of that slice:

```
struct Together {
// ...

    int opIndex(size_t index) const {
        /* Save the index for the error message */
        immutable originalIndex = index;

        foreach (slice; slices) {
            if (slice.length > index) {
                return slice[index];

            } else {
                index -= slice.length;
            }
        }

        throw new Exception(
            format("Invalid index: %s (length: %s)",
                    originalIndex, this.length));
    }
}
```

Note: *This opIndex() does not satisfy the constant time requirement that has been mentioned above. For this implementation to be acceptably fast, the slices member must not be too long.*

This new range is now ready to be used with any number of int slices. With the help of take() and array(), we can even include the range types that we have defined earlier in this chapter:

```
    auto range = Together(FibonacciSeries().take(10).array,
                          [ 777, 888 ],
                          (new SquaresRange()).take(5).array);

    writeln(range.save);
```

The elements of the three slices are accessed as if they were elements of a single large array:

```
[0, 1, 1, 2, 3, 5, 8, 13, 21, 34, 777, 888, 0, 1, 4, 9, 16]
```

We can pass this range to other range algorithms. For example, to retro(), which requires a BidirectionalRange:

```
    writeln(range.save.retro);
```

The output:

```
[16, 9, 4, 1, 0, 888, 777, 34, 21, 13, 8, 5, 3, 2, 1, 1, 0]
```

Of course you should use the more functional `std.range.chain` instead of `Together` in your programs.

81.9 `OutputRange`

All of the range types that we have seen so far are about element access. `OutputRange` represents streamed element output, similar to sending characters to `stdout`.

I have mentioned earlier that `OutputRange` requires support for the `put(range, element)` operation. `put()` is a function defined in the `std.range` module. It determines the capabilities of the range and the element at compile time and uses the most appropriate method to *output* the element.

`put()` considers the following cases in the order that they are listed below, and applies the method for the first matching case. R represents the type of the range; range, a range object; E, the type of the element; and e an element of the range:

Case Considered	Method Applied
R has a member function named put and put can take an E as argument	`range.put(e);`
R has a member function named put and put can take an E[] as argument	`range.put([ e ]);`
R is an InputRange and e can be assigned to range.front	`range.front = e;` `range.popFront();`
E is an InputRange and can be copied to R	`for (; !e.empty; e.popFront())` `put(range, e.front);`
R can take E as argument (e.g. R could be a delegate)	`range(e);`
R can take E[] as argument (e.g. R could be a delegate)	`range([ e ]);`

Let's define a range that matches the first case: The range will have a member function named `put()`, which takes a parameter that matches the type of the output range.

This output range will be used for outputting elements to multiple files, including `stdout`. When elements are outputted with `put()`, they will all be written to all of those files. As an additional functionality, let's add the ability to specify a delimiter to be written after each element.

```d
struct MultiFile {
    string delimiter;
    File[] files;

    this(string delimiter, string[] fileNames...) {
        this.delimiter = delimiter;

        /* stdout is always included */
        this.files ~= stdout;

        /* A File object for each file name */
        foreach (fileName; fileNames) {
            this.files ~= File(fileName, "w");
        }
    }

    // This is the version that takes arrays (but not strings)
    void put(T)(T slice)
            if (isArray!T && !isSomeString!T) {
        foreach (element; slice) {
            // Note that this is a call to the other version
            // of put() below
            put(element);
        }
    }
```

```
    // This is the version that takes non-arrays and strings
    void put(T)(T value)
            if (!isArray!T || isSomeString!T) {
        foreach (file; files) {
            file.write(value, delimiter);
        }
    }
}
```

In order to be used as an output range of any type of elements, put() is also templatized on the element type.

An algorithm in Phobos that uses OutputRange is std.algorithm.copy. copy() is a very simple algorithm, which copies the elements of an InputRange to an OutputRange.

```
import std.traits;
import std.stdio;
import std.algorithm;

// ...

void main() {
    auto output = MultiFile("\n", "output_0", "output_1");
    copy([ 1, 2, 3], output);
    copy([ "red", "blue", "green" ], output);
}
```

That code outputs the elements of the input ranges both to stdout and to files named "output_0" and "output_1":

```
1
2
3
red
blue
green
```

Using slices as OutputRange

The std.range module makes slices OutputRange objects as well. (By contrast, std.array makes them only input ranges.) Unfortunately, using slices as OutputRange objects has a confusing effect: slices lose an element for each put() operation on them; and that element is the element that has just been outputted!

The reason for this behavior is a consequence of slices' not having a put() member function. As a result, the third case of the previous table is matched for slices and the following method is applied:

```
    range.front = e;
    range.popFront();
```

As the code above is executed for each put(), the front element of the slice is assigned to the value of the *outputted* element, to be subsequently removed from the slice with popFront():

```
import std.stdio;
import std.range;

void main() {
    int[] slice = [ 1, 2, 3 ];
    put(slice, 100);
    writeln(slice);
}
```

As a result, although the slice is used as an OutputRange, it surprisingly *loses* elements:

```
[2, 3]
```

To avoid this, a separate slice must be used as an OutputRange instead:

```
import std.stdio;
import std.range;

void main() {
    int[] slice = [ 1, 2, 3 ];
    int[] slice2 = slice;

    put(slice2, 100);

    writeln(slice2);
    writeln(slice);
}
```

This time the second slice is consumed and the original slice has the expected elements:

```
[2, 3]
[100, 2, 3]    ← expected result
```

Another important fact is that the length of the slice does not grow when used as an OutputRange. It is the programmer's responsibility to ensure that there is enough room in the slice:

```
    int[] slice = [ 1, 2, 3 ];
    int[] slice2 = slice;

    foreach (i; 0 .. 4) {    // ← no room for 4 elements
        put(slice2, i * 100);
    }
```

When the slice becomes completely empty because of the indirect popFront() calls, the program terminates with an exception:

```
core.exception.AssertError@...: Attempting to fetch the front
of an empty array of int
```

std.array.Appender and its convenience function appender allows using slices as *an OutputRange where the elements are appended*. The put() function of the special range object that appender() returns actually appends the elements to the original slice:

```
import std.array;

// ...

    auto a = appender([ 1, 2, 3 ]);

    foreach (i; 0 .. 4) {
        a.put(i * 100);
    }
```

In the code above, appender is called with an array and returns a special range object. That range object is in turn used as an OutputRange by calling its put() member function. The resultant elements are accessed by its .data property:

```
    writeln(a.data);
```

The output:

```
[1, 2, 3, 0, 100, 200, 300]
```

Appender supports the ~= operator as well:

```
    a ~= 1000;
    writeln(a.data);
```

The output:

```
[1, 2, 3, 0, 100, 200, 300, 1000]
```

toString() with an OutputRange parameter

Similar to how toString member functions can be defined as taking a delegate parameter (page 475), it is possible to define one that takes an OutputRange. Functions like format, writefln, and writeln operate more efficiently by placing the output characters right inside the output buffer of the output range.

To be able to work with any OutputRange type, such toString definitions need to be function templates, optionally with template constraints:

```
import std.stdio;
import std.range;

struct S {
    void toString(O)(ref O o) const
            if (isOutputRange!(O, char)) {
        put(o, "hello");
    }
}

void main() {
    auto s = S();
    writeln(s);
}
```

Note that the code inside main() does not define an OutputRange object. That object is defined by writeln to store the characters before printing them:

```
hello
```

81.10 Range templates

Although we have used mostly int ranges in this chapter, ranges and range algorithms are much more useful when defined as templates.

The std.range module includes many range templates. We will see these templates in the next chapter.

81.11 Summary

- Ranges abstract data structures from algorithms and allow them to be used with algorithms seamlessly.
- Ranges are a D concept and are the basis for many features of Phobos.
- Many Phobos algorithms return lazy range objects to accomplish their special tasks.
- UFCS works well with range algorithms.
- When used as InputRange objects, the elements of strings are Unicode characters.
- InputRange requires empty, front and popFront().
- ForwardRange additionally requires save.

- `BidirectionalRange` additionally requires `back` and `popBack()`.
- Infinite `RandomAccessRange` requires `opIndex()` over `ForwardRange`.
- Finite `RandomAccessRange` requires `opIndex()` and `length` over `BidirectionalRange`.
- `std.array.appender` returns an `OutputRange` that appends to slices.
- Slices are ranges of finite `RandomAccessRange`
- Fixed-length arrays are not ranges.

We used mostly `int` ranges in the previous chapter. In practice, containers, algorithms, and ranges are almost always implemented as templates. The `print()` example in that chapter was a template as well:

```
void print(T)(T range) {
    // ...
}
```

What lacks from the implementation of `print()` is that even though it requires T to be a kind of InputRange, it does not formalize that requirement with a template constraint. (We have seen template constraints in the More Templates chapter (page 520).)

The `std.range` module contains templates that are useful both in template constraints and in `static if` statements.

82.1 Range kind templates

The group of templates with names starting with `is` determine whether a type satisfies the requirements of a certain kind of range. For example, `isInputRange!T` answers the question "is T an InputRange?" The following templates are for determining whether a type is of a specific general range kind:

- `isInputRange`
- `isForwardRange`
- `isBidirectionalRange`
- `isRandomAccessRange`
- `isOutputRange`

Accordingly, the template constraint of `print()` can use `isInputRange`:

```
void print(T)(T range)
        if (isInputRange!T) {
    // ...
}
```

Unlike the others, `isOutputRange` takes two template parameters: The first one is a range type and the second one is an element type. It returns `true` if that range type allows outputting that element type. For example, the following constraint is for requiring that the range must be an `OutputRange` that accepts `double` elements:

```
void foo(T)(T range)
        if (isOutputRange!(T, double)) {
    // ...
}
```

When used in conjunction with `static if`, these constraints can determine the capabilities of user-defined ranges as well. For example, when a dependent range of a user-defined range is a `ForwardRange`, the user-defined range can take advantage of that fact and can provide the `save()` function as well.

Let's see this on a range that produces the negatives of the elements of an existing range (more accurately, the *numeric complements* of the elements). Let's start with just the InputRange functions:

```
struct Negative(T)
        if (isInputRange!T) {
    T range;

    bool empty() {
        return range.empty;
    }

    auto front() {
        return -range.front;
    }

    void popFront() {
        range.popFront();
    }
}
```

Note: *As we will see below, the return type of* `front` *can be specified as* `ElementType!T` *as well.*

The only functionality of this range is in the `front` function where it produces the negative of the front element of the original range.

As usual, the following is the convenience function that goes with that range:

```
Negative!T negative(T)(T range) {
    return Negative!T(range);
}
```

This range is ready to be used with e.g. `FibonacciSeries` that was defined in the previous chapter:

```
struct FibonacciSeries {
    int current = 0;
    int next = 1;

    enum empty = false;

    int front() const {
        return current;
    }

    void popFront() {
        const nextNext = current + next;
        current = next;
        next = nextNext;
    }

    FibonacciSeries save() const {
        return this;
    }
}
// ...

    writeln(FibonacciSeries().take(5).negative);
```

The output contains the negatives of the first five elements of the series:

```
[0, -1, -1, -2, -3]
```

Naturally, being just an `InputRange`, `Negative` cannot be used with algorithms like `cycle()` that require a `ForwardRange`:

```
    writeln(FibonacciSeries()
            .take(5)
            .negative
            .cycle      // ←  compilation ERROR
            .take(10));
```

However, when the original range is already a `ForwardRange`, there is no reason for `Negative` not to provide the `save()` function as well. This condition can be determined by a `static if` statement and `save()` can be provided if the original range is a `ForwardRange`. In this case it is as trivial as returning a new `Negative` object that is constructed by a copy of the original range:

```
struct Negative(T)
        if (isInputRange!T) {
// ...

    static if (isForwardRange!T) {
        Negative save() {
            return Negative(range.save);
        }
    }
}
```

The addition of the new `save()` function makes `Negative!FibonacciSeries` a `ForwardRange` as well and the `cycle()` call can now be compiled:

```
    writeln(FibonacciSeries()
            .take(5)
            .negative
            .cycle       // ← now compiles
            .take(10));
```

The output of the entire expression can be described as *take the first five elements of the Fibonacci series, take their negatives, cycle those indefinitely, and take the first ten of those elements*:

```
[0, -1, -1, -2, -3, 0, -1, -1, -2, -3]
```

With the same approach, `Negative` can be made a `BidirectionalRange` and a `RandomAccessRange` if the original range supports those functionalities:

```
struct Negative(T)
        if (isInputRange!T) {
// ...

    static if (isBidirectionalRange!T) {
        auto back() {
            return -range.back;
        }

        void popBack() {
            range.popBack();
        }
    }

    static if (isRandomAccessRange!T) {
        auto opIndex(size_t index) {
            return -range[index];
        }
    }
}
```

For example, when it is used with a slice, the negative elements can be accessed by the [] operator:

```
    auto d = [ 1.5, 2.75 ];
    auto n = d.negative;
    writeln(n[1]);
```

The output:

```
-2.75
```

82.2 `ElementType` and `ElementEncodingType`

`ElementType` provides the types of the elements of the range.

For example, the following template constraint includes a requirement that is about the element type of the first range:

```
void foo(I1, I2, O)(I1 input1, I2 input2, O output)
        if (isInputRange!I1 &&
            isForwardRange!I2 &&
            isOutputRange!(O, ElementType!I1)) {
    // ...
}
```

The previous constraint can be described as *if I1 is an InputRange and I2 is a ForwardRange and O is an OutputRange that accepts the element type of I1.*

Since strings are always ranges of Unicode characters, regardless of their actual character types, they are always ranges of dchar, which means that even `ElementType!string` and `ElementType!wstring` are dchar. For that reason, when needed in a template, the actual UTF encoding type of a string range can be obtained by `ElementEncodingType`.

82.3 More range templates

The `std.range` module has many more range templates that can be used with D's other compile-time features. The following is a sampling:

- `isInfinite`: Whether the range is infinite
- `hasLength`: Whether the range has a `length` property
- `hasSlicing`: Whether the range supports slicing i.e. with `a[x..y]`
- `hasAssignableElements`: Whether the return type of `front` is assignable
- `hasSwappableElements`: Whether the elements of the range are swappable e.g. with `std.algorithm.swap`
- `hasMobileElements`: Whether the elements of the range are movable e.g. with `std.algorithm.move`

  This implies that the range has `moveFront()`, `moveBack()`, or `moveAt()`, depending on the actual kind of the range. Since moving elements is usually faster than copying them, depending on the result of `hasMobileElements` a range can provide faster operations by calling `move()`.

- `hasLvalueElements`: Whether the elements of the range are *lvalues* (roughly meaning that the elements are not copies of actual elements nor are temporary objects that are created on the fly)

  For example, `hasLvalueElements!FibonacciSeries` is `false` because the elements of `FibonacciSeries` do not exist as themselves; rather, they are copies of the member `current` that is returned by `front`. Similarly, `hasLvalueElements!(Negative!(int[]))` is `false` because although the int slice does have actual elements, the range that is represented by `Negative` does not provide access to those elements; rather, it returns copies that have the negative signs of the elements of the actual slice. Conversely, `hasLvalueElements!(int[])` is `true` because a slice provides access to actual elements of an array.

The following example takes advantage of `isInfinite` to provide `empty` as an enum when the original range is infinite, making it known at compile time that `Negative!T` is infinite as well:

```
struct Negative(T)
        if (isInputRange!T) {
// ...

    static if (isInfinite!T) {
        // Negative!T is infinite as well
        enum empty = false;

    } else {
        bool empty() {
            return range.empty;
        }
    }

// ...
}

static assert( isInfinite!(Negative!FibonacciSeries));
static assert(!isInfinite!(int[]));
```

82.4 Run-time polymorphism with `inputRangeObject()` and `outputRangeObject()`

Being implemented mostly as templates, ranges exhibit *compile-time polymorphism*, which we have been taking advantage of in the examples of this chapter and previous chapters. (*For differences between compile-time polymorphism and run-time polymorphism, see the "Compile-time polymorphism" section in the More Templates chapter (page 520).*)

Compile-time polymorphism has to deal with the fact that every instantiation of a template is a different type. For example, the return type of the `take()` template is directly related to the original range:

```
writeln(typeof([11, 22].negative.take(1)).stringof);
writeln(typeof(FibonacciSeries().take(1)).stringof);
```

The output:

```
Take!(Negative!(int[]))
Take!(FibonacciSeries)
```

A natural consequence of this fact is that different range types cannot be assigned to each other. The following is an example of this incompatibility between two InputRange ranges:

```
auto range = [11, 22].negative;
// ... at a later point ...
range = FibonacciSeries();    // ← compilation ERROR
```

As expected, the compilation error indicates that `FibonacciSeries` and `Negative!(int[])` are not compatible:

```
Error: cannot implicitly convert expression (FibonacciSeries(0, 1))
of type FibonacciSeries to Negative!(int[])
```

However, although the actual types of the ranges are different, since they both are *ranges of int*, this incompatibility can be seen as an unnecessary limitation. From the usage point of view, since both ranges simply provide int elements, the actual mechanism that produces those elements should not be important.

Phobos helps with this issue by `inputRangeObject()` and `outputRangeObject()`. `inputRangeObject()` allows presenting ranges as *a specific kind of range of specific types of elements*. With its help, a range can be used e.g. as *an InputRange of int elements*, regardless of the actual type of the range.

inputRangeObject() is flexible enough to support all of the non-output ranges: InputRange, ForwardRange, BidirectionalRange, and RandomAccessRange. Because of that flexibility, the object that it returns cannot be defined by auto. The exact kind of range that is required must be specified explicitly:

```
// Meaning "InputRange of ints":
InputRange!int range = [11, 22].negative.inputRangeObject;

// ... at a later point ...

// The following assignment now compiles
range = FibonacciSeries().inputRangeObject;
```

As another example, when the range needs to be used as *a ForwardRange of int elements*, its type must be specified explicitly as ForwardRange!int:

```
ForwardRange!int range = [11, 22].negative.inputRangeObject;

auto copy = range.save;

range = FibonacciSeries().inputRangeObject;
writeln(range.save.take(10));
```

The example calls save() just to prove that the ranges can indeed be used as ForwardRange ranges.

Similarly, outputRangeObject() works with OutputRange ranges and allows their use as *an OutputRange that accepts specific types of elements*.

82.5 Summary

- The std.range module contains many useful range templates.
- Some of those templates allow templates be more capable depending on the capabilities of original ranges.
- inputRangeObject() and outputRangeObject() provide run-time polymorphism, allowing using different types of ranges as *specific kinds of ranges of specific types of elements*.

83 static foreach

We saw compile-time `foreach` earlier in the Tuples chapter (page 513). Compile-time `foreach` iterates the loop at compile time and unrolls each iteration as separate pieces of code. For example, given the following `foreach` loop over a tuple:

```
auto t = tuple(42, "hello", 1.5);

foreach (i, member; t) {
    writefln("%s: %s", i, member);
}
```

The compiler *unrolls* the loop similar to the following equivalent code:

```
{
    enum size_t i = 0;
    int member = t[i];
    writefln("%s: %s", i, member);
}
{
    enum size_t i = 1;
    string member = t[i];
    writefln("%s: %s", i, member);
}
{
    enum size_t i = 2;
    double member = t[i];
    writefln("%s: %s", i, member);
}
```

Although being very powerful, some properties of compile-time `foreach` may not be suitable in some cases:

- With compile-time `foreach`, each unrolling of the loop introduces a scope. As seen with the `i` and `member` variables above, this allows the use of a symbol in more than one scope without causing a multiple definition error. Although this can be desirable in some cases, it makes it impossible for code unrolled for one iteration to use code from other iterations.

- Compile-time `foreach` works only with tuples (including template arguments in the form of `AliasSeq`). For example, despite the elements of the following array literal being known at compile time, the loop will always be executed at run time (this may very well be the desired behavior):

```
void main() {
    enum arr = [1, 2];
    // Executed at run time, not unrolled at compile time:
    foreach (i; arr) {
        // ...
    }
}
```

- Like regular `foreach`, compile-time `foreach` can only be used inside functions. For example, it cannot be used at module scope or inside a user-defined type definition.

```
import std.meta;

// Attempting to define function overloads at module scope:
foreach (T; AliasSeq!(int, double)) {    // ← compilation ERROR
    T twoTimes(T arg) {
        return arg * 2;
```

```
    }
}
void main() {
}
```

```
Error: declaration expected, not foreach
```

- With compile-time `foreach`, it may not be clear whether `break` and `continue` statements inside the loop body should affect the compile-time loop iteration itself or whether they should be parts of the unrolled code.

`static foreach` is a more powerful compile-time feature that provides more control:

- `static foreach` can work with any range of elements that can be computed at compile time (including number ranges like `1..10`). For example, given the `FibonacciSeries` range from the Ranges chapter (page 569) and a function that determines whether a number is even:

```
static foreach (n; FibonacciSeries().take(10).filter!isEven) {
    writeln(n);
}
```

The loop above would be unrolled as the following equivalent:

```
writeln(0);
writeln(2);
writeln(8);
writeln(34);
```

- `static foreach` can be used at module scope.
- `static foreach` does not introduce a separate scope for each iteration. For example, the following loop defines two overloads of a function at module scope:

```
import std.meta;
static foreach (T; AliasSeq!(int, double)) {
    T twoTimes(T arg) {
        return arg * 2;
    }
}
void main() {
}
```

The loop above would be unrolled as its following equivalent:

```
    int twoTimes(int arg) {
        return arg * 2;
    }

    double twoTimes(double arg) {
        return arg * 2;
    }
```

- `break` and `continue` statements inside a `static foreach` loop require labels for clarity. For example, the following code unrolls (generates) `case` clauses inside a `switch` statement. The `break` statements that are under each `case` clause must mention the associated `switch` statements by labels:

```
import std.stdio;

void main(string[] args) {
theSwitchStatement:
    switch (args.length) {
        static foreach (i; 1..3) {
            case i:
                writeln(i);
                break theSwitchStatement;
        }

    default:
        writeln("default case");
        break;
    }
}
```

After the loop above is unrolled, the switch statement would be the equivalent of the following code:

```
    switch (args.length) {
    case 1:
        writeln(1);
        break;

    case 2:
        writeln(2);
        break;

    default:
        writeln("default case");
        break;
    }
```

84 Parallelism

Most modern microprocessors consist of more than one *core*, each of which can operate as an individual processing unit. They can execute different parts of different programs at the same time. The features of the std.parallelism module make it possible for programs to take advantage of all of the cores in order to run faster.

This chapter covers the following range algorithms. These algorithms should be used only when the operations that are to be executed *in parallel* are truly independent from each other. *In parallel* means that operations are executed on multiple cores at the same time:

- parallel: Accesses the elements of a range in parallel.
- task: Creates tasks that are executed in parallel.
- asyncBuf: Iterates the elements of an InputRange semi-eagerly in parallel.
- map: Calls functions with the elements of an InputRange semi-eagerly in parallel.
- amap: Calls functions with the elements of a RandomAccessRange fully-eagerly in parallel.
- reduce: Makes calculations over the elements of a RandomAccessRange in parallel.

In the programs that we have written so far we have been assuming that the expressions of a program are executed in a certain order, at least in general line-by-line:

```
++i;
++j;
```

In the code above, we expect that the value of i is incremented before the value of j is incremented. Although that is semantically correct, it is rarely the case in reality: microprocessors and compilers use optimization techniques to have some variables reside in microprocessor's registers that are independent from each other. When that is the case, the microprocessor would execute operations like the increments above in parallel.

Although these optimizations are effective, they cannot be applied automatically to layers higher than the very low-level operations. Only the programmer can determine that certain high-level operations are independent and that they can be executed in parallel.

In a loop, the elements of a range are normally processed one after the other, operations of each element following the operations of previous elements:

```
auto students =
    [ Student(1), Student(2), Student(3), Student(4) ];

foreach (student; students) {
    student.aSlowOperation();
}
```

Normally, a program would be executed on one of the cores of the microprocessor, which has been assigned by the operating system to execute the program. As the foreach loop normally operates on elements one after the other, aSlowOperation() would be called for each student sequentially. However, in many cases it is not necessary for the operations of preceding students to be completed before starting the operations of successive students. If the operations on the Student objects were truly independent, it would be wasteful to ignore the other microprocessor cores, which might potentially be waiting idle on the system.

To simulate long-lasting operations, the following examples call Thread.sleep() from the core.thread module. Thread.sleep() suspends the operations for the specified amount of time. Thread.sleep is admittedly an artifical method to use in the following examples because it takes time without ever busying any core. Despite being an unrealistic tool, it is still useful in this chapter to demonstrate the power of parallelism.

```d
import std.stdio;
import core.thread;

struct Student {
    int number;

    void aSlowOperation() {
        writefln("The work on student %s has begun", number);

        // Wait for a while to simulate a long-lasting operation
        Thread.sleep(1.seconds);

        writefln("The work on student %s has ended", number);
    }
}

void main() {
    auto students =
        [ Student(1), Student(2), Student(3), Student(4) ];

    foreach (student; students) {
        student.aSlowOperation();
    }
}
```

The execution time of the program can be measured in a terminal by time:

```
$ time ./deneme
The work on student 1 has begun
The work on student 1 has ended
The work on student 2 has begun
The work on student 2 has ended
The work on student 3 has begun
The work on student 3 has ended
The work on student 4 has begun
The work on student 4 has ended

real    0m4.005s    ← 4 seconds total
user    0m0.004s
sys     0m0.000s
```

Since the students are iterated over in sequence and since the work of each student takes 1 second, the total execution time comes out to be 4 seconds. However, if these operations were executed in an environment that had 4 cores, they could be operated on at the same time and the total time would be reduced to about 1 second.

Before seeing how this is done, let's first determine the number of cores that are available on the system by std.parallelism.totalCPUs:

```d
import std.stdio;
import std.parallelism;

void main() {
```

```
    writefln("There are %s cores on this system.", totalCPUs);
}
```

The output of the program in the environment that this chapter has been written is the following:

```
There are 4 cores on this system.
```

84.1 taskPool.parallel()

This function can also be called simply as `parallel()`.

`parallel()` accesses the elements of a range in parallel. An effective usage is with `foreach` loops. Merely importing the `std.parallelism` module and replacing `students` with `parallel(students)` in the program above is sufficient to take advantage of all of the cores of the system:

```
import std.parallelism;
// ...
    foreach (student; parallel(students)) {
```

We have seen earlier in the `foreach` for structs and classes chapter (page 491) that the expressions that are in `foreach` blocks are passed to `opApply()` member functions as delegates. `parallel()` returns a range object that knows how to distribute the execution of the delegate to a separate core for each element.

As a result, passing the `Student` range through `parallel()` makes the program above finish in 1 second on a system that has 4 cores:

```
$ time ./deneme
The work on student 2 has begun
The work on student 1 has begun
The work on student 4 has begun
The work on student 3 has begun
The work on student 1 has ended
The work on student 2 has ended
The work on student 4 has ended
The work on student 3 has ended

real    0m1.005s    ← now only 1 second
user    0m0.004s
sys     0m0.004s
```

Note: *The execution time of the program may be different on other systems but it is expected to be roughly "4 seconds divided by the number of cores".*

A flow of execution through certain parts of a program is called a a *thread of execution* or a *thread*. Programs can consist of multiple threads that are being actively executed at the same time. The operating system starts and executes each thread on a core and then suspends it to execute other threads. The execution of each thread may involve many cycles of starting and suspending.

All of the threads of all of the programs that are active at a given time are executed on the very cores of the microprocessor. The operating system decides when and under what condition to start and suspend each thread. That is the reason why the messages that are printed by `aSlowOperation()` are in mixed order in the output above. This undeterministic order of thread execution may not matter if the operations of the `Student` objects are truly independent from each other.

It is the responsibility of the programmer to call `parallel()` only when the operations applied to each element are independent for each iteration. For example, if it were important that the messages appear in a certain order in the output, calling `parallel()` should be considered an error in the program above.

The programming model that supports threads that depend on other threads is called *concurrency*. Concurrency is the topic of the next chapter.

By the time parallel foreach ends, all of the operations inside the loop have been completed for all of the elements. The program can safely continue after the foreach loop.

Work unit size

The second parameter of parallel() has an overloaded meaning and is ignored in some cases:

```
/* ... */ = parallel(range, work_unit_size = 100);
```

- When iterating over RandomAccessRange ranges:

    The distribution of threads to cores has some minimal cost. This cost may sometimes be significant especially when the operations of the loop are completed in a very short time. In such cases, it may be faster to have each thread execute more than one iteration of the loop. The work unit size determines the number of elements that each thread should execute at each of its iterations:

```
foreach (student; parallel(students, 2)) {
    // ...
}
```

    The default value of work unit size is 100 and is suitable for most cases.

- When iterating over non-RandomAccessRange ranges:

    parallel() does not start parallel executions until *work unit size* number of elements of a non-RandomAccessRange have been executed serially first. Due to the relatively high value of 100, parallel() may give the wrong impression that it is not effective when tried on short non-RandomAccessRange ranges.

- When iterating over the result ranges of asyncBuf() or parallel map() (both are explained later in this chapter):

    When parallel() works on the results of asyncBuf() or map(), it ignores the work unit size parameter. Instead, parallel() reuses the internal buffer of the result range.

84.2 Task

Operations that are executed in parallel with other operations of a program are called *tasks*. Tasks are represented by the type std.parallelism.Task.

In fact, parallel() constructs a new Task object for every worker thread and starts that task automatically. parallel() then waits for all of the tasks to be completed before finally exiting the loop. parallel() is very convenient as it *constructs*, *starts*, and *waits for* the tasks automatically.

When tasks do not correspond to or cannot be represented by elements of a range, these three steps can be handled explicitly by the programmer. task() constructs, executeInNewThread() starts, and yieldForce() waits for a task object. These three functions are explained further in the comments of the following program.

The anOperation() function is started twice in the following program. It prints the first letter of id to indicate which task it is working for.

Note: *Normally, the characters that are printed to output streams like stdout do not appear on the output right away. They are instead stored in an output buffer until a* *line of output is completed. Since write does not output a new-line character, in order to observe the parallel execution of the following program, stdout.flush() is called to send the contents of the buffer to stdout even before reaching the end of a line.*

```d
import std.stdio;
import std.parallelism;
import std.array;
import core.thread;

/* Prints the first letter of 'id' every half a second. It
 * arbitrarily returns the value 1 to simulate functions that
 * do calculations. This result will be used later in main. */
int anOperation(string id, int duration) {
    writefln("%s will take %s seconds", id, duration);

    foreach (i; 0 .. (duration * 2)) {
        Thread.sleep(500.msecs);  /* half a second */
        write(id.front);
        stdout.flush();
    }

    return 1;
}

void main() {
    /* Construct a task object that will execute
     * anOperation(). The function parameters that are
     * specified here are passed to the task function as its
     * function parameters. */
    auto theTask = task!anOperation("theTask", 5);

    /* Start the task object */
    theTask.executeInNewThread();

    /* As 'theTask' continues executing, 'anOperation()' is
     * being called again, this time directly in main. */
    immutable result = anOperation("main's call", 3);

    /* At this point we are sure that the operation that has
     * been started directly from within main has been
     * completed, because it has been started by a regular
     * function call, not as a task. */

    /* On the other hand, it is not certain at this point
     * whether 'theTask' has completed its operations
     * yet. yieldForce() waits for the task to complete its
     * operations; it returns only when the task has been
     * completed. Its return value is the return value of
     * the task function, i.e. anOperation(). */
    immutable taskResult = theTask.yieldForce();

    writeln();
    writefln("All finished; the result is %s.",
             result + taskResult);
}
```

The output of the program should be similar to the following. The fact that the m and t letters are printed in mixed order indicates that the operations are executed in parallel:

```
main's call will take 3 seconds
theTask will take 5 seconds
mtmttmmttmmttttt
All finished; the result is 2.
```

The task function above has been specified as a template parameter to task() as task!anOperation. Although this method works well in most cases, as we have seen in the Templates chapter (page 399), each different instantiation of a template is a different type. This distinction may be undesirable in certain situations where seemingly *equivalent* task objects would actually have different types.

For example, although the following two functions have the same signature, the two `Task` instantiations that are produced through calls to the `task()` function template would have different types. As a result, they cannot be members of the same array:

```d
import std.parallelism;

double foo(int i) {
    return i * 1.5;
}

double bar(int i) {
    return i * 2.5;
}

void main() {
    auto tasks = [ task!foo(1),
                   task!bar(2) ];    // ← compilation ERROR
}
```

```
Error: incompatible types for ((task(1)) : (task(2))):
'Task!(foo, int)*' and 'Task!(bar, int)*'
```

Another overload of `task()` takes the function as its first function parameter instead:

```d
    void someFunction(int value) {
        // ...
    }

    auto theTask = task(&someFunction, 42);
```

As this method does not involve different instantiations of the `Task` template, it makes it possible to put such objects in the same array:

```d
import std.parallelism;

double foo(int i) {
    return i * 1.5;
}

double bar(int i) {
    return i * 2.5;
}

void main() {
    auto tasks = [ task(&foo, 1),
                   task(&bar, 2) ];    // ← compiles
}
```

A lambda function or an object of a type that defines the `opCall` member can also be used as the task function. The following example starts a task that executes a lambda:

```d
    auto theTask = task((int value) {
                       /* ... */
                   }, 42);
```

Exceptions

As tasks are executed on separate threads, the exceptions that they throw cannot be caught by the thread that started them. For that reason, the exceptions that are thrown are automatically caught by the tasks themselves, to be rethrown later when `Task` member functions like `yieldForce()` are called. This makes it possible for the main thread to catch exceptions that are thrown by a task.

```d
import std.stdio;
import std.parallelism;
import core.thread;

void mayThrow() {
    writeln("mayThrow() is started");
    Thread.sleep(1.seconds);
    writeln("mayThrow() is throwing an exception");
    throw new Exception("Error message");
}

void main() {
    auto theTask = task!mayThrow();
    theTask.executeInNewThread();

    writeln("main is continuing");
    Thread.sleep(3.seconds);

    writeln("main is waiting for the task");
    theTask.yieldForce();
}
```

The output of the program shows that the uncaught exception that has been thrown by the task does not terminate the entire program right away (it terminates only the task):

```
main is continuing
mayThrow() is started
mayThrow() is throwing an exception          ← thrown
main is waiting for the task
object.Exception@deneme.d(10): Error message ← terminated
```

`yieldForce()` can be called in a `try-catch` block to catch the exceptions that are thrown by the task. Note that this is different from single threads: In single-threaded programs like the samples that we have been writing until this chapter, `try-catch` wraps the code that may throw. In parallelism, it wraps `yieldForce()`:

```d
    try {
        theTask.yieldForce();

    } catch (Exception exc) {
        writefln("Detected an error in the task: '%s'", exc.msg);
    }
```

This time the exception is caught by the main thread instead of terminating the program:

```
main is continuing
mayThrow() is started
mayThrow() is throwing an exception          ← thrown
main is waiting for the task
Detected an error in the task: 'Error message' ← caught
```

Member functions of Task

- done: Specifies whether the task has been completed; rethrows the exception if the task has been terminated with an exception.

```d
    if (theTask.done) {
        writeln("Yes, the task has been completed");

    } else {
```

```
            writeln("No, the task is still going on");
    }
```

- executeInNewThread(): Starts the task in a new thread.
- executeInNewThread(int priority): Starts the task in a new thread with the specified priority. (Priority is an operating system concept that determines execution priorities of threads.)

There are three functions to wait for the completion of a task:

- yieldForce(): Starts the task if it has not been started yet; if it has already been completed, returns its return value; if it is still running, waits for its completion without making the microprocessor busy; if an exception has been thrown, rethrows that exception.
- spinForce(): Works similarly to yieldForce(), except that it makes the microprocessor busy while waiting, in order to catch the completion as early as possible.
- workForce(): Works similarly to yieldForce(), except that it starts a new task in the current thread while waiting for the task to be completed.

In most cases yieldForce() is the most suitable function to call when waiting for a task to complete; it suspends the thread that calls yieldForce() until the task is completed. Although spinForce() makes the microprocessor busy while waiting, it is suitable when the task is expected to be completed in a very short time. workForce() can be called when starting other tasks is preferred over suspending the current thread.

Please see the online documentation of Phobos for the other member functions of Task.

84.3 taskPool.asyncBuf()

Similarly to parallel(), asyncBuf() iterates InputRange ranges in parallel. It stores the elements in a buffer as they are produced by the range, and serves the elements from that buffer to its user.

In order to avoid making a potentially fully-lazy input range a fully-eager range, it iterates the elements in *waves*. Once it prepares certain number of elements in parallel, it waits until those elements are consumed by popFront() before producing the elements of the next wave.

asyncBuf() takes a range and an optional *buffer size* that determines how many elements to be made available during each wave:

```
    auto elements = taskPool.asyncBuf(range, buffer_size);
```

To see the effects of asyncBuf(), let's use a range that takes half a second to iterate and half a second to process each element. This range simply produces integers up to the specified limit:

```
import std.stdio;
import core.thread;

struct Range {
    int limit;
    int i;

    bool empty() const {
        return i >= limit;
    }
```

```
    int front() const {
        return i;
    }

    void popFront() {
        writefln("Producing the element after %s", i);
        Thread.sleep(500.msecs);
        ++i;
    }
}

void main() {
    auto range = Range(10);

    foreach (element; range) {
        writefln("Using element %s", element);
        Thread.sleep(500.msecs);
    }
}
```

The elements are produced and used lazily. Since it takes one second for each element, the whole range takes ten seconds to process in this program:

```
$ time ./deneme
Using element 0
Producing the element after 0
Using element 1
Producing the element after 1
Using element 2
...
Producing the element after 8
Using element 9
Producing the element after 9

real    0m10.007s      ← 10 seconds total
user    0m0.004s
sys     0m0.000s
```

According to that output, the elements are produced and used sequentially.

On the other hand, it may not be necessary to wait for preceding elements to be processed before starting to produce the successive elements. The program would take less time if other elements could be produced while the front element is in use:

```
import std.parallelism;
//...
    foreach (element; taskPool.asyncBuf(range, 2)) {
```

In the call above, `asyncBuf()` makes two elements ready in its buffer. Elements are produced in parallel while they are being used:

```
$ time ./deneme
Producing the element after 0
Producing the element after 1
Using element 0
Producing the element after 2
Using element 1
Producing the element after 3
Using element 2
Producing the element after 4
Using element 3
Producing the element after 5
Using element 4
Producing the element after 6
Producing the element after 7
Using element 5
Using element 6
Producing the element after 8
```

```
Producing the element after 9
Using element 7
Using element 8
Using element 9

real    0m6.007s    ← now 6 seconds
user    0m0.000s
sys     0m0.004s
```

The default value of buffer size is 100. The buffer size that produces the best performance would be different under different situations.

`asyncBuf()` can be used outside of `foreach` loops as well. For example, the following code uses the return value of `asyncBuf()` as an `InputRange` which operates semi-eagerly:

```
    auto range = Range(10);
    auto asyncRange = taskPool.asyncBuf(range, 2);
    writeln(asyncRange.front);
```

84.4 taskPool.map()

It helps to explain `map()` from the `std.algorithm` module before explaining `taskPool.map()`. `std.algorithm.map` is an algorithm commonly found in many functional languages. It calls a function with the elements of a range one-by-one and returns a range that consists of the results of calling that function with each element. It is a lazy algorithm: It calls the function as needed. (There is also `std.algorithm.each`, which is for generating side effects for each element, as opposed to producing a result from it.)

The fact that `std.algorithm.map` operates lazily is very powerful in many programs. However, if the function needs to be called with every element anyway and the operations on each element are independent from each other, laziness may be unnecessarily slower than parallel execution. `taskPool.map()` and `taskPool.amap()` from the `std.parallelism` module take advantage of multiple cores and run faster in many cases.

Let's compare these three algorithms using the `Student` example. Let's assume that `Student` has a member function that returns the average grade of the student. To demonstrate how parallel algorithms are faster, let's again slow this function down with `Thread.sleep()`.

`std.algorithm.map` takes the function as its template parameter, and the range as its function parameter. It returns a range that consists of the results of applying that function to the elements of the range:

```
    auto result_range = map!func(range);
```

The function may be specified by the `=>` syntax as a *lambda expression* as we have seen in earlier chapters. The following program uses `map()` to call the `averageGrade()` member function on each element:

```
import std.stdio;
import std.algorithm;
import core.thread;

struct Student {
    int number;
    int[] grades;

    double averageGrade() {
        writefln("Started working on student %s",
                 number);
        Thread.sleep(1.seconds);
```

```
        const average = grades.sum / grades.length;

        writefln("Finished working on student %s", number);
        return average;
    }
}

void main() {
    Student[] students;

    foreach (i; 0 .. 10) {
        /* Two grades for each student */
        students ~= Student(i, [80 + i, 90 + i]);
    }

    auto results = map!(a => a.averageGrade)(students);

    foreach (result; results) {
        writeln(result);
    }
}
```

The output of the program demonstrates that map() operates lazily; averageGrade() is called for each result as the foreach loop iterates:

```
$ time ./deneme
Started working on student 0
Finished working on student 0
85                         ← calculated as foreach iterates
Started working on student 1
Finished working on student 1
86
...
Started working on student 9
Finished working on student 9
94

real    0m10.006s    ← 10 seconds total
user    0m0.000s
sys     0m0.004s
```

If std.algorithm.map were an eager algorithm, the messages about the starts and finishes of the operations would be printed altogether at the top.

taskPool.map() from the std.parallelism module works essentially the same as std.algorithm.map. The only difference is that it executes the function calls semi-eagerly and stores the results in a buffer to be served from as needed. The size of this buffer is determined by the second parameter. For example, the following code would make ready the results of the function calls for three elements at a time:

```
import std.parallelism;
// ...
double averageGrade(Student student) {
    return student.averageGrade;
}
// ...
    auto results = taskPool.map!averageGrade(students, 3);
```

Note: *The free-standing averageGrade() function above is needed due to a limitation that involves using local delegates with member function templates like TaskPool.map. There would be a compilation error without that free-standing function:*

```
auto results =
    taskPool.map!(a => a.averageGrade)(students, 3);  // ←  compilation ERROR
```

615

This time the operations are executed in waves of three elements:

```
$ time ./deneme
Started working on student 1   ← in parallel
Started working on student 2   ← but in unpredictable order
Started working on student 0
Finished working on student 1
Finished working on student 2
Finished working on student 0
85
86
87
Started working on student 4
Started working on student 5
Started working on student 3
Finished working on student 4
Finished working on student 3
Finished working on student 5
88
89
90
Started working on student 7
Started working on student 8
Started working on student 6
Finished working on student 7
Finished working on student 6
Finished working on student 8
91
92
93
Started working on student 9
Finished working on student 9
94

real    0m4.007s   ← 4 seconds total
user    0m0.000s
sys     0m0.004s
```

The second parameter of map() has the same meaning as asyncBuf(): It determines the size of the buffer that map() uses to store the results in. The third parameter is the work unit size as in parallel(); the difference being its default value, which is size_t.max:

```
/* ... */ = taskPool.map!func(range,
                              buffer_size = 100
                              work_unit_size = size_t.max);
```

84.5 taskPool.amap()

Parallel amap() works the same as parallel map() with two differences:

- It is fully eager.
- It works with RandomAccessRange ranges.

```
auto results = taskPool.amap!averageGrade(students);
```

Since it is eager, all of the results are ready by the time amap() returns:

```
$ time ./deneme
Started working on student 1    ← all are executed up front
Started working on student 0
Started working on student 2
Started working on student 3
Finished working on student 1
Started working on student 4
Finished working on student 2
Finished working on student 3
Started working on student 6
Finished working on student 0
```

```
Started working on student 7
Started working on student 5
Finished working on student 4
Started working on student 8
Finished working on student 6
Started working on student 9
Finished working on student 7
Finished working on student 5
Finished working on student 8
Finished working on student 9
85
86
87
88
89
90
91
92
93
94

real    0m3.005s    ← 3 seconds total
user    0m0.000s
sys     0m0.004s
```

amap() works faster than map() at the expense of using an array that is large
enough to store all of the results. It consumes more memory to gain speed.

The optional second parameter of amap() is the work unit size as well:

```
auto results = taskPool.amap!averageGrade(students, 2);
```

The results can also be stored in a RandomAccessRange that is passed to amap()
as its third parameter:

```
double[] results;
results.length = students.length;
taskPool.amap!averageGrade(students, 2, results);
```

84.6 `taskPool.reduce()`

As with map(), it helps to explain reduce() from the std.algorithm module
first.

reduce() is the equivalent of std.algorithm.fold, which we have seen
before in the Ranges chapter (page 569). The main difference between the two is
that their function parameters are reversed. (For that reason, I recommend that
you prefer fold() for non-parallel code as it can take advantage of UFCS (page
385) in chained range expressions.)

reduce() is another high-level algorithm commonly found in many functional
languages. Just like map(), it takes one or more functions as template parameters.
As its function parameters, it takes a value to be used as the initial value of the
result, and a range. reduce() calls the functions with the current value of the
result and each element of the range. When no initial value is specified, the first
element of the range is used instead.

Assuming that it defines a variable named result in its implementation, the
way that reduce() works can be described by the following steps:

1. Assigns the initial value to result
2. Executes the expression result = func(result, element) for every
   element
3. Returns the final value of result

For example, the sum of the squares of the elements of an array can be calculated as in the following program:

```
import std.stdio;
import std.algorithm;

void main() {
    writeln(reduce!((a, b) => a + b * b)(0, [5, 10]));
}
```

When the function is specified by the => syntax as in the program above, the first parameter (here a) represents the current value of the result (initialized by the parameter 0 above) and the second parameter (here b) represents the current element.

The program outputs the sum of 25 and 100, the squares of 5 and 10:

```
125
```

As obvious from its behavior, reduce() uses a loop in its implementation. Because that loop is normally executed on a single core, it may be unnecessarily slow when the function calls for each element are independent from each other. In such cases taskPool.reduce() from the std.parallelism module can be used for taking advantage of all of the cores.

To see an example of this let's use reduce() with a function that is slowed down again artificially:

```
import std.stdio;
import std.algorithm;
import core.thread;

int aCalculation(int result, int element) {
    writefln("started  - element: %s, result: %s",
             element, result);

    Thread.sleep(1.seconds);
    result += element;

    writefln("finished - element: %s, result: %s",
             element, result);

    return result;
}

void main() {
    writeln("Result: ", reduce!aCalculation(0, [1, 2, 3, 4]));
}
```

reduce() uses the elements in sequence to reach the final value of the result:

```
$ time ./deneme
started  - element: 1, result: 0
finished - element: 1, result: 1
started  - element: 2, result: 1
finished - element: 2, result: 3
started  - element: 3, result: 3
finished - element: 3, result: 6
started  - element: 4, result: 6
finished - element: 4, result: 10
Result: 10

real    0m4.003s    ← 4 seconds total
user    0m0.000s
sys     0m0.000s
```

As in the `parallel()` and `map()` examples, importing the `std.parallelism` module and calling `taskPool.reduce()` is sufficient to take advantage of all of the cores:

```
import std.parallelism;
// ...
    writeln("Result: ", taskPool.reduce!aCalculation(0, [1, 2, 3, 4]));
```

However, there are important differences in the way `taskPool.reduce()` works.

Like the other parallel algorithms, `taskPool.reduce()` executes the functions in parallel by using elements in different tasks. Each task works on the elements that it is assigned to and calculates a `result` that corresponds to the elements of that task. Since `reduce()` is called with only a single initial value, every task must use that same initial value to initialize its own `result` (the parameter 0 above).

The final values of the results that each task produces are themselves used in the same `result` calculation one last time. These final calculations are executed sequentially, not in parallel. For that reason, `taskPool.reduce()` may execute slower in short examples as in this chapter as will be observed in the following output.

The fact that the same initial value is used for all of the tasks, effectively being used in the calculations multiple times, `taskPool.reduce()` may calculate a result that is different from what `std.algorithm.reduce()` calculates. For that reason, the initial value must be the *identity value* for the calculation that is being performed, e.g. the 0 in this example which does not have any effect in addition.

Additionally, as the results are used by the same functions one last time in the sequential calculations, the types of the parameters that the functions take must be compatible with the types of the values that the functions return.

`taskPool.reduce()` should be used only under these considerations.

```
import std.parallelism;
// ...
    writeln("Result: ", taskPool.reduce!aCalculation(0, [1, 2, 3, 4]));
```

The output of the program indicates that first the calculations are performed in parallel, and then their results are calculated sequentially. The calculations that are performed sequentially are highlighted:

```
$ time ./deneme
started  - element: 3, result: 0  ← first, the tasks in parallel
started  - element: 2, result: 0
started  - element: 1, result: 0
started  - element: 4, result: 0
finished - element: 3, result: 3
finished - element: 1, result: 1
started  - element: 1, result: 0  ← then, their results sequentially
finished - element: 4, result: 4
finished - element: 2, result: 2
finished - element: 1, result: 1
started  - element: 2, result: 1
finished - element: 2, result: 3
started  - element: 3, result: 3
finished - element: 3, result: 6
started  - element: 4, result: 6
finished - element: 4, result: 10
Result: 10

real    0m5.006s    ← parallel reduce is slower in this example
user    0m0.004s
sys     0m0.000s
```

Parallel `reduce()` is faster in many other calculations like the calculation of the math constant *pi* (π) by quadrature.

84.7 Multiple functions and tuple results

`std.algorithm.map()`, `taskPool.map()`, `taskPool.amap()`, and `taskPool.reduce()` can all take more than one function, in which case the results are returned as a `Tuple`. We have seen the `Tuple` type in the Tuples chapter (page 513) before. The results of individual functions correspond to the elements of the tuple in the order that the functions are specified. For example, the result of the first function is the first member of the tuple.

The following program demonstrates multiple functions with `std.algorithm.map`. Note that the return types of the functions need not be the same, as seen in the `quarterOf()` and `tenTimes()` functions below. In that case, the types of the members of the tuples would be different as well:

```d
import std.stdio;
import std.algorithm;
import std.conv;

double quarterOf(double value) {
    return value / 4;
}

string tenTimes(double value) {
    return to!string(value * 10);
}

void main() {
    auto values = [10, 42, 100];
    auto results = map!(quarterOf, tenTimes)(values);

    writefln(" Quarters   Ten Times");

    foreach (quarterResult, tenTimesResult; results) {
        writefln("%8.2f%8s", quarterResult, tenTimesResult);
    }
}
```

The output:

```
 Quarters  Ten Times
    2.50        100
   10.50        420
   25.00       1000
```

In the case of `taskPool.reduce()`, the initial values of the results must be specified as a tuple:

```d
    taskPool.reduce!(foo, bar)(tuple(0, 1), [1, 2, 3, 4]);
```

84.8 TaskPool

Behind the scenes, the parallel algorithms from the `std.parallelism` module all use task objects that are elements of a `TaskPool` container. Normally, all of the algorithms use the same container object named `taskPool`.

`taskPool` contains appropriate number of tasks depending on the environment that the program runs under. For that reason, usually there is no need to create any other `TaskPool` object. Even so, explicit `TaskPool` objects may be created and used as needed.

The `TaskPool` constructor takes the number of threads to use during the parallel operations that are later started through it. The default value of the number of threads is one less than the number of cores on the system. All of the features that we have seen in this chapter can be applied to a separate `TaskPool` object.

The following example calls `parallel()` on a local `TaskPool` object:

```d
import std.stdio;
import std.parallelism;

void main() {
    auto workers = new TaskPool(2);

    foreach (i; workers.parallel([1, 2, 3, 4])) {
        writeln("Working on %s", i);
    }

    workers.finish();
}
```

`TaskPool.finish()` tells the object to stop processing when all of its current tasks are completed.

84.9 Summary

- It is an error to execute operations in parallel unless those operations are independent from each other.
- `parallel()` accesses the elements of a range in parallel.
- Tasks can explicitly be created, started, and waited for by `task()`, `executeInNewThread()`, and `yieldForce()`, respectively.
- The exceptions that are escaped from tasks can be caught later by most of the parallelism functions like `yieldForce()`.
- `asyncBuf()` iterates the elements of an `InputRange` semi-eagerly in parallel.
- `map()` calls functions with the elements of an `InputRange` semi-eagerly in parallel.
- `amap()` calls functions with the elements of a `RandomAccessRange` fully-eagerly in parallel.
- `reduce()` makes calculations over the elements of a `RandomAccessRange` in parallel.
- `map()`, `amap()`, and `reduce()` can take multiple functions and return the results as tuples.
- When needed, `TaskPool` objects other than `taskPool` can be used.

85 Message Passing Concurrency

Concurrency is similar to but different from the topic of the previous chapter, parallelism. As these two concepts both involve executing programs on threads, and as parallelism is based on concurrency, they are sometimes confused with each other.

The following are the differences between parallelism and concurrency:

- The main purpose of parallelism is to take advantage of microprocessor cores to improve the performance of programs. Concurrency on the other hand, is a concept that may be needed even on a single-core environment. Concurrency is about making a program run on more than one thread at a time. An example of a concurrent program would be a server program that is responding to requests of more than one client at the same time.

- In parallelism, tasks are independent from each other. In fact, it would be a bug if they did depend on results of other tasks that are running at the same time. In concurrency, it is normal for threads to depend on results of other threads.

- Although both programming models use operating system threads, in parallelism threads are encapsulated by the concept of task. Concurrency makes use of threads explicitly.

- Parallelism is easy to use, and as long as tasks are independent it is easy to produce programs that work correctly. Concurrency is easy only when it is based on *message passing*. It is very difficult to write correct concurrent programs if they are based on the traditional model of concurrency that involves lock-based data sharing.

D supports both models of concurrency: message passing and data sharing. We will cover message passing in this chapter and data sharing in the next chapter.

85.1 Concepts

Thread: Operating systems execute programs as work units called *threads*. D programs start executing with main() on a thread that has been assigned to that program by the operating system. All of the operations of the program are normally executed on that thread. The program is free to start other threads to be able to work on multiple tasks at the same time. In fact, tasks that have been covered in the previous chapter are based on threads that are started automatically by std.parallelism.

The operating system can pause threads at unpredictable times for unpredictable durations. As a result, even operations as simple as incrementing a variable may be paused mid operation:

```
++i;
```

The operation above involves three steps: Reading the value of the variable, incrementing the value, and assigning the new value back to the variable. The thread may be paused at any point between these steps to be continued after an unpredictable time.

Message: Data that is passed between threads are called messages. Messages may be composed of any type and any number of variables.

Thread identifier: Every thread has an id, which is used for specifying recipients of messages.

Owner: Any thread that starts another thread is called the owner of the new thread.

Worker: Any thread that is started by an owner is called a worker.

85.2 Starting threads

spawn() takes a function pointer as a parameter and starts a new thread from that function. Any operations that are carried out by that function, including other functions that it may call, would be executed on the new thread. The main difference between a thread that is started with spawn() and a thread that is started with task() (page 605) is the fact that spawn() makes it possible for threads to send messages to each other.

As soon as a new thread is started, the owner and the worker start executing separately as if they were independent programs:

```d
import std.stdio;
import std.concurrency;
import core.thread;

void worker() {
    foreach (i; 0 .. 5) {
        Thread.sleep(500.msecs);
        writeln(i, " (worker)");
    }
}

void main() {
    spawn(&worker);

    foreach (i; 0 .. 5) {
        Thread.sleep(300.msecs);
        writeln(i, " (main)");
    }

    writeln("main is done.");
}
```

The examples in this chapter call Thread.sleep to slow down threads to demonstrate that they run at the same time. The output of the program shows that the two threads, one that runs main() and the other that has been started by spawn(), execute independently at the same time:

```
0 (main)
0 (worker)
1 (main)
2 (main)
1 (worker)
3 (main)
2 (worker)
4 (main)
main is done.
3 (worker)
4 (worker)
```

The program automatically waits for all of the threads to finish executing. We can see this in the output above by the fact that worker() continues executing even after main() exits after printing "main is done."

The parameters that the thread function takes are passed to spawn() as its second and later arguments. The two worker threads in the following program print four numbers each. They take the starting number as the thread function parameter:

```d
import std.stdio;
import std.concurrency;
```

```
import core.thread;

void worker(int firstNumber) {
    foreach (i; 0 .. 4) {
        Thread.sleep(500.msecs);
        writeln(firstNumber + i);
    }
}

void main() {
    foreach (i; 1 .. 3) {
        spawn(&worker, i * 10);
    }
}
```

The output of one of the threads is highlighted:

```
10
20
11
21
12
22
13
23
```

The lines of the output may be different at different times depending on how the threads are paused and resumed by the operating system.

Every operating system puts limits on the number of threads that can exist at one time. These limits can be set for each user, for the whole system, or for something else. The overall performance of the system can be reduced if there are more threads that are busily working than the number of cores in the system. A thread that is busily working at a given time is said to be *CPU bound* at that point in time. On the other hand, some threads spend considerable amount of their time waiting for some event to occur like input from a user, data from a network connection, the completion of a Thread.sleep call, etc. Such threads are said to be *I/O bound* at those times. If the majority of its threads are I/O bound, then a program can afford to start more threads than the number of cores without any degradation of performance. As it should be in every design decision that concerns program performance, one must take actual measurements to be exactly sure whether that really is the case.

85.3 Thread identifiers

thisTid() returns the identifier of the *current* thread. It is commonly called without the function parentheses:

```
import std.stdio;
import std.concurrency;

void printTid(string tag) {
    writefln("%s: %s", tag, thisTid);
}

void worker() {
    printTid("Worker");
}

void main() {
    spawn(&worker);
    printTid("Owner ");
}
```

The return type of thisTid() is Tid, which has no significance for the program. Even its toString() function is not overloaded:

```
Owner : Tid(std.concurrency.MessageBox)
Worker: Tid(std.concurrency.MessageBox)
```

The return value of spawn(), which I have been ignoring until this point, is the id of the worker thread:

```
Tid myWorker = spawn(&worker);
```

Conversely, the owner of a worker thread is obtained by the ownerTid() function.

In summary, the owner is identified by ownerTid and the worker is identified by the return value of spawn().

85.4 Message Passing

send() sends messages and receiveOnly() waits for a message of a particular type. (There is also prioritySend(), receive(), and receiveTimeout(), which will be explained later below.)

The owner in the following program sends its worker a message of type int and waits for a message from the worker of type double. The threads continue sending messages back and forth until the owner sends a negative int. This is the owner thread:

```
void main() {
    Tid worker = spawn(&workerFunc);

    foreach (value; 1 .. 5) {
        worker.send(value);
        double result = receiveOnly!double();
        writefln("sent: %s, received: %s", value, result);
    }

    /* Sending a negative value to the worker so that it
     * terminates. */
    worker.send(-1);
}
```

main() stores the return value of spawn() under the name worker and uses that variable when sending messages to the worker.

On the other side, the worker receives the message that it needs as an int, uses that value in a calculation, and sends the result as type double to its owner:

```
void workerFunc() {
    int value = 0;

    while (value >= 0) {
        value = receiveOnly!int();
        double result = to!double(value) / 5;
        ownerTid.send(result);
    }
}
```

The main thread reports the messages that it sends and the messages that it receives:

```
sent: 1, received: 0.2
sent: 2, received: 0.4
sent: 3, received: 0.6
sent: 4, received: 0.8
```

It is possible to send more than one value as a part of the same message. The following message consists of three parts:

```
ownerTid.send(thisTid, 42, 1.5);
```

Values that are passed as parts of a single message appear as a tuple on the receiver's side. In such cases the template parameters of receiveOnly() must match the types of the tuple members:

```
/* Wait for a message composed of Tid, int, and double. */
auto message = receiveOnly!(Tid, int, double)();

auto sender   = message[0];    // of type Tid
auto integer  = message[1];    // of type int
auto floating = message[2];    // of type double
```

If the types do not match, a MessageMismatch exception is thrown:

```
import std.concurrency;

void workerFunc() {
    ownerTid.send("hello");    // ← Sending string
}

void main() {
    spawn(&workerFunc);

    auto message = receiveOnly!double();    // ← Expecting double
}
```

The output:

```
std.concurrency.MessageMismatch@std/concurrency.d(235):
Unexpected message type: expected 'double', got 'immutable(char)[]'
```

The exceptions that the worker may throw cannot be caught by the owner. One solution is to have the worker catch the exception to be sent as a message. We will see this below.

Example

Let's use what we have seen so far in a simulation program.

The following program simulates independent robots moving around randomly in a two dimensional space. The movement of each robot is handled by a separate thread that takes three pieces of information when started:

- The number (id) of the robot: This information is sent back to the owner to identify the robot that the message is related to.
- The origin: This is where the robot starts moving from.
- The duration between each step: This information is used for determining when the robot's next step will be.

That information can be stored in the following Job struct:

```
struct Job {
    size_t robotId;
    Position origin;
    Duration restDuration;
}
```

The thread function that moves each robot sends the id of the robot and its movement to the owner thread continuously:

```
void robotMover(Job job) {
    Position from = job.origin;

    while (true) {
        Thread.sleep(job.restDuration);
```

```
        Position to = randomNeighbor(from);
        Movement movement = Movement(from, to);
        from = to;

        ownerTid.send(MovementMessage(job.robotId, movement));
    }
}
```

The owner simply waits for these messages in an unconditional loop. It identifies
the robots by the robot ids that are sent as parts of the messages. The owner
simply prints every movement:

```
    while (true) {
        auto message = receiveOnly!MovementMessage();

        writefln("%s %s",
                 robots[message.robotId], message.movement);
    }
```

All of the messages in this simple program go from the worker to the owner.
Message passing normally involves more complicated communication in many
kinds of programs.

Here is the complete program:

```
import std.stdio;
import std.random;
import std.string;
import std.concurrency;
import core.thread;

struct Position {
    int line;
    int column;

    string toString() {
        return format("%s,%s", line, column);
    }
}

struct Movement {
    Position from;
    Position to;

    string toString() {
        return ((from == to)
                ? format("%s (idle)", from)
                : format("%s -> %s", from, to));
    }
}

class Robot {
    string image;
    Duration restDuration;

    this(string image, Duration restDuration) {
        this.image = image;
        this.restDuration = restDuration;
    }

    override string toString() {
        return format("%s(%s)", image, restDuration);
    }
}

/* Returns a random position around 0,0. */
Position randomPosition() {
    return Position(uniform!"[]"(-10, 10),
                    uniform!"[]"(-10, 10));
}
```

```
/* Returns at most one step from the specified coordinate. */
int randomStep(int current) {
    return current + uniform!"[]"(-1, 1);
}

/* Returns a neighbor of the specified Position. It may be one
 * of the neighbors at eight directions, or the specified
 * position itself. */
Position randomNeighbor(Position position) {
    return Position(randomStep(position.line),
                    randomStep(position.column));
}

struct Job {
    size_t robotId;
    Position origin;
    Duration restDuration;
}

struct MovementMessage {
    size_t robotId;
    Movement movement;
}

void robotMover(Job job) {
    Position from = job.origin;

    while (true) {
        Thread.sleep(job.restDuration);

        Position to = randomNeighbor(from);
        Movement movement = Movement(from, to);
        from = to;

        ownerTid.send(MovementMessage(job.robotId, movement));
    }
}

void main() {
    /* Robots with various restDurations. */
    Robot[] robots = [ new Robot("A",  600.msecs),
                       new Robot("B", 2000.msecs),
                       new Robot("C", 5000.msecs) ];

    /* Start a mover thread for each robot. */
    foreach (robotId, robot; robots) {
        spawn(&robotMover, Job(robotId,
                               randomPosition(),
                               robot.restDuration));
    }

    /* Ready to collect information about the movements of the
     * robots. */
    while (true) {
        auto message = receiveOnly!MovementMessage();

        /* Print the movement of this robot. */
        writefln("%s %s",
                 robots[message.robotId], message.movement);
    }
}
```

The program prints every movement until terminated:

```
A(600 ms) 6,2 -> 7,3
A(600 ms) 7,3 -> 8,3
A(600 ms) 8,3 -> 7,3
B(2 secs) -7,-4 -> -6,-3
A(600 ms) 7,3 -> 6,2
A(600 ms) 6,2 -> 7,1
A(600 ms) 7,1 (idle)
B(2 secs) -6,-3 (idle)
A(600 ms) 7,1 -> 7,2
```

```
A(600 ms) 7,2 -> 7,3
C(5 secs) -4,-4 -> -3,-5
A(600 ms) 7,3 -> 6,4
...
```

This program demonstrates how helpful message passing concurrency can be: Movements of robots are calculated independently by separate threads without knowledge of each other. It is the owner thread that *serializes* the printing process simply by receiving messages from its message box one by one.

85.5 Expecting different types of messages

receiveOnly() can expect only one type of message. receive() on the other hand can wait for more than one type of message. It dispatches messages to message handling delegates. When a message arrives, it is compared to the message type of each delegate. The delegate that matches the type of the particular message handles it.

For example, the following receive() call specifies two message handlers that handle messages of types int and string, respectively:

```
void workerFunc() {
    bool isDone = false;

    while (!isDone) {
        void intHandler(int message) {
            writeln("handling int message: ", message);

            if (message == -1) {
                writeln("exiting");
                isDone = true;
            }
        }

        void stringHandler(string message) {
            writeln("handling string message: ", message);
        }

        receive(&intHandler, &stringHandler);
    }
}
```

Messages of type int would match intHandler() and messages of type string would match stringHandler(). The worker thread above can be tested by the following program:

```
import std.stdio;
import std.concurrency;

// ...

void main() {
    auto worker = spawn(&workerFunc);

    worker.send(10);
    worker.send(42);
    worker.send("hello");
    worker.send(-1);            // ← to terminate the worker
}
```

The output of the program indicates that the messages are handled by matching functions on the receiver's side:

```
handling int message: 10
handling int message: 42
handling string message: hello
```

```
handling int message: -1
exiting
```

Lambda functions and objects of types that define the opCall() member function can also be passed to receive() as message handlers. The following worker handles messages by lambda functions. The following program also defines a special type named Exit used for communicating to the thread that it is time for it to exit. Using such a specific type is more expressive than sending the arbitrary value of -1 like it was done in the previous example.

There are three anonymous functions below that are passed to receive() as message handlers. Their curly brackets are highlighted:

```d
import std.stdio;
import std.concurrency;

struct Exit {
}

void workerFunc() {
    bool isDone = false;

    while (!isDone) {
        receive(
            (int message) {
                writeln("int message: ", message);
            },

            (string message) {
                writeln("string message: ", message);
            },

            (Exit message) {
                writeln("exiting");
                isDone = true;
            });
    }
}

void main() {
    auto worker = spawn(&workerFunc);

    worker.send(10);
    worker.send(42);
    worker.send("hello");
    worker.send(Exit());
}
```

Receiving any type of message

std.variant.Variant is a type that can encapsulate any type of data. Messages that do not match the handlers that are specified earlier in the argument list always match a Variant handler:

```d
import std.stdio;
import std.concurrency;

void workerFunc() {
    receive(
        (int message) { /* ... */ },

        (double message) { /* ... */ },

        (Variant message) {
            writeln("Unexpected message: ", message);
        });
}

struct SpecialMessage {
```

```
    // ...
}
void main() {
    auto worker = spawn(&workerFunc);
    worker.send(SpecialMessage());
}
```

The output:

```
Unexpected message: SpecialMessage()
```

The details of `Variant` are outside of the scope of this chapter.

85.6 Waiting for messages up to a certain time

It may not make sense to wait for messages beyond a certain time. The sender may have been busy temporarily or may have terminated with an exception. `receiveTimeout()` prevents blocking the receiving thread indefinitely.

The first parameter of `receiveTimeout()` determines how long the message should be waited for. Its return value is `true` if a message has been received within that time, `false` otherwise.

```
import std.stdio;
import std.concurrency;
import core.thread;

void workerFunc() {
    Thread.sleep(3.seconds);
    ownerTid.send("hello");
}

void main() {
    spawn(&workerFunc);

    writeln("Waiting for a message");
    bool received = false;
    while (!received) {
        received = receiveTimeout(600.msecs,
                                  (string message) {
                                      writeln("received: ", message);
                                  });

        if (!received) {
            writeln("... no message yet");

            /* ... other operations may be executed here ... */
        }
    }
}
```

The owner above waits for a message for up to 600 milliseconds. It can continue working on other things if a message does not arrive within that time:

```
Waiting for a message
... no message yet
... no message yet
... no message yet
... no message yet
received: hello
```

85.7 Exceptions during the execution of the worker

As we have seen in the previous chapter, the facilities of the `std.parallelism` module automatically catch exceptions that have been thrown during the execution of tasks and rethrow them in the context of the owner. This allows the owner to catch such exceptions:

```
    try {
        theTask.yieldForce();

    } catch (Exception exc) {
        writefln("Detected an error in the task: '%s'",
                exc.msg);
    }
```

`std.concurrency` does not provide such a convenience for general exception types. However, the exceptions can be caught and sent explicitly by the worker. As we will see below, it is also possible to receive `OwnerTerminated` and `LinkTerminated` exceptions as messages.

The `calculate()` function below receives `string` messages, converts them to `double`, adds 0.5, and sends the result back as a message:

```
void calculate() {
    while (true) {
        auto message = receiveOnly!string();
        ownerTid.send(to!double(message) + 0.5);
    }
}
```

The `to!double()` call above would throw an exception if the string cannot be converted to a `double` value. Because such an exception would terminate the worker thread right away, the owner in the following program can receive a response only for the first message:

```
import std.stdio;
import std.concurrency;
import std.conv;

// ...

void main() {
    Tid calculator = spawn(&calculate);

    calculator.send("1.2");
    calculator.send("hello");  // ← incorrect input
    calculator.send("3.4");

    foreach (i; 0 .. 3) {
        auto message = receiveOnly!double();
        writefln("result %s: %s", i, message);
    }
}
```

The owner receives the response for "1.2" as 1.7 but because the worker has been terminated, the owner would be blocked waiting for a message that would never arrive:

```
result 0: 1.7
                ← waiting for a message that will never arrive
```

One thing that the worker can do is to catch the exception explicitly and to send it as a special error message. The following program sends the reason of the failure as a `CalculationFailure` message. Additionally, this program takes advantage of a special message type to signal to the worker when it is time to exit:

```
import std.stdio;
import std.concurrency;
import std.conv;

struct CalculationFailure {
    string reason;
}
```

```
struct Exit {
}

void calculate() {
    bool isDone = false;

    while (!isDone) {
        receive(
            (string message) {
                try {
                    ownerTid.send(to!double(message) + 0.5);

                } catch (Exception exc) {
                    ownerTid.send(CalculationFailure(exc.msg));
                }
            },

            (Exit message) {
                isDone = true;
            });
    }
}

void main() {
    Tid calculator = spawn(&calculate);

    calculator.send("1.2");
    calculator.send("hello");   // ← incorrect input
    calculator.send("3.4");
    calculator.send(Exit());

    foreach (i; 0 .. 3) {
        writef("result %s: ", i);

        receive(
            (double message) {
                writeln(message);
            },

            (CalculationFailure message) {
                writefln("ERROR! '%s'", message.reason);
            });
    }
}
```

This time the reason of the failure is printed by the owner:

```
result 0: 1.7
result 1: ERROR! 'no digits seen'
result 2: 3.9
```

Another method would be to send the actual exception object itself to the owner.
The owner can use the exception object or simply rethrow it:

```
// ... at the worker ...
                try {
                    // ...

                } catch (shared(Exception) exc) {
                    ownerTid.send(exc);
                }},

// ... at the owner ...
        receive(
            // ...

            (shared(Exception) exc) {
                throw exc;
            });
```

The reason why the shared specifiers are necessary is explained in the next chapter.

85.8 Detecting thread termination

Threads can detect that the receiver of a message has terminated.

OwnerTerminated exception

This exception is thrown when receiving a message from the owner if the owner has been terminated. The intermediate owner thread below simply exits after sending two messages to its worker. This causes an OwnerTerminated exception to be thrown at the worker thread:

```
import std.stdio;
import std.concurrency;

void main() {
    spawn(&intermediaryFunc);
}

void intermediaryFunc() {
    auto worker = spawn(&workerFunc);
    worker.send(1);
    worker.send(2);
} // ← Terminates after sending two messages

void workerFunc() {
    while (true) {
        auto m = receiveOnly!int(); // ← An exception is
                                    //   thrown if the owner
                                    //   has terminated.
        writeln("Message: ", m);
    }
}
```

The output:

```
Message: 1
Message: 2
std.concurrency.OwnerTerminated@std/concurrency.d(248):
Owner terminated
```

The worker can catch that exception to exit gracefully:

```
void workerFunc() {
    bool isDone = false;

    while (!isDone) {
        try {
            auto m = receiveOnly!int();
            writeln("Message: ", m);

        } catch (OwnerTerminated exc) {
            writeln("The owner has terminated.");
            isDone = true;
        }
    }
}
```

The output:

```
Message: 1
Message: 2
The owner has terminated.
```

We will see below that this exception can be received as a message as well.

LinkTerminated exception

spawnLinked() is used in the same way as spawn(). When a worker that has been started by spawnLinked() terminates, a LinkTerminated exception is thrown at the owner:

```d
import std.stdio;
import std.concurrency;

void main() {
    auto worker = spawnLinked(&workerFunc);

    while (true) {
        auto m = receiveOnly!int(); // ← An exception is
                                    //   thrown if the worker
                                    //   has terminated.
        writeln("Message: ", m);
    }
}

void workerFunc() {
    ownerTid.send(10);
    ownerTid.send(20);
} // ← Terminates after sending two messages
```

The worker above terminates after sending two messages. Since the worker has been started by spawnLinked(), the owner is notified of the worker's termination by a LinkTerminated exception:

```
Message: 10
Message: 20
std.concurrency.LinkTerminated@std/concurrency.d(263):
Link terminated
```

The owner can catch the exception to do something special like terminating gracefully:

```d
    bool isDone = false;

    while (!isDone) {
        try {
            auto m = receiveOnly!int();
            writeln("Message: ", m);

        } catch (LinkTerminated exc) {
            writeln("The worker has terminated.");
            isDone = true;
        }
    }
```

The output:

```
Message: 10
Message: 20
The worker has terminated.
```

This exception can be received as a message as well.

Receiving exceptions as messages

The OwnerTerminated and LinkTerminated exceptions can be received as messages as well. The following code demonstrates this for the OwnerTerminated exception:

```d
    bool isDone = false;

    while (!isDone) {
        receive(
```

```
            (int message) {
                writeln("Message: ", message);
            },

            (OwnerTerminated exc) {
                writeln("The owner has terminated; exiting.");
                isDone = true;
            }
        );
    }
```

85.9 Mailbox management

Every thread has a private mailbox that holds the messages that are sent to that thread. The number of messages in a mailbox may increase or decrease depending on how long it takes for the thread to receive and respond to each message. A continuously growing mailbox puts stress on the entire system and may point to a design flaw in the program. It may also mean that the thread may never get to the most recent messages.

setMaxMailboxSize() is used for limiting the number of messages that a mailbox can hold. Its three parameters specify the mailbox, the maximum number of messages that it can hold, and what should happen when the mailbox is full, in that order. There are four choices for the last parameter:

- OnCrowding.block: The sender waits until there is room in the mailbox.
- OnCrowding.ignore: The message is discarded.
- OnCrowding.throwException: A MailboxFull exception is thrown when sending the message.
- A function pointer of type bool function(Tid): The specified function is called.

Before seeing an example of setMaxMailboxSize(), let's first cause a mailbox to grow continuously. The worker in the following program sends messages back to back but the owner spends some time for each message:

```
/* WARNING: Your system may become unresponsive when this
 *          program is running. */
import std.concurrency;
import core.thread;

void workerFunc() {
    while (true) {
        ownerTid.send(42);     // ← Produces messages continuously
    }
}

void main() {
    spawn(&workerFunc);

    while (true) {
        receive(
            (int message) {
                // Spends time for each message
                Thread.sleep(1.seconds);
            });
    }
}
```

Because the consumer is slower than the producer, the memory that the program above uses would grow continuously. To prevent that, the owner may limit the size of its mailbox before starting the worker:

```
void main() {
    setMaxMailboxSize(thisTid, 1000, OnCrowding.block);

    spawn(&workerFunc);
// ...
}
```

The setMaxMailboxSize() call above sets the main thread's mailbox size to 1000. OnCrowding.block causes the sender to wait until there is room in the mailbox.

The following example uses OnCrowding.throwException, which causes a MailboxFull exception to be thrown when sending a message to a mailbox that is full:

```
import std.concurrency;
import core.thread;

void workerFunc() {
    while (true) {
        try {
            ownerTid.send(42);

        } catch (MailboxFull exc) {
            /* Failed to send; will try again later. */
            Thread.sleep(1.msecs);
        }
    }
}

void main() {
    setMaxMailboxSize(thisTid, 1000, OnCrowding.throwException);

    spawn(&workerFunc);

    while (true) {
        receive(
            (int message) {
                Thread.sleep(1.seconds);
            });
    }
}
```

85.10 Priority messages

Messages can be sent with higher priority than regular messages by prioritySend(). These messages are handled before the other messages that are already in the mailbox:

```
    prioritySend(ownerTid, ImportantMessage(100));
```

If the receiver does not have a message handler that matches the type of the priority message, then a PriorityMessageException is thrown:

```
std.concurrency.PriorityMessageException@std/concurrency.d(280):
Priority message
```

85.11 Thread names

In the simple programs that we have used above, it was easy to pass the thread ids of owners and workers. Passing thread ids from thread to thread may be overly complicated in programs that use more than a couple of threads. To reduce this complexity, it is possible to assign names to threads, which are globally accessible from any thread.

The following three functions define an interface to an associative array that every thread has access to:

- `register()`: Associates a thread with a name.
- `locate()`: Returns the thread that is associated with the specified name. If there is no thread associated with that name, then `Tid.init` is returned.
- `unregister()`: Breaks the association between the specified name and the thread.

The following program starts two threads that find each other by their names. These threads continuously send messages to each other until instructed to terminate by an `Exit` message:

```d
import std.stdio;
import std.concurrency;
import core.thread;

struct Exit {
}

void main() {
    // A thread whose partner is named "second"
    auto first = spawn(&player, "second");
    register("first", first);
    scope(exit) unregister("first");

    // A thread whose partner is named "first"
    auto second = spawn(&player, "first");
    register("second", second);
    scope(exit) unregister("second");

    Thread.sleep(2.seconds);

    prioritySend(first, Exit());
    prioritySend(second, Exit());

    // For the unregister() calls to succeed, main() must wait
    // until the workers terminate.
    thread_joinAll();
}

void player(string nameOfPartner) {
    Tid partner;

    while (partner == Tid.init) {
        Thread.sleep(1.msecs);
        partner = locate(nameOfPartner);
    }

    bool isDone = false;

    while (!isDone) {
        partner.send("hello " ~ nameOfPartner);
        receive(
            (string message) {
                writeln("Message: ", message);
                Thread.sleep(500.msecs);
            },

            (Exit message) {
                writefln("%s, I am exiting.", nameOfPartner);
                isDone = true;
            });
    }
}
```

The `thread_joinAll()` call that is seen at the end of `main()` is for making the owner to wait for all of its workers to terminate.

The output:

```
Message: hello second
Message: hello first
Message: hello second
Message: hello first
Message: hello first
Message: hello second
Message: hello first
Message: hello second
second, I am exiting.
first, I am exiting.
```

85.12 Summary

- When threads do not depend on other threads, prefer *parallelism*, which has been the topic of the previous chapter. Consider *concurrency* only when threads depend on operations of other threads.
- Because concurrency by data sharing is hard to implement correctly, prefer concurrency by message passing, which is the subject of this chapter.
- spawn() and spawnLinked() start threads.
- thisTid is the thread id of the current thread.
- ownerTid is the thread id of the owner of the current thread.
- send() and prioritySend() send messages.
- receiveOnly(), receive(), and receiveTimeout() wait for messages.
- Variant matches any type of message.
- setMaxMailboxSize() limits the size of mailboxes.
- register(), unregister(), and locate() allow referring to threads by name.
- Exceptions may be thrown during message passing: MessageMismatch, OwnerTerminated, LinkTerminated, MailboxFull, and PriorityMessageException.
- The owner cannot automatically catch exceptions that are thrown from the worker.

The previous chapter was about threads sharing information through message passing. As it has been mentioned in that chapter, message passing is a safe method of concurrency.

Another method involves more than one thread reading from and writing to the same data. For example, the owner thread can start the worker with the address of a bool variable and the worker can determine whether to terminate or not by reading the current value of that variable. Another example would be where the owner starts multiple workers with the address of the same variable so that the variable gets modified by more than one worker.

One of the reasons why data sharing is not safe is *race conditions*. A race condition occurs when more than one thread accesses the same mutable data in an uncontrolled order. Since the operating system pauses and starts individual threads in unspecified ways, the behavior of a program that has race conditions is unpredictable.

The examples in this chapter may look simplistic. However, the issues that they convey appear in real programs at greater scales. Also, although these examples use the std.concurrency module, the concepts of this chapter apply to the core.thread module as well.

86.1 Sharing is not automatic

Unlike most other programming languages, data is not automatically shared in D; data is thread-local by default. Although module-level variables may give the impression of being accessible by all threads, each thread actually gets its own copy:

```d
import std.stdio;
import std.concurrency;
import core.thread;

int variable;

void printInfo(string message) {
    writefln("%s: %s (@%s)", message, variable, &variable);
}

void worker() {
    variable = 42;
    printInfo("Before the worker is terminated");
}

void main() {
    spawn(&worker);
    thread_joinAll();
    printInfo("After the worker is terminated");
}
```

variable that is modified inside worker() is not the same variable that is seen by main(). This fact can be observed by printing both the values and the addresses of the variables:

```
Before the worker is terminated: 42 (@7F26C6711670)
After the worker is terminated: 0 (@7F26C68127D0)
```

Since each thread gets its own copy of data, spawn() does not allow passing references to thread-local variables. For example, the following program that tries to pass the address of a bool variable to another thread cannot be compiled:

```
import std.concurrency;

void worker(bool * isDone) {
    while (!(*isDone)) {
        // ...
    }
}

void main() {
    bool isDone = false;
    spawn(&worker, &isDone);        // ← compilation ERROR

    // ...

    // Hoping to signal the worker to terminate:
    isDone = true;

    // ...
}
```

A `static assert` inside the `std.concurrency` module prevents accessing *mutable* data from another thread:

```
src/phobos/std/concurrency.d(329): Error: static assert
"Aliases to mutable thread-local data not allowed."
```

The address of the mutable variable `isDone` cannot be passed between threads.

An exception to this rule is a variable that is defined as `__gshared`:

```
__gshared int globallyShared;
```

There is only one copy of such a variable in the entire program and all threads can share that variable. `__gshared` is necessary when interacting with libraries of languages like C and C++ where data sharing is automatic by default.

86.2 shared to share mutable data between threads

Mutable variables that need to be shared must be defined with the `shared` keyword:

```
import std.concurrency;

void worker(shared(bool) * isDone) {
    while (*isDone) {
        // ...
    }
}

void main() {
    shared(bool) isDone = false;
    spawn(&worker, &isDone);

    // ...

    // Signalling the worker to terminate:
    isDone = true;

    // ...
}
```

Note: Prefer message-passing to signal a thread.

On the other hand, since `immutable` variables cannot be modified, there is no problem with sharing them directly. For that reason, `immutable` implies `shared`:

```
import std.stdio;
import std.concurrency;
import core.thread;
```

```
void worker(immutable(int) * data) {
    writeln("data: ", *data);
}

void main() {
    immutable(int) i = 42;
    spawn(&worker, &i);          // ← compiles

    thread_joinAll();
}
```

The output:

```
data: 42
```

Note that since the lifetime of i is defined by the scope of main(), it is important that main() does not terminate before the worker thread. The call to core.thread.thread_joinAll above is to make a thread wait for all of its child threads to terminate.

86.3 A race condition example

The correctness of the program requires extra attention when mutable data is shared between threads.

To see an example of a race condition let's consider multiple threads sharing the same mutable variable. The threads in the following program receive the addresses as two variables and swap their values a large number of times:

```
import std.stdio;
import std.concurrency;
import core.thread;

void swapper(shared(int) * first, shared(int) * second) {
    foreach (i; 0 .. 10_000) {
        int temp = *second;
        *second = *first;
        *first = temp;
    }
}

void main() {
    shared(int) i = 1;
    shared(int) j = 2;

    writefln("before: %s and %s", i, j);

    foreach (id; 0 .. 10) {
        spawn(&swapper, &i, &j);
    }

    // Wait for all threads to finish their tasks
    thread_joinAll();

    writefln("after : %s and %s", i, j);
}
```

Although the program above gets compiled successfully, in most cases it would work incorrectly. Observe that it starts ten threads that all access the same two variables i and j. As a result of the *race conditions* that they are in, they inadvertently spoil the operations of other threads.

Also observe that total number of swaps is 10 times 10 thousand. Since that amount is an even number, it is natural to expect that the variables end up having values 1 and 2, their initial values:

```
before: 1 and 2
after : 1 and 2    ← expected result
```

Although it is possible that the program can indeed produce that result, most of the time the actual outcome would be one of the following:

```
before: 1 and 2
after : 1 and 1    ← incorrect result
```

```
before: 1 and 2
after : 2 and 2    ← incorrect result
```

It is possible but highly unlikely that the result may even end up being "2 and 1" as well.

The reason why the program works incorrectly can be explained by the following scenario between just two threads that are in a race condition. As the operating system pauses and restarts the threads at indeterminate times, the following order of execution of the operations of the two threads is likely as well.

Let's consider the state where i is 1 and j is 2. Although the two threads execute the same swapper() function, remember that the local variable temp is separate for each thread and it is independent from the other temp variables of other threads. To identify those separate variables, they are renamed as tempA and tempB below.

The chart below demonstrates how the 3-line code inside the for loop may be executed by each thread over time, from top to bottom, operation 1 being the first operation and operation 6 being the last operation. Whether i or j is modified at each step is indicated by highlighting that variable:

```
Operation        Thread A                                  Thread B
────────────────────────────────────────────────────────────────────────────

  1:    int temp = *second; (tempA==2)
  2:    *second = *first;   (i==1, j==1)

        (Assume that A is paused and B is started at this point)

  3:                                            int temp = *second; (tempB==1)
  4:                                            *second = *first;   (i==1, j==1)

        (Assume that B is paused and A is restarted at this point)

  5:    *first = temp;    (i==2, j==1)

        (Assume that A is paused and B is restarted at this point)

  6:                                            *first = temp;    (i==1, j==1)
```

As can be seen, at the end of the previous scenario both i and j end up having the value 1. It is not possible that they can ever have any other value after that point.

The scenario above is just one example that is sufficient to explain the incorrect results of the program. Obviously, the race conditions would be much more complicated in the case of the ten threads of this example.

86.4 synchronized to avoid race conditions

The incorrect program behavior above is due to more than one thread accessing the same mutable data (and at least one of them modifying it). One way of avoiding these race conditions is to mark the common code with the synchronized keyword. The program would work correctly with the following change:

```
    foreach (i; 0 .. 10_000) {
        synchronized {
            int temp = *b;
            *b = *a;
            *a = temp;
        }
    }
```

The output:

```
before: 1 and 2
after : 1 and 2        ← correct result
```

The effect of synchronized is to create a lock behind the scenes and to allow only one thread hold that lock at a given time. Only the thread that holds the lock can be executed and the others wait until the lock becomes available again when the executing thread completes its synchronized block. Since one thread executes the *synchronized* code at a time, each thread would now swap the values safely before another thread does the same. The state of the variables i and j would always be either "1 and 2" or "2 and 1" at the end of processing the synchronized block.

Note: *It is a relatively expensive operation for a thread to wait for a lock, which may slow down the execution of the program noticeably. Fortunately, in some cases program correctness can be ensured without the use of a* synchronized *block, by taking advantage of atomic operations that will be explained below.*

When it is needed to synchronize more than one block of code, it is possible to specify one or more locks with the synchronized keyword.

Let's see an example of this in the following program that has two separate code blocks that access the same shared variable. The program calls two functions with the address of the same variable, one function incrementing and the other function decrementing it equal number of times:

```
void incrementer(shared(int) * value) {
    foreach (i; 0 .. count) {
        *value = *value + 1;
    }
}

void decrementer(shared(int) * value) {
    foreach (i; 0 .. count) {
        *value = *value - 1;
    }
}
```

Note: *If the shorter equivalents of the expression above are used (i.e. ++(*value) and --(*value)), then the compiler warns that such read-modify-write operations on* shared *variables are deprecated.*

Unfortunately, marking those blocks individually with synchronized is not sufficient, because the anonymous locks of the two blocks would be independent. So, the two code blocks would still be accessing the same variable concurrently:

```
import std.stdio;
import std.concurrency;
import core.thread;

enum count = 1000;

void incrementer(shared(int) * value) {
    foreach (i; 0 .. count) {
        synchronized { // ← This lock is different from the one below.
            *value = *value + 1;
        }
```

```
        }
    }

    void decrementer(shared(int) * value) {
        foreach (i; 0 .. count) {
            synchronized { // ← This lock is different from the one above.
                *value = *value - 1;
            }
        }
    }

    void main() {
        shared(int) number = 0;

        foreach (i; 0 .. 100) {
            spawn(&incrementer, &number);
            spawn(&decrementer, &number);
        }

        thread_joinAll();
        writeln("Final value: ", number);
    }
```

Since there are equal number of threads that increment and decrement the same variable equal number of times, one would expect the final value of number to be zero. However, that is almost never the case:

```
Final value: -672    ← not zero
```

For more than one block to use the same lock or locks, the lock objects must be specified within the synchronized parentheses:

Note: *This feature is not supported by dmd 2.098.1.*

```
    // Note: dmd 2.098.1 does not support this feature.
    synchronized (lock_object, another_lock_object, ...)
```

There is no need for a special lock type in D because any class object can be used as a synchronized lock. The following program defines an empty class named Lock to use its objects as locks:

```
import std.stdio;
import std.concurrency;
import core.thread;

enum count = 1000;

class Lock {
}

void incrementer(shared(int) * value, shared(Lock) lock) {
    foreach (i; 0 .. count) {
        synchronized (lock) {
            *value = *value + 1;
        }
    }
}

void decrementer(shared(int) * value, shared(Lock) lock) {
    foreach (i; 0 .. count) {
        synchronized (lock) {
            *value = *value - 1;
        }
    }
}

void main() {
    shared(Lock) lock = new shared(Lock)();
    shared(int) number = 0;
```

```
    foreach (i; 0 .. 100) {
        spawn(&incrementer, &number, lock);
        spawn(&decrementer, &number, lock);
    }

    thread_joinAll();
    writeln("Final value: ", number);
}
```

Because this time both synchronized blocks are connected by the same lock, only one of them is executed at a given time and the result is zero as expected:

```
Final value: 0          ← correct result
```

Class types can be defined as synchronized as well. This means that all of the non-static member functions of that type are synchronized on a given object of that class:

```
synchronized class Class {
    void foo() {
        // ...
    }

    void bar() {
        // ...
    }
}
```

The following is the equivalent of the class definition above:

```
class Class {
    void foo() {
        synchronized (this) {
            // ...
        }
    }

    void bar() {
        synchronized (this) {
            // ...
        }
    }
}
```

When blocks of code need to be synchronized on more than one object, those objects must be specified together. Otherwise, it is possible that more than one thread may have locked objects that other threads are waiting for, in which case the program may be *deadlocked*.

A well known example of this problem is a function that tries to transfer money from one bank account to another. For this function to work correctly in a multi-threaded environment, both of the accounts must first be locked. However, the following attempt would be incorrect:

```
void transferMoney(shared BankAccount from,
                   shared BankAccount to) {
    synchronized (from) {          // ← INCORRECT
        synchronized (to) {
            // ...
        }
    }
}
```

The error can be explained by an example where one thread attempting to transfer money from account A to account to B while another thread attempting to transfer money in the reverse direction. It is possible that each thread may have just locked its respective from object, hoping next to lock its to object. Since the from objects correspond to A and B in the two threads respectively, the objects would be in locked state in separate threads, making it impossible for the other thread to ever lock its to object. This situation is called a *deadlock*.

The solution to this problem is to define an ordering relation between the objects and to lock them in that order, which is handled automatically by the synchronized statement. In D, it is sufficient to specify the objects in the same synchronized statement for the code to avoid such deadlocks:

Note: *This feature is not supported by dmd 2.098.1.*

```
void transferMoney(shared BankAccount from,
                   shared BankAccount to) {
    // Note: dmd 2.098.1 does not support this feature.
    synchronized (from, to) {        // ← correct
        // ...
    }
}
```

86.5 shared static this() for single initialization and shared static ~this() for single finalization

We have already seen that static this() can be used for initializing modules, including their variables. Because data is thread-local by default, static this() must be executed by every thread so that module-level variables are initialized for all threads:

```
import std.stdio;
import std.concurrency;
import core.thread;

static this() {
    writeln("executing static this()");
}

void worker() {
}

void main() {
    spawn(&worker);

    thread_joinAll();
}
```

The static this() block above would be executed once for the main thread and once for the worker thread:

```
executing static this()
executing static this()
```

This would cause problems for shared module variables because initializing a variable more than once would be wrong especially in concurrency due to race conditions. (That applies to immutable variables as well because they are implicitly shared.) The solution is to use shared static this() blocks, which are executed only once per program:

```
int a;                // thread-local
immutable int b;      // shared by all threads

static this() {
    writeln("Initializing per-thread variable at ", &a);
    a = 42;
}
```

```
shared static this() {
    writeln("Initializing per-program variable at ", &b);
    b = 43;
}
```

The output:

```
Initializing per-program variable at 6B0120      ← only once
Initializing per-thread variable at 7FBDB36557D0
Initializing per-thread variable at 7FBDB3554670
```

Similarly, shared static ~this() is for final operations that must be executed only once per program.

86.6 Atomic operations

Another way of ensuring that only one thread mutates a certain variable is by using atomic operations, functionality of which are provided by the microprocessor, the compiler, or the operating system.

The atomic operations of D are in the core.atomic module. We will see only two of its functions in this chapter:

atomicOp

This function applies its template parameter to its two function parameters. The template parameter must be a *binary operator* like "+", "+=", etc.

```
import core.atomic;

// ...

        atomicOp!"+="(*value, 1);      // atomic
```

The line above is the equivalent of the following line, with the difference that the += operation would be executed without interruptions by other threads (i.e. it would be executed *atomically*):

```
        *value += 1;                   // NOT atomic
```

Consequently, when it is only a binary operation that needs to be synchronized, then there is no need for a synchronized block, which is known to be slow because of needing to acquire a lock. The following equivalents of the incrementer() and decrementer() functions that use atomicOp are correct as well. Note that there is no need for the Lock class anymore either:

```
import core.atomic;

//...

void incrementer(shared(int) * value) {
    foreach (i; 0 .. count) {
        atomicOp!"+="(*value, 1);
    }
}

void decrementer(shared(int) * value) {
    foreach (i; 0 .. count) {
        atomicOp!"-="(*value, 1);
    }
}
```

atomicOp can be used with other binary operators as well.

cas

The name of this function is the abbreviation of "compare and swap". Its behavior can be described as *mutate the variable if it still has its currently known value*. It is used by specifying the current and the desired values of the variable at the same time:

```
bool is_mutated = cas(address_of_variable, currentValue, newValue);
```

The fact that the value of the variable still equals currentValue when cas() is operating is an indication that no other thread has mutated the variable since it has last been read by this thread. If so, cas() assigns newValue to the variable and returns true. On the other hand, if the variable's value is different from currentValue then cas() does not mutate the variable and returns false.

The following functions re-read the current value and call cas() until the operation succeeds. Again, these calls can be described as *if the value of the variable equals this old value, replace with this new value*:

```
void incrementer(shared(int) * value) {
    foreach (i; 0 .. count) {
        int currentValue;

        do {
            currentValue = *value;
        } while (!cas(value, currentValue, currentValue + 1));
    }
}

void decrementer(shared(int) * value) {
    foreach (i; 0 .. count) {
        int currentValue;

        do {
            currentValue = *value;
        } while (!cas(value, currentValue, currentValue - 1));
    }
}
```

The functions above work correctly without the need for synchronized blocks.

In most cases, the features of the core.atomic module can be several times faster than using synchronized blocks. I recommend that you consider this module as long as the operations that need synchronization are less than a block of code.

Atomic operations enable *lock-free data structures* as well, which are beyond the scope of this book.

You may also want to investigate the core.sync package, which contains classic concurrency primitives in the following modules:

- core.sync.barrier
- core.sync.condition
- core.sync.config
- core.sync.exception
- core.sync.mutex
- core.sync.rwmutex
- core.sync.semaphore

86.7 Summary

- When threads do not depend on other threads, prefer *parallelism*. Consider *concurrency* only when threads depend on operations of other threads.
- Even then, prefer *message passing concurrency*, which has been the topic of the previous chapter.
- Only `shared` data can be shared; `immutable` is implicitly `shared`.
- `__gshared` provides data sharing as in C and C++ languages.
- `synchronized` is for preventing other threads from intervening when a thread is executing a certain piece of code.
- A class can be defined as `synchronized` so that only one member function can be executed on a given object at a given time. In other words, a thread can execute a member function only if no other thread is executing a member function on the same object.
- `static this()` is executed once for each thread; `shared static this()` is executed once for the entire program.
- The `core.atomic` module enables safe data sharing that can be multiple times faster than `synchronized`.
- The `core.sync` package includes many other concurrency primitives.

87 Fibers

A fiber is a *thread of execution* enabling a single thread achieve multiple tasks. Compared to regular threads that are commonly used in parallelism and concurrency, it is more efficient to switch between fibers. Fibers are similar to *coroutines* and *green threads*.

Fibers enable multiple call stacks per thread. For that reason, to fully understand and appreciate fibers, one must first understand the *call stack* of a thread.

87.1 Call stack

The parameters, non-static local variables, the return value, and temporary expressions of a function, as well as any additional information that may be needed during its execution, comprise the *local state* of that function. The local state of a function is allocated and initialized automatically at run time every time that function is called.

The storage space allocated for the local state of a function call is called a *frame* (or *stack frame*). As functions call other functions during the execution of a thread, their frames are conceptually placed on top of each other to form a stack of frames. The stack of frames of currently active function calls is the *call stack* of that thread.

For example, at the time the main thread of the following program starts executing the bar() function, there would be three levels of active function calls due to main() calling foo() and foo() calling bar():

```
void main() {
    int a;
    int b;

    int c = foo(a, b);
}

int foo(int x, int y) {
    bar(x + y);
    return 42;
}

void bar(int param) {
    string[] arr;
    // ...
}
```

During the execution of bar(), the call stack would consist of three frames storing the local states of those currently active function calls:

```
The call stack grows upward
as function calls get deeper.         ▲ ▲
                                      │ │
    Top of the call stack →  ┌─────────────────┐
                             │ int param       │  ← bar's frame
                             │ string[] arr    │
                             ├─────────────────┤
                             │ int x           │
                             │ int y           │  ← foo's frame
                             │ return value    │
                             ├─────────────────┤
                             │ int a           │
                             │ int b           │  ← main's frame
                             │ int c           │
    Bottom of the call stack →  └─────────────────┘
```

As layers of function calls get deeper when functions call other functions and shallower when functions return, the size of the call stack increases and decreases accordingly. For example, once bar() returns, its frame would no longer be needed and its space would later be used for another function call in the future:

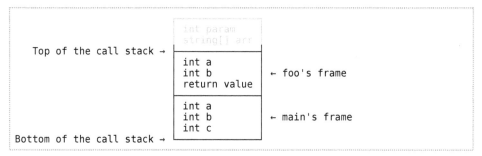

We have been taking advantage of the call stack in every program that we have written so far. The advantages of the call stack is especially clear for recursive functions.

Recursion

Recursion is the situation where a function calls itself either directly or indirectly. Recursion greatly simplifies certain kinds of algorithms like the ones that are classified as *divide-and-conquer*.

Let's consider the following function that calculates the sum of the elements of a slice. It achieves this task by calling itself recursively with a slice that is one element shorter than the one that it has received. The recursion continues until the slice becomes empty. The current result is carried over to the next recursion step as the second parameter:

```d
import std.array;

int sum(int[] arr, int currentSum = 0) {
    if (arr.empty) {
        /* No element to add. The result is what has been
         * calculated so far. */
        return currentSum;
    }

    /* Add the front element to the current sum and call self
     * with the remaining elements. */
    return sum(arr[1..$], currentSum + arr.front);
}

void main() {
    assert(sum([1, 2, 3]) == 6);
}
```

Note: *The code above is only for demonstration. Otherwise, the sum of the elements of a range should be calculated by* std.algorithm.sum, *which uses special algorithms to achieve more accurate calculations for floating point types.*

When sum() is eventually called with an empty slice for the initial argument of [1, 2, 3] above, the relevant parts of the call stack would consist of the following frames. The value of each parameter is indicated after an == sign. Remember to read the frame contents from bottom to top:

```
┌─────────────────────────────┐
│ arr         == []           │  ← final call to sum
│ currentSum == 6             │
├─────────────────────────────┤
│ arr         == [3]          │  ← third call to sum
│ currentSum == 3             │
├─────────────────────────────┤
│ arr         == [2, 3]       │  ← second call to sum
│ currentSum == 1             │
├─────────────────────────────┤
│ arr         == [1, 2, 3]    │  ← first call to sum
│ currentSum == 0             │
├─────────────────────────────┤
│            ...              │  ← main's frame
└─────────────────────────────┘
```

Note: In practice, when the recursive function directly returns the result of calling itself, compilers use a technique called "tail-call optimization", which eliminates separate frames for each recursive call.

In a multithreaded program, since each thread would be working on its own task, every thread gets it own call stack to maintain its own execution state.

The power of fibers is based on the fact that although a fiber is not a thread, it gets its own call stack, effectively enabling multiple call stacks per thread. Since one call stack maintains the execution state of one task, multiple call stacks enable a thread work on multiple tasks.

87.2 Usage

The following are common operations of fibers. We will see examples of these later below.

- A fiber starts its execution from a callable entity (function pointer, delegate, etc.) that does not take any parameter and does not return anything. For example, the following function can be used as a fiber function:

```d
void fiberFunction() {
    // ...
}
```

- A fiber can be created as an object of class core.thread.Fiber with a callable entity:

```d
import core.thread;

// ...

    auto fiber = new Fiber(&fiberFunction);
```

Alternatively, a subclass of Fiber can be defined and the fiber function can be passed to the constructor of the superclass. In the following example, the fiber function is a member function:

```d
class MyFiber : Fiber {
    this() {
        super(&run);
    }

    void run() {
        // ...
    }
}
// ...
```

```
    auto fiber = new MyFiber();
```

- A fiber is started and resumed by its `call()` member function:

```
    fiber.call();
```

Unlike threads, the caller is paused while the fiber is executing.

- A fiber pauses itself (*yields* execution to its caller) by `Fiber.yield()`:

```
void fiberFunction() {
    // ...

        Fiber.yield();

    // ...
}
```

The caller's execution resumes when the fiber yields.

- The execution state of a fiber is determined by its `.state` property:

```
    if (fiber.state == Fiber.State.TERM) {
        // ...
    }
```

`Fiber.State` is an enum with the following values:

- HOLD: The fiber is paused, meaning that it can be started or resumed.
- EXEC: The fiber is currently executing.
- TERM: The fiber has terminated. It must be `reset()` before it can be used again.

87.3 Fibers in range implementations

Almost every range needs to store some information to remember its state of iteration. This is necessary for it to know what to do when its `popFront()` is called next time. Most range examples that we saw in the Ranges (page 569) and later chapters have been storing some kind of state to achieve their tasks.

For example, `FibonacciSeries` that we have defined earlier was keeping two member variables to calculate the *next next* number in the series:

```
struct FibonacciSeries {
    int current = 0;
    int next = 1;

    enum empty = false;

    int front() const {
        return current;
    }

    void popFront() {
        const nextNext = current + next;
        current = next;
        next = nextNext;
    }
}
```

While maintaining the iteration state is trivial for some ranges like `FibonacciSeries`, it is surprisingly harder for some others, e.g. recursive data structures like binary search trees. The reason why it is surprising is that for such data structures, the same algorithms are trivial when implemented recursively.

For example, the following recursive implementations of `insert()` and `print()` do not define any variables and are independent of the number of elements contained in the tree. The recursive calls are highlighted. (Note that `insert()` is recursive indirectly through `insertOrSet()`.)

```d
import std.stdio;
import std.string;
import std.conv;
import std.random;
import std.range;
import std.algorithm;

/* Represents the nodes of a binary tree. This type is used in
 * the implementation of struct Tree below and should not be
 * used directly. */
struct Node {
    int element;
    Node * left;       // Left sub-tree
    Node * right;      // Right sub-tree

    void insert(int element) {
        if (element < this.element) {
            /* Smaller elements go under the left sub-tree. */
            insertOrSet(left, element);

        } else if (element > this.element) {
            /* Larger elements go under the right sub-tree. */
            insertOrSet(right, element);

        } else {
            throw new Exception(format("%s already exists",
                                       element));
        }
    }

    void print() const {
        /* First print the elements of the left sub-tree */
        if (left) {
            left.print();
            write(' ');
        }

        /* Then print this element */
        write(element);

        /* Lastly, print the elements of the right sub-tree */
        if (right) {
            write(' ');
            right.print();
        }
    }
}

/* Inserts the element to the specified sub-tree, potentially
 * initializing its node. */
void insertOrSet(ref Node * node, int element) {
    if (!node) {
        /* This is the first element of this sub-tree. */
        node = new Node(element);

    } else {
        node.insert(element);
    }
}

/* This is the actual Tree representation. It allows an empty
 * tree by means of 'root' being equal to 'null'. */
struct Tree {
    Node * root;

    /* Inserts the element to this tree. */
    void insert(int element) {
```

```
        insertOrSet(root, element);
    }

    /* Prints the elements in sorted order. */
    void print() const {
        if (root) {
            root.print();
        }
    }
}

/* Populates the tree with 'n' random numbers picked out of a
 * set of '10 * n' numbers. */
Tree makeRandomTree(size_t n) {
    auto numbers = iota((n * 10).to!int)
                    .randomSample(n, Random(unpredictableSeed))
                    .array;

    randomShuffle(numbers);

    /* Populate the tree with those numbers. */
    auto tree = Tree();
    numbers.each!(e => tree.insert(e));

    return tree;
}

void main() {
    auto tree = makeRandomTree(10);
    tree.print();
}
```

Note: *The program above uses the following features from Phobos:*

- `std.range.iota` generates the elements of a given value range lazily. (By default, the first element is the `.init` value). For example, `iota(10)` is a range of int elements from 0 to 9.
- `std.algorithm.each` is similar to `std.algorithm.map`. While `map()` generates a new result for each element, `each()` generates side effects for each element. Additionally, `map()` is lazy while `each()` is eager.
- `std.random.randomSample` picks a random sampling of elements from a given range without changing their order.
- `std.random.randomShuffle` shuffles the elements of a range randomly.

Like most containers, one would like this tree to provide a range interface so that its elements can be used with existing range algorithms. This can be done by defining an `opSlice()` member function:

```
struct Tree {
// ...

    /* Provides access to the elements of the tree in sorted
     * order. */
    struct InOrderRange {
        ... What should the implementation be? ...
    }

    InOrderRange opSlice() const {
        return InOrderRange(root);
    }
}
```

Although the `print()` member function above essentially achieves the same task of visiting every element in sorted order, it is not easy to implement an InputRange for a tree. I will not attempt to implement InOrderRange here but I encourage you to implement or at least research tree iterators. (Some implementations require that tree nodes have an additional Node* to point at each node's parent.)

The reason why recursive tree algorithms like print() are trivial is due to the automatic management of the call stack. The call stack implicitly contains information not only about what the current element is, but also how the execution of the program arrived at that element (e.g. at what nodes did the execution follow the left node versus the right node).

For example, when a recursive call to left.print() returns after printing the elements of the left sub-tree, the local state of the current print() call already implies that it is now time to print a space character:

```
void print() const {
    if (left) {
        left.print();
        write(' ');    // ← Call stack implies this is next
    }

    // ...
}
```

Fibers are useful for similar cases where using a call stack is much easier than maintaining state explicitly.

Although the benefits of fibers would not be apparent on a simple task like generating the Fibonacci series, for simplicity let's cover common fiber operations on a fiber implementation of one. We will implement a tree range later below.

```
import core.thread;

/* This is the fiber function that generates each element and
 * then sets the 'ref' parameter to that element. */
void fibonacciSeries(ref int current) {               // (1)
    current = 0;      // Note that 'current' is the parameter
    int next = 1;

    while (true) {
        Fiber.yield();                                // (2)
        /* Next call() will continue from this point */ // (3)

        const nextNext = current + next;
        current = next;
        next = nextNext;
    }
}

void main() {
    int current;                                      // (1)
                        // (4)
    Fiber fiber = new Fiber(() => fibonacciSeries(current));

    foreach ( ; 0 .. 10) {
        fiber.call();                                 // (5)

        import std.stdio;
        writef("%s ", current);
    }
}
```

1. The fiber function above takes a reference to an int. It uses this parameter to communicate the current element to its caller. (The parameter could be qualified as out instead of ref as well).

2. When the current element is ready for use, the fiber pauses itself by calling Fiber.yield().

3. A later `call()` will resume the function right after the fiber's last `Fiber.yield()` call. (The first `call()` starts the function.)
4. Because fiber functions do not take parameters, `fibonacciSeries()` cannot be used directly as a fiber function. Instead, a parameter-less delegate (page 475) is used as an adaptor to be passed to the `Fiber` constructor.
5. The caller starts and resumes the fiber by its `call()` member function.

As a result, `main()` receives the elements of the series through `current` and prints them:

```
0 1 1 2 3 5 8 13 21 34
```

`std.concurrency.Generator` for presenting fibers as ranges

Although we have achieved generating the Fibonacci series with a fiber, that implementation has the following shortcomings:

- The solution above does not provide a range interface, making it incompatible with existing range algorithms.
- Presenting the elements by mutating a `ref` parameter is less desirable compared to a design where the elements are copied to the caller's context.
- Constructing and using the fiber explicitly through its member functions exposes *lower level* implementation details, compared to alternative designs.

The `std.concurrency.Generator` class addresses all of these issues. Note how `fibonacciSeries()` below is written as a simple function. The only difference is that instead of returning a single element by `return`, it can make multiple elements available by `yield()` (*infinite elements* in this example).

Also note that this time it is the `std.concurrency.yield` function, not the `Fiber.yield` member function that we used above.

```d
import std.stdio;
import std.range;
import std.concurrency;

/* This alias is used for resolving the name conflict with
 * std.range.Generator. */
alias FiberRange = std.concurrency.Generator;

void fibonacciSeries() {
    int current = 0;
    int next = 1;

    while (true) {
        yield(current);

        const nextNext = current + next;
        current = next;
        next = nextNext;
    }
}

void main() {
    auto series = new FiberRange!int(&fibonacciSeries);
    writefln("%(%s %)", series.take(10));
}
```

As a result, the elements that are produced by a fiber function are used conveniently as an `InputRange`:

```
0 1 1 2 3 5 8 13 21 34
```

Using Generator, we can easily present the elements of a tree as an InputRange as well. Further, once the tree has an InputRange interface, the print() member function would not be needed anymore; hence it is removed. Especially note how byNode() is implemented as an adaptor over the recursive function nextNode():

```d
import std.concurrency;

alias FiberRange = std.concurrency.Generator;

struct Node {
// ...

    /* Note: print() member function is removed because it is
     * not needed anymore. */

    auto opSlice() const {
        return byNode(&this);
    }
}

/* This is the fiber function that yields the next tree node
 * in sorted order. */
void nextNode(const(Node) * node) {
    if (!node) {
        /* No element at or under this node */
        return;
    }

    nextNode(node.left);     // First, elements on the left
    yield(node);             // Then, this element
    nextNode(node.right);    // Finally, elements on the right
}

/* Returns an InputRange to the nodes of the tree. */
auto byNode(const(Node) * node) {
    return new FiberRange!(const(Node)*)(
        () => nextNode(node));
}

// ...

struct Tree {
// ...

    /* Note: print() member function is removed because it is
     * not needed anymore. */

    auto opSlice() const {
        /* A translation from the nodes to the elements. */
        return byNode(this).map!(n => n.element);
    }
}

/* Returns an InputRange to the nodes of the tree. The
 * returned range is empty if the tree has no elements (i.e.
 * if 'root' is 'null'). */
auto byNode(const(Tree) tree) {
    if (tree.root) {
        return byNode(tree.root);

    } else {
        alias RangeType = typeof(return);
        return new RangeType(() {});    // ← Empty range
    }
}
```

Tree objects can now be sliced with [] and the result can be used as an InputRange:

```d
    writefln("%(%s %)", tree[]);
```

87.4 Fibers in asynchronous input and output

The call stack of a fiber can simplify asynchronous input and output tasks as well.

As an example, let's imagine a system where users sign on to a service by connecting to a server and providing their *name, email*, and *age*, in that order. This would be similar to the *sign-on user flow* of a website. To keep the example simple, instead of implementing an actual web service, let's simulate user interactions using data entered on the command line. Let's use the following simple sign-on protocol, where input data is highlighted:

- `hi`: A user connects and a flow id is generated
- *id data*: The user of flow that corresponds to id enters the next expected data. For example, if the expected data for flow 42 is *name*, then the command for Alice would be 42 `Alice`.
- `bye`: Program exits

For example, the following can be the interactions of Alice and Bob, where the inputs to the simulation program are highlighted. Each user connects and then provides *name, email*, and *age*:

```
> hi                     ← Alice connects
Flow 0 started.
> 0 Alice
> 0 alice@example.com
> 0 20
Flow 0 has completed.    ← Alice finishes
Added user 'Alice'.
> hi                     ← Bob connects
Flow 1 started.
> 1 Bob
> 1 bob@example.com
> 1 30
Flow 1 has completed.    ← Bob finishes
Added user 'Bob'.
> bye
Goodbye.
Users:
  User("Alice", "alice@example.com", 20)
  User("Bob", "bob@example.com", 30)
```

This program can be designed to wait for the command `hi` in a loop and then call a function to receive the input data of the connected user:

```
if (input == "hi") {
    signOnNewUser();    // ← WARNING: Blocking design
}
```

Unless the program had some kind of support for multitasking, such a design would be considered *blocking*, meaning that all other users would be blocked until the current user completes their sign on flow. This would impact the responsiveness of even lightly-used services if users took several minutes to provide data.

There can be several designs that makes this service *non-blocking*, meaning that more than one user can sign on at the same time:

- Maintaining tasks explicitly: The main thread can spawn one thread per user sign-on and pass input data to that thread by means of messages. Although this method would work, it might involve thread synchronization and it can be slower than a fiber. (The reasons for this potential performance penalty will be explained in the *cooperative multitasking* section below.)

- Maintaining state: The program can accept more than one sign-on and remember the state of each sign-on explicitly. For example, if Alice has entered only her name so far, her state would have to indicate that the next input data would be her email information.

Alternatively, a design based on fibers can employ one fiber per sign-on flow. This would enable implementing the flow in a linear fashion, matching the protocol exactly: first the name, then the email, and finally the age. For example, `run()` below does not need to do anything special to remember the state of the sign-on flow. When it is `call()`'ed next time, it continues right after the last `Fiber.yield()` call that had paused it. The next line to be executed is implied by the call stack.

Differently from earlier examples, the following program uses a `Fiber` subclass:

```
import std.stdio;
import std.string;
import std.format;
import std.exception;
import std.conv;
import std.array;
import core.thread;

struct User {
    string name;
    string email;
    uint age;
}

/* This Fiber subclass represents the sign-on flow of a
 * user. */
class SignOnFlow : Fiber {
    /* The data read most recently for this flow. */
    string inputData_;

    /* The information to construct a User object. */
    string name;
    string email;
    uint age;

    this() {
        /* Set our 'run' member function as the starting point
         * of the fiber. */
        super(&run);
    }

    void run() {
        /* First input is name. */
        name = inputData_;
        Fiber.yield();

        /* Second input is email. */
        email = inputData_;
        Fiber.yield();

        /* Last input is age. */
        age = inputData_.to!uint;

        /* At this point we have collected all information to
         * construct the user. We now "return" instead of
         * 'Fiber.yield()'. As a result, the state of this
         * fiber becomes Fiber.State.TERM. */
    }

    /* This property function is to receive data from the
     * caller. */
    void inputData(string data) {
        inputData_ = data;
```

```
    }

    /* This property function is to construct a user and
     * return it to the caller. */
    User user() const {
        return User(name, email, age);
    }
}

/* Represents data read from the input for a specific flow. */
struct FlowData {
    size_t id;
    string data;
}

/* Parses data related to a flow. */
FlowData parseFlowData(string line) {
    size_t id;
    string data;

    const items = line.formattedRead!" %s %s"(id, data);
    enforce(items == 2, format("Bad input '%s'.", line));

    return FlowData(id, data);
}

void main() {
    User[] users;
    SignOnFlow[] flows;

    bool done = false;

    while (!done) {
        write("> ");
        string line = readln.strip;

        switch (line) {
        case "hi":
            /* Start a flow for the new connection. */
            flows ~= new SignOnFlow();

            writefln("Flow %s started.", flows.length - 1);
            break;

        case "bye":
            /* Exit the program. */
            done = true;
            break;

        default:
            /* Try to use the input as flow data. */
            try {
                auto user = handleFlowData(line, flows);

                if (!user.name.empty) {
                    users ~= user;
                    writefln("Added user '%s'.", user.name);
                }

            } catch (Exception exc) {
                writefln("Error: %s", exc.msg);
            }
            break;
        }
    }

    writeln("Goodbye.");
    writefln("Users:\n%(  %s\n%)", users);
}

/* Identifies the owner fiber for the input, sets its input
 * data, and resumes that fiber. Returns a user with valid
 * fields if the flow has been completed. */
```

```
User handleFlowData(string line, SignOnFlow[] flows) {
    const input = parseFlowData(line);
    const id = input.id;

    enforce(id < flows.length, format("Invalid id: %s.", id));

    auto flow = flows[id];

    enforce(flow.state == Fiber.State.HOLD,
            format("Flow %s is not runnable.", id));

    /* Set flow data. */
    flow.inputData = input.data;

    /* Resume the flow. */
    flow.call();

    User user;

    if (flow.state == Fiber.State.TERM) {
        writefln("Flow %s has completed.", id);

        /* Set the return value to the newly created user. */
        user = flow.user;

        /* TODO: This fiber's entry in the 'flows' array can
         * be reused for a new flow in the future. However, it
         * must first be reset by 'flow.reset()'. */
    }

    return user;
}
```

main() reads lines from the input, parses them, and dispatches flow data to the appropriate flow to be processed. The call stack of each flow maintains the flow state automatically. New users are added to the system when the complete user information becomes available.

When you run the program above, you see that no matter how long a user takes to complete their individual sign-on flow, the system always accepts new user connections. As an example, Alice's interaction is highlighted:

```
> hi                          ← Alice connects
Flow 0 started.
> 0 Alice
> hi                          ← Bob connects
Flow 1 started.
> hi                          ← Cindy connects
Flow 2 started.
> 0 alice@example.com
> 1 Bob
> 2 Cindy
> 2 cindy@example.com
> 2 40                        ← Cindy finishes
Flow 2 has completed.
Added user 'Cindy'.
> 1 bob@example.com
> 1 30                        ← Bob finishes
Flow 1 has completed.
Added user 'Bob'.
> 0 20                        ← Alice finishes
Flow 0 has completed.
Added user 'Alice'.
> bye
Goodbye.
Users:
  User("Cindy", "cindy@example.com", 40)
  User("Bob", "bob@example.com", 30)
  User("Alice", "alice@example.com", 20)
```

Although Alice, Bob, and Cindy connect in that order, they complete their sign-on flows at different paces. As a result, the users array is populated in the order that the flows are completed.

One benefit of using fibers in this program is that SignOnFlow.run() is written trivially without regard to how fast or slow a user's input has been. Additionally, no user is blocked when other sign-on flows are in progress.

Many asynchronous input/output frameworks like vibe.d[1] use similar designs based on fibers.

87.5 Exceptions and fibers

In the Exceptions chapter (page 192) we saw how "an exception object that is thrown from a lower level function is transferred to the higher level functions one level at a time". We also saw that an uncaught exception "causes the program to finally exit the main() function." Although that chapter did not mention the call stack, the described behavior of the exception mechanism is achieved by the call stack as well.

Continuing with the first example in this chapter, if an exception is thrown inside bar(), first the frame of bar() would be removed from the call stack, then foo()'s, and finally main()'s. As functions are exited and their frames are removed from the call stack, the destructors of local variables are executed for their final operations. The process of leaving functions and executing destructors of local variables due to a thrown exception is called *stack unwinding*.

Since fibers have their own stack, an exception that is thrown during the execution of the fiber unwinds the fiber's call stack, not its caller's. If the exception is not caught, the fiber function terminates and the fiber's state becomes Fiber.State.TERM.

Although that may be the desired behavior in some cases, sometimes a fiber may need to communicate an error condition to its caller without losing its execution state. Fiber.yieldAndThrow allows a fiber to yield and immediately throw an exception in the caller's context.

To see how it can be used let's enter invalid age data to the sign-on program:

```
> hi
Flow 0 started.
> 0 Alice
> 0 alice@example.com
> 0 hello                   ← the user enters invalid age
Error: Unexpected 'h' when converting from type string to type uint
> 0 20                      ← attempts to correct the error
Error: Flow 0 is not runnable.  ← but the flow is terminated
```

Instead of terminating the fiber and losing the entire sign-on flow, the fiber can catch the conversion error and communicate it to the caller by yieldAndThrow(). This can be done by replacing the following line of the program where the fiber converts age data:

```
    age = inputData_.to!uint;
```

Wrapping that line with a try-catch statement inside an unconditional loop would be sufficient to keep the fiber alive until there is data that can be converted to a uint:

```
    while (true) {
        try {
```

---

1. http://vibed.org

```
                age = inputData_.to!uint;
                break;   // ← Conversion worked; leave the loop

        } catch (ConvException exc) {
            Fiber.yieldAndThrow(exc);
        }
    }
```

This time the fiber remains in an unconditional loop until data is valid:

```
> hi
Flow 0 started.
> 0 Alice
> 0 alice@example.com
> 0 hello                    ← the user enters invalid age
Error: Unexpected 'h' when converting from type string to type uint
> 0 world                    ← enters invalid age again
Error: Unexpected 'w' when converting from type string to type uint
> 0 20                       ← finally, enters valid data
Flow 0 has completed.
Added user 'Alice'.
> bye
Goodbye.
Users:
  User("Alice", "alice@example.com", 20)
```

As can be seen from the output, this time the sign-on flow is not lost and the user is added to the system.

87.6 Cooperative multitasking

Unlike operating system threads, which are paused (suspended) and resumed by the operating system at unknown points in time, a fiber pauses itself explicitly and is resumed by its caller explicitly. According to this distinction, the kind of multitasking that the operating system provides is called *preemptive multitasking* and the kind that fibers provide is called *cooperative multitasking*.

In preemptive multitasking, the operating system allots a certain amount of time to a thread when it starts or resumes its execution. When the time is up, that thread is paused and another one is resumed in its place. Moving from one thread to another is called *context switching*. Context switching takes a relatively large amount of time, which could have better been spent doing actual work by threads.

Considering that a system is usually busy with high number of threads, context switching is unavoidable and is actually desired. However, sometimes threads need to pause themselves voluntarily before they use up the entire time that was alloted to them. This can happen when a thread needs information from another thread or from a device. When a thread pauses itself, the operating system must spend time again to switch to another thread. As a result, time that could have been used for doing actual work ends up being used for context switching.

With fibers, the caller and the fiber execute as parts of the same thread. (That is the reason why the caller and the fiber cannot execute at the same time.) As a benefit, there is no overhead of context switching between the caller and the fiber. (However, there is still some light overhead which is comparable to the overhead of a regular function call.)

Another benefit of cooperative multitasking is that the data that the caller and the fiber exchange is more likely to be in the CPU's data cache. Because data that is in the CPU cache can be accessed hundreds of times faster than data that needs to be read back from system memory, this further improves the performance of fibers.

Additionally, because the caller and the fiber are never executed at the same time, there is no possibility of race conditions, obviating the need for data synchronization. However, the programmer must still ensure that a fiber yields at the intended time (e.g. when data is actually ready). For example, the `func()` call below must not execute a `Fiber.yield()` call, even indirectly, as that would be premature, before the value of `sharedData` was doubled:

```
void fiberFunction() {
    // ...

        func();                // ← must not yield prematurely
        sharedData *= 2;
        Fiber.yield();         // ← intended point to yield

    // ...
}
```

One obvious shortcoming of fibers is that only one core of the CPU is used for the caller and its fibers. The other cores of the CPU might be sitting idle, effectively wasting resources. It is possible to use different designs like the *M:N threading model (hybrid threading)* that employ other cores as well. I encourage you to research and compare different threading models.

87.7 Summary

- The call stack enables efficient allocation of local state and simplifies certain algorithms, especially the recursive ones.
- Fibers enable multiple call stacks per thread instead of the default single call stack per thread.
- A fiber and its caller are executed on the same thread (i.e. not at the same time).
- A fiber pauses itself by *yielding* to its caller and the caller resumes its fiber by *calling* it again.
- `Generator` presents a fiber as an `InputRange`.
- Fibers simplify algorithms that rely heavily on the call stack.
- Fibers simplify asynchronous input/output operations.
- Fibers provide cooperative multitasking, which has different trade-offs from preemptive multitasking.

D is a language that does not require explicit memory management. However, it is important for a system programmer to know how to manage memory when needed for special cases.

Memory management is a very broad topic. This chapter will introduce only the garbage collector (GC), allocating memory from it, and constructing objects at specific memory locations. I encourage you to research various memory management methods as well as the `std.allocator` module, which was still at experimental stage at the time of writing this book.

As in some of the previous chapters, when I write *variable* below, I mean any type of variable including `struct` and `class` objects.

88.1 Memory

Memory is a more significant resource than other system resources because both the running program and its data are located in the memory. The memory belongs ultimately to the operating system, which makes it available to programs to satisfy their needs. The amount of memory that a program uses may increase or decrease according to the immediate needs of a program. When a program terminates, the memory areas that it has been using are automatically returned back to the operating system.

The memory can be imagined like a large sheet of paper where the values of variables are noted down. Each variable is kept at a specific location where its value is written to and read from as needed. Once the lifetime of a variable ends, its place is used for another variable.

The & (address-of) operator is useful when experimenting with memory. For example, the following program prints the addresses of two variables that are defined next to each other:

```d
import std.stdio;

void main() {
    int i;
    int j;

    writeln("i: ", &i);
    writeln("j: ", &j);
}
```

Note: The addresses would likely be different every time the program is executed. Additionally, the mere act of taking the address of a variable disables the optimization that would otherwise make the variable live on a CPU register.

As can be seen from the output, the locations of the variables are four bytes apart:

```
i: 7FFF2B633E28
j: 7FFF2B633E2C
```

The last digits of the two addresses indicate that i lives in a memory location that is right before the location of j: 8 plus 4 (size of `int`) makes 12 (C in hexadecimal notation).

88.2 The garbage collector

The dynamic variables that are used in D programs live on memory blocks that are owned by the garbage collector (GC). When the lifetime of a variable ends (i.e. it's no longer being used), that variable is subject to being finalized according to an algorithm that is executed by the GC. If nothing else needs the memory location containing the variable, the memory may be reclaimed to be used for other variables. This algorithm is called *garbage collection* and an execution of the algorithm is called a *garbage collection cycle*.

The algorithm that the GC executes can roughly be described as the following. All of the memory blocks that can be reached directly or indirectly by pointers (including references) that are in the program roots are scanned. Any memory block that can be reached is tagged as being still in use and all the others are tagged as not being used anymore. The finalizers of objects and structs that live on inaccessible blocks are executed and those memory blocks are reclaimed to be used for future variables. The roots are defined as all of the program stack for every thread, all global and thread-local variables, and any additional data added via GC.addRoot or GC.addRange.

Some GC algorithms can move objects around to keep them together in one place in memory. To preserve program correctness, all of the pointers (and references) that point to such objects are automatically modified to point to the new locations. D's current GC does not do this.

A GC is said to be "precise" if it knows exactly which memory contains pointers and which doesn't. A GC is conservative if it scans all memory as if it were pointers. D's GC is partially conservative, scanning only blocks that contain pointers, but it will scan all data in those blocks. For this reason, in some cases blocks are not ever collected, thereby "leaking" that memory. Large blocks are more likely to be targeted by "false pointers". In some cases it may be recommended to manually free large blocks you are no longer using to avoid this problem.

The order of executing the finalizers is unspecified. For example, a reference member of an object may be finalized before the object that contains that member. For that reason, no class member that refers to a dynamic variable should be accessed inside the destructor. Note that this is very different from the deterministic destruction order of languages like C++.

A garbage collection cycle can be started for various reasons like needing to find space for more data. Depending on the GC implementation, because allocating new objects during a garbage collection cycle can interfere with the collection process itself, all of the running threads may have to be halted during collection cycles. Sometimes this can be observed as a hesitation in the execution of the program.

In most cases the programmer does not need to interfere with the garbage collection process. However, it is possible to delay or dispatch garbage collection cycles as needed by the functions defined in the core.memory module.

Starting and delaying garbage collection cycles
It may be desired to delay the execution of garbage collection cycles during a part of the program where it is important for the program to be responsive. GC.disable disables garbage collection cycles and GC.enable enables them again:

```
    GC.disable();
// ... a part of the program where responsiveness is important ...
    GC.enable();
```

However, `GC.disable` is not guaranteed to prevent a garbage collection cycle from executing: If the GC needs to obtain more memory from the OS, but it cannot, it still goes ahead and runs a garbage collection cycle as a last-ditch effort to gain some available memory.

Instead of relying on garbage collections happening automatically at unspecified times, a garbage collection cycle can be started explicitly using `GC.collect()`:

```
import core.memory;
// ...
    GC.collect();    // starts a garbage collection cycle
```

Normally, the GC does not return memory blocks back to the operating system; it holds on to those memory pages for future needs of the program. If desired, the GC can be asked to give unused memory back to the operating system using `GC.minimize()`:

```
    GC.minimize();
```

88.3 Allocating memory

System languages allow programmers to specify the memory areas where objects should live. Such memory areas are commonly called *buffers*.

There are several methods of allocating memory. The simplest method would be using a fixed-length array:

```
    ubyte[100] buffer;    // A memory area of 100 bytes
```

`buffer` is ready to be used as a 100-byte memory area. Instead of `ubyte`, it is also possible to define such buffers as arrays of `void`, without any association to any type. Since `void` cannot be assigned any value, it cannot have the `.init` value either. Such arrays must be initialized by the special syntax `=void`:

```
    void[100] buffer = void;    // A memory area of 100 bytes
```

We will use only `GC.calloc` from the `core.memory` module to reserve memory in this chapter. That module has many other features that are useful in various situations. Additionally, the memory allocation functions of the C standard library are avaliable in the `core.stdc.stdlib` module.

`GC.calloc` allocates a memory area of the specified size pre-filled with all 0 values, and returns the beginning address of the allocated area:

```
import core.memory;
// ...
    void * buffer = GC.calloc(100);
                         // A memory area of 100 zero bytes
```

Normally, the returned `void*` value is cast to a pointer of the proper type:

```
    int * intBuffer = cast(int*)buffer;
```

However, that intermediate step is usually skipped and the return value is cast directly:

```
    int * intBuffer = cast(int*)GC.calloc(100);
```

Instead of arbitrary values like 100, the size of the memory area is usually calculated by multiplying the number of elements needed with the size of each element:

```
// Allocate room for 25 ints
int * intBuffer = cast(int*)GC.calloc(int.sizeof * 25);
```

There is an important difference for classes: The size of a class variable and the size of a class object are not the same. .sizeof is the size of a class variable and is always the same value: 8 on 64-bit systems and 4 on 32-bit systems. The size of a class object must be obtained by __traits(classInstanceSize):

```
// Allocate room for 10 MyClass objects
MyClass * buffer =
    cast(MyClass*)GC.calloc(
        __traits(classInstanceSize, MyClass) * 10);
```

When there is not enough memory in the system for the requested size, then a core.exception.OutOfMemoryError exception is thrown:

```
void * buffer = GC.calloc(10_000_000_000);
```

The output on a system that does not have that much free space:

```
core.exception.OutOfMemoryError
```

The memory areas that are allocated from the GC can be returned back to it using GC.free:

```
GC.free(buffer);
```

However, calling free() does not necessarily execute the destructors of the variables that live on that memory block. The destructors may be executed explicitly by calling destroy() for each variable. Note that various internal mechanisms are used to call finalizers on class and struct variables during GC collection or freeing. The best way to ensure these are called is to use the new operator when allocating variables. In that case, GC.free will call the destructors.

Sometimes the program may determine that a previously allocated memory area is all used up and does not have room for more data. It is possible to *extend* a previously allocated memory area by GC.realloc. realloc() takes the previously allocated memory pointer and the newly requested size, and returns a new area:

```
    void * oldBuffer = GC.calloc(100);
// ...
    void * newBuffer = GC.realloc(oldBuffer, 200);
```

realloc() tries to be efficient by not actually allocating new memory unless it is really necessary:

- If the memory area following the old area is not in use for any other purpose and is large enough to satisfy the new request, realloc() adds that part of the memory to the old area, extending the buffer *in-place*.
- If the memory area following the old area is already in use or is not large enough, then realloc() allocates a new larger memory area and copies the contents of the old area to the new one.

- It is possible to pass `null` as `oldBuffer`, in which case `realloc()` simply allocates new memory.
- It is possible to pass a size less than the previous one, in which case the remaining part of the old memory is returned back to the GC.
- It is possible to pass 0 as the new size, in which case `realloc()` simply frees the memory.

`GC.realloc` is adapted from the C standard library function `realloc()`. For having such a complicated behavior, `realloc()` is considered to have a badly designed function interface. A potentially surprising aspect of `GC.realloc` is that even if the original memory has been allocated with `GC.calloc`, the extended part is never cleared. For that reason, when it is important that the memory is zero-initialized, a function like `reallocCleared()` below would be useful. We will see the meaning of `blockAttributes` later below:

```d
import core.memory;

/* Works like GC.realloc but clears the extra bytes if memory
 * is extended. */
void * reallocCleared(
    void * buffer,
    size_t oldLength,
    size_t newLength,
    GC.BlkAttr blockAttributes = GC.BlkAttr.NONE,
    const TypeInfo typeInfo = null) {
    /* Dispatch the actual work to GC.realloc. */
    buffer = GC.realloc(buffer, newLength,
                        blockAttributes, typeInfo);

    /* Clear the extra bytes if extended. */
    if (newLength > oldLength) {
        import core.stdc.string;

        auto extendedPart = buffer + oldLength;
        const extendedLength = newLength - oldLength;

        memset(extendedPart, 0, extendedLength);
    }

    return buffer;
}
```

The function above uses `memset()` from the `core.stdc.string` module to clear the newly extended bytes. `memset()` assigns the specified value to the bytes of a memory area specified by a pointer and a length. In the example, it assigns 0 to `extendedLength` number of bytes at `extendedPart`.

We will use `reallocCleared()` in an example below.

The behavior of the similar function `GC.extend` is not complicated like `realloc()`; it applies only the first item above: If the memory area cannot be extended in-place, `extend()` does not do anything and returns 0.

Memory block attributes

The concepts and the steps of a GC algorithm can be configured to some degree for each memory block by enum `BlkAttr`. `BlkAttr` is an optional parameter of `GC.calloc` and other allocation functions. It consists of the following values:

- `NONE`: The value zero; specifies *no attribute*.
- `FINALIZE`: Specifies that the objects that live in the memory block should be finalized.

Normally, the GC assumes that the lifetimes of objects that live on explicitly-allocated memory locations are under the control of the programmer; it does not finalize objects on such memory areas. GC.BlkAttr.FINALIZE is for requesting the GC to execute the destructors of objects:

```d
Class * buffer =
    cast(Class*)GC.calloc(
        __traits(classInstanceSize, Class) * 10,
        GC.BlkAttr.FINALIZE);
```

Note that FINALIZE depends on implementation details properly set up on the block. It is highly recommended to let the GC take care of setting up these details using the new operator.

- NO_SCAN: Specifies that the memory area should not be scanned by the GC.

  The byte values in a memory area may accidentally look like pointers to unrelated objects in other parts of the memory. When that happens, the GC would assume that those objects are still in use even after their actual lifetimes have ended.

  A memory block that is known to not contain any object pointers should be marked as GC.BlkAttr.NO_SCAN:

```d
int * intBuffer =
    cast(int*)GC.calloc(100, GC.BlkAttr.NO_SCAN);
```

The int variables placed in that memory block can have any value without concern of being mistaken for object pointers.

- NO_MOVE: Specifies that objects in the memory block should not be moved to other places.
- APPENDABLE: This is an internal flag used by the D runtime to aid in fast appending. You should not use this flag when allocating memory.
- NO_INTERIOR: Specifies that only pointers to the block's first address exist. This allows one to cut down on "false pointers" because a pointer to the middle of the block does not count when tracing where a pointer goes.

The values of enum BlkAttr are suitable to be used as bit flags that we saw in the Bit Operations chapter (page 446). The following is how two attributes can be merged by the | operator:

```d
const attributes =
    GC.BlkAttr.NO_SCAN | GC.BlkAttr.NO_INTERIOR;
```

Naturally, the GC would be aware only of memory blocks that are reserved by its own functions and scans only those memory blocks. For example, it would not know about a memory block allocated by core.stdc.stdlib.calloc.

GC.addRange is for introducing unrelated memory blocks to the GC. The complement function GC.removeRange should be called before freeing a memory block by other means e.g. by core.stdc.stdlib.free.

In some cases, there may be no reference in the program to a memory block even if that memory block has been reserved by the GC. For example, if the only reference to a memory block lives inside a C library, the GC would normally not know about that reference and assume that the memory block is not in use anymore.

GC.addRoot introduces a memory block to the GC as a *root*, to be scanned during collection cycles. All of the variables that can be reached directly or indirectly through that memory block would be marked as alive. The complement function GC.removeRoot should be called when a memory block is not in use anymore.

Example of extending a memory area

Let's design a simple `struct` template that works like an array. To keep the example short, let's provide only the functionality of adding and accessing elements. Similar to arrays, let's increase the capacity as needed. The following program uses `reallocCleared()`, which has been defined above:

```d
struct Array(T) {
    T * buffer;          // Memory area that holds the elements
    size_t capacity;     // The element capacity of the buffer
    size_t length;       // The number of actual elements

    /* Returns the specified element */
    T element(size_t index) {
        import std.string;
        enforce(index < length,
                format("Invalid index %s", index));

        return *(buffer + index);
    }

    /* Appends the element to the end */
    void append(T element) {
        writefln("Appending element %s", length);

        if (length == capacity) {
            /* There is no room for the new element; must
             * increase capacity. */
            size_t newCapacity = capacity + (capacity / 2) + 1;
            increaseCapacity(newCapacity);
        }

        /* Place the element at the end */
        *(buffer + length) = element;
        ++length;
    }

    void increaseCapacity(size_t newCapacity) {
        writefln("Increasing capacity from %s to %s",
                 capacity, newCapacity);

        size_t oldBufferSize = capacity * T.sizeof;
        size_t newBufferSize = newCapacity * T.sizeof;

        /* Also specify that this memory block should not be
         * scanned for pointers. */
        buffer = cast(T*)reallocCleared(
            buffer, oldBufferSize, newBufferSize,
            GC.BlkAttr.NO_SCAN);

        capacity = newCapacity;
    }
}
```

The capacity of the array grows by about 50%. For example, after the capacity for 100 elements is consumed, the new capacity would become 151. (*The extra 1 is for the case of 0 length, where adding 50% would not grow the array.*)

The following program uses that template with the double type:

```d
import std.stdio;
import core.memory;
import std.exception;

// ...
```

```
void main() {
    auto array = Array!double();

    const count = 10;

    foreach (i; 0 .. count) {
        double elementValue = i * 1.1;
        array.append(elementValue);
    }

    writeln("The elements:");

    foreach (i; 0 .. count) {
        write(array.element(i), ' ');
    }

    writeln();
}
```

The output:

```
Adding element with index 0
Increasing capacity from 0 to 1
Adding element with index 1
Increasing capacity from 1 to 2
Adding element with index 2
Increasing capacity from 2 to 4
Adding element with index 3
Adding element with index 4
Increasing capacity from 4 to 7
Adding element with index 5
Adding element with index 6
Adding element with index 7
Increasing capacity from 7 to 11
Adding element with index 8
Adding element with index 9
The elements:
0 1.1 2.2 3.3 4.4 5.5 6.6 7.7 8.8 9.9
```

88.4 Alignment

By default, every object is placed at memory locations that are multiples of an amount specific to the type of that object. That amount is called the *alignment* of that type. For example, the alignment of int is 4 because int variables are placed at memory locations that are multiples of 4 (4, 8, 12, etc.).

Alignment is needed for CPU performance or requirements, because accessing misaligned memory addresses can be slower or cause a bus error. In addition, certain types of variables only work properly at aligned addresses.

The .alignof property

The .alignof property of a type is its default alignment value. For classes, .alignof is the alignment of the class variable, not the class object. The alignment of a class object is obtained by std.traits.classInstanceAlignment.

The following program prints the alignments of various types:

```
import std.stdio;
import std.meta;
import std.traits;

struct EmptyStruct {
}

struct Struct {
    char c;
    double d;
}
```

```
class EmptyClass {
}

class Class {
    char c;
}

void main() {
    alias Types = AliasSeq!(char, short, int, long,
                            double, real,
                            string, int[int], int*,
                            EmptyStruct, Struct,
                            EmptyClass, Class);

    writeln(" Size  Alignment  Type\n",
            "==========================");

    foreach (Type; Types) {
        static if (is (Type == class)) {
            size_t size = __traits(classInstanceSize, Type);
            size_t alignment = classInstanceAlignment!Type;

        } else {
            size_t size = Type.sizeof;
            size_t alignment = Type.alignof;
        }

        writefln("%4s%8s     %s",
                 size, alignment, Type.stringof);
    }
}
```

The output of the program may be different in different environments. The
following is a sample output:

```
Size  Alignment  Type
=========================
   1        1     char
   2        2     short
   4        4     int
   8        8     long
   8        8     double
  16       16     real
  16        8     string
   8        8     int[int]
   8        8     int*
   1        1     EmptyStruct
  16        8     Struct
  16        8     EmptyClass
  17        8     Class
```

We will see later below how variables can be constructed (emplaced) at specific
memory locations. For correctness and efficiency, objects must be constructed at
addresses that match their alignments.

Let's consider two *consecutive* objects of Class type above, which are 17 bytes
each. Although 0 is not a legal address for a variable on most platforms, to
simplify the example let's assume that the first object is at address 0. The 17 bytes
of this object would be at adresses from 0 to 16:

```
    0   1           16
    ┌───┬───┬ ... ┬───┬───┐  ...
    │<──┼───first object───┼──>│
    └───┴───┴ ... ┴───┴───┘  ...
```

Although the next available address is 17, that location cannot be used for a Class
object because 17 is not a multiple of the alignment value 8 of that type. The
nearest possible address for the second object is 24 because 24 is the next smallest

multiple of 8. When the second object is placed at that address, there would be unused bytes between the two objects. Those bytes are called *padding bytes*:

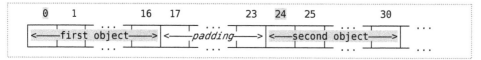

The following formula can determine the nearest address value that an object can be placed at:

```
(candidateAddress + alignmentValue - 1)
/ alignmentValue
* alignmentValue
```

For that formula to work, the fractional part of the result of the division must be truncated. Since truncation is automatic for integral types, all of the variables above are assumed to be integral types.

We will use the following function in the examples later below:

```
T * nextAlignedAddress(T)(T * candidateAddr) {
    import std.traits;

    static if (is (T == class)) {
        const alignment = classInstanceAlignment!T;

    } else {
        const alignment = T.alignof;
    }

    const result = (cast(size_t)candidateAddr + alignment - 1)
                   / alignment * alignment;
    return cast(T*)result;
}
```

That function template deduces the type of the object from its template parameter. Since that is not possible when the type is void*, the type must be provided as an explicit template argument for the void* overload. That overload can trivially forward the call to the function template above:

```
void * nextAlignedAddress(T)(void * candidateAddr) {
    return nextAlignedAddress(cast(T*)candidateAddr);
}
```

The function template above will be useful below when constructing *class* objects by emplace().

Let's define one more function template to calculate the total size of an object including the padding bytes that must be placed between two objects of that type:

```
size_t sizeWithPadding(T)() {
    static if (is (T == class)) {
        const candidateAddr = __traits(classInstanceSize, T);

    } else {
        const candidateAddr = T.sizeof;
    }

    return cast(size_t)nextAlignedAddress(cast(T*)candidateAddr);
}
```

The .offsetof property

Alignment is observed for members of user-defined types as well. There may be padding bytes *between* members so that the members are aligned according to their respective types. For that reason, the size of the following `struct` is not 6 bytes as one might expect, but 12:

```d
struct A {
    byte b;      // 1 byte
    int i;       // 4 bytes
    ubyte u;     // 1 byte
}

static assert(A.sizeof == 12);     // More than 1 + 4 + 1
```

This is due to padding bytes before the `int` member so that it is aligned at an address that is a multiple of 4, as well as padding bytes at the end for the alignment of the entire `struct` object itself.

The `.offsetof` property gives the number of bytes a member variable is from the beginning of the object that it is a part of. The following function prints the layout of a type by determining the padding bytes by `.offsetof`:

```d
void printObjectLayout(T)()
        if (is (T == struct) || is (T == union)) {
    import std.stdio;
    import std.string;

    writefln("=== Memory layout of '%s'" ~
             " (.sizeof: %s, .alignof: %s) ===",
             T.stringof, T.sizeof, T.alignof);

    /* Prints a single line of layout information. */
    void printLine(size_t offset, string info) {
        writefln("%4s: %s", offset, info);
    }

    /* Prints padding information if padding is actually
     * observed. */
    void maybePrintPaddingInfo(size_t expectedOffset,
                               size_t actualOffset) {
        if (expectedOffset < actualOffset) {
            /* There is some padding because the actual offset
             * is beyond the expected one. */

            const paddingSize = actualOffset - expectedOffset;

            printLine(expectedOffset,
                      format("... %s-byte PADDING",
                             paddingSize));
        }
    }

    /* This is the expected offset of the next member if there
     * were no padding bytes before that member. */
    size_t noPaddingOffset = 0;

    /* Note: __traits(allMembers) is a 'string' collection of
     * names of the members of a type. */
    foreach (memberName; __traits(allMembers, T)) {
        mixin (format("alias member = %s.%s;",
                      T.stringof, memberName));

        const offset = member.offsetof;
        maybePrintPaddingInfo(noPaddingOffset, offset);

        const typeName = typeof(member).stringof;
        printLine(offset,
                  format("%s %s", typeName, memberName));

        noPaddingOffset = offset + member.sizeof;
    }

    maybePrintPaddingInfo(noPaddingOffset, T.sizeof);
}
```

The following program prints the layout of the 12-byte `struct A` that was defined above:

```
struct A {
    byte b;
    int i;
    ubyte u;
}

void main() {
    printObjectLayout!A();
}
```

The output of the program showns where the total of 6 padding bytes are located inside the object. The first column of the output is the offset from the beginning of the object:

```
=== Memory layout of 'A' (.sizeof: 12, .alignof: 4) ===
    0: byte b
    1: ... 3-byte PADDING
    4: int i
    8: ubyte u
    9: ... 3-byte PADDING
```

One technique of minimizing padding is ordering the members by their sizes from the largest to the smallest. For example, when the `int` member is moved to the beginning of the previous `struct` then the size of the object would be less:

```
struct B {
    int i;      // Moved up inside the struct definition
    byte b;
    ubyte u;
}

void main() {
    printObjectLayout!B();
}
```

This time, the size of the object is down to 8 due to just 2 bytes of padding at the end:

```
=== Memory layout of 'B' (.sizeof: 8, .alignof: 4) ===
    0: int i
    4: byte b
    5: ubyte u
    6: ... 2-byte PADDING
```

The `align` attribute

The `align` attribute is for specifying alignments of variables, user-defined types, and members of user-defined types. The value provided in parentheses specifies the alignment value. Every definition can be specified separately. For example, the following definition would align S objects at 2-byte boundaries and its i member at 1-byte boundaries (1-byte alignment always results in no padding at all):

```
align (2)                   // The alignment of 'S' objects
struct S {
    byte b;
    align (1) int i;        // The alignment of member 'i'
    ubyte u;
}

void main() {
    printObjectLayout!S();
}
```

When the `int` member is aligned at a 1-byte boundary, there is no padding before it and this time the size of the object ends up being exactly 6:

```
=== Memory layout of 'S' (.sizeof: 6, .alignof: 4) ===
    0: byte b
    1: int i
    5: ubyte u
```

Although `align` can reduce sizes of user-defined types, there can be *significant performance penalties* when default alignments of types are not observed (and on some CPUs, using misaligned data can actually crash the program).

align can specify the alignment of variables as well:

```
    align (32) double d;    // The alignment of a variable
```

However, objects that are allocated by new must always be aligned at multiples of the size of the `size_t` type because that is what the GC assumes. Doing otherwise is undefined behavior. For example, if `size_t` is 8 bytes long, than the alignments of variables allocated by new must be a multiple of 8.

88.5 Constructing variables at specific memory locations

The new expression achieves three tasks:

1. Allocates memory large enough for the object. The newly allocated memory area is considered to be *raw*, not associated with any type or any object.
2. Copies the `.init` value of that type on that memory area and executes the constructor of the object on that area. Only after this step the object becomes *placed* on that memory area.
3. Configures the memory block so it has all the necessary flags and infrastructure to properly destroy the object when freed.

We have already seen that the first of these tasks can explicitly be achieved by memory allocation functions like GC.calloc. Being a system language, D allows the programmer manage the second step as well.

Variables can be constructed at specific locations with `std.conv.emplace`.

Constructing a struct object at a specific location

emplace() takes the address of a memory location as its first parameter and constructs an object at that location. If provided, it uses the remaining parameters as the object's constructor arguments:

```
import std.conv;
// ...
    emplace(address, /* ... constructor arguments ... */);
```

It is not necessary to specify the type of the object explicitly when constructing a struct object because emplace() deduces the type of the object from the type of the pointer. For example, since the type of the following pointer is Student*, emplace() constructs a Student object at that address:

```
    Student * objectAddr = nextAlignedAddress(candidateAddr);
// ...
    emplace(objectAddr, name, id);
```

The following program allocates a memory area large enough for three objects and constructs them one by one at aligned addresses inside that memory area:

```
import std.stdio;
import std.string;
import core.memory;
import std.conv;

// ...

struct Student {
    string name;
    int id;

    string toString() {
        return format("%s(%s)", name, id);
    }
}

void main() {
    /* Some information about this type. */
    writefln("Student.sizeof: %#x (%s) bytes",
             Student.sizeof, Student.sizeof);
    writefln("Student.alignof: %#x (%s) bytes",
             Student.alignof, Student.alignof);

    string[] names = [ "Amy", "Tim", "Joe" ];
    const totalSize = sizeWithPadding!Student() * names.length;

    /* Reserve room for all Student objects.
     *
     * Warning! The objects that are accessible through this
     * slice are not constructed yet; they should not be
     * accessed until after they are properly constructed. */
    Student[] students =
        (cast(Student*)GC.calloc(totalSize))[0 .. names.length];

    foreach (i, name; names) {
        Student * candidateAddr = students.ptr + i;
        Student * objectAddr =
            nextAlignedAddress(candidateAddr);
        writefln("address of object %s: %s", i, objectAddr);

        const id = 100 + i.to!int;
        emplace(objectAddr, name, id);
    }

    /* All of the objects are constructed and can be used. */
    writeln(students);
}
```

The output of the program:

```
Student.sizeof: 0x18 (24) bytes
Student.alignof: 0x8 (8) bytes
address of object 0: 7F1532861F00
address of object 1: 7F1532861F18
address of object 2: 7F1532861F30
[Amy(100), Tim(101), Joe(102)]
```

Constructing a class object at a specific location

Class variables need not be of the exact type of class objects. For example, a class variable of type Animal can refer to a Cat object. For that reason, emplace() does not determine the type of the object from the type of the memory pointer. Instead, the actual type of the object must be explicitly specified as a template argument of emplace(). (**Note:** *Additionally, a class pointer is a pointer to a class variable, not to a class object. For that reason, specifying the actual type allows the programmer to specify whether to emplace a class object or a class variable.*)

The memory location for a class object must be specified as a void[] slice with the following syntax:

```
    Type variable =
        emplace!Type(voidSlice,
                        /* ... constructor arguments ... */);
```

`emplace()` constructs a class *object* at the location specified by the slice and returns a class *variable* for that object.

Let's use `emplace()` on objects of an `Animal` hierarchy. The objects of this hierarchy will be placed *side-by-side* on a piece of memory that is allocated by `GC.calloc`. To make the example more interesting, we will ensure that the subclasses have different sizes. This will be useful to demonstrate how the address of a subsequent object can be determined depending on the size of the previous one.

```
interface Animal {
    string sing();
}

class Cat : Animal {
    string sing() {
        return "meow";
    }
}

class Parrot : Animal {
    string[] lyrics;

    this(string[] lyrics) {
        this.lyrics = lyrics;
    }

    string sing() {
        /* std.algorithm.joiner joins elements of a range with
         * the specified separator. */
        return lyrics.joiner(", ").to!string;
    }
}
```

The buffer that holds the objects will be allocated with `GC.calloc`:

```
    const capacity = 10_000;
    void * buffer = GC.calloc(capacity);
```

Normally, it must be ensured that there is always available capacity for objects. We will ignore that check here to keep the example simple and assume that the objects in the example will fit in ten thousand bytes.

The buffer will be used for constructing a `Cat` and a `Parrot` object:

```
    Cat cat = emplace!Cat(catPlace);
// ...
    Parrot parrot =
        emplace!Parrot(parrotPlace, [ "squawk", "arrgh" ]);
```

Note that the constructor argument of `Parrot` is specified after the address of the object.

The variables that `emplace()` returns will be stored in an `Animal` slice later to be used in a `foreach` loop:

```
    Animal[] animals;
// ...
    animals ~= cat;
// ...
    animals ~= parrot;

    foreach (animal; animals) {
```

```
        writeln(animal.sing());
    }
```

More explanations are inside the code comments:

```
import std.stdio;
import std.algorithm;
import std.conv;
import core.memory;

// ...

void main() {
    /* A slice of Animal variables (not Animal objects). */
    Animal[] animals;

    /* Allocating a buffer with an arbitrary capacity and
     * assuming that the two objects in this example will fit
     * in that area. Normally, this condition must be
     * validated. */
    const capacity = 10_000;
    void * buffer = GC.calloc(capacity);

    /* Let's first place a Cat object. */
    void * catCandidateAddr = buffer;
    void * catAddr = nextAlignedAddress!Cat(catCandidateAddr);
    writeln("Cat address    : ", catAddr);

    /* Since emplace() requires a void[] for a class object,
     * we must first produce a slice from the pointer. */
    size_t catSize = __traits(classInstanceSize, Cat);
    void[] catPlace = catAddr[0..catSize];

    /* Construct a Cat object inside that memory slice and
     * store the returned class variable for later use. */
    Cat cat = emplace!Cat(catPlace);
    animals ~= cat;

    /* Now construct a Parrot object at the next available
     * address that satisfies the alignment requirement. */
    void * parrotCandidateAddr = catAddr + catSize;
    void * parrotAddr =
        nextAlignedAddress!Parrot(parrotCandidateAddr);
    writeln("Parrot address: ", parrotAddr);

    size_t parrotSize = __traits(classInstanceSize, Parrot);
    void[] parrotPlace = parrotAddr[0..parrotSize];

    Parrot parrot =
        emplace!Parrot(parrotPlace, [ "squawk", "arrgh" ]);
    animals ~= parrot;

    /* Use the objects. */
    foreach (animal; animals) {
        writeln(animal.sing());
    }
}
```

The output:

```
Cat address    : 7F0E343A2000
Parrot address: 7F0E343A2018
meow
squawk, arrgh
```

Instead of repeating the steps inside main() for each object, a function template like newObject(T) would be more useful.

88.6 Destroying objects explicitly

The reverse operations of the new operator are destroying an object and returning the object's memory back to the GC. Normally, these operations are executed automatically at unspecified times.

However, sometimes it is necessary to execute destructors at specific points in the program. For example, an object may be closing a File member in its destructor and the destructor may have to be executed immediately when the lifetime of the object ends.

destroy() calls the destructor of an object:

```
destroy(variable);
```

After executing the destructor, destroy() sets the variable to its .init state. Note that the .init state of a class variable is null; so, a class variable cannot be used once destroyed. destroy() merely executes the destructor. It is still up to the GC when to reuse the piece of memory that used to be occupied by the destroyed object.

Warning: When used with a *struct* pointer, destroy() must receive the pointee, not the pointer. Otherwise, the pointer would be set to null but the object would not be destroyed:

```d
import std.stdio;

struct S {
    int i;

    this(int i) {
        this.i = i;
        writefln("Constructing object with value %s", i);
    }

    ~this() {
        writefln("Destroying object with value %s", i);
    }
}

void main() {
    auto p = new S(42);

    writeln("Before destroy()");
    destroy(p);                          // ← WRONG USAGE
    writeln("After destroy()");

    writefln("p: %s", p);

    writeln("Leaving main");
}
```

When destroy() receives a pointer, it is the pointer that gets destroyed (i.e. the pointer becomes null):

```
Constructing object with value 42
Before destroy()
After destroy()    ← The object is not destroyed before this line
p: null            ← Instead, the pointer becomes null
Leaving main
Destroying object with value 42
```

For that reason, when used with a struct pointer, destroy() must receive the pointee:

```
destroy(*p);                          // ← Correct usage
```

This time the destructor is executed at the right spot and the pointer is not set to null:

```
Constructing object with value 42
Before destroy()
Destroying object with value 42    ← Destroyed at the right spot
After destroy()
p: 7FB64FE3F200                    ← The pointer is not null
Leaving main
Destroying object with value 0     ← Once more for S.init
```

The last line is due to executing the destructor one more time for the same object, which now has the value S.init.

88.7 Constructing objects at run time by name

The factory() member function of Object takes the fully qualified name of a class type as parameter, constructs an object of that type, and returns a class variable for that object:

```d
module test_module;

import std.stdio;

interface Animal {
    string sing();
}

class Cat : Animal {
    string sing() {
        return "meow";
    }
}

class Dog : Animal {
    string sing() {
        return "woof";
    }
}

void main() {
    string[] toConstruct = [ "Cat", "Dog", "Cat" ];

    Animal[] animals;

    foreach (typeName; toConstruct) {
        /* The pseudo variable __MODULE__ is always the name
         * of the current module, which can be used as a
         * string literal at compile time. */
        const fullName = __MODULE__ ~ '.' ~ typeName;
        writefln("Constructing %s", fullName);
        animals ~= cast(Animal)Object.factory(fullName);
    }

    foreach (animal; animals) {
        writeln(animal.sing());
    }
}
```

Although there is no explicit new expression in that program, three class objects are created and added to the animals slice:

```
Constructing test_module.Cat
Constructing test_module.Dog
Constructing test_module.Cat
meow
woof
meow
```

Note that `Object.factory()` takes the fully qualified name of the type of the object. Also, the return type of `factory()` is `Object`; so, it must be cast to the actual type of the object before being used in the program.

88.8 Summary

- The garbage collector scans the memory at unspecified times, determines the objects that cannot possibly be reached anymore by the program, destroys them, and reclaims their memory locations.
- The operations of the GC may be controlled by the programmer to some extent by `GC.collect`, `GC.disable`, `GC.enable`, `GC.minimize`, etc.
- `GC.calloc` and other functions reserve memory, `GC.realloc` extends a previously allocated memory area, and `GC.free` returns it back to the GC.
- It is possible to mark the allocated memory by attributes like `GC.BlkAttr.NO_SCAN`, `GC.BlkAttr.NO_INTERIOR`, etc.
- The `.alignof` property is the default memory alignment of a type. Alignment must be obtained by `classInstanceAlignment` for class *objects*.
- The `.offsetof` property is the number of bytes a member is from the beginning of the object that it is a part of.
- The `align` attribute specifies the alignment of a variable, a user-defined type, or a member.
- `emplace()` takes a pointer when constructing a `struct` object, a `void[]` slice when constructing a `class` object.
- `destroy()` executes the destructor of objects. (One must destroy the struct pointee, not the struct pointer.)
- `Object.factory()` constructs objects with their fully qualified type names.

Any declaration (e.g. struct type, class type, variable, etc.) can be assigned attributes, which can then be accessed at compile time to alter the way the code is compiled. User defined attributes is purely a compile-time feature.

The user defined attribute syntax consists of the @ sign followed by the attribute and appear before the declaration that it is being assigned to. For example, the following code assigns the Encrypted attribute to the declaration of name:

```
@Encrypted string name;
```

Multiple attributes can be specified separately or as a parenthesized list of attributes. For example, both of the following variables have the same attributes:

```
@Encrypted @Colored string lastName;     // ← separately
@(Encrypted, Colored) string address;    // ← together
```

An attribute can be a type name as well as a value of a user defined or a fundamental type. However, because their meanings may not be clear, attributes consisting of literal values like 42 are discouraged:

```
struct Encrypted {
}

enum Color { black, blue, red }

struct Colored {
    Color color;
}

void main() {
    @Encrypted              int a;   // ← type name
    @Encrypted()            int b;   // ← object
    @Colored(Color.blue)    int c;   // ← object
    @(42)                   int d;   // ← literal (discouraged)
}
```

The attributes of a and b above are of different kinds: The attribute of a is the type Encrypted itself, while the attribute of b is an *object* of type Encrypted. This is an important difference that affects the way attributes are used at compile time. We will see an example of this difference below.

The meaning of attributes is solely determined by the programmer for the needs of the program. The attributes are determined by __traits(getAttributes) at compile time and the code is compiled according to those attributes.

The following code shows how the attributes of a specific struct member (e.g. Person.name) can be accessed by __traits(getAttributes):

```
import std.stdio;

// ...

struct Person {
    @Encrypted @Colored(Color.blue) string name;
    string lastName;
    @Colored(Color.red) string address;
}

void main() {
    foreach (attr; __traits(getAttributes, Person.name)) {
```

```
            writeln(attr.stringof);
    }
}
```

The output of the program lists the attributes of `Person.name`:

```
Encrypted
Colored(cast(Color)1)
```

Two other `__traits` expressions are useful when dealing with user defined attributes:

- `__traits(allMembers)` produces the members of a type (or a module) as strings.
- `__traits(getMember)` produces a *symbol* useful when accessing a member. Its first argument is a symbol (e.g. a type or a variable name) and its second argument is a string. It produces a symbol by combining its first argument, a dot, and its second argument. For example, `__traits(getMember, Person, "name")` produces the symbol `Person.name`.

```
import std.string;

// ...

void main() {
    foreach (memberName; __traits(allMembers, Person)) {
        writef("The attributes of %-8s:", memberName);

        foreach (attr; __traits(getAttributes,
                                __traits(getMember,
                                         Person, memberName))) {
            writef(" %s", attr.stringof);
        }

        writeln();
    }
}
```

The output of the program lists all attributes of all members of `Person`:

```
The attributes of name    : Encrypted Colored(cast(Color)1)
The attributes of lastName:
The attributes of address : Colored(cast(Color)2)
```

Another useful tool is `std.traits.hasUDA`, which determines whether a symbol has a specific attribute. The following `static assert` passes because `Person.name` has `Encrypted` attribute:

```
import std.traits;

// ...

static assert(hasUDA!(Person.name, Encrypted));
```

hasUDA can be used with an attribute type as well as a specific value of that type. The following `static assert` checks both pass because `Person.name` has `Colored(Color.blue)` attribute:

```
static assert(hasUDA!(Person.name, Colored));
static assert(hasUDA!(Person.name, Colored(Color.blue)));
```

89.1 Example

Let's design a function template that prints the values of all members of a struct object in XML format. The following function considers the Encrypted and Colored attributes of each member when producing the output:

```
void printAsXML(T)(T object) {
// ...

    foreach (member; __traits(allMembers, T)) {          // (1)
        string value =
            __traits(getMember, object, member).to!string; // (2)

        static if (hasUDA!(__traits(getMember, T, member),  // (3)
                           Encrypted)) {
            value = value.encrypted.to!string;
        }

        writefln(`    <%1$s color="%2$s">%3$s</%1$s>`, member,
                 colorAttributeOf!(T, member), value);      // (4)
    }
}
```

The highlighted parts of the code are explained below:

1. The members of the type are determined by __traits(allMembers).
2. The value of each member is converted to string to be used later when printing to the output. For example, when the member is "name", the right-hand side expression becomes object.name.to!string.
3. Each member is tested with hasUDA to determine whether it has the Encrypted attribute. The value of the member is encrypted if it has that attribute. (Because hasUDA requires *symbols* to work with, note how __traits(getMember) is used to get the member as a symbol (e.g. Person.name).)
4. The color attribute of each member is determined with colorAttributeOf(), which we will see below.

The colorAttributeOf() function template can be implemented as in the following code:

```
Color colorAttributeOf(T, string memberName)() {
    foreach (attr; __traits(getAttributes,
                    __traits(getMember, T, memberName))) {
        static if (is (typeof(attr) == Colored)) {
            return attr.color;
        }
    }

    return Color.black;
}
```

When the compile-time evaluations are completed, the printAsXML() function template would be instantiated for the Person type as the equivalent of the following function:

```
/* The equivalent of the printAsXML!Person instance. */
void printAsXML_Person(Person object) {
// ...

    {
        string value = object.name.to!string;
        value = value.encrypted.to!string;
        writefln(`    <%1$s color="%2$s">%3$s</%1$s>`,
                 "name", Color.blue, value);
```

```
    }
    {
        string value = object.lastName.to!string;
        writeln(`  <%1$s color="%2$s">%3$s</%1$s>`,
                 "lastName", Color.black, value);
    }
    {
        string value = object.address.to!string;
        writeln(`  <%1$s color="%2$s">%3$s</%1$s>`,
                 "address", Color.red, value);
    }
}
```

The complete program has more explanations:

```
import std.stdio;
import std.string;
import std.algorithm;
import std.conv;
import std.traits;

/* Specifies that the symbol that it is assigned to should be
 * encrypted. */
struct Encrypted {
}

enum Color { black, blue, red }

/* Specifies the color of the symbol that it is assigned to.
 * The default color is Color.black. */
struct Colored {
    Color color;
}

struct Person {
    /* This member is specified to be encrypted and printed in
     * blue. */
    @Encrypted @Colored(Color.blue) string name;

    /* This member does not have any user defined
     * attributes. */
    string lastName;

    /* This member is specified to be printed in red. */
    @Colored(Color.red) string address;
}

/* Returns the value of the Colored attribute if the specified
 * member has that attribute, Color.black otherwise. */
Color colorAttributeOf(T, string memberName)() {
    auto result = Color.black;

    foreach (attr;
             __traits(getAttributes,
                      __traits(getMember, T, memberName))) {
        static if (is (typeof(attr) == Colored)) {
            result = attr.color;
        }
    }

    return result;
}

/* Returns the Caesar-encrypted version of the specified
 * string. (Warning: Caesar cipher is a very weak encryption
 * method.) */
auto encrypted(string value) {
    return value.map!(a => dchar(a + 1));
}

unittest {
    assert("abcdefghij".encrypted.equal("bcdefghijk"));
}
```

```
/* Prints the specified object in XML format according to the
 * attributes of its members. */
void printAsXML(T)(T object) {
    writefln("<%s>", T.stringof);
    scope(exit) writefln("</%s>", T.stringof);

    foreach (member; __traits(allMembers, T)) {
        string value =
            __traits(getMember, object, member).to!string;

        static if (hasUDA!(__traits(getMember, T, member),
                            Encrypted)) {
            value = value.encrypted.to!string;
        }

        writefln(`  <%1$s color="%2$s">%3$s</%1$s>`,
                 member, colorAttributeOf!(T, member), value);
    }
}

void main() {
    auto people = [ Person("Alice", "Davignon", "Avignon"),
                    Person("Ben", "de Bordeaux", "Bordeaux") ];

    foreach (person; people) {
        printAsXML(person);
    }
}
```

The output of the program shows that the members have the correct color and
that the name member is encrypted:

```
<Person>
  <name color="blue">Bmjdf</name>            ← blue and encrypted
  <lastName color="black">Davignon</lastName>
  <address color="red">Avignon</address>     ← red
</Person>
<Person>
  <name color="blue">Cfo</name>              ← blue and encrypted
  <lastName color="black">de Bordeaux</lastName>
  <address color="red">Bordeaux</address>    ← red
</Person>
```

89.2 The benefit of user defined attributes

The benefit of user defined attributes is being able to change the attributes of
declarations without needing to change any other part of the program. For
example, all of the members of Person can become encrypted in the XML output
by the trivial change below:

```
struct Person {
    @Encrypted {
        string name;
        string lastName;
        string address;
    }
}

// ...

    printAsXML(Person("Cindy", "de Cannes", "Cannes"));
```

The output:

```
<Person>
  <name color="black">Djoez</name>           ← encrypted
  <lastName color="black">ef!Dbooft</lastName> ← encrypted
  <address color="black">Dbooft</address>    ← encrypted
</Person>
```

Further, `printAsXML()` and the attributes that it considers can be used with other types as well:

```
struct Data {
    @Colored(Color.blue) string message;
}

// ...

    printAsXML(Data("hello world"));
```

The output:

```
<Data>
  <message color="blue">hello world</message>      ← blue
</Data>
```

89.3 Summary

- User defined attributes can be assigned to any declaration.
- User defined attributes can be type names as well as values.
- User defined attributes can be accessed at compile time by `hasUDA` and `__traits(getAttributes)` to alter the way the program is compiled.

As we have been using throughout the book, expressions can be *chained* with more than one operator. For example, the following line contains four expressions chained with three operators:

```
a = b + c * d     // three operators: =, +, and *
```

Operator precedence rules specify the order that the chained operators are executed in and the expressions that they use. Operators are executed according to their precedences: first the higher ones, then the lower ones.

The following is D's operator precedence table. Operators are listed from the highest precedence to the lowest. The ones that are in the same table row have the same precedence. (Line wrapping inside table cells is insignificant; for example, == and !is have the same precedence.) Unless specified otherwise, operators are *left-associative*.

Some of the terms used in the table are explained later below.

Operators	Description	Notes
!	Template instantiation	Cannot be chained
=>	Lambda definition	Not a real operator; occurs twice in the table; this row is for binding power to the *left*
. ++ -- ([	Postfix operators	(and [must be balanced with) and], respectively
^^	Power operator	Right-associative
++ -- * + - ! & ~ cast	Unary operators	
* / %	Binary operators	
+ - ~	Binary operators	
<< >> >>>	Bit shift operators	
== != > < >= <= in !in is !is	Comparison operators	Unordered with respect to bitwise operators, cannot be chained
&	Bitwise *and*	Unordered with respect to comparison operators
^	Bitwise *xor*	Unordered with respect to comparison operators
|	Bitwise *or*	Unordered with respect to comparison operators
&&	Logical *and*	Short-circuit
||	Logical *or*	Short-circuit
? :	Ternary operator	Right-associative
= -= += = *= %= ^= ^^= ~= <<= >>= >>>=	Assignment operators	Right-associative
=>	Lambda definition	Not a real operator; occurs twice in the table; this row is for binding power to the *right*
,	Comma operator	Not to be confused with using comma as a separator (e.g. in parameter lists)
..	Number range	Not a real operator; hardwired into syntax at specific points

Chaining
Let's consider the line from the beginning of the chapter:

```
a = b + c * d
```

Because binary * has higher precedence than binary +, and binary + has higher precedence than =, that expression is executed as the following parenthesized equivalent:

```
a = (b + (c * d))    // first *, then +, then =
```

As another example, because postfix . has higher precedence than unary *, the
following expression would first access member ptr of object o and then
dereference it:

```
*o.ptr      // ← dereferences pointer member o.ptr
*(o.ptr)    // ← equivalent of the above
(*o).ptr    // ← NOT equivalent of the above
```

Some operators cannot be chained:

```
if (a > b == c) {      // ← compilation ERROR
    // ...
}
```

```
Error: found '==' when expecting ')'
```

The programmer must specify the desired execution order with parentheses:

```
if ((a > b) == c) {    // ← compiles
    // ...
}
```

Associativity

If two operators have the same precedence, then their associativity determines
which operator is executed first: the one on the left or the one on the right.

Most operators are *left-associative*; the one on the left-hand side is executed first:

```
10 - 7 - 3;
(10 - 7) - 3;   // ← equivalent of the above (== 0)
10 - (7 - 3);   // ← NOT equivalent of the above (== 6)
```

Some operators are right-associative; the one on the right-hand side is executed
first:

```
4 ^^ 3 ^^ 2;
4 ^^ (3 ^^ 2);   // ← equivalent of the above (== 262144)
(4 ^^ 3) ^^ 2;   // ← NOT equivalent of the above (== 4096)
```

Unordered operator groups

Precedence between bitwise operators and logical operators are not specified by
the language:

```
if (a & b == c) {      // ← compilation ERROR
    // ...
}
```

```
Error: b == c must be parenthesized when next to operator &
```

The programmer must specify the desired execution order with parentheses:

```
if ((a & b) == c) {   // ← compiles
    // ...
}
```

The precedence of =>

Although => is not an operator, it takes part in the table twice to specify how it
interacts with operators on its left-hand side and right-hand side.

```
l = a => a = 1;
```

Although both sides of => above have an = operator, => has precedence over = on the left hand side so it *binds stronger* to a as if the programmer wrote the following parentheses:

```
l = (a => a = 1);
```

On the right-hand side, => has lower precedence than =, so the a on the right-hand side binds stronger to = as if the following extra set of parentheses are specified:

```
l = (a => (a = 1));
```

As a result, the lambda expression does not become just a => a but includes the rest of the expression as well: a => a = 1, which means *given a, produce a = 1*. That lambda is then assigned to the variable l.

Note: *This is just an example; otherwise, a = 1 is not a meaningful body for a lambda because the mutation to its parameter a is seemingly lost and the result of calling the lambda is always 1. (The reason I say "seemingly" is that the assignment operator may have been overloaded for a's type and may have side effects.)*

Comma operator

Comma operator is a binary operator. It executes first the left-hand side expression then the right-hand side expression. The values of both expressions are ignored.

```
int a = 1;
foo(), bar(), ++a;

assert(a == 2);
```

The comma operator is most commonly used with for loops when the loop iteration involves mutating more than one variable:

```
for ({ int i; int j; } i < 10; ++i, ++j) {
    // ...
}
```

The Hello World Program (page 1)

1.
```
import std.stdio;

void main() {
    writeln("Something else... :p");
}
```

2.
```
import std.stdio;

void main() {
    writeln("A line...");
    writeln("Another line...");
}
```

3. The following program cannot be compiled because the semicolon at the end of the writeln line is missing:

```
import std.stdio;

void main() {
    writeln("Hello, World!")    // ← compilation ERROR
}
```

writeln and write (page 5)

1. One method is to use another parameter in between:

```
    writeln("Hello, World!", " ", "Hello, fish!");
```

2. write can take multiple parameters as well:

```
    write("one", " two", " three");
```

Fundamental Types (page 8)
We can use other types instead of int:

```
import std.stdio;

void main() {
    writeln("Type           : ", short.stringof);
    writeln("Length in bytes: ", short.sizeof);
    writeln("Minimum value  : ", short.min);
    writeln("Maximum value  : ", short.max);
    writeln("Initial value  : ", short.init);

    writeln();

    writeln("Type           : ", ulong.stringof);
    writeln("Length in bytes: ", ulong.sizeof);
    writeln("Minimum value  : ", ulong.min);
    writeln("Maximum value  : ", ulong.max);
    writeln("Initial value  : ", ulong.init);
}
```

Assignment and Order of Evaluation (page 11)
The values of a, b, and c are printed on the right-hand side of each operation. The value that changes at every operation is highlighted:

```
at the beginning    →    a 1, b 2, c irrelevant
c = a               →    a 1, b 2, c 1
a = b               →    a 2, b 2, c 1
b = c               →    a 2, b 1, c 1
```

At the end, the values of a and b have been swapped.

Variables (page 12)

```
import std.stdio;

void main() {
    int amount = 20;
    double rate = 2.11;

    writeln("I have exchanged ", amount,
            " Euros at the rate of ", rate);
}
```

Standard Input and Output Streams (page 14)

```
import std.stdio;

void main() {
    stdout.write(1, ",", 2);

    // To complete the line if needed:
    writeln();
}
```

Reading from the Standard Input (page 15)

When the characters cannot be converted to the desired type, stdin gets in an unusable state. For example, entering "abc" when an int is expected would make stdin unusable.

Logical Expressions (page 18)

1. Because the compiler recognizes 10 < value already as an expression, it expects a comma after it to accept it as a legal argument to writeln. Using parentheses around the whole expression would not work either, because this time a closing parenthesis would be expected after the same expression.

2. Grouping the expression as (10 < value) < 20 removes the compilation error, because in this case first 10 < value is evaluated and then its result is used with < 20.

    We know that the value of a logical expression like 10 < value is either false or true. false and true take part in integer expressions as 0 and 1, respectively. (We will see automatic type conversions in a later chapter.) As a result, the whole expression is the equivalent of either 0 < 20 or 1 < 20, both of which evaluate to true.

3. The expression "greater than the lower value and less than the upper value" can be coded as follows:

    ```
    writeln("Is between: ", (value > 10) && (value < 20));
    ```

4. "There is a bicycle for everyone" can be coded as personCount <= bicycleCount or bicycleCount >= personCount. The rest of the logical expression can directly be translated to D from the exercise:

```
writeln("We are going to the beach: ",
        ((distance < 10) && (bicycleCount >= personCount))
        ||
        ((personCount <= 5) && existsCar && existsLicense)
        );
```

Note the placement of the || operator to help with readability by separating the two main conditions.

The if Statement (page 24)

1. The statement writeln("Washing the plate") is written indented as if to be within the else scope. However, because the scope of that else is not written with curly brackets, only the writeln("Eating pie") statement is actually inside the scope of that else.

    Since whitespaces are not important in D programs, the *plate statement* is actually an independent statement within main() and is executed unconditionally. It confuses the reader as well because of having been indented more than usual. If the *plate statement* must really be within the else scope, there must be curly brackets around that scope:

```
import std.stdio;

void main() {
    bool existsLemonade = true;

    if (existsLemonade) {
        writeln("Drinking lemonade");
        writeln("Washing the cup");

    } else {
        writeln("Eating pie");
        writeln("Washing the plate");
    }
}
```

2. We can come up with more than one design for the conditions of this game. I will show two examples. In the first one, we apply the information directly from the exercise:

```
import std.stdio;

void main() {
    write("What is the value of the die? ");
    int die;
    readf(" %s", &die);

    if (die == 1) {
        writeln("You won");

    } else if (die == 2) {
        writeln("You won");

    } else if (die == 3) {
        writeln("You won");

    } else if (die == 4) {
        writeln("I won");

    } else if (die == 5) {
        writeln("I won");

    } else if (die == 6) {
        writeln("I won");
```

```
    } else {
        writeln("ERROR: ", die, " is invalid");
    }
}
```

Unfortunately, that program has many repetitions. We can achieve the same result by other designs. Here is one:

```
import std.stdio;

void main() {
    write("What is the value of the die? ");
    int die;
    readf(" %s", &die);

    if ((die == 1) || (die == 2) || (die == 3)) {
        writeln("You won");

    } else if ((die == 4) || (die == 5) || (die == 6)) {
        writeln("I won");

    } else {
        writeln("ERROR: ", die, " is invalid");
    }
}
```

3. The previous designs cannot be used in this case. It is not practical to type 1000 different values in a program and expect them all be correct or readable. For that reason, it is better to determine whether the value of the die is *within a range*:

```
    if ((die >= 1) && (die <= 500))
```

The while Loop (page 28)

1. Because the initial value of number is 0, the logical expression of the while loop is false since the very beginning, and this is preventing from entering the loop body. A solution is to use an initial value that will allow the while condition to be true at the beginning:

```
    int number = 3;
```

2. All of the variables in the following program are default initialized to 0. This allows entering both of the loops at least once:

```
import std.stdio;

void main() {
    int secretNumber;

    while ((secretNumber < 1) || (secretNumber > 10)) {
        write("Please enter a number between 1 and 10: ");
        readf(" %s", &secretNumber);
    }

    int guess;

    while (guess != secretNumber) {
        write("Guess the secret number: ");
        readf(" %s", &guess);
    }

    writeln("That is correct!");
}
```

Integers and Arithmetic Operations (page 31)

1. We can use the / operator for the division and the % operator for the remainder:

```d
import std.stdio;

void main() {
    int first;
    write("Please enter the first number: ");
    readf(" %s", &first);

    int second;
    write("Please enter the second number: ");
    readf(" %s", &second);

    int quotient = first / second;
    int remainder = first % second;

    writeln(first, " = ",
            second, " * ", quotient, " + ", remainder);
}
```

2. We can determine whether the remainder is 0 or not with an if statement:

```d
import std.stdio;

void main() {
    int first;
    write("Please enter the first number: ");
    readf(" %s", &first);

    int second;
    write("Please enter the second number: ");
    readf(" %s", &second);

    int quotient = first / second;
    int remainder = first % second;

    // We cannot call writeln up front before determining
    // whether the remainder is 0 or not. We must terminate
    // the line later with a writeln.
    write(first, " = ", second, " * ", quotient);

    // The remainder must be printed only if nonzero.
    if (remainder != 0) {
        write(" + ", remainder);
    }

    // We are now ready to terminate the line.
    writeln();
}
```

3.
```d
import std.stdio;

void main() {
    while (true) {
        write("0: Exit, 1: Add, 2: Subtract, 3: Multiply,",
              " 4: Divide - Please enter the operation: ");

        int operation;
        readf(" %s", &operation);

        // Let's first validate the operation
        if ((operation < 0) || (operation > 4)) {
            writeln("I don't know this operation");
            continue;
        }

        if (operation == 0){
            writeln("Goodbye!");
```

```
            break;
        }

        // If we are here, we know that we are dealing with
        // one of the four operations. Now is the time to read
        // two integers from the user:

        int first;
        int second;

        write(" First number: ");
        readf(" %s", &first);

        write("Second number: ");
        readf(" %s", &second);

        int result;

        if (operation == 1) {
            result = first + second;

        } else if (operation == 2) {
            result = first - second;

        } else if (operation == 3) {
            result = first * second;

        } else if (operation == 4) {
            result = first / second;

        } else {
            writeln(
                "There is an error! ",
                "This condition should have never occurred.");
            break;
        }

        writeln("        Result: ", result);
    }
}
```

4.
```
import std.stdio;

void main() {
    int value = 1;

    while (value <= 10) {
        if (value != 7) {
            writeln(value);
        }

        ++value;
    }
}
```

Floating Point Types (page 42)

1. Replacing float with double produces an outcome that is surprising in a different way:

```
// ...

    double result = 0;

// ...

    if (result == 1) {
        writeln("As expected: 1");

    } else {
```

```
        writeln("DIFFERENT: ", result);
    }
```

Although the value fails the `result == 1` comparison, it is still printed as 1:

```
DIFFERENT: 1
```

That surprising outcome is related to the way floating point values are formatted for printing. A more accurate approximation of the value can be seen when the value is printed with more digits after the decimal point. (We will see formatted output in a later chapter (page 104).):

```
        writefln("DIFFERENT: %.20f", result);
```

```
DIFFERENT: 1.00000000000000066613
```

2. Replacing the three `int`s with three `double`s is sufficient:

```
        double first;
        double second;

        // ...

        double result;
```

3. The following program demonstrates how much more complicated it would become if more than five variables were needed:

```
import std.stdio;

void main() {
    double value_1;
    double value_2;
    double value_3;
    double value_4;
    double value_5;

    write("Value 1: ");
    readf(" %s", &value_1);
    write("Value 2: ");
    readf(" %s", &value_2);
    write("Value 3: ");
    readf(" %s", &value_3);
    write("Value 4: ");
    readf(" %s", &value_4);
    write("Value 5: ");
    readf(" %s", &value_5);

    writeln("Twice the values:");
    writeln(value_1 * 2);
    writeln(value_2 * 2);
    writeln(value_3 * 2);
    writeln(value_4 * 2);
    writeln(value_5 * 2);

    writeln("One fifth the values:");
    writeln(value_1 / 5);
    writeln(value_2 / 5);
    writeln(value_3 / 5);
    writeln(value_4 / 5);
    writeln(value_5 / 5);
}
```

Arrays (page 49)

1.
```
import std.stdio;
import std.algorithm;
```

```
void main() {
    write("How many values will be entered? ");
    int count;
    readf(" %s", &count);

    double[] values;
    values.length = count;

    // The counter is commonly named as 'i'
    int i;
    while (i < count) {
        write("Value ", i, ": ");
        readf(" %s", &values[i]);
        ++i;
    }

    writeln("In sorted order:");
    sort(values);

    i = 0;
    while (i < count) {
        write(values[i], " ");
        ++i;
    }
    writeln();

    writeln("In reverse order:");
    reverse(values);

    i = 0;
    while (i < count) {
        write(values[i], " ");
        ++i;
    }
    writeln();
}
```

2. The explanations are included as code comments:

```
import std.stdio;
import std.algorithm;

void main() {
    // Using dynamic arrays because it is not known how many
    // values are going to be read from the input
    int[] odds;
    int[] evens;

    writeln("Please enter integers (-1 to terminate):");

    while (true) {

        // Reading the value
        int value;
        readf(" %s", &value);

        // The special value of -1 breaks the loop
        if (value == -1) {
            break;
        }

        // Adding to the corresponding array, depending on
        // whether the value is odd or even. It is an even
        // number if there is no remainder when divided by 2.
        if ((value % 2) == 0) {
            evens ~= value;

        } else {
            odds ~= value;
        }
    }
```

```
    // The odds and evens arrays are sorted separately
    sort(odds);
    sort(evens);

    // The two arrays are then appended to form a new array
    int[] result;
    result = odds ~ evens;

    writeln("First the odds then the evens, sorted:");

    // Printing the array elements in a loop
    int i;
    while (i < result.length) {
        write(result[i], " ");
        ++i;
    }

    writeln();
}
```

3. There are three mistakes (bugs) in this program. The first two are with the
    while loops: Both of the loop conditions use the <= operator instead of the <
    operator. As a result, the program uses invalid indexes and attempts to access
    elements that are not parts of the arrays.

    Since it is more beneficial for you to debug the third mistake yourself, I
    would like you to first run the program after fixing the previous two bugs. You
    will notice that the program will not print the results. Can you figure out the
    remaining problem before reading the following paragraph?

    The value of i is 5 when the first while loop terminates, and that value is
    causing the logical expression of the second loop to be false, which in turn is
    preventing the second loop to be entered. The solution is to reset i to 0 before
    the second while loop, for example with the statement i = 0;

Slices and Other Array Features (page 65)

Iterating over elements by consuming a slice from the beginning is an interesting
concept. This method is also the basis of Phobos ranges that we will see in a later
chapter.

```
import std.stdio;

void main() {
    double[] array = [ 1, 20, 2, 30, 7, 11 ];

    double[] slice = array;      // Start with a slice that
                                 // provides access to all.of
                                 // the elements of the array

    while (slice.length) {       // As long as there is at least
                                 // one element in that slice

        if (slice[0] > 10) {     // Always use the first element
            slice[0] /= 2;       // in the expressions
        }

        slice = slice[1 .. $];   // Shorten the slice from the
                                 // beginning
    }

    writeln(array);              // The actual elements are
                                 // changed
}
```

Strings (page 75)

1. Although some of the functions in Phobos modules will be easy to use with strings, library documentations are usually terse compared to tutorials. You may find especially the Phobos ranges confusing at this point. We will see Phobos ranges in a later chapter.

2. Many other functions may be chained as well:

```
import std.stdio;
import std.string;

void main() {
    write("First name: ");
    string first = capitalize(strip(readln()));

    write("Last name: ");
    string last = capitalize(strip(readln()));

    string fullName = first ~ " " ~ last;
    writeln(fullName);
}
```

3. This program uses two indexes to make a slice:

```
import std.stdio;
import std.string;

void main() {
    write("Please enter a line: ");
    string line = strip(readln());

    ptrdiff_t first_e = indexOf(line, 'e');

    if (first_e == -1) {
        writeln("There is no letter e in this line.");

    } else {
        ptrdiff_t last_e = lastIndexOf(line, 'e');
        writeln(line[first_e .. last_e + 1]);
    }
}
```

Redirecting the Standard Input and Output Streams (page 82)

Redirecting standard input and output of programs are commonly used especially on Unix-based operating system shells. (A shell is the program that interacts with the user in the terminal.) Some programs are designed to work well when piped to other programs.

For example, a file named deneme.d can be searched under a directory tree by piping find and grep as in the following line:

```
find | grep deneme.d
```

find prints the names of all of the files to its output. grep receives that output through its input and prints the lines that contain deneme.d to its own output.

Files (page 84)

```
import std.stdio;
import std.string;

void main() {
    write("Please enter the name of the file to read from: ");
    string inFileName = strip(readln());
    File inFile = File(inFileName, "r");
```

```
    string outFileName = inFileName ~ ".out";
    File outFile = File(outFileName, "w");

    while (!inFile.eof()) {
        string line = strip(inFile.readln());

        if (line.length != 0) {
            outFile.writeln(line);
        }
    }

    writeln(outFileName, " has been created.");
}
```

auto and typeof (page 88)

We can use typeof to determine the type of the literal and .stringof to get the name of that type as string:

```
import std.stdio;

void main() {
    writeln(typeof(1.2).stringof);
}
```

The output:

```
double
```

The for Loop (page 93)

1.
```
import std.stdio;

void main() {
    for (int line = 0; line != 9; ++line) {
        for (int column = 0; column != 9; ++column) {
            write(line, ',', column, ' ');
        }

        writeln();
    }
}
```

2. Triangle:

```
import std.stdio;

void main() {
    for (int line = 0; line != 5; ++line) {
        int length = line + 1;

        for (int i = 0; i != length; ++i) {
            write('*');
        }

        writeln();
    }
}
```

Parallellogram:

```
import std.stdio;

void main() {
    for (int line = 0; line != 5; ++line) {
        for (int i = 0; i != line; ++i) {
            write(' ');
```

```
        }
            writeln("********");
        }
    }
}
```

Can you produce the diamond pattern?

```
    *
   ***
  *****
 *******
  *****
   ***
    *
```

The Ternary Operator ? : (page 96)

Although it may make more sense to use an if-else statement in this exercise, the following program uses two ?: operators:

```
import std.stdio;

void main() {
    write("Please enter the net amount: ");

    int amount;
    readf(" %s", &amount);

    writeln("$",
            amount < 0 ? -amount : amount,
            amount < 0 ? " lost" : " gained");
}
```

The program prints "gained" even when the value is zero. Modify the program to print a message more appropriate for zero.

Literals (page 99)

1. The problem here is that the value on the right-hand side is too large to fit in an int. According to the rules about integer literals, its type is long. For that reason it doesn't fit the type of the variable on the left-hand side. There are at least two solutions.

    One solution is to leave the type of the variable to the compiler for example by the auto keyword:

    ```
    auto amount = 10_000_000_000;
    ```

    The type of amount would be deduced to be long from its initial value from the right-hand side.

    Another solution is to make the type of the variable long as well:

    ```
    long amount = 10_000_000_000;
    ```

2. We can take advantage of the special '\r' character that takes the printing to the beginning of the line.

    ```
    import std.stdio;

    void main() {
        for (int number = 0; ; ++number) {
            write("\rNumber: ", number);
        }
    }
    ```

The output of that program may be erratic due to its interactions with the output buffer. The following program flushes the output buffer and waits for 10 millisecond after each write:

```d
import std.stdio;
import core.thread;

void main() {
    for (int number = 0; ; ++number) {
        write("\rNumber: ", number);
        stdout.flush();
        Thread.sleep(10.msecs);
    }
}
```

Flushing the output is normally not necessary as it is flushed automatically before getting to the next line e.g. by `writeln`, or before reading from `stdin`.

Formatted Output (page 104)

1. We have already seen that this is trivial with format specifiers:

```d
import std.stdio;

void main() {
    writeln("(Enter 0 to exit the program.)");

    while (true) {
        write("Please enter a number: ");
        long number;
        readf(" %s", &number);

        if (number == 0) {
            break;
        }

        writefln("%1$d <=> %1$#x", number);
    }
}
```

2. Remembering that the % character must appear twice in the format string to be printed as itself:

```d
import std.stdio;

void main() {
    write("Please enter the percentage value: ");
    double percentage;
    readf(" %s", &percentage);

    writefln("%%%.2f", percentage);
}
```

Formatted Input (page 113)

Using a format string where the parts of the date are replaced with %s would be sufficient:

```d
import std.stdio;

void main() {
    int year;
    int month;
    int day;

    readf("%s.%s.%s", &year, &month, &day);
```

```
        writeln("Month: ", month);
    }
```

The do-while Loop (page 115)

This program is not directly related to the do-while loop, as any problem that is solved by the do-while loop can also be solved by the other loop statements.

The program can guess the number that the user is thinking of by shortening the candidate range from top or bottom according to the user's answers. For example, if its first guess is 50 and the user's reply is that the secret number is greater, the program would then know that the number must be in the range [51,100]. If the program then guesses another number right in the middle of that range, this time the number would be known to be either in the range [51,75] or in the range [76,100].

When the size of the range is 1, the program would be sure that it must be the number that the user has guessed.

Associative Arrays (page 117)

1. ∘ The .keys property returns a slice (i.e. dynamic array) that includes all of the keys of the associative array. Iterating over this slice and removing the element for each key by calling .remove would result in an empty associative array:

```
import std.stdio;

void main() {
    string[int] names =
        [
            1   : "one",
            10  : "ten",
            100 : "hundred",
        ];

    writeln("Initial length: ", names.length);

    int[] keys = names.keys;

    /* 'foreach' is similar but superior to 'for'. We will
     * see the 'foreach' loop in the next chapter. */
    foreach (key; keys) {
        writefln("Removing the element %s", key);
        names.remove(key);
    }

    writeln("Final length: ", names.length);
}
```

That solution may be slow especially for large arrays. The following methods would empty the array in a single step.

∘ Another solution is to assign an empty array:

```
string[int] emptyAA;
names = emptyAA;
```

∘ Since the initial value of an array is an empty array anyway, the following technique would achieve the same result:

```
names = names.init;
```

2. The goal is to store multiple grades per student. Since multiple grades can be stored in a dynamic array, an associative array that maps from string to int[] would work here. The grades can be appended to the dynamic arrays that are stored in the associative array:

```
import std.stdio;

void main() {
    /* The key type of this associative array is string and
     * the value type is int[], i.e. an array of ints. The
     * associative array is being defined with an extra
     * space in between to help distinguish the value type: */
    int[] [string] grades;

    /* The array of ints that correspond to "emre" is being
     * used for appending the new grade to that array: */
    grades["emre"] ~= 90;
    grades["emre"] ~= 85;

    /* Printing the grades of "emre": */
    writeln(grades["emre"]);
}
```

The grades can also be assigned in one go with an array literal:

```
import std.stdio;

void main() {
    int[][string] grades;

    grades["emre"] = [ 90, 85, 95 ];

    writeln(grades["emre"]);
}
```

The foreach Loop (page 121)

To have an associative array that works the opposite of names, the types of the key and the value must be swapped. The new associative array must be defined as of type int[string].

Iterating over the keys and the values of the original associative array while using keys as values and values as keys would populate the values table:

```
import std.stdio;

void main() {
    string[int] names = [ 1:"one", 7:"seven", 20:"twenty" ];

    int[string] values;

    foreach (key, value; names) {
        values[value] = key;
    }

    writeln(values["twenty"]);
}
```

switch and case (page 127)

1.
```
import std.stdio;
import std.string;

void main() {
    string op;
    double first;
    double second;
```

```
    write("Please enter the operation: ");
    op = strip(readln());

    write("Please enter two values separated by a space: ");
    readf(" %s %s", &first, &second);

    double result;

    final switch (op) {

    case "add":
        result = first + second;
        break;

    case "subtract":
        result = first - second;
        break;

    case "multiply":
        result = first * second;
        break;

    case "divide":
        result = first / second;
        break;
    }

    writeln(result);
}
```

2. By taking advantage of distinct case values:

```
    final switch (op) {

    case "add", "+":
        result = first + second;
        break;

    case "subtract", "-":
        result = first - second;
        break;

    case "multiply", "*":
        result = first * second;
        break;

    case "divide", "/":
        result = first / second;
        break;
    }
```

3. Since the default section is needed to throw the exception from, it cannot be a final switch statement anymore. Here are the parts of the program that are modified:

```
// ...

    switch (op) {

    // ...

    default:
        throw new Exception("Invalid operation: " ~ op);
    }
// ...
```

enum (page 132)

```
import std.stdio;
import std.conv;

enum Operation { exit, add, subtract, multiply, divide }

void main() {
    // Print the supported operations
    write("Operations - ");
    for (Operation operation;
         operation <= Operation.max;
         ++operation) {

        writef("%d:%s ", operation, operation);
    }
    writeln();

    // Unconditional loop until the user wants to exit
    while (true) {
        write("Operation? ");

        // The input must be read in the actual type (int) of
        // the enum
        int operationCode;
        readf(" %s", &operationCode);

        /* We will start using enum values instead of magic
         * constants from this point on. So, the operation code
         * that has been read in int must be converted to its
         * corresponding enum value.
         *
         * (Type conversions will be covered in more detail in
         * a later chapter.) */
        Operation operation = cast(Operation)operationCode;

        if ((operation < Operation.min) ||
            (operation > Operation.max)) {
            writeln("ERROR: Invalid operation");
            continue;
        }

        if (operation == Operation.exit) {
            writeln("Goodbye!");
            break;
        }

        double first;
        double second;
        double result;

        write(" First operand? ");
        readf(" %s", &first);

        write("Second operand? ");
        readf(" %s", &second);

        switch (operation) {

        case Operation.add:
            result = first + second;
            break;

        case Operation.subtract:
            result = first - second;
            break;

        case Operation.multiply:
            result = first * second;
            break;

        case Operation.divide:
            result = first / second;
```

```
            break;

        default:
            throw new Exception(
                "ERROR: This line should have never been reached.");
        }

        writeln("          Result: ", result);
    }
}
```

Functions (page 136)

1.
```
import std.stdio;

void printMenu(string[] items, int firstNumber) {
    foreach (i, item; items) {
        writeln(' ', i + firstNumber, ' ', item);
    }
}

void main() {
    string[] items =
        [ "Black", "Red", "Green", "Blue", "White" ];
    printMenu(items, 1);
}
```

2. Here are some ideas:

   ° Write a function named drawHorizontalLine() to draw horizontal lines.

   ° Write a function named drawSquare() to draw squares. This function could take advantage of drawVerticalLine() and drawHorizontalLine() when drawing the square.

   ° Improve the functions to also take the character that is used when "drawing". This would allow drawing each shape with a different character:

   ```
   void putDot(Canvas canvas, int line, int column, dchar dot) {
       canvas[line][column] = dot;
   }
   ```

Function Parameters (page 168)

Because the parameters of this function are the kind that gets copied from the arguments, what gets swapped in the function are those copies.

To make the function swap the arguments, both of the parameters must be passed by reference:

```
void swap(ref int first, ref int second) {
    const int temp = first;
    first = second;
    second = temp;
}
```

With that change, now the variables in main() would be swapped:

```
2 1
```

Although not related to the original problem, also note that temp is specified as const as it is not changed in the function.

Program Environment (page 185)

1.
```d
import std.stdio;
import std.conv;

int main(string[] args) {
    if (args.length != 4) {
        stderr.writeln(
            "ERROR! Usage: \n    ", args[0],
            " a_number operator another_number");
        return 1;
    }

    immutable first = to!double(args[1]);
    string op = args[2];
    immutable second = to!double(args[3]);

    switch (op) {

    case "+":
        writeln(first + second);
        break;

    case "-":
        writeln(first - second);
        break;

    case "x":
        writeln(first * second);
        break;

    case "/":
        writeln(first / second);
        break;

    default:
        throw new Exception("Invalid operator: " ~ op);
    }

    return 0;
}
```

2.
```d
import std.stdio;
import std.process;

void main() {
    write("Please enter the command line to execute: ");
    string commandLine = readln();

    writeln("The output: ", executeShell(commandLine));
}
```

assert and enforce (page 208)

1. You will notice that the program terminates normally when you enter 06:09 and 1:2. However, you may notice that the start time is not what has been entered by the user:

    ```
    1 hours and 2 minutes after 09:06 is 10:08.
    ```

    As you can see, although the time that has been entered as 06:09, the output contains 09:06. This error will be caught by the help of an `assert` in the next problem.

2. The `assert` failure after entering 06:09 and 15:2 takes us to the following line:

```
string timeToString(int hour, int minute) {
    assert((hour >= 0) && (hour <= 23));
    // ...
}
```

For this `assert` check to fail, this function must have been called with invalid `hour` value.

The only two calls to `timeToString()` in the program do not appear to have any problems:

```
writefln("%s hours and %s minutes after %s is %s.",
         durationHour, durationMinute,
         timeToString(startHour, startMinute),
         timeToString(endHour, endMinute));
```

A little more investigation should reveal the actual cause of the bug: The hour and minute variables are swapped when reading the start time:

```
readTime("Start time", startMinute, startHour);
```

That programming error causes the time to be interpreted as 09:06 and incrementing it by duration 15:2 causes an invalid hour value.

An obvious correction is to pass the hour and minute variables in the right order:

```
readTime("Start time", startHour, startMinute);
```

The output:

```
Start time? (HH:MM) 06:09
Duration? (HH:MM) 15:2
15 hours and 2 minutes after 06:09 is 21:11.
```

3. It is again the same `assert` check:

```
assert((hour >= 0) && (hour <= 23));
```

The reason is that `addDuration()` can produce hour values that are greater than 23. Adding a *remainder* operation at the end would ensure one of the *output guarantees* of the function:

```
void addDuration(int startHour, int startMinute,
                 int durationHour, int durationMinute,
                 out int resultHour, out int resultMinute) {
    resultHour = startHour + durationHour;
    resultMinute = startMinute + durationMinute;

    if (resultMinute > 59) {
        ++resultHour;
    }

    resultHour %= 24;
}
```

Observe that the function has other problems. For example, `resultMinute` may end up being greater than 59. The following function calculates the minute value correctly and makes sure that the function's output guarantees are enforced:

```
void addDuration(int startHour, int startMinute,
                 int durationHour, int durationMinute,
                 out int resultHour, out int resultMinute) {
    resultHour = startHour + durationHour;
```

```
        resultMinute = startMinute + durationMinute;

        resultHour += resultMinute / 60;
        resultHour %= 24;
        resultMinute %= 60;

        assert((resultHour >= 0) && (resultHour <= 23));
        assert((resultMinute >= 0) && (resultMinute <= 59));
    }
```

4. Good luck.

Unit Testing (page 214)

The first thing to do is to compile and run the program to ensure that the tests actually work and indeed fail:

```
$ dmd deneme.d -w -unittest
$ ./deneme
core.exception.AssertError@deneme(11): unittest failure
```

The line number 11 indicates that the first one of the tests has failed.

For demonstration purposes let's write an obviously incorrect implementation that passes the first test by accident. The following function simply returns a copy of the input:

```
dstring toFront(dstring str, dchar letter) {
    dstring result;

    foreach (c; str) {
        result ~= c;
    }

    return result;
}

unittest {
    immutable str = "hello"d;

    assert(toFront(str, 'h') == "hello");
    assert(toFront(str, 'o') == "ohell");
    assert(toFront(str, 'l') == "llheo");
}

void main() {
}
```

The first test passes but the second one fails:

```
$ ./deneme
core.exception.AssertError@deneme.d(17): unittest failure
```

Here is a correct implementation that passes all of the tests:

```
dstring toFront(dstring str, dchar letter) {
    dchar[] firstPart;
    dchar[] lastPart;

    foreach (c; str) {
        if (c == letter) {
            firstPart ~= c;

        } else {
            lastPart ~= c;
        }
    }

    return (firstPart ~ lastPart).idup;
}
```

```
unittest {
    immutable str = "hello"d;

    assert(toFront(str, 'h') == "hello");
    assert(toFront(str, 'o') == "ohell");
    assert(toFront(str, 'l') == "llheo");
}

void main() {
}
```

The tests finally pass:

```
$ ./deneme
$
```

This function can now be modified in different ways under the confidence that its tests will have to pass. The following two implementations are very different from the first one but they too are correct according to the tests.

- An implementation that takes advantage of `std.algorithm.partition`:

```
import std.algorithm;

dstring toFront(dstring str, dchar letter) {
    dchar[] result = str.dup;
    partition!(c => c == letter, SwapStrategy.stable)(result);

    return result.idup;
}

unittest {
    immutable str = "hello"d;

    assert(toFront(str, 'h') == "hello");
    assert(toFront(str, 'o') == "ohell");
    assert(toFront(str, 'l') == "llheo");
}

void main() {
}
```

Note: *The => syntax that appears in the program above creates a lambda function. We will see lambda functions in later chapters.*

- The following implementation first counts how many times the special letter appears in the string. That information is then sent to a separate function named `repeated()` to produce the first part of the result. Note that `repeated()` has a set of unit tests of its own:

```
dstring repeated(size_t count, dchar letter) {
    dstring result;

    foreach (i; 0..count) {
        result ~= letter;
    }

    return result;
}

unittest {
    assert(repeated(3, 'z') == "zzz");
    assert(repeated(10, 'é') == "éééééééééé");
}

dstring toFront(dstring str, dchar letter) {
    size_t specialLetterCount;
    dstring lastPart;
```

```
        foreach (c; str) {
            if (c == letter) {
                ++specialLetterCount;

            } else {
                lastPart ~= c;
            }
        }

        return repeated(specialLetterCount, letter) ~ lastPart;
}

unittest {
    immutable str = "hello"d;

    assert(toFront(str, 'h') == "hello");
    assert(toFront(str, 'o') == "ohell");
    assert(toFront(str, 'l') == "llheo");
}

void main() {
}
```

Contract Programming (page 221)

The unittest block can be implemented trivially by copying the checks that are already written in main(). The only addition below is the test for the case when the second team wins:

```
int addPoints(int goals1, int goals2,
              ref int points1, ref int points2)
in {
    assert(goals1 >= 0);
    assert(goals2 >= 0);
    assert(points1 >= 0);
    assert(points2 >= 0);

} out (result) {
    assert((result >= 0) && (result <= 2));

} do {
    int winner;

    if (goals1 > goals2) {
        points1 += 3;
        winner = 1;

    } else if (goals1 < goals2) {
        points2 += 3;
        winner = 2;

    } else {
        ++points1;
        ++points2;
        winner = 0;
    }

    return winner;
}

unittest {
    int points1 = 10;
    int points2 = 7;
    int winner;

    // First team wins
    winner = addPoints(3, 1, points1, points2);
    assert(points1 == 13);
    assert(points2 == 7);
    assert(winner == 1);
```

```
    // Draw
    winner = addPoints(2, 2, points1, points2);
    assert(points1 == 14);
    assert(points2 == 8);
    assert(winner == 0);

    // Second team wins
    winner = addPoints(0, 1, points1, points2);
    assert(points1 == 14);
    assert(points2 == 11);
    assert(winner == 2);
}

void main() {
    // ...
}
```

Expression-based contracts can be useful for this function:

```
int addPoints(int goals1, int goals2,
              ref int points1, ref int points2)
in (goals1 >= 0)
in (goals2 >= 0)
in (points1 >= 0)
in (points2 >= 0)
out (result; (result >= 0) && (result <= 2)) {
    // ...
}
```

Structs (page 246)

1. One of the simplest designs is to use two dchar members:

    ```
    struct Card {
        dchar suit;
        dchar value;
    }
    ```

2. It would be as simple as printing the two members side by side:

    ```
    void printCard(Card card) {
        write(card.suit, card.value);
    }
    ```

3. Assuming that there is already a function called newSuit(), newDeck() can
    be implemented by calling that function for each suit:

    ```
    Card[] newDeck()
    out (result) {
        assert(result.length == 52);

    } do {
        Card[] deck;

        deck ~= newSuit('♠');
        deck ~= newSuit('♡');
        deck ~= newSuit('◇');
        deck ~= newSuit('♣');

        return deck;
    }
    ```

    The rest of the work can be accomplished by the following newSuit(), which
    constructs the suit by combining the suit character with each value of a string:

    ```
    Card[] newSuit(dchar suit)
    in {
    ```

```
    assert((suit == '♠') ||
           (suit == '♡') ||
           (suit == '◇') ||
           (suit == '♣'));

} out (result) {
    assert(result.length == 13);

} do {
    Card[] suitCards;

    foreach (value; "234567890JQKA") {
        suitCards ~= Card(suit, value);
    }

    return suitCards;
}
```

Note that the functions above take advantage of contract programming to reduce risk of program errors.

4. Swapping two elements at random would make the deck become more and more shuffled at each repetition. Although it is possible to pick the same element by chance, swapping an element with itself does not have any effect other than missing an opportunity toward a more shuffled deck.

```
void shuffle(Card[] deck, int repetition) {
    /* Note: A better algorithm is to walk the deck from the
     *       beginning to the end and to swap each element
     *       with a random one that is picked among the
     *       elements from that point to the end.
     *
     * It would be even better to call randomShuffle() from
     * the std.algorithm module, which already applies the
     * same algorithm. Please read the comment in main() to
     * see how randomShuffle() can be used. */
    foreach (i; 0 .. repetition) {
        // Pick two elements at random
        immutable first = uniform(0, deck.length);
        immutable second = uniform(0, deck.length);

        swap(deck[first], deck[second]);
    }
}
```

The function above calls `std.algorithm.swap`, which simply swaps the values of its two `ref` parameters. It is effectively the equivalent of the following function:

```
void mySwap(ref Card left,
            ref Card right) {
    immutable temporary = left;
    left = right;
    right = temporary;
}
```

Here is the entire program:

```
import std.stdio;
import std.random;
import std.algorithm;

struct Card {
    dchar suit;
    dchar value;
}

void printCard(Card card) {
```

```
    write(card.suit, card.value);
}

Card[] newSuit(dchar suit)
in {
    assert((suit == '♠') ||
           (suit == '♡') ||
           (suit == '◇') ||
           (suit == '♣'));

} out (result) {
    assert(result.length == 13);

} do {
    Card[] suitCards;

    foreach (value; "234567890JQKA") {
        suitCards ~= Card(suit, value);
    }

    return suitCards;
}

Card[] newDeck()
out (result) {
    assert(result.length == 52);

} do {
    Card[] deck;

    deck ~= newSuit('♠');
    deck ~= newSuit('♡');
    deck ~= newSuit('◇');
    deck ~= newSuit('♣');

    return deck;
}

void shuffle(Card[] deck, int repetition) {
    /* Note: A better algorithm is to walk the deck from the
     *       beginning to the end and to swap each element
     *       with a random one that is picked among the
     *       elements from that point to the end.
     *
     * It would be even better to call randomShuffle() from
     * the std.algorithm module, which already applies the
     * same algorithm. Please read the comment in main() to
     * see how randomShuffle() can be used. */
    foreach (i; 0 .. repetition) {
        // Pick two elements at random
        immutable first = uniform(0, deck.length);
        immutable second = uniform(0, deck.length);

        swap(deck[first], deck[second]);
    }
}

void main() {
    Card[] deck = newDeck();

    shuffle(deck, 100);
    /* Note: Instead of the shuffle() call above, it would be
     *       better to call randomShuffle() as in the
     *       following line:
     *
     * randomShuffle(deck);
     */
    foreach (card; deck) {
        printCard(card);
        write(' ');
    }
```

```
        writeln();
}
```

Variable Number of Parameters (page 258)

For the `calculate()` function to be able to take variable number of parameters, its parameter list must include a slice of `Calculation` followed by `...`:

```d
double[] calculate(Calculation[] calculations...) {
    double[] results;

    foreach (calculation; calculations) {
        final switch (calculation.op) {

        case Operation.add:
            results ~= calculation.first + calculation.second;
            break;

        case Operation.subtract:
            results ~= calculation.first - calculation.second;
            break;

        case Operation.multiply:
            results ~= calculation.first * calculation.second;
            break;

        case Operation.divide:
            results ~= calculation.first / calculation.second;
            break;
        }
    }

    return results;
}
```

Each calculation is evaluated inside a loop and their results are appended to a slice of type `double[]`.

Here is the entire program:

```d
import std.stdio;

enum Operation { add, subtract, multiply, divide }

struct Calculation {
    Operation op;
    double first;
    double second;
}

double[] calculate(Calculation[] calculations...) {
    double[] results;

    foreach (calculation; calculations) {
        final switch (calculation.op) {

        case Operation.add:
            results ~= calculation.first + calculation.second;
            break;

        case Operation.subtract:
            results ~= calculation.first - calculation.second;
            break;

        case Operation.multiply:
            results ~= calculation.first * calculation.second;
            break;

        case Operation.divide:
            results ~= calculation.first / calculation.second;
            break;
```

```
        }
    }

    return results;
}

void main() {
    writeln(calculate(Calculation(Operation.add, 1.1, 2.2),
                      Calculation(Operation.subtract, 3.3, 4.4),
                      Calculation(Operation.multiply, 5.5, 6.6),
                      Calculation(Operation.divide, 7.7, 8.8))));
}
```

The output:

```
[3.3, -1.1, 36.3, 0.875]
```

Function Overloading (page 265)

The following two overloads take advantage of the existing info() overloads:

```
void info(Meal meal) {
    info(meal.time);
    write('-');
    info(addDuration(meal.time, TimeOfDay(1, 30)));

    write(" Meal, Address: ", meal.address);
}

void info(DailyPlan plan) {
    info(plan.amMeeting);
    writeln();
    info(plan.lunch);
    writeln();
    info(plan.pmMeeting);
}
```

Here is the entire program that uses all of these types:

```
import std.stdio;

struct TimeOfDay {
    int hour;
    int minute;
}

void info(TimeOfDay time) {
    writef("%02s:%02s", time.hour, time.minute);
}

TimeOfDay addDuration(TimeOfDay start,
                      TimeOfDay duration) {
    TimeOfDay result;

    result.minute = start.minute + duration.minute;
    result.hour = start.hour + duration.hour;
    result.hour += result.minute / 60;

    result.minute %= 60;
    result.hour %= 24;

    return result;
}

struct Meeting {
    string    topic;
    size_t    attendanceCount;
    TimeOfDay start;
    TimeOfDay end;
}
```

```
void info(Meeting meeting) {
    info(meeting.start);
    write('-');
    info(meeting.end);

    writef(" \"%s\" meeting with %s attendees",
           meeting.topic,
           meeting.attendanceCount);
}

struct Meal {
    TimeOfDay time;
    string    address;
}

void info(Meal meal) {
    info(meal.time);
    write('-');
    info(addDuration(meal.time, TimeOfDay(1, 30)));

    write(" Meal, Address: ", meal.address);
}

struct DailyPlan {
    Meeting amMeeting;
    Meal    lunch;
    Meeting pmMeeting;
}

void info(DailyPlan plan) {
    info(plan.amMeeting);
    writeln();
    info(plan.lunch);
    writeln();
    info(plan.pmMeeting);
}

void main() {
    immutable bikeRideMeeting = Meeting("Bike Ride", 4,
                                        TimeOfDay(10, 30),
                                        TimeOfDay(11, 45));

    immutable lunch = Meal(TimeOfDay(12, 30), "İstanbul");

    immutable budgetMeeting = Meeting("Budget", 8,
                                      TimeOfDay(15, 30),
                                      TimeOfDay(17, 30));

    immutable todaysPlan = DailyPlan(bikeRideMeeting,
                                     lunch,
                                     budgetMeeting);

    info(todaysPlan);
    writeln();
}
```

That main() function can also be written with only object literals:

```
void main() {
    info(DailyPlan(Meeting("Bike Ride", 4,
                           TimeOfDay(10, 30),
                           TimeOfDay(11, 45)),

                   Meal(TimeOfDay(12, 30), "İstanbul"),

                   Meeting("Budget", 8,
                           TimeOfDay(15, 30),
                           TimeOfDay(17, 30))));

    writeln();
}
```

Member Functions (page 269)

1. Potentially negative intermediate values make decrement() slightly more complicated than increment():

```d
struct TimeOfDay {
    // ...

    void decrement(Duration duration) {
        auto minutesToSubtract = duration.minute % 60;
        auto hoursToSubtract = duration.minute / 60;

        minute -= minutesToSubtract;

        if (minute < 0) {
            minute += 60;
            ++hoursToSubtract;
        }

        hour -= hoursToSubtract;

        if (hour < 0) {
            hour = 24 - (-hour % 24);
        }
    }

    // ...
}
```

2. To see how much easier it gets with toString() member functions, let's look at the Meeting overload of info() one more time:

```d
void info(Meeting meeting) {
    info(meeting.start);
    write('-');
    info(meeting.end);

    writef(" \"%s\" meeting with %s attendees",
            meeting.topic,
            meeting.attendanceCount);
}
```

Taking advantage of the already-defined TimeOfDay.toString, the implementation of Meeting.toString becomes trivial:

```d
    string toString() {
        return format("%s-%s \"%s\" meeting with %s attendees",
                      start, end, topic, attendanceCount);
    }
```

Here is the entire program:

```d
import std.stdio;
import std.string;

struct Duration {
    int minute;
}

struct TimeOfDay {
    int hour;
    int minute;

    string toString() {
        return format("%02s:%02s", hour, minute);
    }

    void increment(Duration duration) {
        minute += duration.minute;
```

```
        hour += minute / 60;
        minute %= 60;
        hour %= 24;
    }
}

struct Meeting {
    string    topic;
    int       attendanceCount;
    TimeOfDay start;
    TimeOfDay end;

    string toString() {
        return format("%s-%s \"%s\" meeting with %s attendees",
                      start, end, topic, attendanceCount);
    }
}

struct Meal {
    TimeOfDay time;
    string    address;

    string toString() {
        TimeOfDay end = time;
        end.increment(Duration(90));

        return format("%s-%s Meal, Address: %s",
                      time, end, address);
    }
}

struct DailyPlan {
    Meeting amMeeting;
    Meal    lunch;
    Meeting pmMeeting;

    string toString() {
        return format("%s\n%s\n%s",
                      amMeeting,
                      lunch,
                      pmMeeting);
    }
}

void main() {
    auto bikeRideMeeting = Meeting("Bike Ride", 4,
                                   TimeOfDay(10, 30),
                                   TimeOfDay(11, 45));

    auto lunch = Meal(TimeOfDay(12, 30), "İstanbul");

    auto budgetMeeting = Meeting("Budget", 8,
                                 TimeOfDay(15, 30),
                                 TimeOfDay(17, 30));

    auto todaysPlan = DailyPlan(bikeRideMeeting,
                                lunch,
                                budgetMeeting);

    writeln(todaysPlan);
    writeln();
}
```

The output of the program is the same as the earlier one that has been using `info()` function overloads:

```
10:30-11:45 "Bike Ride" meeting with 4 attendees
12:30-14:00 Meal, Address: İstanbul
15:30-17:30 "Budget" meeting with 8 attendees
```

Operator Overloading (page 298)

The following implementation passes all of the unit tests. The design decisions
have been included as code comments.

Some of the functions of this struct can be implemented to run more efficiently.
Additionally, it would be beneficial to also *normalize* the numerator and
denominator. For example, instead of keeping the values 20 and 60, the values
could be divided by their *greatest common divisor* and the numerator and the
denominator can be stored as 1 and 3 instead. Otherwise, most of the operations
on the object would cause the values of the numerator and the denominator to
increase.

```d
import std.exception;
import std.conv;

struct Fraction {
    long num;   // numerator
    long den;   // denominator

    /* As a convenience, the constructor uses the default
     * value of 1 for the denominator. */
    this(long num, long den = 1) {
        enforce(den != 0, "The denominator cannot be zero");

        this.num = num;
        this.den = den;

        /* Ensuring that the denominator is always positive
         * will simplify the definitions of some of the
         * operator functions. */
        if (this.den < 0) {
            this.num = -this.num;
            this.den = -this.den;
        }
    }

    /* Unary -: Returns the negative of this fraction. */
    Fraction opUnary(string op)() const
            if (op == "-") {
        /* Simply constructs and returns an anonymous
         * object. */
        return Fraction(-num, den);
    }

    /* ++: Increments the value of the fraction by one. */
    ref Fraction opUnary(string op)()
            if (op == "++") {
        /* We could have used 'this += Fraction(1)' here. */
        num += den;
        return this;
    }

    /* --: Decrements the value of the fraction by one. */
    ref Fraction opUnary(string op)()
            if (op == "--") {
        /* We could have used 'this -= Fraction(1)' here. */
        num -= den;
        return this;
    }

    /* +=: Adds the right-hand fraction to this one. */
    ref Fraction opOpAssign(string op)(Fraction rhs)
            if (op == "+") {
        /* Addition formula: a/b + c/d = (a*d + c*b)/(b*d) */
        num = (num * rhs.den) + (rhs.num * den);
        den *= rhs.den;
        return this;
    }

    /* -=: Subtracts the right-hand fraction from this one. */
```

```
    ref Fraction opOpAssign(string op)(Fraction rhs)
            if (op == "-") {
        /* We make use of the already-defined operators += and
         * unary - here. Alternatively, the subtraction
         * formula could explicitly be applied similar to the
         * += operator above.
         *
         * Subtraction formula: a/b - c/d = (a*d - c*b)/(b*d)
         */
        this += -rhs;
        return this;
    }

    /* *=: Multiplies the fraction by the right-hand side. */
    ref Fraction opOpAssign(string op)(Fraction rhs)
            if (op == "*") {
        /* Multiplication formula: a/b * c/d = (a*c)/(b*d) */
        num *= rhs.num;
        den *= rhs.den;
        return this;
    }

    /* /=: Divides the fraction by the right-hand side. */
    ref Fraction opOpAssign(string op)(Fraction rhs)
            if (op == "/") {
        enforce(rhs.num != 0, "Cannot divide by zero");

        /* Division formula: (a/b) / (c/d) = (a*d)/(b*c) */
        num *= rhs.den;
        den *= rhs.num;
        return this;
    }

    /* Binary +: Produces the result of adding this and the
     * right-hand side fractions. */
    Fraction opBinary(string op)(Fraction rhs) const
            if (op == "+") {
        /* Takes a copy of this fraction and adds the
         * right-hand side fraction to that copy. */
        Fraction result = this;
        result += rhs;
        return result;
    }

    /* Binary -: Produces the result of subtracting the
     * right-hand side fraction from this one. */
    Fraction opBinary(string op)(Fraction rhs) const
            if (op == "-") {
        /* Uses the already-defined -= operator. */
        Fraction result = this;
        result -= rhs;
        return result;
    }

    /* Binary *: Produces the result of multiplying this
     * fraction with the right-hand side fraction. */
    Fraction opBinary(string op)(Fraction rhs) const
            if (op == "*") {
        /* Uses the already-defined *= operator. */
        Fraction result = this;
        result *= rhs;
        return result;
    }

    /* Binary /: Produces the result of dividing this fraction
     * by the right-hand side fraction. */
    Fraction opBinary(string op)(Fraction rhs) const
            if (op == "/") {
        /* Uses the already-defined /= operator. */
        Fraction result = this;
        result /= rhs;
        return result;
    }
```

```
    /* Returns the value of the fraction as double. */
    double opCast(T : double)() const {
        /* A simple division. However, as dividing values of
         * type long would lose the part of the value after
         * the decimal point, we could not have written
         * 'num/den' here. */
        return to!double(num) / den;
    }

    /* Sort order operator: Returns a negative value if this
     * fraction is before, a positive value if this fraction
     * is after, and zero if both fractions have the same sort
     * order. */
    int opCmp(const Fraction rhs) const {
        immutable result = this - rhs;
        /* Being a long, num cannot be converted to int
         * automatically; it must be converted explicitly by
         * 'to' (or cast). */
        return to!int(result.num);
    }

    /* Equality comparison: Returns true if the fractions are
     * equal.
     *
     * The equality comparison had to be defined for this type
     * because the compiler-generated one would be comparing
     * the members one-by-one, without regard to the actual
     * values that the objects represent.
     *
     * For example, although the values of both Fraction(1,2)
     * and Fraction(2,4) are 0.5, the compiler-generated
     * opEquals would decide that they were not equal on
     * account of having members of different values. */
    bool opEquals(const Fraction rhs) const {
        /* Checking whether the return value of opCmp is zero
         * is sufficient here. */
        return opCmp(rhs) == 0;
    }
}

unittest {
    /* Must throw when denominator is zero. */
    assertThrown(Fraction(42, 0));

    /* Let's start with 1/3. */
    auto a = Fraction(1, 3);

    /* -1/3 */
    assert(-a == Fraction(-1, 3));

    /* 1/3 + 1 == 4/3 */
    ++a;
    assert(a == Fraction(4, 3));

    /* 4/3 - 1 == 1/3 */
    --a;
    assert(a == Fraction(1, 3));

    /* 1/3 + 2/3 == 3/3 */
    a += Fraction(2, 3);
    assert(a == Fraction(1));

    /* 3/3 - 2/3 == 1/3 */
    a -= Fraction(2, 3);
    assert(a == Fraction(1, 3));

    /* 1/3 * 8 == 8/3 */
    a *= Fraction(8);
    assert(a == Fraction(8, 3));

    /* 8/3 / 16/9 == 3/2 */
    a /= Fraction(16, 9);
```

```
    assert(a == Fraction(3, 2));

    /* Must produce the equivalent value in type 'double'.
     *
     * Note that although double cannot represent every value
     * precisely, 1.5 is an exception. That is why this test
     * is being applied at this point. */
    assert(to!double(a) == 1.5);

    /* 1.5 + 2.5 == 4 */
    assert(a + Fraction(5, 2) == Fraction(4, 1));

    /* 1.5 - 0.75 == 0.75 */
    assert(a - Fraction(3, 4) == Fraction(3, 4));

    /* 1.5 * 10 == 15 */
    assert(a * Fraction(10) == Fraction(15, 1));

    /* 1.5 / 4 == 3/8 */
    assert(a / Fraction(4) == Fraction(3, 8));

    /* Must throw when dividing by zero. */
    assertThrown(Fraction(42, 1) / Fraction(0));

    /* The one with lower numerator is before. */
    assert(Fraction(3, 5) < Fraction(4, 5));

    /* The one with larger denominator is before. */
    assert(Fraction(3, 9) < Fraction(3, 8));
    assert(Fraction(1, 1_000) > Fraction(1, 10_000));

    /* The one with lower value is before. */
    assert(Fraction(10, 100) < Fraction(1, 2));

    /* The one with negative value is before. */
    assert(Fraction(-1, 2) < Fraction(0));
    assert(Fraction(1, -2) < Fraction(0));

    /* The ones with equal values must be both <= and >=. */
    assert(Fraction(-1, -2) <= Fraction(1, 2));
    assert(Fraction(1, 2) <= Fraction(-1, -2));
    assert(Fraction(3, 7) <= Fraction(9, 21));
    assert(Fraction(3, 7) >= Fraction(9, 21));

    /* The ones with equal values must be equal. */
    assert(Fraction(1, 3) == Fraction(20, 60));

    /* The ones with equal values with sign must be equal. */
    assert(Fraction(-1, 2) == Fraction(1, -2));
    assert(Fraction(1, 2) == Fraction(-1, -2));
}

void main() {
}
```

As has been mentioned in the chapter, string mixins can be used to combine the definitions of some of the operators. For example, the following definition covers the four arithmetic operators:

```
    /* Binary arithmetic operators. */
    Fraction opBinary(string op)(Fraction rhs) const
        if ((op == "+") || (op == "-") ||
            (op == "*") || (op == "/")) {
        /* Takes a copy of this fraction and applies the
         * right-hand side fraction to that copy. */
        Fraction result = this;
        mixin ("result " ~ op ~ "= rhs;");
        return result;
    }
```

Inheritance (page 328)

1. The member functions that are declared as abstract by superclasses must be defined by the override keyword by subclasses.

   Ignoring the Train class for this exercise, Locomotive.makeSound and RailwayCar.makeSound can be implemented as in the following program:

```d
import std.stdio;
import std.exception;

class RailwayVehicle {
    void advance(size_t kilometers) {
        writefln("The vehicle is advancing %s kilometers",
                 kilometers);

        foreach (i; 0 .. kilometers / 100) {
            writefln("  %s", makeSound());
        }
    }

    abstract string makeSound();
}

class Locomotive : RailwayVehicle {
    override string makeSound() {
        return "choo choo";
    }
}

class RailwayCar : RailwayVehicle {
    // ...

    override string makeSound() {
        return "clack clack";
    }
}

class PassengerCar : RailwayCar {
    // ...
}

class FreightCar : RailwayCar {
    // ...
}

void main() {
    auto railwayCar1 = new PassengerCar;
    railwayCar1.advance(100);

    auto railwayCar2 = new FreightCar;
    railwayCar2.advance(200);

    auto locomotive = new Locomotive;
    locomotive.advance(300);
}
```

2. The following program uses the sounds of the components of Train to make the sound of Train itself:

```d
import std.stdio;
import std.exception;

class RailwayVehicle {
    void advance(size_t kilometers) {
        writefln("The vehicle is advancing %s kilometers",
                 kilometers);

        foreach (i; 0 .. kilometers / 100) {
            writefln("  %s", makeSound());
        }
```

```
    }
    abstract string makeSound();
}

class Locomotive : RailwayVehicle {
    override string makeSound() {
        return "choo choo";
    }
}

class RailwayCar : RailwayVehicle {
    abstract void load();
    abstract void unload();

    override string makeSound() {
        return "clack clack";
    }
}

class PassengerCar : RailwayCar {
    override void load() {
        writeln("The passengers are getting on");
    }

    override void unload() {
        writeln("The passengers are getting off");
    }
}

class FreightCar : RailwayCar {
    override void load() {
        writeln("The crates are being loaded");
    }

    override void unload() {
        writeln("The crates are being unloaded");
    }
}

class Train : RailwayVehicle {
    Locomotive locomotive;
    RailwayCar[] cars;

    this(Locomotive locomotive) {
        enforce(locomotive !is null,
                "Locomotive cannot be null");
        this.locomotive = locomotive;
    }

    void addCar(RailwayCar[] cars...) {
        this.cars ~= cars;
    }

    override string makeSound() {
        string result = locomotive.makeSound();

        foreach (car; cars) {
            result ~= ", " ~ car.makeSound();
        }

        return result;
    }

    void departStation(string station) {
        foreach (car; cars) {
            car.load();
        }

        writefln("Departing from %s station", station);
    }

    void arriveStation(string station) {
```

```
            writefln("Arriving at %s station", station);

            foreach (car; cars) {
                car.unload();
            }
        }
    }

    void main() {
        auto locomotive = new Locomotive;
        auto train = new Train(locomotive);

        train.addCar(new PassengerCar, new FreightCar);

        train.departStation("Ankara");
        train.advance(500);
        train.arriveStation("Haydarpaşa");
    }
```

The output:

```
The passengers are getting on
The crates are being loaded
Departing from Ankara station
The vehicle is advancing 500 kilometers
  choo choo, clack clack, clack clack
  choo choo, clack clack, clack clack
  choo choo, clack clack, clack clack
  choo choo, clack clack, clack clack
  choo choo, clack clack, clack clack
Arriving at Haydarpaşa station
The passengers are getting off
The crates are being unloaded
```

Object (page 342)

1. For the equality comparison, rhs being non-null and the members being equal would be sufficient:

```
enum Color { blue, green, red }

class Point {
    int x;
    int y;
    Color color;

// ...

    override bool opEquals(Object o) const {
        const rhs = cast(const Point)o;

        return rhs && (x == rhs.x) && (y == rhs.y);
    }
}
```

2. When the type of the right-hand side object is also Point, they are compared according to the values of the x members first and then according to the values of the y members:

```
class Point {
    int x;
    int y;
    Color color;

// ...

    override int opCmp(Object o) const {
        const rhs = cast(const Point)o;
        enforce(rhs);
```

```
        return (x != rhs.x
                ? x - rhs.x
                : y - rhs.y);
    }
}
```

3. Note that it is not possible to cast to type const TriangularArea inside opCmp below. When rhs is const TriangularArea, then its member rhs.points would be const as well. Since the parameter of opCmp is non-const, it would not be possible to pass rhs.points[i] to point.opCmp.

```
class TriangularArea {
    Point[3] points;

    this(Point one, Point two, Point three) {
        points = [ one, two, three ];
    }

    override bool opEquals(Object o) const {
        const rhs = cast(const TriangularArea)o;
        return rhs && (points == rhs.points);
    }

    override int opCmp(Object o) const {
        auto rhs = cast(TriangularArea)o;
        enforce(rhs);

        foreach (i, point; points) {
            immutable comparison = point.opCmp(rhs.points[i]);

            if (comparison != 0) {
                /* The sort order has already been
                 * determined. Simply return the result. */
                return comparison;
            }
        }

        /* The objects are considered equal because all of
         * their points have been equal. */
        return 0;
    }

    override size_t toHash() const {
        /* Since the 'points' member is an array, we can take
         * advantage of the existing toHash algorithm for
         * array types. */
        return typeid(points).getHash(&points);
    }
}
```

Pointers (page 425)

1. When parameters are value types like int, the arguments are copied to functions. The preferred way of defining reference parameters is to specify them as ref.

   Another way is to define the parameters as pointers that point at the actual variables. The parts of the program that have been changed are highlighted:

```
void swap(int * lhs, int * rhs) {
    int temp = *lhs;
    *lhs = *rhs;
    *rhs = temp;
}

void main() {
    int i = 1;
```

```
    int j = 2;

    swap(&i, &j);

    assert(i == 2);
    assert(j == 1);
}
```

The checks at the end of the program now pass.

2. Node and `List` have been written to work only with the `int` type. We can convert these types to struct templates by adding (T) after their names and replacing appropriate `int`s in their definitions by `T`s:

```
struct Node(T) {
    T element;
    Node * next;

    string toString() const {
        string result = to!string(element);

        if (next) {
            result ~= " -> " ~ to!string(*next);
        }

        return result;
    }
}

struct List(T) {
    Node!T * head;

    void insertAtHead(T element) {
        head = new Node!T(element, head);
    }

    string toString() const {
        return format("(%s)", head ? to!string(*head) : "");
    }
}
```

`List` can now be used with any type:

```
import std.stdio;
import std.conv;
import std.string;

// ...

struct Point {
    double x;
    double y;

    string toString() const {
        return format("(%s,%s)", x, y);
    }
}

void main() {
    List!Point points;

    points.insertAtHead(Point(1.1, 2.2));
    points.insertAtHead(Point(3.3, 4.4));
    points.insertAtHead(Point(5.5, 6.6));

    writeln(points);
}
```

The output:

```
((5.5,6.6) -> (3.3,4.4) -> (1.1,2.2))
```

3. In this case we need another pointer to point at the last node of the list. The new code is necessarily more complex in order to manage the new variable as well:

```
struct List(T) {
    Node!T * head;
    Node!T * tail;

    void append(T element) {
        /* Since there is no node after the last one, we set
         * the new node's next pointer to 'null'. */
        auto newNode = new Node!T(element, null);

        if (!head) {
            /* The list has been empty. The new node becomes
             * the head. */
            head = newNode;
        }

        if (tail) {
            /* We place this node after the current tail. */
            tail.next = newNode;
        }

        /* The new node becomes the new tail. */
        tail = newNode;
    }

    void insertAtHead(T element) {
        auto newNode = new Node!T(element, head);

        /* The new node becomes the new head. */
        head = newNode;

        if (!tail) {
            /* The list has been empty. The new node becomes
             * the tail. */
            tail = newNode;
        }
    }

    string toString() const {
        return format("(%s)", head ? to!string(*head) : "");
    }
}
```

The new implementation of `insertAtHead()` can actually be shorter:

```
    void insertAtHead(T element) {
        head = new Node!T(element, head);

        if (!tail) {
            tail = head;
        }
    }
```

The following program uses the new `List` to insert `Point` objects with odd values at the head and `Point` objects with even values at the end.

```
void main() {
    List!Point points;

    foreach (i; 1 .. 7) {
        if (i % 2) {
            points.insertAtHead(Point(i, i));

        } else {
            points.append(Point(i, i));
        }
    }
```

```
        writeln(points);
}
```

The output:

```
((5,5) -> (3,3) -> (1,1) -> (2,2) -> (4,4) -> (6,6))
```

Bit Operations (page 446)

1. It may be acceptable to use magic constants in such a short function. Otherwise, the code may get too complicated.

```
string dotted(uint address) {
    return format("%s.%s.%s.%s",
                  (address >> 24) & 0xff,
                  (address >> 16) & 0xff,
                  (address >>  8) & 0xff,
                  (address >>  0) & 0xff);
}
```

Because the type is an unsigned type, the bits that are inserted into the value from the left-hand side will all have 0 values. For that reason, there is no need to mask the value that is shifted by 24 bits. Additionally, since shifting by 0 bits has no effect, that operation can be eliminated as well:

```
string dotted(uint address) {
    return format("%s.%s.%s.%s",
                  address >> 24,
                  (address >> 16) & 0xff,
                  (address >>  8) & 0xff,
                  address          & 0xff);
}
```

2. Each octet can be shifted to its proper position in the IPv4 address and then these expressions can be "*orred*":

```
uint ipAddress(ubyte octet3,     // most significant octet
               ubyte octet2,
               ubyte octet1,
               ubyte octet0) {  // least significant octet
    return
        (octet3 << 24) |
        (octet2 << 16) |
        (octet1 <<  8) |
        (octet0 <<  0);
}
```

3. The following method starts with a value where all of the bits are 1. First, the value is shifted to the right so that the upper bits become 0, and then it is shifted to the left so that the lower bits become 0:

```
uint mask(int lowestBit, int width) {
    uint result = uint.max;
    result >>= (uint.sizeof * 8) - width;
    result <<= lowestBit;
    return result;
}
```

uint.max is the value where all of the bits are 1. Alternatively, the calculation can start with the value that is the complement of 0, which is the same as uint.max:

```
    uint result = ~0;
    // ...
```

foreach with Structs and Classes (page 491)

1. The step size must be stored alongside begin and end, and the element value must be increased by that step size:

```d
struct NumberRange {
    int begin;
    int end;
    int stepSize;

    int opApply(int delegate(ref int) dg) const {
        int result;

        for (int number = begin; number != end; number += stepSize) {
            result = dg(number);

            if (result) {
                break;
            }
        }

        return result;
    }
}

import std.stdio;

void main() {
    foreach (element; NumberRange(0, 10, 2)) {
        write(element, ' ');
    }
}
```

2.
```d
import std.stdio;
import std.string;

class Student {
    string name;
    int id;

    this(string name, int id) {
        this.name = name;
        this.id = id;
    }

    override string toString() {
        return format("%s(%s)", name, id);
    }
}

class Teacher {
    string name;
    string subject;

    this(string name, string subject) {
        this.name = name;
        this.subject = subject;
    }

    override string toString() {
        return format("%s teacher %s", subject, name);
    }
}

class School {
private:
```

```
        Student[] students;
        Teacher[] teachers;

    public:

        this(Student[] students, Teacher[] teachers) {
            this.students = students;
            this.teachers = teachers;
        }

        /* This opApply override will be called when the foreach
         * variable is a Student. */
        int opApply(int delegate(ref Student) dg) {
            int result;

            foreach (student; students) {
                result = dg(student);

                if (result) {
                    break;
                }
            }

            return result;
        }

        /* Similarly, this opApply will be called when the foreach
         * variable is a Teacher. */
        int opApply(int delegate(ref Teacher) dg) {
            int result;

            foreach (teacher; teachers) {
                result = dg(teacher);

                if (result) {
                    break;
                }
            }

            return result;
        }
}

void printIndented(T)(T value) {
    writeln("  ", value);
}

void main() {
    auto school = new School(
        [ new Student("Can", 1),
          new Student("Canan", 10),
          new Student("Cem", 42),
          new Student("Cemile", 100) ],

        [ new Teacher("Nazmiye", "Math"),
          new Teacher("Makbule", "Literature") ]);

    writeln("Student loop");
    foreach (Student student; school) {
        printIndented(student);
    }

    writeln("Teacher loop");
    foreach (Teacher teacher; school) {
        printIndented(teacher);
    }
}
```

The output:

```
Student loop
  Can(1)
  Canan(10)
```

```
  Cem(42)
  Cemile(100)
Teacher loop
  Math teacher Nazmiye
  Literature teacher Makbule
```

As you can see, the implementations of both of the opApply() overrides are exactly the same, except the slice that they iterate on. To reduce code duplication, the common functionality can be moved to an implementation function template, which then gets called by the two opApply() overrides:

```d
class School {
// ...

    int opApplyImpl(T)(T[] slice, int delegate(ref T) dg) {
        int result;

        foreach (element; slice) {
            result = dg(element);

            if (result) {
                break;
            }
        }

        return result;
    }

    int opApply(int delegate(ref Student) dg) {
        return opApplyImpl(students, dg);
    }

    int opApply(int delegate(ref Teacher) dg) {
        return opApplyImpl(teachers, dg);
    }
}
```

Index

A

www.ingramcontent.com/pod-product-compliance
Lightning Source LLC
LaVergne TN
LVHW082143040326
832903LV00006B/258